SOUTHERN BIOGRAPHY SERIES

Titles in the SOUTHERN BIOGRAPHY SERIES

Edited by Fred C. Cole and Wendell H. Stephenson

Edited by T. Harry Williams

BRECKINRIDGE

JOHN C. BRECKINRIDGE

BRECKINRIDGE
Statesman
Soldier
Symbol

WILLIAM C. DAVIS

Louisiana State University Press
Baton Rouge

ISBN 0–8071–0068–4
Library of Congress Catalog Card Number 73–77658
Copyright © 1974 by Louisiana State University Press
All rights reserved
Manufactured in the United States of America
Printed by The TJM Corporation, Baton Rouge, Louisiana
Designed by Albert R. Crochet

*Publication of this book was assisted by the
American Council of Learned Societies under a grant
from the Andrew W. Mellon Foundation.*

Winner of the
Jules F. Landry Award for 1973

In gratitude for the vital parts they played in making it possible, this book is dedicated to
Mary Breckinridge Kirkland
and Pamela S. Davis.
They will both be glad it is done at last.

Contents

Illustrations

Abbreviations Used in Footnotes

CHS	Chicago Historical Society
UC	University of Chicago Library
DU	Duke University Library, Durham, N.C.
FC	Filson Club, Louisville, Ky.
HLH	Houghton Library, Harvard University, Cambridge, Mass.
HL	Henry E. Huntington Library, San Marino, Calif.
ISL	Indiana State Library, Indianapolis
UK	University of Kentucky Library, Lexington
LC	Library of Congress, Washington, D.C.
ConnHS	Connecticut Historical Society, Hartford
MassHS	Massachusetts Historical Society, Boston
CLUM	William L. Clements Library, University of Michigan, Ann Arbor
MHS	Minnesota Historical Society, St. Paul
NA	National Archives, Washington, D.C.
NYHS	New York Historical Society, New York
NYPL	New York Public Library, New York
NCDAH	North Carolina Department of Archives and History, Raleigh
SHC	Southern Historical Collection, University of North Carolina Library, Chapel Hill
HSP	Historical Society of Pennsylvania, Philadelphia
LHAC	Louisiana Historical Association Collection, Howard-Tilton Memorial Library, Tulane University, New Orleans
WRHS	Western Reserve Historical Society, Cleveland, Ohio

Preface

The search for reasons leads inevitably to men. In the continuing span of human events men are at once the materials and the builders of history. Never was this more true than in the troubled yet triumphant years 1850–1877 when America at midcentury was shattered from within, and then began the long struggle to rebuild itself. The agents of its disintegration and rebirth were men of all stripes—radicals, reactionaries, moderates. Within themselves they all bore the potentials of achievement and catastrophe, the reasons of history.

One man, a moderate, was John C. Breckinridge of Kentucky. Like so many others, he charted his course with but a single thought in mind, his devotion to his country's welfare as he saw it; like so many others, he found himself bewildered at how that devotion could guide him and his country to both success and disaster. His story is largely theirs; yet it is unique. Not one of his confused compeers equaled his rise; none suffered a greater fall; and few emerged from their own involvements so unembittered, unbroken, and able to go on with an enhanced devotion to their country. The story of the three worlds through which John C. Breckinridge walked, and upon which he left his mark, is incomplete without his own story. It alone will not provide the reasons for what happened to America in the middle of the nineteenth century. But it will give us clues.

William C. Davis
Mechanicsburg, Pennsylvania
August, 1973

Acknowledgments

I suppose I owe it all to my great-great-grandfather and a careless editor at *Century Magazine*. In the fall of 1863 Josiah Solomon Davis enlisted in the Forty-fifth Virginia Infantry and served in southwestern Virginia until his capture at the Battle of Piedmont the following June. He would be exchanged several months later, already racked with the disease contracted in a northern prison which killed him two days before Lee surrendered. Two decades later, as part of its series of articles titled "Battles and Leaders of the Civil War," *Century* published a table of the opposing forces engaged at the widely touted little Battle of New Market, Virginia, May 15, 1864. Among the Confederate units listed was the Forty-fifth Virginia.

An accompanying article turned up a curious fact. The commander of the Confederate forces in the battle had been vice-president of the United States little more than three years before. Immediately the question arose in my mind: What could have induced a man who had been vice-president —and a presidential candidate, as more reading revealed—to turn and fight against his own country? It seemed an important question, which made all the more surprising the discovery that no one had attempted to answer it seriously in the near-century since his death. I all but forgot great-great-grandfather Josiah Davis and the Forty-fifth Virginia, but for the next nine years I would live with John C. Breckinridge.

Aside from a score or more of brief sketches and profiles, most of them of questionable value, only one attempt at a biography of the Kentuckian ever reached print. Lucille Stillwell's *Born to Be a Statesman: John Cabell Breckinridge* began with an incorrect date of birth for its subject, and thereafter seldom rose above that standard of accuracy. Six pages covered the momentous years of his vice-presidency; fewer than twenty-one were devoted to his services as a Confederate general and secretary of war; his funeral received more attention and detail than his final years as a champion of peaceful reconstruction and reconciliation. From 1936, when *Born to Be a Statesman* appeared, until the present, it was the only readily available source on the life of a very important man.

My nine years with Breckinridge have been busy years but good ones, and they have brought me in contact with a host of kind people who felt, as I did, that Breckinridge deserved a thorough biography. Most helpful to me were his numerous descendants, members of a family which has lost none of the honor and sense of duty that have characterized almost two centuries of participation in American leadership. Mr. and Mrs. John Marshall Prewitt of Mt. Sterling, Kentucky, first introduced me to Mrs. Prewitt's family, the Breckinridges of today, and lent as well their collection of papers, notebooks, diaries, and photographs of her ancestor. Breckinridge's four granddaughters, Mrs. Kenneth Kirkland, Mrs. Jeter Horton of New York, Mrs. George W. Dunn of Oostburg, Wisconsin, and Lee Breckinridge Thomas of Oakland, California, were all most generous with their family mementoes. Mrs. Horton, Mrs. Thomas, and Mrs. Dunn have since died. To Mrs. Kirkland in particular, I am truly indebted. A gracious, charming lady, she made this project her own, tracking down elusive descendants, diplomatically urging those who were slow to respond, providing introductions to others, and she was always ready with anecdotes and insights to illuminate "the General." It would have been most difficult, and perhaps impossible, to produce this book without her.

Mrs. J. C. Breckinridge of Summit Point, West Virginia, was most kind in allowing me to explore the contents of "the trunk" in her attic. Its yield of personal, political, and financial papers was indispensable and comprises a collection previously unknown, which is second in importance only to the extensive Breckinridge Family Papers in the Manuscripts Division of the Library of Congress, where it will soon be deposited. Other lineal and collateral descendants of the family who gave freely of their minds and memorabilia were: Walter R. Agard, Chicago; Robert Breckinridge, New York; Colonel William L. Breckinridge, South Haven, Michigan; Mrs. Wheaton Byers, Bethesda, Maryland; Joseph C. Carter, Elmhurst, Illinois; Mrs. George Roy Hill, New York; Breckinridge T. E. Stoddart, Hartford, Connecticut; Peter H. Ten Eyck, Boston; the Honorable Lady (Louise) Stockdale, Basingstoke, England. Invariably, I met with nothing but courtesy and eager interest from these proud bearers of an illustrious heritage.

A number of friends were most generous with their private collections.

Stanley E. Butcher of Andover, Massachusetts, let me use a number of Breckinridge items in his extensive Confederate collection; Ray Marshall, Clarksville, Tennessee, kindly lent material from his personal collection; Major Chapman Grant, Escondido, California, lent me the regimental order book of the Fourth United States Infantry, the Mexican War unit of his grandfather, General U. S. Grant; Dr. Edward O. Guerrant of Pasadena, California, kindly gave me his permission to use the extensive diaries of Colonel Edward O. Guerrant, which are now in the Southern Historical Collection, University of North Carolina Library, Chapel Hill; Dr. Alfred J. Hanna of Rollins College, author of the excellent *Flight Into Oblivion*, gave valuable comments and pointers, as did Dr. Robert D. Meade of Randolph-Macon Woman's College; Robert J. Younger of Dayton, Ohio, put up with repeated requests for references from Confederate journals and regimentals and very kindly furnished from his collection a previously unpublished photograph of Breckinridge in his last years. A good friend, Darryl Bertolucci, put up with my many overnight stays during research trips to Washington, D.C.

The staffs of a host of libraries and archives were courteous and helpful in my research. I cannot list them all, but those who were of particular assistance include: Archie Motley, Chicago Historical Society; James R. Bentley, Filson Club, Louisville, Kentucky; Jacqueline Bull and Charles C. Hay III, University of Kentucky Library, Lexington; the entire staff of the Manuscripts Division, Library of Congress; Mrs. Ruby J. Shields, Minnesota Historical Society, St. Paul; Elmer O. Parker, National Archives; Clyde N. Wilson, Southern Historical Collection, University of North Carolina Library, Chapel Hill; Haskell M. Monroe, former editor of *The Papers of Jefferson Davis*, Rice University, Houston, Texas; Watt P. Marchman, The Rutherford B. Hayes Library, Fremont, Ohio; Howson W. Cole, Virginia Historical Society, Richmond; and John Large and Virginia R. Hawley, Western Reserve Historical Society, Cleveland, Ohio.

Friends and fellow historians have been exceedingly kind in lending their aid and advice in the preparation of this book. Robert H. Fowler, president of the National Historical Society, and Dr. J. Winston Coleman, Jr., of Lexington, Kentucky, both read large portions of the manuscript, offering comments and suggestions which were invaluable. Dr. Robert W. Johannsen, whose own long awaited biography of Breckinridge's friend and fellow Democrat Stephen A. Douglas has appeared, read and criticized all of Book One. The knowledge and wisdom he has acquired during years of studying this complicated era served more than once to bring a straying line of thought back on the track. Likewise, Dr. Thomas L. Connelly, University of South Carolina, author of a brilliant history of the Confederate Army of Tennessee, reviewed my account of Breckinridge's service with that army, and his perceptive comments illuminated the often confusing command situations of that troubled, tragic organization. Dr. Lowell H. Harrison, himself the author of a biography of a Breckinridge, John C.'s grandfather John, read my account of the family's background and progress in America. Dr. Bell I. Wiley, Emory University, criticized the chapters covering Breckinridge's service as Confederate secretary of war. To these gentlemen, as well as to all of those who so kindly gave of their time and experience, I am most sincerely grateful.

Finally, to my wife, Pamela, who did not aid in the research or writing of this book, who did not type, correct, or edit any portion of the manuscript, and who, by all odds, will never read it, I must express both gratitude and profound wonder at her enduring patience with this "other person" in my life.

And Josiah Davis? He was nowhere near the Battle of New Market. While he served in southwestern Virginia for about six weeks under Breckinridge before the general marched north to battle, there is a good chance that he never even saw the Kentuckian. He and the Forty-fifth Virginia were left behind to garrison Saltville when Breckinridge moved to meet the Federals. The table in *Century* that places them in the battle is wholly in error, but it slipped past, and, in its peculiar yet integral role in the genesis of this book, it is hoped that this is one error which has served a useful purpose. The errors that will, of course, have insinuated themselves into the present book, can in no way be attributed to any of those individuals who have given their aid and counsel. Responsibility can only rest with the author, unless, of course, he can somehow shift the blame to that unfortunate editor at *Century*.

Book I

Statesman

CHAPTER 1

Your Brother Has a Fine Son

The vice-president had a standard answer for each of the surprising number of people who seemed continually to badger him for details on his ancestors and family history. Of course he felt his measure of pride in his illustrious family heritage, and he knew perhaps as much as anyone about his forebears. It was a natural outgrowth of his passionate interest in history and his beliefs in its practical lessons and usefulness. But with the Union appearing to be in mortal danger of disruption in the late 1850s, he had more urgent uses for his time than studying his genealogy. To inquiries received from those he described as "much exercised on the subject of pedigrees," his reply was always the same. "Dr Breckinridge is far more familiar with the subject than I am," he would say, referring them to his uncle, Robert J. Breckinridge.[1] Indeed, despite his pride in his past, John C. Breckinridge never fully understood the impact that it had on his own life and career. His heritage helped mold him, and he built upon it, both the good and the bad.

His recorded heritage went back two centuries to the tumultuous years of England's civil war and interregnum. Thousands of Protestants, their fears for liberty hardly disquieted by the Restoration of Charles II, fled their homes for safety. One such family in the Ayrshire lowlands of Scotland sought refuge for several decades in the higher reaches of Breadalbane. Life there proved hard, the land unyielding, and sometime after 1700 this small clan of Covenanters moved yet again, across the sea to Ulster. Before they left their mountainous Scotland home, they claimed a piece

---

1. John C. Breckinridge to Robert J. Breckinridge, January 10, 1858, in Breckinridge Family Papers, LC, hereinafter cited as B. MSS; John C. Breckinridge to Henry Randall, March 8, 1859, in Alfred W. Anthony Autograph Collection, NYPL. Henceforward in these notes, John C. Breckinridge will be referred to as Breckinridge.

of it, forever their own. They took their name from the land, called "Breckenridge." [2]

Northern Ireland offered a much more hospitable future to the immigrants, but, already uprooted and restless, some Breckenridges saw better prospects farther to the west. America beckoned. By the second quarter of the eighteenth century several had made their way to the colonies, among them Alexander Breckenridge who imported himself, his wife, and six children, into Philadelphia around 1728. A decade later he moved west again, to Augusta County, Virginia. By the time of his death in 1743, Breckenridge had become a well-established, prosperous Presbyterian with five sons. His son Robert managed his late father's holdings and then pursued his own career in which he rose to a variety of civic and military positions before the lure of new land led him to frontier Botetourt County. He became a justice of the new county, colonel of its militia, and kept an "ordinary" or tavern. Here he became probably the first of his family in America to buy Negro slaves. When he died in the early autumn of 1773, he left an estate worth £3,000. He was survived by his wife, Lettice, and seven children, including John for whom he made a special provision in his will that certain of his lands be sold and the proceeds be "put at interest for the use of John, or to give him a learned education." [3]

Young John was indeed a promising boy for a twelve-year-old, but the responsibility thrust on him by his father's death overburdened him. When their money ran out, the help of relatives was required to see the widow and orphans through hard times, and this same source provided the means for young Breckenridge to enter the College of William and Mary at Williamsburg in 1780. With teachers like George Wythe and Bishop James Madison, and classmates like Thomas and Richard Bland Lee, the boy delighted in college. The study of law particularly interested him, and encouraged by Wythe and others, he decided to pursue it as a career. Interruptions plagued him. The Revolution forced the college to close in 1781, and, even before this, Breckenridge saw active service as an ensign in the Botetourt militia, searching out and capturing Tories. Late in 1780, when he was nineteen, the people of Botetourt surprised him by electing him to

2. Lewis Collins, *Historical Sketches of Kentucky* (Cincinnati, 1850), 214; Alvin F. Harlow, *Weep No More My Lady* (New York, 1942), 39; Kilmarnock (Scotland) *Standard*, March 22, 1947.

3. James Malcom Breckenridge, *William Clark Breckenridge: His Life, Lineage and Writings* (Louisville, 1969), 215–18, 120–22; Lowell H. Harrison, *John Breckinridge: Jeffersonian Republican* (Louisville, 1969), 2–4.

represent them in the House of Burgesses. Breckenridge promised to serve his constituents "as well as I am capable of," and for the next five years he did his best, though still working toward his license as a lawyer. He spoke out for separation of church and state, for guarantees of the civil and property rights of citizens, and for a strong central government under the Articles of Confederation. At the same time, however, he made clear his belief that the will of the majority in a democracy should not be allowed to infringe upon the chartered rights of the minority. It was a principle that would haunt his descendants for decades to come.[4]

During these years Breckenridge, for some unknown reason, changed the spelling of the family name to Breckinridge. On June 28, 1785, he married Joseph Cabell's sixteen-year-old daughter Mary, who like most Mary's of the day was called Polly. In the next few years she gave birth to four children, Letitia, Joseph Cabell, Mary, and Robert. Meanwhile, her husband, who was struggling to establish a law practice in a state overcrowded with lawyers, was receiving glowing reports from his two brothers in Kentucky, telling of that state's promise and its flourishing bar.

In 1790 John Breckinridge traveled to Kentucky alone to purchase six hundred acres in Fayette County on the North Elkhorn Creek, seven miles from Lexington in the heart of the Bluegrass region. He called the estate Cabell's Dale. Three years later, when his family joined him, the move to the new country was saddened by the loss of two children, Robert and Mary, in a smallpox epidemic. With his family he brought his twenty or more slaves. Breckinridge had become an antifederalist, aligned with Thomas Jefferson and many other Virginians, and like them he believed the institution of slavery to be evil, but necessary to agrarian economy. He hoped for a gradual emancipation of the Negroes because of what slavery did to white and black alike, and his attitude eventually became family doctrine.

In addition to his successful financial activities in his new home, Breckinridge continued his interest in politics. He had turned down a seat in Congress before he left Virginia, but his influential associations in the Old Dominion marked him for prominence in Kentucky. He officially identified with Jefferson's Republicans and moved more firmly toward a conservative stance on the rights of the minority. Governor Isaac Shelby appointed

4. George Skillern to John Breckinridge, August 12, 1780, in Breckinridge family papers in possession of Mrs. J. C. Breckinridge, hereinafter cited as JCB Papers; James Malcom Breckinridge, *William Clark Breckenridge*, 123; Harrison, *John Breckinridge*, 4–8. Unless otherwise cited, material in this sketch of John Breckinridge is taken from Harrison's excellent biography.

him attorney general, and after an unsuccessful bid for the United States Senate, he won a seat in the state legislature.

In 1798 the administration of President John Adams, in reaction to attacks from Jeffersonians, had passed the Alien Friends Act, the Alien Enemies Act, and other measures commonly called the Alien and Sedition Acts, seriously threatening the freedom of speech and of the press. The legislation was aimed directly at Republicans, and Breckinridge opposed it vehemently. This same year he spent a few months in Virginia and may have conferred on the matter with Jefferson. What went on at that meeting, if it occurred, may never be known, but when Breckinridge returned to Kentucky he came armed with a paper denouncing the Alien and Sedition Acts —the controversial Kentucky Resolutions of 1798. Their authorship was long a mystery. Although his family always claimed that Breckinridge composed the resolves—for years he alone received credit for them—the bulk of the evidence points conclusively to Jefferson as their author.[5] Indeed, the Virginian a quarter of a century later revealed the fact to Breckinridge's son Joseph, though some details were cloudy after the passage of time.[6] Most likely, Jefferson gave Breckinridge a draft which served as the basis for the resolves and allowed the Kentuckian to elaborate somewhat upon this foundation.

Breckinridge presented nine resolutions to the state House of Representatives. In them it was argued that the individual states created the Congress and that as the sources of its authority, they were entitled to pass judgment on its laws and enactments. Should Congress fail to heed the remonstrance of the states, then it was their duty to nullify offending acts and to prevent, by force if necessary, the unjust imposition of such acts upon the people. It was a revolutionary doctrine, and within it lay the seeds of secession, seeds in the fertile ground of fear in a section of the country that could already see itself becoming a minority.

When the Kentucky Resolutions, and similar ones passed in Virginia, failed to gain widespread support, Breckinridge, now speaker of the House, introduced another measure to the legislature in 1799, reaffirming the resolves of the year before. Each of the states, he said, as parties to a contract, possessed the right to judge the legality of congressional measures. Breckinridge never wavered in his devotion to the infant Union, but he would not see the rights and prerogatives of the individual states curtailed or con-

5. Collins, *Historical Sketches*. 215: Breckinridge to Randall, March 8, 1859, in Anthony Collection; Harrison. *John Breckinridge*. 72–88.

6. Thomas Jefferson to J. Cabell Breckinridge, December 11, 1821, in B. MSS.

tained by Congress, especially since his party was then in the minority. "States' rights," ever to be the rallying cry of a minority jealously guarding its powers, was born. Intimately connected with it was slavery. Breckinridge regarded a slave, under the Constitution, strictly as property; only an owner had the right to free a slave. On this basis he opposed official emancipation, preferring individual initiative among slaveholders. But the rise of the new doctrine articulated in his resolutions threw a new light on the institution. Slavery was almost entirely restricted to the South, and already statutes restricting the slave trade were going on the books. Many states outlawed the institution completely, and now he feared that an antislavery majority in Congress could similarly outlaw its spread into new territories that were opened up or acquired in the West. Thus southern slaveholders would not be able to settle the new lands. This meant that, as the country grew and added more states, the South would increasingly find itself a minority. Consequently, the protection of southern rights and southern opportunities demanded the official protection of slavery, however repugnant he might find it personally. Breckinridge offered only one defense in the argument for slavery. It was recognized in the Constitution, and for him that was justification enough. Congress had no right to tamper with it, and the slave states must be vigilant to protect themselves, by nullification if necessary.

In 1800 the Kentuckian finally won his seat in the United States Senate. He went to Washington as one of Jefferson's most trusted friends, as evidenced in part by the name he gave his infant son he left behind with Polly—Robert Jefferson. Almost immediately Breckinridge became a Republican leader in the Senate, trusted with guiding to passage much of President Jefferson's legislative program. When the president presented the treaty for the purchase of the Louisiana Territory, Breckinridge backed it to passage and then fought to insure that the question of importation of slaves, and other domestic matters, be left to the territory's eventual settlers. Unknowingly, he was helping found the doctrine of "popular sovereignty."

In August, 1805, Jefferson rewarded his able friend with an appointment as attorney general. Breckinridge served only a few months, however, before taking a leave to return to Cabell's Dale, and here, late in 1806, he was suddenly bedridden, probably by tuberculosis. In October he was unable to journey back to Washington to resume his duties. Thereafter he grew steadily weaker. On the morning of December 14, 1806, little more than a week after his forty-sixth birthday, Breckinridge breathed his last. His had been a brief but comparatively important political career, one that contemporaries regarded as full of promise at the time of his death. What none could assess, however, was the profound impact that his career would have upon his progeny. Half a century after his passing, as the Union approached its greatest trial, his political legacy would wield, in the hands of one of his descendants, a power and influence of which John Breckinridge never dreamed.

Management of the family now fell to eighteen-year-old Cabell. He had his mother, a sister, Mary, and brothers Robert, James, William, and John, to care for. His father's estate, terribly complicated with claims and demands, was a great burden and would be in litigation of one sort or another for the next forty years. The consequent strain placed on young Cabell affected him for life, giving him a "prudence and grave maturity" beyond his years.[7]

Still he was able to finish his education at the College of New Jersey in Princeton, where, with his roommate James G. Birney, he came under the influence of Dr. Samuel Stanhope Smith, president of the college. An eminent opponent of slavery, Smith agreed with the Breckinridges that it must be abolished only by voluntary emancipation, that government action on the institution was no more allowable than would be interference with any other form of property. Smith's stand was backed by his illustrious father-in-law, the Reverend John Witherspoon. Clergyman, educator, and patriot, Witherspoon was the only cleric to sign the Declaration of Independence. His services in the Revolution were equaled by the eminence he enjoyed in Presbyterian circles, and he passed on a rich intellectual heritage to Smith and his children. One of Smith's daughters, Mary Clay, in turn helped bring this heritage west to Kentucky. On May 11, 1811, she and Joseph Cabell Breckinridge exchanged wedding vows. The union of the two cemented generations of devout Presbyterianism, ancestries resplendant with service in the formation and development of the United States, two lines of almost identical thought on the proper relationship of the states to the federal government, and on sentiments which supported the fact yet deplored the idea of slavery. This was the legacy they would pass on to their

7. Mary H. Breckinridge to Robert J. Breckinridge, March 22, 1841, in B. MSS; Collins, *Historical Sketches*, 279. This sketch of J. Cabell was written by his son John C. Breckinridge; Lewis Collins to Breckinridge, November 11, 1846, quoted in Clifton R. Breckinridge Notebook No. 5, p. 40, in the Breckinridge family papers in possession of Mr. and Mrs. John M. Prewitt, hereinafter cited as Prewitt Collection. This is one of eight notebooks wherein Clifton Breckinridge transcribed some of his father's papers before donating them to the Library of Congress. Included are many documents that are lost in the original. Hereinafter cited as CRB Books.

children, the gift they would give to their several daughters, and to their only son.[8]

Breckinridge graduated from the College of New Jersey in 1810 and, after his marriage, returned to Kentucky to pursue the law. The War of 1812 interrupted him briefly as he served in what he called "a foolish and ineffectual brace of campaigns on the Illinois & Wabash." But he was soon back at the bar, already assuming the influence which henceforth would come naturally to his family. Handsome, nearly six feet tall, and well formed, Breckinridge won a seat in the state legislature in 1817 and held it for two terms, becoming speaker of the House. Meanwhile business prospered, and he formed friendly associations with the most influential men in the state, men like Leslie Combs, John J. Crittenden, Birney, and his near neighbor Robert Todd.[9]

As his fortunes increased, so did his family. By now his brother John was in the ministry, Robert had just graduated from college, and William was well along in school. His sister Mary, who had married David Castleman, died in 1816. The vacancies in the Breckinridge household, however, filled rapidly. Cabell's first daughter, Frances, was born in 1812, and thereafter Mary gave birth to two more girls, Caroline and Mary Cabell. The family now lived in a stylish two-story brick home on the southeast corner of Limestone and Fifth streets in Lexington. They called it Thorn Hill, and here Mary remained with the children when Cabell was away meeting with the legislature in Frankfort.[10]

Even after he left the legislature, Breckinridge remained actively involved in politics, particularly in regard to the controversy over the admission of Missouri to the Union. "We are awaiting with great impatience to

8. Harrison, *John Breckinridge*, 161; Alexander Brown, *The Cabells and Their Kin* (Boston, 1895), 489; Collins, *Historical Sketches*, 279; William Birney, *James G. Birney and His Times* (New York, 1890), 25–27; CRB Book No. 5, pp. 9–10, in Prewitt Collection; Robert J. Breckinridge to Mary C. Breckinridge, April 3, 1832, in B. MSS. For a full account of Witherspoon's career see Vernon L. Collins, *President Witherspoon* (Princeton, 1925).

9. J. Cabell Breckinridge to James Breckinridge, February 2, 1813, photocopy, CRB Book No. 1, p. 26, in Prewitt Collection; Brown, *Cabells and Their Kin*, 489; Collins, *Historical Sketches*, 280; James Allen to Breckinridge, May 4, 1841, John J. Crittenden to J. Cabell Breckinridge, May 31, 1832, James G. Birney to J. Cabell Breckinridge, November, 1822, David Todd to J. Cabell Breckinridge, August 29, 1823, all in B. MSS; Niels Henry Sonne, *Liberal Kentucky, 1780–1828* (New York, 1939), 154.

10. Robert Stuart Sanders, *Sketch of Mount Horeb Presbyterian Church 1827–1952* (Lexington, 1952), 7–9; W. O. Shewmaker, *The Pisgah Book* (N.p., n.d.), 27–30; C. Frank Dunn, "The Breckinridges," *In Kentucky*, VII (Summer, 1942), 42; J. Winston Coleman, Jr., *Historic Kentucky* (Lexington, 1967), 119.

hear the result of the Missouri question," he wrote his brother Robert. "I fear that some of the eastern states and many of the eastern politicians meditate a dissolution of the Union. I can never remember when the bare mention of such an event filled my mind with [more] horror." In 1820 the election of his friend John Adair to the governorship resulted in Breckinridge's appointment as secretary of state. It was a prestigious, albeit not too influential, position and would require his full-time presence at the capital. Tired of being separated from his family, he decided to move from Thorn Hill to Frankfort. There was one obstacle to the move; Mary was pregnant again.[11]

Breckinridge probably remained in Lexington with his wife to await the baby's arrival. There, at Thorn Hill, she gave birth to their fourth child on January 16, 1821. David Castleman set about notifying absent relatives of the event. "Your Brother has a fine son," he wrote to Robert. Overjoyed, the family entertained great expectations for the new boy. "I hope he may make as great a man as his grandfather, for whom I am told he is named," wrote an aunt. Indeed, they did name the baby for his grandfather, and for his father as well, calling him John Cabell Breckinridge.[12]

The family remained in Lexington a few weeks while the baby gained his strength and then in February moved to Frankfort to live with Adair. For Polly Breckinridge, the sudden separation from her husband's namesake and only grandson was too much, and she soon went to the capital to visit. "My dear little babe is adorable well," she found, and soon she discovered that "little Breckinridge" was enchanted by the shrill whistles of the steamboats on the Kentucky River.[13]

The next two years saw Cabell's continued service with Adair, the birth of another daughter, Letitia, and the severe deterioration of his health. By the fall of 1823 his constitution was so weakened that he fell easily susceptible to a raging fever which swept the capital. It hit him late in August, and he sank fast, beyond the help of his physicians. Mary, too, was stricken,

11. J. Cabell Breckinridge to Robert J. Breckinridge, December 19, 1820, in B. MSS; Collins, *Historical Sketches*, 280.

12. Several historians have stated that Breckinridge was born "near Lexington," meaning Cabell's Dale. Fayette County court records reveal clearly, however, that he was born in Lexington at Thorn Hill. Breckinridge himself made reference to it several times in his public speeches. See Dunn, "The Breckinridges," 42; David Castleman to J. Cabell Breckinridge, March 8, 1821, Eliza Lewis to Mary C. Breckinridge, April 16, 1821, both in B. MSS.

13. John Adair to J. Cabell Breckinridge, February 16, 1821, J. Cabell Breckinridge to Robert J. Breckinridge, May 28, 1821, Mary H. Breckinridge to Robert J. Breckinridge, June 12, 1821, all in B. MSS.

and his brother John, now pastor of Lexington's McChord Presbyterian Church, ministered to them both. Cabell confided to his brother a willingness to die if it be God's will, and John sadly wrote that in "the last conversation I ever had with him he spoke with just agitation enough to show the tenderness and illumination of a Christian heart." On September 1, 1823, after a violent illness of little more than a week, Cabell Breckinridge died.[14]

The Breckinridge men seemed always to die young, and now once again a widow was left behind with her orphaned children and a difficult estate. Mary was grief-stricken at Cabell's death. Still ill herself, the tragedy so upset her that she lost yet another child that she was carrying, and John Breckinridge found her "the merest object of hope less woe." Her husband had left debts totaling almost $15,000. She needed time and rest, and to lighten her load she sent her son off to Princeton in October to stay with relatives. Once there he sent back word to "give my love to Aunt Mary, Mama, and everybody," boasted proudly that he was not sick once on the journey to New Jersey, and promised faithfully to write to his mother, quite a mouthful for a boy not yet three. The aunt with whom he stayed wrote that, "as for little Breckinridge, he is as fat and rosy as he ever can be. Breckinridge has won upon all of us already." [15]

The boy soon returned to his mother, and for the next several years they lived with Polly Breckinridge at Cabell's Dale. It was one of the grandest homes of the Bluegrass, its walls lined with portraits by Matthew Jouett and other American masters. The long, kind face of John Breckinridge looked down on his young grandson from one wall, while on another hung a portrait of the father that "little Breckinridge" never came to know. For a little boy, even greater influences lay outside in the estate's thick forest. An ancient Adena Indian village had once been here, and mounds laden with tomahawks and arrowheads lay in abundance on the grounds, food for a boy's imagination. Here began his abiding respect for the American Indian, his fascination with archaeology, and his passion for history.[16]

Here, too, he developed an intense respect for authority which he never

14. Castleman to J. Cabell Breckinridge, December 20, 1821, J. Cabell Breckinridge to Robert J. Breckinridge, June 24, 1821, Mary H. Breckinridge to Robert J. Breckinridge, December 20, 1821, Letitia Porter to J. Cabell Breckinridge, January 4, 1823, J. Cabell Harrison to Robert J. Breckinridge, September 4, 1823, John Breckinridge to Robert J. Breckinridge, September 23, 1823, all in B. MSS; Collins, *Historical Sketches*, 280.

15. Castleman to Robert J. Breckinridge, September 20, 1823, John Breckinridge to Robert J. Breckinridge, September 23, 1823, J. T. Salomon to Mary C. Breckinridge, November 2, 1823, all in B. MSS.

16. John B. Castleman, *Active Service* (Louisville, 1917), 323–24, 332; Collins, *Historical Sketches*, 294–95.

lost. It resulted from an atmosphere of devout Calvinist Presbyterianism. Uncles John and William were both in the ministry, now, and in 1827 Mount Horeb Presbyterian Church was founded in a drawing room at Cabell's Dale. All of the Breckinridges tutored the boy in the Bible and church dogma. He learned his lessons well, for during the rest of his life he exhibited a thorough familiarity with the Scriptures, particularly biblical history.[17]

By far the most profound influence upon little Breckinridge, however, and surely the one most responsible for instilling in him a keen sense of his own history and heritage, was Polly Breckinridge herself. Called Grandma Black Cap for the mourning bonnet she never set aside after her husband's death, this venerable lady was a link with an earlier era. Bad eyesight kept her from walking the grounds by herself, and her grandson was a favorite companion on her walks that always led to John Breckinridge's grave and then to the little law office he once used. "My son," she would say, " 'twas in this office that my husband would write to Tom Jefferson and to his other friends and it was here that my husband wrote the Kentucky Resolutions of 1798. 'Twas here that John Breckinridge transacted his private and public business." This teary-eyed old lady and her talk of the law and politics and the principles for which her husband fought so hard had a profound impact upon "little Breckinridge." [18]

He grew up an extremely sensitive child. Not yet three when Cabell Breckinridge died, he had almost no recollection of his father and would later search avidly to find what sort of man he had been. Then, when he was old enough to feel the pain, he lost two of his sisters, Mary Ann in 1827, and Frances ten years later. He lived in a house without men, subject to the teasing and tricks of older sisters, and to the sometime tyranny of a mother who never fully recovered her emotional stability after her husband's death. This, combined with a naturally sensitive personality, left young Breckinridge easily hurt, easily moved to tears. Years later he would look back on this period and remark that this exaggerated susceptibility "made life almost a burden." As he grew older he learned to conceal his emotions and to control his feelings, though never entirely. Meanwhile he found refuge in a mutually close attachment to his younger sister Letitia. They became friends and confidants. She understood him as did no one else in his young years. He had friends and playmates as well to brighten

17. Sanders, *Sketch of Mount Horeb*, 7–12; Castleman, *Active Service*, 49; Louisville *Courier-Journal*, June 18, 1875.
18. Castleman, *Active Service*, 31.

his days. Cousins Elizabeth and Peter Porter came to play, as did John J. Crittenden's sons Thomas and George. When in Lexington, Breckinridge played with pretty Mary Todd, daughter of his father's old friend Robert Todd.[19]

There was much to learn. Breckinridge's mother taught him to read and write, and when he was ten she sent him to Kentucky Academy, a church boarding school at Pisgah where he received a standard classical education. While he was away a major upheaval took place at Cabell's Dale. Amid a storm of accusation from both sides, his mother left Polly's house and moved in with his sister Mary's family in Danville. There had always been tension between Cabell's widow and the rest of the family, largely due to her haughty manners and sometime irascibility. Robert and Grandma Black Cap became the particular objects of her spite over a period of years. Robert simply washed his hands of Mary and her children, and his mother nearly did the same. "Let them all go," she told him. "Vengeance will overtake them. It makes me thankful their sainted father is in glory and dont know how they all carry on here." She derisively dubbed Mary "Madam," and declared, "Alas what a woman she is." "Madam" Breckinridge's overbearing manner even created a gap between her and Letitia, causing the girl so much difficulty that one uncle suggested that she be taken away from her mother. Fortunately, young John was away at school during much of this troubled time, but still he came in for his share. He and those who knew him best all agreed that his mother was chiefly responsible for shaping his character and purpose in life. Nevertheless, looking back on his childhood, Breckinridge would always regard his happiest days as those spent at school.[20]

In November, 1834, the young Kentuckian was ready to enter the freshman class at Danville's Centre College, also a Presbyterian school, which boasted a beautiful campus and, for a college west of the Alleghenies, a fine

19. Lexington *Kentucky Statesman*, April 19, 1853; Breckinridge to James G. Birney, September 6, 1853, in James G. Birney MSS, CLUM; Brown, *Cabells and Their Kin*, 490; Breckinridge to Ignatius Donnelly, August 14, 1852, in Ignatius Donnelly MSS, MHS; CRB Book No. 3, pp. 20–21, in Prewitt Collection; William H. Townsend, *Lincoln and the Bluegrass* (Lexington, 1955), 13.

20. Lexington *Kentucky Statesman*, May 6, 1853; Coleman, *Historic Kentucky*, 45; Shewmaker, *Pisgah Book*, 27–30; Sonne, *Liberal Kentucky*, 62–65; Mary H. Breckinridge to Robert J. Breckinridge, November 30, 1832, Porter to Robert J. Breckinridge, January 7, 1824, February 9, 1825, Robert J. Breckinridge to Mary C. Breckinridge, April 3, 1832, Robert J. Breckinridge to A. Sophonisba Breckinridge, December 13, 1837, all in B. MSS; CRB Book No. 3, pp. 6, 34, in Prewitt Collection.

library. An uncle, Dr. John Young, was president of the college, and William Breckinridge sat on its faculty. The student lived here with the president, becoming extremely fond of "Uncle Young," who in turn exerted much influence on his nephew. Young's Presbyterianism was heavily Calvinist, and he instilled in Breckinridge a rather fundamental view of man's natural tendency toward evil and the doctrine of original sin. A superb orator from whom Breckinridge learned much on the manner of public speaking, Young also reinforced the boy's ancestral position on slavery and the nature of the Union.[21]

The course of study at Centre was wide, leaning particularly to the classics, which Breckinridge loved. Indeed, he committed many of his readings to memory, particularly the orations of Demosthenes and Pericles. For the rest of his life he maintained a pleasant association with ancient literature and antiquities. He found too that things mechanical fascinated him. He here toyed more than once with the idea of making a career of engineering.[22]

When not in class or studying, Breckinridge spent most of his free time with his friends. Classmates included Thomas Crittenden, his close friend Samuel R. Bullock, a brilliant but restless boy named Theodore O'Hara, and William Birney, the son of his father's old companion James G. Birney. Breckinridge regarded young Birney as "my special friend and playmate," and was often at the Birney home to visit William and his brother David. Theirs was all manner of mischief, from driving ringbolts into the trees in Young's yard to hunting and shooting game on the college grounds. Breckinridge, a general favorite at school, seemed "full of pranks and boyish nonsense," recalled a friend. Yet he could be serious as well. He and William delighted in sitting together under a tree to read novels, particularly Cooper's *The Last of the Mohicans.* Young Birney, as he later said, loved the "blue-eyed, blue boy" Breckinridge as a brother. Meanwhile Birney's father, upon whom young Breckinridge made something of an impression, was vainly trying to start an antislavery newspaper in Danville. Here was Breckinridge's first real contact with an abolitionist, for James G. Birney had moved far away from the gradualism on which he and the Breckinridges once stood in agreement. Even now he was declaring that "It has

21. Collins, *Historical Sketches*, 205–206; Walter A. Groves, "Centre College—The Second Phase: 1830–1857," *Filson Club History Quarterly*, XXIV (October, 1950), 313–15, 325–26; CRB Book No. 3, p. 15, CRB Book No. 2, p. 15, in Prewitt Collection.
22. Centre's curriculum for 1838 is given in Groves, "Centre College," 325.

now become absolutely necessary that slavery shall cease. . . . *Slavery shall be exterminated* or *Liberty destroyed.*" [23]

The student learned much in his four years at Centre, and made a lasting impression on his faculty and fellow students. One of the latter declared to him that, for "brilliancy of parts, readiness of wit, a happy force and luxuriance of imagination, acuteness in argument and felicity of expression, as a gentleman, scholar, statesman or a companion," no one could be compared with him. "For what is remarkable," the friend went on, "your lordship's modesty is exceeded only by your worth." His "lordship" was a fast and able student, and soon discovered the limits of his endurance at study, and the necessity of a sound body for a sound mind. "I knew a young man at college," he would one day write, "who thought he studied sixteen hours a day, when in truth from want of exercise and his bowels being moved only about twice a week he was all the time in a stupid, half conscious condition." Exercise and "daily regularity *in a particular habit*," he decided, held the key to physical and mental fitness. Both served him well at college, and in September, 1838, he received his bachelor of arts degree in a graduating class of fourteen. Sometime before, he made a rare visit to Cabell's Dale, and there Grandma Black Cap was happy to find that "Cabell's John is . . . much grown and I hope will be a credit to the name." [24]

By this time, despite their animosity toward his mother, the student's family began taking a considerable interest in his development. Several had sent him money to help with school expenses, and now his Uncle Robert, pastor of a congregation in Baltimore, came forward. He invited his nephew to come live with him and perhaps do some graduate work at the College of New Jersey in Princeton. Breckinridge accepted and immediately went east. He spent six months at Princeton as a resident graduate, the only non-alumnus in the graduate school, though he neither sought nor received any degree. His mind was already set on a career at the law, and at Princeton

23. "Theodore O'Hara," *Confederate Veteran*, VII (May, 1899), 202; Breckinridge to James G. Birney, September 6, 1853, in Birney MSS; David Birney to Breckinridge, May 21, 1855, William Birney to Breckinridge, January 1, 1853, May 3, 1854, Thomas L. Crittenden to Breckinridge, August 14, 1841, all in B. MSS; Cabell Bullock, "Major General John C. Breckinridge, C.S.A." (MS in Prewitt Collection); Birney, *James G. Birney*, 184–85.

24. Breckinridge to Clifton R. Breckinridge, October 7, 1867, in JCB Papers; Mary H. Breckinridge to Robert J. Breckinridge, April 21, 1836, Joseph B. Townsend to Breckinridge, February 23, 1841, Mary H. Breckinridge to Letitia Breckinridge, February 23, 1838, all in B. MSS; Groves, "Centre College," 325–28; *General Catalogue of the Centre College of Kentucky* (Danville, 1890), 131; *Congressional Globe*, 32nd Cong., Appendix, 383.

he concentrated primarily on a course of study to prepare him to read under some established jurist. He took time, also, to join the largely southern Whig Society, a literary and oratorical group. Already he was developing into an able public speaker. He found that address came naturally to him.[25]

During these months there grew a strong bond of affection between Breckinridge and his uncle. Indeed, Robert eventually came to be almost a father to the young man and a profound influence on his life. Robert Jefferson Breckinridge now was an agent for the American Colonization Society, an organization devoted to the emancipation of slaves and the founding of a separate black nation in Liberia. These were no abolitionists. They believed in voluntary manumission and in raising funds to purchase freedom for others. While John C. Breckinridge would never join the society, still his sympathy for it bred at his uncle's always led him to support its efforts. Meanwhile, Robert's deep religious associations further reinforced Breckinridge's Presbyterian upbringing, though it could not prevent him and the rest of the family some embarrassment over his nonattendance at Danville's First Presbyterian Church. Of course, he had been away at Princeton for several months, and, considering himself "no longer worthy of being a member of the church," he asked that his name be dropped from its rolls. This was not enough for the church elders, though. Instead they officially suspended him "until he gives evidence of penitence." While his rearing had instilled in Breckinridge a deep reverence for the church, the Scriptures, and the Lord, throughout life he would be a sporadic churchgoer, content more with the faith than the forms of religion.[26]

Two other definite areas in which Robert influenced his nephew were law and politics, by now ancestral preoccupations. Robert had served at both before going into the ministry, and immediately upon returning to Kentucky young Breckinridge made arrangements to read law under Judge William Owsley, a prominent Whig jurist and politician. "I always had a preference for the law," the student wrote to his uncle, "and thus far I have no reason to regret my choice." Owsley worked him hard, making him read Blackstone twice then sending him into Kent's *Commentaries*, but after six

25. Breckinridge to Robert J. Breckinridge, October 24, 1838, John Breckinridge to Breckinridge, January 26, 1841, Mary H. Breckinridge to Robert J. Breckinridge, October 26, 1838, L. E. Peterson to Breckinridge, February 9, 1854, all in B. MSS; *Catalogue of the College of New Jersey, 1838–39* (Princeton, 1839), cited by A. H. Thomas in a letter to the author, March 6, 1967; Thomas J. Wertenbaker, *Princeton: 1746–1896* (Princeton, 1946), 206–208, 214.

26. John Carroll to Robert J. Breckinridge, July 14, 1831, in B. MSS; Louisville *Christian Observer*, August 7, 1935.

months Breckinridge could report progress: "I am much pleased with the study of law, and having worked the science with something like shape and symmetry, in my mind, I begin to apprehend with some clearness, the leanings of one part of it upon another, and the great principles which govern the system. Many things, which formerly appeared rough and misty to my mind, are now clearly defined, and accurately understood; but there is still a good deal of mist ahead, which application alone can dissapate [sic]."

Apply himself he did. Seven hours a day he read law, then turned to history and literature for three more hours, all the while suffering from ill health. Later he increased his law to eight hours. "In that length of time, my mind accumulates as much as it can manage and becomes exhausted." No doubt he paid continued attention to daily regularity in his "particular habit" as well.[27]

All the while that he read under Owsley, Breckinridge also kept up on state politics, showing special concern for state appropriations for schools. With the rest of the family he was pleased when a measure to repeal the slave law of 1833 failed, thus insuring the continued ban on importation of slaves into Kentucky. And he seemed particularly interested in the current campaign for the governorship, remarking with perception that Robert P. Letcher, the Whig candidate, owed his popularity to his "lively person and jovial demeanor." This understanding of Letcher would serve him well one day.[28]

When he finished studying with Owsley, Breckinridge decided to add further to his training by spending a year in the law department at Lexington's Transylvania University, one of the finest schools in the West. Its law faculty, including the eminent professors, George Robertson and Thomas Marshall, was among the most distinguished, and Breckinridge found that "The lectures are much more instructive than I anticipated, and the professors express themselves pleased with the class." Robertson was particularly eloquent, often discoursing on his views of the Union and slavery, views which coincided with those of the Breckinridge family.[29]

Finally came February 25, 1841, and graduation. Breckinridge received his LL.B. degree with exceptional marks: 100 in "behavior," 100 in "indus-

27. Breckinridge to Robert J. Breckinridge, February 17, April 20, June 16, 1840, in B. MSS.

28. Ibid., February 17, June 16, 1840.

29. Ibid., August 30, December 24, 1840; Collins, Historical Sketches, 267; Robert Peter, Transylvania University (Louisville, 1896), 168. For a complete account of Robertson's life and thought see George Robertson, An Outline of the Life of George Robertson (Lexington, 1876), and George Robertson, Scrap Book on Law & Politics, Men & Times (Lexington, 1855).

try," and 98 in "scholarship." "This is very fine," wrote Robert, and the next day young Breckinridge went before the Kentucky Court of Appeals and was found "duly qualified to practice as an attorney and counsellor at law." He could take some pride in his progress thus far: a college graduate at seventeen and now a licensed lawyer when barely past twenty. But the fact that he had been forced to rely on support from his family to get through school rankled, and he was anxious to get out on his own and start practicing. Searching for a likely place to hang his shingle, he settled on Frankfort. It had surprisingly few lawyers, most of them had little skill, and Owsley thought it a fine opening. As for Breckinridge, he felt sanguine over his prospects, though hardly boastful. "I think that I am very far from being a fine lawyer," he wrote his uncle, "yet I think I am sufficiently acquainted with the principles of the science and well enough versed in its details to prevent me from committing eggregious [sic] blunders, even at the start. I know that procuring a license will not make a man a lawyer and that when I take out the former I will not be the latter. Indeed long study and much practice alone will make one a skillful and accurate lawyer." [30]

Other aspects of his future vied with the law for Breckinridge's attention. He was in love. The girl is something of a mystery, though her name seems to have been Susan C. Green, regarded by some as Lexington's most lovely belle. He definitely meant to marry her, and she could hardly have been indifferent toward him. John C. Breckinridge had grown into a very handsome young man. He was six feet and two inches tall and carried his 175 pounds on a square-shouldered, slim, well-proportioned frame. His full face was clean-shaven with a firm jaw and a broad forehead from which he brushed back thick, almost black hair. He had a wide, rigid mouth and a nose almost Roman in size and form. His large, deep-set eyes were a shade of blue that sometimes seemed black. Breckinridge himself would say, "I have no beauty," but friends disagreed, remarking on his "tall and manly person, graceful carriage, polite address, impressive countenance and dignified and imposing presence." [31]

Breckinridge announced his intended matrimony to many of his friends and family, and then moved to Frankfort to look for an office and get his practice under way. He soon fell ill again, but he was not too sick to accept

30. Breckinridge to Robert J. Breckinridge, February 1, 1841, Robert J. Breckinridge to Breckinridge, February 28, 1842, License of John C. Breckinridge, February 26, 1841, all in B. MSS.

31. "W. A." to Breckinridge, February 16, 1841, Samuel W. Stevenson to Breckinridge, March 4, 1842, Townsend to Breckinridge, February 23, 1841, all in B. MSS; New York *Turf, Field and Farm*, May 21, 1875; Lexington *Kentucky Statesman*, May 6, 1853; Breckinridge to Donnelly, August 14, 1852, in Donnelly MSS.

a very important invitation. Perhaps because of his widely respected family name, his speaking ability in college, and Owsley's recommendation, Breckinridge was asked to deliver the main address at the state celebration of the Fourth of July. He could hardly refuse—a young man not yet in his majority invited to give the keynote oration of a grand state affair.[32]

On the Fourth, a hot, dry day, several hundred ladies and gentlemen filled the hall of the House of Representatives in Frankfort. They heard a traditional reading of the Declaration of Independence, and then came the principal speaker. For the next half hour "Mr. Breckinridge entertained his audience with a speech characterized alike for its chasteness of diction, its patriotic sentiment, pure morality, and sound philosophy." He disdained the popular "spread eagle" theme and, instead, probed thoughtfully into the origins of freedom and the concept of the rights of man. In particular he stressed the role played by a free press and the absolute necessity for the maintenance of its liberty. "If its *freedom* be destroyed," he declared, "from being the greatest promoter of truth and right—it becomes the strongest engine of terror and oppression. . . . Let the liberty of the press and the liberty of the country hold an equal place in the hearts of all citizens, for the existence of the one is involved in that of the other." [33]

The main thrust of his speech turned around freedom and its component parts, knowledge and virtue. "A nation possessing both these elements," he said, "cannot continue to be slaves, and one wanting them both cannot be free. . . . They are free whom the truth makes free and all are slaves beside." While he never actually touched on Negro slavery in the address, much of his discussion obviously pointed toward it. He spoke not only of political oppression by tyrants, but of physical "unlawful dominion over the *bodies* . . . of men." By now he regarded slavery as a genuine evil visited upon the nation by the Founding Fathers, a mistake which saddled the country with a heavy weight of guilt. This did not necessarily mean that the black and white man were equals. The Negro was inferior by education and, perhaps, by race, but still he was entitled to something better than slavery. It was spiritually and morally degrading. At the same time, however, he believed with all those who so influenced his upbringing that government had no power to interfere with the institution. Slaves were still property, and interference would be tyranny.

The way to avoid tyranny, he said, was for a vigilant, educated public

32. "W. A." to Breckinridge, February 16, 1841, Robert J. Breckinridge to Breckinridge, May 29, 1841, Theodore Prevost to Breckinridge, March 15, 1841, all in B. MSS.
33. Frankfort *Commonwealth*, July 7, 1841; manuscript of speech made on July 4, 1841, in B. MSS.

to choose thoughtfully its leaders. In light of the events of years to come, the views Breckinridge here expressed on the requirements for a public servant are meaningful. "In a public man, industry is desirable—ability not less so—but above all let him be an honest man; he who wants this essential constituent of rectitude is unfit to be entrusted with the interests of others. . . . Seek those for honor and trust who are worthy of your confidence, and consider no man worthy who cannot abide the political test of Mr. Jefferson: 'Is he honest, is he capable, is he faithful?' "

The people must guard against all who sought power for the sake of ambition. They must beware the man whose "fidelity reposes on the brittle thread which binds him to popular opinion." Indeed, though he did not say so, he had definite feelings on the dangers of what he was himself doing before them. Oratory, he felt, could be a dangerous tool. A man's eloquence should be used only to protect rights, reform abuses, and control men's passions; not as an elegant art or entertainment for cultivated minds, for this could give rise to demagoguery. It was a remarkable attitude for one of his blossoming oratorical abilities, and it explains why, throughout life, he rarely ever accepted an invitation to *entertain* an audience with a speech. As he now told his listeners in his final remarks, "The transient honors of him who has no other aim than his own aggrandisement, sear like the leaf and perish away. The breath of the multitude may extinguish, as it can create, the temporary gleam that hovers around the brow of a party leader —but the more abiding renown of the patriot and philanthropist is as enduring as the memory of man, and gathers brightness from time." [34]

Nothing that he said was new. Indeed, as one of his sons would write years later, no man was less revolutionary in his views and temperament than this Kentuckian. He was almost an archetype Jeffersonian, a firm but not inflexible Calvinist, and most of all an optimist. He saw good people ruling themselves by education, enlightenment, and by ruling as little as possible. The good people of Frankfort heartily approved of his initial oration, and the capital press complimented an obvious friend. He stepped down from the rostrum, and with the rest walked down the street to the Mansion House where dinner awaited. There Breckinridge enjoyed the food and drink and the talk about patriots of old and the road to independence, of an age now past which could never die, and of men long dead who lived forever.[35]

34. CRB Book No. 4, pp. 49–50, CRB Book No. 2, pp. 3–4, in Prewitt Collection; Louisville *Courier-Journal*, June 18, 1875.

35. CRB Book No. 2, pp. 2–3, 22, in Prewitt Collection; Frankfort *Commonwealth*, July 7, 1841.

CHAPTER 2

You Are a Glorious Democrat

The Fourth of July speech was about all that went well for Breckinridge that summer. He ran out of money, proved unsuccessful in finding an office in Frankfort, and finally saw his intended Miss Green transfer her affections to another. The cumulative effect of all this was a melancholy which stayed with Breckinridge for several months. A visit to relatives in Virginia in the fall did not help, and when the young lawyer returned to Lexington he did so with farther horizons in mind. For years stories of the richness and beauty of the newly settled Iowa Territory had filtered back to Kentucky. Many of its burgeoning towns, particularly Burlington on the Mississippi River, sounded like good prospects for a fledgling lawyer, and the change could help him forget his sorrow. One who later knew Breckinridge well believed that a strong attraction was that Iowa, under the Missouri Compromise, was free territory where slavery was banned by law. For all of these reasons he decided to try his fortune in the new country. Friends and relatives encouraged him, and an old family friend, Senator John J. Crittenden, lent the young man his personal three-hundred-book law library. Just before Breckinridge's departure, Crittenden also sent him a letter in which, to the young man's astonishment, the statesman predicted that he would one day welcome Breckinridge as a member of Congress.[1]

By October 10, 1841, he was ready to go. After borrowing $100 from his Uncle Young for traveling money, Breckinridge said his goodbyes,

1. Theodore Prevost to Breckinridge, May 15, 1841, Samuel W. Stevenson to Breckinridge, March 4, 1842, W. D. Green to Breckinridge, January 9–10, 1842, P. Cabell Breckinridge to A. Sophonisba Breckinridge, September 14, 1841, John C. Breckinridge, "Catalogue of Books I Have Received from Hon. John J. Crittenden," May 15, 1841, all in B. MSS; Breckinridge to Mrs. C. M. Coleman, April 16, 1869, in John J. Crittenden MSS, DU; James G. Blaine, *Twenty Years in Congress* (Norwich, Conn., 1884), I, 322.

mounted his favorite horse, "Fidler," and headed west. His cousin, Thomas Bullock, a young lawyer just out of school accompanied him. They had intended to go directly to Burlington, but passing through Illinois they were struck by the country around Jacksonville, where Breckinridge had inherited a small piece of land. The two lawyers were tempted to settle there until they learned of Jacksonville's full bar. One of the town's lawyers was the secretary of state at Springfield, Stephen A. Douglas. Another from the area, suffering the pains of a broken engagement to Breckinridge's childhood playmate Mary Todd, was Abraham Lincoln. Bullock and Breckinridge, ambitious and interested in politics, felt they should definitely look elsewhere to begin their careers.[2]

Once in Burlington the lawyers were obviously pleased; "the best position of the West," Breckinridge called it. The courts did a lively business, and Breckinridge was confident. "No doubt I shall suffer many of the trials and hardships incident to a new country," he wrote home, "but if I can preserve my health I have the strongest confidence in attaining my wishes and supporting the honour of our name." He found accommodations expensive and finally took a tiny room in a private home. "I think I have done wisely," he wrote. His furnishings were a straw mattress and a broom, and the room was soon dubbed the "den of iniquity."[3]

The firm of Breckinridge and Bullock was not an overnight success. Business was slow, and relatives back east began trying to get their kinsman an appointment in the federal patronage. Robert thought little of the idea and so did his nephew. "I cannot solicit such a gift for myself," wrote the lawyer. He preferred to establish his career without political favors. Of course, this did not mean he had lost his interest in politics. Indeed, his friends, like Crittenden, continued to see public office in his future. "Will John C. Breckinridge, ten years hence," wrote one, "be [an] honorable representative ... in the Congress of the U.S.? ... Stranger things have happened."[4]

Business did pick up after a time, though when receipts sometimes came in the form of beets, potatoes, and onions, the company coffers hardly bulged. Still Breckinridge was hopeful and determined. "I don't expect to

2. Note of Breckinridge with John C. Young, October 10, 1841, in JCB Papers; Breckinridge to Robert J. Breckinridge, November 14, 1841, in B. MSS.

3. Breckinridge to Robert J. Breckinridge, November 14, 1841, Oliver Cock to Breckinridge, November 5, 1844, Letitia Breckinridge to Breckinridge, December 20, 1841, E. M. Vaughn to Breckinridge, December 26, 1841, all in B. MSS.

4. Mary C. Breckinridge to Breckinridge, November 14, 1841, Robert J. Breckinridge to Breckinridge, December 6, 1841, Breckinridge to Robert J. Breckinridge, January 5, 1842, Stevenson to Breckinridge, December 13, 1841, all in B. MSS.

leave Iowa for several years," he resolved, "even on a short visit." Consequently, the only ties with home were the frequent letters he received. He must write more, they said. He must always put his coat on when going out. He must not let his disposition for fun get him into trouble, and he must absolutely stop calling temperance crusaders "humbugs." Mary Breckinridge was devoted to the temperance cause, and chafed at her son's irreverence. When the movement reached Burlington in 1842, however, his mind changed. "The rude eloquence of these men was every effective," he wrote of reformed sots now stumping for the movement. He never ridiculed them again. Fortunately, not all of the letters from home were full of motherly fussing. Sometimes they brought word of interesting visitors, among them Senator Crittenden. The senator and his family continued to praise Breckinridge's independence and fortitude. The consensus among the Crittendens was that he would one day return from Iowa to flourish in Kentucky, a great man.[5]

The great man would have been contented to flourish a little more in Iowa. Meanwhile, when business was slack and time seemed abundant, he enjoyed what social life Burlington could offer. By March, 1842, when he received word of Susan Green's marriage, he was already enjoying the company of several of the town's young ladies. From one family three sisters showed a great deal of interest in him, but he found one too ugly and the others too old. There were more attractive girls to call on, and he enjoyed himself as the pain of his jilting subsided. Meanwhile, his mother worried, yet unable to accept the fact that her son was now a man in his majority, independent, and on his own. "You may find yourself in a dilemma some of these days," she warned, "if you receive the *attentions* of ladies you don't mean to have." [6]

Robert J. Breckinridge was now editing a journal of religious and anti-slavery tracts called the *Spirit of the XIX Century*, and he suggested that his nephew prepare an article for it about Iowa and its people. Breckinridge agreed to write the piece, and in the April, 1842, issue it appeared: "Iowa Territory—Its Condition, Resources, Population and Wants." It was his

5. Breckinridge to Robert J. Breckinridge, February 4, 1842, Mary C. Breckinridge to Breckinridge, November 14, 1841, January 4, March 7, n.d. [June], 1842, Thomas L. Crittenden to Breckinridge, August 14, 1841, Letitia Breckinridge to Breckinridge, November 25, December 20, 1841, March 29, 1842, all in B. MSS.

6. Mary C. Breckinridge to Breckinridge, December 19, 1841, March 7, 1842, Stevenson to Breckinridge, March 4, 1842, Silas A. Henderson to Breckinridge, March 22, 1842, Letitia Breckinridge to Breckinridge, December 20, 1841, all in B. MSS.

first publication and, with the exception of a few political paragraphs, his last. In it he betrayed his own concerns and feelings for the territory, going far beyond the travelogue his uncle had in mind.

In the article Breckinridge decried the dearth of talented statesmen in the new country, the men needed to organize it, and set its political tone. Good, honest men were needed, for law and order were undependable in this raw frontier. In particular, he lamented over the condition of the Indian, once the monarch of this fertile land; the white man had all but destroyed him. The conquerors' promises had been hollow, but the result was inevitable anyway. Looking back across history, he realized that every people who had stood in the way of the Anglo-Saxon advance had been consumed. With a measure of bitterness—and a thinly veiled reference to slavery—he declared that his race "has established freedom for itself—but it has wrested from others, this, their dearest birth-right; it has founded and maintained the purest principles of civil and religious liberty ... and then has said, worship God as your conscience dictates, but yield up your civil liberty, your prosperity, all your rights, if need be—to our power. It fastens the fetters of oppression, even as the noblest maxims of truth and right are uttered from its lips." He hoped that the good deeds of his race would eventually cover the memory "of the wrong and suffering it has inflicted."

Iowa, he continued, "holds within itself the elements of future greatness, but the direction of their development is as yet uncertain." Along with public leaders who would counteract the evil done by the white man's march west, it also needed religious leaders to build the moral and spiritual fiber of the territory, and preferably Protestant leaders at that. Catholicism had already reached the new land, and the authoritarianism of Rome was anathema to all Breckinridges. The regal hierarchy and kingly decrees of that church ran counter to his nature, and he bemoaned that the Papal minions' "wicked influences are sowing the seeds of evil; error is more zeal-ous than truth; its ministers labour with untiring activity to poison the pub-lic heart." Fortunately this attitude would mellow considerably as Breckin-ridge grew older.

Iowa did not need a superman, he concluded; he did not believe in super-men. "I know that one man, or two, or three cannot mould the destiny of a country; a distinguished man is rather the index than the author of the condition of his times—mankind moves forward, rather by common im-pulse, than by the impelling power of one intellect; and great movements and happy results are produced by a combination of many minds, rather than by the superior efforts of one." He was a true democrat, and in democracy he saw Iowa's future secure.[7]

Robert was very pleased with the article, as were his readers, at least one of whom was persuaded by it to move to the territory. By the time the article appeared, however, Breckinridge was preoccupied with other things than praise for his efforts. Early in April he witnessed a brief verbal encounter at Burlington's post office. There was talk of a duel, and the young lawyer did his best to dissuade one party from challenging another, but to no avail. The two antagonists met again that night, and soon one was dead. Breckinridge, unlike many young men of his time and place, found dueling repugnant, and throughout life, despite insults, he never stooped to a challenge to finish what words began. He was resolved never to engage in such a form to settle his personal differences. Consequently, when a town meeting was called over the affair, Breckinridge attended and was elected to a committee to draft resolutions. After half an hour's deliberation the committee returned, pronouncing that "we consider the practice [of dueling] unchristian, ungentlemanly, and in the highest degree reprehensible." Furthermore, the dead man's antagonist was summarily directed to leave the territory. This frontier justice was harsh, but effective, and Breckinridge concurred wholeheartedly.[8]

The youthful law firm continued to grow, though slowly, and as summer came on John Breckinridge found a new diversion to fill his abundant free time. He was occasionally accused of being indolent, too fond of pleasure, and now he gave his accusers fresh ammunition by accepting an invitation to join a band of Sauk and Fox warriors on what he ever after called "the *Buffaloe hunt!*" His empathy with the Indian led him to befriend those about Burlington, and they returned his kindness. He was taken on a memorable hunt. Its most outstanding moment came when he attended a council meeting and heard an address by the mighty chief Keokuk. Breckinridge understood not a word of it, but remained inspired to the end of his days by the scene of this red man standing on a low mound speaking to his people. After walking among the greatest orators of his century, Breckin-

---

7. Robert J. Breckinridge to Breckinridge, December 6, 1841, in B. MSS; *Spirit of the XIX Century*, II (April, 1842), 184–88.

8. Robert J. Breckinridge to Breckinridge, March 29, 1842, David Smith to Breckinridge, April 9, 1842, in B. MSS; Burlington *Hawkeye and Iowa Patriot*, April 14, May 5, 1842; CRB Book No. 9, pp. 111–12, in Prewitt Collection; Louisville *Courier-Journal*, June 18, 1875.

ridge would still recall, "In person, voice and manner the chief was the most impressive man he had ever seen." [9]

The hunting was poor this trip, and the younger spirits in the group began to seek diversion. In Breckinridge's tent was a cook whom he called "a little dried up Frenchman, or what passed for a Frenchman," who had a mortal fear of rattlesnakes. One night, as the cook fussed over his pots, Breckinridge crept up behind him and shook a rattle just behind the Frenchman. Cookie jumped straight up in the air, ran through the fire, pots and all, and scrambled to safety, all to the tune of Breckinridge's laughter. Only then did the cook realize that his assailant was not a rattler, but a snake in the grass.

The Frenchman was no believer in forgive and forget, and he waited his time for revenge. Soon he had the camp buzzing with rumors that the Sioux were in the vicinity, and for days the hunters were vigilant, unmindful that their Indian companions, mortal enemies of the Sioux, were unruffled by the supposed danger. Guards were posted at night, and the cook told them what to look for—grass shaking around the camp, a furtive head popping up and down in the brush, sure signs that the Sioux were about. Finally Breckinridge's turn came to stand watch one night at 11 P.M., "an hour when good indians are apt to be asleep," he thought. Their camp was surrounded by high grass, and Cookie had warned him that this was "a condition favorable for secret and hostile approach."

As Breckinridge sat his post, musket in hand, the grass waved gently in the night breezes, and the stars gave the whole frontier scene a bluish light. Suddenly a tuft of grass shook, then another, and soon it was rustling in several spots. A small, undiscernible head appeared only to dart back down immediately. More such movements followed. Thoroughly aroused, the Kentuckian raced to the nearest tent, the Frenchman's. "Wake up! Wake up! The Sioux are around the camp. . . . You little fool. Don't you hear me? Wake up I say." Finally the drowsy Frenchman opened his eyes. "You say the Sioux are about the camp?" he asked. "How do you know?"

"I saw the grass shaking in spots and places and heads bob up and down, just as you said they would. Get out of here before they make a rush. Tell the camp."

"Oh! Mr. Breckinridge, dont bother me," the cook exclaimed. "When

9. Breckinridge to Robert J. Breckinridge, April 26, July 12, 1842, Mary C. Breckinridge to Breckinridge, n.d. [June], 1842, Breckinridge to H. T. Hugins, October 10, 1843, in B. MSS; Lexington *Kentucky Statesman*, May 6, 1853; Cabell Bullock, "John C. Breckinridge," CBR Book No. 2, pp. 29–30, in Prewitt Collection.

you have been out here longer you will know the difference between an Indian dog and a Sioux indian!" Suddenly it dawned on Breckinridge. He had been set up, from the false rumors to the customary antics of camp dogs. The cook had his revenge, and the Kentuckian had a story he would love to tell on himself for the rest of his life. Hearing of the hunt, a friend wrote, "I should have liked to have seen John on his prancing Fidler with his bright fusee slung around him and his eyes glancing arrows of death and desolation on all things terrestrial—a perfect terror to beasts and Indians." [10]

It was well for the perfect terror that he was in Iowa this summer and fall, for the family in Kentucky, through rumor and newspapers, learned of his politics. "You have become loco foco," wrote Uncle Young. William Breckinridge reacted more harshly. "I felt as I would have done if I had heard that my daughter had been dishonored." Almost by decree, the Breckinridges were Whigs, descendants of John Breckinridge's Democratic-Republican party of Jefferson. It was a weak party from the start, divided by northern antislavery and the protective tariff on one hand, and southern intrenchment on slavery and free trade on the other. Only interest in the West really united Whigs, that and the greatest Whig of them all, Lexington's Henry Clay. [11]

John C. Breckinridge, however, slipped somewhat from the mold. In his college associations—particularly what William Breckinridge called "the Princeton College influence"—he came into contact with a new generation that had grown away from Whiggery, inspired instead by the greatest living hero and movement of his times, Jackson and his Democracy. Caught up in this new, yet essentially conservative, movement as it swept the South, Breckinridge was an easy convert. "You were two thirds of a democrat before you left [for Iowa]," Bullock told his partner, and Breckinridge himself declared that he was a thorough Democrat when studying under Owsley. His Iowa associations further reinforced his leanings, for Burlington was predominantly Democratic, and the increasingly outspoken attacks of northern Whigs on southern institutions, particularly slavery, served well to drive him further from the old party. Finally, Whiggery had always been somewhat equivocal, well illustrated by Young's admonition that his nephew not align himself so staunchly with any cause or faction for fear that its fall might take him with it. This was not for Breckinridge. While

10. CRB Book No. 4, pp. 24–25, in Prewitt Collection; J. S. Erwin to Breckinridge and Bullock, August 27, 1842, in B. MSS.
11. John Young to Breckinridge, April 25, 1842, in B. MSS.

he did hold fast to some of the more liberal tenets espoused by the Whigs, he was a Democrat for life, now, and proud of it.[12]

Once past the initial shock of Breckinridge's defection, his family and friends felt an earnest concern lest his politics, coupled with his rising popularity in Burlington, tempt him to be reckless. They feared he would run for some office. "I hear that you are very popular & that you will probably soon be in politics," wrote Young. "Do withstand that temptation." The family need not have worried as they did, though Breckinridge's name appeared more and more in the pages of Burlington's Democratic organ, the *Territorial Gazette*. He attended the mass meetings and Democratic rallies, sometimes addressed the assemblies, and even wrote an occasional editorial such as "Clay and Adams Compared." But this was all. He believed that a public man should have "*decision of character*," and for his part he was still decided to succeed first at the law.[13]

All through the hard winter that followed, business increased to the point that success seemed assured. "Mr. Bullock plus myself stand fourth or fifth in the number of suits out of about twenty lawyers," he wrote home, "and our prospects are as flattering as we could hope for." It was about time, too. The winter wind whistled through the cracks in the "den of iniquity" with such intensity that snow often blew in on the floor, forcing Breckinridge deeper within the folds of his buffalo robe. Better business could mean better lodgings. Meanwhile, he prospered socially as well. He took an interest in Masonry, joined Des Moines Lodge No. 41, Grand Lodge of Missouri, Knights Templar, soon rose to senior warden, received his first three degrees in Masonry, and was certified a Master Mason. Political interests kept him active in Burlington society and, of course, there were the ladies. The harsh winter of 1842–1843 passed on into spring.[14]

When Breckinridge first went to Iowa, he intended to remain at least three or four years before visiting Kentucky, wishing, in his youthful pride, to come back a triumphant success. Now, though, his prospects proved better than he originally expected, and this, combined with the an-

12. CRB Book No. 4, pp. 1–29 *passim*, in Prewitt Collection; Bullock to Breckinridge, October 6, 1842, Young to Breckinridge, April 25, 1842, in B. MSS; Lexington *Kentucky Statesman*, April 26, 1851.

13. Mary C. Breckinridge to Breckinridge, May 21, October 4, 1842, Bullock to Breckinridge, October 6, 1842, Stevenson to Breckinridge, June 1, 1842, in B. MSS; CRB Book No. 3, pp. 25, 51, CRB Book No. 4, pp. 15–16, 28, in Prewitt Collection.

14. *New Age Magazine*, n.d., 721–22, copy in CRB Book No. 2, p. 28, in Prewitt Collection; certificate of Breckinridge as a Master Mason, October 23, 1843, Breckinridge to Robert J. Breckinridge, March 16, 1843, Mary C. Breckinridge to Breckinridge, December 19, 1841, all in B. MSS.

guish he knew his absence caused his mother, decided him. He determined to go east for a few weeks in May. At least in part, his determination was influenced by his sister Letitia. For some time now she had been scheming to find her brother a wife, and if he returned to Lexington, she threatened to promptly have him married. That was one challenge that Breckinridge would accept.[15]

Apparently he never had a chance. Before the summer was out Letitia had done her work, and the lawyer found himself postponing his return to Iowa due to "the indulgence of my own feelings." The object of his indulgence was pretty Mary Cyrene Burch, seventeen-year-old cousin of Thomas Bullock. The courtship was a fast one, and by September they were engaged.[16]

Breckinridge and his bride-to-be decided to make their home in Kentucky, and before he could wed, he had to return to Burlington to close out his affairs. Ties to Iowa were strong, however, and painful to break. Friends there urged him to stay, and one competitor at the bar even offered to turn over to Breckinridge all of his business if he would remain. A close friend, Oliver Cock, said that if the Kentuckian would stay, his "private and political horizon" would be unlimited. "You cannot form any just conception of the estimations in which the people of this county hold you," another would write after Breckinridge left. As expressed by many influential Burlingtonians, the likelihood was strong that, if the lawyer remained, Iowa would fulfill Crittenden's prophecy and send Breckinridge to Congress.[17]

He settled his accounts in Burlington, divided the company's assets—sixty-eight dollars—and dissolved the firm of Breckinridge and Bullock, getting back to Lexington in time to set up a new partnership with a classmate from Centre College, Samuel R. Bullock, Thomas' cousin. It was agreed that Bullock would handle the firm's business in Lexington, and Breckin-

15. Breckinridge to Robert J. Breckinridge, November 10, 1842, May 29, 1843, Letitia Breckinridge to Breckinridge, May 8, 1843, in B. MSS.

16. Breckinridge to Robert J. Breckinridge, May 29, August 12–13, October 9, 1843, Letitia Breckinridge to Breckinridge, October 7, 1843, in B. MSS; Mary B. Maltby, *Mary Cyrene Breckinridge* (Georgetown, Ky., 1910), 1; Breckinridge to Henry Asbury, October 19, 1857, in John C. Breckinridge MSS, CHS.

17. Mary H. Breckinridge to Breckinridge, December, 1843, in CRB Book No. 5, pp. 5–6, in Prewitt Collection; Breckinridge to Robert J. Breckinridge, October 9, December 29, 1843, Cock to Breckinridge, February 29, March 10, 1844, James Carr to Breckinridge, March 13, 1845, Enos Lowe to Breckinridge, November 12, 1851, in B. MSS; *Biographical Sketches of Hon. John C. Breckinridge and General Joseph Lane*, Breckinridge and Lane Campaign Document No. 8 (Washington, 1860), 6.

ridge would take their cases in nearby Georgetown, where he and Mary decided to settle. Then, on December 12, 1843, wearing a new twelve-dollar coat, John C. Breckinridge married Mary Burch. The marriage suffered a dismal beginning, however. The lawyer spent the entire honeymoon suffering from chills and fever.[18]

For a note for $1,250 Breckinridge bought a modest house on the southwest corner of Georgetown's Main and South streets, and here they set up housekeeping. It was a small town, but provided enough business for its nine or ten lawyers. For $40 Breckinridge rented an office and announced in the newspapers that the firm of Bullock and Breckinridge was ready to practice. The firm prospered from the start, and the newlywed lawyer found himself in comfortable circumstances for the first time, a far cry from the windswept "den of iniquity." By the end of 1844, after one year, he held over $9,000 worth of notes payable to him, and held assessed taxable property valued at $7,800.[19]

Even though business was brisk, it could never entirely distract his mind from politics. A presidential canvass was under way in 1844, and Breckinridge was more involved than ever. He read all of the Democratic papers, and stood firmly behind the party's candidate James K. Polk of Tennessee. Curiously enough, Polk's running mate was a one-time roommate of Cabell Breckinridge at Princeton, George M. Dallas, and one of Polk's opponents was another roommate, James G. Birney. John C. Breckinridge was a confirmed "Polkat" from the start, and plunged into the campaign with vigor. Thanks in part to his influential family name, he immediately assumed prominence in local politics. On the stump, in debates, and at mass meetings and rallies throughout the campaign, he justified his position. The word was soon around that when Breckinridge debated a Whig or an abolitionist, he could "literally eat him up." A firm measure of his growing notoriety came when he was asked to address one of the largest rallies of the national canvass, to be held in Polk's Nashville. The most important Democrats of the West would be there, perhaps even Jackson himself. Although he could not accept, the invitation was a signal honor for Breckinridge. He

18. Receipt of Thomas Bullock, October 9, 1843, receipt of Boyd and Colwell, December 3, 1843, receipt of G. B. Hale, September 29, 1843, all in JCB Papers; Cock to Breckinridge, January 24, 1844, Breckinridge to Robert J. Breckinridge, December 29, 1843, Enos David to Breckinridge, February 3, 1844, all in B. MSS.

19. Note of Breckinridge with D. Howard Smith, April 19, 1844, J. Henry Powell to Breckinridge, October 7, 1869, "List of Notes Held by John C. Breckinridge, 1844," "List of Notes, 1845," tax receipt for 1844, all in JCB Papers; Lexington *Observer and Reporter*, May 4, 1844.

was behind Polk's positions on the annexation of Texas and the general expansionist mood so aptly labeled "manifest destiny" and his influence was being felt. "You are a glorious Democrat," wrote one associate, and he spoke for many.[20]

Indeed, the exposure Breckinridge received in this canvass would do him far more good than he did for Polk. It made him well known to the people of the Bluegrass, and well versed in meeting opponents on the stump. It also taught him something. The congressional district in which he lived, Henry Clay's Eighth "Ashland" District, had always gone Whig. But Breckinridge now discovered that its counties—Scott, Fayette, Bourbon, Woodford, Franklin, Owen, and Jessamine—contained enough solid Democrats that a few hundred Whig defections could give the seat in Congress to a Democrat. It was useful knowledge.

Caught up in the spirit of the canvass, Breckinridge almost sought office himself, the clerkship of the Scott County Court. The press of business and Bullock's grumblings that his partner was spending too much time at politics persuaded him against running. However, it was just as well. Mary was pregnant, and as the child within her grew, the state of her health became more precarious. On December 29, 1844, she gave birth to a son, Joseph Cabell. But in giving him life, she nearly lost her own. Breckinridge, distraught, found that "I scarcely dare hope she can survive the extraordinary sufferings of her confinement." At times, he lost hope entirely. "Day after day," he wrote to Robert, "I wait." Finally, after hovering near death for a week, Mary began a slow recovery.[21]

As his wife improved, business began to decline in Georgetown. By April, 1845, the partners decided to close their office in that city. Breckinridge remained in Georgetown for a time closing out accounts, but Bullock was anxious for him to move to their Lexington office in Jordan's Row on the Fayette Courthouse square. His partner just would not stay out of politics. A movement was now afoot to get Breckinridge the district's Democratic nomination for Congress. Nothing came of it, but it was one more indication of the welling esteem in which he was held. The year 1845 turned out well after all. He had a fine son, Mary was well again, and the community knew and respected him. Late in December, as the year drew

20. Receipt of M. Lamb, July 31, 1845, in JCB Papers; Charles Parkhill to Breckinridge, May 14, 1844, in B. MSS; CRB Book No. 5, pp. 12–21, in Prewitt Collection.
21. J. T. Johnson to Breckinridge, September 13, 1844, F. C. Mills to Breckinridge, June 17, 1844, Breckinridge to Robert J. Breckinridge, January 4, 1845, all in B. MSS.

to a close, he and Mary celebrated its passing over two bottles of fine champagne.[22]

Early in 1846 a move to Lexington became imperative, and there Bullock and Breckinridge became one of the leading firms in the county. One touchy case nearly resulted in Breckinridge's being challenged to a duel, but fortunately, amicable relations with the offended party were restored. Just as fortunately, Breckinridge had enough free time to reenter Lexington society after an absence of five years. He joined the chess club, the Masonic Lodge, wrote a brief biographical sketch of his father for Lewis Collins' new book *Historical Sketches of Kentucky*, and read voraciously. Although he would years later regret that he squandered much time that could have been spent in reading, he did, in fact, read a number of important books. Two in particular left a lasting impression on him: John Bunyan's *Pilgrim's Progress* and John Milton's *Paradise Lost*. Meanwhile, he read a dozen or more newspapers and literary and political journals.[23]

On July 13 he bought the former home of Congressman Richard H. Menefee, a lovely place on Longwood Avenue near South Broadway, and refurbished it extensively. He and Mary would live in it longer than any other, and in later years both would recall their days spent here as the happiest of their lives. To help run the house, Breckinridge hired a gardener and, on New Year's Day, 1847, he bought a slave girl named Clara. She would help keep house while Mary recovered from having their second child, Clifton Rodes, the previous November 22. Clara brought the number of the lawyer's slave holdings to four, all domestics. They received fine care from him, a physician's attention when ill, new clothes, and carefully chosen working conditions whenever he hired them out to others.[24]

On May 13, 1846, the United States Congress declared war on Mexico.

22. Receipt of Fayette County clerk, March, 1845, receipt of Bullock, November 14, 1845, receipt of H. McCarty, December 29, 1845, all in JCB Papers; Bullock to Breckinridge. April 14, July 9, 1845, John W. Forbes to Breckinridge, September 18, 1845, in B. MSS; Lexington *Observer and Reporter*, January 8, 1848. The *Observer and Reporter* of this date gives the only reference to the supposed congressional bid that has been found, saying: "Mr. Breckinridge is a lawyer of high standing, and, although a Democrat of the straightest sect, has very nearly been elected to Congress in his district, notwithstanding that, politically, there was a strong majority against him."

23. *New Age Magazine*, n.d., 722, copy in Prewitt Collection; Richard A. Buckner to Breckinridge, April 9, 1846, Breckinridge to Buckner, April 10, 1846, Breckinridge to Robert J. Breckinridge, December 23, 1846, Robert J. Breckinridge to Breckinridge, December 28, 1846, all in B. MSS; several receipts for subscription to journals, in JCB Papers; Thomas H. Hines Diary in Thomas H. Hines MSS, UK, January 20, 1866.

24. Letitia Breckinridge to Breckinridge, September 5, 1846, T. Hughes to Breckinridge, August 13, 1845, in B. MSS; agreement between Breckinridge and Frederick Cornar, January 15, 1847, receipt of Ansel and Mary Brockway and Mary Crawford, January 1, 1847, receipt of J. F. Miller & Son, January 19, 1847, receipt of J. R. Hall,

The war enjoyed wide popularity in the West, for it promised territorial acquisition that could expand the representation and power of the pro-slavery Democrats in Washington. Partly for this reason—though he did not believe that slavery would ever really move into the newly acquired land—Breckinridge was behind Polk in the war. Almost immediately after Congress' declaration, he tendered his services to Major General William O. Butler and asked for a position on his staff. Butler, a Democrat from Jessamine County, was forming a brigade of volunteers but, unfortunately, he could not take the lawyer to Mexico with him. For the time being, Breckinridge could only observe from afar and support Polk. When the Wilmot Proviso was introduced in Congress—a measure to ban slavery from any territory acquired whether above or below the Missouri Compromise line—the Kentuckian stood heartily opposed to it. When Polk vetoed an important river and harbor bill Breckinridge, a proponent of internal improvements, supported him on the grounds that it would have taken much needed funds away from the war effort. The lawyer's position earned him respect anew in the Bluegrass. Prominent politicians in Frankfort began consulting with him. And when, in July, 1847, a score of Kentuckians killed at the Battle of Buena Vista were brought to Frankfort for a military burial, Breckinridge was asked to be the principal speaker for the occasion.[25]

It was an impressive ceremony, with fifteen or twenty thousand people assembled, the largest audience in the city's history, and they heard from Breckinridge, "in an eloquent and impressive style, an address, which was received with deep emotion by as many as could hear him." He spoke for nearly an hour in eulogy, stirring the assemblage with patriotic fervor. It was "very well done," thought one listener, and the crowd agreed. Breckinridge's old classmate, Theodore O'Hara, was so moved by the address and the ceremonies that he was inspired to write his immortal poem "The Bivouac of the Dead." [26]

The speech made Breckinridge thousands of friends in Kentucky. Besides his eloquence, he touched a responsive nerve when he spoke a broad

September 10, 1845, bill of sale, July 13, 1846, all in JCB Papers; statement of J. R. Roche, March 2, 1934, as related in Lucille Stillwell, *Born to Be a Statesman: John Cabell Breckinridge* (Caldwell, Idaho, 1936), 68–69; Maltby, *Mary Cyrene Breckinridge*, 1–2.

25. William O. Butler to Breckinridge, June 13, 1846, in CRB Book No. 5, p. 35, in Prewitt Collection; *Congressional Globe*, 32nd Cong., 1st Sess., 383, 33rd Cong., 1st Sess., 441; Lexington *Kentucky Statesman*, July 17, 1851; Leslie Combs to Breckinridge, January 29, 1846, in B. MSS; Lexington *Observer and Reporter*, July 14, 1847.

26. Lexington *Observer and Reporter*, July 28, 1847; Breckinridge, *An Address on the Occasion of the Burial of the Kentucky Volunteers Who Fell at Buena Vista . . .* (Lexington, 1847), 5–14 *passim*; Otto A. Rothert, "A Glimpse of Alfred Pirtle, 1837–

commendation of General Zachary Taylor's conduct of the war. It was one of the earliest major tributes to Taylor to come out of the West, and such praise was hardly lost on the Whigs and Democrats, both of whom saw in Taylor a potential presidential candidate in 1848. The lawyer enhanced his standing a few weeks afterward when he participated in a nonpartisan meeting in Lexington at which he and four others wrote resolutions proposing that General Taylor would be the best man for the White House in the coming election. Of course, Breckinridge's hope was that Taylor would run as a Democrat, and, having read a widely publicized letter of the general's in which he seemed to take Democratic party ground on slavery, the tariff, and internal improvements, he felt secure in endorsing Old Rough and Ready. At a second meeting an attempt was made to nominate Taylor but, to Breckinridge's disappointment, the try failed.[27]

Although turned down on his first application for service with the Kentucky Volunteers, Breckinridge still hoped to get into the war. His chance came when the governor, now William Owsley, called for two more regiments on August 31, 1847. Immediately Breckinridge applied for a commission in one of them, and Crittenden backed his application. This made Owsley, who was fond of his former pupil, favorable toward his entreaty. What decided him, however, was the fact that Breckinridge was a Democrat. All of Owsley's appointments so far had gone to fellow Whigs, and advisors suggested that at least one commission should go to a Democrat. Breckinridge was a natural choice. Young and popular, he stood in high esteem in his party and, thanks to his part in the Taylor meetings, he enjoyed some esteem among the Whigs as well. Consequently, on September 4, 1847, Owsley announced the appointment. Two days later he officially decreed Breckinridge's commission as major of the Third Kentucky Volunteers, the only such appointment Owsley would ever give to a member of his opposition. For the young lawyer from Lexington, the land of the Montezumas awaited.[28]

1926," *Filson Club Historical Quarterly*, XI (July, 1937), 212; Edwin A. Alderman and Joel Chandler Harris (eds.), *Library of Southern Literature* (New Orleans, 1907–1909), IX, 3,827.

27. Breckinridge, *An Address*, 10–11; Lexington *Observer and Reporter*, August 18, September 15, 1847; *Speech of Hon. John C. Breckinridge, Delivered at Ashland, Ky., September 5, 1860* (N.p., 1860), 2, hereinafter cited as *Ashland Speech*; *Congressional Globe*, 32nd Cong., 1st Sess., Appendix, 383; Joseph G. Rayback, *Free Soil: The Election of 1848* (Lexington, 1971), 49–50.

28. Lexington *Observer and Reporter*, September 14, 1847; Crittenden to Breckinridge, September 4, 1847, William Tanner to Breckinridge, September 4, 1847, in B. MSS.

The appointment was popular, even among the Whigs. One of their papers, the Lexington *Observer and Reporter*, credited Breckinridge as a man of "intelligence, honor and chivalry," and applauded his commission. His Uncle Robert was highly pleased. "May God Almighty keep & bless you is the prayer of your faithful and attached uncle." [29]

The two new Kentucky regiments, the Third and Fourth, were mustered into service on October 4 at Louisville, though Major Breckinridge may have signed the roll a day before. Drill and discipline began immediately. The officers, for the most part, were untrained amateurs like the major. Colonel Manlius V. Thompson, commander of the Third, was a handsome old Whig with little military aptitude, and the lieutenant colonel, Breckinridge's old playmate Thomas Crittenden, knew little more. So it was with the Fourth as well. In spite of their inexperience, however, they produced two surprisingly well-trained regiments. By October 28 the Frankfort press declared that they "exhibit great progress and proficiency at drill," presenting "a fine appearance." The volunteers were delighted to find that they were to be assigned to Butler's division. Their official designation was the Kentucky Brigade, their destination Winfield Scott's army in the captured city of Mexico.[30]

By the end of October they were ready. On November 1 the volunteers broke camp on the banks of the Ohio and boarded their transports for the long trip to New Orleans. The Third was divided among three steamboats, Major Breckinridge taking command of the three companies aboard the *Horner*. Shortly after noon they pulled away from shore and headed down the river. A pleasant but uneventful trip followed, though even before they reached New Orleans word went out concerning the capability and popularity of the Kentucky officers, those of the Third in particular. "Maj. Breckinridge is the soul of chivalry," wrote a correspondent, "bold, brave and dignified—and still very affable in his manners. He is a man, too, of great energy and perseverance—firm in his commands, but lenient in his requirements." When they arrived at the Crescent City, the Kentuckians "at-

---

29. Robert J. Breckinridge to Breckinridge, September 23, 1847, in CRB Book No. 5, p. 45, in Prewitt Collection; Lexington *Observer and Reporter*, September 8, 1847; Frankfort *Yeoman*, July 13, 1847. Breckinridge's commission is in B. MSS.

30. Compiled Service Record of John C. Breckinridge, Third Kentucky Infantry, Record Group 94, NA. Hereinafter Record Group is cited as RG. "Statement of Service of John C. Breckinridge," Adjutant General's Office, Frankfort, Ky.; Lexington *Observer and Reporter*, September 3, 25, October 6, 16, 1847; Charles F. Hinds (ed.), "Mexican War Journal of Leander M. Cox," *Register of the Kentucky Historical Society*, LV (January, 1957), 29; Frankfort *Yeoman*, October 28, November 5, 1847.

tracted universal admiration for their appearance; probably no two regiments were ever formed of better material." After a day or two in New Orleans, Breckinridge loaded his command onto the transport *California* and steamed out into the Gulf toward Vera Cruz.[31]

The trip took ten days, and Breckinridge found the sea voyage envigorating. When he reached Vera Cruz on November 18, he felt better than he had for months. Once ashore, the Third continued its drill and routine until Butler gave the order to march. On the twenty-sixth they set out for Mexico City. As the march began, Breckinridge opened a notebook and began making notations of the distances between each village they passed, where there was water and wood, and the quantity available, and suitable campsites along the way. It would be useful information for the return trip. He was thinking like an officer.[32]

Thanks to his concern, the major's popularity with his men soared despite his possible performance of such unpleasant tasks as bringing stragglers back to the column at bayonet point. He was easily the best-liked man in the regiment. Reports filtered back to Lexington that Breckinridge "did not ride two days on the march, [but] gave his horse to the sick and tired." One soldier wrote home, "Of courage, talent and all the generous qualities, requisite to make a noble soldier, Breckinridge . . . is in an eminent degree possessed. On our march from Vera Cruz to this place [Mexico City], I do not believe he rode a whole day during the march. On his war-breathing steed I noticed every day a worn down soldier unable to walk mounted and he himself on foot." Private James Shackleford of the Fourth later recalled that when he lagged behind his regiment, sick, footsore, and broken down, the major came up and made him ride while he dismounted and walked. Yet another weary Kentuckian had the major ride up to him and ask where he was from. "Bath County," the private replied. "Well," said Breckinridge, "get on my horse and give me your musket," and thereafter the major nursed the soldier along on the march. He stayed close to the men in camp, too. One captain noted in his diary that the major was the only one of the field officers who came among the men looking to their

31. Hinds, "Mexican War Journal," 34–35; Lexington *Observer and Reporter*, November 13, 1847; New Orleans *National*, November 9, 1847; New Orleans *Picayune*, November 20, 1847; Frankfort *Yeoman*, November 26, 1847.

32. Breckinridge to Robert J. Breckinridge, April 8, 1848, "Table of Distances from Vera Cruz to the City of Mexico," B. MSS; Hinds, "Mexican War Journal," 38–45, 46–49, 50; Charles F. Hinds (ed.), "Mexican War Journal of Leander M. Cox, Part II," *Register of the Kentucky Historical Society*, LV (July, 1957), 213; Lexington *Observer and Reporter*, December 15, 1847; Jacob Oswandel, *Notes of the Mexican War, 1846–47–48* (Philadelphia, 1885), 412.

needs. While the volunteers did suffer some from the inexperience of their commanders in matters of supply and equipment, they never found in Breckinridge a lack of concern.[33]

The march to join Scott was uneventful, with only a false alarm from Mexican guerrillas to excite the column. Once they passed Puebla ("water and wood") the trip became much more interesting for the major, for now they tramped through country studded with ancient Aztec ruins. Then they moved under the shadow of the mountains, ascended to a narrow pass, and walked down the steep road into the Valley of Mexico.[34]

They reached Mexico City on December 18, 1847, and pitched their tents beside the *entrado*, the gateway San Lazaro, main entrance to the city. Three days later they moved into the capital, taking up quarters in two large convents, while Breckinridge found a bed in the Masonic Lodge with Thompson. For the next three months life in the captured city was peaceful, the war all but over. The major saw as much as he could, and formed a low opinion of Mexicans. "This is a hesitating, tardy people," he said. He preferred the company of his own kind of Americans. He and Butler, already acquaintances, became fast friends, which the general thought rather unusual "with men differing so much as we do in point of age." Breckinridge joined the touted Aztec Club formed by many of the officers who originally took the city, and in it he met many of the army's outstanding officers; his cousin Captain John B. Grayson, Lieutenants P. G. T. Beauregard, Richard S. Ewell, Ulysses S. Grant and George B. McClellan, Captains William J. Hardee, Robert E. Lee and John C. Pemberton; Major Earl Van Dorn, Lieutenant Colonel Joseph E. Johnston, and Brigadier General Franklin Pierce. He moved in good company.[35]

Oddly enough, Breckinridge's chief, if unofficial, service here was as a lawyer. Without fee he often voluntarily defended soldiers charged with breaches of discipline ranging from drunkenness to murder. One case, how-

33. CRB Book No. 5, p. 48, in Prewitt Collection; J. S. Chrisman to Breckinridge, October 26, 1848, Mary Clay Breckinridge to Mary Cyrene Breckinridge, March 20, 1848, Breckinridge to Robert J. Breckinridge, April 8, 1848, B. MSS; Lexington *Observer and Reporter*, April 12, 1848; Lexington *Kentucky Statesman*, August 3, 1860; Hinds, "Mexican War Journal, Part II," 221, 227.

34. Hinds, "Mexican War Journal, Part II," 224, 229-31.

35. *Ibid.*, 231; Lexington *Observer and Reporter*, May 13, 1848; John George to Breckinridge, December 29, 1852, Breckinridge to Robert J. Breckinridge, April 8, 1848, in B. MSS; Oswandel, *Notes*, 431; Lexington *Kentucky Statesman*, August 17, 1856. J. F. R. Landis to Mrs. Roy W. McKinney, April 18, 1921, quoted in *Confederate Veteran*, XXIX (June, 1921), 232, says that Breckinridge was a primary member of the Aztec Club, while *Constitution of the Aztec Club of 1847 and the List of Members, 1893* (Washington, D.C., 1893), does not mention him.

ever, proved decidedly out of the ordinary. For months a conspiracy had been brewing to topple Scott from his position as general in chief, inspired largely by a desire to thwart his obvious ambitions for the presidency. The chief conspirator was Major General Gideon J. Pillow, a Tennessee Democrat and former law partner of President Polk's. They produced a scurrilous letter giving Pillow credit for the victories at Churubusco and Contreras, barely mentioning Scott's presence as commander. Other letters followed. Pillow composed at least one of the letters, but persuaded a subordinate to confess to writing it. Scott, however, was not fooled and brought charges against Pillow and others. Considerable machinations ensued, influenced by Polk himself, who disliked the Whig Scott and hoped, instead, to see the Democrat Pillow succeed him in the White House. Finally a court of inquiry was appointed, all of its members good friends to Polk and Pillow.[36]

Major Breckinridge stepped into the controversy when, at Pillow's seemingly urgent request, he agreed to defend him before the court. That the major had any knowledge of the details of Pillow's chicanery other than hearsay is most unlikely. He found political and military scheming contemptible. Nevertheless, he accepted a position as defense counsel, though this in no way interfered with the amicable relations which had grown up between the major and General Scott. Several times now he had been a dinner guest of the general's. He found Scott charming, though decidedly egotistical, and lamented his apparently consuming ambition for the presidency.[37]

The court finally began hearing testimony on March 21, 1848. For a month Breckinridge examined witnesses, among them promising officers like Lee, James Longstreet, Joseph Hooker, and George Cadwalader. Even Polk's in again-out again peace commissioner Nicholas Trist came to the stand. Most of the testimony told against Pillow, but circumstances and the favorable court eventually adjourned without making a decision. Breckinridge's part had little influence on the outcome of the affair, but it did him a great deal of good. He met and came to know the most prominent officers of the army, while the newspaper coverage given to the court of inquiry

36. Lexington *Kentucky Statesman*, May 6, 1853; *Senate Executive Documents*, 30th Cong., 1st Sess., No. 65 *passim*; Charles Winslow Elliott, *Winfield Scott, the Soldier and the Man* (New York, 1937), 575.

37. Lexington *Kentucky Statesman*, May 6, 1853; Louisville *Courier-Journal*, June 18, 1875; Charles F. Hinds (ed.), "Mexican War Journal of Leander M. Cox, Part III," *Register of the Kentucky Historical Society*, LVI (January, 1958), 58.

spread his name throughout the United States. The renown thus gained would prove useful one day.[38]

In spite of heavy legal duties, the major found plenty to do with his regiment. As always, the volunteers maintained regular drill, and the officers of the Third and Fourth put their units in such admirable shape that one of the ablest officers, General Persifor F. Smith, pronounced them the finest troops in the volunteer service. Even more pleasing for Breckinridge was news from his family in Kentucky. He had not been able to get word from them since he left Louisville, and his anxiety had been heightened when, shortly after leaving, a bulletin reached him, indirectly, informing him that Mary was pregnant again. Knowing how difficult her previous pregnancies had been, he worried. "I cannot describe the trouble and anxiety I have felt," he wrote.[39]

With the good news that Mary and the children were well, the major could also rejoice in his own good health. The climate was stimulating, and unlike many in the army, he was careful of what he ate. After his first month in Mexico, he rarely purchased the notoriously unsavory army beef from the commissary. Instead he lived off the land, drank copious amounts of coffee—ten pounds or more per month—and had much of his food prepared by Mexican cooks. To pass the empty evening hours, he read a great deal, as evidenced by the fact that during his stay there he burned fifty-six pounds of candles.[40]

The best news of all was the rumor of impending peace. After some delay, Trist finally negotiated a treaty ceding California and much of the New Mexico territory to the United States in return for recognition of the Rio Grande as the southern boundary of Texas, and a remuneration of $15 million. More delays followed, but, by April, 1848, Breckinridge found the outlook for peace good, though he feared it might come too late for the army to leave Mexico that summer. There was talk of the volunteer officers being allowed to go home early, but he dismissed the idea of abandoning his regiment, "for I will not leave it." On May 19, word came that the Mexican

38. Cadmus M. Wilcox, *History of the Mexican War* (Washington, D.C., 1892), 595; Elliott, *Winfield Scott*, 581–83; Lexington *Observer and Reporter*, April 26, 1848; *Senate Executive Documents*, 30th Cong., 1st Sess., No. 65, pp. 32, 389–91; John Sedgwick, *Correspondence of John Sedgwick, Major General* (New York, 1902–1903), I, 166; Justin H. Smith, *The War with Mexico* (New York, 1919), II, 436–38.

39. Lexington *Observer and Reporter*, April 8, 1848; Breckinridge to Robert J. Breckinridge, April 8, 1848, Mary Clay Breckinridge to Mary Cyrene Breckinridge, March 20, 1848, in B. MSS.

40. "Account of Provisions Sold Major Breckinridge," January 13–February 7, February 8–March 6, March 7–31, April–May, June, 1848, in B. MSS.

Congress had begun to vote on the Treaty of Guadalupe-Hidalgo. Five days later it was ratified, the war was over, and the volunteers were celebrating. "We Are Coming Home," they sang, and on May 30 they began the march back to Vera Cruz. The march was hot and plagued with sickness in the ranks, but by the end of the month they reached the coast and boarded their transports. On June 29 they set out for New Orleans. At dawn on July 16 Breckinridge and his regiment, aboard the *Missouri*, pulled in to the wharf at Louisville. After eight and one half months the Kentuckians touched their native soil.[41]

Major Breckinridge immediately obtained permission to go to Lexington, for he had word of illness in the family, and the birth of a baby girl, Frances. He found all well at home, and a few days later he returned to Louisville to assist in mustering the regiments out of service. The whole city turned out to honor the returned heroes. They had not been in a single fight, but Kentucky was proud of them. There were speeches, a final march, the discharge ceremonies, and a grand banquet. "The Mexicans heard my young nephew was coming," Robert J. Breckinridge would quip, "and straightway they made peace." The major would in turn retort to his warhawk relative that "if my uncle had been in my place . . . the war would be going on yet." There was a sense of elation over the grand adventure so successfully concluded, and the Breckinridges and thousands like them could joke and frolic in their exuberance. John C. Breckinridge's first war had been a good one. His next would not prove so pleasant.[42]

41. Breckinridge to Robert J. Breckinridge, April 8, 1848, "Invoice of public property turned over to Major J. C. Breckinridge," June 12, 1848, in B. MSS; Oswandel, *Notes*, 557–61; Orders, No. 112, May 29, 1848, Regimental Order Book, Fourth United States Infantry, 33–35, in possession of Major Chapman R. Grant, Escondido, Calif.; Lexington *Observer and Reporter*, July 15, 1848; Louisville *Journal*, July 17, 1848.

42. Louisville *Journal*, July 17, 1848; Lexington *Observer and Reporter*, July 19, 22, 1848; Discharge of John C. Breckinridge, July 21, 1848, in B. MSS; CRB Book No. 1, pp. 20–21, in Prewitt Collection.

CHAPTER **3**

My Eloquent Young Friend

A lot had changed since Breckinridge left home. For one thing, Zachary Taylor was no longer his man for the presidency. Unknown to Breckinridge, the supposedly nonpartisan meetings of the year before had been carefully arranged by Crittenden and other powerful Whigs. They disguised any party affiliation in order not to offend the Bluegrass supporters of another Whig presidential hopeful, Henry Clay. The strategy proved successful, for Taylor men came to rule the state convention, denying Clay his own state's support in the contest for the Whig nomination. Beyond this, Taylor himself had finally shown his colors, definitely Whig. It is no surprise, then, that immediately upon returning to Lexington, Major Breckinridge came out for the Democratic nominee, Lewis Cass. It helped that Cass's running mate was to be the major's friend from Mexico, Major General William O. Butler.[1]

Days after resuming domestic life, Breckinridge took the stump for Cass and Butler. On July 27 he spoke at the courthouse in Lexington, and in the next month delivered at least four more addresses, sustaining the candidates "to the best of my ability." He campaigned continuously throughout the remaining weeks before the election, but he laughingly regarded his greatest service to the cause to be his actions on election day itself. He did not vote. At that time Kentucky allowed a citizen to vote anywhere in the state, regardless of his place of residence. At the end of the canvass, then, when the major went on his annual hunting trip to the mountains in the eastern part of the state, he felt no worry over being able to cast his vote for Cass and Butler. On election day, however, his half dozen or more companions—all Whigs—proposed that they spend the day hunting instead

1. Lexington *Observer and Reporter*, August 18, 1847; George R. Poage, *Henry Clay and the Whig Party* (Chapel Hill, N.C., 1936), 156–57.

41

of traveling fifteen miles to the nearest polling place. Breckinridge agreed heartily, reasoning that if they went to vote, Taylor would get six or seven ballots whereas Cass got only his own. "If every man had done as well as myself," he later boasted, "we would have carried the State by forty thousand majority." Few others did so well, though, and Cass lost by a narrow margin.[2]

With the election out of the way, Breckinridge still found it hard to keep his mind off politics. For one thing, business could hardly be stimulating when his case load consisted largely of matters like a client's complaint that a neighbor's privy was filthy and offensive. Besides, in spite of the recent defeat, politics hung heavy in the air, and its smell was sweet and promising to a young Democrat. The Whig party, despite its national victory, was dying. Factionalism and personal animosities were destroying it, and the prospects for the opposition, even in the overwhelmingly Whig Fayette County, looked brighter than ever before. Breckinridge received a steady flow of letters from old comrades of the Third Kentucky assuring him of their support. And he already knew from his own experience in two campaigns that he and his ideas enjoyed considerable approval even among many Whigs. His war service was an added advantage, and the Breckinridge name still had magic in the Bluegrass. The Democratic managers in Fayette stood convinced that the major was a vote getter. Thus it came as no surprise to most—surely not to Breckinridge—when on June 11, 1849, a committee composed of both Whigs and Democrats nominated him for a Fayette seat in the Kentucky House of Representatives. Now, for a change, instead of campaigning on behalf of others, John would speak for himself.[3]

As the new candidate faced his own canvass, he saw only one real issue before him, emancipation. For years attempts to enact gradual emancipation into law had been made by the Whigs without success. They failed to get it into either of the two constitutions so far adopted by Kentucky. Instead, in early 1849 they saw the legislature repeal some of the most important provisions of the Nonimportation Law of 1833, seriously undermining their cause. The only hope on the horizon was the new state constitutional convention called for October, 1849. Throughout the months preceding it

2. *Ashland Speech*, 2. The invitations to speak will be found throughout July and August, 1848, in the B. MSS.

3. Samuel McCullough to Breckinridge, July 6, 1848, in JCB Papers; Poage, *Henry Clay*, 171; Lexington *Observer and Reporter*, June 13, 1849. For the numerous letters from comrades of the Third Kentucky see July–August 1848, in B. MSS.

they gathered in mass meetings, nominating delegates who would stand for election to the convention. Among those nominated from Fayette was the Reverend Robert J. Breckinridge. Their goals were basically humanitarian, principally their support of the Liberian experiment, but many others simply wanted the slaves freed to get them out of Kentucky. Freedmen were socially, economically, and politically undesirable.[4]

All of the influences of his childhood and school days led John C. Breckinridge to oppose slavery as a moral wrong. Many of his friends, men like Cassius M. Clay, Garrett Davis, and Orville H. Browning, were prominent emancipationists, not to mention his several uncles. Breckinridge was a good Mason, member of an organization officially opposed to the "peculiar institution." His church, Lexington's First Presbyterian, denounced slavery from the pulpit as he sat in his rented pew No. 69. As a result, the major was now, as in his youth, an ardent enemy of slavery. He never defended it for its own sake or on racial grounds.

His attitude was slowly changing now, though. He had traveled, seen the often degrading condition imposed upon freedmen by unfriendly whites, and campaigned in Mexico to win lands which were sought to come under southern domination. But this last could only be achieved if southern men could move into the new territory, and they would not move without their "property." Enforced emancipation in existing states like Kentucky would hardly encourage such an exodus. If it did, it would only be in a negative way. Prominent men, unwilling to see their property manumitted forcefully, would leave the state instead, robbing the commonwealth of much of its first-rate talent. As for emancipation's effects on the Negro, Breckinridge had no doubts. Unlike many in the Bluegrass, he had very free personal dealings with former slaves both professionally and privately. He lent money to some, borrowed from others, gave and accepted legal advice, and took a keen interest as a lawyer in seeing that they received as much justice as possible in the courts. In some cases he even paid for a freedman's defense by another counsel. When William Fishback, a freedman, allegedly murdered a slave belonging to the major's Uncle David Castleman, a Lexington court brought him to trial. The prosecution asked Breckinridge to speak in its behalf, but he refused. He found prosecuting distasteful and would take cases only for the defense. Besides, Breckinridge believed that Fishback was unjustly charged. The major visited the accused in his cell,

4. Asa Earl Martin, *The Anti-Slavery Movement in Kentucky, Prior to 1850* (Louisville, 1918), 13–17, 31–32, 88–97, 121–23; *Ashland Speech*, 3; Lexington *Observer and Reporter*, April 28, 1849.

told him of the apparent injustice, and was asked to bring the case to the attention of Governor Crittenden, which he may have done. Fishback's fate is unknown, but Breckinridge agreed with the boy's father that "Owing to the strong pro-Debel pro-Slavery feeling in the community a free negro and my Self are verry odious and that can be the only cause why he was convicted." A free black man simply had too many forces operating against him. The major was convinced that unless freedmen could leave the state—better yet the country—"the interests of both races in the Commonwealth would be promoted by the continuance of their present relations." It was for the good of all. In his mind, Liberia was still perhaps the best solution, and this also reveals that he felt the black man not to be so inferior that he could not exercise judgment and responsibility, for Liberia was ruled by former slaves.[5]

Looking toward achieving his own office in government, Breckinridge faced a tough campaign. His chief competitor was Hugh C. Pindell, an experienced Whig from Fayette whom he would meet on the stump several times in coming months. Another Democrat, Dr. D. L. Price, was also nominated by the committee which put forward Breckinridge, in the hope that the Democrats could capture both of the county's seats in Frankfort. An interesting situation arose from the nominations because the committee presenting Breckinridge and Price actually contained sixty more Whigs than the all-Whig committee that nominated Pindell. Dissatisfied with their party, these men had turned to Democrats for the protection of their interests. It was a sign of things to come.[6]

Breckinridge began campaigning one week after the nomination. Thereafter he stumped vigorously, speaking at least once or twice a day anywhere people would gather. The rigors of the canvass only eased during a cholera epidemic which, in two months, killed 342 people in Lexington alone. To the major's great sorrow, one of the victims was his partner, Samuel Bullock. Nevertheless, he wound up the campaign in high spirits. When the polling began on August 7, he dutifully cast his votes for himself and against his uncle, while Robert Breckinridge voted against his nephew. They would joke about it afterward. Although they represented

5. Martin, *Anti-Slavery Movement*, 90; receipts of R. Long, May, November, 1849, November, 1850, "Rent of Pew No. 69," untitled note, March 7, 1840, in JCB Papers; *Ashland Speech*, 3; Rogers to Breckinridge, January 8, 1850, Henry Wood to Breckinridge, January 11, 14, 1850, Samuel Fishback to Breckinridge, February 20, 1850, all in B. MSS; Order Book No. 35, October 17-18, 1849, Fayette County Clerk's Office, Lexington, Ky.

6. Lexington *Observer and Reporter*, July 18, 1849.

antagonistic political principles, public matters never interfered with their affection for each other.[7]

Even without his uncle's vote, Breckinridge discovered the next day that he had a handsome victory. With 1,481 votes, he was far ahead of his nearest competitor, Pindell, while Price was out of the running. There was much of significance in this election, for this was the first time in all its history that Fayette had sent a Democrat to the legislature, and it was sending him with 43 percent of its vote. More important was what had been learned about Breckinridge. He was a vote getter, a man whose appeal and ideas could pull votes across party lines. From now on the watchful eyes of leading men in the state would be fixed upon him. As for Breckinridge, it was a doubly joyous occasion, for this same day of his first political victory, Mary gave birth to another son, John Milton.[8]

Before the legislative session opened in December, the major had much to do. It had been a good year for the firm of Bullock and Breckinridge. Now, to maintain business, he needed a new partner, particularly since he would be away in Frankfort for two months, unable to transact the affairs of his practice. Two weeks after the election, he brought George B. Kinkead into the firm, and then moved his offices to Short Street, opposite Megowan's Hotel. Business continued brisk, the long hours pleasantly broken now by the frequent visitors who walked into the office to trade stories and talk politics. Here for the first time he met the Illinois legislator whose district included Breckinridge's land near Jacksonville, the man who finally managed to marry Mary Todd. Abraham Lincoln was visiting with his wife's family in Lexington, and liked to look in on the town's lawyers. He formed several lasting friendships here, and one was with the major. Although they never became intimates, they did form a mutual fondness which would last for years.[9]

December came at last. Just after Christmas, Breckinridge went to Frankfort where the legislature opened its session on the last day of the year. The first task before the lawmakers was the election of a speaker of the House, and here the impact of the major's election upon the state's Democrats first manifested itself. In the months preceding the session, speculation ran wild in the press as to who would become speaker. Breckinridge's name

7. *Ibid.*, June 13, 20, 27, July 11, 14, 16, 28, 1849; Frankfort *Commonwealth*, August 21, 1849; *Ashland Speech*, 3.
8. Lexington *Observer and Reporter*, August 8, 1849; Frankfort *Yeoman*, August 9, 1849; Lexington *Kentucky Statesman*, March 20, 1850.
9. Tax receipt, 1849, in JCB Papers; Lexington *Observer and Reporter*, August 22, 1849; Townsend, *Lincoln and the Bluegrass*, 137, 183.

was never mentioned. Now, however, a Democrat from Mercer County placed his name in nomination. Two Whigs were nominated as well, and then the balloting began. Breckinridge received his party's solid vote. With thirty-nine votes, he led both competitors for three ballots, lacking only eight votes for a majority. Another nominee entered the race, and, realizing that he was stalemated, Breckinridge asked that his name be withdrawn in favor of another Democratic nominee. Despite this, a Whig, Thomas Reilly, finally won. Still, the major's nomination was a striking token of the early prominence he was expected to take in state politics.[10]

The months to come proved active and exciting, and as the session progressed, Breckinridge grew steadily more popular and influential. Appointments to the committees on the judiciary and federal relations came to him, and immediately he took an active part in the debate. He first attracted attention for his liberal stand on internal improvements, a not entirely Democratic program. He helped form and bring before the House bills for a geological survey, the opening to navigation of the Kentucky River, chartering a turnpike, incorporating a steamboat company, a homestead exemption law, provision of state funds for a lunatic asylum, establishment of the *Kentucky School Journal*, and better salaries for state employees. Most important was his work for bank reform. By the end of the session Breckinridge's championing of improvements earned him the honor of presiding over debate on an act to incorporate the Louisville & Bowling Green Railroad.[11]

In spite of legion service for internal improvements, the major attracted more attention by his outspoken stand for states' rights, the new constitution, and the Union. On January 16, 1850—his twenty-ninth birthday—Breckinridge presented to the house a lengthy set of resolutions on the Union and slavery. Settlement of the question of slavery in the newly acquired territories rightfully belonged with their future inhabitants, he declared, but he admitted tacitly that the federal government could settle the question "in a manner just and equal to all the states." Should Congress legislate on the matter, then Kentucky's senators and representatives should be instructed to oppose any bills for territorial governments that would exclude slavery south of the Missouri Compromise line or north of it, unless

10. Frankfort *Commonwealth*, October 9, December 11, 25, 1849; *Journal of the House of Representatives of the Commonwealth of Kentucky* (Frankfort, 1849), 4–34 *passim*; Lexington *Observer and Reporter*, January 2, 1850.

11. *Journal of the House, Kentucky*, 51–52, 54, 70, 85, 95, 113, 132, 150, 192, 249, 302, 312, 321, 385; CRB Book No. 5, pp. 12, 56–60, in Prewitt Collection; Lexington *Kentucky Statesman*, February 16, 1850.

slaveholders were guaranteed that they would not be excluded from moving to those territories with their "property." He also opposed abolition of slavery in the District of Columbia, the common property of all the states. "Kentucky does not look to disunion as a remedy for any of the evils which threaten our peace," he declared in conclusion. Similar resolutions were being introduced in statehouses throughout the land, and later this month Henry Clay would propose much the same thing in Congress. Indeed, Breckinridge may have consulted with Clay in the formulation of these resolves. It would be important that Clay's state be behind him in the months to come.

Reaction to the resolutions proved immediately favorable, even from the opposition. "I am glad to see him [Breckinridge] take so decided a position for the Union," wrote the editor of the Whig Louisville *Journal*; "I think he will carry with him the better part of his party." Even William Breckinridge, who had felt dishonored when his nephew turned Democrat, wrote that he was "gratified to see the stand you have taken in the legislature." [12]

Other stands were equally outspoken, and none moreso than his fight for the new constitution which had been framed the previous October. The question, of course, was slavery. Breckinridge still opposed mandatory manumission, but at the same time he actively supported the Liberian experiment. His very first motion as a legislator was to allow the Kentucky Colonization Society to use the representatives' hall for an address. Later he supported a resolution calling on Congress to require a settlement on Africa's coast for a freedmen's state, and to provide freed slaves transportation to their new home. Just the same, however, the major opposed increasing the number of freedmen in Kentucky and, since the new constitution was wholly in line with his views, he promoted its adoption. Among other things, it decreed that any emancipated slave must be removed from the state immediately, that freedmen could not immigrate to Kentucky, and that "the right of property is before and higher than any constitutional sanction; and the right of the owner of a slave, and its increase, is the same and is as inviolable as the right of the owner to any property whatever." [13]

He fought actively for the constitution's adoption, objecting only to

12. *Journal of the House, Kentucky*, 103, 117–23, 179–80, 215–17; Lexington *Kentucky Statesman*, January 23, 1850; Lexington *Observer and Reporter*, January 26, 1850; William L. Breckinridge to Breckinridge, February 7, 1850, in B. MSS; Holman Hamilton, *Prologue to Conflict: The Crisis and Compromise of 1850* (Lexington, 1964), 52–54.

13. *Journal of the House, Kentucky*, 67, 384–85; Martin, *Anti-Slavery Movement*, 137; *Constitution of Kentucky, 1850*, Art. X, Secs. 1–3.

its inadequate provision for amendment. A charter of the people must be amendable speedily by them, he argued, or else the population might go to other means to change their law. "Whenever a majority of the whole people resolved to amend or change their organic law," he declared, "they would overthrow whatever obstacle was interposed, and in that case many men present might live to see the dangerous spectacle of irregular change, a forcible revolution." Indeed, many men present would live to see it. For now, though, they were more concerned with the remarkable ability of the young Kentuckian speaking before them. "His manner was earnest and his arguments clear and forcible," wrote one paper. It was, they said, "One of the ablest speeches of the session." [14]

A measure of recognition for his services came on February 1, when he was nominated and unanimously elected a director of the Kentucky Lunatic Asylum. It made him understandably proud, the moreso since the asylum was one of Kentucky's most significant improvements, one that he heartily endorsed. "Neatness, kindness, discipline, and mental development are here exhibited," he wrote. The asylum was, in his eyes, a positive social reform. But even more envigorating to the young legislator than this honor was the esteem and respect he found he had earned among his fellow lawmakers. Three years later one of them, J. P. Metcalf, looked back to declare that Breckinridge "was emphatically the *leader* of the Democracy in that General Assembly . . . a gifted, eloquent, able and influential legislator." [15]

Whatever happiness Breckinridge felt that spring over his rise to prominence was soon destroyed. The legislature adjourned on March 7, 1850, but he took a leave of absence three days before to return to Lexington. His seven-month-old son John was sick. Young Clifton thought his younger brother "a child of infinite beauty and promise," but this March, with Mary pregnant yet again, the baby took ill. Nothing could be done for him, and on March 18 he died. The family were grief-stricken, so much so that even the younger children never forgot the sadness of that spring.[16]

Breckinridge found that throwing himself anew into politics helped him through his grief. There was a stiff fight ahead before the people voted on the new constitution, and he jumped into it determined to keep himself too

14. Lexington *Observer and Reporter*, February 2, 6, 1850; Lexington *Kentucky Statesman*, February 6, 9, 1850.

15. *Journal of the House, Kentucky*, 187–88; *Journal of the Senate of the Commonwealth of Kentucky, 1849–50* (Frankfort, 1849), 134–35; Wallace B. Turner, "A Rising Social Consciousness in Kentucky During the 1850's," *Filson Club History Quarterly*, XXXVI (January, 1962), 23, 25; J. P. Metcalf to Franklin Pierce, February 28, 1853, in B. MSS.

16. *Journal of the House, Kentucky*, 385, 435; Lexington *Kentucky Statesman*, March 20, 1850.

busy to grieve. He spoke, debated, shook hands, and appeared personally throughout the Bluegrass, and played no small part in the constitution's resounding victory at the polls in May. The day after the charter passed, the major joined Governor Crittenden on a widely publicized trip to Indianapolis to visit with Indiana's governor, Joseph A. Wright, and on June 7 the Fayette Democrats proposed his nomination for reelection to the legislature. Breckinridge was flattered, but in an open letter published in the press he declined. He had repeatedly refused to make another campaign for office now; considerations "of a private and imperative character" made it impossible. Although he would not say so publicly, his problem—besides continuing sadness over his son's death—was money. Overinvestment, absence from Lexington, and a host of other problems, had seriously eroded his income. It was time to turn his attention to private life once more.[17]

Retirement, however, meant no lapse of interest in public affairs. The blossoming railroad industry, always of interest to Breckinridge, received much of his attention. He recognized its financial future as well as the part it could play in building the nation. He had investments in several lines, and actively promoted railroad interests by speaking at charter meetings and serving on committees. And he kept abreast of political developments in the state and the nation. He read three Lexington newspapers, two from Frankfort, one from Georgetown, two from Louisville, the New York *Observer*, and the principal Democratic organ in the country, the Washington *Union*. With these and more than half a dozen political and literary monthlies, not to mention his frequent and intimate associations with legislators and other statesmen, Breckinridge kept in close touch with what was happening in Frankfort, and the nation.[18]

Just as the major stayed informed on public affairs, so did Kentucky's public men keep an eye on him. The Democrats did their best to keep his

17. *Journal of the House, Kentucky*, 385, 435; Lexington *Kentucky Statesman*, February 27, March 2, 27, April 6, 20, 24, June 1, 5, 8, 12, 1850; Lexington *Observer and Reporter*, March 27, 1850; P. B. Shepard to Breckinridge, April 10, 1850, B. MSS; receipt of H. Samuels, November 1, 1850, Tax Receipts, 1849, 1850, "List of Notes &c of JCB at his Law Office," January 23, 1851, "Memorandum of Notes &c Held by J. C. Breckinridge," 1850–51, all in JCB Papers.

18. Lexington & Frankfort Railroad Co. to Breckinridge, May 1, 1849, "Memorandum of Notes &c Held by J. C. Breckinridge," 1850–51, stock certificate in the Maysville & Lexington Railroad, September 22, 1851, receipt of Joseph Ficklin, January 1, 1850, receipt of D. C. Wickliffe, December 26, 1851, receipt of J. Cunningham. October 1, 1849, receipt of William Tanner, March 8, 1850, receipt of Pane Seymour, December 2, 1848, receipt of Sidney Mase, July 4, 1853, receipt of Harney Hughes, September 8, 1851, receipt of James Holland, December 17, 1849, receipt of W. Ramsay, March 7, 1850, receipt of E. Stevenson, March 13, 1849, all in JCB Papers; Lexington *Kentucky Statesman*, July 3, September 6, November 12, 1850, January 8, 1851.

name in print around the state, hoping that he could be coaxed out of his retirement. Finally they did it. Their vehicle was a speech, and it all sprang from that portentious year 1850, and the return to Kentucky of a congressman who had passed a more than normally active session in Washington City, the Honorable Henry Clay.

Eighteen-fifty had been a momentous year for Clay, culminating a career that spanned half a century. On January 29 he stepped into Congress armed with a set of proposals in close harmony with Breckinridge's resolutions of two weeks before. With the southern states on the brink of secession in the face of the increasing power of the antislavery "Free Soilers," he sought to salve the differences between the two. For the South he proposed a more effective fugitive slave law, a guarantee that Congress would not tamper with the slave trade between the southern states, and that recent territorial acquisitions would not be bound by restrictions either for or against slavery—the inhabitants would decide for themselves. For the North he proposed abolition of slavery in the District of Columbia, the immediate admission of California as a free state, and that the public debt of the former Republic of Texas be paid off to its primarily northern creditors. Eventually presented as an "omnibus bill," these proposals ultimately met with success, thanks largely to the fervid support of influential Northern politicians like Daniel Webster, Lewis Cass, and Stephen A. Douglas.

Breckinridge stood heartily in accord with Clay's bill. He had never expected California to be anything but a free state anyhow, and the number of slaves who yearly escaped Kentucky into Ohio made him firmly in favor of the new Fugitive Slave Law. In particular, he liked the opportunity given the inhabitants of new territories to decide for themselves the slavery question. And, of course, he took pardonable pride in the knowledge that this Compromise of 1850 had been based on principles that he advocated even before Clay's resolutions were introduced.[19]

Now Clay, at seventy-three, was coming home to Lexington. The public men of Kentucky of all parties planned a festival in his honor on October 17, 1850, and a committee of invitation was formed which included Breckinridge. He also served on a committee on resolutions and toasts. At the request of this latter body, and reportedly with the unanimous approval of the legislature, he agreed to make the principal toast to Clay.[20]

The appointed day dawned gloomy. In spite of the incessant rain, thou-

19. For a full discussion of the compromise and Clay's activities, see Hamilton, *Prologue to Conflict.*

20. Lexington *Kentucky Statesman,* October 12, 19, 1850; Ed. Porter Thompson, *History of the First Kentucky Brigade* (Cincinnati, 1868), 303.

sands of spectators gathered at the fairgrounds, and at noon Leslie Combs finally called the meeting to order. The toasts followed almost immediately, Breckinridge's coming last. He was fulsome. "Kentucky, with one heart and one voice," he said, "places Henry Clay where, during the late session of Congress, he placed himself, *high above the platform of party*. . . . Nobly has he won the honor—long may he wear it." Breckinridge followed with a brief address tracing Clay's career, concluding with the hope "that Heaven will shed its richest blessings on his declining years, and that it may be his happy fortune to close his long and eventful life amidst the general applause of his countrymen." [21]

Clay was visibly moved by this testimonial. In a voice betraying his emotion, he thanked those present, and then turned his attention to the major. "My welcome has been made all the more grateful," he said, "from being pronounced by my eloquent young friend, the son of an eloquent father, the grandson of a still more eloquent grandfather, both of whom were in days long gone my cherished companions, my earnest supporters." Complimenting Breckinridge on his talent and promise, Clay startled many of his hearers by expressing the hope and belief that the young Democrat would "employ both for the benefit of his country." Before this had its full impact on the audience, Clay then stepped over to the major. In an entirely unexpected move, accompanied by the cheering of the crowd, he threw his arms around Breckinridge in a fatherly embrace. Out in the crowd Will Hood of Scott County cried out: "Old Hall [sic] is passing the leadership to John." Others said the same thing, and for those who witnessed it, Clay's act seemed of profound significance. Whether or not Clay really intended to give the impression of endorsing Breckinridge is conjecturable. But thousands of Kentuckians, Whig and Democrat, so interpreted it, and in their eyes, Clay's wish could not be denied. [22]

The Democrats of Fayette did not wait long to take advantage of Clay's apparent endorsement, and Breckinridge, his financial troubles settled, did not object. He was appointed a delegate to the state party convention in Frankfort, and, meanwhile, a meeting in Fleming County recommended him as a nominee for lieutenant governor. The Whig press, seeking to justify Clay's interest, began referring to the major as "a sort of a half-way Whig," trying to imply that he had voted for Taylor in 1848. Of course,

21. Lexington *Kentucky Statesman*, October 19, 1850.
22. *Ibid.*, June 24, 1853; Blaine, *Twenty Years*, I, 322–23. The account of Will Hood is taken from an unnumbered notebook of Clifton Breckinridge's in the Prewitt Collection. Breckinridge's opinion of Clay as an orator was related by Tom Clay to Lucille Stillwell, December 13, 1934, and is in Stillwell, *Breckinridge*, 43–44.

Breckinridge did not get the lieutenant governor's nomination, nor did he want it. Better things lay within his grasp.[23]

He came to the opening of the Democratic state convention on January 8, 1851 swelled with pride. Another son had been born to him a few days before. They called him John for his father—and perhaps for another baby John who had left them—and Witherspoon for his venerated ancestor. But the elation he felt over the new birth was nothing compared to what came that afternoon. When the delegates reassembled after a meal break, Robert Wickliffe, Jr.—who got the lieutenant governorship nomination—took the stand. In a brief speech he offered the convention the name of John C. Breckinridge for the Eighth "Ashland" Congressional District's seat in Washington. There was an immediate uproar, followed by cries for the major to come forward. The nomination was his.[24]

The press met the news of the nomination with undisguised enthusiasm, even outside the Ashland District. "There is probably no man in Kentucky, so young in years, who possesses more talent, or who is better qualified to discharge the important duties of the statesman," claimed one paper. "He is a gentleman of fine talents," said another. Even the Whig Louisville *Courier* declared, "We rejoice that the people of this district have the opportunity to elect a gentleman so admirably qualified for this station." He was, they said, "a man of the highest order of talents." Within the Eighth District, the reaction was even more heartening. The Georgetown *Herald* compared him to Clay and the late Vice-president Richard M. Johnson, saying he was "capable of equaling either of these two distinguished worthies." [25]

None approached the effusive fervor of the major's own, the Lexington *Kentucky Statesman*. He had promoted its charter when a legislator, and was a stockholder from its founding the year before. Now his name would sit at the head of its editorial page throughout the campaign to come. Although understatement would never be one of the *Statesman*'s virtues when it came to the major, there were few complaints. The man in the flesh lived up to the man in print, though the *Statesman* did not make it easy.

> Major Breckinridge ... has not his superior as a man of talents in Kentucky, among men of his age; we even doubt whether, among young men, he has his equal. His judgment is strong; his intellect keen, vigorous and active;

23. Lexington *Kentucky Statesman*, October 30, November 13, 27, 1850; Louisville *Democrat*, November 25, 1850.
24. Lexington *Kentucky Statesman*, January 8, 15, 1851.
25. *Ibid.*, January 15, 18, 22, 25, April 26, June 21, July 26, 1851.

his perception clear; his apprehension quick, and all his mental operations performed with a vigor and energy, a boldness, firmness and decision, which evince an affirmative character of a superior order. To all these characteristics he adds a high consideration for the rights and feelings of others, sympathies alive to every generous impulse, and manners bland and conciliatory.

The *Statesman* would do its best to elevate the major to Homeric proportions, and place its Ajax among the gods in Washington City.[26]

Indeed, a god would be needed to unseat the Whigs in this district. It had been their bailiwick for decades, a party stronghold in Kentucky. Henry Clay made it so with his election to Congress in 1811, and in the following forty years only two Democrats won its seat, the second in 1827. For a quarter century now it had been their undisputed domain. They knew, however, that they faced a new threat in Breckinridge, a Democrat who enjoyed some favor among many Whigs in the district. Consequently, they responded by opposing him with one of their strongest sons, General Leslie Combs. A hero of William Henry Harrison's campaigns in the Northwest, Combs had been an ardent supporter of the Texas Revolution, and a longtime member of the Kentucky legislature. He enjoyed a warm friendship with Clay and wide popularity in the district. Some claimed that he had Clay's endorsement in this campaign, though the compromiser himself never said so. Still, it seemed to matter little. The Whigs had a safe 1,000–1,500 vote majority out of a voting population of 11,000, and to many it seemed an insurmountable advantage.[27]

Breckinridge planned a backbreaking campaign to overcome that majority. He would speak daily for five and six weeks at a time without letup —throughout the district's seven counties, Fayette, Franklin, Woodford, Scott, Owen, Jessamine, and Bourbon. The canvass would last six months, and he studied hard for it, preparing himself to meet every question Combs might raise on the stump. For subjects such as the tariff, he reread Adam Smith, familiarized himself with the course of free trade abroad to use as an example. He then formulated the position he would take: that government interference with commerce hindered trade and business morals, that free thought needed free trade. Thus prepared for battle, Breckinridge awaited the opening of the campaign in February.[28]

26. *Ibid.,* July 2, 1851.

27. Collins, *Historical Sketches,* 277; *Sketches of Breckinridge and Lane,* 7; W. W. Stapp to Breckinridge, April 28, 1851, in B. MSS.

28. Typewritten manuscript of a speech by Edward C. Marshall, 1877, JCB Papers. Lists of Breckinridge's stump engagements were carried in the *Kentucky Statesman* throughout the campaign, February–August, 1851.

The antagonists first met at the courthouse in Lexington. Following Combs's speech, Breckinridge proved himself an able opponent. "Mr. Breckinridge is more than a fine speaker," wrote a correspondent, "he is an eloquent and able man. . . . No one could mistake or misunderstand him. His mind, thought and mode of expression are clear, explicit and intelligent, his manners dignified, courteous and pleasing. His diction is that of a scholar and man of taste, always selecting the appropriate word and placing it in the right position, all of which give to his speaking efforts the air of a finished and eloquent composition." Breckinridge showed himself to be a strict constructionist of the Constitution. He spoke in reiteration of the position he had taken on the issues settled by the Compromise of 1850, and defended the line which separated the powers of the federal government from those of the several states. And he loved the Union. "I shall not attempt its eulogy," he declared. "It is above and beyond my powers." It was an excellent maiden speech, and set the tone for the remainder of his campaign.[29]

The canvass gathered momentum rapidly, and the major blossomed as a campaigner. He told stories, shook hands, attended barbecues, passed out cigars, and provided drinks on occasion. His greatest article of persuasion, however, proved undoubtedly to be his oratory. By mid-April the *Statesman*—surprisingly fair toward Combs—warned that he might as well not come to Fayette again. The Whigs were so mortified at his lack of eloquence that they feared to hear him speak for fear that "they should be compelled to vote for Breckinridge." [30]

After the first few weeks, the major proceeded with abundant confidence. He discovered that he could match Combs fact for fact, wit for wit. He could meet him on his own ground, and even trip up Combs on his own past. When the general accused him of having been a Whig in his youth, Breckinridge put down the charge and then countered with the revelation that when Taylor had been nominated by the Whigs over Clay in 1848, Combs declared that he was glad of it, and that the party had been tied to Clay for too long. To speak thus of Clay was, in the Ashland District, suicide.[31]

Sensing the threat posed by Breckinridge, Combs's fellow Whigs began an organized attack to aid their lagging nominee. Ignoring the major's fine

29. Lexington *Kentucky Statesman*, February 12, 1851.

30. Receipt of A. J. Lovely, March 29, 1850, receipt of W. K. Higgins, March 27, 1851, in JCB Papers; Castleman, *Active Service*, 32; Lexington *Kentucky Statesman*, April 12, 1851.

31. Lexington *Kentucky Statesman*, April 26, 1851.

legislative record on internal improvements, they brought up his support of Polk's rivers and harbors veto. The major was taken aback by this. He had discussed the matter with Combs before the canvass, explained his reason for supporting Polk, and his opponent had found it entirely satisfactory, agreeing not to bring up the subject. But now here it was. Breckinridge answered the charge in an open letter published in the press. Once again he explained the situation, ending with the declaration: "I have argued in favor of internal improvements of a *national character*, including the great navigable rivers of the West, as well as the rivers on our coasts. Let us conduct this canvass, to its close, with candor and fairness." [32]

As election day approached the Whigs grew more desperate. They circulated a leaflet in the district stressing the goodness of past Whig administrations, hinting that disunion was at the root of the Democratic party. "Our opponents are completely organized," it said, "while we, confident of our numbers and strength, are idle and supine." All Whigs were urged to support Combs, if for no other reason than the fact that he was a Whig.[33]

By late July, Combs was obviously tiring. He still spoke for prodigious lengths of time, but his vigor and wit were gone. Audiences now listened to him "with great attention and profound courtesy," but precious little enthusiasm. On the other hand, Breckinridge's equally long speeches were frequently interrupted by cheering and applause. Sensing his advantage, the major went in for the kill at every opportunity, often leaving Combs obviously angry and embarrassed. Yet Breckinridge himself remained calm and casual. "He can be decisive without violence," wrote one correspondent, "and energetic without ranting." By the evening of August 2, 1851, at the grand rally in Lexington, which both candidates attended, Breckinridge had moved from a decidedly disadvantaged position at the start of the canvass to one equal, if not better, than his opponent's. The morrow's polling would tell.[34]

The voter turnout was heavy. Balloting took two days, and as the votes were counted they revealed a close race. Breckinridge carried Lexington but lost Fayette. He lost Bourbon, Woodford, and Jessamine as well, but at the same time won populous Franklin and Scott. With these six counties totaled, he trailed Combs 4,491 to 4,631. But then came the results from Owen, and forever afterward it would be "Sweet Owen" to the major and his friends. The county turned in an even 500 for Combs, and 1,177 for

---

32. *Ibid.*, June 11, July 26, 1851.
33. Circular in the B. MSS, n.d. [June–July, 1851].
34. Lexington *Kentucky Statesman*, July 26, August 2, 8, 1851.

Breckinridge, giving him an overall majority in the district of 537, and with it Ashland's seat in Congress.[35]

He accomplished what had seemed impossible; he lured over 1,000 Whig voters away from Combs. It was a harbinger of great change for the district, and for Kentucky; the Whig era was nearing its end. Breckinridge's opponents were not dead yet, however, and his election mortified them, particularly since their own party members secured his victory. More galling were the rumors that Clay himself had voted for the major, though in fact he did not. Many Whigs simply regarded the whole affair as an unhappy accident. Others tried to save face by calling Breckinridge an "independent" or "moderate Democrat," thus explaining his appeal to Whig voters. Some were simply bitter. State Attorney General James Harlan, disdainfully referring to Breckinridge as the "young gentleman," predicted that the incumbent would not make a ripple in Congress and that this election would be the last anyone would ever hear from him.[36]

The reaction among the Democrats was electric. From as far as Virginia and Iowa the congratulations came. "We are proud of your success," wrote a friend from Burlington. Indeed, people of that city now declared that they would regard him as their Congressman as well as Ashland's. Already predictions were being made of even higher offices to come. Meanwhile, in far off Washington City the election made the news, though not with such fanfare. There it was variously reported that "J. C. Brackenridge" or "F. C. Breckenridge" had been elected to Congress. One thing that his new position could not—would never—change was the constant misspelling of his name. He seldom objected, though; it was one of those sacrifices that the public required from its servants.[37]

Breckinridge's new constituents were ecstatic. "Veni, vidi, vici," said letters from Sweet Owen and elsewhere. Democrats promised never to forget the man "by whose mighty efforts our flag has been carried aloft, and victory perched upon our banners." There were barbecues, grand illuminations, dinners, and testimonials all around. The major was the man of the year. Indeed, the only one not entirely elated was his mother. While she believed that "my boy has an old head on young shoulders," she feared that

35. The final vote is in the *Kentucky Statesman* for August 29, 1851, but it contains a typographical error that gives Breckinridge's majority as 528 instead of 537.

36. Lexington *Kentucky Statesman*, August 8, 13, 20, 1851; Louisville *Courier-Journal*, June 8, 1875; Lexington *Herald*, October 8, 1911.

37. John Steele to Breckinridge, September 5, 1851, Enos Lowe to Breckinridge, November 12, 1851, Martin McCarver to Breckinridge, October 5, 1851, all in B. MSS; Lexington *Kentucky Statesman*, August 20, 1851; Washington *Daily National Intelligencer*, August 8, 9, 11, 1851.

"having tasted political life, he will never be willing to return to the monotous [sic] tread to, and from his office." A friend teased him in the same vein. When it was all over in Congress, he said, it would be hard for Breckinridge to come back to "a dingy little office where you sit by the hour and talk with a client as to who owes $2.50." [38]

Breckinridge was both proud of and humbled by his success. One of his first actions after the election was to ask a friend of Henry Clay's how the elder statesman would receive him if he should call. "As a gentleman and a Kentuckian," came the reply, and the major accordingly paid a visit to Ashland. With Clay at the time was his son James, a friend of Breckinridge's since childhood. He later recalled the major's words to his father. " 'Mr. Clay,' said Mr. Breckinridge . . . 'I have been elected from your old district, and am about to go, quite a young man, to Washington City. We have always differed, sir, in politics, but I have ever entertained the highest respect for you. I have no doubt but I shall often have occasion for good advice, and if you will allow me, sir, to do so, it will afford me great satisfaction to call freely upon you at Washington, and to be enabled to avail myself of your wisdom and great experience.' "

Clay replied at first in an equally formal manner. "Major Breckinridge, I congratulate you. You are worthy to represent the people of this district, whose esteem and favor have been the chief objects of my ambition, and the most precious rewards of my long and laborious life." This done, he dropped his voice and spoke in a warm, almost fatherly tone. "My dear John, be true to your name. Never forget that you are a Kentuckian and a Breckinridge, and the highest honors of the Republic, or, what is more valuable, the consciousness of having served well your country, will be your glorious reward." [39]

These two men, statesmen of different eras, were already good friends. In the months ahead they would be drawn closer still. The major's reverence for Clay was undisguised, and yet, in turn, Breckinridge so impressed the old patriot that, a century later, the Great Compromiser's descendants recalled that Henry Clay regarded John C. Breckinridge as the brightest, most promising young man of his day.[40]

38. Lexington *Kentucky Statesman*, August 6, 1851; Richard Williams and others to Breckinridge, August 18, 1851, in B. MSS; CRB Book No. 7, p. 30, in Prewitt Collection; Mary C. Breckinridge to Abraham W. Venable, January 28, 1852, in Abraham W. Venable MSS, SHC.

39. Cincinnati *Daily Enquirer*, July 29, 1856; James B. Clay in *Old Line Whigs for Buchanan & Breckinridge* (N.p., 1856), 16; Lexington *Kentucky Statesman*, August 3, 1861.

40. Henry Clay's opinion of Breckinridge is taken from an interview with Tom Clay, December 13, 1934, by Lucille Stillwell, and quoted in Stillwell, *Breckinridge*, 43.

CHAPTER 4

Go On, You Cannot Fail

In the three months between his election and his departure for Washington City in mid-November, 1851, Breckinridge was swamped by solicitations for patronage jobs, pension claims, and all the other favors that constituents expected. Even as he boarded the coach in Lexington to begin his journey, office seekers tugged at his sleeve. He lost them quickly, and few if any saw the coach take him to the outskirts of the city to Ashland. Here, from its lovely garden, he took a single rose. He would take it to the capital with him, to give to Henry Clay.[1]

Breckinridge had his first glimpse of Washington City in the cold winter of late November. He took a room in the National Hotel, and while he awaited the opening of the first session of the Thirty-second Congress on December 1, friends took good care of him. From Kentucky they sent him bacon, hams, shoulders, and, to take some chill out of the season, some eighteen gallons of whiskey that was guaranteed to be sixteen years old and to have passed around Cape Horn twice.

Their interest was not just for his culinary welfare. Shortly after his election Breckinridge found his friends talking of him for speaker of the House. He was a likely candidate; a westerner, a moderate, the supposed successor of Clay, a man with cross-party appeal, he had many advantages in his favor. But Breckinridge never believed that he could win the post, and so expressed himself to Lazarus Powell, a close friend and governor-elect of Kentucky. Before leaving for the capital, he had told Powell his chances were slim. If his name were put in nomination, he felt it would only hurt another Kentuckian, who could win, the Democrat Linn Boyd.

1. Breckinridge to C. C. Rogers, January 21, 1852, Autograph Collection of the Historical Society of Pennsylvania, HSP; John Darby to Breckinridge, December 1, 1851, in B. MSS; Interview of Lucille Stillwell with Tom Clay, December 13, 1934, quoted in Stillwell, *Breckinridge,* 44.

Consequently, even before leaving Lexington, Breckinridge decided not to allow his name to be put forth. At the same time he predicted to Powell that Boyd, if successful, would show little or no gratitude when it came time for the new speaker to make committee appointments. Breckinridge proved to be a prophet. When the session opened, and he withheld his name, Boyd won the speakership handily on the first ballot. Whereas Powell and the Democratic managers back in Kentucky felt that the major should have received a first-rate chairmanship in reward, Boyd gave him an inconsequential post on the then unimportant foreign affairs committee. "It was your withholding your name from the contest for speaker that elected Boyd," Powell complained to Breckinridge, "and he should have recollected it." [2]

With Boyd's election out of the way, Breckinridge familiarized himself with his new roles and those around him. There were old friends. Presley Ewing, a Centre classmate, sat with him in the Kentucky delegation. Obadiah Bowne, a friend from Princeton, represented New York. An intimate from Burlington, Augustus C. Dodge, sat across the Capitol building in the Senate, and the major's near cousin Edward C. Marshall came from far off California as a representative. There were new friends to make, as well, and almost immediately Breckinridge formed one friendship in particular. John W. Forney, alcoholic, brilliant journalist, chief promoter of the political interests of his fellow Pennsylvanian, James Buchanan, was the new clerk of the House. The Kentuckian fascinated Forney. "Never have I met a man more adapted by nature, by education, and by rearing, to be a favorite among men and women," Forney would say. The two talked much and often. Frequently their discussion turned to slavery, and they found that they were agreed upon its abhorrence. Breckinridge repeatedly told Forney of the expatiations of Sam Houston on the evils of the institution, and Forney easily saw the same line of thinking in the congressman's mind. "At that time," he said of the Kentuckian, "if he had a conscientious feeling, it was hatred of slavery, and both of us, 'Democrats' as we were, frequently confessed that it was a sinful and an anti-Democratic institution, and that the day would come when it must be peaceably or forcibly removed." Breckinridge and Forney would go through a great deal together before that day came. [3]

2. William O. Smith to Breckinridge, December 1, 13, 1851, January 8, 1852, R. Long to Breckinridge, December 13, 1851, Lazarus Powell to Breckinridge, January 5, 1853, J. W. Cleland to Breckinridge, December 4, 1851, all in B. MSS; *Congressional Globe*, 32nd Cong., 1st Sess., Pt. 1, pp. 9, 47.

3. John W. Forney, *Anecdotes of Public Men* (New York, 1873), I, 41; Samuel M. Wilson, *History of Kentucky* (Chicago, 1928), II, 356.

The new congressman dug into his new duties with determination. He devoted the first three months of the session entirely to trying to meet the needs and requests of his constituents. Throughout the weeks of debate, he remained silent, biding his time as he learned his trade. Often new members took every opportunity, however inconsequential, to speak up for the record, to prove to those back home that they were doing their job. Consequently, Breckinridge's discreet silence made him conspicuous in contrast, and earned him the growing respect of many of the senior representatives. John Bragg of Alabama was impressed. Despite the major's reticence and the fact that his youth made him "barely eligible to a seat in that body," wrote Bragg, "there was something about him that placed him at once, *facile princeps* among the leaders of the House." The potential lay there awaiting the catalyst.[4]

The work, at first stimulating, soon grew commonplace, even dreary. The endless petitions, pension claims, bounty land disputes, and applications for patronage positions, took up all of his time, the moreso since he was anxious to please as many as possible. Already a move had begun in Frankfort to gerrymander decisive Owen County out of his district. It would seriously damage, or even cripple, any reelection attempt in 1853, and Breckinridge needed all the friends he could find. His supporters in the legislature, led by Thomas Marshall, put up a stiff fight against the Whigs. This nephew of Chief Justice John Marshall fought earnestly, declaring that he would rather have his right hand cut off than see Breckinridge defeated. The closeness of the fight was evident when the gerrymander came to a vote. It deadlocked at forty-seven for and forty-seven against, and thus failed to pass. By this slim margin Breckinridge could hold his seat with some security. "Your constituents are very sanguine they can return you," wrote one soon after. Kinkead, more exuberant, advised Breckinridge to acquire a taste for Washington City, "as we anticipate you will be required to stay there four or five years longer."[5]

With this crisis at home out of the way, the major focused more attention on national affairs, and there was much to draw his notice. The young men of the nation were on the move. A salient feature of this Congress—one

4. Mobile (Ala.) *Daily Register*, May 30, 1875.
5. *Congressional Globe*, 32nd Cong., 1st Sess., Pt. 1, p. 150; L. B. Dickerson to Breckinridge, December 27, 1851, George Marshall to Breckinridge, December 31, 1851, R. R. Bolling to Breckinridge, January 7, 1852, J. P. Metcalf to Breckinridge, February 23, 1852, W. W. Stapp to Breckinridge, January 7, 1852, S. M. Moore to Breckinridge, February 6, 1852, George B. Kinkead to Breckinridge, December 26, 1851, several petitions 1851–1852, all in B. MSS.

which Breckinridge himself ably represented—was the comparative youth of its members. The median age among the 233 representatives was forty-three. Breckinridge was only thirty, and there were seven other members younger than he. The concentration of youthful members was principally from the western and border states, which also reflected the trend toward according greater responsibility to younger men in these less urban areas. In contrast, the average representative from Massachusetts in this Congress had been born in 1798.

Largely expressive of this new preoccupation with youth was an equally new movement styling itself Young America. Its chief exponent was a Kentuckian and casual friend of Breckinridge's, George N. Sanders. With the Democratic party fragmented over a variety of issues and leaders, Sanders hoped to unite it on a policy of further annexation, active support of European revolutionary movements, free trade, and aggressive foreign commerce. This international expansionist outlook was calculated to draw attention away from the growing sectional controversy. Since Stephen A. Douglas' plans for westward expansion and a transcontinental railroad were largely based on the same goal, Sanders seized on the "Little Giant" as a torchbearer for Young America's political aspirations. To promote the cause of Douglas and Young America, Sanders also purchased the widely respected *United States Democratic Review* to serve as an official organ.

Breckinridge might have seemed a natural adherent of the movement, but he was not. He firmly opposed American interference in the affairs of other nations, sympathizing with the cause of European revolutionaries like Louis Kossuth—whom he saw on the Hungarian's touted trip to America in 1851. But John Breckinridge believed that only force could establish, maintain, or change the rules of international law, and he could not countenance the use of force. His constituents backed him in this. As for further annexation, that would come with or without Young America, and so would free trade and international commerce, all of which Breckinridge favored. What disturbed him most about Young America, however, was its appeal to emotionalism and its repudiation of the nation's elder statesmen. Sanders regarded men like Butler and Cass with contempt, and Breckinridge's instinctive respect for authority—in this case authority through the wisdom of experience—was too great for him to find common ground with Young America.[6]

All this came to a head in the presidential campaign of 1852. A variety of favorites were in the running—Cass, Houston, Buchanan, Butler—all older

6. CRB Book No. 8, p. 2, in Prewitt Collection; Kinkead to Breckinridge, January 20, 1852, in B. MSS.

men. Young America, of course, backed Douglas, and though he began campaigning for the nomination in 1851, by January Butler appeared to be the most likely nominee. Sanders determined to aim his sights first at this fellow Kentuckian and, despite Douglas protestations, began work on a scathing attack to appear in the *Democratic Review*. Breckinridge, meanwhile, was reporting regularly to Butler on the feeling in Washington City. He was committed to the general's candidacy, confident that Butler was sound on slavery and the territorial question. When rumors sprang up that Butler was secretly a Free-Soiler, Breckinridge got from him a letter denying the charge. Before he could circulate it, however, Representative Edward C. Cabell of Florida arose in the House and repeated the rumor, asserting that Butler was "a man whose opinions are not known." The growing threat to Butler was clear.[7]

Clearly a rejoinder was required to counteract the slanders on Butler. No one saw this better than old Francis Preston Blair, editor of the *Congressional Globe*, and father of Francis, Jr., who attended the College of New Jersey with Breckinridge. The elder Blair, though a Free-Soiler himself, had decided to support Butler if he were nominated. At the same time he felt an almost paternal regard for his cousin, John Breckinridge. He thought he saw a way to help both of them. Writing to Breckinridge, he suggested that, since Kentucky had officially endorsed Butler, "You may ... break a lance with her assailants in defense of her principles and her candidate." Breckinridge should answer Cabell on the House floor, he said, not in advocacy of Butler's presidential hopes, but in defense of Kentucky's endorsement. This would make the speech a defense rather than a campaign address. "If I did not think you could enrich my naked thoughts and adorn them with eloquence," Blair went on, "I would not give you even the cue."[8]

Breckinridge did not need prompting, for he already contemplated some rejoinder. Immediately after Cabell's attack, he began trying to get the floor. Unsuccessful for some days, still he tried, now with an added impetus. Sanders had published the first number of the *Democratic Review*, and it sent a jolt through the party. Thoroughly disparaging the elder statesmen —old fogies—he launched a vigorous assault on Butler in particular, using

7. Robert W. Johannsen, *Stephen A. Douglas* (New York, 1973), 360–61; William O. Butler to Breckinridge, February 3, 1852, B. MSS; *General Butler—the Democratic Review—Judge Douglas—The Presidency: Speech of John C. Breckinridge, of Kentucky, Delivered in the House of Representatives, Mar. 4, 1852* (Washington, 1852), 5–6, hereinafter cited as *General Butler*.

8. Francis P. Blair to Breckinridge, February 6, 1852, in B. MSS.

faulty judgment and vicious generalizations. Although Sanders nowhere mentioned Douglas by name, it was clear that the Little Giant was the only alternative to the fogies so far as the *Democratic Review* was concerned.[9]

Not long after the appearance of this article, Breckinridge was conversing with Douglas and others near the Senate chamber. The Little Giant drew Breckinridge aside and confided that the next issue of the journal would contain further attacks on Butler. Breckinridge replied that he would denounce them, suggesting that Douglas try to stop Sanders first. Douglas did try, but without success, and a joint effort by Breckinridge, Douglas, and others, met with the same failure. Sanders could not be stopped, and the February issue of his journal produced the anticipated assault on Butler. A day or two before its official publication, a copy of the issue was handed to the major by Sanders himself. He wanted Breckinridge's opinion, and the Congressman frankly told him that he intended to denounce the article publicly. It now remained only for Breckinridge to prepare his address, and to get the floor of the House. He found the whole affair shameful. "There is little of interest going on here," he wrote his uncle Robert, "but much scheming, and a great deal of rascality generally." He was determined that his own contribution to the melee should be dignified and nonpartisan. As he worked on his speech, his friends in Kentucky—particularly Butler—grew anxious. Finally, on March 4, 1852, the House resolved itself into a committee of the whole and gave Breckinridge the floor.[10]

There was an air of anticipation in the House that day as Breckinridge arose, and he presented an aspect well calculated to add emphasis to his words. Tall and graceful, he wore his usual suit of black broadcloth. A simple velvet cravat encircled his high collar, set off by a gold serpentine stickpin. His eyes shone in his clean-shaven face. Watching the Kentuckian as he spoke was Congressman Bragg, who marveled. "Nature seemed to have favored him far beyond most men. Of a mein and presence vouchsafed to few, an eloquence rarely ever equalled, an address and bearing

9. *General Butler*, 4; George N. Sanders, "1852 and the Presidency," *United States Democratic Review*, XXX (January, 1852), 1–12.

10. *Judge Douglas—the Democratic Review, etc., Remarks of Mr. Breckinridge in Reply to Mr. Richardson of Illinois, Delivered in the House of Representatives, Mar. 10, 1852* (Washington, 1852), 6–7, hereinafter cited as *Judge Douglas*; Stephen Douglas to Sanders, February 10, 1852, Sanders to Douglas, February 11, 1852, in Robert W. Johannsen (ed.), *The Letters of Stephen A. Douglas* (Urbana, Ill., 1961), 239–40; *Democratic Review*, XXX (February, 1852), 183 (March, 1852), 207; Breckinridge to Robert J. Breckinridge, February 23, 1852, W. Tanner to Breckinridge, February 26, 1852, Butler to Breckinridge, March 1, 1852, all in B. MSS; *Congressional Globe*, 32nd Cong., 1st Sess., Pt. 1, pp. 670–71.

truly inimitable, an harmonious blending of the *suaviter in modo* with the *fortiter in re*. These, with the lofty integrity and proud disdain of all the mean tricks 'of low ambition,' marked him as the very best type of Southern character, and the fittest representative of the people who loved and trusted him so well." [11]

Breckinridge began with a reply to Cabell's insinuations, avowing, "It is our custom in Kentucky to defend and honor all our worthy public men." He ably stood up for Butler, asserting that the general's opinions were widely known and that he was not at all a Free-Soiler. Citing Butler's past record, Breckinridge quickly dispensed with Cabell's charges. There was larger game to go after.

"Mr. Chairman," Breckinridge said, "I have been defending this gentleman against a Whig attack. It now becomes my disagreeable duty to notice one proceeding from a Democratic source—if that can be called a Democratic source which traduces all the best and most honored names in the party." He meant, of course, Sanders and the *Review*. Immediately he launched into an unimpassioned examination of the charges in the January issue, focusing on Sanders' announcement of a new generation of young statesmen with young ideas. "Now, sir," said the congressman, "I am in favor of progress. I like young blood, and I like young ideas, too, (at a certain time of life,) but I do not like this course." And the February *Review*, he continued, was even more objectionable, both in its attacks on Butler and in its break with the journal's conventional unbiased approach to potential party nominees. The *Review*, he lamented, had been "converted into a mere partisan sheet." In answer to the course taken by Sanders and his journal, Breckinridge gave his own views on progress and statesmanship in one of the most lucid expressions of his conservatism that he would ever make.

> Let me say a word now upon this question of progress. I profess to be a friend of rational progress; but I want no wild and visionary progress that would sweep away all the immortal principles of our forefathers—hunt up some imaginary genius, place him on a new policy, give him "Young America" for a fulcrum, and let him turn the world upside down. That is not the progress I want. I want to progress in the line of the principles of our fathers; I want a steady and rational advance—not beyond the limits of the Federal Constitution—but I am afraid that such progress as is now talked about would carry us clear away from that sacred instrument. I want to progress by ameliorating the condition of the people by fair, just, and equal laws, and by sim-

11. Mobile *Daily Register*, May 30, 1875.

plicity, frugality, and justice marking the operations of the Federal Government. Above all, I hope to see the Democratic party adhere with immovable fidelity to the ancient and distinguished land-marks of its policy.

Breckinridge went on to summarize Sanders' course, and to expose completely the connection—however tenuous—with Douglas. The Little Giant's chief lieutenant in the House, William Richardson, now arose to speak briefly in defense of Douglas. He and Breckinridge had agreed the day before that he should have such an opportunity. Richardson declared that Douglas had no interest in, or control over, the *Review*, and he spoke the truth. He also denied that Douglas had signed a paper endorsing the *Review* after having seen the offensive January issue. Breckinridge accepted Richardson's defense and then made his main point. Just as Douglas, an honorable man, should not be held personally accountable for the excesses of such supporters as Sanders, so Butler ought not to be condemned because some of his adherents were Free-Soilers. "Again, I say, let us be just," he concluded, "let us be fair; let no man, by himself or through his friends, attempt to promote individual interests by traducing others. If this course is continued, we will not succeed, we cannot succeed, we ought not to succeed." [12]

It was an outstanding maiden speech. Those who heard it in the House stood impressed. Thomas Ritchie, editor of the party organ, the Washington *Union*, wrote, "I admire your speech. It was a fine first effort— luminous in its views, beautiful in its style, moderate in its tone." Breckinridge's cousin, Edward Marshall, himself an ardent Young American, would go farther. "I do not remember any one speech which produced more effect," he said later. When Breckinridge took the floor "he was almost unknown, at the expiration of the one hour he was recognized among the most formidable debaters in the house." The party press also approved. Papers all over the Union scrambled to reprint his address, spreading his name through every state. One Richmond correspondent wrote that the congressman "was heard with great effect.... Mr. Breckenridge's speech is admitted to have been among the best delivered in the House for some time, and produced a great sensation." Breckinridge received letters of compliments from all over the country. Prominent men like Caleb Cushing, Charles Ingersoll, and J. L. M. Curry, wrote to offer their praise. Charles L. Woodbury of Boston, himself a noted orator, wrote to say that "Your speech has created much sensation.... I hear it continually spoken of as the best speech of the session." Even some emancipationists admired it. "All

12. *General Butler*, 1–7 *passim*.

hail to J. C. Breckinridge of the Fayette district," one Free-Soiler wrote to the congressman, "go on, you cannot fail." Kentucky, of course, was delirious with pride. "I am in sincere friendship rejoiced at the impression your first speech has made," wrote Kinkead. "I have no doubt that future events likely or at least not unlikely to arise will make you feel it the happiest & most fortunate day of your life." Whereas in some parts of the state people had said, "Well, who is Breckenridge?" he was now known throughout the state. The speech, said one, "has certainly immortalized you in this section of Kentucky." Butler, of course, was profoundly grateful. "It does not need my praise," he told the congressman of his speech, "for all praise it, but it has placed me under a sense of obligation to you, which I will not attempt to express in words, but which I feel assured will never be forgotten." [13]

Just as Butler would not forget the speech, neither would Young America, nor those Whigs like Cabell who hoped to reelect Millard Fillmore in 1852. Even as he praised Breckinridge, Ritchie had cautioned, "You have not passed the rock. Your danger now commences." Indeed, for three straight days those burned by the fire he had stirred tried to put the torch to him. It started on March 9 when fellow Kentuckian Humphrey Marshall —a Whig—took the floor to defend Fillmore against the major's charge that the president was not as sound on slavery as the supposedly opinionless Butler. The speech attracted little notice, but the next day the Douglas forces took the floor, their strategy being to discredit Breckinridge's speech by characterizing it as a blatant attack on Douglas and an electioneering appeal for Butler. Richardson continued his line of defense that Douglas was innocent of Sanders' indiscretions, and then accused Breckinridge of assaulting the Little Giant in full knowledge of that innocence.

Breckinridge was ready for him. He proceeded to prove Richardson a liar. On March 4, when Breckinridge brought up the matter of the endorsement of the *Review* which Douglas signed, Richardson declared that the Little Giant affixed his signature to the document before knowing of or reading the January number's opening assaults. Now, producing testimony backed by witnesses, Breckinridge proved conclusively that Douglas had signed the endorsement fully a month after the January issue appeared and

13. Thomas Ritchie to Breckinridge, March 4, 1852, Charles J. Ingersoll to Breckinridge, March 23, 1852, J. L. M. Curry to Breckinridge, July 21, 1852, Caleb Cushing to Breckinridge, July 28, 1852, Charles L. Woodbury to Breckinridge, April 13, 1852, Samuel Osborne to Breckinridge, April 20, 1852, Kinkead to Breckinridge, March 15, 1852, John Eaker to Breckinridge, April 12, 1852, Butler to Breckinridge, March 15, 1852, all in B. MSS; manuscript of speech by Edward Marshall, 1877, in JCB Papers; Richmond *Enquirer*, March 9, 10, 16, 18, 1852.

caused its furor. Even if he had not read the offending article, after a month of controversy over it Douglas could not have been ignorant of its contents. Breckinridge brought this out, not to damage Douglas, but to aid in discrediting Sanders, though it served both purposes. As for Richardson, confronted with proof of his false denial, he hedged, backed down, and finally admitted the truth, adding that Breckinridge could "make the most of it." This seemed to end the threat to Breckinridge, but March 11 brought the worst attack of all, and it came from his own cousin, Edward C. Marshall.[14]

Marshall's speech that day was a perfect example of what seasoned statesmen most disliked in freshman representatives. Forney characterized Marshall as "impetuous, blind, reckless," and this speech was much the same. Ignoring Richardson's exposure of the day before, Marshall charged that all of his cousin's allegations had been proved false. He went on to accuse the congressman of currying favor with the old fogies, of having made a bargain with Butler to support him in return for the attorney general's portfolio. Since Breckinridge had pointed up some inconsistencies in other men in his speech, Marshall declared that "I would rather, upon my honor, undertake to defend the inconsistencies of General Cass or Mr. Buchanan than those of that young gentleman." Once again Breckinridge's involvement in the Zachary Taylor meeting in 1847 was brought up. When he arose to offer a defense against the charge, Marshall cut him off: "Oh, I can't give you time to defend yourself, it would take all of my hour, and more hours than I ever mean to consume upon this floor, to defend yourself from that charge. I want to know if the charge is true."

Again Breckinridge arose, betraying his indignation, and his hurt. "I will answer the question," he said, "though I do not admire the taste that prompts it." Because of his speech a few days before, he now found himself the object of attacks from several points, and he heard rumors that an attempt to discredit him would be made, its goal being to show that he had once been a Whig. "It is not true," he declared, and followed with a full explanation of the circumstances of the Taylor meeting and his involvement. Marshall ignored him, uttered a few more barbs, and then launched into a half-hour phillippic on Douglas. That ended it.[15]

Although he could by now well conceal his feelings when angry or hurt, Breckinridge's mortification at this attack from his kinsman was evident.

14. Ritchie to Breckinridge, March 4, 1852, in B. MSS; *Congressional Globe*, 32nd Cong., 1st Sess., Appendix, 373–76, Pt. 1, pp. 710–14; *Judge Douglas*, 3–7.
15. Forney, *Anecdotes*, I, 315; *Congressional Globe*, 32nd Cong., 1st Sess., Appendix, 383–85.

Forney saw it. "You have no cause to feel deserted," he told the major. "Marshall has helped himself by ruining his friend." Forney could not have been more wrong. After this speech, Marshall never made another ripple in Congress; he served out his one term and was never heard of politically again. Breckinridge, far from being ruined, survived the attack with his newly made reputation unharmed, even enhanced. The entire affair had been blown out of proportion, and the real loser was Douglas. Sanders' ill-advised attacks seriously crippled the Little Giant's chances of nomination. Finally aware of what he had done, Sanders tried to win Breckinridge over. "I beg that you do not separate yourself from the young men any more than very absolutely necessary to defend Genl. Butler," he wrote. When solicitations and even the threat of publishing an attack on Breckinridge in the *Review* failed to win him over, Sanders resorted to the absurd. Through a relative he leaked to Breckinridge the preposterous intelligence that the Douglas ticket had already been made up and that Breckinridge was to be the nominee for vice-president. The fact that the congressman was constitutionally four years too young to be eligible for the office apparently never occurred to him.[16]

While Douglas would continue to work for the nomination, Butler's once bright prospects dimmed before long, and the whole *Democratic Review* controversy slowly died out, kept alive only by Sanders' continued but ignored editorials. Breckinridge, however, grew steadily in the public eye, assuming now the responsibilities attendant to his new position of leadership in the House. He spoke more often and more aggressively, particularly regarding legislation touching slavery. He voted against Andrew Johnson's homestead bill, fearing that it would create new territories that would exclude slaveholders. When the Fugitive Slave Law came under discussion, Breckinridge engaged Joshua Giddings of Ohio in a heated debate, winning a constitutional—if not a moral—argument on its legality.[17]

Breckinridge visited briefly in Lexington this April, bringing Mary back with him to Washington City. But there was a sad spring ahead. Only days after he left Kentucky his beloved sister Letitia died. She had been as close to him as anyone alive, his friend and confidante. He, in turn, represented her ideal of a true man. She had been married briefly, to a man Breckinridge thought a little insane, and when he died suddenly, she never recovered

16. John W. Forney to Breckinridge, March 11, 1852, George N. Sanders to Breckinridge, n.d. [March, 1852], James B. Breckinridge to Breckinridge, April 24, 1852, all in B. MSS; Johannsen, *Douglas*, 362; *Democratic Review*, XXX (March, 1852), 202–204.
17. *Congressional Globe*, 32nd Cong., 1st Sess., Pt. 2, p. 1350, Appendix, 384, 774–75.

from the loss. Now her brother was distraught. Despite the soothing sympathy of Forney and others, he grieved hard. For some days his seat in the House was vacant.[18]

Worse was in store for him and the nation. On leaving Lexington, Breckinridge took another rose from the garden at Ashland, but when he reached the capital to present it to Clay, he found the aged man dying. Clay was seventy-five, weak, bed-ridden, nearly helpless. Throughout May and early June, Breckinridge was at his bedside almost daily, talking about politics, Kentucky, family, and friends. When Clay could not speak, the congressman read to him. "I am not afraid to die, sir," he told Breckinridge. "I have hope, faith, and confidence. I do not think any man can be entirely certain in regard to his future state, but I have an abiding trust in the merits and mediation of our Savior." Once, just after Breckinridge had left him, the failing statesman said something else. "That young man is serving now his first term in Congress," he told a friend; "I perceive in him so much judgment and talent, so many of the elements of true statesmanship, that I clearly foresee he will yearly grow in the confidence and esteem of his countrymen, and eventually receive the highest honors it is in their power to bestow." On June 29, 1852, he was dead, and on that day it was John C. Breckinridge who smoothed down his last pillow.[19]

Even in death Clay advanced Breckinridge's career. Following custom, the House resolved itself into a committee of the whole on June 30 to hear the deceased eulogized. Clay, no ordinary congressman, would require more than an ordinary eulogist. It was testimony to the esteem in which he was held both by Clay and by his fellow representatives, that Breckinridge was singled out for this honor, and his colleagues were not disappointed. His elegy on Clay surpassed his defense of Butler. Keeping in mind the "severely simple" oration of Pericles over the dead of Athens, which he had read as a boy, Breckinridge kept his own words simple, but moving and reverent. He treated Clay's career as a whole, praising not the deeds but the fact of Henry Clay, his honesty. The great man's life, he said, was a

18. Brown, *Cabells and Their Kin*, 490; Mary C. Breckinridge to Breckinridge, October 4, 1842, Forney to Breckinridge, May 23, 1852, Breckinridge to Robert J. Breckinridge, February 23, 1852, all in B. MSS; Mary C. Breckinridge to Joseph Desha, June 1, 1852, in Joseph and John R. Desha MSS, LC; interview of Lucille Stillwell with Tom Clay, December 13, 1934, in Stillwell, *Breckinridge*, 44; *Congressional Globe*, 32nd Cong., 1st Sess., Pt. 2, p. 1637; Breckinridge to Woodbury, June 19, 1852, in Grenville H. Norcross Collection, MassHS.

19. *Congressional Globe*, 32nd Cong., 1st Sess., Pt. 2, p. 1637; *Sketches of Breckinridge and Lane*, 19; Lexington *Kentucky Statesman*, May 2, 1853.

reproach to the scheming and petty. If Breckinridge were allowed to compose an epitaph, he concluded, it would read: "Here lies a man who was in the public service for fifty years, and never attempted to deceive his countrymen." [20]

For all its simplicity, this speech would be remembered as one of the most eloquent and moving memorials ever pronounced in the House. Again the compliments poured in. By fulfilling his final obligation to a departed friend, Breckinridge had secured as well his own place as what one Massachusetts Democratic leader termed, "one of the most prominent & able leaders of the Democratic Party and the Union." Beyond cavil, John C. Breckinridge now stood as the most widely known, respected, and promising young man in the nation.[21]

Perhaps because of his own youthful success, Breckinridge now and always took an interest in the encouragement and advancement of other young men. His rise in esteem and fame was already something of a model for others to emulate and, conscious of this, he never turned a deaf ear to the entreaties of youth. One of his most interesting such cases came in the wake of the Clay eulogy when he received a letter from a twenty-year-old Philadelphia law student, Ignatius Donnelly. The boy, fascinated by Breckinridge's rise, had written an article on him which, though complimentary, described the congressman as somewhat less than handsome. Breckinridge, pleased and amused, comforted Donnelly with the admission that "I am aware that I have no beauty except in the eyes of a devoted wife." Indeed, Breckinridge was impressed with the boy, and hoped they might become friends. Donnelly would have none of it. He wanted no friendship with the congressman or any other prominent man until he had won some laurels himself. "I *shall* be something," he declared, "and when I am, then, and not till then, shall I be happy, very happy, to take you by the hand and call you my dear, dear friend." One day Donnelly would be "something." [22]

Just three days after the Clay eulogy, Breckinridge followed it with another widely read and well-received address, this time on government spending and involvement with private enterprise. His particular object was the heavily subsidized E. K. Collins and Company steamship line. The firm was already getting $385,000 per year to carry U.S. mail, and now it

20. Breckinridge to Ignatius Donnelly, August 14, 1852, Donnelly MSS; *Sketches of Breckinridge and Lane*, 15; *Congressional Globe*, 32nd Cong., 1st Sess., Pt. 2, p. 1637.

21. *Sketches of Breckinridge and Lane*, 14; Edward Hamilton to Breckinridge, June 25, 1852, in B. MSS.

22. Donnelly to Breckinridge, August 11, 17, 1852, in B. MSS; Breckinridge to Donnelly, August 14, 1852, in Donnelly MSS.

was asking for an additional $473,000 via an amendment to a deficiency bill. Breckinridge, a strict laissez faire advocate, was not about to let the amendment go by without a fight. He disliked monopolies, subsidies, and unreasonable spending, and the Collins case involved all three.

Breckinridge began with the fact that Great Britain's steamship lines carried mail throughout the world at thousands of dollars less per voyage than Collins was already receiving. At the same time, while the government financed these mail voyages entirely, Collins realized extra commercial profits from them by carrying passengers and cargo. Congress had originally become involved with the Collins subsidy on the condition that in time of war the navy could take over Collins' ships and convert them to war vessels. But Breckinridge produced a statement from Commodore Matthew G. Perry declaring that the ships were inferior in construction and could not be outfitted even as second-rate warships without a tremendous investment, and at that they would not be suitable for extended service. Finally, to Collins' argument that the mail would wind up being carried in foreign hulls unless his amendment was approved, Breckinridge offered a statement by Cornelius Vanderbilt that he would build the ships to carry the mails, seek no government funds for their construction as Collins had, and then operate them at four million dollars less than Collins for an eight-year contract period.

The real rub here, he went on, was that if the government could make such a princely endowment to a private steamship monopoly, then it could also do it for telegraphs, railroads, canals, stage lines, and a host of other companies. The power of the government had already spread beyond the limits of the Constitution, and he feared to see it go farther into the private business world, particularly since it used the tax monies of all the people to the great advantage of select private enterprises. "I am opposed to every scheme of national plunder by which the people are to be bought up with their own money," he declared. "I am opposed openly and forever to any system which would plunder one half of my country for the emolument of the other." Asking that Congress make a formal investigation of the Collins case, he promised again to fight every such excess. "It is time again to inscribe on our banners *Economy—Retrenchment—Reform*," he concluded, "and for one, I will labor faithfully with those who, instead of constantly seeking for new sources of expenditures, shall strive to curtail the already enormous cost of this Government." [23]

23. *Congressional Globe*, 32nd Cong., 1st Sess., Appendix, 820–26.

Once more the praise came in. The major's cousin Marshall later declared —in an interesting about-face from his invective on the *Democratic Review* affair—that it was a speech "full of sound democratic doctrine and common sense, and fully sustained the reputation he had won." The Boston *Post* declared that the speech "has already become a textbook for those who take his side of the question." Most gratifying, though, was the knowledge that most of Breckinridge's party stood behind him. And, though the amendment passed the House in July, three years later, on March 3, 1855, President Franklin Pierce vetoed another such bill in favor of Collins, in so doing taking precisely the same ground that Breckinridge had expounded.[24]

Breckinridge had another interest in Pierce, the governor of New Hampshire, in this summer of 1852, for the "Young Hickory of the Granite Hills" had emerged as perhaps the darkest horse in party history to capture the Democratic presidential nomination in June.

Breckinridge attended the Democratic National Convention at Baltimore that month as a delegate from Kentucky. He was still earnestly for General Butler's nomination and had been working behind the scenes for some months to build support for his candidate. He laid some plans with such Butler men as Governor Hannibal Hamlin of Maine, perhaps aiding in convention strategy. When June arrived, however, things looked bad. Support for Butler had fallen off badly; Hamlin and many others had gone over to Pierce. Breckinridge's own delegation was seriously divided between the "hot bloods," those anxious to put Butler's name in nomination early, and those who believed with Breckinridge that their best course lay in waiting, hoping for a deadlock between the other candidates, a situation in which Butler could become a compromise candidate. Breckinridge managed to keep the general out of the fray for the first twenty ballots, but then the vote for Lewis Cass of Michigan sharply declined, and the "hot bloods," seeing a void that Butler might fill, became almost violent. Breckinridge regretted that he could not get the delegation into a room by themselves for half an hour to explain the necessity of further patience, for out on the confused convention floor, he barely stood a chance. A quick poll of the Kentucky delegates gave the "hot bloods" a narrow decision, and Butler's name went in nomination on the twenty-first ballot. The movement for him never got off the ground, and Pierce captured the convention instead. Breckinridge was hardly morose, however, for Pierce had been his second choice. He thought the nomination a "sublime rebuke" to those

24. Franklin Pierce to the House of Representatives, March 3, 1855, in James D. Richardson (comp.), *A Compilation of the Messages and Papers of the Presidents, 1789–1897* (Washington, D.C., 1897), V, 322–25.

who had intrigued—particularly Sanders—and it is apparent that he was also pleased that Douglas had been rejected, for he despised the cliques like Young America that had grown up in the party. Breckinridge considered the election of the ticket a certainty and looked forward to the end of the session of Congress, that he might return to Kentucky and help in the campaign.[25]

Once back in Washington after the convention, the congressman sat through the rest of a dull session until adjournment on August 31. Then he returned to Kentucky in triumph. His performance had spread his fame throughout the nation, and the Bluegrass was proud of him. Even a newly developed variety of garden pea was named for him—the Breckinridge Double Blossom Prolific. He stumped the district for Pierce, making nearly twenty appearances, and the crowds were so large and enthusiastic that on occasion the town halls and courthouses could not accommodate them. Breckinridge brought in outside speakers like Jesse D. Bright of Indiana to help in the fight. He tried, unsuccessfully, to get Douglas as well, but still he was sure of the result in November. Pierce won handily, and the only sour note for Breckinridge was the fact that Kentucky was one of only four states that went for the Whig candidate.[26]

No sooner was Pierce elected than Breckinridge's friends began intimating that the congressman deserved a higher station in government. His Whig admirers, unhappy over the defeat of their candidate Winfield Scott, expressed to Breckinridge the hope that "your new Democratic President will offer you some high office worthy your acceptance. There ought to be some talent around the Presidency when there is so little in it." At the same time, the major's party supporters wished to see him "placed in a position once occupied by your illustrious grandsire." For his own part, however, the Kentuckian would be quite content to win reelection to Congress.[27]

He had been a good, attentive representative so far, acting on his constituents' petitions, sending them government documents, and trying his best to secure a few appointments for friends in the district. But the federal

25. Breckinridge to Woodbury, June 9, 1852, in Norcross Collection; Woodbury to Breckinridge, February 10, 1852, in B. MSS; Washington *Union*, January 12, 1854; H. Draper Hunt, *Hannibal Hamlin of Maine* (Syracuse, 1969), 75–76.

26. *Congressional Globe*, 32nd Cong., 1st Sess., Pt. 3, pp. 1964–65, 2015, 2132, 2220; William Pettit to Breckinridge, July 17, 1852, John Morten to Breckinridge, August 15, 1852, Thomas Metcalf to Breckinridge, November 22, 1852, Jesse D. Bright to Breckinridge, September 23, 1852, Rankin Revill to Breckinridge, December 2, 1852, all in B. MSS; Lexington *Kentucky Statesman*, October 8, 12, 19, 1852, April 19, 1853.

27. William Callander to Breckinridge, November 27, 1852, T. B. Moore to Breckinridge, November, 1852, in B. MSS.

patronage proved difficult, especially for a Democrat during the Whig Fillmore administration. Try as he did, he secured very few positions. Some Democrats were disappointed, as were many more Whigs. Indeed, he received so many applications for favors from the opposition in the district that, frustrated, he injudiciously wrote to one of them, "The intolerable labor imposed upon me by you and other Whigs like you has almost determined me never again to be a Candidate." The letter was published in an attempt to hurt him, but gradually his opposition receded, and friends could again report that he had a good chance of reelection.[28]

Breckinridge himself remained undecided. Once again money was a problem. His share of the proceeds from his practice had not increased noticeably, but his expenses had. Mary was expecting another baby in early 1853. He had invested heavily in land near Chicago, predicting to Kinkead that it would one day be "a great place," and he had to borrow several hundred dollars from the influential pro-Democrat Washington banking firm of Corcoran and Riggs to make his down payments. Friends owed him money and they were not paying. These and other concerns were with him when he returned to Washington City for the second session and took a room in the boardinghouse of William Peterson at 453 Tenth Street Northwest, across the street from the First Baptist Church.[29]

There was a somewhat different Washington awaiting him. The nation in general seemed recovering from the exertions of the past campaign. The variety of defeated Democratic factions were regrouping, realigning, largely in favor of Douglas and Buchanan. Young America was in its death throes and the Whig party was hardly more alive. The Free-Soilers continued to gain strength from disaffected northerners of both parties, and an astute observer might have seen here hints of a new and more perfect antislavery party on the horizon. Equally portentious, the southern rights extremists were gathering strength, and, despite their apparent acquiescence in Pierce's platform, they were not content. But this winter was a time for waiting and troubled rest; 1853 would be an election year, too, and national policy had to wait.

28. D. Watson to Breckinridge, November 25, 1851, Stapp to Breckinridge, December 26, 1851, Kinkead to Breckinridge, March 29, 1852, N. M. O. Smith to Breckinridge, April 1852, Breckinridge to Robert J. Breckinridge, December 22, 1852, S. D. Jacobs to Breckinridge, December 12, 1851, James Monroe to Breckinridge, December 17, 1852, C. C. Rogers to Breckinridge, December 22, 1852, all in B. MSS.

29. Kinkead to Breckinridge, August 11, 1852, Breckinridge to Robert J. Breckinridge, February 12, 1853, in B. MSS; Tax receipt, 1852, list of notes, November 27, 1852, in JCB Papers.

Mary Clay Smith Breckinridge, mother of John C. Breckinridge, *ca.* 1863. Her husband, Joseph Cabell Breckinridge, became speaker of the House in Kentucky. She was widowed in 1823. (Courtesy Mr. and Mrs. John M. Prewitt)

John Breckinridge, grandfather of John C. Breckinridge, moved from Virginia to Kentucky in 1790. He was attorney general of Kentucky when this portrait was painted. (Courtesy Walter R. Agard)

John C. Breckinridge in 1850 as Fayette representative in the Kentucky legislature at Frankfort. (Author's collection)

The earliest known photograph of John C. Breckinridge, *ca.* 1845, was made about two years after his marriage to Mary Cyrene Burch. (Courtesy Mr. and Mrs. John M. Prewitt)

The second session of the Thirty-second Congress proved a dull one. Aside from an unsuccessful attempt to push a trade settlement with Canada, Breckinridge's chief action in the House was to declare himself irrevocably opposed to the erection of any more statues showing George Washington in Roman costume. He attracted the public eye outside the Capitol this time, thanks to one of his favorite themes, transportation and domestic commerce. Speaking before the Southern and Western Commercial Convention in Baltimore on December 18, 1852, he decried the fact that the great trade of the Mississippi Valley was so isolated from the eastern cities and seaboard. Then he revealed to his audience how just eighty miles of track, laid between Parkersburg, Virginia, and the mouth of the Big Sandy River near Catlettsburg, Kentucky, would connect the Baltimore and Ohio with the commerce of the entire West, Northwest, and Southwest. "Gentlemen," he said, "this is no visionary scheme," and indeed it was not. Lexington was already linked by river and rail with the Mississippi, and even now a rail line from that city to the Big Sandy was on the drawing tables. A connection between it and the Baltimore and Ohio at Parkersburg could have become the lifeline of a growing nation. Breckinridge did not need to point out to his friends and constituents in Lexington what such a line could mean to them. Lamentably, though, the realization of his "scheme" would not come when he hoped, and lay too far in his future even for his rather unusual powers of presentiment.[30]

Breckinridge's main efforts at prophecy this winter were focused upon the coming canvass in his district. Word had gone out among the Whigs that he "must be beat cost what it will." There was talk of running Crittenden against him. The only encouraging news by the end of September came from Combs, still a good friend despite his defeat. Although a Whig, Combs warned Breckinridge away from a trap being set to embarrass him over a certain patronage job, giving the congressman his assurance that "I rely more on you than anyone in HR." Further moral support came from William Birney, who now resumed the friendship begun in their childhood. He wrote to compliment Breckinridge's reputation as "a Congressman, said to stand six feet in his boots and still higher for laws and order." [31]

30. *Congressional Globe*, 32nd Cong., 2nd Sess., Pt. 1, pp. 19, 244, 993, 1154; Baltimore *Weekly Sun*, December 25, 1852; Lexington *Kentucky Statesman*, December 10, 31, 1852.

31. Kinkead to Breckinridge, December 16, 1852, D. Vanderslice to Breckinridge, December 28, 1852, Robert Wickliffe, Jr., to Breckinridge, December 27, 1852, Leslie Combs to Breckinridge, December 4, 25, 1852, William Birney to Breckinridge, January 1, 1853, all in B. MSS.

Better news came after the New Year, when Crittenden was nominated for the Senate. In Georgetown, D. Howard Smith got roaring drunk and was carried out of town while yelling that he would be Breckinridge's opponent. If so, Breckinridge's reelection was certain. Smith, said a fellow Whig, Thomas Marshall, was a "reel-footed, bandy-shanked scrub"; not a high recommendation. Meanwhile, a friendly steamboat captain promised to "burst two boilers" paddling up votes for Breckinridge. By mid-February Breckinridge was nearly decided to make the race. "I know the power of the [Whig] rally in that district," he wrote his Uncle Robert. "It is formidable, but I see no alternative but to run again, or be kicked ignominiously off the track. . . . It would be better to be beaten in fair and open fight, than to refuse the race." But he withheld a while yet before declaring himself a candidate.[32]

He held back because of the newly organized Territory of Washington. When Pierce took office he would have to appoint a governor, and Breckinridge had decided to seek the office. It would insure his place in public life should he be defeated in Kentucky. He asked Mary's advice. She had just given birth to their second daughter, Mary Desha, and she wrote back leaving the decision entirely up to him. He then asked Powell and Butler for letters of recommendation, and both complied in gratifying terms. "*I would hate like thunder*, John, to lose you," said Powell, "We want you in Kentucky." Although these recommendations, along with one by Kentucky Secretary of State J. P. Metcalf, were sent to Breckinridge for presentation to Pierce, it is likely that the president-elect never saw them. Breckinridge stayed in the capital for a week after Pierce's inauguration, met with the president, and was offered the appointment. But by then he had decided to run for reelection to Congress at all hazards. He arrived in Lexington on March 18, and four days later announced his candidacy.[33]

The Whigs in Ashland were more divided than ever. In convention they had nominated state Attorney General James Harlan to oppose Breckinridge, but the candidate was received unhappily in some factions of the

32. Lazarus Powell to Breckinridge, January 5, February 4, 1853, Wickliffe to Breckinridge, January 18, 1853, Mary C. Breckinridge to Breckinridge, February 3, 1853, James G. Leach to Breckinridge, February 14, 1853, Robert J. Breckinridge to Breckinridge, February 7, 1853, Breckinridge to Robert J. Breckinridge, February 12, 1853, all in B. MSS.

33. Paul Rankin to Breckinridge, February 25, 1853, Butler to Pierce, February 28, 1853, Powell to Pierce, February 28, 1853, Metcalf to Pierce, February 28, 1853, Powell to Breckinridge, February 28, 1853, Robert J. Breckinridge, Jr., to Robert J. Breckinridge, March 7, 1853, E. C. Hibben to Breckinridge, August 4, 1853, all in B. MSS; Lexington *Kentucky Statesman*, March 22, 25, 1853.

party. "It has fallen upon the Whigs like a vast pancake," one Democrat said of Harlan's nomination. Still rumors spread that the Whigs would bring to bear every cent they had to beat the incumbent. Beriah Magoffin wrote to him: "You can beat Harlan, but you have not a moment to spare." The picture changed abruptly late in March when Harlan withdrew his name, and the Whigs nominated Robert P. Letcher, former governor, who had wanted to make the canvass from the start. He was the toughest campaigner of his party in the state. If anyone could beat Breckinridge, Letcher was the man.[34]

Breckinridge now faced the distinct possibility of being a one-term congressman though, unlike many such, defeat need not bring with it obscurity. He had made his mark in Washington. During the session just past his name was increasingly mentioned in connection with higher offices. Shortly before the adjournment a reporter for the Boston *Post*, seeing Breckinridge for the first time, asked another Congressman about the tall, graceful young Kentuckian. "That man," came the reply, "is John C. Breckinridge, of Kentucky, who will one day, if he lives, be President of the United States." There was something about the major that invited prophecy.[35]

34. Lexington *Kentucky Statesman*, February 22, April 5, 1853; Dickerson to Breckinridge, February 22, 1853, George W. Johnson to Breckinridge, February 23, 1853, Charles Wheatley to Breckinridge, February 23, 1853, Beriah Magoffin to Breckinridge, March 30, 1853, Powell to Breckinridge, March 30, 1853, all in B. MSS.
35. *United States Review*, IV (September, 1856), 150.

CHAPTER 5

Beat Breckinridge, D—n Him

Breckinridge did not feel well when he returned to Lexington. He had already developed the habit of working feverishly, with no letup for periods of several days at a time, forsaking sleep. When either his work or his endurance ran out, he would collapse in his bed and sleep for a day and a half or more. It was an impractical and unhealthy mode of living, but his myriad duties as a congressman required long hours, especially towards the close of the Thirty-second Congress. He had felt so fatigued throughout the months of the second session that he neglected his correspondence with his constituents and had to publish an apology in the *Statesman*.[1]

While resting and spending a good deal of time in bed, Breckinridge had a visit from his opponent Letcher. It was a courtesy call, during which the Whig supposedly offered to delay opening his campaign until the congressman was well. The sick man would have none of that, however, and replied to Letcher, "No, sir, do not delay your canvass on my account; take the stump, and I will meet you as soon as my strength will allow." As it turned out, Breckinridge did not regain his health until well into April, and even then began the fight in a weakened condition.[2]

The candidate had made good use of his "rest" time, and with his friends laid out a remarkable plan of action for the canvass, taking care of even the most minute details. In choosing the dates for his coming speeches, he was careful to schedule them, whenever possible, on either the day before or

1. Lexington *Kentucky Statesman*, March 29, 1853; J. Stoddard Johnston, "Sketches of Operations of General John C. Breckinridge," *Southern Historical Society Papers*, VII (1879), 387, hereinafter cited as *SHSP*. Complaints about Breckinridge's impunctuality as a correspondent are found throughout B. MSS.

2. *Sketches of Breckinridge and Lane*, 7; J. P. Metcalf to Breckinridge, April 9, 1853, in B. MSS.

the day after county court days. Lazarus Powell, as governor, called up the state militia regiments for drill on these court days, and Breckinridge would find ready-made audiences. He exercised care in selecting the places for his speeches, and, once he picked the dates and sites for his appearances, he would make full use of the local newspapers for advertising them. Of course, the *Statesman* and the Frankfort *Yeoman* carried his name at the head of their editorial pages, and announced in every issue his forthcoming speeches. However, Breckinridge bought space in other papers as well, and even in the Whig press. As in his first campaign, he would need Whig votes to win. Indeed, when the friendly Democrat editor of the Covington *Kentucky Flag* made up his mind to move out of the district just before the canvass, the candidate persuaded him to stay in the newspaper business. Breckinridge needed all the help he could get.[3]

Already the Democratic press, chiefly the *Statesman*, had begun printing an occasional letter signed "An Old Line Whig" or "An Independent Clay Whig" or other such sobriquets, purportedly written by loyal Whigs who were supporting Breckinridge and urging all others to do the same. Undoubtedly many of these letters were authentic—late in the canvass the *Statesman* would carry one in almost every issue—but several were from Democratic pens, one of which may have belonged to Governor Powell himself. The opposition soon followed suit, with Democrats renouncing their faith and proclaiming for Robert Letcher. As the campaign progressed, one or the other of Lexington's two rival tabloids, the *Statesman* or the *Observer and Reporter*, often ran its own letters on the same page with an editorial denouncing the other for printing spurious correspondence. Breckinridge took no part in concocting the letters, but he was well aware of what was going on. It was one of the games of politics, as both he and Letcher well knew.[4]

Breckinridge's chief concern in preparing for the canvass was, of course, Letcher himself, and even from his sickbed he dug into the subject. At the recommendation of Metcalf and others, Breckinridge began studying his record in the state legislature. On his own, he wrote to John C. Rives, publisher of the *Congressional Globe*, and set him looking through its back files for Letcher's voting and speaking record during 1823–1835, the years that

---

3. Metcalf to Breckinridge, April 15, 1853, Paul Rankin to Breckinridge, June 29, 1853, in B. MSS; Receipt of D. C. Wickliffe, October 15, 1853, receipt of S. Pike, April 14, 1853, in JCB Papers.

4. Lazarus Powell to Breckinridge, February 10, 1853, in B. MSS. The Lexington *Kentucky Statesman* and the *Observer and Reporter* for April–July 1853 carry the "Independent Clay Whig" letters.

he was a congressman. The major obtained copies of the federal commerce and navigation reports for the previous eight years, looked deeply into Letcher's course as governor of the state, 1840–1844, and familiarized himself with his opponent's previous stands on virtually every issue that had faced the nation for the past thirty years.[5]

The sixty-five-year-old Whig was commonly called Black Bob or Greasy Bob, partly because of his swarthy complexion, but more so because of his wiles as a politician. Large and rather rotund, he had an extremely winning manner, a pleasant and convivial personality, and an inexhaustible fund of humorous stories. Breckinridge was warned by more than one observer that Letcher "will not attempt to meet you in sober argument but will run off on appropriate anecdotes." He had seen this himself back in 1840, when he observed that Letcher's "lively person and jovial demeanor" would probably win him the governorship, as indeed it did. Worse yet, whenever Greasy Bob finished a speech, he generally withdrew some distance from the stand and, taking up his violin, drew away the audience with its music. More than once Letcher fiddled while his opponents burned, and Breckinridge would have to dream up a few of his own tricks if he expected to hold and win his listeners. One thing was sure, Breckinridge stood resolved to carry the battle to Letcher at every opportunity. He told Rives that he would make the Whig "lard the lean earth" by August, and he meant it. It might well be his only hope of victory.[6]

Breckinridge held one trump that might prove decisive. In 1848 Letcher and another former Whig governor, Thomas Metcalfe, had stumped Indiana in behalf of Zachary Taylor's bid for the presidency. In the course of their tour, they stopped at Indianapolis, and there both delivered addresses that smacked of Free-Soilism. Letcher declared, "It is only the ultra men of the extreme South who desire the extension of slavery. . . . Kentucky did not desire its extension." He went on to predict that in the coming constitutional convention in Kentucky (1849), some enactment would be included for gradual emancipation.[7]

This speech attracted little, if any, notice in Kentucky at the time, but in November, 1852, when Breckinridge's Indiana friend John F. Robinson came to the district to make a few addresses, he brought up the subject of

---

5. Metcalf to Breckinridge, April 9, 1853, John C. Rives to Breckinridge, April 13, 1853, R. McKner to Breckinridge, April 14, 1853, in B. MSS.

6. Rives to Breckinridge, April 13, 1853, in B. MSS.

7. Indianapolis *Indiana State Sentinel*, September 14, 1848; Indianapolis *Indiana State Journal*, September 18, 1848.

Metcalfe's Free-Soil utterances, and he may have mentioned Letcher's as well. Within two days after the announcement of Black Bob's nomination, Breckinridge was in touch with Robinson, requesting him to furnish a copy of Letcher's Indianapolis speech. Not content with this, Robinson went to Indiana in person to obtain signed statements from the editors of its papers that carried the speech, the Whig *Indiana State Journal* and the Democrat *Indiana State Sentinel*, and from those who heard Letcher speak. It would take him nearly one month to get what he sought, and in the meantime he gave Breckinridge his own copies of several pertinent documents. One was a transcript of the report of Letcher's speech taken from the *Journal* and verified as accurate by the Indiana state librarian. At Robinson's suggestion, a copy of the report of the speech was sent to the friendly press in the district, and almost from the beginning of the canvass they printed it in every issue under such headlines as "Letcher Gems." [8]

The contest finally began on April 18 at Nicholasville, in Jessamine County. This was a model of stump politics that Kentucky would never forget, and over half a century later, when old men looked back on the political past, they invariably recalled Breckinridge and Letcher and 1853.

It was the custom on the stump for each opponent to speak twice, with no rebuttal, and since Breckinridge was the incumbent, he took the stand first. He had not yet fully recovered his health, and his friends feared that he might not speak "with his usual eloquence and spirit." Apparently he had little difficulty. He opened by reviewing his course in Congress, his votes and speeches, and followed with a narrative of his tour of the district the previous year in advocacy of Pierce. Proceeding into a discussion of national politics in general, he concentrated on the tariff, comparing the high duties of the Whig tariff of 1842 with the much more reasonable, and therefore profitable, rates imposed by the Democratic Walker Tariff Act of 1846. This done, he sat down, as Letcher arose to make his opening remarks. He made no reply to any of the arguments offered by the incumbent on national affairs, but instead simply announced himself a candidate and then embarked upon a lengthy defense of his term as governor, an equivocal denial of the Indianapolis speech, an implication that Breckinridge had an unfair advantage in this contest since he was a college graduate whereas Letcher was of humble origins, "graduated in a brick yard,"

8. Thomas Metcalf to Breckinridge, November 22, 1852, Breckinridge to Thomas Metcalf, November 27, 1852, John F. Robinson to John R. Desha, April 7, 1853, Robinson to Breckinridge, April 15, 1853, all in B. MSS. The letters that Robinson gave Breckinridge are in the JCB Papers.

and concluded with the injunction to all Whigs that they must maintain control of the district "to protect the grave of Mr. Clay from the impious tread of Democracy."

Breckinridge retook the stand now, and tore into his opponent. He pointed out that Letcher did not answer one of the arguments that he had proposed, but instead introduced the subject of the newspaper charges about the Indianapolis speech. Since the Whig brought up the matter, Breckinridge felt justified in pursuing it and, holding in his hand the papers that Robinson had given him, read the *Journal*'s report of Letcher's speech. Breckinridge digressed for a moment to note that, although such appeals to emotion distressed him, his own origins and background were hardly more patrician than his opponent's, and then went on to attack Letcher's weak defense against the Free-Soil charge. Finally, he concluded with the remark that he did not believe that Henry Clay's will contained a provision that "his ashes be exhumed from the tomb in order to be thrown into the scale to influence the result of the present Congressional contest." While Breckinridge spoke, the *Statesman*'s reporter wrote that Letcher "exhibited unmistakable signs of discomfiture, perplexity and ill temper." When it came time for Black Bob's final remarks, he could only plead that he was an old man "whose race was run," and repeated his denial of the Free-Soil speech. At this, Breckinridge interrupted to thank him for this firm denial, and asked Letcher what he had said in Indianapolis. The Whig could only answer that he did not remember.[9]

This first meeting set the tone for the remainder of the canvass. Breckinridge would cite his record in Congress, defend Democratic national policy, and tear into the inconsistencies in Letcher's political past. Greasy Bob would avoid answering the challenges whenever possible, defend himself simply by saying that he was an old man and should be forgiven for earlier mistakes, and call upon his friends to maintain Whig sanctity in Clay's home district. Breckinridge, he said, was bound to misrepresent the district no matter how he voted in the House. When asked why, Letcher's sage reply was, "Because he is a Democrat." When taken to task by fellow Whigs for not replying to Breckinridge's thrusts, he remained silent, only remarking that Breckinridge was "the prettiest demagogue" he ever saw.[10]

Letcher left the scene of this first debate almost immediately. The crowd remained for some time, and a number of Whig supporters swore that he should not meet with Breckinridge in open battle again, but should instead

9. Lexington *Kentucky Statesman*, April 19, 22, 1853.
10. *Ibid.*, June 3, 1853; Rankin to Breckinridge, April 23, 1853, in B. MSS.

"still-hunt" and "bush dash whack" by speaking alone, thus denying Breckinridge the opportunity to answer any charges made. On the other hand, the Democrats were elated. They congratulated the major upon drawing from his opponent the denial of the Free-Soil expressions, and enjoined, "Do not spare him. As *he* has opened up the *charges and specifications against himself* give him gooses upon them in every speech you make." Breckinridge intended to do just that.[11]

Letcher did "bush dash whack" a little, showing up unannounced somewhere so that the incumbent would not be there to defend himself, but for the most part he met openly with Breckinridge, who published well in advance listings of when and where he would speak. The two next met in debate at Paris, Bourbon County, on May 2, where Black Bob repeated his performance at Nicholasville. He still declined to point out anything objectionable in Breckinridge's congressional record and did not fail to proclaim himself the guardian of Clay's bones. The congressman, not a little irritated, sternly rebuked Letcher. "Why sir can you not let this great shade rest in peace! I will not compare my honorable opponent's conduct to that of the hyena—for that would be discourteous—but let him [Clay] alone in his charnel house, where to disturb him is sacrilege." To show that Henry Clay might not turn in his grave should Breckinridge be elected, he related the friendly feelings that he and the great statesman had felt for each other, and concluded that "I reckon, without making it a matter of boast, that the relations between us were quite as kindly, as those between him and certain gentlemen who now for certain personal ends are constantly vexing and fretting his manes." [12]

Had Letcher been more imaginative, he might have made one or two telling arguments against Breckinridge, though this was a contest in which manner and deportment were speaking almost as persuasively as the issues. Instead, he relied on his well-known wit, but he won more laughs than votes, especially when his arguments degenerated to the ridiculous like his accusation that Breckinridge had stolen watermelons as a boy! It did not help that the congressman met him wit for wit and replied to this charge: "Well, if I get the vote of all the boys who have ever taken any watermelons to eat, I'll elected by a big majority." [13]

11. Lexington *Kentucky Statesman*, April 19, 1853; Metcalf to Breckinridge, April 21, 1853, in B. MSS.

12. William Martin to Breckinridge, April 27, 1853, in B. MSS; Lexington *Kentucky Statesman*, May 3, 1853.

13. Stillwell, *Breckinridge*, 52.

The only time that Breckinridge was free of his opponent's redundant whining, was on those occasions that he spoke alone, and they were few. One, however, stayed in his memory for the rest of his life, and he never tired of retelling its story. He had been scheduled to speak in a county in which the vote stood rather evenly divided, and he naturally hoped to make a good showing. On the day of the affair, he arrived early with a friend, James Cohen, and began mixing with the audience, but his friend disappeared. The two did not meet again until they mounted the speaker's stand for Cohen to introduce Breckinridge to the assembly.

After the congressman had begun his address, and stood well on his way to winning over the audience, one "tall, burly, hard-featured, sarcastic-looking 'cuss' " started interrupting him, making it quite obvious that he was not what the hill people of the district called a "Brackenridge man." The crowd became uneasy, then surly, and Cohen arose to threaten to expel the troublemaker.

"You shet your damn head, Jim Cohen," came the reply. "I reckon this air a free country and I've got a right to talk."

At this the audience seemed ready to jump on the offender, but Breckinridge interposed, condemned their anger, and asked that the rude individual be allowed to hear him out, announcing that if the heckler did, he would be converted. The crowd, cowed by Breckinridge's scolding, and its curiosity aroused by his self-confident prediction, remained docile, while its near-victim warned, "You'll have a hell of a time convertin' of me." Breckinridge continued.

It was soon obvious that the speaker's whole effort was now aimed at this one man, who still displayed his disdain with a variety of grunts and defiant looks. Shortly, however, he began to soften. "His corrugated brow relaxed, the smile of scorn faded from his lip, he shifted from one foot to the other, like a bear on hot plates, and turned once or twice as if seeking to escape, but the dense crowd held him in his place." Those around him saw tears creeping out of his eyes, then a sob, and finally the exclamation rang out, "By hell, Brackenridge! You kin beat 'em all. I'm fer you agin' the worl'!"

The effect was startling, and soon it appeared that Breckinridge had won the whole assemblage. That evening, as he and Cohen rode home in the latter's carriage, Breckinridge remarked with pride, "I must have been making a pretty good speech, to affect that fellow the way I did."

Cohen, giving him a queer look, replied, "You think you did it, do you?"

Breckinridge suddenly felt struck by "an indescribable dismay . . . an awful feeling that some cherished conviction was about to be dissipated."

"Why, what do you mean," he gasped. Cohen then revealed how, while the major was mixing with the crowd, he saw the supposed convert, "the rankest bummer unhung," and, knowing that the fellow was a stranger to the area, went over to him and asked, "Bill, how do you stand in this race?" Bill had not yet taken a side and, hearing this, Cohen offered him ten dollars to "go to work for Breckinridge." He thought for a moment, then said, "Jim Cohen, if you'll make it twenty-five dollars, I'll act a piece afore that crowd to-day which 'ull fetch every dad-burned son of a gun in it; git 'em all. I'll jes' have a whoopin' fer Brackenridge." Bill started to outline his plan of action but, before he finished, Cohen closed the deal. "I felt sure you would show up well," he told Breckinridge, "do the magnanimous, and all that, and I believed we had the work done." The poor congressman felt stunned, but before long the humor of the situation, and admiration for the performance he had seen, took over. Whenever he told the story thereafter, he never failed to conclude, "Now, don't you think I did pretty well?" [14]

The news reporting of the campaign was most flattering to Breckinridge. A Whig correspondent for the Erie, Pennsylvania, *Gazette* noted how Breckinridge and Letcher canvassed the district, speaking together once, and sometimes twice, a day. "I have often heard of Gov. Letcher as an unrivalled stump orator," he wrote, "but he must be heard to be appreciated. His forcible style and manner, and his inexhaustible fund of anecdotes, are inimitable, and the effect upon a promiscuous crowd indescribable." However, when it came to Letcher's opponent, "Although I can seldom see anything in a Democrat I can approve, much less applaud, I am constrained to say that Major Breckinridge is one of the most gifted men of the nation. . . . And in every respect he is certainly a model of beauty, manliness and eloquence. I have heard many speakers, from Daniel Webster down to zealous Democratic leaders in Erie, but for pure, soul stirring eloquence, John C. Breckinridge stands unrivalled." The *Indiana Madisonian*, with the directness typical of the Old Northwest, stated its opinion much more simply. "We cannot imagine, for a moment, that the people of that district [Ashland] . . . could record a verdict in favor of a broken down old hack over such a distinguished, accomplished and talented gentleman as John C. Breckinridge." A singular feature of nearly all of these reports was the conclusion that the major deserved, and soon would wear, "the mantle of Henry Clay." Perhaps equally significant, and surely gratifying to Breckinridge, was the fact that now they were spelling his name right. Beyond this, there were

14. Basil W. Duke, *Reminiscences of General Basil W. Duke, C.S.A.* (New York, 1911), 436–38.

a number of newborn male children in the district being named "John C. Breckinridge ————." [15]

Naturally, the Whig press was not quite as kind, but it had its mavericks, probably the most embarrassing one being the influential Louisville *Journal*. After indiscreetly averring that "Mr. Breckinridge is a thorough democrat . . . and most certainly one of the very ablest men in the body to which he belongs," the *Journal* committed near-treason by saying that "There is in his speeches a clearness, a force and a condensation of thought that strongly reminds us of John C. Calhoun." [16]

As the canvass progressed, and Letcher steadily lost ground in the debates, he turned more and more to his fiddle, playing while Breckinridge spoke, and often drawing away an embarrassingly large portion of the audience. Finally the congressman, knowing the people, and seeing some capital to be made out of the situation, devised a plan that put an effective check on Greasy Bob's further musical exploits. Before one of their meetings in the more backward section of the district, Breckinridge let out a rumor which resulted in an uproar as soon as Letcher took up his fiddle. As the music began, a lank backwoodsman much like Cohen's unhung "bummer" Bill, called out, "Why don't you fiddle with that t'other hand o'yourn?"

Immediately the cry went up, "T'other hand!"

Poor Letcher, left-handed since birth, did not at first understand what they meant, until the fellow in a coonskin cap who began the scene bellowed, "T'other hand! We've heard about you! You fiddle down thar in that d—n Bluegrass country, 'mong rich folks, with your right hand and think when you git up in the hills 'mong pore folks, left-handed fiddlin's good enuf for us; you've cussedly missed it. Left-handed doin's won't run up hyar." Letcher, the victim both of Breckinridge's ingenuity and the yeomen's unbending democracy, had no reply.[17]

Indeed, Black Bob had few replies as the canvass wore on. Robinson finally sent Breckinridge copies of the Indianapolis papers that ran Letcher's indiscreet Free-Soil speech, and in a debate at Lexington's courthouse the major read them to the crowd, along with his letter to the editor of the *Sentinel* and that gentleman's reply. Breckinridge's friends regarded this as

15. Erie *Gazette*, as quoted in Richmond *Examiner*, August 12, 1853; Lexington *Kentucky Statesman*, June 3, 1853; Richard Ridgeley to Breckinridge, n.d. [1853], in B. MSS.

16. Frankfort *Yeoman*, June 24, 1853; Lexington *Observer and Reporter*, May 11, 1853.

17. Clement Eaton, *The Mind of the Old South* (Baton Rouge, 1967), 142–43.

"the most terrific blow" he had yet dealt, and its importance hardly escaped him. For the remainder of the campaign, he read from those papers at almost every speech, and gave them such good service that they literally fell apart. The congressman had to tape them back together to finish the canvass.[18]

The fight reached its peak in June and early July. In June alone the antagonists met each other at least thirteen times on the stump, and each made several single speeches in addition. Breckinridge made at least nine such appearances and always invited Letcher to attend. In the month of July they met on fifteen more occasions, all in Owen County, a testament to the decisive role that all knew "Sweet Owen" would play in the August election. The weather was hot, partisanship fierce, and the whole aspect of the canvass presented a marked contrast to the tranquil scene depicted in the popular painter George Caleb Bingham's latest work, "The County Election," then being shown free of charge in Dr. Browning's rooms in Lexington.[19]

Their meetings were generally festive occasions, and by far the best entertainment available to the voters of Ashland. The barbecues and "burgoos" —so called because of the thick, stewlike, and highly seasoned vegetable and meat soup that was prepared for the occasion—drew crowds from a wide area, and with such audiences as this Breckinridge shone. One such meeting was held within the very Indian "fort" at Cabell's Dale where he had played in his childhood. As was his custom, he arrived several hours early and began moving among the crowd. He brought his young cousin John Breckinridge Castleman with him, and let the boy sit on the edge of the stand during the speaking. The youth was fascinated: "From miles around a great throng of people came to listen to the debate. Interest in young Breckinridge was remarkable, and to me everyone seemed to favor and cheer him. When the debate was finished, he held me by the hand, and together we walked through the multitude. He seemed to know almost everyone and to ask about the personal affairs of many to whom he spoke. He seemed to call everyone by name and to know who was sick and who was convalescent. No wonder that, when personal association with the electorate was possible, this man was invincible." Another young man who witnessed these "pick-nick" meetings between Breckinridge and Letcher was the fifteen-

18. Lexington *Kentucky Statesman*, May 10, 1853. Breckinridge's copies of these Indiana papers are in the JCB Papers.

19. Frankfort *Yeoman*, June 2, 1853; Lexington *Kentucky Statesman*, May 20, June 28, 1853.

year-old Basil W. Duke, who would later testify that, "It is scarcely necessary to say that at that time John C. Breckinridge had no peer as a stump speaker in Kentucky—it is a matter of history. But those who never saw or heard him can form no conception of his wonderful magnetism. It resided as much in his look and gesture as in his voice. Often a mere glance over the crowd, while he remained seated and silent, would elicit wild cheers and a tumult that could with difficulty be stilled." [20]

Without doubt the most vivid first-hand portrayal of the battle between the congressional hopefuls, came from the pen of, strangely enough, one of the most outspoken Whigs in the country, the abolitionist Cassius M. Clay. Despite his party leanings, he gave his full support to Breckinridge in this canvass and personally arranged a meeting between the candidates at Little Hickman, Jessamine County, late in June. Clay, living proof of the wide appeal that Breckinridge enjoyed among the Whigs of the district, was not disappointed by his favorite's performance.

> The contrast between the men was itself an argument. Breckinridge was tall, well-formed, with fair complexion, regular face of great mental power, large blue eyes, and auburn hair, intellectual, composed, and full of conscious genius and future prowess. Letcher had grown so corpulent by age and heavy eating, that he seemed at times on the very verge of suffocation or apoplexy. The weather was very warm. Breckinridge went at him with the coolness of a skilled swordsman; making home thrusts and coolly observing the effect of each. Letcher was very much confused, greatly angry and fought as one who had lost all muscular power, and even eyesight. The perspiration poured off him; and he literally "larded the earth." His voice was guttural and ejected from his lungs as a badly charged fuse of wet and dry powder. The boys shouted, "Cut the halter, and give him air!" It was a pitiable sight! Letcher had no friends. By invitation all joined us, and down we went to the celebrated spring at Boone's Creek. The "Black Horse" was already beaten. That was the last of Letcher.[21]

Breckinridge came to the speaker's stand well armed to meet his opponent. He always had a well-marked copy of Pierce's inaugural with him, and used it to illustrate his own and his party's position and goals. In addition, since Letcher's past record was especially vulnerable on the tariff question, the major generally held in his hand a copy of the country's *Commerce and Navigation Report* for 1852, as well as copies of the New Hampshire Democrat Edmund Burke's famous "Bundlecund" essays on the protective system. The *Congressional Globe* and the *Journal* of Kentucky's

---

20. Castleman, *Active Service*, 45–46; Duke, *Reminiscences*, 436–37.
21. Cassius M. Clay, *Cassius Marcellus Clay, Life and Memoirs, Writings and Speeches* (Cincinnati, 1886), I, 218.

legislature usually sat close at hand, and a copy of the Constitution always lay within reach.[22]

Breckinridge did not write out his speeches beforehand. He had little patience or discipline for lengthy writing, and besides, he preferred to speak spontaneously, with only as much reading as was necessary. As Cassius Clay observed, the major liked to make witty and pointed thrusts at Letcher, and he hastily wrote down his ideas before each lunge while listening to Greasy Bob. He never tired of poking fun at his opponent's complaint that he was running against his will, but did so in response to the universal request of the voters of the district. Breckinridge, taking a less exalted view of Letcher's candidacy, preferred to say that the Whigs had "trotted out the old horse," and then asked Letcher to explain the contradiction between this first complaint, and a later one that he was laboring through the campaign without even the support of his own party. This was strange indeed. The Democrats certainly did not stand behind Letcher, and if the Whigs did not as well, then who was it that raised the popular clamor for him to run? [23]

One of Letcher's weakest points was his uncontrollable temper. While the major played with him Black Bob would grow steadily more angry, much to the crowd's delight. Interrupting constantly, "fairly foaming at the mouth," Letcher once accused Breckinridge of denouncing the Whig party. To the congressman's reply that he had spoken in none but parliamentary tones of his opponents, Letcher exclaimed, "Oh, confound your parliamentary language, Major Breckinridge, and you too." Old Crittenden, sitting nearby, had to pull Letcher to his seat by his coattails every time he stood up to interrupt. To the Whigs's dismay, the audience seized on a good thing, and began crying "coattails" every time Breckinridge made a good point.[24]

In going at Letcher, Breckinridge was careful not to attack the Whig party itself, for fear of offending any friendly Whigs whose votes he would need to win. Indeed, he made overt gestures to win their admiration, particularly by requesting fair hearings for Letcher. In so doing he made "Breckinridge," or "Whippoorwill" Whigs out of several who had formerly been "Letcher-ous." [25]

The Whigs knew that even without campaigning, they could count on

22. These items are in the JCB Papers.   23. *Ibid.*

24. Louisville *Courier-Journal*, June 19, 1875.

25. Metcalf to Breckinridge, May 30, 1853, John B. Stout to Breckinridge, May 7, 1853, in B. MSS; Lexington *Kentucky Statesman*, June 7, 1853.

the vote of a majority of the Whigs in the district, simply because Ashland had always been a Whig bailiwick, and these voters always stuck by the party regardless of the issues involved in the canvass. However, there was no hope of a victory unless the recalcitrants who were supporting Breckinridge could be brought back into the fold, and in this endeavor Letcher proved sadly lacking. In the opening of the fight he had been shown culpable for the Indiana speech and was then held up as a liar for denying it after the major produced positive proof. Worse yet, though he avidly sought the nomination, he declared on the stump that he had not wanted to run. To his supporters' dismay, Black Bob made it appear as if he really did not care about making the canvass, for he came to the stump totally unprepared to meet his opponent. His attacks on Breckinridge—those that were not based upon the major's being a Democrat and therefore unfit to represent—were mostly of a personal nature, founded on either ignorance or disregard of the real facts, and generally outside the realm of what statesmen regarded as tasteful. He accused Breckinridge of begging for Whig votes, wanting them whether the voters agreed with him or not, and denounced those who voted for the Democrat. Besides, there were too many Democrats in Congress, and Letcher thought he should go there as "ballast." With Letcher as their standard-bearer, the Whigs found themselves left with no motto better than "*we must beat Breckinridge, d—n him!*" Greasy Bob himself apparently entertained little optimism for his success and was heard to say that though most of the Whigs stood in his favor, "the result is doubtful." [26]

With their arguments meeting a generally stiff and successful defense and their candidate doing as much harm as good, the Whigs of Ashland were driven to their last, and most dangerous argument—money. As early as April, Breckinridge had been warned that his enemies might attempt to carry the election by fraud and bribery, and as the canvass progressed, it became increasingly obvious that they were trying to do just that. By June they were raising money in Louisville and other cities outside the district, and one month later funds were being sent from as far off as New York to aid in the major's defeat, testament to the nationwide interest and importance to the Whig party of this election. Breckinridge later declared that he knew that at least $30,000 was used in the attempt to beat him, and his old professor, the Whig George Robertson, then boasted that over $100,000 was being devoted to buying votes for Letcher.[27]

26. John C. Breckinridge, notes on speeches of Robert P. Letcher, 1853, in JCB Papers; Lexington *Kentucky Statesman*, May 13, July 29, 1853.
27. Metcalf to Breckinridge, April 21, 1853, Rankin Revill to Breckinridge, June 6,

Exactly how much money the Whigs did bring to bear in the campaign is unknown, but the fact that they were trying to buy the election was a badly kept secret. Breckinridge's friends warned him from every county in the district that "The Whigs are using money here very freely." Scott was reported to be flooded with cash, Woodford much the same, and Fayette as well. Letcher's friends went door-to-door in many precincts, attempting to buy votes. In crucial Owen County, they paid men $20 to $25 to stay at home on election day, and offered as much as $30 to $50 for a Letcher vote. As one friend told Breckinridge, the Whigs were "buying up every slubberdedegullion they can possibly purchase." [28]

Breckinridge and his supporters did not stand idly by while their opponents attempted to buy the election out from under them. They took matters into their own hands before he was able to organize a fund-raising campaign. The first major contributor was none other than W. W. Corcoran, perhaps the most widely known and respected financier in the nation. Corcoran authorized Breckinridge to draw on him for one thousand dollars if it would "strengthen your arm in the glorious fight you are making." Other smaller contributions came in throughout the campaign, perhaps as much as four or five thousand dollars in all, which, added to what could be raised among the Democrats of the several counties in the district, allowed Breckinridge's friends to counteract the damage the Whigs were doing.[29]

As August approached, it became obvious that the whole nation was interested in the contest in the Ashland district. Richardson reported from Illinois, "It is really the only canvass now going on that excites the least interest"; Emanuel B. Hart, representative from New York, expressed a like conviction; and an observer in Washington City told Breckinridge that "No congressional canvass has excited in this city, so much interest as yours." This interest ran in high places. Secretary of the Navy James C. Dobbin, who held "the most exalted opinions" of Breckinridge, said that

---

24, 1853, William Moss to Breckinridge, July 23, 1853, John A. McClure to Breckinridge, July 19, 1853, T. P. Moore to Breckinridge, July 19–20, 1853, all in B. MSS; Daniel Sickles and Emanuel B. Hart to B. B. Taylor, July 26, 1853, all in Lexington *Kentucky Statesman*, August 2, 1853.

28. John Lovely to Breckinridge, July 16, 1853, Wheatley to Breckinridge, July 19, 24, 1853, William Moss to Breckinridge, July 23, 1853, John A. McClure to Breckinridge, July 25, 1853, Revill to Breckinridge, July 29, 1853, A. Tarrant to Breckinridge, July 21, 1853, James G. Leach to Breckinridge, July 23, 1853, all in B. MSS.

29. W. W. Corcoran to Breckinridge, in W. W. Corcoran MSS, LC; Jesse D. Bright to Breckinridge, May 10, 1853, in W. W. Corcoran, *A Grandfather's Legacy* (Washington, 1878), 114; Bright to Breckinridge, June 5, 1853, John W. Forney to Breckinridge, June 17, 1853, in B. MSS; *Congressional Globe*, 32nd Cong., 1st Sess., Pt. 1, p. 763.

his election "seemed to be a subject of greater interest than that of any other man." Franklin Pierce, no doubt mindful of Breckinridge's prestige, and grateful for the outspoken support of his appointments and policies that the congressman voiced on the stump, stood foremost among Breckinridge's well-wishers in the capital, and frequently expressed his concern for the Kentuckian's success.[30]

In spite of his own forebodings before the canvass opened, Breckinridge maintained a judicious optimism throughout the months of speeches and stump meetings. Back in May he told Corcoran of the money being spent in Letcher's behalf, but confided, "I am confident that he can be beaten, and have entered the canvass with the purpose to expend the last atom of my strength in the effort to do it." A month later he expressed his belief that *he* could beat Letcher, and by mid-July he could tell Forney that "My contest is very severe and exhausting, but thank God, it draws to a close, and I am very hopefull of the result." Indeed, in estimating his opponents' chances of electing Letcher, he now declared that "the Whigs cant come it." In a desperate effort to achieve victory, they had been circulating leaflets which sought to hurt the congressman by showing that the abolitionist Cassius Clay supported him. The Whigs's final act may have been the formulation of a plan to place a committee in every community of twenty-five or more people throughout the district, and have them each buy one Democratic vote, whatever the price. By this they hoped to gain three hundred votes. None of these efforts produced significant results, however, and by late July some of the Whigs admitted that "the thing looks a little bad." The only serious threat to Breckinridge votes was his friends' extravagant betting on the outcome of the election. Ten thousand dollars was wagered in Lexington alone, and it was costing him the support of a few high-minded citizens, even though he apparently took no part in the betting. Still, he remained optimistic. He spent the last few days of the canvass in Frankfort, visiting with Senator-elect Crittenden and making a few more speeches. On the evening of July 31, 1853, the eve of the election, with the campaign against Letcher at a close, he returned to his hotel, dismounted his horse, and told a nearby friend, "I have beaten him." [31]

30. William A. Richardson to Breckinridge, July 1, 1853, Hart to Breckinridge, August 4, 1853, Perry E. Brocchus to Breckinridge, August 6, 1853, W. V. McKeun to Breckinridge, June 17, 1853, all in B. MSS.

31. Breckinridge to Corcoran, May 23, 1853, in Corcoran, *A Grandfather's Legacy*, 114; Breckinridge to Forney, July 15, 1853, in Ferdinand J. Dreer Collection, HSP; A. G. Brown to Breckinridge, July 26, 1853, Revill to Breckinridge, July 25, 1853, John Crittenden to Breckinridge, July 27, 1853, all in B. MSS; Lexington *Kentucky States-*

August 1 dawned cloudy, and rain drenched much of the district during the day. Telegrams flew in and out of Frankfort as Breckinridge's managers throughout the district advised him of the progress of the balloting. At eight o'clock that evening the results began coming in, and they showed a close race. The voting also revealed the keen interest that the canvass had excited in the district, for over 1,700 more voters turned out this day than had voted two years before when Breckinridge stood against Leslie Combs, and this in spite of the rain—and the money—that kept many at home. There were other differences between the two races; the tallies showed that where Breckinridge won Franklin County and lost Jessamine in 1851, he now lost the former and won the latter, both by majorities of less than 60. However, as in his first bid for election, he definitely lost Bourbon, Fayette, and Woodford, this time by majorities of 405, 211, and 284. Scott County kept him in the running with a 525 plurality, but, as everyone had known from the beginning, Owen would decide the issue, and the Democratic rally there had been phenomenal. The total votes cast there in 1851 had been 1,677, but this year it jumped to 2,071, with 1,473 of the ballots for Breckinridge. " 'Sweet Owen'—God bless and forever protect her," declared Metcalf. "She deserves to be a *state* instead of a county." The Owen vote gave Breckinridge an 875 majority in the county, 526 plurality in the election, and another two years in Washington City. Breckinridge never forgot her loyalty and, as a token of his appreciation—supposedly at the request of the county's citizens—he gave his infant son John Witherspoon a nickname that he would carry throughout life; he called him Owen.[32]

Kentucky's Democrats were ecstatic. The celebration began at eleven o'clock on the night of the election when the congressman's victory was announced, and continued throughout the following day. In Frankfort, Democrats began speaking of purchasing Ashland from Henry Clay's heirs and presenting it to Breckinridge. "If this must be the 'Ashland' district," wrote Metcalf, "you are the man to live there." Otherwise, Breckinridge must name his Lexington home "Young America," and the district must take the same name. Influential Democrat John White Stevenson of Covington could not find words to express the "unbounded joy of a thousand

man, August 2, 5, 1853; *Buchanan and Breckinridge. Lives of James Buchanan and John C. Breckinridge, Democratic Candidates for the Presidency and Vice-Presidency of the United States with the Platforms of the Three Political Parties in the Presidential Canvass of 1856* (Cincinnati, 1856), 83.

32. Lexington *Kentucky Statesman*, August 29, 1851, August 5, 1853; Metcalf to Breckinridge, August 2, 1853, in B. MSS.

democratic hearts" at the result, and Powell, returning to Frankfort on August 10 from an extended absence, found Breckinridge's friends still rejoicing. "The *fogies* here still look sadly mournful," he told Breckinridge.[33]

The reaction was much the same throughout the nation. From New York came word that "Your return to Congress is hailed as a great national triump." A Washington City friend reported that jubilation reigned among the capital's Democrats and, from far off Iowa came news that the major's friends were making the prairies "ring with triumphal shouts of exultation on your election." Newspapers from Richmond to Boston to Indiana and beyond carried editorials celebrating his victory, and letters of congratulations came in from nearly all of the leading Democrats of the day. Even some Whigs sent their regards, including the wife of Linn Boyd, though Boyd himself—no doubt seeing in the congressman's reelection and increased popularity a threat to his own reelection as speaker—did not see fit to congratulate the man who helped to make him speaker in the first place. Francis P. Blair wrote to his cousin, calling his victory "the triumph of purity over 'lechery,' " and even the old abolitionist James G. Birney offered his compliments and renewed his former acquaintance with Breckinridge. However, there was one Whig who certainly had no kind words for Breckinridge. Poor old Robert P. Letcher chafed severely over his first political setback and would later admit that he could have borne his defeat better had he been beaten "by any one but a *mere boy*." [34]

One of the last to congratulate Breckinridge, and the one who surely wrote from the greatest distance to do so, was Senator Stephen A. Douglas. He was touring Europe, and it was September 9, in Vienna, before he heard of the victory. "I have this moment learned from the [Washington] *Union* the fact of your reelection," he wrote. "I congratulate you & especially the Democratic party on this brilliant triumph." It was a letter from one friend to another; from the acknowledged Democratic leader in one branch of Congress, to a newly risen leader of the other. As friends and as Democrats, Stephen A. Douglas and John C. Breckinridge would go through much together during the next eight years, in company with the Union that both loved so dearly.[35]

33. Metcalf to Breckinridge, August 2, 1853, John W. Stevenson to Breckinridge, August 2, 1853, Powell to Breckinridge, August 10, 1853, all in B. MSS.
34. Hart to Breckinridge, August 4, 1853, Brocchus to Breckinridge, August 6, 1853, E. C. Hibben to Breckinridge, August 4, 1853, Francis P. Blair to Breckinridge, August 20, 1853, James G. Birney to Breckinridge, August 22, 1853, all in B. MSS; *United States Review*, IV (September, 1856), 150.
35. Stephen A. Douglas to Breckinridge, September 9, 1853, in B. MSS.

CHAPTER **6**

I Thought It Had to Be Met

It was late in November when Congressman Breckinridge entrained once more for Washington City, taking with him not only the love of his family and the trust of his district, but a destiny as well. Forney stated it best when he wrote Breckinridge: "What a position is yours! You are the living personification of 'excelsior,' and hereafter when Democratic progress wants an illustration, your face and form must be used." No man was more talked of in the capital, he said, and while much of the talk smacked of flattery, he was confident that the young congressman would not be swayed by it. "If you but persevere," urged Forney, "and boldly go on in the way you have begun, nothing can keep you back from the highest places." [1]

Indeed, many people were interested in the "way" Breckinridge would go. In the previous Congress he had established himself as one of the leaders of the House, and now, as one of only eighty of the Thirty-second Congress' two hundred and thirty-four representatives to be reelected, his leadership and the direction it would take assumed added importance. In his first term he aligned himself with no faction, took no one side consistently against any other, but stood instead as a national—sometimes nonpartisan—representative. He appeared in Washington that winter as a man who had not yet cast his lot.

It would seem obvious that, considering himself a southerner, Breckinridge would align himself with the South, but thus far this had not entirely been the case. Socially and politically, he was one of the most atypical southerners of his time. Whereas the typical born-to-the-purple southerner took a certain pride in casual, even careless, dress, Congressman Breckin-

1. Lexington *Kentucky Statesman*, November 25, 1853; John W. Forney to Breckinridge, September 21, 1853, in B. MSS.

ridge invariably took pains with the neatness and stylishness of his attire. He also did his best by what James B. "Champ" Clark's father called Breckinridge's "two-story-and-a-half head." He never let a growth of fashionable whiskers mar his face, but he did allow his dark hair to grow long and flowing. His appearance was a first-rate political, business, and social asset, and Breckinridge gave it the attention it deserved. It was already commonplace this winter of 1853–1854, and it would become more so in the years ahead, for people to repeat the words of "Champ" Clark himself when he called the major "the handsomest man, the most majestic human being, I ever clapped eyes on." [2]

As for the other traditional characteristics of a southern aristocrat, Breckinridge seldom fell in place, though this was somewhat typical of the border state Democrats. He condemned the time-honored *code duello*, and never carried a weapon in civil life. He was most attentive to women, and gallant in the best southern manner but, unlike his more chivalric compeers, did not set them so high on a pedestal that, when a single man in Burlington, he would not keep several young ladies on his string at the same time. In Kentucky, where it had been said that to "offer a Kentuckian cents in change would be deemed almost an insult," Breckinridge kept a tight eye on every penny. And though the customary aristocrat favored romantic, unintellectual reading, he thrived on history and the classics.[3]

Even in his political beliefs and practices, Breckinridge sometimes stood at odds with the prevalent attitudes of his section, though not so much Kentucky. Southerners looked down on the practice of exciting hostility among the poor against the rich to make political capital or to get votes, yet Breckinridge was capable of it, in a mild form, as the left-handed Letcher had recently learned. Contrary to the general feeling in the South, Breckinridge had shown himself a friend of internal improvements, pension and land reform, and "democratization" of Kentucky's judicial system. Most contrary of all, of course, were his views on slavery, though they were not generally known.[4]

In spite of all this, John C. Breckinridge would, in this new Congress about to convene, take the first steps toward political alignment with his "section." These steps put him on the road that would, in future years establish him, in the eyes of much of the nation, as a southerner first, and an

2. Champ Clark, *My Quarter Century of American Politics* (New York, 1920), I, 47–48.
3. Eaton, *Mind of the Old South*, 290.
4. Forney, *Anecdotes*, I, 41.

American second. This development was in large part due to his peculiar relationships with two powerful men, President Franklin Pierce and Senator Stephen A. Douglas.

After seeing William O. Butler's chances for the nomination fall through, Congressman Breckinridge gave Pierce his wholehearted support at the Baltimore convention and stumped Kentucky for him. He received from hundreds—the *Statesman* said "thousands"—of Whigs, their assurances that if they were satisfied that his representations of the New Hampshirian's views on the Compromise of 1850 and southern rights were correct, they would give him their votes. Breckinridge heard the rumor that he might expect a cabinet position because of his aid in the election. Sensing that in Breckinridge he had a friend—and Franklin Pierce, as president, had few enough friends—he kept a close eye on the Kentuckian. Following Breckinridge's reelection, Forney could write him, "You stand no. 1 with the President, and you can have what you want for the asking." Even before Breckinridge left Lexington, rumors began to fly around the capital that the Pierce administration would be backing him for speaker. The president recognized that the congressman, in his new position of leadership in the House, could be a potent ally.[5]

The friendship between Breckinridge and Pierce lay on an austere plain, only slightly personal; but the friendship linking the Kentuckian with Stephen A. Douglas was of an altogether different nature. Aside from their political viewpoints, and their respective successes through perseverance, they did not have a great deal in common. Physically, of course, they presented a study in contrasts, the Illinoisian's stocky trunk, stubby legs, and stern features presenting a pugnacious aspect quite at odds with the grace and calm of Breckinridge's appearance. Indeed, their temperaments fitted their physiques, Douglas being an instinctive fighter in debate, sharp, quick, vicious when need be, while Breckinridge was much more restrained, slower to anger, and more diplomatic in relations with his adversaries.

In 1853 Douglas inaugurated an ingenious opportunity for winning over the influence and support of important Democrats to himself and his ambitions. The country was about to embark on an unparalleled run of land speculation in the northwestern territories, and he took a special interest in the area at the western tip of Lake Superior in Wisconsin. He was part of a syndicate, organized by, among others, the financier, W. W. Corcoran.

5. Breckinridge to Charles Woodbury, June 15, 1852, Norcross Collection; Lexington *Kentucky Statesman*, April 12, 1853; Forney to Breckinridge, September 20, 1853, R. H. Bacon to Breckinridge, August 16, 1853, in B. MSS.

They had the town of Superior City laid out, and began selling shares in the operation. Superior, being a natural terminus for a northern transcontinental railroad, was a project close to the investors' hearts and of much importance in Washington City. The land prices in their six-thousand-acre holdings would probably soar out of sight. Offering shares in this lucrative plum to certain important people would win Douglas not only earnest, interested, support for his railroad dream, but gratitude as well, and perhaps loyalty. It is significant that the first to whom he offered interests were Forney and Breckinridge. Douglas discovered Breckinridge's power during the affair with the *Democratic Review* and saw what it did to thwart his own chances in the Baltimore convention. Indeed, the erratic Sanders claimed that Breckinridge and he himself were the two men most responsible for nominating Pierce, so Douglas seriously needed that kind of influence.[6]

Thus Breckinridge, already fully committed to Pierce, and now strongly tied to the Little Giant, came to Congress with his support and his sympathies largely devoted to two men who, though they had little else in common, were united in one respect: they were, for all intents and purposes, "doughfaces," northern politicians whose principles catered to, or sought the favor and support of, the South. Douglas needed the sympathy of southern politicians and voters if he hoped to win the presidency, and President Pierce had to have the backing of the South, and especially its senators, if he wished to make a success of his administration.

Even before the House opened on December 5, Breckinridge's course in the coming session was much under discussion. In all corners of the capital, and throughout the nation, rumors flew that he would assume the speakership. Indeed, back in August one Washington observer declared that if the election were to be held then, Breckinridge would win handsomely. Old Blair wrote to his young cousin, "It seems only a matter of course that, like Clay, you are to take one step from the floor of the House of Representatives to the speaker's chair." Speculation that Pierce was trying to exert some influence for Breckinridge's election may not have been entirely conjecture. As for Breckinridge himself, he remained entirely aloof. Obviously, Boyd would again seek the position, and for one Kentuckian to attempt actively to unseat another, might not appear in a favorable light back in the Bluegrass. When the time came to vote, Breckinridge, seeing the general disposition among the party to reelect Boyd, cast his vote with them.

6. Allan Nevins, *Ordeal of the Union* (New York, 1947), II, 86–87; George Fort Milton, *The Eve of Conflict* (Boston, 1934), 104–105; George N. Sanders to Breckinridge, May 2, 1853, in B. MSS; Forney, *Anecdotes*, I, 19–20.

Boyd won, but in the balloting one representative refused to abandon his champion, and the final tally recorded the single vote of Augustus R. Sollers of Maryland for Breckinridge.[7]

From the very beginning of the session Congressman Breckinridge continued his defense of the Pierce administration that he began on the stump the summer before. Although he had not been elected speaker, and though his membership on the Ways and Means Committee was not the chairmanship that many expected the jealous Boyd to give him, Breckinridge, before the first month of the session was out, gave ample proof to Pierce that he would be a staunch friend and able confederate in the House.[8]

The major attracted nationwide attention to his endorsement of the president when, shortly after New Year's on January 8, 1854, he responded to one of numerous toasts proposed during a dinner in celebration of the anniversary of Jackson's victory over the British at New Orleans in 1815. Breckinridge directed his chief comments at a faction of the New York Democrats called the "hards," or "hard-shells," whose attacks on Pierce had been particularly galling and embarrassing since they came from within the party. Six years before, the Free-Soil wing of the party in New York had bolted. By 1852 they stood ready to return to the ranks, but a considerable opposition to them sprang up among anti-Free-Soil Democrats. This group, the "hards," opposed the reunion, while others, "softs" or "soft-shells," favored it. The fight was still on during the presidential canvass, and since all three groups backed Pierce, each felt entitled to a representative in the new cabinet. When Pierce appointed William L. Marcy, a "soft," as his secretary of state, and Robert McClelland, a supposed abolitionist, secretary of the interior, the "hards" felt betrayed, and bolted.[9]

In reply to these attacks, but without pointing a finger at the "hards," Breckinridge condemned those who would impugn Pierce simply because of his cabinet appointments. Adding that it would be "gross sycophancy" to say that all of Pierce's appointments, including those at lower levels, had been good ones, Breckinridge forthrightly asserted that the president had,

7. Bacon to Breckinridge, August 16, 17, 1853, Francis P. Blair to Breckinridge, August 20, 1853, Lazarus Powell to Breckinridge, August 19, 1853, R. H. Stanton to Breckinridge, August 7, 12, 1853, all in B. MSS; Lexington *Kentucky Statesman*, November 25, 1853; *Congressional Globe*, 33rd Cong., 1st Sess., Pt. 1, p. 2.

8. *Congressional Globe*, 33rd Cong., 1st Sess., Pt. 1, pp. 15, 38, 56–61, 173; Roy F. Nichols, *Franklin Pierce, Young Hickory of the Granite Hills* (Philadelphia, 1931), 315–17; Charles Wheatley to Breckinridge, December 21, 1853, in B. MSS.

9. Washington *Union*, January 11, 12, 1854; Nichols, *Pierce*, 218–19; John Payne to Breckinridge, January 19, 1854, in B. MSS.

nevertheless, been true to the Baltimore platform. Speaking for an end to factionalism in the party, he declared: "I am in favor of the union of the Democratic party. I believe it can exist, and believe that it ought to exist." [10]

Reaction to Breckinridge's speech was varied, and largely partisan. His Uncle Robert remonstrated him for falling in line behind Pierce and his cabinet in the New York controversy, and for not taking a powerful position of his own. He thought the speech was costing the congressman instead of profiting him. He appears to have been right to some degree, for Breckinridge's enemies in the state legislature at Frankfort began making a great deal of noise about the speech, and already another resolution was under discussion to gerrymander his district. [11]

Breckinridge himself was somewhat displeased by his address, but only from an oratorical standpoint. He had not planned to speak at the dinner, and his remarks were thrown out on the spur of the moment. However, he believed them to be quite independent. He denied any intention to fall into rank and pointed out that he had expressed the same feelings in his last canvass. This defense was a good one, borne out by his record on the stump and in his course thus far in the present session. His Democratic friends saw this. Pierce's confidant, Sidney Webster, applauded him for "eloquence such as seldom falls from the lips of man." In Kentucky he met with exultant approval from the Democrats who were, in his words, beginning to "see the top of the hill." It put an end to accusations from the Whigs that Breckinridge favored the "hards," and bolstered his friends in Frankfort who were striving to kill the gerrymander. By this time, however, he was already embarked upon something much greater, something that transcended the rumors, the accusations, or the acclaim. He had begun the most important single week of his legislative career and, in terms of its impact upon both his own future course and that of the nation, probably the most signal action of his life. Stephen Douglas had reported to the Senate a bill to organize the Territory of Nebraska. [12]

Douglas, now chairman of the Senate Committee of Territories, had long been interested in the organization of Nebraska and introduced the subject on several occasions, but with little success. On January 4, 1854, he re-

10. Washington *Union*, January 11, 12, 1854; Lexington *Kentucky Statesman*, January 20, 1854.

11. Lexington *Kentucky Statesman*, January 31, 1854; Robert J. Breckinridge to Breckinridge, February 22, 1854, A. Tarrant to Breckinridge, January 9, 1854, in B. MSS.

12. Breckinridge to Robert J. Breckinridge, March 6, 1854, Payne to Breckinridge, January 19, 1854, Paul Rankin to Breckinridge, January 24, 1854, all in B. MSS; Washington *Union*, January 11, 1854.

ported another bill to the Senate. The bill arose from a complex set of causes, no one of which was really preeminent. The nation, and particularly the Northwest, wanted a Pacific railroad, and a northern route required the organization of Nebraska since its path would lie across the territory. All sections were anxious to begin the settlement of the virgin land, and many families had already moved there in anticipation of territorial organization. The Democratic party was sorely divided and needed a unifying program. And Douglas wanted to be president. The organization of Nebraska would go a long way toward achieving all of these goals. However, their achievement via a Nebraska bill also required something in return. The territory lay north of the old Missouri Compromise line of 1820. This meant that the territory could not be organized with slavery, and that, under its territorial status, slaveholders could not settle there with their "property." The South stood to gain nothing by this, and the lack of southern support had killed previous bills, one of them during last session. Douglas needed to do something to win southern backing, and he made his try while the bill was in his committee. He inserted a clause stating that the question of whether slavery was to be countenanced in Nebraska should be settled by Congress at the time the territory applied for statehood, and according to the provisions of its constitution at the time of its admission. This and Douglas' accompanying report called into question the constitutionality of the Missouri Compromise—which he felt had been made inapplicable by the Compromise of 1850—though he made no concrete statement as to whether that enactment should be repealed. This left the question hanging in the air, and pressed hard by David Rice Atchison and other southern politicians, Douglas six days later added an extra section to the bill, explaining that it had been omitted from the first version by mistake. This new section gave the people of Nebraska, not Congress, the right to decide the slavery issue for themselves, and not only upon achieving statehood, but while in the territorial stage as well. This was a direct application of the "popular sovereignty" principle that Douglas had drafted into the Compromise of 1850, and the implication that this later enactment abrogated the Missouri restriction was unmistakable. Douglas had opened a volcano.[13]

Breckinridge's part in all this is conjecturable. There is no doubt that he favored organizing Nebraska. An ardent expansionist, he wanted the territory opened. Friendly toward the Pacific railroad idea, he now, thanks to

13. Nevins, *Ordeal*, II, 94–107; Nichols, *Pierce*, 318–20; Milton, *Eve of Conflict*, 107–109.

Douglas' shrewd use of his Superior property, had a vested interest in a northern route which must go through Nebraska. He also wanted to see the party reunited. And, because of his political and business friendship with Douglas, he was no longer opposed to the idea of the Little Giant becoming president.

It is equally certain that Breckinridge stood totally opposed to the Missouri Compromise. He had admitted that Congress might have the power to decide the matter of slavery in the territories, but only in a manner "just and equal to all the states." He cited the Missouri Compromise as an example of such Congressional action, so far as it went, but kept to himself his opposition to it on the grounds that the compromise line of 36°30′ should have been extended to the Pacific. This would have guaranteed that slavery could move into all of the territory acquired from Mexico below that line. Now, however, exactly four years later, his views were somewhat changed. He felt that Congress definitely did not have the power to decide domestic issues in the territories, and was convinced that the Missouri restriction was unconstitutional. Indeed, he later stated that at this time his conviction of its illegality was so great that "I never would have voted for the Territorial organization of Kansas and Nebraska while that odious stigma remained on the statute book." The search for the reasons behind his shift to a more conservative position need go no farther than Breckinridge's naturally defensive reactions—as a southerner—to the constant and ever-increasing attacks upon slavery by northern abolitionists, and his own sincere desire to see such agitation over the institution come to an end. He felt that, with the Missouri line abolished and the settlers in the territories free to decide upon slavery for themselves, the aggravating question of its extension would cease to be a national problem and become, instead, a local one. This was augmented by his belief that due to the geographical location and features of much of the new territory to be organized—especially Nebraska—slavery would neither spread to nor take hold in them. However, he did not recognize a fine line of difference which separated himself and the other southerners from Douglas. The Little Giant's popular sovereignty admitted the right of a territorial legislature to rule on slavery. Southerners, knowing that the major influx of settlers would come from free states, could not afford to have the question decided prior to statehood. If a territorial legislature banned slavery, then slave interests would be unable to settle in the territory, and consequently would be unrepresented when the time came to decide for or against the institution in a state constitution.[14]

In consequence of the position he now held toward the Missouri Compromise, Breckinridge was dubious about the proposed Nebraska bill and Douglas' January 10 revision of it. With the Missouri restriction still in effect, it seemed still to deny the rights of slaveholders to immigrate into the common territory with their property, while free state men could do so at will. The result would be the exclusion of slavery without its ever having had a chance. Douglas believed that the repeal of the Missouri Compromise line was implicit in his bill; Breckinridge did not. "While the bill struck at the spirit of the Missouri prohibition," said Breckinridge, "it did not meet the question fully." He told his Uncle Robert, "I thought it had to be met." Clearly he felt the time had come for repeal.[15]

Others were setting out to accomplish just that. Philip Phillips, an Alabamian serving his only term in the House, conceived of a repeal the day after Douglas' revised bill appeared. He presented it to Atchison, which resulted in a meeting with Douglas himself and a series of meetings in the next few days which included the most prominent southern men in the capital. Now that Breckinridge stood as one of the most important southerners in the House, it is almost certain that he participated in one or more of these discussions, especially as Phillips regarded him a particularly close personal and political friend.[16] However, Henry Clay's successor, Senator

14. *Journal of the House, Kentucky,* 103; *Ashland Speech,* 4; *Substance of a Speech by Hon. John C. Breckinridge, Delivered in the Hall of the House of Representatives, at Frankfort, Kentucky, December 21, 1859,* Breckinridge and Lane Campaign Document No. 10 (Washington, 1860), 2; *Congressional Globe,* 33rd Cong., 1st Sess., Pt. 2, p. 1239.

15. Nevils, *Ordeal,* II, 95–96; Mrs. Archibald Dixon, *The True History of the Missouri Compromise and Its Repeal* (Cincinnati, 1899), 437–39.

16. Philip Phillips to the editor, Washington *Constitution,* August 25, 1860; Philip Phillips, "A Summary of the Principal Events of My Life," June 10–20, 1876, Philip Phillips MSS, LC; S. K. Phillips to W. T. Walthall, December 22, 1881, in Dunbar Rowland (ed.), *Jefferson Davis: Constitutionalist* (Jackson, Miss., 1923), IX, 30–31. Only five accounts of the doings of this week in 1854 are known; of them all, only Breckinridge's March 6 letter to his uncle Robert is at all contemporaneous. One other narrative has been found, however, and it largely bears out what Breckinridge says. This is that of the Washington correspondent of the New York *Herald,* in its January 24, 1854 issue. Both Nichols and Nevins accept his statements (*Pierce,* 322; *Ordeal,* II, 99), and H. B. Learned, "The Relation of Philip Phillips to the Repeal of the Missouri Compromise," *Mississippi Valley Historical Review,* VIII (March, 1922), 303–17, proposes that the correspondent must have had inside information. Significantly, the *Herald* account agrees more closely with Breckinridge's than any of the others, and

Archibald Dixon of Kentucky, stole a march on all of them when on January 16, without having consulted Douglas, he gave notice to the Senate that he would offer an amendment to the Nebraska bill which, without using the word *repeal*, clearly nullified the slavery restrictions of the Missouri Compromise so far as the organization of Nebraska or any other territory was concerned. Dixon later stated that on the morning of January 16, before presenting his amendment, he showed it to Breckinridge and one or two other southern men, seeking their opinion. Their reply was hearty endorsement "from a belief that it would put a stop to agitation and preserve peace and harmony to the country." There was now a definite proposition for repeal to be put before the Senate, and for John C. Breckinridge, his week had begun.[17]

The next day, Tuesday, January 17, 1854, Breckinridge called at Dixon's home to thank and congratulate him for his bold stroke. Indeed, the majority of Kentucky's men in Congress approved of Dixon's course, and they crowded his parlor all day along with exultant members from other states. Among the callers on the next day was Douglas himself, still unconvinced of the propriety of direct repeal and fearful of its effect on the bill's chances for passage. He and Dixon went for a carriage ride. Up to this time, Atchison, Phillips, and Breckinridge, had been working to convince the Little Giant that repeal by implication was not enough. Dixon added his weight—and that of an impressive bloc of proslavery Senators who had rallied behind him—to the argument. Douglas, at last, gave in, and told Dixon that he would incorporate a repeal into his bill, "though I know it will raise the hell of a storm." [18]

Now there was work to be done. Thursday evening, January 19, Breckinridge and Douglas paid a visit to Phillips. Douglas asked Phillips to write out a form of repeal of the Missouri line that would be satisfactory to southern ultras; he read it and then received the Alabamian's promise to

---

these two contemporary sources have, consequently, been used as primary authorities for this narrative. The other sources available are: Phillips' letter in the Washington *Constitution*, August 25, 1860; Phillips' memoir in the Phillips MSS; Jefferson Davis to Mrs. Archibald Dixon, September 27, 1879, in Dixon, *True History*, 457–60; and Jefferson Davis, *Rise and Fall of the Confederate Government* (Reprint; New York, 1958), I, 28.

17. Dixon, *True History*, 593–94. Mrs. Dixon believed that her husband did not show Breckinridge his repeal before introducing it, claiming that after its introduction the major exclaimed, "Governor, *why did none of us ever think of this before?*" (p. 444). This is highly unlikely, since the repeal had been talked of for a full week, and could hardly have surprised him.

18. Phillips, "Principle Events of My Life"; Dixon, *True History*, 444–45.

sound out his southern friends on its acceptability. Phillips reported back to Douglas on Saturday. Meanwhile, probably unknown either to Douglas or Phillips, Breckinridge began some sounding of his own.[19]

President Franklin Pierce, from all accounts, knew nothing about the report Douglas delivered on January 4 until he saw it in print, nor did he give it much thought after its appearance. He believed that the Missouri line was unconstitutional, but was dubious about the advisability of repealing it, and was therefore pleased to see that Douglas planned to circumvent it by way of the Compromise of 1850. Both Pierce and the administration newspaper, the Washington *Union*, favored the bill and anticipated little trouble in passing it. However, Dixon spoiled everything. His amendment and the instantaneous favor it received from the southern men promised to split the party over the issue of repeal, for the northern Democrats were unenthusiastic. Consequently, on Friday, January 20, the *Union* came out with a condemnation of Dixon's amendment. It must have been obvious to Pierce that this would not win him the southern friends he desperately needed, and he set about trying to appease both factions. In this he sought inside help from Breckinridge.[20]

Just as the congressman acted as a go-between for Douglas and Phillips, he now took on the responsibility of liaison between Pierce—the administration—and the repealers. Among those prominent in the work for repeal thus far, Breckinridge was the only one close to the president. Also, since Pierce knew on Friday that Douglas had a repeal amendment in hand, the information could only have come from Douglas, Breckinridge, or Phillips. The Alabamian was busy polling the southern men in Congress, and the Little Giant, no friend to Pierce, certainly would not have disclosed his plans to the president. Scanty evidence and logic point to Breckinridge. Of all the repealers, he was the only one who truly believed in Pierce, felt him to be an honest man, and was earnestly solicitous for the success of his administration. Should the president arbitrarily oppose any form of repeal, he would alienate the most powerful Senators and forfeit any hope of their approving his appointments and backing his administration. Therefore, Breckinridge probably went of his own volition to see Pierce, outlined what Phillips had written the night before, and urged the president either to accept it, or propose an amendment of his own that would be acceptable to the ultras.[21]

19. Phillips, "Principle Events of My Life."   20. Nichols, *Pierce*, 320–21.

21. New York *Herald*, January 24, 1854; Breckinridge to Robert J. Breckinridge, March 6, 1854, Henry M. Rice to Breckinridge, March 26, 1854, in B. MSS; Nichols, *Pierce*, 323.

Pierce chose the latter course. Saturday he met with his cabinet, with Breckinridge perhaps in attendance, and together they drafted an amendment to be proposed which would put the whole question of the validity of the Missouri Compromise line in the hands of the Supreme Court. Since Pierce was certain that it was unconstitutional, he thought this move would satisfy the South. Breckinridge, feeling the same as Pierce, approved of this substitute amendment. The president gave it to him that same day and asked him to present the document to Douglas. Douglas, who apparently still felt that his bill abrogated the restriction, found nothing objectionable in the cabinet amendment and tentatively agreed to accept it if the South did not object. Breckinridge went over to Ninth and F streets to the boardinghouse occupied by Atchison's "mess"; four of the most powerful southerners in Washington City. Besides Atchison himself, there resided James M. Mason and R. M. T. Hunter of Virginia, and Andrew P. Butler of South Carolina. They did not control the Senate, but they could block almost any legislation introduced if they put their backs to it. Breckinridge found that they would not accept the cabinet substitute; they insisted upon outright repeal. They had already seen Phillips and approved his amendment and were not about to settle for something less from the president, especially since they knew they had him in a tight corner. Breckinridge reported the result to Pierce.[22]

Now was the time for decision. Pierce and the ultras stood deadlocked over the repeal. The following Monday, January 23, was the appointed day in the Senate for reports, and the Nebraska bill was on the calendar. Douglas did not want any debate on it until it was in its finished form, but a postponement until such time as general party support could be mustered might keep it from being passed during the present session, perhaps a fatal delay. The bill could not pass without a repeal, and from all indications and the attitude of the *Union*, a bill with the repeal would be opposed by Pierce and the northern Democratic senators. At the same time, the future of the administration stood jeopardized. The only way out of the problem—to organize Nebraska, keep the party together, and get Pierce his southern support—seemed to be to put a repeal into the bill and get the president's endorsement, thereby making it an administration measure. This would mollify all parties, and this is what Breckinridge set out to do.[23]

He determined to assemble several of the most interested senators and

22. Nichols, *Pierce*, 304–305; Phillips, "Principle Events of My Life"; New York *Herald*, January 24, 1854.
23. Nichols, *Pierce*, 322.

John C. Breckinridge, by 1853 a prominent Democratic congressman from Kentucky. This photograph was made in Washington by Mathew Brady. (National Archives)

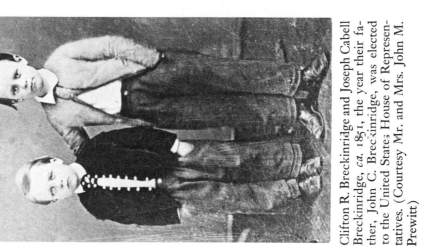

Clifton R. Breckinridge and Joseph Cabell Breckinridge, *ca.* 1851, the year their father, John C. Breckinridge, was elected to the United States House of Representatives. (Courtesy Mr. and Mrs. John M. Prewitt)

This Currier and Ives cartoon portrays John C. Breckinridge's reluctance to enter the race for the presidency in 1860 against fellow Democrat Daniel Webster. The cartoon's caption read: "Between the 'Illinois Bantam' and the 'old Cock' of the White House."

representatives and have them meet with the president that Saturday night, Sunday, or both. Out of such a meeting might come a solution. Undoubtedly the first person that he contacted was Douglas who, perhaps thinking that Breckinridge had Pierce's consent to such an interview, told Phillips Saturday evening that a meeting with Pierce would not be unacceptable. Phillips had objected to calling on the president on Sunday—the only day left for such a meeting—because of the Young Hickory's well-known aversion to doing any political business on the sabbath. Phillips, too, was asked to come, and Breckinridge enlisted Atchison, Hunter, and Mason, probably Jesse D. Bright, and perhaps one or two others. They were to gather and call on the president on the following afternoon.[24]

It is apparent that the major had not consulted Pierce about the proposed meeting—or, at least, had not received his permission—for the next morning before the hour of church, Douglas, Breckinridge, and the others, called on the secretary of war, and the man who in all the government was closest to the president, Jefferson Davis. They told him that the Senate and House committees on the territories had agreed upon a bill to be presented simultaneously in both houses of Congress, showed Davis the bill, and asked that

24. Breckinridge to Robert J. Breckinridge, March 6, 1854, in B. MSS; Phillips, "Principle Events of My Life"; New York *Herald*, January 24, 1854. Nichols (*Pierce*, 322) and Milton (*Eve of Conflict*, 115–16) assume that Douglas assembled the lawmakers to meet the president. Other sources claim that Pierce did it, but it is evident from Breckinridge's March 6 letter that it was his work. This letter deserves to be quoted more fully.

My Dear Uncle,
...You may think I have committed a great error, yet I say to you that I had more to do than any other man here, in putting it in its present shape. Originally, while the bill struck at the spirit of the Missouri prohibition, it did not meet the question fully—I thought it had to be met, and accordingly got some Northern and Southern Senators and Members of the House to go see the President, where, after conference, it was put substantially in its present shape....
Perhaps I ought to add that I did not fall into rank in the above business, but proceeded of my own motion—indeed 'inter nos" the President hesitated, but after taking his course, has very boldly adhered to it,—it will pass the House.
Breckinridge's hint of more than one northern Senator being present may confirm the *Herald*'s statement that Bright also attended, which Phillips contradicts. It is worthy of mention that Phillips is not to be too heavily relied on. He put Edward Stanly in the meeting when, in fact, Stanly had failed to be reelected and in January, 1854, was in San Francisco, California.
There is also a strong probability that Breckinridge met with Pierce on Saturday night. Henry Wilson, *Rise and Fall of the Slave Power in America* (Boston, 1875), II, 382, says so on authority of Reuben Fenton, who heard it from Marcy. Also, in the JCB Papers there is an undated 1854 note from R. M. T. Hunter headed "Sunday Morning," which asks Breckinridge the details of "your conference last night." There is at least the possibility that this refers to a Saturday meeting with Pierce.

he procure them an audience with Pierce.[25] Just what state the repeal amendment was in at this time is conjecturable, but Davis clearly understood that their purpose was to do away with the Missouri restriction, and heartily approved.[26] Consequently, he took them—probably Davis, Douglas, and Atchison rode in a carriage while the others walked—to the White House where, leaving them in the audience chamber, he went to see Pierce. The president, still miffed over the rejection of his substitute amendment, at first declined to see the gentlemen on account of the sabbath. The repealers, not about to be put off by this, replied through Atchison that if Pierce declined to talk with them, they would assume that he favored the repeal, and proceed as though the amendment abrogating the Missouri restriction were an administration measure.[27]

At this, the president grudgingly gave in and received his callers in the library. It is possible that Douglas and Atchison went in first, the others not having finished their walk to the White House, but in any event, when all were together in the library, they found, as Phillips described it, a "cold formality" prevailing. The president did not like to be threatened and apparently he gave them some trouble before settling down to the issue at hand. "Gentlemen," he said, "you are entering a serious undertaking, and the ground should be well surveyed before the first step is taken." There followed a conference over the repeal which lasted two hours or more.[28] There is no record of the conversation, but after considerable discussion, Pierce finally gave his approval to a repeal, whereupon they began composing the language of the amendment. Douglas, fearing that the president would change his mind after they left, persuaded Pierce to draft the amendment himself. The document stated that the Missouri Compromise had been superseded by the Compromise of 1850, and was hereby declared "inoperative and void." It left the inhabitants of a territory or state free to decide the slavery issue for themselves through their representatives in their legislatures and their constitutional conventions, whereas, in cases of title to slaves and questions of personal freedom, special provision was made for reference to the Supreme Court. The language of the bill itself represented

---

25. Davis to Dixon, September 27, 1879, in Dixon, *True History*, 458.

26. The *Herald* says that the final form of the repeal was decided upon before meeting with Pierce, while Breckinridge indicated that it came about during the meeting. The author is more inclined to accept the latter version.

27. Davis to Dixon, September 27, 1879, in Dixon, *True History*, 458; New York *Herald*, January 24, 1854.

28. Phillips, "Principle Events of My Life." Indications point to the meeting having lasted at least two hours.

several compromises. Pierce had a fear of the word *repeal*, and it appears that the Atchison mess gave in and allowed the substitution of *inoperative and void*, a difference only of semantics and not practical meaning. At the same time, while Breckinridge and the other southern men did not believe that a territorial legislature or Congress, possessed the power to exclude slave property from a territory prior to the formation of its constitution, Douglas and his northern backers believed that such power did exist. The result was the clause allowing referral to the Supreme Court, and both sides agreed to abide by its decision. There is something ironic in the fact that this portion of the bill, which was to do so much toward making sectional compromise near-impossible in the coming years, apparently arose from such a dispassioned spirit of mutual conciliation.[29]

Upon leaving the White House, the major and the others called at Secretary of State Marcy's home, at Pierce's request, to show him the bill. Marcy was out; they apparently made no further attempt to see him, and Breckinridge's week was over. His efforts had great impact. He helped Atchison and the others persuade Douglas to accept an explicit repeal, consulted with Douglas and Phillips over the preliminary form of such an enactment, acted as go-between for Pierce in his first attempt at compromising with the repealers, and he was the one man most responsible for bringing Douglas, Atchison, and the president together to put the bill in final form in time to be reported the next day as an administration measure. It was with much pride that the congressman wrote his Uncle Robert shortly afterward: "You may think I have committed a great error, yet I say to you that I had more to do than any other man here, in putting it [the Nebraska bill] in its present shape." He confided, *inter nos*, that Pierce was at first hesitant to take the step but finally came around, while Breckinridge himself, following no one's lead, "proceeded of my own motion." Although he could not foresee the effect the bill would have upon the domestic tranquility both of the territories and the nation, the major had no illusions about what would happen if it failed to accomplish its intended purpose. "To me," he said, "it is clear . . . that if the Union cannot abide upon it, it cannot last under any form of settlement." As a consequence, Breckinridge resolved to exert "such influence as I can command" for the bill. In fighting for its passage, he would come precariously close to risking his life.[30]

Douglas reported his bill as scheduled on January 23, complete with the

29. *Ibid.*; Nichols, *Pierce*, 323; *Ashland Speech*, 4.
30. Wilson, *Slave Power*, II, 382–83; Breckinridge to Robert J. Breckinridge, March 6, 1854, in B. MSS.

repeal and another amendment dividing the Nebraska territory in two, Nebraska and Kansas. From that day on, a hot debate raged in the Senate, while the friends of the bill in the House began marshalling their forces for the fight they knew would come. In the interim Breckinridge reaped the benefits of Pierce's gratitude for the part he played in bringing the president into accord with the southern senators and thereby gaining their support for the administration programs. Breckinridge successfully solicited presidential pardons; in an interview with Pierce, he managed to get back for his friend General John McCalla the land agency in Washington City that he had lost during the Fillmore administration; and, just two days after the White House conference, the Young Hickory appointed Breckinridge to a commission to test the correctness of the assay of the coinage at the mint at Philadelphia, one of those pleasant junkets, at government expense, with which a president could reward a faithful congressman.[31]

All the while that the Kansas-Nebraska Bill bounced around the Senate, Breckinridge received reassuring reports from home that Kentucky approved of the measure. However, many friends presented grave fears for the outcome of the Missouri repeal, and urged him not to lend his hand to the passage of the dangerous legislation. Of course they hoped in vain, but their entreaties and warnings must have given Breckinridge some idea of the opposition the bill would face and the reaction that its enactment might set off. Nevertheless, his resolve never wavered, nor his conviction that this act would cure, and not aggravate, the nation's ills over the extension of slavery. He was never more wrong in his life.[32]

The Kansas-Nebraska Bill passed the Senate thirty-seven to fourteen in the early hours of March 4, 1854, and by March 21 was in the House and ready for referral to a committee. It had undergone one significant change in the Senate, the addition of an amendment by John M. Clayton of Delaware, which aroused considerable ire among the northern senators. While the original bill provided for the privileges of suffrage and officeholding for all citizens of the United States, or those immigrants who had taken an oath to uphold the Constitution and the nation's laws, and who planned to become citizens, Clayton managed to pass an amendment restricting such rights solely to bonafide citizens, thus excluding several large immigrant

31. Charles S. Morehead to Breckinridge, January 29, 1854, George McCalla to Breckinridge, January 31, 1854, James Guthrie to Breckinridge, January 24, 1854, all in B. MSS.

32. Benjamin Crowther to Breckinridge, January 10, 1854, Robert J. Breckinridge to Breckinridge, February 22, 1854, John M. Morgan to Breckinridge, February 22, 1854, all in B. MSS.

groups from participation in the territories' affairs. Many southerners, who saw in both immigration and homesteading a threat to the well-being of the slave system, favored the amendment, but Breckinridge was not one of them.[33] He saw in it one of the first congressional murmurs of a "Native American" movement which had lain in secrecy for five years, and now was taking advantage of the Kansas-Nebraska agitation to come out into the open. He would hear much more from it before long.

Breckinridge, William Richardson—the man charged with putting the bill through the House—and others had worked hard to gather support for the measure. Indeed, some of its opponents thought they intended to drive the bill to victory with the weight of the administration because "They are so deep in the mud there is no backing out." [34] The major hardly agreed, however. When the bill came up for referral that day, he was relatively sure that, after its anticipated reference to the committee on territories, there would be a safe majority in its favor. He was bolstered in this hope by the fact that there would actually be two bills organizing the territories, for a House version of the bill identical to the Senate's had already been introduced and referred to the committee of the whole. This was a safeguard so that, in case the Senate passed a bill with some dangerously offensive amendment such as Clayton's, the House could reject it, then pass its own bill and refer it to the Senate. Thus the House would have two bills to consider, an excellent situation for the friends of Douglas and the repealers. One fear, however, was that, should something happen to the Senate bill, the House version might not be passed—it was far down on the slow-moving committee calendar—and sent to the Senate in time for its passage before the end of the session. This would present an unfortunate, perhaps fatal, delay, and it very nearly came to pass.[35]

The plan agreed upon by Richardson, Breckinridge, Alexander H. Stephens, and the more important of the bill's managers, was to bring the House into committee of the whole while the Senate bill lay on the speaker's table awaiting referral. With it there within easy reach at any time, they would then, in a radical yet precedented move, attempt to postpone the eighteen bills ahead of the House bill on the committee calendar and take it up first. Should it fail for some reason, then the Senate bill could be

---

33. In fact, no statement of Breckinridge's has been found concerning his opinion of the Clayton amendment, but his rigid stand against the Know-Nothing movement makes it clear that he opposed the measure.
34. John S. Williams to Gideon Welles, March 20, 1854, in Gideon Welles MSS, LC.
35. *Congressional Globe*, 33rd Cong., 1st Sess., Pt. 1, p. 762.

brought out immediately, and the friends of Nebraska would have two chances. It all hinged on resolving the House into the committee of the whole, but when Richardson made the motion, it lost. Then Francis Cutting of New York, a "hard" who had voted against going into committee, moved that the House proceed to the business lying on the speaker's table. Primarily by the aid of Nebraska's opponents, his motion passed, and then, bill by bill, they assigned everything on top of the Kansas-Nebraska Bill until, finally, it came up for referral. Then Cutting obtained the floor. Before this day he had been considered a friend of the bill, and still maintained that he favored the organization of the territories and the repeal of the Missouri restriction, but now he declared that there were certain provisions of the bill, most notably the Clayton amendment, which he found objectionable, and which he felt should be fully discussed by the committee of the whole. Consequently, he moved to refer the bill to that committee. It was well known that when a gentleman wished to kill a bill midway through the session, the way to do it was by reference to this committee, for its calendar now had fifty bills for consideration, more than it could possibly handle in the time remaining before adjournment in August.

Seeing this happen, Breckinridge and the bill's friends prepared to take the floor at Cutting's conclusion to warn the House against the effect his motion would have. However, when he finished speaking, Cutting moved the previous question, closing off all debate in spite of Breckinridge's earnest entreaties that he withdraw the motion. Breckinridge, Richardson, and the others, then sat helplessly as, by a vote of 110 to 95, the Nebraska bill was placed at the bottom of the calendar, apparently out of reach for the remainder of the session. The next day the opponents of the bill were exultant. "Nebraska is as dead as mutton," wrote one, "and cannot by any chance pass before the close of the session." [36]

Breckinridge was at first shocked, as much by the action of Cutting as by the state of the bill. Whether Cutting acted out of animosity toward Pierce and a desire to hurt his first administration measure, or out of some corrupt pact with the abolitionists, Breckinridge did not know, but he intended to expose this treachery as soon as possible. He managed to obtain the floor on March 23, though he was nearly too ill at the time to speak, and delivered one of the best, most logical, and well-reasoned speeches of his congressional career. Out of the hour allotted him, he devoted only about ten minutes to Cutting. Breckinridge declined to speculate upon, or

36. *Ibid.*, 760–62, Appendix, 439; T. Green to Simon Cameron, March 22, 1854, in Simon Cameron MSS, LC.

assail, the New Yorker's motives for his act, but declared that "the movement the other day was a movement to kill the bill, and a stab aimed at it by a professed friend." As for the major pretext offered by Cutting for his action—that referral to the committee of the whole would insure that the bill received full discussion—Breckinridge thought it most strange, since everyone present knew that the bill was now so far back on the calendar that it could never be reached, much less discussed.

The remainder of Breckinridge's speech was an able presentation of his view of the nature of the Missouri Compromise, the Compromise of 1850, and his own conviction that the latter superseded the former. Following the lead of other southern members, and particularly Alexander H. Stephens of Georgia, he made a brief exposition of some of those occasions when the North violated or refused to abide by the Missouri decision, and its "plighted faith" to it, the same charge which that section had leveled at the South. As he saw it, the reason for these violations was the same one that lay behind the opposition to the Nebraska bill, the pervading antislavery sentiment. In recent days enemies of the bill had charged that its express purpose, in repealing the Missouri line, was to legislate slavery into the territories and, in reply to this, Breckinridge declared: "Sir, if the bill contained such a feature, it could not receive my vote. The right to establish involves the correlative right to prohibit, and denying both, I would vote for neither." The bill merely sought to return to the settlers of a territory the same control over slavery that they enjoyed before the Missouri Compromise.

Breckinridge gave over the remainder of his time to a discourse on his own fears of overcentralization of the government and a warning against congressional despotism. Here, more than anywhere else in his House speeches, he revealed himself as a very strict constructionist of the powers, express and implied, which the Constitution bestowed upon the states and the general government. Political power over the territories, being nowhere expressly granted to anyone, rightfully belonged to the states. "The States are supreme as to all subjects not granted to the common Government. They establish their own institutions, at their own pleasure; they regulate within themselves all the relations of society; they are complete, self-sustaining, political communities; and they created the Federal Government, not to fix for them and their posterity the relations of society and the various elements that make up a complete social and political community, but to execute for the common good certain specified grants of power." Breckinridge argued that, just as the District of Columbia belonged to the separate states, and Congress could not abolish slavery in it without their consent, so, since the territories also belonged to the states, neither could that body abolish slavery from these future states. Yet this is what the Missouri restriction did, so far as land north of 36°30′ was concerned. For one who held the major's strict view of the Constitution, and who did not countenance the higher, or "natural," law of humanity against any further spread of slavery, these arguments were difficult indeed to dispute.[37]

Breckinridge's speech met with considerable response, most of it highly favorable. Among the most impressed observers was the Washington *Star*, a Democratic sheet which, nevertheless, did not hesitate to balk at administration policies from time to time. However, its praise of Breckinridge was unrestrained, especially toward his manner of delivery. The *Star* saw fit to compare his style of oratory to Clay's, complimenting his deep-toned voice, fine modulation, unerring attention to the rules of grammar and choice of language. Indeed, it concluded, "As a popular orator, he is, perhaps, with the best now in Congress; being exceedingby [*sic*] adroit in making his points, and persuasive in the *cast* of his eloquence." Forney, now with the *Union*, saw this too. He found in the speech, much both of Clay and Crittenden, and regarded the congressman as one of the few true orators in the capital.[38]

There was one person, however, who had no praise for Breckinridge's address. Cutting chafed violently under the brief denunciation and on March 27 obtained the floor to make a "personal explanation." In fact, it was an undisguised attack upon Breckinridge, riddled throughout with half truths, equivocation, and outright falsehoods, which did no honor to the New Yorker. Finally, in the most specious charge of all, Cutting asked what reason there could be for Breckinridge to attack him, a friend of the bill, and then speculated that it was actually the congressman's purpose to drive him and his supporters away from the measure.

Breckinridge was thus far unperturbed by Cutting's remarks, for they cast far more dishonor on the accuser than on the accused, and he began his reply in a jocular vein. However, after quickly exposing the prevarications Cutting had performed upon his speech of four days before, he showed obvious contempt as he replied to the insinuation that he and the administration wished to drive Cutting from the Nebraska bill. He denied

37. Nevins, *Ordeal*, II, 100; *Congressional Globe*, 33rd Cong., 1st Sess., Appendix, 439–43.
38. Washington *Star*, March 24, 1854; Forney, *Anecdotes*, I, 57–58.

having any special connection with the administration that did not exist with any other Democratic member, adding that he owed it nothing but fidelity, and that no administration, or president, or cabinet, could make him do what Cutting was implying. "Sir," he said, "my personal pretensions are humble enough; but I tell him that, clothed with the majesty of the people I represent, I stand here in my place to-day the peer of Presidents and of Cabinets."

As the applause from the galleries died down, Breckinridge went on to one final point. Cutting had accused him of proscribing the "hards" of New York and then had said that the congressman should be the last man to assault him, a "hard," because in the day of Breckinridge's "greatest need," the "hards" of New York had come to his aid. The matter was left unexplained—perhaps intentionally—and now Breckinridge called upon Cutting for an explanation.

Cutting, after hearing his trickery exposed for about twenty minutes, was in a surly, spiteful mood. He answered that during Breckinridge's last canvass information reached the "hards" that money was needed for the congressman's success. Consequently, he was "informed," some fifteen hundred dollars was collected "for the benefit of the gentleman who is now the 'peer of Presidents and Cabinets.' "

"Yes, sir," Breckinridge shot back at him, "and the peer of the gentleman from New York; fully, and in every respect, his peer."

The galleries exploded with applause, echoed by members on the floor, and the chair had to make several calls for order. Both men were excited now, and the listeners felt the tension. After some inconsequential remarks against Cutting from a fellow New Yorker, Breckinridge, composed, but obviously agitated, denied that he had received any such money. However, the real outrage, he said, was that such a subject should be brought before the House, and especially when based only upon rumor. He had thought of calling Cutting severely to account, but decided against it. "Perhaps the advantage I have gained, and the united condemnation of all honorable men, will be punishment enough, if, indeed, he has the sensibility to feel it."

Cutting, wounded, exposed, perhaps not a little humiliated, and left with barely a shred of defense, now went too far. He chose to read into Breckinridge's speech a fear to discuss the House bill, for when the New Yorker sought to bring it into the controversy, Breckinridge refused to be swayed from the subject under discussion. Now, in his anger and frustration, Cutting declared that Breckinridge "retreats, and escapes, and skulks behind the Senate bill."

Breckinridge arose to speak—a reporter in the gallery thought he hissed. "I will ask the gentleman from New York—I suppose we are nearly at the end of this personal explanation—to withdraw that last word." [39]

"I withdraw nothing that I have uttered," replied Cutting. "What I have said has been in answer to the most violent and the most personal attack that has been witnessed upon this floor."

Breckinridge had reached his limit. He would take no more.

"If the gentleman says I skulk, he says what is false, and he knows it."

A sensation ran through the House. Southern members rushed to gather around Breckinridge, while Boyd pounded his gavel, and several present shouted for order. Cutting continued for perhaps another ten minutes, and the major let him. He did not have that obsession for the "last word" that characterized Douglas' debates. Breckinridge had stated his case, and he stood content with that.[40]

The news of the verbal encounter raced throughout the Union, and to most it was evident that Breckinridge had been the victor. Even the generally hostile New York *Herald*, from Cutting's own state, condemned the "worst possible taste" shown in introducing the supposed money sent from the "hards," and declared that "Mr. Cutting's evasions" were painful to witness. Its Washington correspondent reported that Breckinridge's expression was "the quintessence of contempt," and that since the major had accused Cutting of stating a falsehood, it was expected that the New Yorker would demand reparation for the slur to his honor. The *Herald* added, "It is generally conceded that [that] is his only chance of squaring accounts." James C. Van Dyke, influential machine Democrat in Pennsylvania, thought Cutting's action "about as disgraceful and contemptible a piece of puppyism as has come to my knowledge in some time—mean and dishonorable in the extreme." Cutting's fellow New York Democrat, Emanuel Hart, regarded his conduct as unbecoming "a sensitive high-minded gentleman," and the administration papers generally agreed that Breckinridge had exposed and prostrated him beyond recovery.[41]

Of course, there were attacks on Breckinridge's conduct as well, and they reflected a disheartening trend. Instead of displaying mere partisanship, many of the assaults attempted to play up sectional feelings. Thus the

39. Ben Perley Poore, *Perley's Reminiscences of Sixty Years in the National Metropolis* (Philadelphia, 1886), I, 441.

40. *Congressional Globe*, 33rd Cong., 1st Sess., Pt. 1, pp. 760–64.

41. New York *Herald*, March 28, 1854; Washington *Union*, March 28, 1854; Emanuel Hart to Breckinridge, March 28, 1854, J. C. Van Dyke to Breckinridge, n.d., B. MSS.

Democratic New York *Herald* tried to invoke northern feeling against him, a southerner, while southern Whig journals spoke out in his favor. The rigid old party lines were disintegrating in favor of geographical divisions, an ill omen.[42]

For the moment, the future of Cutting and Breckinridge seemed indistinct. On the afternoon or evening of March 27, still flush with the heat of the day's debate, Cutting sent Representative James Maurice of New York to see Congressman Breckinridge, armed with a note demanding that Breckinridge retract his accusation of falsehood, or "make the explanation due from one gentleman to another." Breckinridge refused to withdraw his accusation, and introduced a friend, Colonel T. T. Hawkins, who would act in his behalf "to embrace the alternative offered by your note," and arrange their meeting. Thus, most reluctantly, he accepted the challenge.[43]

That same day, while rumors flew about the capital that a challenge had been made and accepted, Cutting appointed another New York member, Colonel Joseph Monroe, to act as his second in arranging the details. Since Breckinridge was the challenged party, he and Hawkins consulted on the terms of the proposed meeting, and Breckinridge called for most unusual conditions. He named as weapons "the ordinary rifle, commonly known as the western rifle," and set the distance at sixty paces. Cutting, fearful of being done out of his only chance to repay the wounds Breckinridge had inflicted, once more resorted to equivocation. In spite of the fact that it was he who introduced the subject of the "explanation due from one gentleman to another," he now claimed that he was the challenged party, and because he was a good pistol shot, but knew nothing of rifles, called for pistols at ten paces. This outraged even his second, Monroe, who later told Breckinridge that "The truth is, I was *for you*, all the time." [44]

At this point, outside moderators stepped in. The Democrats in the capital, whatever their personal feelings in regard to the two principals, knew that a duel between Breckinridge and Cutting would do no good for the Nebraska bill, the image of the party, and especially for the future prospects of Breckinridge, for whom they all held great hope. Consequently, Boyd, Thomas Hart Benton, and, said one observer, Pierce himself intervened to bring about an amicable settlement. Despite rumors that the an-

42. Washington *Union*, March 31, 1854; Hart to Breckinridge, March 28, 1854, Grant Green to Breckinridge, April 6, 1854, in B. MSS.
43. The correspondence between Breckinridge and Cutting is in Lexington *Kentucky Statesman*, April 11, 1854. Louisville *Courier-Journal*, June 18, 1875.
44. Lexington *Kentucky Statesman*, April 11, 1854; Joseph Monroe to Breckinridge, April 26, 1854, in B. MSS.

tagonists finally met at Bladensburg, the peacemakers did their work well and, by late on the thirtieth, the affair was settled with mutual expressions of regret.[45]

Breckinridge, who came out of the difficulty with increased prestige, ever after referred to it as "my affair with Mr. Cutting." The day after the settlement, Guthrie wrote John W. Stevenson that "Our friend Major Breckinridge has enhanced his character & reputation as a debater and has [earned] the confidence of [the] democratic party in the House & country, and I think has a fine future before him." The major's childhood playmate, and now a Philadelphia editor, abolitionist William Birney, assured him that "Your present position is an enviable one—on the whole rather improved by the late difficulty, since it has attracted to you the eyes of the nation." Of course, the reaction in Kentucky was wildly favorable, and that throughout much of the North was equally hostile. Unswayed by either point of view, Breckinridge secretly resolved never again to engage in an affair of honor.[46]

All during the Cutting affair and throughout the month of April, Pierce, Douglas, Davis, and others, applied pressure to bring into line the northern Democrats whose votes had made possible the referral of the Senate bill to the committee of the whole. By May 8 the administration forces felt they had a safe majority, and on that day Richardson moved that the House go into that committee. Then, in a move that required unwavering support from Nebraska's friends, he began proceedings to lay aside all the legislation on top of the House bill on the committee's calendar. Eighteen roll-call votes on as many bills were taken, Breckinridge voting to lay aside each of them, until the House bill was finally reached. Two weeks of debate followed, some of it as heated as that between himself and Cutting, but Breckinridge took almost no part in it. He was too busy making a show of confidence by striding up and down the House lobby arm-in-arm with Douglas, helping to keep the wavering in line. And he was working behind the scenes with Davis.[47]

The loss of only a half dozen southern votes could kill the bill and, in

45. Lexington *Kentucky Statesman*, March 31, April 11, 1854; Poore, *Reminiscences*, I, 441; Frank Hunt to Welles, in Welles MSS; New York *Herald*, March 30, 31, 1854; Washington *Union*, April 1, 1854.

46. Guthrie to John W. Stevenson, April 1, 1854, in Andrew and John W. Stevenson MSS, LC; William Birney to Breckinridge, May 3, 1854, in B. MSS; Louisville *Courier-Journal*, June 18, 1875.

47. Milton, *Eve of Conflict*, 142; Nichols, *Pierce*, 337; *Congressional Globe*, 33rd Cong., 1st Sess., Pt. 2, pp. 1128–32; Frank E. Stevens, "Life of Stephen Arnold Douglas," *Journal of the Illinois State Historical Society*, XVI (1923–24), 459.

the face of this threat, Davis entrusted much of the problem to Breckinridge, asking him to confer with various members, "or take such other course as you may deem best." Exactly what Breckinridge did do is unknown, but when, on March 22, the House bill finally came up for its third and final reading, and a vote, only two of the fifty-nine southern Democrats voted against it, Benton of Missouri, and John Millson of Virginia. Forty-four of the eighty-six northern Democrats said "Yea" as well, along with twelve of nineteen southern Whigs. The bill received not one northern Whig vote, but nevertheless, it passed 113 to 100, and for Breckinridge a great struggle had ended. The Senate quickly passed the House bill, and on May 30 President Pierce signed it into law. Alexander H. Stephens of Georgia, one of the principal movers behind the bill in the House, would some years later look back on Breckinridge, whom he regarded as "a man of a high order of talents, of most fascinating manners," and reflect upon his part in the campaign now ended. "Very few," Stephens said, "contributed more than he did in the House, to the Kansas-Nebraska legislation of 1854." [48]

For John C. Breckinridge, the formation of the bill and fight for the organization of the Nebraska Territory, was a turning point. Six months before, in the eyes of most of the nation, he was a promising young politician, moderately liberal, moderately prosouthern, but definitely a national man. Now this image had changed. The promise was still there, to be sure, but the specter of sectionalism had arisen to significantly tint his actions for viewers North and South. With Douglas and a small body of southern men, he helped form the Missouri repeal; almost on his own he made it an official measure of an administration decidedly in sympathy with the South; his speeches in the House had defended the southern view on slavery extension in the territories; and his affair with Cutting won him widespread affection and respect in that section. Even though Breckinridge might still regard himself as politically a national man—and his future actions would show a sincere desire to play the part—his national image was changing because of recent events. As time went on, Breckinridge would find himself in the peculiar position of being judged, not by the fact of his record, but by the prevailing interpretation of it, and year by year thereafter, that interpretation would draw his image inexorably deeper into the soft white hands of the land of cotton, and with it his fortunes.

48. Davis to Breckinridge, May 15, 1854, in JCB Papers; James A. Rawley, *Race and Politics: "Bleeding Kansas" and the Coming of the Civil War* (Philadelphia, 1969), 54–56; Alexander H. Stephens, *A Constitutional View of the Late War Between the States* (Philadelphia, 1868–70), I, 274.

CHAPTER 7

The Power Behind the Throne

The Nebraska bill was surely the most absorbing question of the session, but it was not the only one. Breckinridge continued to personally serve his constituents. He looked after the interests of Kentucky hemp growers in the making of government rope, helped keep up some patronage jobs despite federal cutbacks in funds, and worked long hours over pension and land bounty applications from veterans. In the House he continued his support of the Pierce administration, no easy task since both parties were now so fragmented that legislation was being passed by coalitions among the various groups rather than by party vote. This made a steady administration stance dangerous, but he stayed with it almost unfailingly. Thus, now that the Nebraska bill promised an end to the trouble over slavery in the new territories, Breckinridge supported a new homestead measure. It was still unpopular in the South, but he felt the measure now served the national interest. At the same time, he was no slave to Pierce. When a minor incident in March, 1854, provided a new pretext for the clamor to annex Cuba, Breckinridge spoke out against some members of the cabinet—and perhaps Pierce himself—in their willingness to jump at the opportunity without proper investigation to see if there was truly just cause. Breckinridge was also a careful observer of Pierce's military appropriations, firmly opposing any that he considered excessive.[1]

The greater part of his efforts, however, were expended for the administration. Next to the Nebraska bill, the most important legislation to feel his

1. Breckinridge to James C. Dobbin, August 15, 1853, in Charles J. and George E. Hoadley Collection, ConnHS; Dobbin to Breckinridge, October 2, 1854, C. C. Rogers to Breckinridge, May 9, 1854, in B. MSS; Lexington *Kentucky Statesman*, August 4, 1854; *Congressional Globe*, 33rd Cong., 1st Sess., Pt. 1, pp. 41, 548–49, 670, Pt. 3, p. 2125; "Cases of Maj. Breckinridge," June, 1854, in John C. McCalla MSS, DU; Nichols, *Pierce*, 326–27, 335, 353.

influence was Pierce's bill providing for deficiencies in appropriations for the fiscal year ending June 30, 1854. It had been introduced in February but was recommitted to Breckinridge's Ways and Means Committee. The chief problem was the number of expensive customs buildings that it called for. Breckinridge did not favor such extravagance, but he supported the bill on the ground that, since the buildings were under construction, they should at least be completed. The rest of the committee opposed him in this, whereupon he submitted a substitute bill of his own, to no avail. Now, with the deficiency bill back in committee, the major's fellow members put its management entirely in his care. He restructured the bill so that it covered all deficiencies except the customs houses, placing them in a separate bill, and on March 14 he presented both pieces of legislation to the House. For three days he carefully managed and maneuvered the debate, clarifying points, cutting off speeches by friends who might harm the bills, and meeting the arguments of its enemies. On March 17 the House voted 138 to 111 to pass that main deficiency bill. It was the only piece of major legislation officially trusted to his management during Breckinridge's congressional career, and its passage was a source of some pride to him, particularly since it passed by one of the largest majorities given to any administration measure by this House.[2]

A lull came in April, and Breckinridge took advantage of it in order to attend to some personal matters. He brought Mary back to Washington City, rented a house on C Street, and devoted a good deal of time to a private interest of ever-growing importance—his investments in Wisconsin. Prospects for land profits in the territory had soared since Breckinridge and Forney bought their first share. The prospect of a railroad had made Breckinridge's half share jump from $1,250 to a value of $10,000 or more. Great pressure was being applied to have the eastern terminus of the proposed transcontinental railroad located at Superior, there to connect with the great eastern lines. Powerful influences, from Governor Isaac I. Stevens of Washington Territory, to former Secretary of the Treasury Robert J. Walker, pressed themselves on Breckinridge, Douglas, and other legislators to gain support in Congress. As an interested party, Breckinridge was not hard to convince. Consequently, when the Minnesota legislature chartered the Minnesota & Northwestern Railroad Company, Douglas and Breckin-

2. *Congressional Globe*, 33rd Cong., 1st Sess., Pt. 1, pp. 318–19, 370, 410–11, 626, 633–35, 654, 676; *Sketches of Breckinridge and Lane*, 8. It is obvious that Breckinridge took great pride in his deficiency bill activity, since it received unusually full coverage in the 1860 campaign biography which he personally approved.

ridge gave territorial delegate Henry M. Rice their full support when he helped introduce a bill granting public lands to aid in the line's construction. The Senate passed it, but the bill was defeated in the House where there were objections to the fact that some legislators would profit by Superior and the new road.[3]

Even though the measure failed, Breckinridge knew that a rail line to Superior was inevitable, and he saw nothing objectionable about his profiting from it. Thousands of others would profit as well and, wherever its terminus, the transcontinental railroad was a subject of national significance. Back in Lexington Breckinridge discussed Superior with a number of political friends, and an idea was forthcoming. Anticipating the railroad, they would buy up bounty land warrants from veterans at the current rates—forty-four dollars—and hold them until the rail line made their value skyrocket. Kinkead would do the buying so that it would not appear that Breckinridge, as a representative, was getting his veteran constituents bounty lands only to buy them to make a profit. However, little came of the plan.[4]

By this time, in early August, 1854, a new furor raged over the second Minnesota railroad bill. It was much the same as the first, except that by its wording the Minnesota & Northwestern would be ineligible to receive any grants from the government. This was the result of efforts by a rival railroad faction in the territory headed by Governor Willis A. Gorman. Still it passed the House, and Douglas pushed it through the Senate. Finally, Pierce signed it into law, and only then was it discovered that two words had been changed sometime between its submission to the House and its passage. The effect was to allow Rice's corporation to receive grants after all. Repeal proceedings began immediately. In the House, Breckinridge and two others composed a committee to investigate the case, and he himself

3. Breckinridge to Joseph Lane, April 1, 1854, in Joseph Lane MSS, OHS; Robert J. Breckinridge, Jr., to Robert J. Breckinridge, June 6, 15, 1854, Mary C. Breckinridge to Breckinridge, n.d., Stephen Douglas to Breckinridge, September 7, 1854, Isaac I. Stevens to Breckinridge, December 5, 1853, Robert J. Walker to Breckinridge, February 6, 1854, all in B. MSS; receipt of A. O. P. Nicholson, July 15, 1854, Charles M. Butler to Breckinridge, May 9, 1854, in JCB Papers; Milton, *Eve of Conflict*, 105; Philip R. Cloutier, "John C. Breckinridge, Superior City Land Speculator," *Register of the Kentucky Historical Society*, LVII (January, 1959), 13.

4. *Congressional Globe*, 33rd Cong., 1st Sess., Pt. 1, p. 601; Beriah Magoffin to Breckinridge, April 26, 1854, George B. Kinkead to Breckinridge, May 25, 30, 1854, "Memorandum of Land Warrants given to Hon H M Rice," August 5, 1854, in JCB Papers; James B. Beck to Breckinridge, May 22, 1854, Paul Rankin to Breckinridge, May 28, 1854, in B. MSS; Cloutier, "Superior City," 13.

prepared its report. They found no intentional chicanery involved, but heartily condemned the alterations, accidental or otherwise. Although it stood to hurt Breckinridge financially to take such a stand, he would not tolerate such proceedings. However, the exoneration of Rice from intentional tampering rankled his enemies in Minnesota. The investigation, they said, "was a whitewashing affair. . . . Breckinridge . . . is one of Rice's men." Despite later efforts of Breckinridge and Douglas to salvage it, the bill was repealed.[5]

The session ended four days after Breckinridge delivered his report, and he and Mary returned to Lexington. His performance so far had enhanced his growing reputation. State Senator John S. Preston of South Carolina observed the Washington scene in some depth, and he declared that by now Breckinridge attracted more attention than anyone else in Congress. The opposition New York *Times*, just after the adjournment, said in an editorial:

> Surely there is no man in Congress of brighter promise or higher destiny than him. His career has been marked by brilliant success. Until now he is the acknowledged leader of the party in the house of which he is a member. . . . His general expression is one of lofty pride and conscious power of intellect. As an orator, he has few, if any, equals in the present Congress, and no superior. He speaks seldom, but always, when he does, with perfect ease and fluency. His gestures are few and graceful; his language terse and well chosen; his style eminently classic. Like the late Daniel Webster, he seldom uses a wrong word, or a word too much. Personally, Mr. B. is universally popular, and unless spoiled by too much adulation, ar [or] by the contamination of political intrigue, his friends may confidently anticipate for him a brilliant and honorable future.

Clearly Breckinridge still enjoyed a national reputation as a national man. But lurking within the *Times*'s praise, as within the minds of many of the major's friends, were fears for his future.[6]

Breckinridge himself had fears, too. On a private level, his finances were in a sorry state, and his partnership with Kinkead teetered on the brink of dissolution. "The truth is your politicks have broken me up," his partner complained back in February, "and have made the practice here irksome to

5. Magoffin to Breckinridge, March 6, 1855, in JCB Papers; Nichols, *Pierce*, 403; Cloutier, "Superior City," 14; *Congressional Globe*, 33rd Cong., 1st Sess., Pt. 3, p. 2090; St. Paul *Daily Times*, September 29, 1854.

6. Mary C. Breckinridge to Breckinridge, March 3, 1854, in B. MSS; Lexington *Kentucky Statesman*, August 19, 1854.

me instead of a very great pleasure as it was while we were together." Of course, the two remained close friends, but their business was faltering and Kinkead was beginning to look westward for new prospects.[7]

Worse yet for his public career, Breckinridge found that the Whigs had finally succeeded in gerrymandering his district out from under him. Claiming that Breckinridge had "debauched" the district, his enemies passed a reapportionment bill on February 17–18, 1854, which took away from him Jessamine and Owen counties, replacing them with Harrison and Nicholas. The effect was to reduce the number of Democrats in the district by over five hundred, while adding several hundred new Whig voters, making his reelection nearly impossible.[8]

This left Breckinridge in a quandary. His friends still wanted him to run again, and he had tried hard after the gerrymander to keep the favor of his constituents. Yet he knew that his chances were dim. When the ink on the gerrymander was not yet dry the Whigs had begun their search for a candidate to *"dethrone John C. Breckinridge*," and they were reasonably well organized against him. This, added to his uncertain financial condition, Mary's opposition to his making another canvass, and his growing family, left him perplexed, uncertain. "I am sorely puzzled as to the future—must think of it," he told Robert. "On one side I am poor, with a growing family etc. On the other it is hard to surrender just at this point, what it has cost such efforts to secure." He still felt his reelection to be possible, but against a good opponent it would require "an amount of labour frightful to anticipate." By late August he had about decided not to make another race.[9]

When he returned to Kentucky, Breckinridge found the Whig party to be almost dead, destroyed by division over the Nebraska bill. "I have never known the Whig party of Ky so thoroughly disorganized," he told Guthrie. "In an old fashioned race it would in my opinion be easily beaten." But a new party had emerged to replace them. It called itself American, but already it had achieved national notoriety as the Know-Nothings. Begun in New York in 1849, it earned its sobriquet by its preoccupation with secret

7. Kinkead to Breckinridge, February 16, May 18, 1854, in B. MSS.
8. Charles Wheatley to Breckinridge, January 3, February 17, 1854, Lucien B. Dickerson to Breckinridge, February 6, 1854, Robert J. Breckinridge to Breckinridge, February 22, 1854, all in B. MSS; Breckinridge to D. Howard Smith, March 5, 1854, John C. Breckinridge MSS, FC.
9. Lazarus Powell to Breckinridge, February 28, 1854, Dickerson to Breckinridge, March 12, 1854, Smith to Breckinridge, February 26, 1854, Wheatley to Breckinridge, March 16, 1854, Rankin to Breckinridge, March 26, 1854, Breckinridge to Robert J. Breckinridge, March 6, 1854, all in B. MSS.

oaths and signs, and the fact that party members answered all questions about it by saying "I don't know." It was an intolerant, rabidly nativist movement, chiefly opposed to immigrants and Catholics—a natural outgrowth of prejudice against the two largest immigrant groups in the country, the Irish and Germans. The Nebraska bill brought the Know-Nothings out of the woodwork in 1854, and gave them a strong foothold in the South by opening up territory that would likely be settled by these non-Protestant, nonslaveholding foreigners, thus creating more free states. After May, 1854, the movement spread through the South like a whirlwind, and bid fair to capture several state and national offices. It posed a serious threat to the Democrats in that section, whereas in the North its repugnance drove thousands of former Whigs and antislavery Democrats into the fold of the rising Republican party.[10]

Of Republicans, Breckinridge knew little yet, but the Know-Nothings were of immediate concern, for Kentucky, with its large percentage of foreign-born inhabitants, was fertile ground for the insidious movement. By the end of June they controlled much of the old Whig press, including the *Observer and Reporter* and the Frankfort *Commonwealth*, and the Democrats were preparing to launch an attack. By the time of Breckinridge's return in August, they had already won several minor offices and made a noisy but unsuccessful showing in the Eighth District. In the North it was much worse. New York, Maine, New Hampshire, Pennsylvania, Ohio, New Jersey, and Delaware, all fell to what Breckinridge saw as a coalition of "Native American" and Whig forces. To Douglas he lamented, "The fusionists are playing the D——l in the north East." He hoped that Illinois and Indiana could be saved and thus stem the Know-Nothing tide, but they fell too. The fall elections destroyed the Democratic majority in the House and left the party facing disaster.[11]

To combat the menace in Kentucky, Breckinridge organized a mass meeting in Lexington to affirm its support for Pierce's administration. A number of party luminaries were invited to attend, but when meeting day came on October 26, 1854, Breckinridge had the crowd entirely to himself. He explained a lengthy justification of the Nebraska bill, defending Doug-

10. Breckinridge to James Guthrie, September 27, 1854, Breckinridge MSS, FC; See W. Darrell Overdyke, *The Know-Nothing Party in the South* (Baton Rouge, 1950).
11. Overdyke, *Know-Nothing Party*, 27, 64, 297; P. H. Cooney to Breckinridge, June 17, 1854, Kinkead to Breckinridge, June 27, 1854, Powell to Breckinridge, July 3, 1854, John W. Forney to Breckinridge, September 13, 1854, all in B. MSS; Breckinridge to Guthrie, September 27, 1854, Breckinridge MSS, FC; Nichols, *Pierce*, 363–65; Breckinridge to Douglas, September 26, 1854, Stephen A. Douglas MSS, UC.

las against the widespread charge that he introduced the repeal solely to make political capital for his presidential aspirations. In fact, said Breckinridge, the repeal had been forced on Douglas, and no one knew this better than he. He then tried to show that the only reason the Whigs and Know-Nothings raised such an outcry over Nebraska was that there was a Democratic administration in power to embarrass. If he could convict them of purely partisan motives, he felt he might save the state, or part of it at least. He made several other such addresses in the coming weeks, but they were in vain. He met with Douglas in Chicago to discuss what could be done in the crisis and took a brief time away from politics to lend his moral support to Crittenden, who was under severe censure for defending a murderer in court. Despite his opposition to Crittenden's Whiggery—soon to be his Know-Nothingism—Breckinridge signed a letter endorsing the old statesman's conduct and professional propriety. Unlike an increasing number of southern politicians in these trying days, Breckinridge still judged men on their actions and motives, not their politics.[12]

The opening of the second session called the Kentuckian back to Washington, where he found a possible solution to his dilemma over reelection. Expansionists in the capital still coveted Cuba, and Pierce had tried acquisition through negotiation. Failing in this, his minister in Spain, Pierre Soulé, resigned in early January, 1855, after disgracing himself and the administration by promulgating with James Buchanan and John Y. Mason the so-called "Ostend Manifesto." It was the *coup de grâce* to Pierce's hopes for acquisition, stating that unless Spain would sell the island, the United States would be fully justified in taking it. The president needed a new minister to begin over again, and he turned to Breckinridge. He had for some time been anxious to reward the congressman for his fidelity, particularly on Nebraska. "I wish to oblige Breckinridge if it can be done with any propriety," he told Secretary of the Interior Robert McClelland. The Kentuckian's liaison work between Pierce and the repealers had revealed a talent for diplomacy, and the president could reasonably hope that Breckinridge would have success in Madrid. Without notifying Breckinridge of

12. Breckinridge to Guthrie, September 27, 1854, Breckinridge MSS, FC; Powell to Breckinridge, October 18, 1854, Wheatley to Breckinridge, October 18, 1854, David Disney to Breckinridge, October 24, 1854, George Pugh to Breckinridge, October 24, 1854, Jesse D. Bright to Breckinridge, October 30, 1854, John W. Stevenson to Breckinridge, October 27, 1854, Douglas to Breckinridge, September 14, 1854, all in B. MSS; Lexington *Kentucky Statesman*, October 31, November 3, 1854; Breckinridge and others to John J. Crittenden, September 12, 1854, in H. H. Crittenden (comp.), *The Crittenden Memoirs* (New York, 1936), 108–109.

his intentions, Pierce sent his nomination to the Senate for confirmation, and on January 16 it was approved. Breckinridge was allowed a few days to consider before accepting.[13]

His immediate reaction was to accept. It was the only way for him to stay in public life without risking another canvass. His friends and supporters throughout the country wrote urging him to take the post, particularly since their unsolicited efforts to get him other positions—a cabinet post and the governorship of Minnesota Territory—had failed. Word came from New Orleans that "Mr. Breckinridge's appointment gives universal satisfaction," and Cassius Clay wrote to say that "I rejoice in your good fortune." Indeed, the only discouraging advice came from his Virginia friend, A. Dudley Mann. A veteran of more than one foreign mission, he spoke with Breckinridge on January 17 and urged him not to accept. "You [have] too *fine a future* to admit of your going abroad," he told him. Mann believed that if Breckinridge remained in the country, he would be very likely nominated for the vice-presidency at the Democratic convention in 1856.[14]

It was everywhere assumed that Breckinridge would accept as minister, and he himself fully expected to. He attended dinner meetings with Marcy and other cabinet officers to discuss his duties. People with claims against the Spanish government began submitting their cases to him, and the Madrid press carried notices that "M. Bree-Kembridge" would be succeeding Soulé. He was convinced now that his reelection was almost impossible. Besides, the change in climate and scenery might help Mary's always precarious health. By late January he stood definitely resolved to accept the appointment, and even began arrangements to sell off some of his land holdings.[15]

13. Lexington *Kentucky Statesman*, January 2, February 16, 1855; Nichols, *Pierce*, 393–96; Franklin Pierce to Robert McClelland, August 29, 1854, in Franklin Pierce MSS, Dickinson College Library, Carlisle, Pa.; Breckinridge to Pierce, February 8, 1855, appears in the *Statesman* for February 16.

14. Powell to Breckinridge, January 12, 22, 1855, Charles Woodbury to Breckinridge, January 17, 1855, H. V. Willson to Breckinridge, January 18, 1855, Daniel Sickles to Breckinridge, January 26, 1855, William Birney to Breckinridge, January 16, 1855, Cassius M. Clay to Breckinridge, February 9, 1855, Ambrose D. Mann to Breckinridge, July 18, 1856, all in B. MSS; C. G. Baylor to Marcy, January 17, 1855, in William Marcy MSS, LC.

15. Breckinridge to Alexander H. Odell, January 23, 1855, in Charles J. Ingersoll Collection, HSP; James Campbell to Breckinridge, January 16, 1855, William Marcy to Breckinridge, January 23, 1855, James G. Leach to Breckinridge, February 5, 1855, Beck to Breckinridge, January 17, 1855, Robert J. Breckinridge to Breckinridge, January 18, 1855, all in B. MSS; C. Croswell to Marcy, January 18, 1855, Horatio G. Perry

Then, compelling considerations changed his mind. Consular pay was low, though the service itself was expensive. "No gentleman can represent the United States sufficiently at Madrid and save a dollar of his pay," declared the Washington *Evening Star*, and with the growing Breckinridge family this was hardly an alluring aspect. Then too, Soulé had practically destroyed any hope of getting Cuba in the near future, and that left little of interest or importance for a minister to do. And for some time now Mary had been trying to get her husband to leave national politics. By February 8 these and other considerations decided his course. On that day he wrote to Pierce declining the mission. His friends in Kentucky were both happy and sad. To many it indicated that he would seek reelection after all, whereas the more astute saw in it his intention to retire from politics. His enemies were despondent. "Their faces look twelve inches at least longer than the week before," wrote one who hoped Breckinridge would run again. William O. Butler, however, implored him not to make another canvass. However, he said, "If you would like to be governor of Kentucky, the case is very different." But Breckinridge did not want to be governor. Meanwhile, faraway in Madrid a member of Pierce's legation wrote Marcy, "I cannot but regret that decision," he said, "as the most favorable impressions concerning that gentleman have preceded his expected arrival here . . . where his reception would have been excellent." [16]

While he pondered his decision, Breckinridge kept his seat in the House, continuing to take an active part in the last debates. On February 6 he delivered his final full address, this time on a Ways and Means bill providing for payment of the debts owed the creditors of the former Republic of Texas. Since annexation of the Lone Star State, this had been a point of contention, the creditors claiming that the United States must make good on Texas' debts. Breckinridge's interest in the matter came largely at the prompting of his friend Leslie Combs and from the Corcoran-Bright financial combine which owned a considerable quantity of Texas bonds still payable.[17] The result was this bill, and in his address Breckinridge drove

---

to Marcy, March 2, 1855, in Marcy MSS; Lexington *Kentucky Statesman*, March 20, 1855; Magoffin to Breckinridge, March 6, 1855, in JCB Papers.

16. George N. Sanders to Breckinridge, June 30, 1854, Rankin to Breckinridge, February 13, 1854, George W. Johnson to Breckinridge, February 18, 1855, William O. Butler to Breckinridge, February 26, 1854, all in B. MSS; Lexington *Kentucky Statesman*, February 16, 1855; *Congressional Globe*, 33rd Cong., 2nd Sess., Pt. 1, p. 650; Perry to Marcy, March 2, 1855, in Marcy MSS.

17. *Congressional Globe*, 33rd Cong., 2nd Sess., Pt. 1, p. 650, Appendix, 155–58; Leslie Combs to Breckinridge, January 3, February 25, May 28, 1854, in B. MSS.

home the point that, since the federal government had assumed Texas' chief sources of revenues—custom duties—it must also rightfully take on the state's prior debts, but only those debts related to the powers that Texas had surrendered to Congress an annexation. Any encumbrances connected with the sovereign powers still held by the state were not eligible. Finally, after some change and compromise, the Texas Debt Bill passed. It was one of the few times when the Corcoran financial empire had success with Congress.[18]

For the remainder of the session Breckinridge acted as chief spokesman for Ways and Means on a variety of bills. He fought a new appropriation for the Collins line and, though it passed, he had the satisfaction of seeing Pierce veto it, and he stood up in the House to defend the president's action. This satisfaction was tempered by the failure of another appropriation for which he fought, one to live up to an 1839 contract with the Sioux Indians to pay them $12,000 for the purchase of an island in the upper Mississippi. The island was taken, but the money was not forthcoming, nor would it be now, despite Breckinridge's stand.

On March 3, 1855, the last day of the Thirty-third Congress, Breckinridge briefly took the floor for the last time to oppose a bill introduced that same day. A clear reflection of the Know-Nothing mania, it would require all immigrants to obtain from an American consul a certificate stating that they were not insane, lunatics, idiots, poor, blind, and that for five years previous they had not been afflicted by any of these maladies. Ridiculing the bill, Breckinridge suggested that its authors should have added as a further qualification, "nor derangement of the bowels." Despite the laughter around him, he was deadly serious. He went on to become the first congressman to declare himself firmly against the bill and the sentiment it represented, upon the floor of Congress.

> I regard this bill as one of the fruits of the proscriptive feeling which is just now pervading this country. I know it is popular, and I know it is sweeping like a hurricane from one end of the country to the other; but it is in conflict with the fundamental principles of our system of Government, and I am willing to oppose my hand to it, and await the time when there shall be a reaction in the public sentiment, as I know there will be. I want the gentlemen of this House to know that, if they vote for this bill, they draw a distinction between the rich and the poor, and allow only the latter class to come—nor

18. *Congressional Globe*, 33rd Cong., 2nd Sess., Pt. 2, p. 863; Nichols, *Pierce*, 351; Henry Cohen, *Business and Politics in America from the Age of Jackson to the Civil War: The Career Biography of W. W. Corcoran* (Westport, Conn., 1971), 136–38.

can they come except—with a pass in their hands, like a negro going from one plantation to another.

This was just now a dangerous attitude for a southern politician to assume, but so far as he knew, Breckinridge's political career was at an end. A few hours later the final gavel fell, and this Congress and Breckinridge's service in the House, passed into history.[19]

He returned to Lexington immediately, to make public his decision not to run again. His friends were greatly disappointed, but he had made his choice and they could not persuade him otherwise. One glimmer of hope for continuing in political life now appeared, however. Not unexpectedly, it came from Franklin Pierce, still anxious to reward his faithful friend. Before Breckinridge left Washington, the president met with him and said that, "in a certain contingency," he might be able to offer the Kentuckian the governorship of Minnesota Territory.[20]

It was largely Rice's idea. He hated the present governor, Gorman, and at the same time recognized the advantages that could come to the Superior project and the Minnesota and Northwestern by having Breckinridge in office. Predictably, Douglas, Bright, Forney, and Hunter all came to Rice's aid in the project. Their motives varied. Besides the financial possibilities, Bright saw in it a way to deny Minnesota's future vote to Douglas, whom he hated. All the others, excepting the Little Giant, recognized the governorship as a good stepping-stone for Breckinridge should he seek the presidency. As would happen frequently from now on, his prosouthern friends sought to use him for their own goals.

This powerful lobby went to work on Pierce to remove Gorman. Francis P. Blair joined, too, out of an interest in his cousin's advancement. Pierce, very much wanting to help, sought repeatedly to find some proof of incompetence which would justify Gorman's replacement. Soon Guthrie joined the crusade, and through March and April the president had repeated meetings with these men. On April 11 they talked with Pierce for four hours. Douglas, Rice told Breckinridge, was "for you all the time." Pierce asked Guthrie to find out if there was any other position which the major would like to have. There was no way to relieve Gorman; Rice, dejected, called the president "a miserable weak squirt." A week later Forney wrote that Pierce was "full of kindness" toward the Kentuckian despite his

19. *Congressional Globe*, 33rd Cong., 2nd Sess., Pt. 1, p. 778, Pt. 2, pp. 978–79, 1156–57, 1185; Nichols, *Pierce*, 379.

20. Lexington *Kentucky Statesman*, March 17, 1855; Wheatley to Breckinridge, February 18, 1855, Forney to Breckinridge, April 17, 1855, in B. MSS.

inability to give him the appointment. Later that month an erroneous report went out that Breckinridge had been appointed, and it gave a hint of a beginning change in public opinion toward him. "Mr. Breckinridge is a conspicuous and unscrupulous agitator on the side opposed to the sentiments of the people of Minnesota," one New York paper said in regard to his part in the Nebraska bill and the Missouri Compromise repeal. Already a small portion of the northern press was attacking Breckinridge for his part in that crucial legislation which, he mistakenly thought, would put at an end forever the agitation over slavery. Henceforward he would be viewed increasingly as a southerner. Now was opened the small but growing gap between his image in public opinion, and that in his own mind. The difference between the two would one day prove crucial.[21]

But for now most observers, North and South, still saw Breckinridge as a Union man, and as one who had exerted a profound influence in the capital. He had been Pierce's foremost champion in the House, supporting and helping put through virtually every important administration measure, including the vital deficiency bill. He had served as a peacemaker between factions of the administration and, most important, played a role second to none in the formation, passage, and defense, of the greatest administration measure, the Nebraska bill. He was one of the Young Hickory's few genuine friends in Congress. It is enough to say that four years later Washingtonians still spoke of the effects of Congressman Breckinridge's service. A correspondent for the opposition New York *Times* put those words in print when he said that it was tacitly admitted in the capital that Breckinridge had been "the 'power behind the throne' in PIERCE'S Administration." [22]

Almost immediately upon his return to Kentucky, the "power" sought a new partner to replace Kinkead, who would soon move west. He found him in James Burnie Beck. A native of Scotland, just a year younger than Breckinridge, he had come to Lexington in 1843, received a degree from Transylvania, and begun to practice law. As a member of the Kentucky bar, he soon formed a close friendship with Breckinridge and became an ideal partner. He was young, capable, just as interested in land speculation in the Northwest as Breckinridge, and a Democrat. They announced the formation of their partnership in April.[23]

21. Henry N. Rice to Breckinridge, March 18, 20, 24, 26, 28, April 1, 12, 15, May 6, 1855, Francis P. Blair to Breckinridge, March 26, 1855, Guthrie to Breckinridge, March 30, 31, 1855, in B. MSS; Nichols, *Pierce*, 404–405; New York *Courier and Enquirer*, April 30, 1855; Cohen, *Corcoran*, 190.
22. New York *Times*, February 8, 1859.
23. Lexington *Kentucky Statesman*, April 3, 1855.

Although Breckinridge apparently dug into work with as much will as he could concentrate upon it, his retirement from active politics was singularly short-lived, as not a few of his friends had predicted. Dating from the announcement of his partnership with Beck, it lasted eighteen days. On April 21 he addressed a Democratic meeting in Cynthiana, and delivered what would be the first of a series of blows against the Know-Nothings, whose ranks numbered, among others close to him, his Uncle Robert. Admitting that he favored a few of the principles of the American party—he approved of repelling foreign influence in the country's affairs—Breckinridge denounced its exclusion of foreigners and Roman Catholics from suffrage and officeholding. Then he served as a member of Ashland's district congressional convention ten days later and acted on the committee which presented Lucien B. Dickerson as nominee for the succession.[24]

Breckinridge would have doubtless continued his "retirement" had he not had to make a trip to the Northwest to look into his holdings there. In the speculative mood of the time, he probably hoped to alleviate his financial stress by investing still more in the newly opened lands. All the while that Breckinridge was in the Northwest, entreaties from Lexington urged him to come back home and help in the canvass then underway. The Know-Nothings were giving the Democratic party the fight of its life. From all over the district came the cry, "We need help," and one county reported its Democrats *almost crazy* to hear you on the great questions of the day." He hurried his return somewhat on this account and sent word ahead that he would devote the remaining weeks of the canvass to stumping for the Democratic candidates.[25]

The Know-Nothing proliferation in Kentucky posed a serious threat to the future of the Democrats, though it did, at least, drive several capable Whigs like William Preston, Archibald Dixon, Thomas F. Marshall, and Thomas B. Stevenson, into the Democratic ranks where they would serve well in times to come. The Know-Nothings had carried the municipal elections in Louisville back in April, and were now making an all-out effort for the state elections everywhere except in the mountainous eastern counties. Their gubernatorial candidate was Charles S. Morehead, well known and well liked, and a seasoned campaigner, and in the Ashland district they ran Alexander K. Marshall, relatively unknown, but backed by an able-bodied

24. *Ibid.*, April 27, May 4, 1855.

25. Rice to Breckinridge, April 25, May 6, July 17, 30, 1855, Beck to Breckinridge, June 25, 27, 1855, Leach to Breckinridge, July 21, 1855, James Caldwell to Breckinridge, July 23, 1855, all in B. MSS; Lexington *Kentucky Statesman*, July 17, 1855.

Know-Nothing machine. To combat them both, Breckinridge took the stump at Owenton on July 26, and spoke once or twice daily thereafter in every county in the district until election day. He declared that the policy of the American party was not an American policy. It was at war with true Americanism, he said, and he bore out his arguments with a history of the nation, the Democratic party, and the growth of religious and civil freedom. Some years later he said that the principle underlying his opposition to the Know-Nothings was a simple one; "that the condition of citizenship being once obtained, no question either of birth or religion should be allowed to mingle with political considerations." Though the *Statesman* reported that he drubbed them repeatedly, it mattered very little, for election day in August saw the Know-Nothings sweep the field. They won every state office from governor on down, and six of the ten Congressional districts, including Ashland.[26]

Breckinridge was mortified. It was a "damnable political miscarriage," he complained, "Poor old Ky has at last sifted herself down to an isolated & detestable position." He believed that the Democrats should have carried the election, and laid the blame on some bad district nominations, "together with the reign of terror established at Louisville." In that city, on what Democrats afterward styled "Black Monday," rioting broke out at the polls. Breckinridge and others believed it the work of the Know-Nothings, and some held the disturbances accountable for the defeat of William Preston, running as a Democrat for the congressional seat of the Seventh District. It left in Breckinridge and his party a grim determination. They had worked for years to make Kentucky a Democratic state, only to have it snatched from them just short of their goal by bullies and toughs who intimidated the voters. Breckinridge resolved that it would not happen again.[27]

Despite a serious illness suffered throughout most of late July and August, he began the work all over again. To Pierce and others he promised that Kentucky would go Democratic in 1856, with its crucial presidential election, or he would expatriate himself. Promptly he set about redeeming the pledge. Believing that the best way to rally the Democrats from their crushing defeat would be an impressive show of party strength, Breckinridge determined to organize a mass meeting in Lexington, featuring the

26. Overdyke, *Know-Nothing Party*, 105–106; Lexington *Kentucky Statesman*, July 31, August 3, 1855; *Ashland Speech*, 3.

27. Breckinridge to John S. Cunningham, August 18, 1855, in Breckinridge MSS, FC; Breckinridge to Pierce, September 1, 1855, in B. MSS; Overdyke, *Know-Nothing Party*, 106; James R. Robertson, "Sectionalism in Kentucky, 1855–65," *Mississippi Valley Historical Review*, IV (June, 1917), 53–54; Lexington *Herald*, October 8, 1911.

greatest Democratic lights in the country. From Kentucky, he marshaled Powell, Preston, Albert Gallatin Talbot, one of the four successful Democratic congressional candidates, also John M. Elliot and perhaps a score of lesser luminaries. Douglas himself would be a guest at Breckinridge's home for the occasion, and the two of them planned the rally well in advance.[28]

On the appointed day, October 5, 1855, four or five thousand gathered on the lawn in front of Morrison College. At 10 A.M. Breckinridge called the gathering to order, moved that Powell be appointed president of the assembly, oversaw the appointment of several secretaries and vice-presidents, and finally saw himself and four others placed on a committee to draw up resolutions to present to the Cincinnati convention. Then Douglas began a three-hour speech in the rain. Breckinridge sat by him all the while, patting him on the back at every good lick against the opposition, and frequently standing up to call for "three cheers for the 'little giant.' " When Douglas finished the committee conferred and shortly after reported a series of fifteen resolutions. They affirmed devotion to the Constitution and the Union (along with states' right), the Compromise of 1850 and the Nebraska bill, and the position against legislating slavery into or out of the territories. The chief target was the Know-Nothing party, and four resolutions proscribed them severely as "bigoted enemies to religious liberty, foes to our constitution, our laws and our free government." The resolutions stood behind Pierce, praised those Whigs who fought with the Democrats in the late canvass, and gave plaudits to the northern wing of the party, which had kept fighting in spite of the loss of state after state to the Know-Nothing tide. These resolutions would prove to be an important preliminary to the Democratic platform in 1856, and showed the Douglas touch significantly. Here he and Breckinridge laid the groundwork for the program that he hoped to run on the following summer.

The long day wore on, and enthusiasm in the crowd swelled as Breckinridge had hoped it would. Soon it spread throughout Lexington. By evening the crowd was so large that an overflow meeting was held in the courthouse. Being the host, Breckinridge left the serious oratory to his guests, delivering only a brief speech to report the resolutions adopted by his

28. Breckinridge to Cunningham, August 18, 1855, in Breckinridge MSS, FC; Breckinridge to Pierce, September 1, 1855, Joseph Wright to Breckinridge, September 12, 1855, Guthrie to Breckinridge, September 17, 1855, George Pugh to Breckinridge, September 17, 1855, A. P. Willard to Breckinridge, September 18, 1855, Jesse D. Bright to Breckinridge, September 20, 1855, Douglas to Breckinridge, September 18, 22, 1855, all in B. MSS; Lexington *Kentucky Statesman*, September 4, 28, 1855; Johannsen, *Douglas*, 482.

committee. But every time he arose or appeared on the stand, cheers went up. Plainly, it was his meeting, and just as clearly it was a success. An earnest supporter, A. J. Shiddell, recently presented with a bottle of seven-year-old whiskey, resolved never to uncork the precious "article" until the day John C. Breckinridge was elected president.[29]

Breckinridge did not rest. The fifteenth of his resolutions called on him and a few others to superintend publication of the minutes of the meeting. He did so, asking Douglas to provide a written exposition of his position on Nebraska to add to it. Douglas circulated copies in Illinois and elsewhere, though he, Breckinridge, and the others, agreed that authorship of the resolutions and their place of origin should remain unpublicized. Thus, they might be accepted as "original" everywhere they were heard before a meeting, North or South, indicating that the Democrats were unanimous and universal in their creed. Breckinridge distributed the document throughout Kentucky in the months following the rally. By the end of October he found that the state's Democrats were standing firm on the resolutions, and he took special pleasure in the way that the territorial question was being met. The party was advancing to face it squarely. "All things plainly tend to a great issue touching the true character and principles of the govts, State and Federal," he wrote Douglas; "for one, I welcome it, as a real and searching solution of our troubles." [30]

Certainly a solution was needed. Kansas was in turmoil. No one could have forseen that the passage of the Kansas–Nebraska legislation would have opened such a Pandora's box of controversy. Almost instantaneously a bitter contest over the newly opened lands began between proslavery and antislavery factions among the settlers. The territory was immediately divided into two antagonistic—and armed—camps. It did not help that in the first territorial elections, the slavery men brought in aid from across the Missouri river to help swing the contest in their favor by illegal voting. As a result, the new territorial legislature was heavily proslavery, and passed a territorial slave code without difficulty. To make matters worse, Pierce's appointed governor, Andrew J. Reeder, promptly became embroiled in land speculation frauds and proved totally unfit to keep order in the terri-

---

29. Lexington *Kentucky Statesman*, October 9, 1855; Lexington *Herald*, October 8, 1911; Emerson D. Fite, *The Presidential Election of 1860* (New York, 1911), 95; Cincinnati *Commercial*, November 17, 1887.

30. Breckinridge to Douglas, October 30, 1855, in B. MSS; Douglas to Walker and Charles Lanphier, October 15, 1855, Douglas to George W. Jones, October 15, 1855, in Johannsen, *Letters*, 344.

tory. In July, 1855, Reeder was dismissed and, a month later, Pierce appointed Wilson Shannon of Ohio in his place.

Shannon would fare no better. The influx of Free Staters had not been stopped by the proslavery control of the territorial government, and now they outnumbered their antagonists. In September they formed their own Free-State party and began a movement for statehood. This stirred smoldering hostility, and "Bleeding Kansas" was born. Shannon would soon be replaced by John W. Geary who, at last, managed to control the near border war. Meanwhile, the Free-Staters set up their own territorial government and asked recognition from Congress.

Breckinridge, who was a spectator through all of this, stayed reticent while the controversy raged. For one thing, like many another participant in the Kansas-Nebraska legislation, which was supposed to end the sectional strife, he was wondering how it all could have happened. Toward Reeder, with whom he was on only casual terms, he felt contempt because of his chicanery. He recognized and admitted that border men from Missouri, slavery men, were the cause of much of Kansas' trouble, and was confident that charges of illegal voting and provocation held some truth. He deplored the violence that ensued, but was equally opposed to the unconstitutional efforts of the Free-State party to take control. Breckinridge stood firmly behind Congress' refusal to recognize the rump government. In the absence of any decision from the Supreme Court on the right of a territorial legislature to embrace or proscribe slavery prior to being admitted to statehood, he still rigidly defended the constitutional rights of southerners to enter Kansas with their slave property inviolate.

But Breckinridge viewed neither illegal proslavery voting nor the incompetence of Reeder and Shannon as the real cause of the Kansas troubles. He blamed the rise of another new "sectional" party given birth by the agitation over the passage of the Kansas-Nebraska Bill. In a meeting at Ripon, Wisconsin, on February 28, 1854, a local group adopted the name "Republican" in honor of the republicanism of Jefferson and his party. Other organizations quickly adopted the title, and the new party grew rapidly, their platform being the containment of slavery within its present limits. Immediately, anti-Nebraska movements were begun throughout the North, and outspoken sympathy with the Free-Staters in Kansas became party policy. In the 1855 elections, they captured several northern states, among them New York, and by 1856 the infant party was obviously a menace to the White House.

Breckinridge genuinely feared the impact Republicans could have on the nation. They would not be content to abide by the constitutionality of the Kansas-Nebraska settlement; he learned that from their interference and encouragement in the Kansas turmoil. Instead, he believed that their purpose was to abolish slavery entirely by using the power of the federal government to expunge it from the South by a nefarious combination of political action and crafty use of public opinion. The party was purely sectional —as the Democratic party was rapidly becoming—and he feared it more than he feared the Know-Nothings. The fate, not only of slavery, but of the Union as well, seemed to him to be teetering on a scale, and the presidential election of 1856 would be the measure of all things.[31]

Breckinridge began working toward the coming election almost before the cheers of the Lexington mass meeting fell quiet in the cold autumn. On January 8, 1856, the Kentucky Democrats would hold a state convention in Louisville to choose delegates to the national convention in Cincinnati the following June. It was also possible that the Louisville gathering might commit its delegates to a particular individual in advance of the nominations. On this account, especially, Breckinridge sounded the opinion of the prominent party leaders in the state. In view of the disastrous losses to the Know-Nothings at the North, he felt that the nomination ought rightfully to go to a northern Democrat, and Pierce best fitted his idea of a good president: a proponent of states' rights rather than centralization; a cooperator with rather than a dominator of Congress; one who left domestic affairs largely in the hands of the national and the state legislatures while he concentrated on foreign affairs. However, Breckinridge soon found that Pierce's chances of winning the endorsement of the Louisville convention were indeed slim, for it appeared that Kentucky might have two of her own in the race. Over a year before, Metcalf had begun a slow, silent, movement for Powell as an 1856 presidential candidate, while old Linn Boyd was actively seeking support for his own aspirations. Faced with this, Breckinridge decided that it would be better if no endorsement whatever came out of the Louisville assembly. A rejection would hurt his favorite, Pierce, while the party as a whole could not afford to have the various state delegations come to Cincinnati precommitted. The Democrats would have to fight two parties in 1856—the Republicans in the North and the Know-Nothings throughout the nation, but primarily in the South. Nothing must

31. Paris (Ky.) *Flag*, August 4, 1858; draft of speech at Tippecanoe, September 1856, in B. MSS; Louisville *Daily Times*, September 9, 1856; "Notes," 1856, in JCB Papers. For more on the Kansas conflict, see: Rawley, *Bleeding Kansas*, Overdyke, *Know-Nothing Party*, Nichols, *Pierce*, and Nevins, *Ordeal*, II.

stand in the way of party unity; the nomination must be decided in convention, by the Democrats as a whole, and not by the premature action of some of the states. To this end, Breckinridge set several of his friends to work on the delegates as they gathered in Louisville early in January, 1856. Even the loyal Powell put personal considerations aside and joined the effort, and it appears that Breckinridge himself finally went to Louisville to lend his weight. They prevailed over Boyd's forces, adopted resolutions similar to those of the October meeting, and had the pleasure of seeing Breckinridge appointed a state elector and delegate to Cincinnati. Thus far he had not missed a step on the road to fulfilling his prophecy to Pierce that Kentucky would go for the party of Jackson in 1856.[32]

Somehow, with all this, Breckinridge managed to carry on a private life as well, but it must have been hectic. He was in full practice at the bar, though the brunt of the work probably fell on Beck. Indeed, as he told Rice, he had no choice but to work at the law again; he was desperate for money. He tried to sell a lot that he owned in Burlington, borrowed from friends, and even looked into current prices for his treasured investments at Superior. At the same time, however, he remained outwardly unaffected by his financial troubles. In society he was as convivial as ever. Breckinridge called often on Senator Crittenden in Frankfort, where the aged statesman's family found that Breckinridge, "whilst not an intrusive, presumptious man, yet had the most delightful powers of conversation, choice in the use of language and expressive phrases, having a voice so resonant and well toned, that others gathered closer and closer to hear the handsome and brilliant Kentuckian." [33]

But John C. Breckinridge was only fooling himself if he thought he could lead a normal private life, forsaking the excitement and involvement of a public one. More than a year before, one of his most earnest supporters in Kentucky had told him privately, "You I think are a doomed man—doomed to a political life." Rice wrote him the previous October that "your political future is growing bright and brilliant and should your life be spared your friends will place the National Banner on your head." It is unlikely that anyone at the time he left Congress, least of all Breckinridge, enter-

32. Wheatley to Breckinridge, February 18, 1855, Willson to Breckinridge, February 3, 1856, Robert M. Johnson to Breckinridge, February 28, 1856, Guthrie to Breckinridge, November 22, 1855, Lucius Desha to Breckinridge, December 27, 1855, J. P. Metcalf to Breckinridge, June 19, 1854, R. R. Bolling to Breckinridge, January 3, 1856, Powell to Breckinridge, January 5, 1856, all in B. MSS.

33. Rice to Breckinridge, January 23, 1856, Benjamin Thompson to Breckinridge, October 16, 1855, in B. MSS; Crittenden, *Crittenden Memoirs*, 32.

tained definite plans for bringing him again to the capital, but everyone knew that he would be back.[34]

Meanwhile he remained hyperactive in Democratic councils. Even before the New Year, several candidates were in the field, seeking the support of influential party members who might be able to swing votes at Cincinnati. Forney and Guthrie advised Breckinridge that Pierce would allow his name to go before the convention; Forney himself was working actively for his perennial favorite, James Buchanan; old Lewis Cass, approaching seventy-four and senility, had a few friends currying votes; and Breckinridge found his name being mentioned by a few, though he refused to take it seriously. A Democrat from New York, after an extensive trip through the crucial West, wrote that from his observations it appeared that none of the older party candidates could be promoted successfully. However, over an eight-month period he had mentioned Breckinridge's name to a number of party people, and none had expressed anything but approval. "If the matter could be properly managed," he concluded, "*you* could call forth and unite the strength of the party in 1856." Breckinridge's reaction was, "Humbug." [35]

Douglas' friends worked hard to get the nomination for him, and they particularly sought Breckinridge's support. The reason was simple. In the coming convention the South would very likely vote as a unit. Party unity required that the nominee be the choice of that section, and those close to Douglas believed that "Kentucky holds the helm." The South would go with her, and she, so they thought, would follow Breckinridge. Consequently, in January, 1856, the Douglas men began currying Breckinridge's favor. The Little Giant had one of them write to ask that he become one of his two chief advisors for the West. The correspondent added that Douglas "has more confidence in your friendship, sagacity & ability, than that of any other man living." That other similar letters were sent to other prominent Democrats, and the fact that the "more confidence" plaudit was repeated almost word for word to Breckinridge two weeks later, suggest strongly that the passage was contrived. Breckinridge replied simply that he preferred Pierce for the nomination. He added that if Pierce should seem unacceptable to the convention, he would then go for the Little Giant. Douglas was reported to be "pleased" at his honesty but preferred outright

---

34. Leach to Breckinridge, July 10, 1854, Rice to Breckinridge, October 14, 1855, in B. MSS.

35. Forney to Breckinridge, November 15, 1855, Guthrie to Breckinridge, November 22, 1855, H. W. Beers to Breckinridge, August 18, 1855, in B. MSS.

support. What effect this may have had on the friendship between the two is unknown, but after February, Douglas' lieutenants stopped writing their persuasive missives to Breckinridge.[36]

By that time, however, Breckinridge's own friends were writing to him, extremely concerned over the part he would play in the coming convention. Rice in particular showed his anxiety, and though he still hoped that Breckinridge would go for Douglas, the advice he offered was geared strictly to the Kentuckian's future. "You are now placed personally in a very delicate position & politically in a very responsible one. I hope after the convention that no one will be able to say that *you prevented* the *nomination of any one.*" Take no risks, he advised. "Four years hence or eight years hence—I do not wish to have it said that Breckinridge *defeated such a one or such a one.*" His conduct as a delegate at this convention might well make or break him as a candidate at the next.[37]

It is possible that Breckinridge did not take too seriously Rice's anticipations of his future presidential possibilities, but as the winter of 1856 passed into spring, he could not take lightly the suggestions from all sides that his name might go before the convention at Cincinnati as a candidate for the vice-presidency. In many quarters observers saw indications that Douglas would be unable to capture the nomination. In that event, many seemed to agree that Pierce would be beaten out by his own minister to England, James Buchanan, a crafty but unimaginative career politician who, with characteristic candor, had written the year before that "*I shall not again be a candidate.*" Should Buchanan get the nomination, he would be expected to carry the key northern state, his own Pennsylvania, in the November election. He would need a key southern state like Kentucky, which had not gone Democratic in decades, to guarantee success. This, combined with the old party policy of picking a vice-presidential candidate from the South if the presidential nominee was a northerner, pointed directly at Breckinridge.[38]

The movement for him—if it may be called a movement—began in New Orleans back in the previous November. Louisiana's Governor Robert C. Wickliffe had declared that his favorites for the nominations were "*Buchanan & Breckenridge,*" and among those who agreed with him was the state's powerful Senator John Slidell. The senator further declared that no

36. Rice to Breckinridge, February 12, 1856, Willson to Breckinridge, January 21, February 3, 1856, in B. MSS.
37. Rice to Breckinridge, January 23, 1856, in B. MSS.
38. James Buchanan to Jeremiah Black, March 9, 1855, in Jeremiah S. Black MSS, LC.

name would be more acceptable to him than Breckinridge's. By January, Alexander G. Penn, one of Louisiana's delegates to Cincinnati, was asking a friend to write to Breckinridge to see if he would be willing to have his name used in the convention for the vice-presidency. At the same time, in Gettysburg, Pennsylvania, the editor of the *Republican Compiler* endorsed the nomination of a ticket composed of Buchanan and Breckinridge, saying that it would be invincible. While all this was going on that January, John Breckinridge turned thirty-five, the minimum age constitutionally required for a vice-president.[39]

Breckinridge was not sure what to do. On the one hand, his natural ambition as a politician drew him toward seeking the nomination. On the other, he disdained the scrambling for office that characterized most conventions, believing that a man who sought a position too avidly was not entirely trustworthy. Then too, in order to placate Boyd, the Kentucky delegation was tentatively committed to promoting him for the vice-presidency, and for Breckinridge to put his own hat in the ring would not be well received in some quarters of the state. He asked several close friends what they thought he should do, and late in March he went east to Washington City for more advice. At Forney's home, "The Waverley" on Eighth Street, he dined with the editor, Slidell, Douglas, and others. Forney was encouraged to find him "eager to conciliate Northern anti-slavery men," since the "doughface" Buchanan, if elected, would need people in his administration who would be friendly to the North as well as the South. He and Breckinridge also spoke privately, and Forney told him, "I presume nobody cares more for you in this ten mile square than myself." [40]

Breckinridge returned to Lexington still undecided, but by this time the matter was no longer entirely in his hands. Thanks probably to Forney and Breckinridge's friend and relative George H. Martin, both intimates of Buchanan's, the "Sage of Wheatland" was now paying particular attention to the Kentuckian's course. In May, Buchanan asked that his kindest remembrances be extended to Breckinridge, though there is no evidence that the two had ever yet met or even exchanged letters. Martin wrote, "I cannot

39. Logan McKnight to Breckinridge, November 21, 1855, Charles C. McHatton to Breckinridge, January 24, 1856, J. McHatton to Breckinridge, June 18, 1856, Daniel Sheffer to Breckinridge, June 10, 1856, A. L. Shotwell to Breckinridge, January 17, 1857, all in B. MSS.
40. Henry C. Harris to Breckinridge, April 7, 1856, Forney to Breckinridge, March 31, 1856, in B. MSS; Forney, *Anecdotes*, 15–17. Forney does not actually date this dinner, but circumstances surrounding it indicate that it took place in March or May, 1856.

resist telling you your movements are looked on by your friends in Penna. with the deepest anxiety—for God's sake Breckinridge—don't fail or falter in the struggle, *the future* my dear fellow *the future*." Still uncertain, Breckinridge journeyed east again, stopping in Philadelphia to visit Martin. In Baltimore he saw a friend from Kentucky, Charles G. Baylor, who predicted that he would receive the nomination. Breckinridge only smiled. Going on to Washington, he attended a lavish dinner party at the home of Senator Robert Toombs of Georgia. Also present were Cass, Douglas, Congressman Howell Cobb, and the convention delegation from Georgia. The purpose of the evening was to win support for Douglas, and perhaps Breckinridge as well.[41]

By the time Breckinridge returned to Lexington, the Cincinnati convention was almost upon him, and a decision was imperative. He decided not to put his name into active competition. Thus resolved, he spent a few quiet days at home with Mary and the children. On the eve of his departure, they had a grand dinner, with pies, five kinds of cakes, strawberries, and ice cream for desert. That same day Breckinridge paid the Lexington agent of the Aetna Insurance Company of Hartford, Connecticut, one year's premium on a $3,700 life insurance policy which, curiously enough, took effect on June 2, the opening day of the Cincinnati convention. If he thought he was taking his life in his hands, he never admitted it.[42]

The convention opened in Nixon's Hall early June 2, and it was obvious from the start that Buchanan's people were in charge, thanks largely to the efforts of Slidell, Bright, Judah P. Benjamin of Louisiana, and James A. Bayard of Delaware. A "Buchaneer" was elected chairman, Buchanan men won control of all the committees, and Slidell and the others flew from one delegation to another gathering votes. By the second day of the convention, one Tennessee delegate found that there was "more triggering going on than one who really loves his country liked to see." More Buchanan influence was felt on June 4 when the committee on resolutions reported the platform. Here, however, Breckinridge and Douglas showed the top hands. The resolutions were largely identical to those which the major had written —with the hidden collaboration of Douglas—for the Lexington mass meeting the previous October, and which had been circulated anonymously and

41. George H. Martin to Breckinridge, May 18, 22, 1856, Charles G. Baylor to Breckinridge, June 7, 1856, in B. MSS; William Y. Thompson, *Robert Toombs of Georgia* (Baton Rouge, 1966), 112.

42. Receipt of William Scott, May 30, 1856, receipt of Aetna Insurance Co., May 30, 1856, in JCB Papers.

adopted in several other states before the convention. A declaration of non-interference by Congress with slavery in the territories was also included. It was ambiguous, leaving the question of legislative authority over the subject prior to statehood open to interpretation, a deft move to keep both Douglas and southern Democrats on the platform. It was the culmination of a long campaign to control the convention, the first step toward victory for the Little Giant and for Breckinridge. Breckinridge was determined to back him should Pierce prove unviable, and the Kentuckian was more than once seen conversing with Douglas' floor manager, Richardson. Breckinridge, and the delegation of which he was chairman, voted unanimously in favor of the platform, as did every other state. Otherwise, while the other members of his delegation took an active part in the convention proceedings, he was conspicuously silent, serving on no committees, never addressing the assembly.[43]

Thursday, June 5, 1856, was the day appointed for making the nominations, and the convention met early, only to get bogged down in debate over troubles with hards and softs in New York's delegation. It was well into the afternoon before they got around to the nominations. Buchanan, Pierce, Cass, and Douglas were quickly put into the field, the balloting began, and it was obvious that it would be a long night. None of the candidates even approached the two-thirds vote necessary. Kentucky divided its vote between Buchanan, Pierce, and Douglas on the first four ballots, Breckinridge casting for the president. When, after the sixth ballot, it became obvious that Pierce strength was waning, Breckinridge turned his vote to Douglas. Late that night, at the end of fourteen ballots, Buchanan was far out in front, but still nearly fifty votes short of a nomination. The convention adjourned until the next morning. Breckinridge had stayed loyal to Douglas after Pierce began his decline, and that night, in the room he shared with Magoffin, he received a visit from Martin and others of the Pennsylvania delegation. They proposed a coalition of Buchanan's friends with Breckinridge's, with a view to putting both of them on the ticket. The major refused.[44]

43. Roy F. Nichols, *The Disruption of American Democracy* (New York, 1948), 17; Herschel Gower and Jack Allen (eds.), *Pen and Sword: The Life and Journals of Randall W. McGavock* (Nashville, 1959), 369; Lexington *Kentucky Statesman*, June 10, 1856; Johannsen, *Douglas*, 517.

44. Lexington *Kentucky Statesman*, June 10, 1856; Magoffin to Breckinridge, July 2, 1856, in B. MSS; *Lives of the Present Candidates for President and Vice-President of the U.S.* (Cincinnati, 1856), 120.

On the first ballot the next morning, the Pierce men, by prearranged agreement, went over to Douglas, the hopeful beginning of a landslide that didn't come. Breckinridge's delegation went unanimously for Douglas on the sixteenth ballot but then, unexpectedly, the Little Giant's floor manager William A. Richardson arose and withdrew him. On the next ballot Buchanan received the nomination by acclamation. Shortly afterward the convention adjourned for dinner, to reconvene that afternoon. Breckinridge went back to the Spencer House, and there had his meal with a friend from Iowa, W. F. Coolbaugh. As they ate, the Iowan stated that he had initiated a movement among his fellow delegates, and that Iowa would vote for Breckinridge for vice-president whether he wished to be a candidate or not. At the same time, as a concession to the Douglas men for their candidate's withdrawal, Richardson was asking Slidell to accept Breckinridge as Buchanan's running mate, and to have someone in the already friendly Louisiana delegation nominate him. Slidell agreed, and persuaded General J. L. Lewis to take the assignment.[45]

Once back in the convention hall, the delegates passed a resolution endorsing a Pacific railroad, paid a backhanded compliment to Pierce's administration, and then got to the nominations for vice-president. Shortly after Boyd was nominated, Lewis arose and presented Breckinridge. To many, like Randall McGavock of Tennessee, it came as a complete surprise, and ample proof that the major had not sought it. Slidell and Richardson had been counting on his general popularity and perhaps some fast legwork of their own to bring the other delegations in line behind Louisiana. Of course, there would be some favorite son voting, and General John Quitman, of Mississippi, and Boyd had drummed up a good number of followers, but in general the Douglas delegations would be glad to vote for Breckinridge. The Buchaneers, prodded by Slidell and the other managers, would do pretty much as they were told.[46]

Breckinridge did what few, if any, had counted on. As soon as the applause died down after Lewis' words, Breckinridge stood on his chair and, addressing the assembly, declined the honor. He was already a candidate in Kentucky as elector, he said, and planned to canvass the state for Buchanan and the platform. His own delegation, with his hearty concurrence, had already presented Boyd to the convention, and he would not consent that

45. Lexington *Kentucky Statesman*, June 10, 1856; W. F. Coolbaugh to Breckinridge, July 23, 1856. John Slidell to Breckinridge, June 17, 1856, in B. MSS.

46. Louisville *Daily Times*, June 7, 1856; Gower and Allen, *Pen and Sword*, 370; Cohen, *Corcoran*, 204.

his name be placed in opposition to that of his fellow Kentuckian. He asked that his name be withdrawn.[47]

Out in the audience, serving as an alternate from Arkansas, sat Mary's cousin-by-marriage, J. Stoddard Johnston. What happened after Breckinridge's withdrawal young Johnston thought to be "The most impressive sight I ever witnessed."

> The scene which the convention presented when listening to him was most striking. They had not heard him speak before though all were anxious. And his manner, his severely simple style of delivery with scarcely an ornament of [or] gesture and deriving its force and eloquence solely from the remarkably choice ready flow of words, the rich voice and intonation. Every member seemed riveted to his seat and each face seemed by magnetic influence to be directed to him without an effort of will on the part of its owner. When he finished, brief though he was, I was sure the matter was settled. That speech was irresistible and though sincerely declining made him more votes on the first ballot than Lynn Boyd secured after a year or two's active electioneering and wire pulling.

Of course Johnston knew nothing of what Slidell and Richardson had done backstage, but it cannot be denied that the speech won more votes than it lost. Indeed, John C. Rives of the *Congressional Globe*, later told Breckinridge half in jest and half in earnest that the little address smacked of Caesar refusing the crown.[48]

After Breckinridge sat down, several other nominations were made until, at the time of the first ballot, there were nine candidates in the field—Quitman, Boyd, Benjamin Fitzpatrick of Alabama, Aaron V. Brown of Tennessee, navy secretary Dobbin, Herschel V. Johnson of Georgia, Bayard, Trusten Polk of Missouri, and Benjamin F. Butler of Massachusetts. However, the first two states to be called, cast their votes for yet another Democrat, Breckinridge. Following Maine and New Hampshire, the chairman of the Vermont delegation arose, said his members had instructed him that no Democrat had a right to decline to serve when his country called, and then, too, gave his votes to Breckinridge. Other states did the same. Virginia with fifteen, Louisiana with six, Ohio with seven, Iowa with four, and Wisconsin with five, added their votes to the eighteen he received at the beginning of the ballot. When it was finished, Breckinridge had fifty-one, only eight behind the leader, Quitman, and eighteen ahead of the third-placed Boyd. The second ballot began, and with it near-pandemonium as

47. Cincinnati *Commercial*, May 18, 1875; *Buchanan & Breckinridge*, 84–85.
48. J. Stoddard Johnston to "Dear Aunt," June 10, 1856, transcript in JCB Papers; John C. Rives to Breckinridge, October 10, 1856, in B. MSS.

Massachusetts, Rhode Island, and New York began to shift their votes to the Kentuckian. The convention began cheering, outside a cannon boomed, the chairmen of half a dozen delegations stood up at once to change their votes. Delegates crowded around Breckinridge until he was hidden from sight and, Johnston thought, "must have been nearly suffocated." At the end of the ballot every competitor had been withdrawn, Breckinridge had received the whole 296 votes of the convention, and the chairman announced him as the party's nominee for the vice-presidency.

The applause was deafening, outside the cannon still thundered, the delegates waved their handkerchiefs and cheered, and cries went up of "Breckinridge! Breckinridge! Take the stand." He came forward, waited quietly for the din to subside, and then spoke with much the same simplicity that had characterized his attempt to decline. The honor came to him as a great surprise, he said, and he took satisfaction from the knowledge that he had voted and acted in the convention as he wished, seeking nothing from anyone. To be associated with Buchanan, the last survivor of an earlier breed of noble statesmen and orators, was an honor beyond estimation. Their platform and their cause were just, and he would devote all his mind and heart to the duty here conferred on him, to strive for victory. Finished, he sat down to the tune of nine hearty cheers, and Johnston would remark that "Such enthusiasm and admiration for a man I do not think I ever saw." [49]

Apparently Breckinridge's first thought upon finishing his brief speech was to find Bright, whom he knew much more intimately than any of the other Buchanan managers, and find out just what had happened. They had not had either the time or the inclination to let him know of the agreement with Richardson. Indeed, apparently no one in the Kentucky delegation had been alerted, for it voted as a unit for Boyd on the first ballot. Breckinridge would find Bright and get his explanation, but first he had to pay the price of glory. Democrats were notorious handshakers, and in the wake of this nomination, which had been as exciting and seemingly spontaneous as Buchanan's had been drawn out and contrived, the delegates felt extra gusto in their arms. They so pulled and squeezed and wrenched his poor hand that two days later he was barely able to wield a pen and write. Perhaps he had known what he was doing after all when he took out that insurance policy.[50]

49. Lexington *Kentucky Statesman*, June 10, 1856; Louisville *Daily Times*, June 8, 1856; Johnston to "Dear Aunt," June 10, 1856, in JCB Papers.

50. Slidell to Breckinridge, June 17, 1856, John W. Stevenson to Breckinridge, June 9, 1856, in B. MSS.

CHAPTER 8

Go It

The reaction to the nominations was enthusiastic throughout the party, particularly for Breckinridge. At ratification meetings all over the country the party leaders expressed their satisfaction. Virtually every city that had a cannon fired salutes to him, Buchanan, and the thirty-one states. One of the most impressive meetings took place in Washington City, where a succession of Democrats paid tribute to the Kentuckian. Old Cass spoke of his "true democracy, his high and honorable character, his eminent talents, and his claims upon the public confidence." Pierce was there to pay a compliment, as well, but Douglas outdid them all, saying that Breckinridge was too well known to a Washington audience to require much praise. Most knew him personally, and to know him was to love him. Breckinridge, he said, possessed the highest qualities for the office for which he was nominated, "or for a higher station in future years when his experience should be more fully matured." Pierre Soulé, the man he was once to have replaced in Spain, was equally pleased. "He is beyond the age of boldness," he declared, "but has anticipated that of wisdom." [1]

Even the opposition expressed respect, if not joy, at Breckinridge's nomination. His association with Buchanan was characterized on all sides by, curiously enough, almost always the same words—"It is a strong ticket." Indeed, many Know-Nothings were pleased by his nomination in particular, despite his being one of their most outspoken opponents. After all, he was from all appearances a southern rights man, though not a radical, and since there was little hope of their candidate former President Millard Fillmore being elected, they would infinitely prefer a ticket with Breckinridge to any composed of the Free-Soilers that the Republicans would nominate. Indeed, one of these Know-Nothings, Vespacian Ellis, wrote to Breckin-

---

1. Louisville *Daily Times*, June 11, 12, August 17, 1856; Joseph Coleman to Breckinridge, June 10, 1856, in B. MSS.

ridge expressing his pleasure. "There is no man in the anti American ranks, for whom I entertain a more profound regard, than yourself." Saying that "If you have any assailable points, I do not yet know them," Ellis promised nevertheless to do his best to defeat the Democratic ticket, though he thought the country would be safer under Buchanan and Breckinridge.[2]

Outside of the natural lack of enthusiasm of the Republicans toward the Democratic nominees, the only real objection to Breckinridge's nomination for the vice-presidency came from some of the younger members of his own party. "The young men of the Democratic party," said the Columbus *Ohio Statesman*, "are exorted to try and swallow Buchanan because Breckinridge is on the ticket." Indeed, with sarcastic reference to the fact that Breckinridge was only second on the Democratic list instead of first, some of these friends and a host of opponents began to characterize it as the "Kangaroo ticket." Know-Nothing Henry W. Allen, addressing a Louisiana state party convention, declared it a "very singular ticket—a kind of kangaroo ticket, with its longest and strongest legs behind. The Old Fogy, its head, and Young America for its tail. For Mr. Breckinridge, I have a very high regard. He is a man of intellect, a man of genius—a man of mark. But Mr. Buchanan will not do." Plainly, many Know-Nothings would have preferred to see the Kentuckian running for the presidency. The only Democrat disappointed with Breckinridge's name on the ballot was Andrew Johnson of Tennessee. Johnson felt that the nominee had little or no national reputation to add strength to the ticket, a clear misconception. His other objection was over the Kentuckian's seeming inconsistency on the homestead issue, Johnson's pet bill.[3]

Beyond cavil, Breckinridge himself was pleased with his nomination, though his handshaking experience at Cincinnati might have inspired in him some misgivings of being able to survive the campaign. He returned to Lexington immediately after the convention, only to be called out to address a ratification meeting on June 9. Breckinridge spoke briefly, lauding Buchanan and the platform, and then emphasized two particular points on which he felt that, thanks to Cincinnati, "the Democracy cannot hereafter be misunderstood or misrepresented." One was endorsement of the civil and

2. J. McCallum to John Bell, June 7, 1856, John Bell in MSS. LC; Charles G. Baylor to Breckinridge, June 7, 1856, Vespacian Ellis to Breckinridge. June 7, 1856, in B. MSS.

3. Columbus *Ohio Statesman*, June 10, 1856; Lexington *Daily Press*, May 18, 1875; Vincent H. Cassidy and Amos E. Simpson, *Henry Watkins Allen of Louisiana* (Baton Rouge, 1964), 47; Andrew Johnson to A. O. P. Nicholson, June 27, 1856, in Leroy P. Graf and Ralph W. Haskins (eds.), *The Papers of Andrew Johnson, Volume 2, 1852-1857* (Knoxville, 1970), 388.

religious liberties granted in the Constitution. The other was the touchy question of slavery in the territories. He presented the position that he took on the platform, the same that he had favored during the negotiations over the Nebraska bill, that Congress had no power to interfere, and that the people of the territories could decide the question for themselves upon achieving statehood, but not before. During the coming canvass, many northern Democrats, even Buchanan, would give an opposite cast to this plank, currying the votes of antislavery people by tacitly declaring that the territorial legislatures could decide the matter at their will. Breckinridge, however, never deviated from his position. For one thing, he believed in it, and besides, it was the guarantee most sure to rob the Republicans of southern Know-Nothing votes.[4]

Late in June the Republicans met and nominated John C. Frémont and William L. Dayton, while the Americans put forth Fillmore and Andrew Jackson Donelson. The northern Know-Nothings had split, as many predicted, and gone over to Frémont, just as a portion of southern Whiggery abandoned their northern brethren and endorsed Fillmore instead of the "Pathfinder." And the campaign was on. From the beginning it stood obvious to Breckinridge and most others that, nationally, the contest would be between Buchanan and Frémont. In Kentucky, however, it would be between Buchanan and Fillmore. Of course, winning the Bluegrass State would not return the former president to office, but it would deny the Democratic ticket much-needed electoral votes. Frémont would run well in the free states, and his electoral vote might be high enough that if Fillmore should carry a few key states, Buchanan would be denied a majority in the electoral college. Thus the outcome in Kentucky, lost to the Know-Nothings in 1855, assumed a primary importance.[5]

Thanks to the custom of inactivity on the part of the national candidates in presidential elections, neither Buchanan nor Breckinridge was expected to do more than remain at home, perhaps write a few letters for publication, and lend a restrained hand with the fight in their home states. "Buck" did his part, and "Breck" set out to do the same, after first writing to Buchanan and expressing his pleasure at being associated with him on the ticket. For publication, Breckinridge addressed a formal letter of acceptance upon the official notification of his nomination, in which he endorsed Buchanan, the platform—"the only basis on which the Union can be preserved in its original spirit"—and those Whigs who were joining the Demo-

---

4. Lexington *Kentucky Statesman*, June 10, 1856; Nichols, *Disruption*, 49–50.
5. Nichols, *Disruption*, 18.

cratic ranks. Then he set about winning Kentucky, a state which had not gone Democratic in a presidential contest since 1828.[6]

One of the first considerations facing Breckinridge was the Old Line, or Clay, Whigs. By late 1855 the party was dead in Kentucky. Early in 1856 one of its former leaders, Thomas B. Stevenson, devised a plan to revive it, and actually consulted Breckinridge in the matter, though he had been one of the instruments of the Whigs's downfall. The Know-Nothing storm in Kentucky had blown the Democracy and many of its traditional enemies a little closer together. Indeed, Stevenson even proposed to Breckinridge that he come over to the new Whig party as one of its leaders. Breckinridge, however, sensing that a coalition with the Old Liners was rapidly becoming a viable proposition, had suggested instead that Stevenson and his friends hold off any definite action until after the results of the Cincinnati convention. Now Stevenson, pleased with the nominations and the platform, pledged himself to work for Buchanan and Breckinridge. There were also indications that Henry Clay's own son James would join the Democratic fold, and these two men and others brought a considerable portion of their followers with them.[7]

Other, harder work lay ready for the Kentuckian. Some of the smaller cities in the state had no Democratic newspaper to champion the cause, and he gave his counsel to a movement for forming one in Danville, hoping apparently to model it along the lines of the *Statesman*. Meanwhile, and throughout the canvass, that paper hammered unceasingly at the Know-Nothings, no doubt aided considerably by Breckinridge. Then too, the Democracy did not have central committees in every county, and if they were to carry the state both in the August congressional election and in November, they needed every bit of organization. In this, Breckinridge lent his influence, as well as in another, perhaps more vital, enterprise. There had never been a state poll of Democratic voters. His friend James G. Leach proposed that such a poll be taken, asserting that the knowledge thus gained might increase their vote by 10 percent, and indeed it had already begun in a few counties. Breckinridge quickly assumed partial management, making sure that poll books were prepared, and probably reviewing the results. The knowledge thus gained would be of special use to him in the most important of his activities in the state canvass, the selection and

6. Breckinridge to James Buchanan, June 12, 1856, in James Buchanan MSS, HSP; *Buchanan & Breckinridge*, 86–87.

7. Thomas B. Stevenson to Breckinridge, February 2, 20, April 18, May 3, July 23, 1856, in B. MSS; Breckinridge to Buchanan, July 1, 1856, in Buchanan MSS.

arrangements for Democratic orators to make the rounds of the whole of Kentucky, and especially those areas with a heavy representation of Democratic voters. He even extended his efforts to bringing in out-of-state speakers when possible, like Governor Joseph A. Wright of Indiana.[8]

One of the chief methods of reaching the voters in Kentucky, as well as every other state, was through the extensive distribution of campaign documents, pamphlets, and other related materials. The Democrats at large, especially in the rural areas of the state, prized these tokens of their own individual importance to the party. A committee was set up in Washington City to mail the documents to lists sent in from the various states, and Breckinridge kept the mailers well supplied with names. The things sent to the voters ranged from any of a number of campaign biographies of "Buck & Breck," prepared tracts by Forney and other powerful Democratic writers, and published speeches by party leaders, to satires, venomous attacks on both Frémont and Fillmore, and even light musical literature like the "Breckinridge Polka" and the "Buchanan and Breckinridge Songster." A special item of importance for distribution throughout Kentucky was a pamphlet titled *Old Line Whigs for Buchanan & Breckinridge*, composed of letters and speeches by former Clay men, among them James B. Clay, who did come out heartily for the Democratic ticket. Even campaign badges came into the field, and one agent in Philadelphia was mailing 30,000 weekly as the campaign wore on. It was this sort of personal contact between the voters and the party managers, and in Kentucky with one of the candidates himself, that won not only the support, but the hearts, of the Democrats at large. In Kentucky, as well as other states, it was manifested most obviously by another, and larger, crop of newborn males named "John C. Breckinridge ————." [9]

Beyond these private activities, Breckinridge did appear publicly on occasion at the request of Democratic mass meetings. In early July, whether by purpose or accident, he happened to be in Louisville at the time of a

8. Thomas Morrow and Van Carter to Breckinridge, June 12, 1856, Carter to Breckinridge, June 17, 1856, James G. Leach and W. D. Reed to Breckinridge, July 18, 1856, Leach to Breckinridge, July 17, 1856, Simeon Garfield to Breckinridge, July 18, 27, 1856, John Lovely to Breckinridge, July 21, 1856, in B. MSS; Breckinridge to John W. Stevenson, July 12, 1856, in Stevenson MSS; Breckinridge to Joseph A. Wright, July 14, 1856, in Joseph A. Wright MSS, Indiana State Library, Indianapolis.

9. Nichols, *Disruption*, 42–43; Breckinridge to John C. Rives, July 4, 1856, in Simon Gratz Collection, HSP; Louisville *Daily Times*, June 8, 1856; B. M. Coulogue to Breckinridge, August 15, 1856, Henry M. Rice to Breckinridge, October 6, 1856, B. C. Harley to Breckinridge, July 30, 1856, Samuel Murrey to Breckinridge, October 3, 1856, all in B. MSS.

rally in Democratic Hall. Even as the meeting was in session a crowd began gathering outside the Galt House. Upon the adjournment of the rally, its audience repaired en masse to join them, and soon repeated calls for Breckinridge brought him out of his room to a balcony. The wisdom of his making an appearance in Louisville was apparent to any Democrat who knew the temper of the Know-Nothings in the city. The latter were strong here, and their strength and sometimes unscrupulous methods had been greatly exaggerated by the Democrats in the state. Later in the campaign Breckinridge himself would express the belief that Louisville was governed by mob rule. Now, speaking from the Galt House, he experienced something which surely added to his apprehension over the state of the city. As he spoke, a band of "rowdies" gathered on the fringe of the crowd and did their best to shout him down. Everyone assumed that they were Know-Nothings and the civil authorities did nothing to quell their disturbance. In this kind of situation, the city's Democrats needed all the help they could get from prominent party men. Although Breckinridge made only a short address here, in keeping with the general quietude required of a candidate, he made a favorable impression which helped the party. Testimony to this came from the more than 5,000 people who called within a three-day period to see an ambrotype of him on exhibit at a Louisville photographer's shop.[10]

As the August elections neared, the vice-presidential nominee grew more and more confident of success in Kentucky, and he was not let down. The Know-Nothings lost their majority in the congressional delegation, and with the results of the balloting not entirely tabulated, he tendered to Buchanan the prediction that four out of five counties in the state would go Democratic in November. Nevertheless, he warned, "We may have a hot and embittered contest yet in this state." [11]

While he was worrying Kentucky through the first months of the campaign, Breckinridge paid no less attention to the progress of the canvass in the country as a whole, and it was in this sphere that he would eventually make his greatest contribution toward victory in November. From the very day of his nomination, he was kept advised of party affairs in every southern state, and most of those in the North as well. He helped to salve the wounded feelings of state managers who felt slighted by Buchanan, for the presidential nominee had reportedly adopted a policy of not writing to any of the major party figures, even Douglas and Cass, to thank them for their

10. Louisville *Daily Times*, July 11, 15, 1856; New York *Times*, July 12, 1856; Breckinridge to James Buchanan, September 21, 1856, in Buchanan MSS.
11. Breckinridge to Buchanan, August 10, 1856, in Buchanan MSS.

efforts. Even Pierce complained of Buchanan's ingratitude, and this made the letters that Breckinridge wrote appreciated all the more. At the same time, Breckinridge found himself in need of occasional defense against charges calculated to disaffect strong supporters. In Washington several questionable sources attempted to turn Douglas against him by intimating that he formed a coalition with the Buchanan men at Cincinnati, agreeing to help defeat Douglas in return for the second spot on the ticket. Thanks to Magoffin's repeating Breckinridge's refusal to Martin the night before the nomination, and to the Little Giant's own trust in his friend's loyalty, no harm was done.[12]

Ohio, Michigan, Illinois, and especially Indiana and Pennsylvania, presented a major concern. Without them the Democrats would lose the election. From his position in Lexington, Breckinridge's chief concern was directed toward Indiana. Forney had told him, "You should look after Illinois and Indiana," and Breckinridge took his advice. Early in the canvass he helped persuade Preston to make one or more appearances in the latter, and enjoined Governor Wright to keep him posted on progress in the state. However, always mindful of his position, he declined making any appearances there, or elsewhere, himself.[13]

By the end of July, circumstances forced Breckinridge to reassess his role in the campaign. Never very well organized, it was going badly in Indiana, and party leaders in the state implored him to come and speak. Both that state and Pennsylvania were absolutely necessary to the party's success. Great efforts were being expended in the Keystone State and nothing less should be done in Indiana. Consequently, the needs of the situation far outweighing the usefullness of decorum, Breckinridge decided to make a radical break with tradition. When an invitation came to attend a great mass meeting in Indiana on the old Tippecanoe battleground, he accepted. And, once the break was made, there were other invitations that could not be turned down. Cass wanted him to come and speak in Michigan; several requests came from Ohio; the Democrats of Pittsburgh wanted him for a mass meeting; and even Buchanan asked him to come to Philadelphia for a great rally. Breckinridge's friends urged him to accept. Bright enjoined him to "Lay aside those feelings of false modesty if you have them," and Guthrie

12. Simeon B. Jewett to Breckinridge, July 25, 1856, Franklin Pierce to Breckinridge, July 22, 1856, Beriah Magoffin to Breckinridge, July 2, 1856, all in B. MSS; Howell Cobb to Buchanan, July 14, 1856, in Ulrich B. Phillips (ed.), *Correspondence of Robert Toombs, Alexander H. Stephens and Howell Cobb* (Washington, 1913), 375.

13. John W. Forney to Breckinridge, July 5, 1856, in B. MSS; Breckinridge to Wright, July 14, 1856, in Wright MSS.

advised him to take the stump, seeing no reason for delicacy. Before he heard from either of them, however, he had made the decision on his own. By mid-August he stood committed to make campaign speeches at Tippecanoe, Dayton, Ohio, Pontiac and Kalamazoo, Michigan, Pittsburgh, and perhaps Philadelphia. This did not take into account those impromptu speeches that would await him at rail stops and other Democratic meetings he chanced to attend. He had undertaken a stump tour that would keep him speaking almost daily for over two weeks.[14]

Breckinridge began his tour late in August, starting off with some unscheduled talks in Kentucky. He traveled to Ohio, stopping briefly in Covington, Kentucky, for another speech which left him slightly hoarse. At Cincinnati, on September 1, he looked in on a Democratic meeting, was discovered, and amid shouts and huzzas was carried on the shoulders of his admirers to the platform where, to an audience of 20,000, he spoke again. The same scene was repeated the next day at a great meeting in Hamilton, Ohio.[15]

By September 3, after more unscheduled speeches along the way, Breckinridge finally reached Lafayette, Indiana, escorted the last sixty-five miles from Indianapolis by the three hundred or more young men of the "Breckinridge Rangers." Also along were Douglas, Cass, Preston, Clay, John Van Buren, and thousands of others who had come for the largest political meeting in the history of the West. Reaching Tippecanoe, he met a huge crowd. Upon their appearance, Breckinridge, Douglas, and the others, found themselves rushed and borne almost over the heads of the multitude to the platform. After few formalities, the Kentuckian was presented as the first speaker.[16]

Breckinridge obviously anticipated this to be an occasion of the first importance, for contrary to his usual practice, he came prepared with a several-page rough draft of his address. At the same time, the important day's proceedings aggravated his hoarseness, and the exertion was telling

14. H. S. McCollum to Breckinridge, July 23, 31, 1856, Lewis Cass to Breckinridge, July 31, August 12, 1856, David Campbell and others to Breckinridge, August 18, 1856, Simeon Garfield to Breckinridge, September 19, 1856, Buchanan to Breckinridge, September 2, 1856, Jesse D. Bright to Breckinridge, July 26, 1856, James Guthrie to Breckinridge, August 1, 1856, all in B. MSS.

15. James Tandy Ellis, *The Old Ellum Tree Whar Breckinridge Spoke*, undated leaflet published by the Kentucky Historical Society; Louisville *Daily Times*, September 5, 1856; New York *Times*, September 2, 1856.

16. Gordon Tanner to Breckinridge, August 13, 1856, in B. MSS; Louisville *Daily Times*, September 6, 1856.

on his general health. He had been ill off and on throughout the summer, but here the occasion demanded, and he gave what he could.

Breckinridge went straight to the heart of the Union's ills—slavery. All of the country's dissidence, sectional hatred, and uncertain future, stemmed from that cataclysmic issue, and to it each must eventually return for a solution. He showed that he still thought and felt with moderation, but he was a worried moderate, his once-fervent optimism now guarded and restrained. Where five or even three years before, his speeches were given over primarily to the glories of the party and the Union, now the elation was gone, replaced by sober reflections on what had happened to divide the nation into sections and stern warnings of what was to come if it proceeded on its present course.

"He must be blind indeed, and given over to fatal delusion, who does not see that the union of the states is in imminent peril," he began. A geographical line had been drawn, the two sections stood arrayed against each other, and the South—including Breckinridge—was on the defensive. He repudiated the charge that the South sought to control the government in order to propagate slavery in the territories, and proclaimed on his own, "For myself, I have no connection with any party that proposes to legislate slavery into the territories—nor on the other hand with any party, that proposes to expel the people of the Southern States from the common territory, or to employ the Fed Govt to restrain the new communities from establishing their own institutions." Indeed, he said, had the Nebraska bill—the catalyst of all this uproar—excluded the people of the North from the territories, he would not have given it his vote.

In a theme more and more recurrent in his speeches during the past two years, he entered into a detailed examination of the powers granted the federal government by the Constitution, and their historical antecedants. He went back to the colonial era and the governing bodies that ruled it, then moved forward step by step, showing always how the powers of the central government were held applicable only to the common ground, leaving the local and municipal interests of the states to their own people. The Republicans, seeking to abolish slavery, at least from the territories, would thereby exclude one-half of the nation from the enjoyment of the common ground, denying the equality of the South. He went on to expound the well-known doctrine of strict nonintervention. Everyone had heard it before, and there was probably little new in his presentation, but Douglas, delighted with Breckinridge's arguments and logic, stood up behind him and told him to "go it." That any such decision to exclude the peculiar institution would be the result of a majority vote of the elected representatives of all the people, mattered little to the South—and, to a degree, to Breckinridge—for it would be a majority over which the slave states had no control. "But, fellow citizens, long—long before these purposes could be accomplished, the last spark of affection between the North and the South would be extinguished and the Union would be to each, as hateful and intolerable, as its past has been beneficent and glorious." [17]

Throughout his speech Breckinridge's logic was, as always, that of a lawyer, point by point, in natural progression, seemingly irrefutable. The relationships between slavery and the Constitution, the Union, the South and the territories were, as he showed them, fixed, immutable, beyond the realm of lawful change. That someone like Douglas, who had few expressed feelings on the morality of black bondage, could accept this strict, simplistic, view of the situation, was not uncommon. But it must have been difficult in the case of Breckinridge, who felt a deep-seated conviction from childhood that slavery was wrong. Like the party he championed, Breckinridge was made up of principles, and was in some degree their victim. They restricted his vision to one gradually narrowing direction. They kept him from seeing that when a nation is faced with a moral issue of the magnitude of slavery, principles and logic are sometimes simply not enough.[18]

Others spoke that day at Tippecanoe, but none of them, Douglas included, saw his speech so widely quoted and reproduced as Breckinridge. Democratic papers in every state and territory carried as much of it as the telegraph could supply, and as Breckinridge rode north into Michigan it was already acquiring stature as one of *the* speeches of the campaign. That a large share of its notoriety was due simply to the unorthodox fact of its being delivered by one of the major candidates, cannot be denied, but much as well was due to the sentiments and oratory of the speaker. They were well calculated both to warn and reassure Indiana and the North of the import of the November election.

Breckinridge spoke in Kalamazoo on September 5, went the next day for his address at Pontiac, and then took the cars once more, this time for Philadelphia. He was expected to arrive in Philadelphia on the ninth, but when

17. Fite, *Presidential Campaign*, 95; rough draft of speech at Tippecanoe, 1856, in B. MSS. This draft of the speech is not dated in Breckinridge's hand but, since the paper matches exactly that used for other notes during the campaign—now in the JCB Papers—the dating is obviously correct.
18. All of his biographers have labored valiantly to show that Douglas felt some genuine moral compunction over slavery, but their evidence falls far short of proof.

by that evening he still had not shown up, it was discovered that he was laying over a night in Lancaster, Pennsylvania. At last he and Buchanan had met.[19]

From the beginning of the canvass "Buck" and "Breck" had been anxious to see each other. On more than one occasion Buchanan offered the hospitality of his home, should the vice-presidential nominee come east. Throughout the summer Breckinridge received testimony of the elder statesman's high regard for him while, at the same time, his friends, especially Martin, gave Buchanan repeated assurances of the Kentuckian's frankness and honesty.[20]

In appearance the two seemed not unalike. Both were tall, dignified, and courtly, though Buchanan was stouter. In age, of course, they plainly differed, Breckinridge being little more than half as old as the sixty-five-year-old Pennsylvanian. Breckinridge was vibrant, alive; all sides conceded that his presence was stimulating. Buchanan, on the other hand, acted and thought like a man even older than his years. He was steady, predictable, unfailingly mediocre both in personality and character. No one ever accused him of being exciting.

Differences much deeper than appearance and manner made it unlikely that the two would ever become intimates, if even friends. Buchanan was by nature suspicious, standoffish, even petty. He had a way of holding personal grudges against any who opposed him personally or politically. Indeed, this may have put him on his guard against Breckinridge from the very first, though he seems not to have showed it. At Cincinnati, Breckinridge had voted consistently for Pierce, then just as consistently for Douglas, and only accepted "Buck" on the last ballot. He had refused a proposed coalition with Buchanan's forces, and though there is no evidence that the Pennsylvanian ever knew of this, it seems likely that some member of his state's delegation would have told him. Finally, in his acceptance speech before the entire convention, Breckinridge, without actually mentioning his running mate's name, drew everyone's attention to the fact that he had followed his preferences and opposed Buchanan throughout the proceedings. Forney, as close to the cold, aloof Buchanan as anyone, believed that

19. New York *Times*, September 9, 10, 18, 1856; A. G. Pratt to Breckinridge, August 25, 1856, George H. Martin to Breckinridge, August 19, 1856, in B. MSS. Breckinridge to Buchanan, July 1, 1856, in Buchanan MSS., indicates that the two may have met prior to this meeting, but there is nothing to corroborate it.

20. Buchanan to Breckinridge, June 20, 1856, in Breckinridge MSS, FC; Martin to Breckinridge, June 17, 1856, A. W. Churchwell to Breckinridge, July 7, 1856, in B. MSS.

Breckinridge fell under the suspicion of the Pennsylvanian from the very moment of his nomination. Some time later an observer in Washington commented that this suspicion was tempered by not a little jealousy.[21]

Buchanan's suspicion and jealousy had fed on the widespread rumors that Breckinridge, and not he, would be the next president. They stemmed initially from Buchanan's unacceptability to a large body of the southern Know-Nothings who, nevertheless, found Breckinridge much to their liking. They would prefer, they said, to vote for Fillmore for president and Breckinridge for vice-president. This was mild, however, compared to the story that sprang up in the New York *Herald* in mid-July. It stated that a conspiracy had been discovered among the friends of Pierce, Cass, and Douglas, whose aim was to throw the election into the House of Representatives by giving Fillmore enough southern states to deny Buchanan an electoral majority. In such a situation, by provision of the Constitution, Buchanan, Frémont, and Fillmore would go before the House, where it was supposed that the election of a speaker, long-winded personal explanations, filibustering speeches, and unending roll-call votes, would prevent that body from electing a president before its adjournment on March 4, 1857. This would throw the decision into the Senate, which would choose between the two vice-presidential candidates with the highest electoral votes, almost surely Breckinridge and Dayton. Thanks to the safe Democratic majority in the upper house Breckinridge would be declared president, whether he came before it with the higher or lower electoral count. However, just to make sure that he did have a good vote in the electoral college, so the rumor went, several leading southern Know-Nothings had been enlisted to stump for Fillmore and Breckinridge.[22]

It did not help that the possibility of the election going into Congress had gained wide credence, and was even being discussed by Democratic orators on the campaign trail, with Breckinridge coming out the unquestioned victor. In Nashville, Andrew Johnson openly committed himself to opposing any election in the House, should the election go there, in order that Breckinridge might be designated by the Senate. "So far as I am con-

21. Nicholson to Pierce, June 3, 1857, in Pierce MSS; Louisville *Dai'y Times*, June 8, 1856; Forney, *Anecdotes*, 63–64; New York *Times*, February 8, 1859. The best study of Buchanan's character is Nichols, *Disruption*, 75–78. Buchanan's most recent biographer, Philip S. Klein, *President James Buchanan: A Biography* (University Park, Pa., 1962), is rather too sympathetic.

22. Leroy Cord to Caleb Cushing, July 3, 1856, in Caleb Cushing MSS, LC; New York *Herald*, July 16, 1856; Cleveland *Leader*, October 3, 1856; B. Williams to Breckinridge, July 22, 1856, J. A. Woodward to Breckinridge, September 15, 1856, in B. MSS; A. J. Cass to Butler, September 25, 1856, in Benjamin F. Butler MSS, LC.

cerned, if we cannot get the head of the ticket, I am perfectly willing to take the tail." Rives of the *Congressional Globe* spoke of the possibility and was not above encouraging it. He even wrote to Breckinridge on the subject, suggesting that "by so managing, by luck or design," the Kentuckian might become president. The whole thing hinged on Pennsylvania. If it went Democratic in its October congressional elections, then "Buck" would carry it and the presidency in November. However, if he lost his own state, then the election would surely go into the House.[23]

Perhaps Buchanan's suspicion was allayed somewhat by the fact that Breckinridge had come to help in the fight in Pennsylvania. Surely the Kentuckian would not have come if he personally wished to see the contest decided in Congress. Furthermore, the canvass still had two months to go, and a cold reception at Wheatland might jeopardize the good work that his campaign tour was doing. Whatever happened the night that Breckinridge spent at Lancaster, he and Buchanan parted the next day on apparent good terms.

On September 10 Breckinridge spoke at Pittsburgh, and then, with several more scheduled appearances at Philadelphia, Dayton, and other points yet unfulfilled, he cancelled the remainder of his tour. After two weeks of constant traveling and speaking, aggravated by continual illness, he was worn out, physically unable to go on. Immediately after the Pittsburgh speech he wrote to James B. Clay, "I . . . am thoroughly broken down, having talked nearly every night for a week." Despite the disappointment at Philadelphia and elsewhere, and his fear that Pennsylvania was still uncertain, he returned to Kentucky to recuperate, though not to retire from active participation in the campaign. As he rode the cars back to Lexington, he left behind him a new precedent. Never before in the nation's history had a presidential or vice-presidential candidate taken the stump to advocate his own election. Breckinridge, however, had made a major tour through four states—five, counting Kentucky—delivered four principal campaign addresses, and made as many as a dozen or more unscheduled appearances. By later standards it was a modest tour, but it was a beginning.[24]

Several new developments awaited Breckinridge's arrival at home. For one thing, the Know-Nothing press in some southern states was grossly

23. Andrew Johnson, "Speech at Nashville, July 15, 1856," in Graf and Haskins (eds.), *Papers of Andrew Johnson*, II, 421–22; Rives to Breckinridge, October 10, 1856, in B. MSS.

24. Garfield to Breckinridge, September 19, 1856, A. Pratt to Breckinridge, September 25, 1856, in B. MSS; Breckinridge to James B. Clay, September 10, 1856, in Thomas J. Clay MSS, LC.

misrepresenting his statements at Tippecanoe. Some accused him of saying that the Democratic party was opposed to slavery extension, while others came right out and called him a Free-Soiler, charging that he had admitted the power of a territorial legislature to exclude slavery prior to its admission as a state. To meet this, the editor of the *Statesman*, who had traveled with Breckinridge during part of his campaign tour, published an account of what the candidate had actually said as he heard it. This declamation was widely republished throughout the South. Breckinridge, on his own, answered the charges to those who inquired, asserting, "Hands off the whole subject by the Federal Government." He would not do anything more to counteract the allegations, considering them "so absurd as to be unworthy of further notice." However, since the whole affair arose as a result of misreporting of his speech—whether accidental or deliberate—he acquired a distrust of newspaper reporters that he did not soon lose.[25]

Perhaps the most disheartening news to arrive that September was of the Republican victory in the Maine election. This brought the Republican threat home to the Democrats as nothing else in the canvass had. Governor Henry Wise of Virginia immediately sent out letters to other southern governors, calling a convention to ponder the South's course should Frémont be elected; no one needed to be told that he had secession in mind. Meanwhile, northern Democrats redoubled their efforts in Indiana and Pennsylvania. Breckinridge, barely home from his tour, and still sick, wrote Forney to say, "Your state is now indeed the Key Stone of the arch. It will ruin Mr Buchanan—his party, and what is worse, the country, if the state is lost in October." His sense of urgency was augmented by his misgivings over Indiana. If Pennsylvania was lost, he said, "I fear that violence will not be confined to the plains of Kansas." At Buchanan's request, Breckinridge persuaded Clay to go to Pennsylvania to make several addresses before the election there. To Buchanan himself, he confided that if the Keystone State went Republican, all was perhaps not lost, but "we must gird ourselves for a desperate struggle, and no democrat must take off his clothes until the 5 of Nov." [26]

25. Lexington *Kentucky Statesman*, October 14, 17, 1856; John B. Breckinridge to Breckinridge, October 10, 21, 1856, W. R. Miles to Breckinridge, October 13, 1856, in B. MSS; *Ashland Speech*, 3–5. This distrust of newsmen remained with Breckinridge as late as 1864 (William Simms to Breckinridge, November 4, 1864, in John C. Breckinridge MSS, DU).

26. Nichols, *Disruption*, 44–45; Breckinridge to Forney, September 17, 1856, in John C. Breckinridge MSS, HSP; Breckinridge to Buchanan, September 21, 29, 1856, in Buchanan MSS; Buchanan to Breckinridge, September 2, 25, 1856, Forney to Breckinridge, September 30, 1856, Garfield to Breckinridge, September 30, 1856, all in B. MSS.

Meanwhile Breckinridge had to work against the renewed efforts of the Know-Nothings in his own state. Upon returning from his tour, he found the contest in Kentucky "bitter and unnatural." The American party was unusually active, distributing money freely, especially in the eastern mountain counties, and resolved again, so it appeared, to disrupt Democratic voting in Louisville. In this state of affairs, Breckinridge resolved to remain in the state until November. He began again selecting speakers to cover Kentucky and kept poor Powell speaking every day except Sundays. At the same time, he and his managers arranged to keep their papers filled with news on the fusion between Republicans and Know-Nothings in Pennsylvania, the object being to blame that state's loss—should it occur—upon Know-Nothing treachery rather than Democratic weakness.[27]

In October the Pennsylvania election went for Buchanan, as did Indiana, and the Democrats were elated. Preston wrote to Breckinridge, "Now is the winter of our discontent made glorious summer by this son of Lancaster," while Breckinridge, foregoing Shakespeare's temptations, expressed his joy to Buchanan: "What a grand Democracy you have when there is opposition enough to awaken its majestic power! If the mischief makers destroy the Union in my time, I shall remove my household goods for safety into the heart of 'Old Bucks.'" Victory in November seemed assured.[28]

Breckinridge's happiness was not what it might have been. There were troubles in the family that dampened his spirits. Mary's health was unstable, as usual, her malady undiagnosed; his son Clifton had somehow managed to get a serious powder burn, "happily in his behind"; and Uncle Robert and his wife Virginia were having severe marital problems, she wanting a separation, and Robert engaging Breckinridge as his counsel. More disturbing, however, was the portent of more trouble to come in politics. The Know-Nothings were now bent on violence in Lexington itself.[29]

Breckinridge's hometown had passed a relatively uneventful campaign. However, as its final contribution to victory in November, the city's Democrats planned a grand mass meeting and parade for October 23. Ashbel Willard of Indiana was brought in as one of the principal speakers, along with the dependable Powell, and twenty thousand gathered for the event.

27. Breckinridge to Forney, September 17, 1856, in Breckinridge MSS, HSP; Breckinridge to Buchanan, September 21, 29, 1856, in Buchanan MSS; Isaac Cardwell to Breckinridge, October 18, 1856, Lazarus Powell to Breckinridge, September 31, 1856 (misdated—probably October 1), in B. MSS.

28. William Preston to Breckinridge, October 18, 1856, in B. MSS; Breckinridge to Buchanan, October 18, 1856, in Buchanan MSS.

29. Breckinridge to Robert J. Breckinridge, October 22, 1856, Robert J. Breckinridge to Breckinridge, September 28, October 20, 1856, in B. MSS.

They formed a giant procession in the morning, preceded by several brass bands, and marched down the main streets of Lexington. With them they hauled a model "ship of state" with "Direct for the White House" emblazoned in bold letters. There followed a huge wagon loaded with three hundred of the faithful—so the *Statesman* reported—and drawn by thirty-one horses: fifteen black ones to represent the slave states, and sixteen white, symbolizing the free states. Behind it came yet another wagon drawn by another thirty-one horses. The first bore great portraits of "Buck & Breck" and the second a flagpole forty feet high from which the Stars and Stripes flew. Behind it, one more followed, but this time drawn by only thirty horses. It was prepared by the members of the "Dog Fennel" precinct of Fayette County, and they preferred not to represent the obnoxious, abolitionist Massachusetts at the festive proceedings.

That evening a Democratic boys' torchlight parade marched through the streets, carrying torches, banners, flags, and illuminated color transparencies, accompanied by fireworks and more brass bands. Then, unexpectedly, several of the boys were struck down and perhaps beaten by unknown assailants. The next night the home of an Irish immigrant was stoned, as was a Democratic speaker, and thereafter armed mobs roamed the streets beating lone victims and cursing the immigrants, yelling "Americans shall rule America." Breckinridge himself saw weapons of all kinds brandished openly, especially "brass knucks," and sadly observed that the city authorities did nothing to stop the disturbances. If they would not, however, he would. Lexington would not become another Louisville; there would be no more Black Mondays.[30]

Breckinridge had already been in touch with Preston about the possibility of forming a corps of perhaps two hundred men for the purpose of guarding the polls, probably in Louisville. Preston was not optimistic. He wrote, "I fear it will all end in smoke." Breckinridge now felt the same way about affairs in Lexington. "There is great danger of hot work here next week," he told his Uncle Robert on October 26. "Now, it is my immovable purpose not to submit to their outrages. I will resist them as long as I can raise an arm in defense. I regard all considerations of personal advancement as utterly insignificant in this issue. I will not be robbed of my legal rights, nor humiliated and dishonored in the town where I was born—and I regard as my own case that of the humblest of my supporters." He stood determined to call a number of friends together "and make the issue in the public streets" if need be, though he abhorred the idea of such violence, and felt

30. Lexington *Kentucky Statesman*, October 24, 1856.

a personal sense of outrage that this should be happening in his own town. If Breckinridge was aware of the effects that such an encounter could have on his political future, he did not show it. The image, well publicized and managed, of a candidate for the vice-presidency standing cudgel in hand, with blooded brow, bravely defending with his life the rights of free men to vote as they chose, would be political dynamite.[31]

Supposing that Robert might have some pacifying influence on the Know-Nothing trouble makers in Lexington, Breckinridge asked his uncle to try to discourage them, and then went on with his work. As the final days of the campaign wore on toward the finish, renewed attacks sprang up here and there. In Kentucky the Fillmore men tried to persuade the voters not to support the Democratic ticket because Breckinridge was only second on it. Throughout the South misrepresentations of the Tippecanoe declarations on slavery were circulated again and again, and in Virginia a political cartoon went the rounds, depicting Uncle Sam playing the banjo and singing a parody on the tune "John Anderson, My Joe, John."

> John Breckinridge, my Joe John,
> When we were first aquaint,
> You were an abolitionist,
> And now you say you ain't.

The rhyme may have been a little crude, but it was perceptive and appropriate. Throughout the campaign, as always, Breckinridge carefully avoided any mention of his personal views on the morality of slavery, views he had held almost unchanged from youth. As a southerner needing southern votes, he now confided his opposition to slavery only in private to friends, while in public proclaiming himself opposed to abolition. Strictly speaking, this was not a lie, for he was against abolition, whether by state or federal edict, preferring a mode of gradual emancipation. Still, he was begging the question, telling from his point of view a semantic truth, but not a moral one.[32]

These last-minute attacks on the two candidates probably had little effect as November 4 approached. And when that day came Breckinridge was ready. His friends and supporters all over the state kept him apprised throughout the day of the progress of the voting, which precincts and counties were going well, and which were not. Fillmore won Lexington by 29 votes, and Fayette County by 398, whereas "Buck & Breck" took Sweet

31. Preston to Breckinridge, October 20, 1856, Breckinridge to Robert J. Breckinridge, October 26, 1856, in B. MSS.

32. Lexington *Kentucky Statesman*, November 3, 1856; John S. Wise, *Recollections of Thirteen Presidents* (New York, 1906), 55.

Owen by a majority of 1,048. Returns for the whole state would take time to tally, but it was obvious at the end of the day that the Democrats had carried it for the first time in twenty-eight years. Their majority would eventually add up to 6,118, short of Breckinridge's prediction, but safe enough. Kentucky was saved.

In the rest of the nation, it went much as the party had hoped. Pennsylvania and Indiana fell in line, as did the entire South except Maryland, and added to New Jersey, California, and a somewhat unexpected victory in Illinois, this ensured success. The Democratic ticket received 1,838,169 popular votes, and thereby 174 in the electoral college, as opposed to 1,341,264 and 114 for Frémont, and 874,534 and 8 for Fillmore. There would be another four years of Democratic rule in Washington City, and Breckinridge had become the youngest vice-president in the history of his country. At thirty-five, he was seven years younger than his nearest rivals, Daniel D. Tompkins and John C. Calhoun.[33]

If a story that later circulated through the South can be believed, Breckinridge, though surely satisfied at his success, did not let it go to his head. Immediately after the election, so the story goes, he took his mother shopping in Lexington. After visiting several shops, she made her last purchase, a large one. Turning to the vice-president-elect, she said, "Here, John, take this bundle." Reportedly with "the gentle placidity of a girl," he took the bundle and said, "It is yours to command, mine to obey." However, there were others who took the victory with much less humility. On the evening of the election, in Philadelphia, Forney—"in ecstasy" at the favorable results—Senator William Bigler of Pennsylvania, and several of that state's campaign managers gathered for dinner. Among the party, as they celebrated the victory, the wish was general that Breckinridge should succeed Buchanan in the presidency. At almost the same time, with the results barely tallied, some newspapers in the Northwest raised Breckinridge's name for the nomination in 1860. With the Kentuckian barely elected to one office of the nation's executive branch, the movement was already underway to place him in the other.[34]

---

33. Lexington *Kentucky Statesman*, December 2, 1856; Rankin Revill to Breckinridge, November 4, 1856, in B. MSS. Breckinridge's record still stands, and since he was only nine months eligible when elected, it is not likely ever to be broken. The next youngest vice-president was Richard M. Nixon (as of this writing). He was elected at the age of thirty-nine years and nine months.

34. New York *Times*, January 9, 1876; John S. Cunningham to Breckinridge, November 7, 1856, Theodore Holt to Breckinridge, November 8, 1856, Rice to Breckinridge, November 16, 1856, all in B. MSS.

CHAPTER 9

I Like Him God Damn Him

The fall of 1856 was a good one for John C. Breckinridge. He found himself finally able to settle down to a few peaceful weeks with his family and his business. With the cares of the canvass over, he seemed happy to those around him, relaxed and cheerful. A fellow Kentuckian, meeting him for the first time at a breakfast party, found Breckinridge easy, genial, pleasant in conversation, and a man of "extraordinary individuality." He got back to work to some degree, attending court in Georgetown, and taking cases elsewhere. His standing was now such that he received an offer of $100 to deliver a closing summation to a jury. He would not have been required to do any other work before or after the summation, and if he obtained a favorable verdict, the fee would be doubled. This fall was a very good time.[1]

Breckinridge had an opportunity to do a last service for his good friend Franklin Pierce late in November. The president, wishing to replace the almost criminal chief justice of Kansas Territory, Samuel Lecompte, sought to give the position to a Kentuckian who would be less inclined to show flagrant favoritism to proslavery interests. He settled on James O. Harrison, and asked Breckinridge to consult Harrison to find if he would accept the post. Breckinridge did so, reporting back to the president, but meanwhile Pierce had already decided on another.[2]

The Christmas holidays were barely over before politics intruded once more. For Powell, who must have set a record for stump endurance in the

1. Alexander McClure, *Col. Alexander McClure's Recollections of Half a Century* (Salem, Mass., 1902), 159; Breckinridge to A. O. P. Nicholson, November 18, 1856, in John C. Breckinridge MSS, NYHS; J. W. Moore to Breckinridge, January 20, 1857, in B. MSS.

2. James Guthrie to Breckinridge, November 27, December 4, 1856, Eliza McHatton to Mary Breckinridge, December 10, 1856, in B. MSS.

final weeks of the campaign, Breckinridge hinted at the possibility of a cabinet post. Kentucky was entitled to a place in the cabinet, and Powell, too dignified to jump at the hint and too interested to refuse it, allowed that he would not turn it down if proffered. Not forgetting the able assistance from a phalanx of Whigs, Breckinridge declared in a brief speech in Frankfort in January, 1857, that it would be a good idea for Buchanan to include one or two of the old followers of Henry Clay in the administration. The Whigs should be treated like brothers, he said, and the implication was obvious that he felt the Old Liners should be represented by a Kentuckian.[3]

There were many who did not wait for Breckinridge to come to them with rewards. Instead, they flooded him with petitions for office and appointment. However, because he did not know what Buchanan's policy would be on appointments, he determined not to make any recommendations until he saw the president-elect in Washington. And to avoid the further intrigue in Washington City, he decided not to go there until as late as possible.[4]

Breckinridge and Mary left Lexington for Philadelphia on February 19, arriving there two days later. They took up quarters at McKibbon's Merchants' Hotel, and while Mary shopped about for a gown to wear to the inaugural ball, Breckinridge saw to his own wardrobe for the occasion. Before leaving Kentucky, he had written to Martin inquiring about the proper mode of dress, fearful lest his friend would laugh at his "country simplicity." It seems that he proposed wearing a common frock coat, whereas a cutaway or swallowtail coat was the custom. Martin promised to outfit him properly.[5]

March 4 was a sunny spring day, and by noon the inaugural procession was ready to march down Pennsylvania Avenue to the Capitol. Both Breckinridge and Buchanan joined it at the National Hotel, and after someone remembered that they had forgotten to pick up Pierce, they rode on. Breckinridge rode in an open barouche with a few other gentlemen, and to one observer appeared very quiet and "business like." After they arrived at the Capitol, the inaugural party gathered in the Senate Chamber to see Breck-

3. C. W. Wooley to Breckinridge, January 16, 1857, Lazarus Powell to Breckinridge, January 1857, Thomas B. Stevenson to Breckinridge, January 21, 1857, James H. Garrard to Breckinridge, January 26, 1857, all in B. MSS.

4. Breckinridge to Nicholson, November 18, 1856, in Breckinridge MSS, NYHS; Breckinridge to Jesse Durbin Ward, February 17, 1857, in Jesse Durbin Ward MSS, Ohio Historical Society, Columbus.

5. Breckinridge to James Buchanan, February 25, 1857, in Buchanan MSS; Philadelphia *Pennsylvanian*, February 23, 1857; George H. Martin to Breckinridge, February 5, 1857, in B. MSS.

inridge sworn in by Senator James M. Mason of Virginia, president pro tempore of the body. After taking the oath, he addressed the Senate briefly, affirming his respect for its members, admitting his inexperience, and invoking their aid with exercise of the rules of the House, and concluding with a remark that might have been interpreted as a declaration of policy; indeed, the only such declaration of his tenure. "It shall be my constant aim, gentlemen of the Senate," he said, "to exhibit at all times, to every member of this body, the courtesy and impartiality which are due to the representatives of equal States." [6]

John C. Breckinridge was vice-president of the United States, proud holder of what an illustrious predecessor, John Adams, called "the most insignificant office that ever the invention of man contrived or his imagination conceived." The office was, indeed, an anomaly. Difficult to define at first, its duties were never entirely clear, beyond serving as president of the Senate, and assuming the presidency in case of incapacity or death of the chief executive. In its early years it had consistently been occupied by men of talent, thanks to the constitutional provision that the first runner up in the presidential election should assume the vice-presidency. John Adams, Thomas Jefferson, and Aaron Burr graced the office, and two of them found it a springboard to a higher position. However, since the passage of the Twelfth Amendment in 1804, providing for a separate election of the vice-president, few men of genuine talent had occupied the seat, excepting John C. Calhoun. The vice-president was not included in cabinet meetings, was given little or no responsibility by the president, and assumed a passive, unimportant role as president of the Senate. Even his vote in the event of ties was often used to support the administration rather than his own views. And as the office degenerated, so did the relations of president and vice-president, until it became almost traditional that there be no rapport between the two. With few exceptions, the traditional vice-president was consulted by no one, respected by few, and almost powerless. Calhoun had actually resigned to become a Senator, such was his contempt for his post, and others had given thought to the same move. Even the vice-president's staff was insignificant, and Breckinridge's would be limited to one private secretary. This was the auspicious position and heritage that he now assumed.[7]

6. Klein, *Buchanan*, 271–72; Nichols, *Disruption*, 71; New York *Harper's Weekly*, March 14, 1857; Washington *Daily Globe*, March 5, 1857; Lexington *Kentucky Statesman*, January 30, 1857.

7. John Peebles to Breckinridge, April 4, 1857, in JCB Papers; John D. Feerick, *From Failing Hands: The Story of the Presidential Succession* (New York, 1965), 67–100 *passim*.

He felt some uncertainty on accepting his new office, especially since he was the first genuine vice-president to sit before the Senate in almost seven years. When Taylor died in July, 1850, Millard Fillmore moved to the White House, leaving his office vacant, and Pierce's vice-president, William R. King, died before ever taking his seat. In the meantime, the Senate had been ruled by several presidents pro tempore, including Atchison, Cass, Bright, and Mason, and they, especially Atchison, often acted with less than commendable impartiality. Two were southerners, the others doughfaces, and their interpretation of the rules and order of debate often betrayed their partisan interests. It might well have been expected, in spite of his declaration of "courtesy and impartiality," that Breckinridge, another southerner, would act the same. He did not say what he thought about the office, and his feelings about it can only be inferred.

A special session of the Senate was called for March 4, and Breckinridge began his duties immediately. They were light, since the session only lasted ten days, and had been called mainly for the usual purpose of considering and approving the president's cabinet appointments. Contrary to the hopes expressed by Breckinridge, no Whigs found a place in that cabinet, nor did Powell or any other Kentuckian. Cass was made secretary of state, while the vice-president's distant cousin, John B. Floyd, of Virginia became secretary of war. The only item of note regarding the new vice-president came up when he laid before the Senate resolutions from the Ohio legislature relative to recognizing the independence of Liberia. Breckinridge, always a friend of the Liberian colonization program, asked that action be taken to approve the Ohio resolutions and pass a measure to that effect. Since John Adams, vice-presidents had faced the problem of whether they were to act in the Senate as statesmen, or simply as moderators of debate. Most settled on the latter, being content to rely on interpreting the rules as a means to aid legislation they favored. Breckinridge, too, would be primarily a moderator, but from the first he spoke his thoughts if he felt it necessary.[8]

Others were speaking their minds in Washington City this winter, among them Chief Justice Roger B. Taney and his associates on the Supreme Court. Ever since the passage of the Kansas-Nebraska Act, the country had awaited a decision of the Court on the power of Congress to interfere with slavery in the territories. The heat of the issue had grown steadily, and the uproar in Kansas after its admission to territorial status only added fuel to the flame. The Dred Scott case seemed to afford an op-

8. Nichols, *Disruption*, 72; Washington *Daily Globe*, March 10, 1857; New York *Harper's Weekly*, March 21, 1857.

portunity to pass judgment on intervention at last, and Taney hoped that
it might settle the issue and ease tensions. Accordingly, Taney passed down
a decision shortly after Buchanan's inauguration. Congress, it was decided,
did not have the authority to interfere with slavery in the territories, or to
restrict it in any way.

Breckinridge did not get the opportunity—or, perhaps, the inclination—
to air his opinion of the Dred Scott decision and its attendant, portentious
implications, but he approved heartily, nevertheless. Two years later he
would declare with gusto that "I accept the decision of the Supreme Court
of the United States, on every question within its jurisdiction, whether it
corresponds with my private opinion or not. I accept it the more cordially
when, as in the case of Dred Scott, it accords with my own convictions."
He had hoped that the 1850 compromise, and later, the Kansas-Nebraska
Act might settle the sectional controversy over slavery. Now he hoped
that this Court ruling and its implied decision on the Missouri line would
succeed where the other two had failed. Subsequent events would show he
could not have been more wrong.[9]

During the special session, while reaction to the Court decision was echo-
ing through the country, the vice-president found his advice solicited from
an unexpected quarter: President Buchanan. Breckinridge had made a resolution never to initiate an appointment for Whig or Democrat unless first
asked for his counsel by the president. "Buck" generally kept his own counsel in almost all affairs, but now he had questions regarding Kentucky, and
the vice-president was the logical choice for answers. Buchanan, having
ignored the Bluegrass in his cabinet appointments, sought to give it one or
two diplomatic posts. After consulting Breckinridge, he offered James B.
Clay the mission to Berlin, and now he wanted to send Cassius M. Clay's
name before the Senate for the Peruvian mission. Three days after their
inauguration, Buchanan asked the vice-president what effect the appointment of Clay would have in Kentucky. Ever mindful of his struggle to
make the Bluegrass a Democratic state, Breckinridge replied that an appointment to an Old Line Whig, if not matched by equal recognition to
the state's true Democrats, would be hurtful to the cause. To be safe, he
advised that Buchanan first offer Clay the mission by letter before submitting his name to the Senate. Otherwise the opposition might raise the cry
of corrupt bargain, accusing Clay of having made a deal with Buchanan to
refrain from attacking him during the late canvass in return for the appoint-

9. Speech . . . at Frankfort, Kentucky, December 21, 1859, 1.

ment. The president took Breckinridge's advice and wrote to Clay, but the story got into the newspapers, including the hostile Know-Nothing press. Clay visited the vice-president to seek his counsel, and in the end, he did not accept the mission.[10]

During his first three weeks as vice-president, Breckinridge began once more to move in Washington's social life. Percy Walker, lately a representative from Mobile, Alabama, who lived at the same hotel as the Breckinridges—Willards—wrote: "There was a wonderful magnetism about him. You felt instinctively drawn to him. Meet him where you might—in the privacy of his chamber—among his chosen associates—with strangers, or in crowded assemblies, there was the same rare power of attraction." Walker believed that everyone felt this same power. He found a social dignity and agreeability which, in others the result of tact, "was in Breckinridge the expression of his inborn courtesy, the charm of which was irresistible." Although the vice-president was the youngest man of distinction in their hotel, he was regarded as a peer, "And perhaps it is not too much to say, that he was the central figure in this brilliant circle. In the presence of his grand personality party spirit lost its asperity." In spite of the momentous issues before the country, and in spite of Breckinridge's known affinity for frank discussion on such issues, the statesmen boarding with him found in the Kentuckian's conversation and manner so much to suggest pleasant topics for conversation that they rarely discussed these serious matters in his presence. One who opposed Breckinridge on almost every political question of the day found that "there was something about his magnificent physique, frank courtesy, his charming manner, free from all touch of condescension, as it was from every trace of arrogance, that was irresistably attractive." [11]

His happy situation lasted less than three weeks. On March 14, a few days after the special session adjourned, Breckinridge asked the president for a private audience. Buchanan, cold, aloof, replied in what Breckinridge thought an insulting tone that he might, instead, call some evening and see Miss Harriet Lane. There is no record of what the vice-president said to this, but he hardly concealed his mortification from his friends. He told the story to Forney, Rice, Floyd, Bright, and J. C. Van Dyke, in the next few

10. Nichols, *Disruption*, 72; Breckinridge to Buchanan, March 8, 1857, in Buchanan MSS; Breckinridge to John W. Forney, April 1, 1857, in Breckinridge MSS, HSP; John W. Stevenson to James B. Clay, March 29, 1857, in Clay MSS.

11. Receipt of W. M. Morrison & Co., April 3, 1857, in JCB Papers; J. C. Vaughn to Breckinridge, March 23, 1857, in B. MSS; Mobile *Daily Register*, May 30, 1875; Lexington *Herald*, April 25, 1909.

days. All tried to persuade him that he had the wrong impression of Buchanan's intentions. Floyd, Bright, and Van Dyke all brought the subject up in conferences with the president, and he explained that his only object had been to grant Breckinridge free access to him without going through the usual red tape attendant to official appointments and interviews. It was established policy at the White House, Buchanan said, that when a person invited to visit Miss Lane (his niece) was announced, the president broke off all other affairs to devote himself to the caller. Since Buchanan himself is the only person known ever to have made first-hand reference to this unusual procedure, and since he had been in the White House less than three weeks, just how he expected Breckinridge to understand the cryptic reference to Harriet Lane is a mystery. The breach thus opened, widened rapidly.[12]

Some of the failure to smooth over this affair must rest with the vice-president. While he was forgiving, even quite friendly, with outspoken political enemies, he could be righteously indignant when he felt insulted. If he did nothing to bring about the break between himself and Buchanan, he did little in the coming years to mend it.

Buchanan, on the other hand, deserves the lion's share of the blame. Now that he was president, he was giving the runaround to a number of those who supported him during the campaign. A. O. P. Nicholson, retiring owner and manager of the administration paper, the Washington *Union*, found in Buchanan an animosity towards former Pierce supporters which he called repulsive. Another disillusioned supporter declared that "Mr. Buchanan's hatred is as bitter as it is causeless towards every Pierce man, & he never appoints a man til he asks whether he supported his *nomination* —not his election only." Even Forney, who as much as any man made Buchanan president, found himself out in the cold. In the light of this, it is not unlikely that Breckinridge, one of the most ardent Pierce men at Cincinnati, had in the eyes of the president served out his usefulness when the campaign of 1856 came to a close. As with Nicholson, Forney, and a score of others in the coming months, Buchanan no longer felt a need for the friendship or favor of John C. Breckinridge. In later years Forney would write that Breckinridge stood second only to George M. Dallas as the most ignored and neglected vice-president in the nation's history. Dallas, however, enjoyed a good relationship with his chief James K. Polk, was often

12. Henry M. Rice to Breckinridge, March 23, 1857, John Floyd to Breckinridge, March 25, 1857, Jesse D. Bright to Breckinridge, March 30, 1857, John C. Van Dyke to Breckinridge, April 9, 1857, all in B. MSS.

consulted on policy, and was asked to comment on the president's messages and other important public policies. On the other hand, by Breckinridge's own admission, in the entire course of Buchanan's administration, not once did the president consult him on any important matter. It would be more than three and a half years before Buchanan invited him to a private interview. As the vice-president rode home to Lexington late in March, 1857, he may well have pondered that a triumph begun so auspiciously, could have turned so sour in so short a time.[13]

While in Washington City, Breckinridge had looked around for a house in which to lodge his family during his vice-presidency. He sought first to rent Bright's home, and failing in that, he fell into a deal with Rice and Douglas to buy two town blocks in the capital, build on one, and sell the other by lots to pay for the land and the houses combined. Breckinridge's third of the purchase price came to $17,000. In addition to this, Rice estimated that the houses would cost $14,000 or more. His wife and Douglas' new bride, Adele Cutts, did most of the planning of the buildings. Breckinridge had no hand in the design of the house he contracted for, though Rice agreed to take it off his hands if he didn't like it. The houses were to be built on square 560, on I Street near New Jersey Avenue, four floors high, with library, two parlors, a dining room, seven bed chambers, and a bathroom.[14]

Breckinridge's house was no sign of prosperity, however. The Panic of 1857 hit Breckinridge hard. His $666 monthly salary barely covered his needs, but somehow he managed to scrape together the money to meet his obligations. He was forced to sell probably his last remaining "property" in slaves, a domestic, Malvina, and her six-week-old baby. They brought $1,100. He might have gotten more from the sale of another Negro, an old man named James, but he had given him away a few months before in order that the old man might be happier living with his wife in nearby Paris, Kentucky. And finally, hard though it was to do, he sold his home in Lexington. He would miss the delightful morning music of the birds in his yard. During the presidential campaign, he had been particularly amused

13. Nicholson to Franklin Pierce, June 3, 1857, J. M. Brodhead to Pierce, October 6, 1857, in Pierce MSS; Klein, *Buchanan*, 281–82; Forney, *Anecdotes*, 63–64; Lexington *Kentucky Statesman*, March 27, 1857; Feerick, *From Failing Hands*, 99–100; undated clipping from an unidentified newspaper, relating Adlai Stevenson's anecdote about Breckinridge and Buchanan's poor relationship, in JCB Papers.

14. Rice to Breckinridge, March 23, April 6, 14, 28, May 13, July 28, 1857, in B. MSS; Lexington *Kentucky Statesman*, May 8, 1857; Rice to Breckinridge, June 29, 30, 1857; Baldwin Brothers to Breckinridge, September 28, 1857, in JCB Papers.

by the story of a little fellow bragging to another boy about his father's new house. "It's got a cupola, and it's going to have something else." When asked what it was, he replied, "Why, I heard father tell mother this morning, that it's going to have a *mortgage* on it!" The joke must have lost a good deal of its humor for Breckinridge this hard summer.[15]

With all this, he was due for still more blows. Following his brush with Buchanan, he resolved to abstain entirely from attempting to influence any appointments. "My reasons are imperative," he would say to applicants, "and do not proceed from indifference to the wishes of my friends." The word soon got around, and some old supporters were embittered. Before long the opposition press picked up the story, and by June some of them were running the story that Breckinridge had no influence with the administration. The fact that the charge was true hardly lessened his discomfort. The prospect for the coming years was a gloomy one.[16]

Somehow, amidst all these troubles, Breckinridge still managed to take some enjoyment during the stay in Lexington. His correspondence kept him in touch with friends far away, and brought him their continuing expressions of regard, though seldom in quite the terms used by Richardson of Illinois, who asked James B. Beck to write to Breckinridge and "*Tell him that I like him God damn him.*" The major also found some time to read, and varied his fare from a new history of the Mormon Church, to Richard Rush's latest book, *Washington in Domestic Life.* One of the pleasures closest to the vice-president's heart this summer was his ever-increasing rapport with the nation's youth. As the most outstanding example thus far in the country's history of what a young man could achieve in public life, Breckinridge became a symbol and ideal for much of the talented young manhood of the day, North and South. He encouraged their ambition, complimented their talents, and expressed his faith in their future. This was especially true of the now twenty-six-year-old Ignatius Donnelly, by this time almost a protégé, even though the two had not yet met each other

15. This anecdote is taken from a clipping found enclosed in Breckinridge's "Notes 1856" in the JCB Papers; Fayette County Deed Book, 33, p. 409, Fayette County courthouse, Lexington.

16. Breckinridge to Charles Buford, December 28, 1857, in Charles Buford MSS, LC; Breckinridge to William A. Duer, September 16, 1857, in Breckinridge MSS, NYHS; Paul Rankin to Breckinridge, April 3, 1857, James B. Beck to Breckinridge, April 4, 1857, clipping from Newton (N.J.) *Herald*, June 20, 1857, Breckinridge to Robert J. Breckinridge, June 23, 1857, all in B. MSS; Ellen Chambers to Breckinridge, June 23, 1857, Joshua Bell to Breckinridge, June 23, 1857, in JCB Papers; Breckinridge to Ignatius Donnelly, April 19, 1857, in Donnelly MSS; Stevenson to Clay, May 13, 1857, in Clay MSS.

During the presidential campaign, Donnelly pledged to "neglect every other occupation" in his active support of Breckinridge, while seeking Breckinridge's advice as to the best mode of promoting the cause. The candidate, most impressed with the youth's literary style in his letters, had advised him to both write and speak in the canvass, and Donnelly did just that. This summer of 1857 the vice-president could not know, though he might well have guessed, that the example he had set for Donnelly to follow would lead his young friend down a long road of public service. The service would begin two years later, when Donnelly, at twenty-eight, would be elected as Minnesota's second, and youngest, lieutenant governor.[17]

On a broader scale, Breckinridge took considerable interest in the movement for young men's Democratic clubs throughout the country. They were, he believed, "well calculated to extend sound principles, and to promote a healthy political intercourse between the different parts of the Union." In these perilous times, he thought it especially desirable that the people of the South have a free and friendly expression of opinion and communication with the "constitutional element" of the North. He had never known an intelligent man who had traveled and traded thoughts in all parts of the country who was not a Union man, and he hoped that these clubs would contribute to this necessary interchange of ideas.[18]

Of course, state politics occupied some of Breckinridge's time, but, in spite of heavy Know-Nothing campaigning, he was confident of Democratic victory in the congressional election from the first. The August election proved him correct, and the destruction of the American party in Kentucky was complete. Where they had enjoyed a six-to-four majority in the congressional delegation in the Thirty-fourth Congress, now they held only two seats to the Democrats' eight. Most pleasing to Breckinridge was the election of James B. Clay and John W. Stevenson. The result of this election went far toward cementing the Democratic control of Kentucky which remained always one of Breckinridge's chief interests.[19]

17. Breckinridge to Richard Rush, May 7, 1857, in Breckinridge MSS, NYHS; Breckinridge to Clay, June 21, 1857, in Clay MSS; George W. Ranck, *History of Lexington, Kentucky* (Cincinnati, 1872), 377: Beck to Breckinridge, July 5, 1857, E. W. Bartow to Breckinridge, April 16, 1857, Donnelly to Breckinridge, June 18, September 1, 3, 1856, April 8, 23, 1857, all in B. MSS; Breckinridge to Bartow, April 27, 1857, in Gratz Collection; Breckinridge to Donnelly, June 22, September 15, 1856, in Donnelly MSS; George S. Hage, *Newspapers on the Minnesota Frontier* (St. Paul, 1967), 76–78.

18. Breckinridge to Oliver Stevens, August 24, 1857, in John H. Fogg Collection, Maine Historical Society, Portland.

19. J. Dalley to Breckinridge, April 12, 1857, J. P. Metcalf to Breckinridge, July 22, 1857, Lucien B. Dickerson to Breckinridge, September 16, 1857, all in B. MSS; Ann McCallander to Breckinridge, August 25, 1857, Clay to Breckinridge, n.d., in JCB Papers; James B. Clay, "Memoir," December 14, 1862, in Clay MSS.

With the good and the bad Breckinridge passed 1857, somehow, and he looked forward to resuming his duties in Washington City. He went east by way of Baton Rouge, leaving Mary there with friends, and then across the Deep South. Although put out somewhat from the knowledge that he would miss the opening of the session, Breckinridge must have welcomed this opportunity to see some new country and people. There is no evidence that he had ever before been in the Deep South. The trip took him across Mississippi, Alabama, Georgia, and into South Carolina. In South Carolina he had an experience that, judging from its subsequent retelling, must have affected his thinking on the security of the Union.

Craving some company, Breckinridge went to the smoking car and sat down with the only passenger who had boarded the train in that country. Dressed in full regimental uniform, the man wore, in the vice-president's words, "a cocked hat, with three ostrich plumes in it dyed a golden hue. His epaulettes were as goldenly superb as his sash and sword. His martial mien of defiance would have humiliated Job's proudest war-horse snuffing the battle from afar."

Rather meekly, Breckinridge offered the gentleman a cigar and then said, "May I ask, what is going on in this state?" The answer was more than he had bargained for.

"Going on, sir? We won't stand it no mo', sir! The governor has sent for his staff to meet him and consult about it in Columbia, sir! I am one of his staff, sir! We won't stand it any longer, sir! No, sir! It is intolerable, sir! No, sir!"

In surprise, "not unmixed with dread," Breckinridge replied, "Stand what? What is going on?"

"Stand the encroachments on our Southern institutions, sir! The abolitionists must be crushed, sir! We will do it, sir! South Carolina is ready, sir!"

The vice-president thought for a moment, and then told his companion quietly, with the mordant wit that generally characterized his conversation, that "there was a custom in the Indian Office at Washington, to *tote* at the public cost, a band of big Indian chiefs over the North and its marvelous cities; so that they would not go to war, when they saw what a big country they would have to whip!" The joke may well have been lost on the hotspur, but the incident could hardly have failed to alert Breckinridge to the danger facing the Union. Indeed, while he could bandy humorously with this Galahad of South Carolina, the implications in the soldier's ominous declaration of readiness served to heighten Breckinridge's belief in the urgent need for reason, statesmanship, and compromise. Just this same year he had written to a New Jersey Republican that "We may not agree in all respects in our theories of the constitution, but I fear that the differences would not amount to much if the opposing views should ever come to the arbitration of the sword." [20]

He reached the capital two weeks after the opening of the session and made his first appearance in the Senate on December 21, 1857. There sat before him a distinguished body of gentlemen. Men from the South, like Robert Toombs of Georgia, Breckinridge's casual friend Jefferson Davis of Mississippi, Mason and Hunter of Virginia, and old Sam Houston from Texas, rested at their desks. From the North there came the Democrat-turned-Republican Hannibal Hamlin of Maine, New York's controversial William H. Seward, William Bigler, and Simon Cameron from Pennsylvania. Massachusetts, too, was represented, by Henry Wilson and an empty seat, the powerful reminder of Charles Sumner, still ailing from the caning he received from South Carolina's Preston Brooks the year before. The West was here as well, with William Gwin of California. And, of course, there were Douglas, Bright, and Breckinridge's old friend Crittenden. The aged Kentuckian must have been pleased to see the height achieved by his young countryman, despite their political differences. Nearly all were distinguished men, good politicians, and able speakers. However, there was a singular lack in the Senate, well symbolized by Sumner's empty chair: the spirit of true compromise and lofty statesmanship did not abide in this chamber. As subsequent events would show so vividly, Henry Clay was truly dead.

Once more Kansas became a problem, though in fact it had never really been otherwise during the nearly four years since Dixon proposed the Missouri repeal. The near war had been stabilized, and the situation brought under control when Pierce appointed John W. Geary territorial governor in 1856.

Buchanan's choice as successor was doomed to controversy. Robert J. Walker, Polk's secretary of the treasury, was a truly able man with a deep interest in statesmanship for the sake of the country rather than the statesmen. He had almost been appointed secretary of state by Buchanan, but lost the post to Cass. A secret opponent of slavery—much like Breckinridge—

20. Breckinridge to Duer, January 5, 1857, in Breckinridge MSS, NYHS. At least two friends later retold this story, Forney in his *Anecdotes*, I, 283–84, and Samuel S. Cox in his *Union—Disunion—Reunion: Three Decades of Federal Legislation, 1855 to 1885* (Providence, 1885), 410–11. Poore also told the story in his *Reminiscences*, II, 47. The account by Cox is the fullest, and it has been used here.

Walker accepted the governorship only on the condition that Kansans be allowed to decide the slavery question for themselves without fraud or violence. In fact, he sincerely believed that Kansas was destined to be a free state. He, like Breckinridge, saw soil, climate, and population stacked against the profitable operation of the plantation system in the territory.

Meanwhile, the Free-Soilers in Kansas, in convention, adopted a policy of nonparticipation with the proslavery territorial legislature. When they met in their own rump legislature at Topeka in June, Walker narrowly averted trouble by persuading them not to pass their own laws or to try to enforce them. The proslavery element was not so easily controlled, however. The very day of his inauguration, Walker was told in unequivocal terms that they had no intention of letting the people pass on the constitution to be framed later that year. Difficulties were compounded when the election for constitutional convention delegates was held. Through fraud, gerrymandering, and importation of voters from Missouri, the coming convention was guaranteed to be proslavery before the first polling place opened. It did not help that Free-Staters boycotted the polls and, predictably, the result was an overwhelmingly proslavery convention which convened on September 7 to frame the constitution under which Kansas would seek statehood.

Then came the election for a new territorial legislature, and here the proslavery men went too far. Free-Soilers, seeing their chance to win control, turned out full force, but the returns showed a victory for the slave interests. Inspection by Walker revealed gross frauds in the voting in some precincts, and he threw them out, thus giving the Free-Staters a majority in the new legislature. Seeing their hold on the territory slipping, the proslavery members of the constitutional convention resolved to make a last effort. Despite strong opposition, they managed to pass a document through the convention without requiring that it be submitted to a vote of the people. However, this came only as part of a compromise whereby a separate clause allowing a choice between this constitution with slavery, or without it, would go before the people. This, of course, gave Kansans no opportunity to approve or reject the constitution proper; only the slave clause. Walker, refusing to accept this, went east to see the president and remind him of his promise that Kansas should have the opportunity to a popular acceptance or rejection of the constitution. Instead, he found that, even before he left, this Lecompton Constitution had been endorsed by Buchanan—under some duress from the southern hierarchy in the party—and that the administration now stood firmly behind it. Indeed, it would become a test of party faith, said Buchanan. It split the Democrats instead, and a disappointed Walker resigned on December 15. Six days later came the referendum on the "with" or "without" constitution in Kansas.

Breckinridge, from the reserved position that his office seemed to require, made no expression of opinion during the controversy that raged over Kansas during 1857, partly because the position of the administration remained undefined. Any statement on his part might seem to represent Buchanan when, in fact, their relations were such that he hardly knew what the president's position was at any given time. But his own feelings were nonetheless decided. He admitted that there had been illegal voting on both sides in the election in 1855 which determined the proslavery cast of the Kansas legislature, but still he felt that the basic will of the people of Kansas had been enforced. As for the election for convention delegates, since it had been called by a legal legislature and conducted under its regulations—blatant gerrymandering and all—he felt that its results were binding, if not fair. If the Free-Soilers boycotted the polls, that was their fault, and their responsibility; they had had their chance. He freely admitted that the frauds Walker had uncovered in the December elections were genuine, but that did not relate to the legality of the Lecompton Constitution. The chief question there was over submission—submission of the slavery clause only as he saw it—the only requirement being that, in voting for or against it, a vote had to be given for the rest of the constitution, "a perfectly innocent qualification." To it, he felt, there were no legitimate grounds for objection. After all, it had not been common practice to submit state constitutions to popular vote, though in view of the prevailing circumstances and tensions in the territory, he did think that the constitution as a whole should have been put before the people. Thus, when Buchanan sent his annual message to the newly convened Congress in December, the vice-president approved of the Pennsylvanian's recommendation that the Lecompton Constitution be accepted and approved as soon as the results of the December 21 Kansas referendum were known.[21]

Despite this controversy, the vice-president learned a lot in his first days as presiding officer, and reinforced those hints he had given the previous March as to the kind of president he would be in this Senate. As soon as the president's message was received, southerners in the Senate began worrying for fear that Douglas would attack it and the Kansas doings before the Lecompton Constitution, with or without slavery, came before them. He

21. D. M. McNair to Breckinridge, October 17, 1857, in JCB Papers; *Congressional Globe*, 35th Cong., 1st Sess., Pt. 1, p. 111; Paris *Kentucky State Flag*, August 4, 1858.

did just that. Starting on December 9, the Little Giant condemned this violation of popular sovereignty repeatedly until December 21, the day of the Kansas vote, and Breckinridge's first day in his seat. Now Douglas launched into it again. His antagonist was Buchanan's henchman Bigler, and the debate was long and heated. As moderator and arbiter of the rules of the Senate, the vice-president fully displayed that impartiality which he had promised. Even though Douglas was taking a stand against the administration and the president, Breckinridge made sure that he received his rights, even to the point of denying Bigler the floor on one occasion when a strict interpretation of the rules decreed that it belonged to the Illinoisian. When the debate was renewed the next day between Douglas and Indiana's Graham Fitch, Breckinridge continued as he had begun. He might easily have managed the debate and exercised the rules in the administration's favor had he wished.[22]

Other problems, other decisions, came his way during the session. For the most part, he declined drawing to himself any more power than was necessary to preserve the order of the Senate. When in the course of debate a senator who legally held the floor digressed from the subject at hand, and was called to order by Douglas, Breckinridge declared that he did not feel himself authorized to judge the relevance of any member's remarks. However, as he showed on another occasion, he was willing to decide on what was a suitable topic for discussion when the validity of that topic, under the rules, was questionable. Thus, he denied that it was in order to discuss a question which was not an actual bill or amendment, but merely a motion. Acts were acceptable for debate; actions were not. Ever mindful of the limitations of the Constitution upon the powers and assigned tasks of the branches of government, he also declared that it was improper for him to decide on the constitutionality of a proposed amendment, especially when the question arose as a point of order. In general, his practice was to conform his decisions to the accepted usages of the Senate. When his own mind was satisfied as to the accepted practice of the Senate, he declared, he would follow that practice without regard to parliamentary law or his own opinion. Because Breckinridge displayed this sort of prudence and impartiality, it was not unexpected that the press began to notice favorably his course when he had been in office only a month. "The Vice President is said to preside with much dignity and aptitude," wrote one correspondent; "the deep respect and native courtesy of Mr. Breckinridge combine

22. *Congressional Globe*, 35th Cong., 1st Sess., Pt. 1, pp. 112–22, 135, 158; Nichols, *Disruption*, 153–58.

well with his intellectual ability and penrtration [*sic*] to make him a first rate presiding officer. With equal firmness and fervor, he has less impetuosity and more grace than John C. Calhoun. . . . The Vice President will be a favorite in his new position." [23]

As 1858 progressed, the vice-president continued to be a social favorite. He was to be found at dinner parties—with what *Harper's Weekly* called the *"creme de la creme"*—at Postmaster General Aaron Brown's establishment on Ninth Street, at the Toombs's, the Cobb's, and often at Forney's. Now that he felt Buchanan had forsaken him, Forney had gone back to Philadelphia to edit the *Press*, and Breckinridge heartily approved his conduct. It is not surprising that the vice-president shone his best at Forney's parties. The editor usually had the Kentuckian's best friends in attendance, friends who, he told Breckinridge, "are legion . . . and do not hesitate to say how much they esteem and love you." They included Douglas, Bright, Slidell, Lawrence Keitt of South Carolina, and Samuel S. "Sunset" Cox of Ohio. Their dinner conversations with Breckinridge so impressed Forney, Cox, and others, that they still wrote and spoke of his anecdotes and repartee twenty years later. At one such party, Keitt went on at some length poking fun at Kentucky brag, obviously aiming it at Breckinridge, who "was in his happiest mood, and received it with abundant drollery." Then the vice-president replied with an account of his recent encounter with the South Carolina hotspur on the train. The humor at the expense of Keitt's state paid him back in full, and he laughed along with the rest of the company at the suggestion that perhaps South Carolina's governor and staff, like the Indian chiefs, should be brought at public expense to the North to see, as he told it, "what an almighty big country they will have to whip before they get through." Indeed, Breckinridge was found to be almost equally pleasant company at the tables of his political opponents. At one dinner that winter, he and House Speaker James Orr were the only Democrats at a party given as a practical joke in honor of some "non-descript Englishman" who had been pulled in off the street. Others at the board were the Know-Nothing Humphrey Marshall; another Kentucky friend, Lieutenant William Nelson; the Whig and prominent Masonic leader Albert Pike; a Whig Representative from Ohio, Lewis D. Campbell; and the arch-Republican William H. Seward, in politics Breckinridge's greatest enemy. Despite their differences, Breckinridge's conduct in the Senate won Seward's respect. Typical of the vice-president's refusal to confuse political

23. *Congressional Globe*, 35th Cong., 1st Sess., Pt. 1, pp. 500, 625, 642, Pt. 3, p. 2083; Lexington *Kentucky Statesman*, January 22, 1858.

animosity with his personal relations, the two were friends, though not intimates. The wine flowed freely, Breckinridge probably told his South Carolina story again, and humor and goodwill held dominion through the evening. Seward was especially impressed by the conviviality and the lack of any of the heated sectional arguments which lately broke up so many dinner parties. He proposed a toast: "May many such pleasant banquets as this hereafter occur among us, and may none of them be interrupted or rendered less agreeable by the introduction of sectional topics." Breckinridge was in hearty accord.[24]

At least a part of the vice-president's social activity was on behalf of the Buchanan administration. Relations between him and the president did not improve, and Breckinridge's name was conspicuously absent from almost every guest list that Buchanan and Miss Lane prepared for their weekly state dinners. The vice-president's unconcealed sympathy toward Forney did not help; nor, with the president's narrow vision, was it likely that he appreciated the vice-president's impartiality in the Senate. Consequently, Buchanan appears to have tried, through Secretary of State Cass most likely, to use Breckinridge to some advantage with visiting dignitaries. When Turkish Admiral Mehmet Pasha came to the United States in February, 1858 in the hope of having a warship for Turkey built in the United States, the vice-president was among those who took the task of keeping him entertained. Although who arranged it is unknown, plans were made by Breckinridge, Rice, Fitch, Marcy, and others, to take the admiral on a hunting trip for elk and buffalo along the Red River between Minnesota and the "Dakotah" territory in July. It fell through when the Turk left the country in disgust at not getting his warship. Later, Breckinridge attended a ball given in honor of Queen Victoria by her minister, Lord Napier, at the British Embassy. He went, not as vice-president of the United States, nor even as a simple dignitary, but as an "official" guest, the head of a Senatorial delegation. He would be used as administrative host in the years to come, but Breckinridge never made any objection.[25]

Interest in social and other events in Washington faded when, on February 2, the Lecompton Constitution came before Congress. The December 21 election under questionable circumstances and with another Free-Soil

24. New York *Harper's Weekly*, February 20, 1858; Forney to Breckinridge, March 24, August 12, 1857, in B. MSS; Cox, *Union—Disunion—Reunion*, 410–11; Forney, *Anecdotes*, I, 284–85; Henry S. Foote, *A Casket of Reminiscences* (New York, 1874), 130–31.

25. Klein, *Buchanan*, 274; New York *Harper's Weekly*, April 3, 10, June 12, July 31, 1858.

boycott, had produced a vote overwhelmingly in favor of the constitution with the slavery clause. The next month the new Free-State legislature met in special session and called another referendum on the whole constitution, and this one—boycotted by the proslavery men in protest—showed an even more overwhelming rejection. Nevertheless, the election of state officers to take over in the event that Lecompton should be accepted by Congress went ahead, and the slavery interests won by the most gross frauds yet. Breckinridge freely admitted the irregularity of the January elections, but felt with Buchanan that the January referendum did not supersede the December 21 vote as authorized. Buchanan accepted Lecompton as passed with slavery in December, mainly to keep his southern support.[26]

After a good deal of speaking, and an unsuccessful attempt at compromise by Crittenden, the Lecompton Constitution passed the Senate on March 23, thirty-three to twenty-five. However, with a rough road ahead of it in the House, there was a possibility that it could only pass that body with a form of the amendment proposed by Crittenden, calling for submission of the entire constitution to the people. If this happened, then the bill would come back to the Senate, where the renewed fight would be even hotter and closer, and where the decision might even wind up in the hands of the vice-president. Thus far in the Lecompton battle, one of the best-kept secrets in Washington City was Breckinridge's position on the issue. He stayed absolutely quiet in the capital, as he felt a vice-president should, but many speculated that his silence resulted from concealed sympathy with Douglas and a desire not to come into open conflict with his own administration. In fact, there is evidence that Breckinridge and Douglas met to attempt a compromise between the latter and Buchanan. It hardly subdued the guessing game when, in the midst of the battle with all signs pointing toward an important decision in the Senate, the vice-president suddenly left on March 29 for the South. Before this, he had not missed a day at his post since the previous December 21. That he would pick just this time to absent himself from the Senate smacked, to some, of either shrewd reasoning, or cowardice.[27]

Two considerations made Breckinridge leave Washington so suddenly. One was Mary's health, which had apparently improved sufficiently for her to leave Baton Rouge and join him at the capital. The other was the news that, on March 26, after fifty-two years of widowhood, Grandma

26. Nichols, *Disruption*, 155–58; *Congressional Globe*, 35th Cong., 1st Sess., Pt. 1, p. 521; Paris *Kentucky State Flag*, August 4, 1858.

27. *Congressional Globe*, 35th Cong., 1st Sess., Pt. 2, pp. 1263, 1400; Nichols, *Disruption*, 164; Stevens, "Douglas," 524; Lexington *Kentucky Statesman*, March 30, July 27, 1858.

Black Cap had died at the home of her son William, in Louisville. The vice-president was gone for a month, and, meanwhile a great deal took place in the Senate. The House had, as feared, attached the Crittenden measure to the Lecompton bill and sent it back across the Capitol to the Senate, where it was rejected. Expecting this, the administration had put its hopes on obtaining a committee of conference from both houses to reconsider the bill and rewrite it in a form acceptable to each. Such a rewrite would depend on a good administration majority in the committee, which would consist of three members from each house, chosen by the presiding officers.

Had Breckinridge been there to choose the Senate members, his personal feelings on Lecompton could no longer have been considered secret. Pressure would have been applied to him—as it was to the president pro tempore Benjamin Fitzpatrick—by Buchanan's managers Slidell and Bigler, and regardless of his intentions or private views, the appointment of an administration majority from the Senate would be construed as an endorsement by the vice-president. In fact, the pro-Lecomptonites did control the committee, which, in itself, required no little maneuvering, and they soon reported a compromise bill fathered primarily by William English. It proposed to Kansans that, if they so voted, a grant of nearly four million acres of public land would be made along with 5 percent of the profits from the sale of an additional two million which would be disposed of in July. However, along with the grant came the submission of the Lecompton Constitution to the people of the territory. Buchanan needed submission to save face, but he could not offer it straightforward. Most anti-Lecomptonites rejoiced at the bill, for its submission of the constitution to the people of Kansas guaranteed the death of the odious charter. However, Douglas and his backers, after much soul-searching, still could not accept it, for it offered only an indirect submission. He demanded an open, undisguised, submission to Kansans; nothing less. Despite his opposition to the bill, it passed both houses just a few days before Breckinridge arrived back in Washington City.[28]

The vice-president was reticent about the English Bill. He had favored submission of the Lecompton Constitution to the people, and his view on this had not changed, even though he knew with everyone else that the English Bill doomed Lecompton. Like other administration southerners, he was happy to see the troublesome question about to be resolved and the administration relieved of a measure of its embarrassment, yet he was sad to witness the certain loss of the only new slave state that could be expected for years to come, perhaps indefinitely.

28. Lexington *Kentucky Statesman*, March 30, April 27, 1858; Louisville *Courier*, April 24, 1857.

Again his timing aroused speculation, the assumption being that he wished to remain noncommittal, with an eye toward the main chance and, perhaps, a nomination in 1860. The gossips could not know, and the vice-president did not tell them, that his sudden trip had nothing to do with Lecompton. As far back as January, even before the constitution was sent to Congress, he had tentatively planned to go South in April. This was rushed somewhat by the unexpected news of Grandma Black Cap's death. As for the speculation that he sought to avoid the responsibility of appointing members of the conference committee by absenting himself, the fact was that the administration plan for such a committee, and the report to come out of it, did not emerge until March 29, while Breckinridge was on a train heading South. Nevertheless, the charges that he was either a trimmer, or worse yet a Douglas man on Lecompton, went on uncontradicted for the next three months.[29]

The remainder of the session was anticlimactic in comparison with what had already transpired. Finally, in the last weeks of the session, Breckinridge had opportunity to exercise his only constitutional voice in the Senate, a casting vote to break a tie. Three of these ties came his way. The first was on a motion to postpone until December a bill on the tariff on cod-fishing. John Bell of Tennessee was opposed to the bounties imposed on the industry and had moved for the postponement. Besides, he and other senators felt that all considerations related to the tariff, a financial matter, belonged within the province of the House. Breckinridge, concerned with the funds needed by an administration that was already characterized by heavy spending, killed the motion with his tie-breaking vote. Likewise, when Douglas wanted to take up a bill for the admission of Oregon as a state, and Iverson of Georgia wanted instead to proceed on some business from several days before, the vice-president broke a tie in favor of Douglas' motion. And, early in June, on an amendment by Toombs to limit military pensions to fifty dollars a month, Breckinridge again broke a deadlock by voting in the affirmative. This, like his fishing bounties decision, was a move toward economy.[30]

One final controversy involving Breckinridge did arise from the final days of the session. Minnesota was admitted as a state on May 11, and the next day some consideration was given to its elected senators, Rice and General James Shields. On May 14 the two came forward to be assigned

29. Nichols, *Disruption*, 164–75; Lexington *Kentucky Statesman*, July 27, August 13, 1858; Breckinridge to George H. Martin, January 29, 1858, in Dreer Collection.

30. *Congressional Globe*, 35th Cong., 1st Sess., Pt. 2, p. 2013, Pt. 3, pp. 2084, 2200, 2728–29, 2896.

their terms of office. Breckinridge had the secretary of the Senate, Asbury Dickins, put two slips of paper into a ballot box, one of them numbered *1* and the other blank. Whoever drew the numbered slip would have the term ending in March, 1859. Shields drew this. Then two more pieces of paper were put into the box, this time numbered *2* and *3*. If Rice drew the former, his term would end in March, 1861; if the latter, he would remain in office until March, 1863. He drew *3* and thereby received the longest possible term. Not long after this several opposition papers in the Northwest, who had always been opposed to Rice, Breckinridge, and their combined speculative efforts, insinuated that Breckinridge had tampered with the slips of paper in order to ensure Rice the long term, "with a view to some dishonorable object to be accomplished or promoted by his votes." Not until in July, when Dickins saw the accusations, were they refuted. Since he had handled the entire operation, he was able to say, in an open letter to the Washington *Union*, that the vice-president had never touched either the slips of paper or the ballot box. Breckinridge, who sometimes exhibited a lamentable disinclination to speak out publicly and deny false charges, sincerely appreciated Dickins' refutation of the "slander." [31]

June 14, 1858, was the last day of the session. As was the custom, Breckinridge vacated the chair in favor of an appointed presiding officer, Mason of Virginia, and the last business of the Senate ground on toward the adjournment. Then Seward arose and submitted a resolution to which he asked the unanimous approval of the body: "*Resolved*, That the thanks of the Senate are unanimously tendered to the Hon. John C. Breckinridge for the dignity and impartiality with which he has discharged the duties of presiding officer of this body." This, too, was custom, as was the unanimous agreement which followed, but it was not traditional for the most ultra leader of the party opposed to the vice-president to make such a proposal. Indeed, this was the first such motion that Seward had made for any presiding officer in his nine-year senatorial career. It certainly came, and was then interpreted, as a mark of esteem for Breckinridge's "dignity and impartiality." A man who could win such plaudits from his most bitter political enemy was one to be reckoned with. An acquaintance, seeing the vice-president as the session ended, wrote home, "He is a fine-looking man, universally esteemed and respected, deemed and taken to be a son of fortune, destined to rise." [32]

31. Washington *Union*, May 13, 15, July 23, 1858; Breckinridge to Asbury Dickins, August 3, 1858, Miscellaneous Papers (John C. Breckinridge), in NYPL.

32. *Congressional Globe*, 35th Cong., 1st Sess., Pt. 3, p. 3041; Robert M. Myers (ed.), *The Children of Pride: A True Story of Georgia and the Civil War* (New Haven, Conn., 1972), 325.

CHAPTER **10**

Let Justice Be Done

A week after the adjournment, Breckinridge was back in Kentucky, with a variety of impulses operating on him. He had just finished a period of six months as a paid listener, a professional master of ceremonies—although a good one—who had no right or opportunity to engage in the momentous debates going on before him on the floor of the Senate. This alone was enough to make him want to speak out upon reaching Lexington. He was not the kind of man who could sit and listen. There were insinuations that he wished to avoid committing himself on Lecompton, with a view to being eventually on the *right* side so far as the Democratic National Convention in 1860 was concerned. And it cannot be denied that with the constant linking of his name with a presidential nomination, coupled with his own natural ambition, he was fully conscious that the pursuit of the proper course might make him Buchanan's successor. All of this, plus his stated belief that the people had "a right to expect that public men should be prepared to give their views upon public matters at all convenient times," decided Breckinridge to take the stump.[1]

No vice-president before Breckinridge had ever done so during his tenure, in his own behalf or for any other program or candidate. His pretext for speaking out would be promoting the election of his friend Rankin Revill for clerk of the Kentucky Court of Appeals.[2]

The real meat of Breckinridge's speeches, as everyone expected, was his stand on Lecompton. It was not an easy stand to take, and the complexities of the issue and the times showed clearly in its expression. He first used an argument that previously had been entirely foreign to him, and which strongly suggests that his desire to prove Lecompton to be fair and legal

1. Lexington *Kentucky Statesman*, June 25, October 29, 1858; Paris *Kentucky State Flag*, August 4, 1858.
2. Paris *Kentucky State Flag*, August 4, 1858; Washington *Union*, August 14, 1858.

outweighed somewhat his own convictions. He proposed simply that the president, the cabinet, all the congressional Democrats from the South and a majority of them from the North, as well as a majority of the southern Know-Nothings, were in favor of Lecompton; in short, might made right.[3]

There were a variety of charges concerning Kansas that Breckinridge felt obliged to answer. He made no denial that a considerable number of unlawful ballots were cast in every election that had been held in Kansas, and he placed the blame almost equally on proslavery "border ruffians" from Missouri, and antislaveryites from New England who were shipped into the territory to vote. The legislature was legal, he argued, largely because of the number of its acts that were recognized as binding; therefore, the constitutional convention which it had called was also lawful. He rigidly denied that any people had been refused their right to vote, or that they had been required to take an odious test oath before casting their ballots. Thus, with a legislature *legally* elected under *legal* voting practices, the convention which it called and the constitution thereby produced were also genuine expressions of the will of Kansas.

Having, he felt, undermined the accusations of fraud, Breckinridge proceeded to one of the Republican arguments against the Lecompton Constitution, the fact that it would admit Kansas without the benefit of a congressional enabling act. He needed merely to point out that California had been admitted—"the Free State interest forced her into the Union," he said—without such an act, and for the opposition to demand one now at the prospect of the admission of a slave state, was sheer hypocrisy. He dispensed with the complaint that the Lecompton Constitution had been accepted without the vote of the Free-Soilers in Kansas by the simple and legalistic statement that they had had their chance to express their will. If they chose to boycott the referendum and let the slavery clause pass, they had no one to blame but themselves. Until legal action to the contrary took place, the acceptance of the slavery clause must stand as the lawful expression of the wishes of Kansas voters.

He unequivocally expressed his desire that Congress might have accepted the Lecompton document back when it was first proposed, and he loosed a shaft at Crittenden for his part in the rejection. This, of course, would have meant that the people of Kansas would not have had the opportunity to vote on the constitution itself, a violation of the popular sovereignty dogma which was the main bulwark of Douglas' violent opposition to the

3. Paris *Kentucky State Flag*, August 4, 1858; Lexington *Kentucky Statesman*, July 16, 20, 27, 1858.

whole affair. Still Breckinridge would have accepted this, though he declared that if he had been a member of the Lecompton convention, he would have favored and voted for submitting the constitution to the people before sending it to congress.

Breckinridge declared that the whole controversy over submission of the constitution was a sham; the real issue was the slavery clause. Kansans did not want it. But, he said, they had had a fair and legal opportunity to vote it down, and passed it up. They had, he felt, no grounds for complaint. He did not deny the argument that, even without the offensive clause, there would still have been slaves in Kansas. He reckoned their number at about three hundred, and their value at perhaps $150,000. At the same time, armed with the fact that provision had been made for the emancipation of those slaves and the payment to their owners of a just remuneration, should the clause fail, he put to the lie the charge that the evil institution would still be practiced in Kansas with or without Lecompton. Indeed, he felt personally that to admit Kansas to the Union as a free state, and then let these few slaveholders continue to do "just exactly as they pleased" would be reprehensible. "What an outrage!" he declared.[4]

Of course, the whole Kansas-Lecompton question, he said, was but part of a much larger issue, the program of the Republican party of the North. The object of that organization was to prevent the admission of any more slave states and, eventually, to abolitionize the entire Union. Breckinridge doubted that Kentucky fully realized the power of this party. He believed that it was now the dominant political body in the Union—unless the Democratic party was perhaps a little stronger—and certainly the Democrats were the only ones who could challenge its bid for supremacy. To back up his views on the objects of the opposition, he read passages from the Senate speeches of Henry Wilson of Massachusetts and one whom he believed to be "greater than Wilson," Seward. Of course, they merely stood on the perimeter of the Republican whirlpool; the man at the center was William Lloyd Garrison. He admired Garrison more than any of his cohorts because the editor of the *Liberator* manfully admitted that the United States Constitution stood between him and general abolition; Seward and the others, said Breckinridge, did not.

After urging the remnant of the Know-Nothings to come over and join the Democrats in the great fight ahead, Breckinridge closed with a final expostulation of the Democratic creed, why his party alone had survived all

4. *Speech . . . at Frankfort, Kentucky, December 21, 1859*, 1–3; Albert D. Kirwan, *John J. Crittenden: The Struggle for the Union* (Lexington, 1962), 332.

others, and why it was the only hope of destroying Republicanism. The contest in 1860, he said, would be between a "straight out" Republican and a solid Democrat, and the issue would be the doctrines of the former's party, "the most dangerous, atrocious, and baneful organization" which had ever taken root in America.[5]

They were curious speeches, these, on the surface quite simple, but rife with conflict beneath. He endorsed the administration's position on Lecompton and applauded Buchanan, yet not without several subtle reservations. The overwhelming majority of the Lecompton Democrats, however, overlooked or ignored the reservations, and read into the speech a firm, unequivocal, endorsement of the president. It is doubtful that Buchanan felt this way, and to many others, Breckinridge must have seemed to be straddling a fence. No one could deny that he had honestly spoken his views, but his presentation was well calculated to offend as few as possible, excepting of course the Republicans.[6]

The press reaction to the speeches was no more partisan than might have been expected. Probably the most violent critic was the Pittsburgh *Gazette*, which said, "It is the first time in our national history, we believe, that the *vice-president* has lowered his dignity by taking the stump and making partizan speeches." No one outside of Kentucky seemed concerned that Revill won.[7]

All the papers failed to catch in Breckinridge's statements the conspicuous absence of any mention of Stephen A. Douglas. His nearest reference to the Illinoisian was when he lamented the bitterness and strife that Lecompton had caused "between men who should have made common cause for peace." By this time, the Little Giant had made himself almost as big an issue as Lecompton itself, and for Breckinridge not to follow the lead of scores of other Democrats who were denouncing Douglas in every state, seemed indeed strange.[8]

The vice-president could find several reasons to speak against Douglas. For one thing, he was sowing dissension in the party at a time when unanimity was more essential than ever to combat the Republicans. Worse yet, just a few days before Breckinridge concluded his series of appearances, Douglas had begun his own campaign for reelection to the Senate

5. Paris *Kentucky State Flag*, August 4, 1858; Lexington *Kentucky Statesman*, July 20, 27, 30, 1858.
6. Rawley, *Race and Politics*, 250–51.
7. Lexington *Kentucky Statesman*, July 27, 30, August 6, 13, November 5, 1858; Cleveland *Leader*, July 30, 1858.
8. Paris *Kentucky State Flag*, August 4, 1858.

against a Republican opponent, Abraham Lincoln. It was no secret that Douglas would be denouncing Lecompton and Buchanan from every stump in Illinois.

Despite these inducements, however, Breckinridge could find many more reasons not to sail into his friend. For one thing, they agreed on the fact that the Lecompton Constitution should have been submitted to the people of Kansas, and that Congress did not have the power to command its submission. Also, Breckinridge felt some personal sympathy with Douglas. In a characteristic move Buchanan began a systematic persecution of the Little Giant as soon as it became apparent that Douglas would oppose Lecompton. Breckinridge saw fully what the president did not: in the face of the growing Republican leviathan, the only hope for victory in 1860, the preservation of the party, and perhaps for the Union itself, lay in remaining united. In the face of what Douglas had done so far, Breckinridge could hardly endorse his course even though friends urged him to do so, but neither would he condemn him. Forney believed that this refusal to assist in the persecution of the Little Giant cost the vice-president even more of Buchanan's confidence in him.[9]

Matters with Douglas came to a head as the weeks passed. Although the voters of Kansas decisively rejected the Lecompton Constitution on August 2, Kansas was not much of an issue in the senatorial campaign in Illinois. Both Lincoln and Douglas were agreed on Lecompton. The two candidates were now engaged in a series of seven debates, and, at Freeport on August 27, Lincoln backed his antagonist into a corner and forced from him an admission that he did not feel bound by the Supreme Court's decision in the Dred Scott case. Douglas declared that regardless of what that Court said, the power to embrace or prohibit slavery rested only with the people of the territories. This is how southern Democrats viewed the speech, though Douglas genuinely did not believe that the Court's ruling applied to territorial jurisdiction over slavery. He had said as much before, but now the nation seized upon this speech and the supposed "Freeport Doctrine" which Douglas announced. It won him favor in the North, but cost him terribly in the South, and in Kentucky. Stevenson declared, "That speech cooled the ardor of our people." To counteract this, Douglas sought endorsements from prominent party men, North and South, and sent Breckinridge's friend J. A. McHatton to Kentucky to see what, if anything, the vice-president would contribute. Breckinridge told him *"unqualifiedly"*

9. Milton, *Eve of Conflict*, 325; Forney, *Anecdotes*, I, 41–42.

that he earnestly desired Douglas' success, and that McHatton might repeat his declaration "to the world." [10]

McHatton began to do just that and saw to the publication, in at least one paper, of a statement that Breckinridge even desired to come into Illinois to stump in Douglas' behalf. Faced with this, the Little Giant sent his friend an invitation to visit his state and speak for him. Sensing that this would be going too far away from the administration, Breckinridge decided to decline. However, on October 21 he sent to Illinois an open letter in which he firmly advocated Douglas' election. He had often said in conversation that he wished to see his friend reelected, the vice-president began, though he did not plan to mix himself in the political contests in other states. In all fairness, he had to say that he did not favor Douglas on account of his course on Lecompton, nor did he approve of all of the positions assumed by the Little Giant in his present canvass, almost surely a reference to the Freeport Doctrine. Nevertheless, now that the Kansas discussion was dead, since Douglas had recently given assurances of his fidelity to the Democratic party, because he was the one most able to defeat Lincoln, and due to his lifelong defense of the Union and the rights of the states, the Little Giant should, in Breckinridge's opinion, be given all the support necessary to send him back to the Senate. One of the concluding sentences of the letter is indicative of the vice-president's concern for what Douglas and Buchanan were doing to the party. "I have not desired to say anything upon this or any other subject," he wrote, "about which a difference may be supposed to exist in our political family." [11]

Some of the opposition chose to regard the vice-president's letter as rather a backhanded endorsement, and even Douglas may have been somewhat piqued at it, but there was no denying that it helped the senator toward his victory. Illinois' administration Danites, a term applied by Douglas to those who supported Buchanan against him, had been so confident of Breckinridge's assistance in their war on Douglas that they distributed leaflets advertising his appearance at a Danite mass meeting in Springfield on September 7. There was no little embarrassment when he did not show, and his letter of the following month was salt in the wound. In the largely pro-Buchanan "Egypt" district, one Danite found the endorsement doing Douglas so much good that he wrote to the president complaining of Breckin-

10. Milton, *Eve of Conflict*, 347–48; Stephenson to Alexander H. Stephens, October 8, 1858, in Alexander H. Stephens MSS, LC.

11. New York *Harper's Weekly*, November 6, 1858; Lexington *Kentucky Statesman*, October 26, 1858.

ridge's treachery. The Chicago *Democrat* went much further in speaking of the vice-president's part in this canvass, stating "He alone dismembered the Buchanan party in this State, and left it almost without a semblance of existence." Needless to say, the son of Lancaster did not appreciate his vice-president's course.[12]

It could not have made the president any happier to hear Douglas, on a tour down the Mississippi following the close of his campaign, ardently denying his own pretensions to the White House in 1860, but paying a number of high compliments to Breckinridge as a good man for the Charleston convention. It appeared that some sort of unwritten, unspoken alliance may have arisen between the two, and immediately the opposition press —as well as a very few administration papers—began to charge that Breckinridge wrote his letter for Douglas with the understanding that he would receive the Little Giant's support for the nomination in 1860.[13]

None of this was calculated to make Breckinridge any more welcome at the White House. Indeed, even before he wrote the Douglas letter, the vice-president received the greatest insult yet. Buchanan asked him to accept an appointment as minister to Spain, the same position that Breckinridge turned down three and one half years before. Of course there was nothing dishonorable in such a diplomatic post, but John Adams had established a precedent more than a half century before that diplomatic missions and errands were definitely beneath the dignity of the vice-president. This was the first time that a president had ever asked such a thing of his second in command, and in Buchanan's offer, which Breckinridge refused, the implication was obvious that the vice-president's services were no longer desired or appreciated.[14]

The cold within the tortured Buchanan court was well matched by the winter of 1858–1859. Breckinridge, his new home still unfinished, took a house with Clay and Stevenson for the duration of the second session of the Congress. These short sessions were generally the scene of often shameless party politicking, for the time did not allow much serious discussion or legislation, and from the first sounding of the gavel it became apparent that the primary purpose of the southern and administration men was the further chastisement of Douglas. Their first move was a vicious one; they met

12. Cleveland *Leader*, October 27, 1858; Chicago *Democrat*, November 9, 1858.
13. Allan Nevins, *The Emergence of Lincoln: Douglas, Buchanan, and Party Chaos, 1857–1859* (New York, 1950), 348–49, 370, 420; Lexington *Kentucky Statesman*, November 2, 1858.
14. Nichols, *Disruption*, 229; Feerick, *From Failing Hands*, 70–71.

in caucus and took away his chairmanship of the Committee on Territories. It was clear that there was more to come.[15]

Early in 1859 came a brief interruption in the vice-presidential routine. At last Breckinridge would have the floor of the Senate to speak. For years a new Senate chamber had been under construction, as the present one steadily grew more cramped with the addition of new states. Now it was completed and ready for its occupants. It was only natural that the vice-president be invited to give a farewell address to the old chamber where so much of the nation's history had been made, and Breckinridge readily accepted.

As expected, Breckinridge's speech was primarily historical, tracing the origins and development of the Senate and the Capitol. Only as he neared its conclusion did he leave the past and reflect upon the present state of the Union. "The career of the United States cannot be measured by that of any other people of whom history gives account," he said. It now stood happier, more powerful, more prosperous, than any other nation of comparable size on the globe. "In a word, behold present greatness, and, in the future, an empire to which the ancient mistress of the world in the height of her glory could not be compared. Such is our country; ay, and more—far more than my mind could conceive or my tongue could utter. Is there an American who regrets the past? Is there one who will deride his country's laws, pervert her Constitution, or alienate her people? If there be such a man, let his memory descend to posterity laden with the execrations of all mankind."

He pointed to the seats of Calhoun, Webster, and Clay, and declared, "What models were these!" All of the states might point with pride to their sons in this old chamber. And then it was time to leave. The senators bore with them, he said, a Constitution unimpaired, to be cherished for all time. "The structures reared by men yield to the corroding tooth of time. These marble walls must moulder into ruin; but the principles of constitutional liberty, guarded by wisdom and virtue, unlike material elements, do not decay. Let us devoutly trust that another Senate, in another age, shall bear to a new and larger Chamber, this Constitution vigorous and inviolate, and that the last generation of posterity shall witness the deliberations of the Representatives of American States still united, prosperous, and free."[16]

15. Nichols, *Disruption*, 222–26; James B. Clay, Sr., to James B. Clay, Jr., December 7, 1858, Clay to Susan M. Clay, December 7, 1858, in Clay MSS.
16. *Address of Hon. John C. Breckinridge, Vice President of the United States, Preceding the Removal of the Senate from the Old to the New Chamber* (Washington, 1860), 3–8.

So saying, Breckinridge led the Senate out of the old chamber and into the new, called them to order, heard a prayer read by the Reverend P. D. Gurley, and inaugurated the spacious new hall with the words, "Petitions are now in order." [17]

His address was well received and widely spoken of. Years later, Senator Henry W. Blair of New Hampshire would reflect on the vice-president's stirring Union speech. Considering the shaky state of the Union in January, 1859, Blair said, "It seems to me that Vice President Breckinridge was in that address giving utterance to an exalted and prophetic condition of the national mind. . . . It seems to me as something more than the individual John C. Breckinridge could have done, yet as belonging to him as fully as Webster is entitled to the credit of his own inspired peroration in his historic reply to Senator Hayne. There is more than Breckinridge or Webster in this sort of work." [18]

Before the fires had warmed the new chamber, the war on Douglas continued, helped somewhat by his absence in Illinois. A host of the southern men, their own ambitions for the presidency pressing them onward, conceived several insults to his reputation and standing. As a consequence, it was no surprise that on January 10, when the Little Giant did make his first appearance of the session, he was roundly spurned and ignored. This made even more conspicuous the vice-president's own action, as he alone of the southerners took Douglas by the hand and greeted him with undisguised warmth.[19]

In mid-January Breckinridge had to return to Kentucky briefly, and he was not back in the Senate until February 10. With just three weeks of the short session left, he found himself so burdened with work that he was forced to let all of his correspondence go and concentrate his energies entirely on the Senate. It was a hurried and troubled three weeks. For one thing, the senators themselves lacked discipline. One day, at the hour of meeting, the vice-president took his seat to find fewer than ten of them in theirs. With most of them absent in the committee rooms working over a variety of special interests, there was not a quorum in the Senate. The difficulty with absentees continued, and brought about one of the most tense votes of the session, and Breckinridge's most important vote. Andrew John-

17. *Congressional Globe*, 35th Cong., 2nd Sess., Pt. 1, pp. 202–204.
18. Clay to Susan M. Clay, January 6, 1859, in Clay MSS. Blair's characterization of Breckinridge's speech is taken from "History Builders," a column by Dr. E. J. Edwards, clipping from an unidentified newspaper, in JCB Papers.
19. Allan Nevins, *The Emergence of Lincoln: Prologue to Civil War, 1859–1861* (New York, 1950), 282.

son, as usual, was still working on his bill, the only bill so far as he was concerned, a homestead act. It commanded support among western Democrats, whose states and territories stood to gain greatly from the influx of settlers and capital that it would bring. Thus, the bill had passed the House 120 to 76, and when it came before the Senate it appeared that it would pass there as well, unless some administration absentees were brought in. The antihomestead men were called in and, on February 17, on a motion to postpone consideration of the bill—which would kill it for this session— the vote tied at 28 to 28. The vice-president then decided the matter, voted in the negative, and postponed the bill.

Breckinridge's motives for this important vote are difficult to discern from the variety of influences acting on him. It has been suggested that it may have been arranged by the administration to win over southern support for his presidential aspirations. True, the move was calculated to gain approval from the southern managers, who saw in the homestead act only another means to intrude the central government on state and territorial affairs, while also promoting abolition through the Free-Soil sentiments of a majority of the potential homesteaders. And after his refusal to take part in the Douglas purge, Breckinridge did need to get back into the good graces of some of the more powerful southern men like Slidell. However, Breckinridge's presidential ambitions at this time were dormant, though it cannot be denied that he knew his vote could help his chances in 1860. This was the general interpretation given his action by opposition editors, who maintained that "Vice President Breckenridge and Senator [R. M. T.] Hunter, both aspirants for the Presidency, should be held responsible for defeating the people's great measure." [20]

Better clues, however, can be found in Breckinridge's past votes on homestead acts. In 1852, as a congressman, he had voted against Johnson's bill. Then, with the Missouri Compromise still in effect, he would merely have been helping the settlement of more free states to upset the precarious balance in Congress. Two years later, however, he voted in favor of a similar homestead bill. Then the offensive compromise had been superseded by the Kansas-Nebraska Act, all of the territories were open to settlers, free or slave and, since Breckinridge believed that climate and soil would dictate slavery from Kansas south to the Mexican border, he saw no threat to south-

20. Breckinridge to S. I. Prime, March 5, 1859, in Breckinridge MSS, HSP; Lexington *Kentucky Statesman*, February 8, 1859; *Congressional Globe*, 35th Cong., 2nd Sess., Pt. 1, pp. 573, 920, 1051, 1076; Nichols, *Disruption*, 252; Cleveland *Leader*, February 27, 1859.

ern interests from a homestead act. Now, five years later, faced with a gigantic new antislavery party in the North which had hardly a name in 1854, and which had shown in Kansas that it would import settlers in order to influence Free State constitutions, the situation was reversed. Southern interests in the new territories of the West were more threatened than ever, and Breckinridge voted to protect them.

Through several emergencies the session wore on to adjournment on March 4. The Senate had been meeting until after midnight more often than not, but still they could not rest because of a special six-day session for swearing in new senators. Once more Breckinridge received the unanimous compliments of the members for his conduct. Once more it came on the motion of a Republican, this time Senator Solomon Foot of Vermont. Then, in the special session, Breckinridge had the pleasure of swearing in Lazarus W. Powell, and appointing him to the committee on commerce. In general, Breckinridge's appointments were just as fair and impartial as his service as presiding officer had been. To the Democratic stronghold committee on territories, he nevertheless appointed a Republican, James Grimes of Iowa.[21]

With half of his tenure as vice-president now done, Breckinridge's impression on the senators and the nation was considerable. Albert Gallatin Riddle of Ohio, soon to be a representative, but now just an interested Republican observer, characterized his conduct as president of the Senate as "inflexibly impartial." James G. Blaine, another Republican future hopeful, agreed with Riddle, believing that Breckinridge had been fair and just, while exhibiting great poise and dignity. Henry L. Dawes, Republican congressman from Massachusetts during the preceding two years, saw the vice-president in even closer perspective. He found Breckinridge, especially in appearance and manner, "youthful and dashing—more like a Highland chieftain than a grave legislator." As for the vice-president's service in the Senate, Dawes declared, "He was an honorable and (if there is any distinction in the two words) an honest man, and was conscientious in the discharge of every official duty, never betraying a trust and never doing a mean thing to advance a cause, however infatuated and blinded in its espousal." The votes of confidence from Seward, Foot, and others, testified to the feeling for the vice-president even among his bitterest enemies. During the last days of the session, the New York *Times'* Washington City correspondent wrote to his Republican journal, "Vice President Breckin-

21. *Congressional Globe*, 32nd Cong., 2nd Sess., Pt. 2, pp. 1652, 1685–86.

ridge stands deservedly high in public estimation, and has the character of a man slow to form resolves, but unceasing and inexorable in their fulfillment." He felt that the Kentuckian was just now beginning to exercise some influence on the administration, and that, while it "falls lower every hour in prestige and political consequence, the star of the Vice President rises higher above the clouds and drifting scud—the one fixed point in the Administration sky, which may be steered by securely under all changes and variations of the popular trade winds." [22]

The people, too, felt the steadiness, the honesty of their vice-president, especially as it stood out in an administration characterized largely by craft and half truths. Settlers named their new towns Breckinridge—though they nearly always misspelled his name—and his namesakes appeared on the maps of Colorado, Texas, Minnesota, and Michigan. In troublesome Kansas there was a county named for him, and with the name spelled correctly. He was more in demand as a speaker than ever and, more often than before, he declined. Breckinridge was especially careful not to accept any of the invitations to deliver lectures. "I have no experience in, and I fear, no aptitude for that kind of intellectual effort," he said.[23]

Other recognition came, and the vice-president was flooded with honorary and real memberships in a number of organizations. Although he had little time to keep up with his Masonic affiliation, the organization kept well up with him. During the past session, the sovereign grand commander, Albert Pike, conferred on him as an honorarium, the Scottish Rite degrees from the fourth through the thirty-second, and in March he received the thirty-third degree and was made sovereign grand inspector general of Kentucky. This made him one of the very early Kentuckians to receive the thirty-third degree, and be elected a member of the Supreme Council as well. Pike counted the order fortunate to have one "so intelligent and industrious" on the council. Another honor close to the vice-president's heart was his membership on the Board of Regents of the Smithsonian Institution. He found the natural and physical sciences fascinating, enjoyed friendships with several scientific men, including Benjamin Franklin's grandson, A. D. Bache, and took considerable interest in modern invention, including Cyrus Field's so far unsuccessful transatlantic telegraphic cable. Among the gifts

22. Albert G. Riddle. *Recollections of War Times* (New York, 1895), 5; Blaine, *Twenty Years,* I, 281; Henry L. Dawes, "Two Vice Presidents." *Century Magazine,* L (July, 1895), 463; Memphis *Appeal,* May 18, 1875; New York *Times,* February 8, 1859.
23. George R. Stewart, *American Place Names* (New York, 1970), 59; Breckinridge to Prime, March 5, 1859, in Breckinridge MSS, HSP; Lexington *Kentucky Statesman,* February 2, 1858, January 15, March 29, 1859.

he received was a gold-headed ebony cane, inscribed with his initials, presented to him by the Negro steward of the Senate.[24]

Breckinridge did not tarry long in Washington City. Mary did not particularly like living in rented quarters in the capital. It was only her deep—almost reverential—love for her husband that made her come to Washington City at all, and, not yet able to occupy their I Street home, both longed to be back in Lexington. Breckinridge did not go directly to Kentucky; he went north to New York and Philadelphia. Ostensibly, he was traveling on personal and business matters, but many knew the real object of his visit. Now, at last, it was time to think of the presidency. It would be foolish to say that Breckinridge had not thought of it before. Indeed, it may have been constantly in his thoughts ever since Cincinnati, and it could hardly be otherwise when his name had been continually linked with the office since his congressional days. And a residence in the White House seemed a natural culmination of a political career that was in many respects the most meteoric in the nation's history. In the face of all this, only a blind man or a fool could fail to see that Breckinridge should at least look into, if not actually try for, the party's nomination at Charleston in 1860.

Looking is just what the vice-president was doing. It was much too early to begin a public campaign for support of the influential, and there were too many things to find out. Everyone knew that Douglas would be in the field; how much support could he command? Lecompton and the Freeport Doctrine had cost him much, if not all, of the South, whereas those of the prominent southern hopefuls who could command the support of their region were considered too ultra to hope for success in the North. In this state of affairs moderates from the border states began to look promising. As early as December, 1858, there was speculation that the administration wing of the party would turn to Guthrie, while Young America—presumably including the Douglas men—would turn to Breckinridge. Virginians like Hunter and Wise were spoken of as well. For any of these men, all of whom could more or less count on the South, the real question was whether or not they could carry Pennsylvania and New York. Success in these two states plus their own section would guarantee the presidency. Of course, an ever present concern was what Douglas would do if faced with minority support for his candidacy. Would he gracefully yield as he had at Cincinnati, or would his adamant stand on Lecompton make it impossible for him

24. *New Age Magazine* (n.d.), 721–22, clipping in JCB Papers; Lexington *Transcript*, May 3, 1881; Breckinridge to A. D. Bache, December 27, 1853, in William J. Rhees Collection, HL; Roswell S. Ripley to Breckinridge, December 7, 1856, in B. MSS.

to support a southern, or administration, nominee? These were, indeed, important questions, and Breckinridge sought answers.[25]

Nearly two years before, his friend R. C. Wintersmith had written to him: "It is not worth while to deal in inuendoes [sic], or attempt to disguise the fact, that you would like to be the next candidate for the Presidency, and that you will have most of the politicians to contend with, but the 'peops' [Kossuth's engaging pronunciation of "people"] are for you certain." [26] By January, 1859, there were several in Washington City who believed that Breckinridge was actively seeking the nomination, and Senator James H. Hammond of South Carolina ranked him high on a list of eleven such aspirants.[27]

Thus it came as no surprise that the vice-president, stopping first in New York, paid calls on several of the leading "business Democrats," men with enough political influence—and the money to back it—to sway their state at Charleston. Fernando Wood, mayor of New York City, Augustus Schell, collector of the Port of New York, Charles O'Connor, perhaps the country's leading trial lawyer, and William M. "Boss" Tweed, power behind Tammany Hall, the city's most important political organization, all showed marked courtesy to Breckinridge. Indeed, they got together and proposed a public dinner in his honor, saying in their letter to him that "no public servant more than yourself is justly and honorably entitled by his public services, as well as by [the] integrity and honor of his private life, to the compliment proposed to be rendered." Since Breckinridge did not wish to be considered as actively seeking the nomination, a public dinner such as this would have been imprudent, and he turned it down. Nevertheless, the powerful support that the invitation implied was too good for him to let it go wasted. A week later the invitation, accompanied by his adroit declension, appeared prominently in the *Statesman* and other tabloids, perhaps even before he arrived back in Kentucky. "To command, by deserving it, the confidence of his fellow citizens," the vice-president wrote to the New Yorkers, "is, or should be, the highest aim of a public man." [28]

In his letter turning down the invitation, written on March 22, 1859, Breckinridge stated that his "private business" was finished and that he in-

25. Maltby, *Mary Cyrene Breckinridge*, 2; Breckinridge to Henry M. Rice, March 21, 1859, in Lee Kohns Collection, NYPL; New York *Times*, March 1, 1859; Lexington *Kentucky Statesman*, December 31, 1858.
26. R. C. Wintersmith to Breckinridge, September 28, 1857, in JCB Papers.
27. Edmund Ruffin Diary, January 17, 1859, LC.
28. Fernando Wood and others to Breckinridge, March 21, 1859, Breckinridge to Wood and others, March 22, 1859, in Lexington *Kentucky Statesman*, March 29, 1859.

tended to return immediately to Kentucky. However, he probably stayed in New York City for at least one or two more days and then, instead of going directly to Lexington, paid a visit in Philadelphia. There he consulted Forney, and surely found out that his friend was bound to support Douglas because of Lecompton. He also saw, among others, Congressman Joseph McKibbin of California, a native of Pennsylvania. McKibbin had already received strong assurances of the vice-president's strength in Pittsburgh and adjoining counties. Some there regarded Breckinridge as "the *only man* on whom we can rely," and the congressman probably relayed this to the vice-president.[29]

In terms of its immediate object—to sound out feeling for him in these crucial states—Breckinridge's trip was a success. He had received the vocal and written approval of the managers in New York, and even more positive encouragements were coming out of Pennsylvania. McKibbin had written to Hendrick B. Wright, state Democratic mogul, suggesting that it was time to get a Breckinridge movement going in the state, and strongly suggesting that Pennsylvania might be turned toward the vice-president at Charleston. Within a few weeks an organized campaign was underway in Philadelphia to replace the postmaster with a man more friendly to Breckinridge, and one friend of Buchanan's wrote to the president, "I shall not be surprised to see Douglass [sic] & Forney run up the Breckinridge Flag at no distant day." By late April, with the vice-president's name already being mentioned in connection with the nomination throughout the nation, the New York Republicans began counting him as definitely a potential adversary in 1860. It was felt that he would be willing to accept the support of the naughty Douglas, though no one was sure if Breckinridge would go for the Illinoisian if he should prove the stronger at Charleston. Already Douglas stood as the measure of things in 1860: no matter what happened, it could not happen without him.[30]

The most significant indication of the interest that the vice-president aroused in Pennsylvania on his trip was the reaction of Buchanan's sometime Senate spokesman William Bigler. In April, Bigler wrote to Breckinridge twice in the same week about the presidency. And only in the reply

29. *Ibid.*; Joseph C. McKibbin to Hendrick B. Wright, April 11, 1859, in Hendrick B. Wright MSS, Wyoming Historical and Geological Society, Wilkes-Barre, Pa., furnished through the courtesy of Dr. Daniel J. Curran and Ralph L. Hazeltine.

30. McKibbin to Wright, April 11, 1859, in Wright MSS, Wyoming Historical and Geological Society; Vincent Bradford to Buchanan, May 2, 1859, in Buchanan MSS; Lexington *Kentucky Statesman*, April 5, 1859; Preston King to John Bigelow, April 11, 1859, in John Bigelow, *Retrospections of an Active Life* (New York, 1905), I, 224.

does it appear that Breckinridge himself may not have been sufficiently impressed with the results of his stay in New York and Philadelphia. As befit a hopeful but undecided candidate for a nomination, he affected surprise that Bigler should think of him in connection with the White House, noted that he had received many other such letters but usually did not answer them, and then went on to "give you my present and future position frankly. . . . I have not thought that the attention of the people would be seriously turned to me in connection with that office. I have not at any time, and do not intend to take one step towards promoting myself in that direction—and indeed, I infer from your letter that you would not yourself consider such a course proper in any public man. I have not the folly to affect perfect indifference on such a subject, but I have the will to execute just what I have said above." As for the sentiment of Kentucky on the matter, he declined to comment, saying only that a Democratic victory in the races for the legislature would be a good sign. To a possible question regarding the necessity of a slave code to protect southern property in the territories, Breckinridge cited the position of Magoffin—now a candidate for governor—that it was not yet needed. The implication was strong that he held this opinion himself, though he did go on to say that the judiciary should be guaranteed sufficient power to carry out "constitutional decrees" —by which he surely meant the Fugitive Slave Law and the Dred Scott decision. There is no reason to suppose that Breckinridge—a consistent moderate—did not really believe in what he was saying here, but it was certainly a good middle-of-the-road declaration, well calculated to offend neither the North nor the South—a very politic statement for one who declined to "take one step" towards promoting himself.[31]

Although Breckinridge's reply to Bigler hardly closed the door on any presidential possibilities, it did not betray the enthusiasm that a great success in New York and Pennsylvania might have been expected to produce in him. Of course, there were other factors operating on the vice-president at the same time. For one thing, the large number of southern men who hoped for the nomination could neatly cleave up the South at Charleston, and almost certainly deny him the nearly unanimous vote that he would need from that region. Then there was Buchanan. His favorite, Slidell, was among the aspirants, and administration weight would almost certainly be used in the Louisianian's favor. Not a few southern men simply did not believe that Breckinridge possessed enough positive strength to get and hold

31. Breckinridge to William Bigler, May 7, 1859, in William Bigler MSS, HSP.

the nomination. Breckinridge knew the absolute necessity of unanimity at Charleston. As he told Bigler, "I would not have one fourth of a convention to dissent," and in the light of the above, it was obvious that such a unanimous support was not likely to come his way. Faced with this, Breckinridge shelved, at least temporarily, any presidential ambitions.[32]

There was yet another, perhaps decisive, influence working on his thoughts as the summer of 1859 approached. Old Crittenden had announced some time before that he would not seek reelection to the Senate. His retirement would leave an inviting vacuum for Kentucky's Democrats, a chance to send another one of their own to Washington City. Speculation had run rampant for over a year as to whom the legislature would elect to succeed him in the coming December, and Boyd, Guthrie, and John W. Stevenson were mentioned continually in the Democratic press. However, almost from the beginning it was clear that the party nomination was his if he wanted it.

As far back as January, 1858, Breckinridge's friends were discussing what he could, or should, do in regard to Crittenden's seat. Some openly pitted him against Boyd for the nomination, and this disturbed others. The vice-president was already near the peak in public life; it would be ungraceful for him to jump into this race if by doing so he would ruin the chances of some of those who had long supported him. Of course, if none of his friends showed the strength necessary to win, then Breckinridge might step in, and well he should. Now, in mid-1859, more of his unthinking supporters in the press were urging him toward the Senate and the presidency. This could be especially injurious, since it made him—or his followers at least—appear greedy. Besides, there were other prominent Kentucky Democrats, and party men still wanted to keep Guthrie in the capital in some capacity. It appears that Buchanan or his chief lieutenants were partially behind this, having sent Bright to stir up Guthrie's ambitions, and Rice to prod Breckinridge or his followers. Buchanan did not care which of the two Kentucky backed in 1860, just so long as it was not Douglas. By the time the vice-president returned from his brief northern trip, the case was boiled down in many minds to a simple formula: If Breckinridge wanted the Senate seat, would he and his friends then support Guthrie at Charleston; or if the state sent a delegation committed to Breckinridge to the 1860 convention, would the vice-president then back Boyd or Guthrie for the Senate? [33]

32. *Ibid.*; James G. Buret to R. M. T. Hunter, May 18, 1859, in Charles H. Ambler (ed.), *The Correspondence of R. M. T. Hunter, 1826–1876* (Washington, 1918), II, 272.

33. Thomas Stevenson to John W. Stevenson, January 21, 1858, R. W. Murdy to Stevenson, April 21, 1859, in Stevenson MSS; Breckinridge to Bigler, May 7, 1859, in Bigler MSS; Milton, *Eve of Conflict*, 374.

While the degree to which Breckinridge really wanted the presidency is debatable, there is no question that he avidly desired this Senate seat. Indeed, the latter largely explains the former. In his concept of American government, the real power in the federal system belonged with Congress, and in the Capitol it was the Senate which commanded the greatest importance and attention. Indeed, a senator could, and many times did, wield more influence than a president in domestic affairs. On the other hand, a president, outside of his work in foreign relations, could seem as nothing more than a man with a veto and a big white house. Looking at the matter more particularly from Breckinridge's point of view, a senator was a speaker, an orator, and a president was not. Since Breckinridge was young, and considering the perilous conditions facing the Charleston convention, it probably appeared to him as it did to others, including Jefferson Davis, that he could wait for better times to seek a presidential nomination, and lose nothing.[34]

Although it would be unbecoming for him to actively seek the party nomination for the Senate, there was no reason Breckinridge should not curtail those who were hurting his chances. As soon as he reached Lexington in April, he immediately set about discouraging the well-meaning editors who were loudly advancing his name. Thereafter, he left the behind-the-scenes work in his behalf largely in the hands of his friends. It was not until August that his candidacy was announced. Then, in order to counter charges from the opposition that he was also seeking the presidency in 1860, Breckinridge authorized several statements in the *Statesman* that he did not want the Charleston nomination. However, he would not renounce it beforehand, either, even to secure the support of Boyd and Guthrie. If Charleston offered, senator or not, he would be bound to accept. He could not, and would not, make any bargains.[35]

It was no coincidence that Breckinridge's candidacy for the Senate was not announced officially until late August, for the state elections occurred earlier that month, and they had brought overwhelming victory for the Democratic party. The Democrats now held substantial majorities in both houses at Frankfort, and Breckinridge's old friend Magoffin won the governorship. Revill was clerk of the Court of Appeals, and Powell was senator-elect. There was a strong party majority in the representatives in Congress, and now Breckinridge would seek the succession to Crittenden. The August landslide gave added impetus to the already swelling support for him,

34. Davis, *Rise and Fall*, I, 52.
35. Lexington *Kentucky Statesman*, May 6, 10, 24, August 26, November 9, 25, 1859; Breckinridge to Bigler, May 7, 1859, in Bigler MSS.

and the party press, especially the *Statesman*, fed Kentucky a steady diet of Breckinridge throughout the remaining months of 1859. If he could win, Kentucky would, at last, be a Democratic state.[36]

Other than the standard partisan arguments of the opposition, there had never really been a serious obstacle to the vice-president. The only potential danger came suspiciously late in November when a letter signed "Kentucky Gentleman" appeared in the Frankfort press. It was written in reaction to the recent—October 16–18—raid of the abolition zealot John Brown on the Federal arsenal at Harpers Ferry, Virginia, and voiced the opinion that Brown should not be hanged, for it would make him a martyr and rallying point for the treasonable abolitionists of the North. Although the letter made good sense, the reactionary flame that swept across the southern proslavery world demanded vengeance and death for John Brown. To hint that he should be spared could draw immediate suspicion, and the "Kentucky Gentleman" may have sought to make use of this, for the rumor was soon let out that the letter's author was Breckinridge. He denied any knowledge of it immediately, through the *Statesman*, and that ended the matter with no appreciable damage to him.[37]

On December 5, while Breckinridge was back in Washington City for the opening of the Thirty-sixth Congress, the Kentucky legislature opened its session in Frankfort. Three nights later the Democratic members met in caucus to make their nomination. Breckinridge's chief competitor, Lieutenant-governor Linn Boyd, had been too ill to preside over the opening of the state senate, and was now sinking rapidly towards his death on December 17. Although he had been sometimes a friend, sometimes a helper, to Breckinridge, Boyd had never been able to conceal his consuming jealousy —some said hatred—of the younger Democrat. Indeed, Boyd's supporters agreed to the bargain that Breckinridge had disdained, by publicly promising their support for Guthrie in 1860. Now that Boyd was out of the way, there was no obstacle to Breckinridge's nomination, and he won it on the first ballot. On December 9 the *Statesman* accurately prophesied, "The election of Mr. Breckinridge on Monday next is almost a fixed fact." Joshua F. Bell, Magoffin's unsuccessful Whig opponent of the previous August, accepted another defeat when the legislature gave Breckinridge the senatorship by a vote of eighty-one to fifty-two.[38]

36. Lexington *Kentucky Statesman*, August 26, October 21, 25, 28, November 4, 8, 25, 29, 1859.

37. *Ibid.*, November 20, 1859.

38. *Ibid.*, October 4, December 9, 13, 1859; Thomas Stevenson to John W. Stevenson, January 21, 1858, in Stevenson MSS; Lewis Collins, *History of Kentucky* (Louisville, 1924), I, 81.

The word went to the vice-president immediately, and within a few days he was on his way to Frankfort to accept the office. For Breckinridge, this was a much greater victory than it appeared on the surface. It was the culmination of eight years of work to make Kentucky a Democratic state. In December, 1851, when he first took his seat in Congress, the state had a Whig governor, a Whig-dominated legislature, two Whig senators, and a delegation of representatives evenly divided between the two parties. Breckinridge had attacked, and been largely responsible for the downfall of, Whiggery in its own home territory, Ashland. For three years he fought it as it died a lingering death, only to see his work set back by the shattering Know-Nothing earthquake of 1854–55. He began again, worked and campaigned for party candidates for every office, helped build up the party press, personally took charge of Democratic speakers and their engagements, contributed funds when needed and when he could, found his vice-presidential candidacy a big boost to his crusade, and neglected his business, his family, and even his health for the cause. In 1857 he finally saw the "top of the hill," as he called it, and now his own election at last put his party on the summit where, on every side, there stood the exhilarating view of a Democratic Kentucky as a reward. Wholly aside from any personal satisfaction at being made a senator, Breckinridge felt a profound sense of pride and accomplishment. Now, no state in the Union was more in the hands of the Democratic party than Kentucky. Of course, Breckinridge had not done it all himself, but it would not, could not, have been done without him. It had been a long, hard journey to reach the top of the hill. What Breckinridge did not know, though, was that there would soon be another, rougher, road ahead of him. It would come to a fork, and he and Kentucky would have to face the agonizing decision of which way to go.

CHAPTER 11

I Trust I Have the Courage

Breckinridge went first to Lexington upon arriving in Kentucky, and then on December 20, 1859, he boarded the train for Frankfort. The next night he strode into the hall of the House of Representatives and, in an address lasting one hour and a half, gave his thanks for his recent election to the Senate. The vice-president proceeded to deny the rumors that he had entered into any sort of bargain to obtain his new-found honor. "This trust was your free gift," he declared, "and when it came to my hands, I received it unstained by the slightest taint of bargain or intrigue." [1]

With the preliminaries out of the way, Breckinridge went on to answer questions asked in a blanket letter which the legislature had sent to all of the senatorial hopefuls before the election. It had asked if he upheld the Dred Scott decision; did he believe that Congress had the power to pass laws for the protection of a citizen and his property in the territories; and, if so, would he as senator introduce and promote such laws, if the territorial legislatures failed to enforce such property rights? After declaring his firm adherence to the Supreme Court ruling, especially since it agreed with his own opinion in the case, Breckinridge entered into a lengthy study of the history of Congress, the territories, slavery, and how the question could properly come before the courts. The Kansas–Nebraska Act had accomplished this last, he said, and the Dred Scott decision was an example of the principle in action. The question of slavery had thus been taken out of Congress. [2]

The vice-president went on at some length to prove that Congress did not have the constitutional power to legislate over the rights of person and property, either to exclude such property from the territories, or to confis-

1. Lexington *Kentucky Statesman*, December 20, 23, 1859; *Speech ... at Frankfort, Kentucky, December 21, 1859*, 1–8.
2. Lexington *Kentucky Statesman*, December 9, 1859.

cate it. At the same time, he asserted, also in line with Taney's decision, that the judiciary stood duty-bound to protect these rights whenever the question should come before a tribunal. There was nothing new in this so far as Breckinridge was concerned. It was the same doctrine of nonintervention that he had espoused since 1854 and even before. However, what followed was new, for he publicly affirmed those attitudes that he had implied to Bigler seven months before. Slaveholders, he said, were entitled to federal protection of their title to their slaves in the territories. At the same time, as if to temper his most radical statement yet on the slavery question, Breckinridge hastened to add that he saw no need at present for a slave code, believing that the existing machinery of the government was sufficient to execute judicial decisions. But, he added, should that machinery fail to do the job, then such a code should be enacted and enforced.

The slavery question was not presently before Congress, he went on, and it should stay that way. "Its agitation there has been productive only of evil to us, and that continually." To show that the controversy had been largely unnecessary, he declared that climate and soil had decided the matter before men ever took it up. "No man of sense and observation ever supposed that the institution would penetrate into Minnesota, Nebraska, and other Northern Territories." As for that land to the south where slavery could be profitable, "and where the interests of both races seem to harmonize in this relation," he did not doubt that environment, the Constitution, and the proximity of other slave states, would make "Southern States out of Southern soil."

Breckinridge gave over the great bulk of his speech to an attack on the Republican party. As usual, he quoted from its manifestos, this time the party platform of 1856, Seward's celebrated "irrepressible conflict" speech, and Hinton R. Helper's controversial book *The Impending Crisis of the South*, which had been endorsed by a host of Republicans. He had read the book, but seemed unconvinced that the North Carolinian Helper was really its author. As for Seward, Breckinridge declared him to be the most influential public man in the country. But now, to his assertion of an irrepressible conflict until the South emancipated its slaves either by volition or violence, Breckinridge stood indignant. "It is idle to shut our eyes to the nature of the issue offered by this party. It is folly to attempt to turf over a volcano. It is vain to cry peace, peace, when there is no peace!"

The natural result of the Republican program, he said, was alienation, discord, and fanaticism, all leading up to a collision. Indeed, such a collision had already occurred at Harpers Ferry and, while the major did not say that it was part of the plan of the Republicans, still he felt that it came as a result of their policy. For his own part, the vice-president regarded Brown's raid as "the most atrocious act of treason, murder and rapine combined that ever polluted the soil of Virginia."

Breckinridge charged the Republicans with the "present and ulterior" purposes of establishing the doctrine of Negro equality, exclusion of slavery from the territories, prevention of the admission of any more slave states, the repeal of the Fugitive Slave Law and making the obeyance of it a crime, abolition of slavery in Washington City and the District of Columbia and all Federal installations, and the curtailment of the interstate slave trade. By all of this, he said, the Republicans would seek to wear down the South until it submitted to emancipation. He added, "Resistance in some form is inevitable." While some states might seek comfort in secession, he prayed that Kentucky would resist within the Union. In the capital he had seen for some time a growing alienation, a lessening of the spirit of brotherhood, which had once bound the sections together. Now, the representatives of South Carolina, Georgia, Alabama, Mississippi, and other states, spoke freely of the secession spirit at home. "God forbid that such an event should occur!" he cried. "God forbid that the step shall ever be taken!"

He made a final plea for unanimity within the party, North and South. He did not deny that on one or two well-known points they stood at odds, but these differences were petty in comparison to the task that lay before them. They must stand united against the Republicans, he said with unerring prophecy, for "to fall to pieces on questions of less magnitude than its defeat, is to surrender to its domination, and all the fatal consequences that may ensue."

This speech marked a significant—though not quite radical—departure for Breckinridge. Although, as in every such speech he had made in the past, the vice-president delivered an eloquent, even stirring, appeal for the Union, still there was much that was new to his public address, and not a little disturbing to some. Breckinridge, who eight years before had agreed with Forney that slavery must be abolished either by peaceful means or by force, now asserted that slave property must be protected in the territories, even by a new Federal slave code if necessary. For the first time in any of his public utterances, he had made reference—fleeting though it was—to the relative positions of the white and black races. His attack on the supposed Republican doctrine of "negro equality" was the first revelation of his belief in the inherent inferiority of the blacks, a subject he had scrupulously ignored in every prior address. Finally, his prediction of blazing border war and the possible dissolution of the Union, showed an appeal to emotionalism and suspicion which had not previously characterized his speeches.

What brought about these changes in Breckinridge's attitudes? In his last addresses in Kentucky, a year and a half before, he gave no hint or sign of such thoughts. Of course, his attack on the Republicans was much the same, and couched in some of the identical statements and metaphors, but even here he had now added a touch of fervor, of fear, that had not been there before. As was to be expected, his supporters received the speech with enthusiasm, and even the Republican New York *Times* found it not unacceptable, but there were those who were not so pleased. On January 9, 1860, Robert J. Breckinridge wrote his nephew an open letter in which he expressed displeasure over some of the subjects covered in the address. He decried all the talk of the disunion and civil war. It could produce nothing but harm.[3]

A great deal had happened in the eighteen months since the vice-president's last speech in Kentucky, and in those troubled days and weeks lay the primary causes for his still moderate, but increasingly militant, positions. For one thing, where in 1858 the party still seemed ascendant, he now said straight out that the enemy was the strongest political organization in the country. He could see it first hand in Washington City. The once-powerful Democratic majority had crumbled under the attack of increased Republican strength from the North, and Democratic hatred of Douglas in the South. The threat of Republican victory in 1860 was now a clear danger, and Breckinridge had no reason to believe that, once in power, they would not carry out their threats to use the federal government to restrict slavery. This imminent threat drove him back even farther into his strict constructionist view of the Constitution; showed him that the only hope of the Democrats, and personal property rights in slaves or anything else, lay in a united and unyielding South; and may even have led him to believe that the opposition would somehow use its doctrine of "negro equality" to overpower the South by weight of numbers, white and black. All of this was catalyzed by John Brown's raid just two months before the Frankfort speech. In this state of affairs, it appeared to him, as to many others, that if the Republicans continued in their present vein unchecked, and if the South did not receive some assurance that its rights would be honored, dis-

3. *Ibid.*, December 23, 27, 1859, January 20, 1860; Ollinger Crenshaw, *The Slave States in the Presidential Election of 1860* (Baltimore, 1945), 154–55, 250–60; Robert J. Breckinridge to Breckinridge, January 9, 1860, in Robert J. Breckinridge Scrapbook 1860–63, Breckinridge to Robert J. Breckinridge, January 30, 1860, in B. MSS.

union and civil war must surely ensue. Although he may not have recognized it himself, Breckinridge, and much of the nation with him, was beginning to be motivated by fear, and it was coloring his thoughts ever closer to a peculiar butternut gray.[4]

Yet one more reason behind his shift in position may lie in the suggestion advanced by opponents that he was unwittingly maneuvered into it by fellow conservatives who would later turn into ardent Union men. What their motives were in doing so, and who they were, is conjecturable, but it is certain that a number of Douglas' friends were happy to see Breckinridge take this stand. It would cost him dearly in the North, freeing much-needed Democratic votes for the Little Giant. Just how Breckinridge could have been persuaded into such a move is a knotty question. He was too astute a politician to be fooled easily, and Douglas himself would not have countenanced such a move. It is possible that a promise of support for constitutional guarantees from some of Douglas' managers would have gone a long way toward this result. Breckinridge was nearly convinced that such guarantees were the only hope against disunion, and the intimation that strong northern Democrats felt the same way might have made such a declaration as his at Frankfort seem to be a strong appeal for the Union. If this was really the reason behind his new stand, then the subsequent refusal of the Douglas men to countenance guarantees, and the realization that he had been hoodwinked and used, must have been a bitter pill indeed. It is a fact that less than a month after his speech, he lamented to a friend over the scheming and low character prevalent in the men among whom he lived and worked at Washington City. If it is true that Breckinridge was tricked into making his stand with the ultras of the South for guarantees, then it is truly tragic that, discovering the mistake he had made, he did not immediately admit it. Intimates, among them Forney, were agreed that Breckinridge was soon cognizant of his error in the Frankfort speech, but that, as the Pennsylvanian put it, "having taken the one wrong step, he was too proud to retract." [5]

That these were the influences which primarily accounted for his shift in position, is largely borne out by the vice-president's own refutation of the motive which most of his opponents ascribed to the new stand in his Frankfort speech. His old mentor, George Robertson, put the charge against him

4. Nichols, *Disruption*, 273–76.
5. Cincinnati *Commercial*, November 15, 1887; Forney, *Anecdotes*, I, 41; Wilson, *History of Kentucky*, II, 356; Blaine, *Twenty Years*, I, 322–23; Frank H. Heck, "John C. Breckinridge in the Crisis of 1860–1861," *Journal of Southern History*, XXI (August, 1955), 318. Breckinridge's opinion of the politicians in Washington is in Breckinridge to John W. Forney, January 19, 1860, in Frederick M. Dearborn Collection, HLH.

succinctly when he said that Breckinridge had been hoping for the Charleston nomination prior to December, 1859, "until finding that Douglas would overwhelm him in the North, he changed his creed, and in his Frankfort speech last January [*sic*], turned Southerner and advocated protection by Congressional intervention." [6] However, it is clear that Breckinridge had given up whatever hopes he may have entertained for the presidency in 1860. Little more than a month after the speech, he wrote to his Uncle Robert: "I find my name a good deal discussed in connection with the Presidency, yet I have neither said or done any thing to encourage it—and am firmly resolved not to do so. I do not think that I will be nominated, for . . . I know of no organization for me anywhere, and many of the friends of other gentlemen are actively whistling me down the wind. The old chieftains will never allow it—and for myself I am astonished at the indifference I feel to the personal aspect of the matter." [7] Nearly two weeks earlier, on January 19, 1860, Breckinridge had been even more explicit in estimating his chances, and his ambitions, for the Charleston nomination. Writing to Theodore O'Hara, he said: "Thanks for your good wishes about the White House. I fancy they spring chiefly from personal friendship. I do not anticipate being in the way of any body; for my old resolution is unchanged, to take no step to promote myself in that direction. If I were taken up it would be such an accident as does not occur in ages. I am in a good public position now, and am content." [8]

These were much the same sentiments that he had expressed to Bigler the previous May. However, where he could be coy or flirtatious with the Pennsylvanian, he could not with Robert or O'Hara. There can be no doubt that presidential ambition, consciously or unconsciously, influenced Breckinridge's course at Frankfort in some degree, but it is equally certain that, in view of the forces against him and the disrupted state of the party, he no longer entertained serious thoughts of a nomination in 1860. As he told O'Hara—probably in reference to the Senate seat he would assume on March 4, 1861—he had "a good public position." That was enough for now. There would be other nominations. [9]

In his letter to Robert, Breckinridge continued the arguments he had

6. George Robertson to "Mr. Alexander," August 23, 1860, in *Ashland Speech*, 2–3.

7. Breckinridge to Robert J. Breckinridge, January 30, 1860, in B. MSS. This letter, in a box marked Breckinridge Papers 1860-, is published in full, with several errors in transcription, in Dorothy Garrett Melzer, "Mr. Breckinridge Accepts," *Register of the Kentucky Historical Society*, LVI (July, 1958), 226–27.

8. Breckinridge to Theodore O'Hara, January 19, 1860, in Dearborn Collection.

9. Mobile *Daily Register*, May 30, 1875; Louisville *Courier-Journal*, May 26, June 18, 1875, November 17, 1887; William Preston Johnston, *The Life of Gen. Albert Sidney Johnston* (New York, 1879), 297.

advanced at Frankfort. He did not deny that the present state of the country was gloomy, "and almost tempts me to turn my back on the Capital in indignant despair." Indeed, he now believed that a time was nearly in sight "at which some of the states will go off, or employ the State Governments to paralyze the regular action of the Federal Gov't—and a sad day it will be when it comes." The only remedy, he felt, was a radical change of feeling among the "moral or fanatical element" in the North. However, if that element was too predominant in that section, "then according to all human experiences the present system is destined to fail." If the Republicans and their policy could be beaten in 1860, then he hoped for another decade or so of peace, and that should satisfy any statesman. He had observed that nothing lasts as an active political issue which could not make a president. Consequently, if the opposition could be defeated, then their dogmas might die with them. However, in a statement which showed that the vice-president may finally have begun to realize the force and power of a moral idea like emancipation, he added that this observation "may not apply to moral as to political questions. . . . The duty, it seems to me of a public man now, is to proclaim honestly the dangers that threaten the country, and yet to cling to the constitution and the Union to the last. I am not conscious of being influenced by the scenes around me. I look calmly and mournfully at the unhappy tendency of things—and if I had the capacity—and opportunity would make at least a manly effort to restore the feeling for a Constitutional Union." [10] Few doubted that Breckinridge had the capacity to make such an effort; whether or not he would get the opportunity would depend on Charleston and Stephen Douglas.

While Douglas was most grateful for the aid given by Breckinridge against Lincoln in 1858, the gap between them was growing because of Breckinridge's hinted endorsement of a slave code. This the Little Giant firmly opposed. Apparently, the vice-president had gone over to his extreme southern opponents. Added to this were apprehensions that he might present an obstacle in the coming convention. Then too, there is a suggestion that Breckinridge, discovering too late the supposed trick played on him by Douglas' friends in promoting his hard line stance at Frankfort, charged the Little Giant with the treachery, after which a "violent personal quarrel" ensued. Whatever happened, the breach between the two was clearly open and widening by January, 1860. Breckinridge was reticent, but Douglas hardly concealed his feelings, and freely told Toombs that Breckinridge was his last choice for the nomination. Indeed, to many he

10. Breckinridge to Robert J. Breckinridge, January 30, 1860, in B. MSS.

proclaimed a determination to prevent the convention from choosing the vice-president, even if it meant sacrificing his own pretensions by supporting Alexander H. Stephens of Georgia. However, in an obvious retort to Breckinridge's letter in 1858, Douglas did say that if the vice-president were nominated, *"rather than see a black Rep. elected he would vote for him."* [11] Consideration of the Illinoisian's determination, and the divisive consequences it could have at Charleston were uppermost among the reasons that Breckinridge decided not to seek the nomination. Indeed, he could see this division in Kentucky, where the state Democratic convention on January 9 and 10 was divided over whether to instruct its Charleston delegates for him or Douglas. As a compromise, it settled on Guthrie, whom Breckinridge had already resolved to support, while endorsing the vice-president's Frankfort declaration on the slavery question. If he had tried to secure the delegation to himself, the state would very likely have sent a divided group to Charleston. It was obvious that the determination of the Douglas men would cause the same thing in the nominating convention if Breckinridge tried to go before it. The whole situation he characterized as a "mess." [12]

As the vice-president resumed his duties in the Senate on January 16, 1860, not a few politicians felt much more optimistic about his chances at Charleston than he. Toombs, who seems to have favored Hunter for the nomination, found "decided indications" in the North that pointed toward Breckinridge. "Penn. is certainly for him as well as N. York *if she can carry him,*" he wrote Stephens. J. D. Hoover, confidant of Franklin Pierce, saw the same signs. "Breckinridge is unquestionably thought [of], for he can, in my opinion, get the Southern vote... Penn. is for him, and so will be New Jersey, and other scattering votes in the North, as against Douglas, I regard his chances as much the most certain. So thinks Douglas too." [13]

From the press, too, it was obvious that the vice-president commanded support, and not just in the South. The preponderance of advocacy for him in Pennsylvania was undeniable. "In Pennsylvania ... our fixed opinion is that there will be, virtually, no contest if Mr. Breckinridge be nominated,"

11. Robert Toombs to Alexander H. Stephens, January 11, 1860, in Phillips, *Correspondence*, 455; J. D. Hoover to Franklin Pierce, December 25, 1859, in Pierce MSS; Cincinnati *Commercial*, November 15, 1887.

12. Nichols, *Disruption*, 28; Heck, "Breckinridge in the Crisis," 319; Frankfort *Yeoman*, January 12, 1860; Lexington *Kentucky Statesman*, December 13, 1859; Breckinridge to S. L. M. Barlow, January 12, 1860, in S. L. M. Barlow MSS, HL.

13. *Congressional Globe*, 36th Cong., 1st Sess., Pt. 1, p. 447; Thompson, *Toombs*, 140; Toombs to Stephens, January 11, 1860, in Phillips, *Correspondence*, 455; Hoover to Pierce, December 25, 1859, in Pierce MSS.

wrote one editor. Yet another wrote that "the feeling in behalf of his nomination has reached the point of uncontrollable enthusiasm. . . . He is neither a bully nor a fire-eater. He detests fanaticism and [the] absurdities into which it has driven Seward Republicans." [14]

Now the Washington correspondent of the Cincinnati *Enquirer* even declared that Breckinridge was the favorite of the president, though by whose authority he made the statement, he did not say. There were appearances that Buchanan was softening toward his vice-president, and for some time he had been aware of the feeling in his home state for Breckinridge. However, at the moment the president actually leaned more toward Howell Cobb of Georgia as a nominee. Of course, he would support anyone who could beat Douglas, and this could include Breckinridge. With over three months to go before the convention assembled at Charleston, almost anything might happen and, despite his own views, Breckinridge certainly was not to be counted out. [15]

The vice-president passed those months eventfully. In the Senate the atmosphere grew intense as the convention approached, for with it rested the fate of the party, perhaps slavery, and the presidential aspirations of more than a dozen senators. It was no wonder tempers were hot. Harpers Ferry was discussed and rediscussed almost endlessly, often to the accompaniment of a tumult in the galleries, and the rapping of Breckinridge's gavel. The members campaigned for the nomination shamelessly on the floor, while their personal differences became increasingly violent. Senators were coming to the chamber with pistols in their pockets now, and Hammond of South Carolina could write of the northern and southern men that "No two nations on earth are or ever were more distinctly separate and hostile than we are here." Even Breckinridge could not avoid these calamities, and late in February he chanced to be nearby in Washington City when two Representatives, John Hickman, Republican of Pennsylvania, and Henry Edmundson, Democrat of Virginia, collided. Only his stepping in personally and separating them prevented violence. [16]

Except for witnessing the scenes in the chamber, and casting one more inconsequential vote on postponement of prior orders to take up a patent

14. Lexington *Kentucky Statesman*, December 27, 1859, January 6, 13, 16, 20, 27, February 10, 1860.

15. *Ibid.*, February 21, 1860; James Buchanan to John B. Floyd, August 5, 1859, in Philip G. Auchampaugh, *James Buchanan and His Cabinet on the Eve of Secession* (Boston, 1965), 57; Klein, *Buchanan*, 341.

16. *Congressional Globe*, 36th Cong., 1st Sess., Pt. 1, pp. 447, 480, 553; Nichols, *Disruption*, 286–87; Lexington *Kentucky Statesman*, February 28, 1860.

bill, Breckinridge's days in the Senate were not busy. He still did not get any favors out of Buchanan, however, and had to operate through his cabinet members. Buchanan was still using his vice-president as something of an official host to visiting dignitaries. In March it was Baron Salomon de Rothschild, young member of the Paris branch of the famous European banking family. The youth was introduced to Breckinridge by Sam Ward, powerful Democratic lobbyist, and thereafter the vice-president gave him a tour of the Capitol, showed him the two houses, the Supreme Court—which now met in the old Senate chamber—and introduced him around among the members. Rothschild met most of the presidential aspirants, and was duly impressed, but Breckinridge struck him particularly. "The . . . Vice President," he wrote back to France, "has all my sympathies. He is a young man, charming, full of fire, intelligent, and, what is rare, a perfect gentleman." [17]

But neither visitors nor Senate votes could compete with the coming Charleston convention. After March 15, when Georgia's state convention failed to instruct its delegates for Cobb, Buchanan began to look more favorably on Breckinridge, Guthrie, and Joseph Lane as potential candidates. Soon rumors flew that Breckinridge was his favorite. At the same time, Douglas' outspoken bitterness against the vice-president was actually winning Breckinridge favor. Some pundits now felt that Breckinridge, Jefferson Davis, Slidell, or Hunter, could beat Douglas in the North, and the feeling ran strong that the South should have the next nominee, Davis being perhaps first in line, and then Breckinridge. In Kentucky, despite the state party's official commitment to Guthrie, the elder statesman appeared to have few real friends, while the vice-president "is silently growing stronger every day, and every night, and every hour, and every moment." Some of his friends there now actually thought Douglas would be entirely out of the running at Charleston, believing that it would come down to a contest between the vice-president and Hunter. As early as March 13, Magoffin had resolved to go to the convention, though not as a member of the delegation, to work in Breckinridge's behalf "if it is thought advisable to enter him in the race." [18]

17. Lately Thomas, *Sam Ward, "King of the Lobby"* (Boston, 1965), 243; Salomon de Rothschild to Nathaniel Rothschild, March 30, 1860, in Jacob R. Marcus (ed.), *Memoirs of American Jews, 1775–1865* (Philadelphia, 1956), III, 81–82.

18. Klein, *Buchanan,* 341; Beriah Magoffin to John W. Stevenson, March 12, 1860, Thomas Stevenson to John W. Stevenson, April 13, 1860, in Stevenson MSS; J. G. Dickerson to Jefferson Davis, March 17, 1860, in Jefferson Davis MSS, LC; William H. Oldham to Hunter, March 16, 1860, Ambler, *Correspondence of . . . Hunter,* 302.

In the face of this apparent shift in public sentiment, the vice-president was forced to revise his thinking. Of course, he was committed not to stand in Guthrie's way; it would have been a violation of several pledges he had made and, equally important to him, a breach of the courtesy due to the older Kentuckian. Consequently, he instructed his two closest friends on the Kentucky delegation, Beck and Robert M. Johnson, to insist that all of his supporters from every delegation should stand behind Guthrie.[19] In addition, he placed the same charge on Powell, Magoffin, William Preston, and Henry Burnett, who would attend the convention in an unofficial capacity. He asked James B. Clay to go to Charleston as a favor, specifically to guard his name and interests. He allowed his friends no discretion in the matter, insisting that they stand for Guthrie through the entire convention.[20]

However, should Douglas prove to be weakening as rumor implied, and should the convention in general show a disinclination for Guthrie, then Breckinridge could expect to be a natural choice. Although it would be improper for Kentucky to make the initial move for him if this deadlock occurred, and Guthrie be withdrawn, there would be nothing wrong in presenting his name. Of course, this depended entirely upon how persistent Guthrie's managers might be in the face of adversity. This, or similar reasoning, was behind a dinner which Breckinridge gave for a portion of the Massachusetts delegation on April 16, less than a week before the delegates were to gather at Charleston. Pennsylvania was already friendly towards him, New York was a good possibility, and the addition of part of Massachusetts might form a northern bloc—admittedly small—which could

19. Beck, in the Louisville *Courier-Journal*, November 17, 1887, says:

I well recollect how earnestly he urged me to go to the Charleston Convention and insist that all his friends should cordially support Mr. Guthrie for the Presidency, and under no circumstances allow his name to come before the convention. and how earnestly he assured me the night after the final rupture of the party at Baltimore, that he would not accept a nomination which meant the disruption of the Democracy, and probably of the Union, and when he changed his mind so suddenly and I saw him the next night, he not only assured, but convinced me, that his acceptance was the only possible way of securing the withdrawal of both Judge Douglas and himself, and the nomination and probable election of Mr. Guthrie or Mr. Hunter, of Virginia.

William Preston, also at Charleston, says in the Louisville *Courier-Journal*, June 18, 1875, that Breckinridge "did not wish the nomination for the Presidency at Charleston, and urged his friends not to suffer his name to be presented." Robert M. Johnson says the same thing, Johnson to Stevenson, May 27, 1860, in Stevenson MSS.

20. Louisville *Courier-Journal*, June 18, 1875; William B. Hesseltine (ed.), *Three Against Lincoln: Murat Halstead Reports the Caucuses of 1860* (Baton Rouge, 1960), 30; James B. Clay to Susan M. Clay, April 13, 17, 1860, in Clay MSS.

thwart Douglas. As if to add silent, but impressive, weight to his bid for the Bay Staters, Breckinridge's master of ceremonies for the dinner was Slidell, himself a prominent candidate, and generally accepted as an administration spokesman. The implication that there was more power than met the eye behind the vice-president could not have been mistaken. Indeed, since even the rumors that Slidell would withdraw and support Breckinridge did not hit the press until April 23, he was still considered an aspirant, which gave added impact to his appearance at the dinner.[21]

The delegations began gathering at Charleston two days after Breckinridge's dinner. The Massachusetts men arrived three days later, long after machinations had already begun, even though the convention would not officially open until April 23. The Douglas men came in a large, tightly organized bloc that posed a greater threat than current rumor had indicated. Administration men, led by Slidell, immediately went to work to find someone, anyone, who could beat the Little Giant. Although Breckinridge was considered, his refusal to go before the convention as long as Guthrie's name was in nomination put a stop to any thoughts on Slidell's part, at least temporarily. Yet the support for the vice-president did materialize. On April 20 Toombs declared that Breckinridge could get Pennsylvania, and two days later another observer agreed. The Gulf states showed a good deal of interest in him, and one of the two delegations from New York—an anti-Douglas group which hoped to be admitted and given half of the state's vote in the balloting—could be cajoled or bought without too much effort, though Toombs thought that Breckinridge's character "is too good for them." A correspondent for the New York *Herald* found that the vice-president "has a host of friends, being personally very popular, and they feel confidant of success if he can but receive the nomination." [22]

No one got the nomination at Charleston. Despite the labors of Slidell and his henchmen, the Douglas men had a very slight majority and managed to control the rules and the platform, which simply reaffirmed Cincinnati, but conceded to the South the referral of the slavery question to the Supreme Court. This was basically a reaffirmation of his popular sovereignty tenet of 1854 and before, and was calculated to get southern votes

21. Lexington *Kentucky Statesman*, March 23, 1860; Milton, *Eve of Conflict*, 419; New York *Herald*. April 23, 1860.

22. Nichols, *Disruption*, 293–94; Toombs to Stephens, April 20, 1860, in Phillips, *Correspondence*, 467; Hesseltine, *Three Against Lincoln*, 16, 30; Lexington *Kentucky Statesman*, April 24, 1860.

by showing a willingness to accept a court ruling. The southern states would not accept him, however, and refused to take part in the final votes on platform planks. Instead, they discussed walking out of the convention, and finally six did, to set up their own convention. Some Douglas men viewed their withdrawal as a boon, since most of the delegates who left were opposed to him, but their elation soon turned more sober when the rest of the convention passed a ruling that a nominee would have to receive a vote totaling two-thirds of the original membership of 303, instead of a like proportion of the remaining 253. On May 1 the balloting began.[23]

It appears that Magoffin, Preston, Burnett, and Powell, unlike Clay, were not too exacting in fulfilling their promises to prevent Breckinridge's name from going before the convention. Indeed, they worked actively for him. Nevertheless, he was not mentioned as, on the first thirty-five ballots on May 1 and 2, Douglas led consistently with as many as 151½ votes, while the second-place Guthrie never went above 47½. On the twenty-fifth ballot, North Carolina began fidgeting with its 10 votes, wishing mightily to cast them for Breckinridge. Only the exertions of Robert Johnson, and perhaps Clay, prevented it from doing so as, during the next ten ballots, the state fluttered from one candidate to another. Then, on the thirty-sixth, when the lone remaining member of the Arkansas delegation rose and cast his vote for Breckinridge, Beck dutifully asked that it be withdrawn, explaining that Breckinridge did not desire that his name should be used in opposition to Guthrie's.[24]

Breckinridge and Guthrie's managers were each guilty of misjudgment. The vice-president, by his strict instructions to his representatives at Charleston, had made it impossible for his name to be used so long as Guthrie was in the race, yet by now it was obvious that Guthrie was no contender against Douglas. In spite of this, the elder Kentuckian's people apparently gave no thought to withdrawing him. If they had, then Kentucky, North Carolina, the delegate from Arkansas, the anti-Douglas Massachusetts men, the pro-Breckinridge Pennsylvanians who were spreading their votes among half a dozen other candidates, and a number of others would have been free to vote for Breckinridge. Also, with Guthrie withdrawn, most of the other votes that had been going for him would have switched to Breckinridge. Then there was Hunter, who actually believed that the southern and border state men had "an outside preference for

23. Nichols, *Disruption*, 296–309.
24. Hesseltine, *Three Against Lincoln*, 30, 103–104; Johnson to Stevenson, May 27, 1860, in Stevenson MSS.

Breckinridge." Lane felt warmly toward the vice-president, and the twelve to fourteen votes that he was receiving on each ballot might have gone over if there appeared to be a general movement toward the Kentuckian. Indeed, it is not reckless to suppose that—Guthrie withdrawn—Davis, Lane, Hunter, Daniel S. Dickinson, and perhaps even Andrew Johnson, would have been withdrawn in Breckinridge's favor. However, even if the shift to the vice-president began to look like the landslide that nominated him in 1856, and in its enthusiasm managed to carry away those members of un-committed delegations who were voting for Douglas, still the highest possible vote that Breckinridge could have received was 138, far short of the 202 needed, and only twenty-three ahead of the Little Giant. This was hardly enough to persuade Douglas to withdraw, especially since it would have left the vice-president the nominee. Even if the seceding delegations, already favorable to Breckinridge, came back and voted for him, he would have had only 188, and the Douglas men would probably have attempted to prevent the bolters from voting.[25]

In no way could Breckinridge have captured the Charleston nomination. He might have provided a rallying point as a compromise candidate for all of the dissident anti-Douglas delegates, thus presenting the Little Giant with a strong, united opposition, to show him that he was not, and could not be, the choice of the whole party. The result of even this would have been doubtful, but it is not inconceivable that it could have brought about the withdrawal of both in favor of a mutually agreed upon border state Union man, perhaps Hunter or Johnson.

In fact Breckinridge entertained some faint hopes of being nominated. On the evening of May 2, 1860, the second day of the balloting, he and Mary joined Hammond, Cobb, Milton Latham of California, W. W. Boyce of South Carolina, and Albert G. Brown of Mississippi, for dinner with Senator and Mrs. Gwin. As they were eating, the lobbyist Ward came into the room and handed Gwin the news that Douglas had withdrawn, and that Guthrie was only six votes short of a majority. Just where the false report came from is unknown. Gwin, disgusted, announced the news to the rest of the diners, who heard it with shocked silence. Latham believed that he could hear Mary's heart beating and the vice-president grew visibly pale. Now, considering the loyalty and steadfastness with which he had instructed his friends for Guthrie, this turning of the tables must have been hard to swallow. It was probably not until the next day that he found out

25. Charles Mason to Hunter, April 30, 1860, in Ambler, *Correspondence of . . . Hunter*, 312; Johnson to Stevenson, May 27, 1860, in Stevenson MSS.

that the Charleston convention, deadlocked after fifty-seven ballots, had in fact voted to adjourn and reassemble in Baltimore on June 18.[26]

Breckinridge was quite disturbed. "The proceedings at Charleston threaten great calamities," he wrote Clay, "unless there is wisdom and forbearance enough to redeem errors, at Baltimore." While he believed that his friends approved of his motives and conduct thus far, it was clearly time for him to reassess his position. Clay and others felt that only two courses of action lay before him: to leave his interests entirely in the hands of his representatives at Baltimore, unencumbered by the restrictions placed on them at Charleston; or to refuse the use of his name under any circumstances. They were divided in their feelings on his chances. Clay believed that Breckinridge could not be nominated without the cooperation of the Douglas men and saw some evidence that Guthrie's supporters would be as adamant as the Little Giant's in refusing to go over to Breckinridge. On the other hand, Robert Johnson saw decided indications throughout the South of favor for the vice-president, and was optimistic about the North. Breckinridge himself saw such indications. On May 5 he, Ward, Calhoun Benham of California, and others, joined Latham on what the latter called a "little bender." After a ride in the country they dined with Magoffin, Powell, and Alfred Gilmore, a Pennsylvania delegate to the Charleston convention. Magoffin and Powell reaffirmed that the entire Kentucky delegation was still for Breckinridge, and Gilmore intimated that the Keystone State wanted him as well.[27]

Everything depended on Breckinridge's attitude. By late May he made his decision. He would not interpose any further for Guthrie. However, out of fairness, he would ask that his friends not present his own name so long as Guthrie maintained the vote he had had at the adjournment in Charleston. This was the best he could do and remain true to the pledges he had made, and to his own conscience. He found in Washington City a desire among the Hunter men to unite the South on himself; Lane was vociferous in his declarations that Breckinridge should have the nomination; the crucial New York delegation was not unfriendly, though preferring native son Horatio Seymour; Stevenson had just spent two days in Philadelphia and found that Breckinridge was regarded as the strongest man in

26. Edgar Eugene Robinson (ed.), "The Day Journal of Milton S. Latham, January 1 to May 6, 1860." *Quarterly of the California Historical Society*, XI (March, 1932), 17; Hesseltine, *Three Against Lincoln*, 104–10.

27. Breckinridge to Clay, May 9, 1860, in Clay MSS; Clay to Stevenson, May 28, 1860, Johnson to Stevenson, May 27, 1860, in Stevenson MSS; Robinson, "Journal of Milton S. Latham," 18. The letters by Breckinridge and Clay are published in full in Melzer, "Mr. Breckinridge Accepts," 227.

the state; Connecticut and New Jersey were friendly; and it was obvious to everyone that Douglas had lost ground.[28]

Breckinridge agreed with Stevenson that if Pennsylvania, New Jersey, New York, or any two of the three, went for Guthrie, then Kentucky ought to stand by him. At the same time, the same two states, combined with the South, could give Breckinridge the nomination. If this appeared to be their preference, then Guthrie's friends "should not refuse to recognize the greater strength of another Kentuckian, if indeed it should exist and be distinctly developed." The vice-president clearly saw that Douglas was bitter toward him and would struggle to the death; he saw equally well that he himself was losing valuable support thanks to the general impression that Buchanan was behind him. "The President is not for me except as last necessity," he told Clay, "that is to say not untill [sic] his help will not be worth a d—n; meantime I suffer under the imputation of being his favorite." Under these circumstances, while Breckinridge believed that his chances were good if his name should get on the floor—he instructed Clay to buttonhole two or three members of the Kentucky delegation when, and if, the right time came—he was not optimistic over the prospects at Baltimore. "I have some hope, but no great confidence in the general result at Baltimore. If we can unite, *we will elect the nominees.*" [29]

Now, with more of a will, Breckinridge's followers began working for him, though still on a limited scale, and principally in Kentucky and the other border states, Tennessee, Missouri, and Maryland. The southern states already stood much on his side, and signs from the North were good. In Philadelphia, Benjamin Rush, namesake and grandson of one who had signed the Declaration with Witherspoon, wrote a week before the convention that "Mr. Breckinridge could carry *this state,* I firmly believe.... He has hosts of warm friends and admirers in Pennsylvania, and there would be a wide spread enthusiasm in his favor *among us,* the moment he were nominated, for which his high character, abilities and patriotism, and his early promise, would be an ample guaranty." Much the same news came from Connecticut, where it was reported that he "would carry this state without a doubt." [30]

28. Johnson to Stevenson, May 27, 1860, in Stevenson MSS; Breckinridge to Clay, May 31, 1860, Stevenson to Clay, June 1, 1860, in Clay MSS. With some transcription errors, the Breckinridge and Clay letters are published in full in Melzer, "Mr. Breckinridge Accepts," 228–29.

29. Breckinridge to Clay, May 31, 1860, in Clay MSS.

30. Johnson to Stevenson, May 27, 1860, Colin M. Ingersoll to Stevenson, June 4, 1860, in Stevenson MSS; Benjamin Rush to James M. Wayne, June 9, 1860, Rush to _____ (identified only as a close friend of Breckinridge), June 7, 1860, in James

In June the delegations reassembled in Baltimore. The night before the convention opened, Breckinridge dined with several other friends at Toombs's and, midway through dinner, heard John Cochrane, Democrat Congressman from New York, announced. The vice-president and his host left the table and joined Cochrane in the hall, where both asked about the prospects for the next day's proceedings. The New York delegate was favorably impressed with both the fervor and the cordiality with which they expressed their concern that the factions within the party might be reconciled, and that a candidate might be found who was acceptable to the whole party.

Several of the recalcitrant southern men, rather than take further part in the debacle, had resigned, and now their places were filled largely by Douglasites who had cleverly managed to be chosen after Charleston. From the first, it would be Douglas' convention in Baltimore, and as Caleb Cushing called the delegates to order in the Front Street Theater, the air was filled with apprehension over what the remaining supporters of other men would do. Another question was whether the Douglas majority would admit those southern delegations who sought to return. Eventually, the Little Giant's followers passed a majority report admitting the Charleston delegations from most of the southern states, excluding only Alabama and Louisiana as punishment for their withdrawal. When this report was promulgated on June 22, Virginia withdrew from the convention in protest, and once again a walkout was under way. Eventually it numbered 105 delegates from twenty-two states, including 16 from Massachusetts, 10 from Kentucky—Beck among them— and the full delegations of California, Oregon, Arkansas, Texas, Louisiana, Mississippi, and Alabama. Behind them they left Douglas in control of the Front Street meeting, and on June 23 it proceeded to give him 181½ votes for the nomination. That morning, now that it was too late, Guthrie had withdrawn. If he had done so a day earlier, Douglas might have been stopped, the walkout prevented by the knowledge that Breckinridge would definitely be in the race, and a compromise candidate found to hold the party together. This distinct possibility was obvious, especially since Douglas had actually authorized his manager, Richardson, to withdraw his name. Now, even though Douglas did not have a two-thirds majority of the original delegation—Breckinridge received 7½ votes on the second ballot—the convention declared him its nominee, and designated Benjamin Fitzpatrick as his running mate.[31]

Moore Wayne MSS, Georgia Historical Society, Savannah.
31. Nichols, *Disruption*, 314–19; Hesseltine, *Three Against Lincoln*, 241–50; John

Meanwhile, the seceders had not been idle. Gathering in the hall of the Maryland Institute, they quickly made Caleb Cushing their president, and adopted a platform not unlike the one at Cincinnati four years before. The principal difference was a resolution declaring the duty of the Federal government to "protect the rights of persons and property in the Territories, and wherever else its constitutional authority extends." Then came the time for nominations.[32]

Sometime before June 23, 1860, and probably before the gathering of delegates in Baltimore, a group of northern men led by Benjamin F. Butler of Massachusetts stopped in Washington City to consult with Breckinridge. Thinking him a viable candidate, they sought his views, and received from him a firm assurance of his desire to maintain party unity. He pledged his devotion to the Constitution and the Union, and firmly condemned the feeling in the South that the election of the Republican nominee—an old friend, Abraham Lincoln—would bring on the secession of those states from the Union. Thus fortified, Butler and other northerners now in the Maryland Institute meeting believed that a vote for Breckinridge would be a vote against secession, and this view was reflected in the speech of George Loring of Massachusetts when he arose and nominated Breckinridge for the presidency.[33]

Dickinson, Lane, and Davis, were also put in nomination, but at the end of the first ballot the vote stood divided only between Breckinridge, with eighty-one, and Dickinson, with twenty-four. The ovation that greeted Breckinridge's nomination indicated that he was the first choice of the convention, and in rapid succession the Dickinson votes changed over until John C. Breckinridge was declared the unanimous nominee. The friendly, unselfish Lane was made his running mate. Shortly thereafter, a meeting of southerners, in Richmond, who had left the Charleston convention and not shown up in Baltimore, ratified the Breckinridge and Lane ticket.[34]

When he received the news of his nomination—probably late on June 23—the vice-president was mortified. He had not wanted his name used at all in the seceders' convention, but control over that had passed from his

Cochrane, "The Charleston Convention," *Magazine of American History*, XIV (August, 1885), 150–51.

32. New York *Times*, July 19, 1860.

33. Benjamin F. Butler, *Autobiography and Personal Reminiscences of Major-General Benj. F. Butler: Butler's Book* (Boston, 1892), 144–46, 148; Hesseltine, *Three Against Lincoln*, 273. Butler's autobiography is not entirely trustworthy in many points, but it appears that he was telling the truth regarding this meeting with Breckinridge. Nichols, *Disruption*, 319, accepts the story as genuine.

34. Hesseltine, *Three Against Lincoln*, 273–74, 278.

hands now that Guthrie was out of the running. The instructions for discretion that he gave his friends on the Kentucky delegation worked against him, though Beck, fully cognizant of the ruinous possibilities of the Maryland Institute action, did not promote Breckinridge's name. Now it had placed him in the midst of perhaps the greatest dilemma he had yet faced. For him to accept the nomination would be to split the party hopelessly. It would ensure Lincoln's election, especially since yet another ticket was in the field, a "Constitutional Union" package made up of *status quo* northern Whigs and moderates who shut their eyes to the sectional issue and put forward John Bell of Tennessee and Edward Everett. In the face of a united Republican party, these three other tickets were self-defeating. On the other hand, refusal of the nomination was equally difficult. First, it would have been a betrayal of his promises to those representing him at Baltimore, who would not have taken kindly to his fickle response to their work in his behalf. Furthermore, he quite approved of the platform adopted at the institute, and it would be difficult to withdraw from a program he supported.[35]

He made up his mind quickly. The night after the nominations he assured Beck that he would not accept. It would split the party and most likely the Union.[36] But that same evening or the next day, something turned up that indicated the party might actually be kept intact if Breckinridge accepted. On Monday, June 25, Jefferson Davis invited him to his house for dinner at five o'clock. Significantly, the invitation was also extended to Cushing.[37] Toombs was probably present as well, and surely it was here that Davis made one of the few genuinely statesmanlike proposals of this troubled summer. With the opposition divided between three tickets, it was obvious to all that Lincoln was a sure bet in November. Davis now suggested that Breckinridge, Bell, and Douglas, all withdraw if someone else more generally acceptable to the whole Democratic party could be found. Thus the party could be united, success in November reasonably

35. *Ashland Speech*, 1.

36. Louisville *Courier-Journal*, November 17, 1887.

37. Davis to Caleb Cushing, June 25, 1860, in Cushing MSS. The dating of this episode at this time is based on the fact that this last week of June is the only time that Douglas, Bell, Breckinridge, and Davis were all in the same place at the same time. Since no written proposals survive, it must be surmised that Davis made his overtures in person. The fact that he, Breckinridge, Cushing, and Toombs were all together on the evening of June 25, 1860, makes it most likely that Davis here made his move on Breckinridge. This is confirmed by Beck's recollection that two nights after the nomination—June 25—Breckinridge had decided to accept in order to secure his own and Douglas' withdrawal (Louisville *Courier-Journal*, November 17, 1887).

assured, and the Union preserved. In 1875, six years before Davis first made public this proposal in 1881, the Louisville *Courier-Journal* flatly stated that Breckinridge was its author and that he suggested to Douglas that both withdraw in favor of Fitzpatrick. Breckinridge himself never claimed credit for the plan and, in the face of all the evidence, Davis was almost certainly its originator.[38]

Of course, Breckinridge could hardly withdraw what he had not yet accepted, but here Toombs took a hand. Trying to play on the vice-president's ambitions, he asserted that Breckinridge would carry the South like a storm, and that, if he accepted, Douglas would be forced into withdrawal within forty days.[39] Although unimpressed with the personal aspects of Toombs's argument, the vice-president saw some sense in this method of securing Douglas' withdrawal. Consequently, he decided to accept formally his own nomination, while pledging to Davis his withdrawal if Bell and Douglas should prove willing to go along. It is possible that Davis had already consulted Bell, but in any event he, too, agreed, leaving only Douglas. Since all three of the candidates were then in Washington City, Congress having adjourned that very afternoon, Davis could have his answers in a very short time.[40]

Their dinner completed, Breckinridge, Davis, and Toombs went to the Breckinridge home on I Street. Shortly they heard the sound of a brass band and a crowd of friendly marchers, as a procession moved up Pennsylvania Avenue, onto New Jersey, and finally gathered in front of the vice-president's house. After serenading him, they called for him to come out, and he did, with Davis and Toombs. Breckinridge spoke briefly, and the other two added some remarks. The vice-president expressed his personal regret over what had happened to the party and reaffirmed his own desire not to stand in the way of harmony, but added that he believed the Maryland Institute convention to be the expression of the true national party. Unwilling to admit the indecision and turmoil he felt, Breckinridge declared that he had made up his mind to accept almost immediately. Then, after outlining his platform and asserting that he and his supporters sought to lengthen and strengthen the Union instead of breaking it up, he closed

38. Davis, *Rise and Fall*. I, 52; Louisville *Courier-Journal*, May 18-19, 1875. Damon Wells. *Stephen Douglas: The Last Years, 1857–1861* (Austin, Tex., 1971), 246, questions that Davis—or anyone—ever made this proposal. However, the weight of the evidence here presented as the case relates to Breckinridge confirms Davis' account.
39. J. Henly Smith to Stephens, August 18, 1860, in Stephens MSS.
40. Davis, *Rise and Fall*, I, 52.

with words which scarcely concealed his inner feelings. "It sometimes [happens] that men are placed in a position where they are reluctant to act and expose themselves to censure, if not to execration they do not merit. But we must be prepared for such occurrences in this life. All men can move forward with dignity and purpose, to pursue that course." Without hatred or animosity, he said, he accepted the nomination.

One fact left little doubt that his acceptance was a strategem to bring about Douglas' withdrawal: This show of enthusiasm for Breckinridge was being held in front of the house on I Street, even though the inner walls of the house were still unplastered and unpapered. The vice-president had not yet moved in, and never would. But Douglas was in his house next door, and such a demonstration outside the Little Giant's very windows was calculated to impress on him Breckinridge's strength and the futility of his own candidacy in a split party.[41]

Later that evening Beck called again, baffled by Breckinridge's sudden change from his resolve of the night before. The vice-president, said Beck, "not only assured, but convinced me, that his acceptance was the only possible way of securing the withdrawal of both Judge Douglas and himself, and the nomination and probable election of Mr. Guthrie or Mr. Hunter, of Virginia." [42] Now Toombs and Davis went to work to effect this result. The Georgian struck first. With some administration help, he began trying to convince Fitzpatrick that accepting his own nomination would be suicide; on the other hand, if he should decline, Douglas would be forced to follow suit. This would open the way for Breckinridge and Lane to withdraw also, and then a new choice could be made. Toombs unscrupulously assured Fitzpatrick that he would be that new man. Toombs's motives are not easy to discern. In his conversation with Breckinridge, he declared his intention to leave the vice-president a clear field. In talking with Fitzpatrick, however, he spoke of Breckinridge withdrawing. Yet these two conversations surely occurred either on the same day or within a very few days of each other. It was also suspected that he had actually conspired to bring about the rupture at Baltimore. In four months he would be standing at the forefront of the Georgia secessionists, and this may explain the cross-purposes toward which he worked this week.[43]

41. Washington *Daily National Intelligencer*, July 25, 1860; Washington *Constitution*, June 27, 1860; *Lives of the Present Candidates for President and Vice-President of the U.S.* (Cincinnati, 1860), 122–24; Hal H. Smith, "Historic Washington Homes," *Records of the Columbia Historical Society, Washington, D.C.*, XI (1908), 263.

42. Louisville *Courier-Journal*, November 17, 1887.

43. Smith to Stephens, August 18, 1860, Stephens MSS; Nichols, *Disruption*, 318, 334–35. Toombs's biographer, William Y. Thompson, is disappointingly silent on all aspects of Toombs's role in the affairs of the week after the Baltimore split.

Fitzpatrick withdrew, but Douglas refused to cooperate. Instead, his national committee promptly selected Herschel V. Johnson of Georgia to replace him, and then, to Davis' proposition that the Little Giant withdraw in favor of a compromise candidate, Douglas turned a deaf ear. No one could replace him in the eyes of northern Democrats, he said. His supporters would go over to Lincoln if he withdrew. In fact, while they would hardly accept Breckinridge, his backers—Douglas withdrawn—would almost certainly have accepted a compromise nominee before turning to the Republican. It was a weak argument.[44]

Now Breckinridge had to face the full consequences of his situation. Instead of one unified Democratic ticket, there would be three—though unsuccessful attempts at fusion would continue. He, as well as everyone else, could plainly see that he was bound for the first defeat of his career. It was also obvious that from the bitterness that had so far characterized the campaign, he would be the recipient of assaults upon his personal and political character, perhaps unparalleled. His eyes were open; he knew what was coming. The fatalistic resignation that he hinted at in his brief address in front of his house now became pronounced, and would remain so. To a friend in Pennsylvania he lamented on June 28 that "My course has been surrounded by difficulties for which I am wholly blameless. We must each pursue what seems to be the path of duty." Two days later, surely in the knowledge that Douglas had refused Davis' proposition, he was even more resigned. "I fear there is nothing left but a square fight," he wrote. "I deeply regret the state of things, but shall do my duty quietly & firmly." It was soon rumored that Breckinridge felt he had been lied to and cheated, probably a reference to Toombs's influence on his acceptance, but he did not complain publicly. Sometime during this terrible week in June, Mrs. Jefferson Davis heard him say: "I trust I have the courage to lead a forlorn hope."[45]

44. Davis, *Rise and Fall*, I, 52; Stephen Douglas to Charles Lanphier, July 5, 1860, in Johannsen, *Letters*, 408. Douglas was clearly deluded about his exclusive claim to the loyalty of northern Democrats. In 1864 the much less popular George B. McClellan polled 500,000 more presidential votes than did Douglas, and his vote came solely from the North whereas one-third of Douglas' came from the South.

45. Breckinridge to G. Nelson Smith, June 28, 1860, in JCB Papers; Breckinridge to Barlow, June 30, 1860, in Barlow MSS; Smith to Stephens, August 18, 1860, in Stephens MSS; Varina H. [Mrs. Jefferson] Davis, *Jefferson Davis, Ex-President of the Confederate States of America: A Memoir by His Wife* (New York, 1890), I, 685.

CHAPTER 12

Pour On, I Can Endure

So Breckinridge must run for president. Until November the rumors would fly as to why he had been nominated. The defensive South maintained that it was because he was the true representative of national interests—as they interpreted those interests; the Douglas men saw in it the culmination of the administration campaign to kill the Little Giant; staunch Union men, and not just Republicans, found in the southern walkout at Charleston and Baltimore, and the vice-president's nomination, a deliberate conspiracy led by William L. Yancey of Alabama and his South Carolina cohorts to split the party, ensure Lincoln's election, and thereby provide the shaky reason for secession and a new southern confederacy. Breckinridge himself, whatever his disappointment with his nomination, believed that his designation by the southern ultras was a sign that they were abandoning any designs at disunion, and were willing to take their chances within the framework of the existing government. He reasoned, and his Uncle Robert and scores of other friends agreed, that true secessionists would hardly be fools enough to give their nomination to a man whose devotion to the Union was as sincere and widely known as his.[1]

The reactions to Breckinridge's nomination and acceptance were as varied as the shades of political opinion in 1860. Among his firm supporters like Senator James A. Bayard of Delaware, or old General Butler, there was, as with most southern Democrats, unrestrained glee at this "regular" nomination. Others who would support it were less enthusiastic, and these included two former presidents, John Tyler and Franklin Pierce. Tyler, whose convictions were more in line with Bell's candidacy, was somewhat

1. For a full examination of the motives charged to Breckinridge's nomination, see Crenshaw, *Slave States*. For his own beliefs on his nomination's relation to the Union feeling of his supporters, see "Rev. R. J. Breckinridge on the Political Crisis, Louisville, Kentucky, 1860," clipping in B. MSS, and Robert J. Breckinridge, "The Civil War, Its Nature and End," Danville *Quarterly Review*, I (December, 1861), 653.

uncomfortable being in the company of the ultras of the South who backed Breckinridge, but saw in him the only chance of denying Lincoln an electoral victory, and perhaps throwing the election into the House. Pierce, who felt that neither Democratic ticket was really regular, expressed the hope that Democrats would unite on Breckinridge. Among the Douglas men, of course, Breckinridge did not meet with much approval. One, Charles Buford, who was a friend of Breckinridge's, wrote before hearing of his acceptance that "He has too much sense and prudence, to suffer himself to be used by a desperate faction, to defeat the regular nominee of his party. Such an act would be suicidal in Mr. B." Douglas' good friend Stephens of Georgia felt the same way, though he believed that his favorite's nomination against Breckinridge would make possible the election of the Kentuckian by throwing the contest into the House of Representatives. Forney, now behind the Little Giant even though the Republican party was looking more and more attractive to him, saw Breckinridge's candidacy at the head of what he termed "the extremists" as a singular thing, "a curious sequel in a life which opened in 1851 in Congress in avowed sympathy with the anti-slavery idea." Another old friend, Abraham Lincoln of Illinois, saw in Breckinridge's nomination a near guarantee that he, a Republican, would be the sixteenth president of the United States. Among Breckinridge's backers, the sensible, party-minded men, there was little said. They despaired for the Democrats and the election. Giving up hope for 1860, sixteen of those who had supported Breckinridge at the Maryland Institute, including Butler and James Whitney of Massachusetts, gathered at the Winthrop House in Washington City, where they made plans to reconvene in December, reorganize the party, and begin laying plans for Breckinridge for 1864.[2]

2. James A. Bayard to Thomas F. Bayard, June 24, 1860, in Thomas F. Bayard MSS, LC; Edmund Ruffin Diary, June 24, 1860, in LC; Charles I. duPont to George Fisher, May 20, 1861, quoted in Leon de Valinger, Delaware Public Archives Commission, Dover, to the author, November 30, 1967; Robert Seager, *And Tyler too: A Biography of John and Julia Gardiner Tyler* (New York, 1963), 441; Franklin Pierce to B. F. Hallett, June 29, 1860, in Pierce MSS; Nichols, *Pierce*, 512–13; Charles Buford to "Charles," June 25, 1860, in Buford MSS; Alexander H. Stephens to J. Henly Smith, July 4, 1860, in Phillips, *Correspondence*, 470; U.S. War Department, *War of the Rebellion: Official Records of the Union and Confederate Armies* (Washington, 1880–1901), Ser. II, Vol. II, 606, hereinafter cited as *O.R.*; Forney, *Anecdotes*, I, 325; Abraham Lincoln to Anson G. Henry, July 4, 1860, in Roy P. Basler (ed.), *The Collected Works of Abraham Lincoln* (New Brunswick, N.J., 1953), IV, 82; James Whitney to Benjamin F. Butler, June 28, 1860, in Butler MSS; Butler to William Schauler, July 10, 1870, in Benjamin F. Butler, *Private and Official Correspondence of Gen. Benjamin F. Butler* (Norwood, Mass., 1917), I, 7.

Few gave much thought to what the "forlorn hope" would do to Breck-inridge personally. Of course, Buford expressed some concern. G. Nelson Smith of Pennsylvania, who had remained in the Douglas convention at Baltimore, implored him not to accept "the nomination of the Seceders' convention, it will be fatal to the party and ruinous to you. I beseech you to consider well the step you are about to take. Evil will most assuredly follow acceptance." But now the step had been taken; the evil had a clear track ahead of it. There were a few who genuinely felt for the vice-president and what lay in store for him. James L. Petigru, one of South Carolina's outspoken Union men, said with sorrow that "Mr. Breckinridge is likely to fill a place among the folks that are remembered as examples of the sport of fortune. The split in the Democratic party comes in the nick of time to mar all his hopes. His friends, who endorse his own declarations of his devotions to the Union, say that it is impossible for him to bear the load of South Carolina's friendship with Yancey upon it." [3]

Breckinridge had little time for self-pity now, for in the three weeks between his nomination and his departure for Lexington there was much work to be done. Unlike Douglas, who had had an active organization working for some time, the vice-president had little or nothing. He must start from the beginning, and start fast. On July 1, 1860, he made an appointment with his friend Isaac I. Stevens of Washington Territory, and both Stevens and Cushing called. There they placed matters of organization in Cushing's hands, and he promptly selected a sixteen-man Democratic National Executive Committee, of which Stevens would be chairman. It is also probable that at this meeting were laid the preliminary plans for a series of twenty or more "Breckinridge and Lane Campaign Documents," primarily to be speeches and essays in defense of the platform and the regularity of the nomination. Two early concerns would be Breckinridge's formal letter of acceptance, and an address outlining the reasons for the Baltimore rupture and defending the nominations. Beyond that, there must be campaign biographies; the portion of the northern press that was friendly must be cultivated, state organizations needed to be set up, youth groups should be created, and the old Breckinridge clubs of 1856 reactivated and speakers engaged to spread the word. [4]

Breckinridge took a hand in much of this, but his very first concern was

3. G. Nelson Smith to Breckinridge, June 26, 1860, in JCB Papers; James P. Carson, *Life, Letters and Speeches of James Louis Petigru, the Union Man of South Carolina* (Washington, 1920), 356.

4. Isaac I. Stevens to Caleb Cushing, July 1, 1860, in Cushing MSS; Nichols, *Disruption*, 337–40.

with his letter of acceptance. Unlike his conduct of the campaign four years before, he intended to act as a candidate should, making no speeches, writing no letters, in no way publicly promoting his cause. Since it was likely to be his only public expression of the canvass, this one letter of acceptance was all the more important. He worked on it for several days and did the actual composition in three separate sessions, dictating to a different secretary each time. Since it would be extensively published, there should be no mistakes in its transcription by the press, and for this his own handwriting was out of the question. On July 6 it was completed and ready for his signature.[5]

He wrote moderately of the rights of property in the territories, reasserting his Frankfort statement that there was no need for a slave code, and then addressed himself to the question of union and disunion. There was, he felt, not a taint of sectionalism in the platform he stood on. It simply upheld the equality of the states and nothing was better calculated to preserve the Union. "The Constitution and the equality of the states!" he concluded. "These are the symbols of everlasting union. Let these be the rallying cries of the people." [6]

For Breckinridge, who did not consider himself an exceptional letter writer, it was an excellent production, lucid, concise, and, within the frame of reference of the Democratic Breckinridge, logical. Judge George W. Woodward, a lawyer of national repute, and an unsuccessful appointee of Polk's to the Supreme Court, regarded Breckinridge's letter as the best exposition in short compass of the conservative position on the territories that he ever saw.[7] Even the Republican New York *Times* characterized the letter as able, distinct, and clear, in its positions, and credited Breckinridge with the disinterest and lack of ambition for this nomination which he professed. "Indeed," it said, "his conduct challenges a certain degree of admiration from the spirit of self-sacrifice which it indicates." [8]

Part of the letter reflected the principal charge which the vice-president's opponents would lay at his door in the coming months, that of disunion. The fact that his leading backers were ultras like Yancey, Toombs, Davis, Louis T. Wigfall of Texas, and a host of other proponents of southern nationalism, and even separation, made it easy to assume that Breckinridge, too, was a secessionist. The knowledge that he was not hardly deterred his

5. Breckinridge to Cushing, July 6, 1860, in Cushing MSS.
6. *Ibid.*
7. John C. Breckinridge Diary, September 21–26, 1867, in Prewitt Collection.
8. New York *Times*, July 11, 1860.

opponents from making capital on his associations. His reply to the charge was now and would be for the remainder of the campaign, disappointing. He stated it succinctly when he wrote to a friend, "Whatever may be done by individuals or in particular states, we cannot ... be responsible for. ... The cry that we are disunionists is a bald absurdity. It cannot affect reflecting men. We are the true union men. We stand for the Union on the principles of the Constitution, and this canvass will explode many loose ideas, and beget much sober thought upon the character of our political system."

It is indeed unfortunate that, from the outset, Breckinridge did not repudiate the support of at least the more outspoken secessionists like Yancey. Of course, his political makeup and his very character made it impossible for him to do this. The San Antonio *Alamo Express* summed up the situation when it said: "Mr. Breckinridge claims that he isn't a disunionist. An animal not willing to pass for a pig shouldn't stay in the stye [*sic*]." [9]

Although both Breckinridge and Douglas seemed bound for a political burial, another possibility was proposed now for the preservation of the party and the defeat of Lincoln. At the same time that Davis was trying to bring about their mutual withdrawal, others began trying to work out a fusion arrangement whereby a Breckinridge ticket would be run in those states where he could command the most support, and a Douglas ticket would be run in states where he was strongest. When this was found impractical, it was then proposed that the two Democrats, plus Bell, be fused on one ticket in the key northern states of New York, Pennsylvania, New Jersey, and perhaps one or two others, and that the states would then cast their electoral vote for the candidate who was revealed in November to have the best chance of beating Lincoln. To everyone's dismay, Douglas refused this, too, and his national committee issued a manifesto that repudiated fusion in any form. "Let the war of the Democratic factions go on," it declared. "The country will be benefitted by it." Despite this irresponsible stand, fusion did come about in a few states, though with it there also came separate, irregular electoral tickets precommitted to Douglas. Still Breckinridge felt that he must have some sort of ticket in these northern states. "We must be represented in any case," he told S. L. M. Barlow. "Every thing must not be yielded. I fear that the friends of Mr. D despairing of success are striking for the organization." [10]

9. Breckinridge to E. Griswold, July 4, 1860, in John C. Breckinridge File, Compiled Service Record, RG 109, NA; Donald E. Reynolds, *Editors Make War: Southern Newspapers in the Secession Crisis* (Nashville, 1970), 86.

10. Nichols, *Disruption*, 341–43; Fite, *Campaign of 1860*, 223; Cleveland *Leader*, July

While everything else seemed to be going sour, at least Breckinridge's national committee operated smoothly, largely under his guidance. At last, after much prodding from Breckinridge, Cushing and Stevens issued the address on the conventions, and thereafter the "Breckinridge and Lane Campaign Documents" came out regularly. They included the Frankfort speech, as well as the vice-president's address on the removal of the Senate to the new chamber, the latter surely to help counteract the disunion charges. Since campaign biographies were needed, the committee hired two writers to prepare them, one to do Breckinridge and the other Lane. The vice-president objected strongly to the profile of himself, declaring that if it were published, it would bring ridicule down upon him. Breckinridge rejected it out of hand, and turned the assignment over to John S. Edwards, who had written the Lane biography. The result, while laudatory, was a rather complete sketch of which the candidate approved. Of course, the sheet-music mongers, who with a polka or quickstep managed to turn a few dollars on every public triumph or calamity, promptly issued the "Breckinridge Schottische," a melody whose unwieldy complexity mirrored the complications of the campaign that sired it.[11]

Finally, after this hectic three weeks spent creating an organization and a movement out of nothing, Breckinridge was ready to go home. He would take with him the greatest burden he had ever borne, and the gnawing uncertainty of a future, which, though he was not wholly blameless for its direction, was almost entirely out of his control.[12]

He made speeches on his return trip, all with a similarity of composition that indicated Breckinridge probably expected to be asked to speak. Indeed, he was probably glad of the opportunity, for responding to spontaneous calls would be the only way he could speak out, without breaking the decorum of silence which he had officially assumed. The speeches themselves were mild, fulsome in their praise of the Union and the Constitution, and largely outgrowths of his acceptance letter. Breckinridge refused to defend in detail his nomination and acceptance, saying only, "To those who take advantage of the position of a silent man, to heap upon him execrations, I say, pour on, I can endure." As for the charges of disunion, he

---

12, 1860; New York *Herald*, June 29, 30, 1860; Breckinridge to S. L. M. Barlow, July 12, 1860, in Barlow MSS.

11. Stevens to Cushing, July 7, 1860, Breckinridge to Cushing, n.d. [July 1860], in Cushing MSS; *Speech of President Buchanan on the Evening of Monday, July 2, 1860* (Washington, 1860), 8; John S. Edwards to Breckinridge, February 28, 1874, in JCB Papers; "Breckinridge Schottische," copy in author's possession.

12. *Congressional Globe*, 36th Cong., 1st Sess., Pt. 4, p. 3297.

was equally evasive. "I am an American citizen—a Kentuckian who never did an act or cherished a thought that was not full of devotion to the Constitution and the Union." But, he warned, if the Constitution were violated for the sake of party policy—excluding property in slaves from the territories by congressional sanction of territorial edict—then the Union ceased to be the government that the Founding Fathers had passed down to them. This did not mean secession, but what it did mean was that certain states would be discriminated against. He did not have to say that secession would follow. He was only warning, not advocating.[13]

These "impromptu" speeches were widely criticized as electioneering appeals, especially by the opposition in Kentucky. Although speaking only in general terms, he had never before seemed quite so militantly conservative. It was well known in the state that his real sympathies were with the Union and gradual emancipation. "His prejudices and his own judgment are averse to the teachings and tendencies of the Yancey school," wrote one critic. "He is conscious whither he is drifting, and he would, if he could, resist the fatal tide. But, from want of decision, the Yanceyites have bound him hand and foot, and he manifestly feels it." This same criticism was in large part voiced by one of the Yanceyites, Albert G. Brown. "If he has a fault as a statesman," Brown wrote of Breckinridge, "it is in being too cautious. Prudence is a virtue, but too much is a fault." Of course, the nominee could not be faulted for his acceptance of his nomination; it was an act of genuine, unselfish statesmanship, for the good of the party and the Union. However, once it became clear that he would be forced to see the canvass through largely as the candidate of the outspoken opponents—by now almost enemies—of that Union, the indecision, the caution, took hold. He did not want this nomination, this campaign, and he said so repeatedly. But neither would he now decline it, once accepted; nor would he sweep the rotten secession apples from among his following. With a social, psychological, and political revolution going on all about him, Breckinridge could not be a revolutionary. An acceptance was a pledge; a trust accepted, even from disunionists, was a trust to be honored; and the loyalty and support received from friends, whatever their political stripe, could not be met with anything less than a full return. The very manly qualities which made him so engaging, so admirable, personally, now conspired against him. He was backed by men whose political views had once been the same as his, but which had now gone beyond him by far. As their can-

13. New York *Times*, July 17, 23, 25, 26, 1860; Washington *Daily National Intelligencer*, July 21, 1860; Lexington *Kentucky Statesman*, July 20, 1860.

didate, he would have to give voice to their beliefs, or stay quiet. He preferred silence.[14]

The vice-president announced at Frankfort that he did not intend to speak again during the canvass, and thereafter he set out to live up to his promise. He took up residence in Lexington at the Phoenix Hotel. Through the next seven weeks of the campaign he ran like a dry stream, wishing not to speak out, waiting to accept defeat manfully. His course was assailed from all sides. Linn Boyd's widow accused him of being "all ruffles and no shirt." He was called a coward, a "mountebank." He was charged with sympathy for John Brown, with being an emancipationist, of having been a Know-Nothing, of supporting Taylor in 1848, and with abandoning the position that he had held with Douglas in 1854 and 1856 on the territorial question. Breckinridge had said "pour on," and they did. There was even personal ridicule. "The subject of our story was born on the day of his birth, on the Cincinnati platform," wrote one wit, "and is chiefly noted for his eloquent silence on all public occasions. . . . Being of a fiery disposition, the Breckinridge coal was appropriately named after him; and it is a question with us whether he is the more noted as a duelist or a fuelist. We can say little more of him than he was born of Southern, but honest parents, and has acquired some fame as an artillerist by his management of the celebrated Buchanan, which will be discharged on the 4th of March next."[15]

Through all of it, regardless of what he felt inside, Breckinridge managed to maintain the same affability, the same humor, that always characterized his manner. But humor was not enough. As the weeks wore on, the vice-president became more and more restive under the weight of a score of pressures. For one thing, the administration was operating with a heavy hand in his favor, and it was costing him. Buchanan, Holt, Black, and others all received many solicitations to use the patronage in Breckinridge's behalf, and they gave in. Buchanan, who was concentrating chiefly on winning Pennsylvania for him, began removing officeholders who favored Douglas. In public he denied it, of course, but men in Tennessee, Massachusetts, Vermont, Indiana, Ohio, and New York lost their jobs and were replaced by Breckinridge men.[16]

14. New York *Times*, July 26, 1860; James B. Ranck, *Albert Gallatin Brown* (New York, 1937), 194.

15. Milton, *Eve of Conflict*, 495; Richmond *Examiner*, August 7, 10, 1860; Crenshaw, *Slave States*, 25–26; Lexington *Kentucky Statesman*, July 21, August 10, 1860; Cleveland *Weekly Plain Dealer*, August 1, 1860.

16. Klein, *Buchanan*, 351; Fite, *Campaign of 1860*, 224–25; Nichols, *Disruption*, 339–40; Breckinridge Committee to Joseph Holt, September 17, 1860, in Breckinridge

On top of this, the Bell and Everett men in Kentucky and the border states were turning their fire increasingly upon Breckinridge, forming a silent partnership with Douglasites in many parts of the Bluegrass. Their campaign, heralded appropriately by crowds of young men ringing bells, hurled the secession charge at Breckinridge unceasingly, unmercifully. In Kentucky alone, their gains were alarming. Revill had died in late June, and the Frankfort convention the next month had nominated an unknown Democrat named Clinton McClarty. To oppose him, the Bell men nominated his old rival Combs. The Douglasites in the state, who had been denied much say in the Frankfort deliberations, turned the lion's share of their support over to Combs, and a hard race was on. It was a minor office, which an August election would fill, but it was recognized throughout the nation as a test of Breckinridge's strength in his own bailiwick.[17]

Combs and Breckinridge, despite their hard fought battle in 1851, had remained close friends. They had enjoyed each other's humor and jest, and dined together not infrequently. One time at the board Breckinridge remarked to his companion: "Leslie, you have done more for your party and received less from it than any man I know of." "Yes, John," replied Combs, "and you have done less and received more from your party than any man I know of." The joke was on Breckinridge and he laughed along with it, but the laughter now no longer rang true. The campaign for clerk was a short one, and through it all Breckinridge had a hard time making his friends realize the significance it held outside the state. As a result, he told Stevens on the eve of the election that "many democrats hundreds, my devoted friends, cannot be pulled from Combs, while hundreds of opposition men who are for B & L will vote for C." What made it all the worse was that Guthrie gave the vice-president almost no help and even used his influence against him. "This is shamefull [sic]," wrote Breckinridge, "for he well knows that I would have supported him with zeal." [18]

He continued to appear optimistic, saying that a defeat would not alarm him unless it was by six or eight thousand votes. In a painful surprise on August 6 Combs carried the state by over twenty-three thousand, a brutal demonstration of what the disunion accusations, coupled with the backing

MSS, NYHS; J. Hooper to Jeremiah S. Black, July 9, 1860, Hiram Perry to Black, September 1860, in Black MSS.

17. Crenshaw, *Slave States*, 134–37; Lexington *Kentucky Statesman*, July 20, August 3, 10, 1860; Heck, "Breckinridge in the Crisis," 325–26.

18. Lexington *Herald*, October 8, 1911; Breckinridge to Stevens, August 3, 1860, in Isaac I. Stevens MSS, University of Washington Library, Seattle.

of the Yanceyites, had done to Breckinridge's standing in his home state. His friends throughout the country were mortified. Buchanan dug his heels deeper into Pennsylvania; Yancey began plans for a northern tour to show Free-State people that a southern man didn't have horns and a tail; and Breckinridge's close friends in Kentucky searched for a solution to their problems. Now it was even rumored, primarily among the Douglas men, that the vice-president would withdraw from the canvass. Instead, perhaps at his own suggestion, his Kentucky friends found their answer. They would ask him to come out of his retirement and address them and the country in answer to the calumnies heaped upon him. Surely it would not be undecorous for a candidate simply to defend himself.[19]

A formal invitation was addressed to him, and just as formally he accepted. He made it quite clear that his speech would be only a defense. "I feel that it would be unjust to my principles, my friends, and myself, to remain longer in silence beneath this torrent of defamation." Once his acceptance was known—and it was widely published throughout the Union—James B. Clay offered the use of his father's estate, Ashland, for a grand barbecue on the occasion of the address. The offer was taken up, and September 5 was set for one of the most important, and in some degrees the most disappointing speeches of Breckinridge's career.[20]

A crowd estimated at between eight and fifteen thousand gathered in the warm sunshine at Ashland to hear him speak. Breckinridge was not well, but he took the stand and held it for three hours, the longest speech of his life.[21] He started out by denying a string of charges against him, all of which were, in whole or in part, untrue. He had been charged by George Robertson and other Bell men with not being a slaveholder. This was a sore point, for, as the candidate of the slave states, it would not be seemly to be an employer of free labor. The fact was that he did not own any, or at least he was not paying taxes on any, and the fact that he no longer owned a home in Lexington makes it likely that he only hired domestic blacks. Since this was a personal matter, he indignantly avoided the issue by saying that he would "not merit the contempt of this audience, by

19. Breckinridge to Stevens, August 3, 1860, in Stevens MSS; Smith to Stephens, August 18, 1860, C. P. Cilver to Stephens, August 18, 1860, in Stephens MSS; Breckinridge to Clay and others, August 21, 1860, in New York *Times*, August 28, 1860.

20. New York *Times*, August 28, 1860; Lexington *Kentucky Statesman*, August 24, 1860.

21. James B. Beck and others to Cushing, August 1860, in Cushing MSS; Committee of Invitation to Pierce, August 25, 1860, in Pierce MSS; Lexington *Kentucky Statesman*, September 4, 7, 1860.

entering into details in regard to my private affairs." He was rewarded by a voice in the crowd: "That is manly." [22]

Breckinridge then began on one of the main objects of his speech, the denial that he and his portion of the party had abandoned the position they held in 1854 and 1856 on slavery in the territories. This first required him once more to define just what he had said in the celebrated Tippecanoe speech, especially since Douglas himself was now misrepresenting the views he had expressed. The Little Giant was claiming on the stump that Breckinridge had admitted the doctrine of "squatter sovereignty," wherein the people of a territory could accept or abolish slavery "just as a State would." Breckinridge had actually advocated nonintervention, the mode by which neither Congress nor its creature the territorial legislature could interfere with slavery one way or the other until the territory's application for statehood, at which time the people could decide the matter. The shade of difference between the two doctrines was elusive, but already it had split the most powerful political party the nation had ever known.[23]

Breckinridge explained that groups representing two sides of the question appeared during the Kansas-Nebraska legislation and that both had agreed to submit the question to the Supreme Court. With Dred Scott, the court had made its decision, and now the vice-president was more than ready to abide by it. He demonstrated effectively, if a little smugly, that he had been consistent, literally so. He attempted to show—inconclusively—that it was Douglas who was inconsistent.

This done, the speaker went on to his final, and most important, topic, disunion. His voice was giving him trouble and he was feeling the strains of extended speaking, but he continued. He cited several persons who had made charges against him, among them Crittenden who, absolving Breckinridge of being personally a disunionist, avowed that he was supported by disunionists, and should be regarded and judged accordingly. Here Breckinridge devoted his remaining energies to a lengthy, profuse, yet somehow unimpressive, defense.

A Kentucky audience did not require his denial. Yet he made it, and backed it up with a treatise of Lane's character; the fact that their platform was based largely upon the words of the Constitution and the Su-

22. L. R. Glass to Williams and others, August 20, 1860, in New York *Times*, September 7, 1860. *Ashland Speech* has been the source for this account of the September 5 address.

23. Crenshaw, *Slave States*, 25–26, agrees that Breckinridge was not inconsistent in his position on nonintervention.

preme Court, and that the candidates for governor during the last canvass, as well as those for the legislature, had endorsed the doctrine of congressional protection; he pointed out that a majority in the Senate and two-thirds of the party men in the House approved of the doctrine. It was his old argument that might makes right. Breckinridge, like most southerners now, was perfectly willing to abide by the will of the majority when it agreed with him. This, however, was a false majority, for the opinion in the nation as a whole was against his posture. Knowing it, he was being forced deeper into the states' rights dogma, where lay protection from an unfavorable majority. Breckinridge chose to accept the will of the men the people had elected to represent them, rather than the will of the people themselves.

Finally, in a last burst of eloquence, in a speech notable for its style, Breckinridge replied to a voice in the audience that cried out "The truth will prevail" in response to his declaration of principles: "Yes, the truth will prevail. You may smother it for a time beneath the passions and prejudices of men, but those passions and prejudices will subside; and the truth will reappear as the rock reappears above the receding tide. I believe this country will yet walk by the light of these principles. Bright and fixed, as the rock-built lighthouse in the stormy sea, they will abide, a perpetual beacon, to attract the political mariner to the harbor of the Constitution."

The address won great applause, and wide praise, but it was, nevertheless, a disappointment. Breckinridge said nothing that he had not said before, and he left too many questions unanswered. For one thing, he did not touch at all on a major issue, the relative claims to regularity of the two Democratic tickets. In fact, according to party custom prior to Charleston, both Douglas and Breckinridge were regularly nominated, for it had been the rule that a two-thirds majority of the delegates present could make a nomination. At Charleston, however, the administration forces had passed their resolution that a nomination required the same proportion of all delegates, whether they were all present or not. Under this ruling, neither of the two Baltimore nominees was regular.[24]

Unfortunately, Breckinridge had also given in, though moderately, to the emotionalism of the campaign and to the fervent fear of plots of all kinds. Of course, he had been accused of plotting for some time, even to the point of being charged with membership in the Knights of the Golden Circle, a secret society of militaristic disunion sentiments. In return, he found it easy to believe Douglas guilty of plotting against the party, and

24. Fite, *Campaign of 1860*, 112.

the Republicans of like intentions against the Union. That Breckinridge, who with clearheadedness and moderation almost invariably omitted rumor and emotionalism from his speeches, would give voice to this, shows that the vicious campaign propaganda had affected even him.[25]

Most disappointing of all in the Ashland speech was his conspicuous failure to answer the celebrated "Norfolk Questions," two interrogatories that one of his managers had put to Douglas during a stump speech at Norfolk, Virginia. The Little Giant was asked: "If Abraham Lincoln be elected President of the United States, will the Southern states be justified in seceding from the Union?" "If they, the Southern states, seceded from the Union upon the inauguration of Abraham Lincoln, before he commits an overt act against their constitutional rights, will you advise or vindicate resistance by force to their secession?" Douglas answered without hesitation. He said no to the first and yes to the second. There followed a challenge to Breckinridge to answer the same questions, and many had hoped he would do so at the Ashland rally. He did not. Under his interpretation of his candidacy, he could not answer them. The first would have been no problem; he would have agreed with Douglas. However, answering the first would require that he answer the second, and the reply would have cost him dearly in the free states. The very day of the speech, Breckinridge was interviewed by the Montgomery, Alabama, *Mail*'s editor, who later reported that the nominee had said that the secession of any state "ends the Federative system; all the delegated powers revert." If this was an accurate report—and there is no reason to suppose that it was not—then Breckinridge had admitted that the abstract right of secession existed. He had believed this all along, though hardly advocating it, and thus he could hardly agree with Douglas on the second question. If a state had the right to secede, then the Federal government had no right to try to force that state back into the Union against its will. The *Statesman* would later attempt to answer the questions for Breckinridge in a roundabout fashion and some supporters would commend him for his silence on them, but by and large the country was not pleased with his lack of a response.[26]

The public reactions to the Ashland speech were varied. Randall Mc-Gavock, a Breckinridge and Lane man in Tennessee, believed that it would be of great importance in the campaign. In Virginia, the vice-president's friends began toying with the idea of inviting him to come and speak in

25. Crenshaw, *Slave States*, 92–97, 107–10, 287.
26. Fite, *Campaign of 1860*, 180–81; Montgomery (Ala.) *Mail*, n.d., quoted in Milton, *Eve of Conflict*, 495; Lexington *Kentucky Statesman*, October 26, 1860; New York *Times*, September 10, 1860; Crenshaw, *Slave States*, 79.

those places where Douglas had already given speeches, though some of the party press were actually sorry he had spoken out. Stephens of Georgia was anxious to see the Ashland speech, as was Douglas himself. Characteristic of the partisan press during the campaign, the Little Giant's newspapers attacked Breckinridge for stooping from his position as a Senator-elect and vice-president to make a partisan stump speech, ignoring the fact that Douglas had been doing just that all summer. When the Illinoisian himself finished an address in Baltimore on September 7, the first thing he did was retire to his hotel, wrap himself in a blanket, light a cigar, and sit down to read his opponent's speech. Meanwhile, genuine disunionists like Edmund Ruffin disliked the vice-president's address. It was "a union-saving speech," said Ruffin. "By the general union-lauding tenor of Breckinridge's speech . . . I consider that he has placed himself with Douglas in that respect, but wants the boldness to avow that position." [27]

Breckinridge's lengthy, but not altogether convincing, protestations of love for the Union fell on deaf ears in several quarters. The attacks against him continued. In the weeks following the Ashland speech, his name was linked with disunion more often than before, and the rumored plots became legion. It was thought that if Lincoln were elected, southern state legislatures would convene, declare a Republic of the South with Breckinridge as president, and begin confiscating property from all opponents. Buchanan believed that a plot was afoot to kidnap him, thereby making Breckinridge president, and enabling the South to take control of Washington City. Even Douglas, poor Douglas, whose exertions in the campaign combined with his frustration over the unfulfilled promise of a great career, had broken his health and set him on the road to an early grave—even Douglas began to believe the rumors. He would later declare that he knew it to be a fact that Buchanan, Davis, Toombs, Floyd, and others had entered into a contract that, if they could carry all the slave states plus Oregon and California, then Buck would retire, handing over the government—army, navy, and all—to Breckinridge who, with this power behind him, would deny Lincoln his election, and be himself inaugurated. As president, Buchanan may not have been a mental giant, but neither did he have the stomach for treason. The whole country was on the verge of hysteria.[28]

27. Gower and Allen, *Pen and Sword*, 578; New York *Herald*, September 6, 7, 1860; Stephens to Smith, September 12, 1860, in Phillips, *Correspondence*, 406; Lexington *Kentucky Statesman*, August 31, 1860; Edmund Ruffin Diary, September 6, 1860, LC.

28. New York *Times*, September 8, October 2, 18, 1860; Theodore C. Pease and James G. Randall (eds.), *The Diary of Orville Hickman Browning* (Springfield, Ill., 1925–33), I, 466.

Breckinridge did have his defenders. His Uncle Robert, believing that his nephew's election was the only hope of averting disunion, declared a month after the Ashland speech that those who now abused the vice-president as a traitor would be sorry. He predicted that the South would consolidate on Breckinridge in 1864. Even the vice-president's cousin, Edward Marshall, a Douglas man, would deny that Breckinridge ever advised secession as a remedy to the election of Lincoln. Following the address of September 5, his leading speakers turned the secession guns against Douglas and Bell and made some telling, if not conclusive, hits. The Little Giant had grudgingly admitted that not every Breckinridge man was a disunionist; at the same time he asserted that there was not a secessionist in the country who was not for Breckinridge. To counter this, the vice-president's managers began exposing the past records of some of Douglas' people, and especially his running mate, Johnson, who was embarrassingly vulnerable, since four years before he had declared that Frémont's election would be grounds for secession. Even old enemies like Humphrey Marshall now stumped Kentucky and the South proclaiming against the disunionists behind the Little Giant. And Bell was equally open for attack. He too favored congressional protection of slavery, and had actually declared in 1850 "Give me disunion," when faced with the proposition of a Union held together only by power instead of mutual respect for the rights of the states.[29]

Besides the disunion charges, there was yet one more mode of attack on Breckinridge introduced during the last months of the canvass. The Bell men promulgated it, and, curiously enough, its contention was that he was unacceptable because of his antislavery record. Even before the Ashland speech, the accusation had gone out that Breckinridge was not a slaveholder, and a letter from Lexington's sheriff to that effect was widely republished. Feverishly, Powell and others vainly exerted themselves to show that the vice-president was, indeed, an owner of slaves. By October, "Parson" William B. Brownlow was delivering Bell speeches whose whole premise was an attack on Breckinridge's supposed neoabolition record. He pointed out the vice-president's willingness in 1854 that Kansas be allowed to become a free state on entering the Union if its people willed, misinterpreted a bit of the Tippecanoe speech, and then fell into the disunion arguments. Asserting that Bell owned, with his wife, no less than 166 slaves,

29. Robert J. Breckinridge to W. F. Warner, October 20, 1860, in B. MSS; speech of Edward C. Marshall [1877], in JCB Papers; Fite, *Campaign of 1860*, 185; Lexington *Kentucky Statesman*, October 2, 1860.

Brownlow was incensed that Breckinridge should be chosen and regarded "as the only man prepared to do justice to the South upon the question of the everlasting nigger!" [30]

Of course, the Bell argument against the vice-president's antislavery views was as much an artifice as charges of disunion against Douglas, but it did unwittingly capture some of the spirit of Breckinridge's feeling on the institution. It also pointed up a curious fact in this campaign. Only two of the candidates were heavily attacked for their antislavery views, the two at the opposite extremes of the spectrum, Breckinridge and Lincoln. Bell, of course, was "solid" on slavery. Douglas affected indifference. "I don't care whether slavery is voted up or voted down," he had said. Only Lincoln and Breckinridge entertained deep-seated feelings against black bondage, and, in the absence of more extensive evidence, it is not at all unlikely that the degrees of their respective prejudices were nearly the same. Indeed, if Forney can be believed, in 1851 Breckinridge had been willing to countenance even force to abolish slavery, a step one or two degrees more radical than the platform on which Lincoln was now running.[31]

The remarkable campaign was drawing to a close. Breckinridge enlarged his personal role only slightly. Alarmed by the August disaster and conscious of the need to carry the state in November, he began a limited tour of some of the mountain counties. He spoke only briefly at his few stops, no longer than half an hour, and with good reason. This was Bell territory, and he wanted to be on the stand only long enough to offer some defense, without being subjected to questions from the independent "sovereigns." Even so, at Owingsville in early October, someone in the audience called out to ask if he had ever answered the "Norfolk Questions." Breckinridge ignored the question.[32]

Meanwhile, the campaign in the rest of the nation ground on, characterized by greater tensions, increased hatreds, and even less hope for compromise or Democratic success. Once again, the subject of mutual withdrawal was proposed, this time by Pierce, but to no avail. Some friends still begged Breckinridge to bow out of the race regardless. The fusion movement had met with a little success in New York, New Jersey, Rhode Island, and

30. Glass to Williams and others, August 20, 1860, in New York *Times*, September 7, 1860; Crenshaw, *Slave States*, 26; "Constitutional Union Speech," by G. Brownlow, Knoxville, Tennessee, October, 1860, in Fite, *Campaign of 1860*, 330–41.

31. Fite, *Campaign of 1860*, 184.

32. Lexington *Kentucky Statesman*, September 28, 1860; Washington *Daily National Intelligencer*, October 6, 1860.

Pennsylvania, but the Douglas men were still uncooperative, and the prospects were slim for the success of the fusion tickets.[33]

One last hope remained, but no one attempted to organize a movement for it. There was a distinct possibility that none of the candidates would receive an electoral majority, in which case the election would be thrown into the House of Representatives. There, it was assumed, Lincoln could command fifteen states, Breckinridge thirteen, Douglas one, Bell one, and three undecided, among them Kentucky. Douglas seemed almost completely out of the running if the House should choose the president. If the Bell and undecided states could be brought around to Breckinridge—recognizing that he was the only candidate who could possibly beat Lincoln by this mode—then Breckinridge would be president. However, if the House failed to decide on a candidate, then the election would go to the Senate for that body to choose between the vice-presidential aspirants. In this safely Democratic body, Lane was a sure bet to be picked. Breckinridge's cousin Montgomery Blair was certain that Breckinridge would be chosen if the election went into Congress, and not a few others agreed, though his real prospects were doubtful. Besides, the whole project turned upon Lincoln being denied the 152 electoral votes needed to elect a president in the college, and to do that one of the other candidates had to carry New York, Pennsylvania, or a combination among Ohio, Indiana, and Illinois. This assumed that the South would go solidly against the "rail-splitter." There was some hope that the fusion tickets would effect this result, but from the lack of organized planning for sending the election into Congress, it does not appear that Breckinridge's managers, or those of Bell or Douglas, seriously looked to this method of blocking Lincoln.[34]

On election day men all over the nation went to the polls to cast their ballots. Ruffin, still believing that "Breckinridge does not come up to my standard of what a southern candidate should be," voted for him anyhow. A colonel of cavalry, Robert E. Lee—who felt that Douglas should long ago have withdrawn—gave his vote to the vice-president, as did another Virginian in the Shenandoah Valley, Thomas J. Jackson. In Ohio, Edwin M. Stanton, who regarded Breckinridge's election as the only hope of averting

33. Pierce to James Campbell, October 17, 1860, in Pierce MSS; Milton, *Eve of Conflict*, 494; Nichols, *Disruption*, 347; Benjamin O. Tayloe letter to Breckinridge, October 11, 1860, Virginia Historical Society, Richmond.

34. Crenshaw, *Slave States*, 60; Lexington *Kentucky Statesman*, October 9, 1860; Montgomery Blair to ————, October 15, 1860, in Blair Family MSS, LC; Nichols, *Disruption*, 341.

secession, voted for him, and, of course, Benjamin Butler did the same in Massachusetts. Down in the Deep South, Judah P. Benjamin, Jefferson Davis, William L. Yancey, Robert Toombs, and a host of others followed suit. In all, 849,781 people voted for Breckinridge, but they were not enough. Douglas polled 1,376,957, and Lincoln received 1,866,452. Bell got 588,879.[35]

Just over 60 percent of the people had shown that they did not want Lincoln in the White House; yet, thanks to the electoral college, he would be president. The results by state were, indeed, strange. Poor Douglas, second in the popular vote, won only the 9 electoral votes of Missouri, and 3 from the fusion ticket in New Jersey, making him dead last. Bell carried Virginia, Tennessee, and to Breckinridge's humiliation, Kentucky, winning 39 electoral ballots. Breckinridge, the only candidate to capture states from more than one section of the country, won Texas, Louisiana, Arkansas, Mississippi, Alabama, Georgia, Florida, and South Carolina in the South, and Maryland, Delaware, and North Carolina among the border states. His electoral total was thus 72, but Lincoln stood far out in front with 180, having carried the entire North, as well as California and Oregon.

The distribution of the vote was of considerable importance. Lincoln had polled two to one against Douglas in the North, but nothing in the South, and only a few thousand in the border states. Bell's popular vote was primarily centered in the states that he had carried, though his total in the slave states, combined with Douglas', actually made more than Breckinridge's. Just as most of the nation was opposed to Lincoln, so were most of the southern and border states opposed to Breckinridge, more particularly, to the hard-line and widely touted disunion tendencies of his most vocal supporters.

From all these totals emerged an interesting and significant fact, which can be regarded as reflecting more on Breckinridge personally than on the men and ideas he had allowed himself to represent. Lincoln's popular vote was wholly northern; Bell's was primarily in the border and the South; Douglas' total was divided almost three to one between the free and slave states. Breckinridge alone, of all the candidates, showed an almost equal appeal in all the different sections. He received approximately 259,000 in

35. Edmund Ruffin Diary, November 1, 1860, LC; Avery Craven, *Edmund Ruffin, Southerner: A Study in Secession* (New York, 1932), 192; Douglas S. Freeman, *R. E. Lee* (New York, 1934), I, 413; Richmond *Times-Dispatch*, June 18, 1958; Benjamin P. Thomas and Harold Hyman, *Stanton: The Life and Times of Lincoln's Secretary of War* (New York, 1962), 87; Butler, *Butler's Book*, 148.

the Deep South, 312,000 in the seven border states, and 279,000 in the free states. Clearly, he was not regarded everywhere as a disunionist.[36]

Even more significant was the distribution of his vote in the slave states. In Louisiana his vote came primarily from the poor white nonslaveholders, and the same held true throughout the lower South. "I & myriads others voted for Breckenridge as *ardent Union* men," wrote one Alabamian. In Kentucky, the proslavery vote went overwhelmingly for Bell. At the same time, Breckinridge lost those counties with the highest concentration of disunion sentiment. The vice-president carried only three of the border states, two of which, Maryland and Delaware, had the smallest slave populations of any in the Union. In the slave states that he carried, his pluralities only exceeded 50 percent in five. In all the others he won less than a majority of the votes. Clearly, he was not regarded as *the* guardian of slave interests.[37]

By and large, what Breckinridge did represent in this election was the spirit of moderation and conciliation. Those who stood most to lose by emancipation or abolition, and the most to gain by disunion, had gone for Bell. The vice-president's vote, especially in the North and in the border states, manifested a willingness to grant the South its protection of property, and thereby avoid disunion. Of course, disunionists voted for Breckinridge, just as they voted for Bell and Douglas, but the greater part of the vice-president's support came from those who, like Edwin M. Stanton, believed that only his election could prevent the downfall of the Union.

On November 7, 1860, when the results became generally known, all this mattered little. Lincoln was the next president; Breckinridge had suffered his first political defeat. He had not expected victory, but being rejected by his own state hurt deeply, and it did not help that the principal reason for it was the incessant Bell–Douglas charge of disunion. Kentucky stood to lose more by civil war than any other border state. Its border with the North, seven hundred miles in length, was the longest of any slave state. It stood as a prime target for invasion from both North and South and, no

36. Crenshaw, *Slave States*, 197–98; Fite, *Campaign of 1860*, 233; Roy F. Nichols, *The Stakes of Power, 1845–1877* (New York, 1961), 85; Nichols, *Disruption*, 370–71; Nevins, *Prologue to Civil War*, 312–13; Heck, "Breckinridge in the Crisis," 329–30.
37. Robert D. Meade, *Judah P. Benjamin, Confederate Statesman* (New York, 1943), 143; George J. F. Walker to Robert J. Breckinridge, March 18, 1861, in B. MSS; David Y. Thomas, paper in *Annual Report of the American Historical Association, 1910* (Washington, 1912), 39; Heck, "Breckinridge in the Crisis," 330; Wilson Porter Shortridge, "Kentucky Neutrality in 1861," *Mississippi Valley Historical Review*, IX (March, 1923), 284; Crenshaw, *Slave States*, 196, 298.

matter who won, Kentucky would lose. Thus, the cry of disunion carried particular weight in the Bluegrass State, and it had weighed heavily against Breckinridge. But even this did not matter now. Three weeks before, Alexander H. Stephens had predicted that if Lincoln carried the entire North, and Breckinridge the entire South, then "no earthly power could prevent civil war." For the most part, with the exception of the states that went for Bell, this is exactly what had taken place in the election, and as soon as the results were known, machinery in South Carolina was put in motion that could lead to secession and the fulfillment of Stephens' prophecy. There was a storm coming, and Breckinridge would face his greatest decision.[38]

38. Stephens to Smith, October 13, 1861, in Phillips, *Correspondence*, 501.

CHAPTER **13**

Iron Beneath the Glove

Breckinridge received the news of his defeat calmly in Lexington. Although it was what he had expected, it left him in a predicament, and voters and politicians watched closely to see what he would do. A week after the election, Robert declared that his nephew could not maintain a doubtful position for long without hurting himself and ruining his party in Kentucky. He must take positive action quickly or the drift of public opinion, already heavily against him, would destroy his career. The old Presbyterian was still proud of Breckinridge, "from whose lips not even a hypothetical case of justifiable dissolution was ever heard," and he was anxious about his future. Others were solicitous of some action by the vice-president. General John Dix, postmaster of New York City, wrote to him pleading that he "come out boldly against secession." The friendly Washington *Evening Star* declared on November 23, "We are among those who believe it to be the duty of Mr. Breckinridge to go South promptly and lend his influence to the discouragement of the current revolutionary schemes in that quarter." [1]

In varying degrees, he disappointed them. The only word to come out of Lexington was that "Mr. Breckinridge counsels moderation, forbearance and compromise." Beyond this, he made no overt move to give direction either to Kentucky or the South. However, in the three weeks between the election and the convening of the second session of the Senate on December 3, 1860, the vice-president certainly was not idle. Kentucky, traditionally the home of national compromise, was at it again. South Carolina had called a convention for December 17 to discuss whether to remain in the

---

1. Robert J. Breckinridge to William C. P. Breckinridge, November 15, 1860, and "Rev. R. J. Breckinridge on the Political Crisis," manuscript, 1860, in B. MSS; Horatio King to James Buchanan, November 25, 1860, in Horatio King, *Turning on the Light* (Philadelphia, 1895), 27.

Union, and other southern states were doing likewise. Faced with this, old Crittenden began considering some means to achieve a mutually agreeable compromise that would keep the Union whole. He solicited the advice of fellow Kentuckians of every political stripe. His chief consultants were Breckinridge, Madison C. Johnson, and probably Powell. While there is some testimony that a definite plan of action was arrived at between them before Congress convened, it is more likely that Crittenden waited until he could speak with senators from other states before proposing any definite action toward compromise. So the vice-president was working for peace and conciliation as his friends had hoped. It is unfortunate that he chose to do it so unobtrusively during weeks when outspoken moderation was so desperately needed, but his position was a difficult one. Besides the distrust that might meet any action of his in that part of the North where he was regarded as a disunionist, there was the attitude of Kentucky to consider. Until he had an idea of just how the Republicans would react to their new-found power, he was hesitant to try to commit himself, or his state, to unqualified support for the Union under Lincoln.[2]

When Breckinridge arrived in Washington City he found a party almost completely disintegrated by internal factions. The election had destroyed the Democratic party of old. The southern representatives, mostly men who supported Breckinridge in the late canvass, were working openly and vigorously for a peaceful separation and were trying to take the border state men with them. These latter, including Powell and Crittenden, sought instead to follow Buchanan's advice in his first message to Congress on December 4, calling for guarantees of their rights to slaveholders and the South. The next day a House committee of thirty-three was called for, and the day after, Powell made a similar motion in the Senate for a committee of thirteen to consider the plan which Crittenden was still working on. An acrimonious debate postponed a vote on the motion, and it had to carry over for several days.[3]

In this state of affairs, it was obvious to Breckinridge and others that, with the men from the slave states so divided, there was little chance of getting any guarantees at all from the Republicans. Only a united southern and border front of fifteen states, in his opinion, would be sufficient to per-

2. New York *Times*, December 1, 1860; John J. Crittenden to Larz Anderson, March 20, 1861, in John J. Crittenden MSS, LC; Lexington *Kentucky Statesman*, February 1, 1861; Heck, "Breckinridge in the Crisis," 331. The *Statesman* says that Breckinridge and Johnson drew up the compromise. Crittenden, in his letter to Anderson, merely says he consulted some "friends" in preparing the document.

3. Nichols, *Disruption*, 392–99.

suade the Radicals to compromise. But the fire-eaters from the South were going too far, arousing further animosity, and jeopardizing the chances of any settlement at all. Consequently, on the evening of December 8, Breckinridge, Powell, Reuben Davis of Mississippi, probably Crittenden, and a number of other concerned senators met to consult. They decided not to let the secessionists speak for them. Instead, Breckinridge and Powell urged for some means to seek guarantees, declaring secession to be only a last resort if the northern men refused to acknowledge and enforce their constitutional rights. The vice-president's caucus was immediately successful in bringing the secessionists and moderates together on a single plan. They would submit to the Committee of Thirty-three a list of demands specifying protection of property in the territories, that those territories should decide the slavery question only upon entering the Union as states, that fugitive slaves not returned from the North should be paid for, and that Congress could not interfere with slavery in either the territories or the District of Columbia. As a concession to the fire-eaters, Breckinridge and the other moderates agreed that, should these demands be refused, then a declaration might be dispatched to the southern states saying that secession was the only other alternative. Indeed, the vice-president agreed that the South would have no other choice.[4]

In the midst of this most crucial month, Breckinridge was stunned by a complete surprise. He had been vocally defending Buchanan against increasingly bitter attacks, and now, two or three days after the meeting of his caucus, he received an urgent summons to come to the White House. For the first time in their administration, Buchanan was inviting him to a personal interview. What the vice-president's thoughts were as he hurried immediately to see the president are unknown, but he was excited, believing that at last Buchanan wished to consult him on the momentous issues of the day. His anticipation must have been heightened when he was shown into Buchanan's room and the president, sitting alone, instructed his secretary to see that they were not disturbed during their important conference. When the secretary had left them, Buchanan took a key, unlocked a private drawer in his desk, and drew out a manuscript. Solemnly he sat down and addressed Breckinridge with deep gravity. "I have sent for you for the purpose of consulting with you, as the second officer in the government, upon the expediency, in the present lamentable condition of the country, of issuing a Proclamation appointing a day of *Humiliation* & *Prayer*. What would you advise?"

4. *Ibid.*, 401.

The vice-president sat in mute shock, fighting with his facial muscles to conceal the anger and frustration that he felt. He listened quietly, respectfully, made a few complimentary remarks, and then smiled and bowed his way out. In time he would be able to laugh over the incident, repeating it to friends with "inimitable narration," but now it was but one more example of the stupidity and disarranged priorities on all sides that had led the country into its difficulty, and a hallmark of Buchanan's singular incapacity for his office.[5]

Breckinridge had little time to worry about his relations with the president, however. Even though the Senate had not yet voted on the proposed Committee of Thirteen, it surely would, and he would have to pick its members. When the committee was finally ordered on December 18, he may still have been undecided, but two days later he was ready to announce his decision. "The Chair has found a great deal of difficulty in framing the committee," he told the Senate, "but has tried to compose it in the spirit which he believes actuated the Senate in ordering its appointment." He was eminently successful, for every faction in the Senate was represented. The Republicans had Seward, Collamer, Wade, Doolittle, and Grimes; Powell and Hunter were border Democrats, and Crittenden from the opposition there; Toombs and Davis sat for the radical southerners; and Douglas, Rice, and Bigler stood for the northern Democrats. Powell was made chairman, and his committee would begin almost immediately the consideration of compromise proposals. An ill omen for its future was South Carolina's formal secession from the Union on the very day the committee was announced. If it had been appointed three weeks before when Powell first made his motion, something might have been done before it was too late.[6]

On December 18 Crittenden had finally announced his proposed compromise. It consisted of precisely the same proposals agreed upon at Breckinridge's caucus meeting of ten days before, though adding a reactivation of the Missouri Compromise line, and a provision for the improvement and enforcement of the Fugitive Slave Law. The Crittenden compromise clearly showed the influence of both its acknowledged author and Breckinridge. Even though he believed the Missouri line was a violation of noninterven-

5. Hines Diary, January 20, 1866, in Hines MSS; "A Great Occasion: When a President Consulted with a Vice-President," undated clipping, probably from New York *Mail & Express*, in JCB Papers. In this latter source, the story is told by Adlai E. Stevenson as Breckinridge related it to him.

6. Nevins, *Prologue to Civil War*, 374; *Congressional Globe*, 36th Cong., 2nd Sess., Pt. 1, p. 159.

tion, he supported the measure wholeheartedly, and that is why he was particularly anxious to appoint a representative committee to consider it. The committee would deliberate over Crittenden's and other proposals, and then report its recommendations, if any, to the Senate. The friends of compromise waited tensely.[7]

During the following days that the Committee of Thirteen sought a solution, even more troubles beset Washington City, this time in Buchanan's cabinet. Floyd, never a good administrator, had to be dismissed. Buchanan lacked the courage to do it himself. He asked Black, who refused, and then somehow persuaded Breckinridge to do the job for him. It was one more meaningless, trivial errand on which Buchanan misused his vice-president, and it was the last. Breckinridge went to see Floyd on Christmas Day, apparently, and later told the president that the secretary had been surprised at the news, but agreed to resign. In actuality, Floyd had no intention of resigning until he had defended himself. That same night, the confused Virginian was pulled in yet another direction when he reportedly received a visit from Wigfall, who had a plan to kidnap Buchanan, thus making Breckinridge president, the expected result being that he would allow the South to secede peacefully. The rumor was current that such a plot had been laid, but, if so, it had little chance. "If there had been," wrote a close friend of the Kentuckian's, "Breckinridge would not have consented to be party to it." Floyd supposedly declined to take any part in this, and, after a stormy cabinet meeting the next day, he resigned in disgrace.[8]

Even as Floyd was brought to account, another disaster was taking place in Washington. Butler and others who had resolved after Baltimore to meet in December to reorganize the party, met during the Christmas holidays. There were several representatives of the states present, including Davis, Slidell, Black, Mason, Rice, Sickles, and others. Breckinridge attended on behalf of Kentucky. They had hoped to issue an address to the country for a regrouping of forces for 1864, but too much had happened in the past six months. Lincoln was elected, South Carolina had seceded, and other states were making motions toward the same action. Now some of the southern members of the conference declared that they were bent on secession and would never consider reunion. "As soon as we came together," Butler

7. Nichols, *Disruption*, 406–407.

8. *Ibid.*, 224–26; Auchampaugh, *Buchanan and His Cabinet*, 95; Frank Maloy Anderson, *The Mystery of "A Public Man"* (Minneapolis, 1948), 197–98; Henry Watterson, *"Marse Henry," An Autobiography* (New York, 1919), I, 76.

stated, "it was evident that the Breckenridge wing of the Democratic party was wholly disrupted." [9]

Hard upon this came worse news. The Committee of Thirteen reported to the Senate on December 31 that it had been unable to agree on any of the proposed methods of compromise. This left Breckinridge especially distressed. He had placed his best hopes for peace and union in the Crittenden resolutions, but even they were rejected by the Republican members of the committee. The very fairness of representation with which he had composed the committee had defeated any possibility of agreement. Immediately the rumors began. One declared that the Crittenden measures had been defeated at Breckinridge's recommendation, or that he had composed the committee specifically with defeat in mind. Another hinted that Breckinridge actually wrote the compromise and "fell upon the old man, and beguiled him to father the resolutions which [he] had contrived," giving them to Crittenden upon arriving in the capital. It is doubtful that either rumor held much truth, but they typified the wild speculation and confusion reigning in Washington. [10]

Like many others, Breckinridge was reeling from the shock of this chaotic December. The party, the administration, and the nation, were crumbling to pieces all around him. It became clear to him that the Republicans were bent on a policy of ignoring all efforts at compromise, even those including great concessions by the South. He was convinced that "no thorough and satisfactory plan will be proposed to the states by Congress." The country was left with two alternatives, peace or war. It no longer mattered whether secession was a genuine constitutional right, for the act had been committed, and he believed that within a few weeks seven or eight more states would join South Carolina. To attempt by force to hold them in the Union would mean war, the unification of southern resistance, destruction of any remaining hopes of reunion, and a conflict that "would exceed anything yet recorded in the annals of human madness and folly." If, in such a war, the South should win its independence, the hatreds and animosities engendered by the conflict would continue for generations, while he felt that a Federal victory would lead to subjugation and eventual military dictatorship. Such a war must be prevented, and the events of December further convinced him that the only means of doing so was to pre-

9. Benjamin F. Butler to William Schauler, July 10, 1870, in Butler, *Private and Official Correspondence*, I, 7; Butler, *Butler's Book*, 149–51.
10. W. P. Buckner to Crittenden, January 17, 1861, in Crittenden MSS; Lexington *Kentucky Statesman*, February 1, 1861; New York *Harper's Weekly*, March 16, 1861, 162.

sent Lincoln with fifteen states united in the resolve not to surrender their constitutional rights. This would also strengthen the voice of the true northern men. Of course, he did not mean by this that Kentucky and the other border states should join the Deep South in secession, but that they should declare their resolve not to be trampled upon. Since Congress had failed, it was time for the states to take matters in their own hands through sovereign conventions from the people, empowered to commit the states to specific courses of action. On December 27 Magoffin had issued a call for a special session of the legislature to meet on January 17, 1861, with a view toward calling a convention. Breckinridge, who earlier thought a convention unnecessary, decided to support the move.[11]

He would go even farther. Since the border states were really the key to the success or failure of either union or disunion, and stood to lose the most in the event of war, the vice-president decided that a border state convention was needed. Probably on the evening of the day that the Committee of Thirteen reported its failure, he sat down and drew up a paper directing the "Governors & people of Dela, Md, Va, Tenn, N. C., Ky & Mo, for the purpose of avoiding civil war & to secure united councils, by conventions or legislatures to send commissioners to Baltimore on Feb. 13 to confer." It was a bold move, assertive, original, the most statesmanlike act of his career. It received the signatures of Crittenden and others, and then he gave it to Senator A. O. P. Nicholson of Tennessee, to solicit further endorsements. Like all other moves it was doomed to failure. Mason and Hunter of Virginia refused to sign. Thomas Bragg of North Carolina wanted to, but his fellow Senator, Thomas Clingman, would not. Without those two states, a convention would be meaningless. On New Year's Day, 1861, his plan failed almost as soon as it had begun. Consequently, on January 6 he wrote Magoffin a public letter outlining his thoughts on the hopelessness of compromise, and openly advocating a call of the legislature. The general assumption among Union men was that such conventions were mere devices to promote the secession of more states. Breckinridge's letter was interpreted by many as an open endorsement of disunion. Robert was greatly pained by it, and found a "general disgust" among all but Breckinridge's most firm partisans. He lamented that his nephew "seems to be incapable of

11. Lexington *Kentucky Statesman*, January 15, 1861. Heck, "Breckinridge in the Crisis," 331, says that Breckinridge probably consulted with the *Statesman*'s editor, Thomas Monroe, advising in favor of a state convention. However, since Monroe wrote his endorsement of a convention on December 15, while there was still hope for the Crittenden Compromise, it is unlikely that Breckinridge concurred. Only after the futility of compromise became evident did he advocate a sovereign convention.

breaking the circle of 'national democracy'—as they [the Yanceyite seces-
sionists] call it." By now, the vice-president was accustomed to being
misunderstood.[12]

The special session of Kentucky's legislature was no more successful
than Breckinridge had been. When it convened on January 17, Magoffin
included in his message the vice-president's border state conference proposal, suggesting that this body should issue the call, but it was met with
little enthusiasm. However, two days later, when a message was received
from the Virginia legislature proposing a conference of delegates from all
thirty-three states, it brought approval on all sides. The Kentucky legislature promptly appointed six delegates to the conference, two from the
Bell men, two Douglasites, and two Breckinridge supporters, Clay and
General Butler. The conference met in Washington on February 4 and was
a signal failure, with many states not bothering to send delegations. Meanwhile, the Kentucky legislature, seeing secession the possible result of such
a convention, rejected the proposal decisively. It is significant that the faction which gave the Bell and Douglas supporters their majority at the convention, was none other than a substantial group of Breckinridge men who,
contrary to the accusations leveled at their candidate the previous fall, were
now working for union.[13]

Of course, Breckinridge took no active part in all this, for he was too
busy in Washington. Within five days after he wrote to Magoffin, three
more states passed ordinances of secession, Mississippi, Florida, and Alabama. At the same time, it was obvious that Georgia, Louisiana, and probably Texas, would soon follow. This presented the senators of those states
with a dilemma over whether to remain in the Senate, or withdraw leaving
the Republicans a majority. A caucus was called on the evening of January 12 to decide the matter, and every state was represented by one or both
of its senators as they gathered in the rooms of Brown of Mississippi. They
had invited the vice-president to attend and give his counsel as well, but
before the meeting was organized he heard some loose talk around the
room on the subject of organizing a provisional government for the seceded
states. He interrupted, reminding the senators of the stated purpose of the
gathering, and refused to take part in such a discussion. His position as vice-

12. Thomas Bragg Diary, January 3, 1861, SHC; Robert J. Breckinridge to William C. P. Breckinridge, January 17, 1861, in B. MSS; Nichols, *Disruption*, 436–37.
Nichols interprets Breckinridge's letter as open aid to the secessionists.

13. E. Merton Coulter, *Civil War and Readjustment in Kentucky* (Chapel Hill, N.C.,
1926), 34; Nevins, *Prologue to Civil War*, 411; Shortridge, "Kentucky Neutrality in
1861," 286–88, 290; Heck, "Breckinridge in the Crisis," 333.

president made his participation, even his presence, improper. Immediately the subject was changed. After much deliberation it was decided that the senators from seceded states should withdraw on the following Monday, January 14, and in this decision Breckinridge concurred. It was the wisest course for them to pursue, he felt, "let the consequences be what they may." The seceding states would suffer more by their presence in the capital, he said, than by their withdrawal. He did not say that it would be a relief to have the hotspurs out of Washington, but surely he felt it. They were beginning to act as much like obstructionists as the Republicans. On January 3 Crittenden had offered a novel resolution to submit his compromise to the whole people for a vote, since it could not get through the Senate, but Toombs aroused northern passions by following with a violent speech, and the resolution never got to a vote. Crittenden would move for reconsideration on the sixteenth, and Breckinridge, knowing this, would be relieved to have the fire-eaters out of the Senate two days before. Only a few days before he had received a visit from a Massachusetts delegation bringing petitions in favor of the Crittenden Compromise. Its leader, Edward Everett, had long been respected by the vice-president, who regarded him as "the acknowledged master" in one of their mutual interests, oratory. Breckinridge agreed wholeheartedly with Everett's mission, knowing that the ultras held the key to success or failure.[14]

If this was his plan it, too, went awry. Only Alabama, Mississippi, and Florida had left the Senate on the appointed day, though they had not yet officially withdrawn, while those remaining—perhaps thinking their action would be more effective with their presence—refused to vote on Crittenden's motion. It lost by only two votes. Apparently, no one had expected this, least of all Breckinridge, but it effectively sealed the fate of compromise.[15]

Meanwhile, the states continued to secede, Georgia on January 19, Louisiana a week later, and Texas on February 1. Then, on February 4, came one of the most moving scenes of the session. That morning Breckinridge had been sitting in his office in the Capitol with a fellow Mason, the Reverend Dr. Worrall, when the Kentucky delegates to a hastily called and ill-fated peace convention began to file in. Breckinridge met each of them

14. Bragg Diary, January 12, 1861, SHC; Nevins, *Prologue to Civil War*, 401–402; Thomas H. O'Connor, *Lords of the Loom: The Cotton Whigs and the Coming of the Civil War* (New York, 1068), 148–49; Breckinridge to Edward Everett, October 9, 1857, in Edward Everett MSS, MassHS.
15. Nevins, *Prologue to Civil War*, 402–403.

at the door—Clay, Butler, Guthrie, Morehead, Joshua Bell, and Charles Wickliffe—welcomed them warmly, and then sat down with them to consult over their course in the conference they would attend later in the day. Crittenden and other border state men may have been present as well, and they entered solemnly into their discussion, no one showing more concern over their success than Breckinridge. Shortly afterwards, even as the Peace Convention was organizing down at Willard's, the Senate was in session, and Slidell and Benjamin were saying their farewells. Benjamin was particularly moving. During his address, the hall heard the cheers of the ultras who applauded his every word, the angry mutterings of his enemies, and the eloquent silence of those whose sadness had momentarily left behind their sectional prejudices. Breckinridge sat in his chair, quiet, unmoving, with only his face giving expression to the pain he felt within. The Reverend Dr. Worrall, sitting nearby, looked at his friend and thought, "I never saw a man whose charm of manner and self-negation seemed more attractive; whose dignity and power in the presiding chair were more commanding; or whose absorbing sorrow more touched my heart than did these things in Mr. Breckinridge." As Benjamin and Slidell concluded their farewells and took leave of their old comrades in the Senate, many were unable to contain their tears. Worrall, glancing once more at the Chair, saw the drops flowing freely down the vice-president's face.[16]

There were more difficult scenes to come. As the appointed day for counting the electoral votes approached, Breckinridge, according to rumor, would tamper with them to somehow defeat Lincoln or disrupt the election. The vice-president met with General Winfield Scott to discuss the rumors, as well as the general danger of violence, and pledged that he would do his best to maintain peace. "His word is reliable," said Scott. Still, Breckinridge's declaration that all the votes were safe and intact did not quell speculation. As the Congress assembled on February 13 for the counting, Scott felt it necessary to place numerous guards around the Capitol and even within the House chamber.[17]

Shortly after noon, Breckinridge declared in the Senate that it was time to repair to the House for the tally. He rose and led the senators across the Capitol, taking his seat on the right of Speaker William Pennington. He

16. Louisville *Courier-Journal*, June 18, 1875; Bragg Diary, February 4, 1861, SHC; *Congressional Globe*, 36th Cong., 2nd Sess., Pt. 1, pp. 720–21; Meade, *Benjamin*. 152–54.
17. Dawes, "Two Vice-Presidents," 463–64; Forney, *Anecdotes*, 362; Lucius E. Chittenden, *Recollections of President Lincoln and His Administration* (New York, 1891), 38–39, 46; Bragg Diary, February 12–15, 1861, SHC; Lexington *Kentucky Statesman*, February 15, 1861.

waited for the tellers to take their positions. Declaring the purpose of the occasion, he called the assemblage to order. He was aware that many of those on the floor before him were armed, that feeling in the chamber was high and needed little to enflame it, but he was determined, wrote Lucius Chittenden, a Treasury Department official who witnessed the affair, "that the result of the count should be declared, and his purpose was manifested in every word and gesture." When a southern member arose on the floor, Breckinridge refused to entertain any motions or other business except points of order. The congressman then stated that he wished to raise such a point, and proceeded to shout: "Shall the members be required to perform a Constitutional duty before the Janizaries of General Scott are withdrawn from the hall?" [18]

This was a crucial moment. If Breckinridge saw fit to act on the point of order, an effort to eject Scott's guards might well have disrupted the session, an end much desired by the southern elements in Washington. However, with what Republican Representative Henry L. Dawes of Massachusetts, called "Roman fidelity," Breckinridge stopped the southerner cold, and refused to sustain the point. Looking down from the gallery, another Republican, the Treasury man Chittenden, believed that "Jupiter never ruled a council on Olympus with a firmer hand." "It was gloved," he wrote, "but there was iron beneath the glove." The count proceeded.

There were no more difficulties in the count, except a brief outburst of applause mixed with a mild titter when the vote of South Carolina was announced for Breckinridge. The vice-president quickly cut it off. Then, when the ballots had all been tallied, he arose in the silent chamber. Dawes thought Breckinridge was a little pale and nervous, "but firm on his feet and unfaltering in his utterance." In a clear voice, he announced that Abraham Lincoln, having received a majority of the electoral votes, was duly elected president. His duty concluded, he then led the Senate back across the Capitol, leaving behind a much relieved Scott, and a number of political enemies whose admiration for his conduct temporarily set aside their partisan differences. Even Chittenden, who would soon regard the Kentuckian as a traitor, felt it. "There is an unmeasured, latent energy in the personal presence of a strong man. If he could be remembered only for his services on that day, Vice-President Breckinridge would fill a high place in the gallery of American statesmen, and merit the permanent gratitude of the American people." [19]

18. *Congressional Globe*, 36th Cong., 2nd Sess., Pt. 1, p. 894; Chittenden, *Recollections*, 43–44; Washington *Evening Star*, February 13, 1861.
19. Dawes, "Two Vice-Presidents," 464; Chittenden, *Recollections*, 43.

The rest of the session passed quickly. Breckinridge appointed commissioners to officially notify Lincoln of his election, appointed a superintendent to oversee the inaugural preparations, and he paid a courtesy call on Lincoln and Mary on February 24, the day after the president-elect's arrival in Washington City. Both may have been uncomfortable at first, but it could not have lasted for long, for there was friendship, though not intimate, which bound them too firmly for politics to break it up. On the twenty-seventh, when the Peace Conference finally submitted the meager fruits of its deliberations—a proposed amendment to the Constitution much akin to Crittenden's defunct compromise—the old Kentucky senator got it referred to a select committee which Breckinridge packed in its favor. Appointing Crittenden, Bigler, and the Democrat John R. Thomson of New Jersey, from among those who favored the original Crittenden compromise, he gave the opposition its representation through Seward and Lyman Trumbull. Predictably, the committee endorsed the amendment three to two. At this late stage in the crisis, the vice-president may have decided that his widely touted nonpartisan detachment should take second place to the need for compromise to avoid calamity. If so, it did him no good, for a few days later the Senate rejected the amendment overwhelmingly. And on March 3, Breckinridge cast his final tie-breaking vote; it concerned the wording of a resolution that would preclude any amendment to the Constitution empowering Congress to abolish or interfere with domestic institutions in the states, namely slavery. The vote came up nineteen to nineteen, and Breckinridge cast in favor of the word substitution, even though it would mean recommitting the resolution to the House, where its supporters feared time would not permit action on it. In view of the fact that the vice-president surely favored the resolution, his vote is hard to explain. though it is likely that he, like others, believed the House would have time, and he always liked things as well worded as possible. Eventually the Senate reconsidered the vote, rejected the amendment, and passed the resolution, and a final vote of thanks to Breckinridge as well.[20]

Two days later, on March 4, 1861, Lincoln and Buchanan entered the

20. *Congressional Globe*, 36th Cong., 2nd Sess., Pt. 1, pp. 895–96, Pt. 2, pp. 1364, 1396–97, Appendix, 350; Earl S. Miers (ed.), *Lincoln Day by Day: A Chronology* (Washington, 1960), III, 22; Robert G. Gunderson, *Old Gentlemen's Convention: The Washington Peace Conference of 1861* (Madison, Wis., 1961), 94. Henry B. Learned, "Casting Votes of the Vice-Presidents," *American Historical Review*, XX (April, 1915), 571, says that Breckinridge made ten such votes. The author has been able to find only seven among the 9,500 triple-columned pages of *Congressional Globe*, 1857–61. He would hardly deny that he might have missed two or three, but, if so, they must have been inconsequential, or else collateral research would have uncovered some mention.

Senate and took seats in front of the secretary's desk, while Hamlin came in and declared himself ready to be sworn in. Breckinridge arose and made a few final remarks of farewell, thanking the Senators for their resolution of approval, their courtesy to him, and their forbearance with him when in error. "The memory of all this will ever be cherished among the most gratifying recollections of my life," he said, and he expressed the hope that Hamlin would meet with the same treatment. "And now, gentlemen of the Senate, officers of the Senate, from whom I have received so many kind offices," he concluded, "accept my gratitude and my cordial good wishes for your prosperity and happiness." So saying, he swore in Hamlin, adjourned the Senate *sine die*, and then stepped down to the floor, took Hamlin by the hand, and led him to the chair. Hamlin called the body back to order for the special session to commence immediately. The first business was the swearing in of the new senators. Breckinridge's credentials of election had been presented by Crittenden. Now, Hamlin administered his oath to Breckinridge, the second vice-president ever to proceed directly from the chair to the floor of the Senate. Breckinridge walked across the chamber to extend his greetings and shake hands warmly with Seward, who was retiring to take a place in Lincoln's cabinet. Then they all went outside to hear the new president address his dissatisfied fellow countrymen, some of whom had already formed a new "Confederate" government and chosen another man of Kentucky birth, Jefferson Davis, as their president.[21]

After four years of enforced silence, Breckinridge sat again in a position where he could speak out, and he had stored up much that he wanted to say. Even now, however, he waited to see what policy the new administration would adopt during the first week of the special session. Before going ahead with anything, he must be firmly resolved on his own course, as well as affirming the line that Kentucky would have him pursue.

The cornerstone of his policy was peace, and at almost any price, even dismemberment of the Union. Already Federal arsenals in the South had been seized by the new Confederates. Fort Sumter in Charleston Harbor was bottled up and denied provisioning, and the relief ship *Star of the West* was fired on when she attempted to get through to the garrison. In this tense situation the least spark could start a war that he sought to avoid. At the same time, he was anxious that nothing be done to make the secession of the southern states permanent, and to this end he believed that Federal forts

21. *Congressional Globe*, 36th Cong., 2nd Sess., Pt. 2, pp. 1374, 1413, 1433, 1435; Earl S. Miers, *Lincoln Day by Day*, III, 24; New York *Harper's Weekly*, March 16, 1861.

in the South should not be reinforced. Instead, all Federal troops should be withdrawn, "so that peace in any event may be *really* the policy." [22]

In Kentucky the Unionists believed that the state would have to stand by Lincoln because of vital economic links with the North during the current fiscal slump. The secessionists felt that Kentucky's business depression came about because the state did not stand with the South, whose planters were the chief customers of Kentucky merchants. Still others, among them Breckinridge's friend Clement Vallandigham of Ohio, saw another course, a "middle confederacy," in case the Union were permanently dissolved. This could possibly divert the attention of the state's radical "Southrons" from immediate secession, while using the border states as a buffer to prevent conflict between North and South. [23]

Breckinridge rejected the idea of a border confederacy and also the idea of Kentucky forming the lower end of a northern nation. Geography, a factor in many ways more powerful than popular sentiment, naturally aligned Kentucky with the South. For it to adhere to the North, dangling as it did below the Ohio River within easy reach of Confederate arms, would be too hazardous to chance. He still hoped for a border state convention; he saw some indications that Virginia might call one; and he believed that Kentucky's delegates to it should adhere to his position: no coercion of the South, in any form, to bring it back into the Union; and a just settlement which could bring all of the recalcitrants back into the fold or, failing in that, a united southern republic which—though he did not yet say it outright—should include Kentucky. He wanted Clay, George Johnson, and others, to go to Frankfort when the legislature convened in a few days, to organize "all true men" along these lines. Clearly, he had not entirely given up hope for compromise, or for the maintenance of the Union. If he can be faulted at this point, it is for misjudging the Union temper of his state. [24]

Breckinridge's first action in the Senate was, characteristically, a step for moderation. On March 5 Mason of Virginia attacked Lincoln's appointment of Breckinridge's Virginia-born cousin Montgomery Blair as postmaster general. No southern man should hold office under Lincoln, said Mason. Breckinridge retorted, calling Mason's charge unjustified, and gave

22. Breckinridge to Clay, March 10, 1861, in Clay MSS; Christopher Chancellor (ed.), *An Englishman in the American Civil War: The Diaries of Henry Yates Thompson, 1863* (New York, 1971), 71.

23. Shortridge, "Kentucky Neutrality in 1861," 288–89.

24. Breckinridge to James B. Clay, March 10, 1861, in Clay MSS.

his support to Blair's appointment. Soon thereafter he joined the fight againt a resolution which would strike from the Senate roll the names of the senators from Mississippi, Florida, Alabama, Georgia, and Louisiana. He believed that they had withdrawn because the action of their states forbade their voting or taking part in the deliberations of the Senate. They had not resigned and, therefore, were still legally members. On the subject of those seceded states, he did his best to aid Douglas in bringing up a motion to consider a resolution asking information on the arms, armament, men, and installations presently within the limits of the Confederacy. In so doing, the opportunity arose for him to make his first substantive speech in Congress in over six years.[25]

Breckinridge addressed his fellow senators for nearly an hour, outlining the condition of the country, strongly averring that the Republican party was not disposed to pursue a course designed to maintain peace, and advancing his own position of troop withdrawal and thorough negotiation. He declared his love and devotion for the Union, though guardedly, and asserted, "For myself, neither in public nor in private life, will I ever consent to sacrifice the principles of constitutional freedom, of municipal liberty, and of State equality, to the naked idea of Federal unity." Digressing to the subject of the last session, he went over the attempts at compromise by a number of senators, himself among them, speaking particularly of Crittenden's resolutions, thus enforcing the idea that he had some hand in their formation. This same compromise could still hold together the crumbling Union, he believed, if the Republicans would set aside sectional prejudices and grant the southern states equal rights in and to the territories. Then, in closing, he warned of "what I think Kentucky will do." His state understood the issue at hand, he said, and would try its best to reunite the states. But, failing in that, the Bluegrass would turn to the southern states, "unite with them to found a noble Republic, and invite beneath its stainless banner such other States as know how to keep the faith of compacts, and to respect constitutional obligations and the comity of a confederacy." [26]

Breckinridge had publicly declared himself. He revered and would protect the Union if he could, but, and even though he abhorred the idea of breaking up the country that he loved so dearly, he would accept secession as a last resort. It seemed not to matter to his listeners—and he did not now make it clear—that even in the united secession of the entire slave-state

---

25. *Congressional Globe*, 36th Cong., 2nd Sess., Pt. 2, pp. 1453–55; Nichols, *Disruption*, 499.
26. *Congressional Globe*, 36th Cong., 2nd Sess., Pt. 2, pp. 1466–69.

complex he still saw some hope of reuniting the Union, or at least of preventing war, by presenting Lincoln with an adversary whose might would preclude conflict and encourage compromise. Instead, his critics saw in his newly declared position merely a confirmation of the different motives which their various prejudices had ascribed to him in the campaign the year before. Among Republicans and Douglas Democrats, his speech was near-treason. To pro-Union border state men like Joseph Holt, a fellow Kentuckian, it was an assurance that, although "Kentucky voted against him on the *suspicion* merely that he was a disunionist—after this avowal, I doubt not, her condemnation of him will be far more decided." Among those already committed heart and soul to the new Confederacy, Breckinridge's words found a joyful reception. The very day of his speech, Wigfall, remaining in the Senate primarily as an obstructionist, wrote to President Davis that "Breckinridge has made a magnificent speech, bold, open, definite, wholly right, and unmistakably with us." Thus were the lines drawn. With the senator himself still committed to working for reunion within the Constitution, his every utterance would be anathema to the North and succor for the South. Through misunderstanding on all sides, would he be judged. It was the penultimate triumph of the extreme conservatives of the South in their campaign to make the Kentuckian one of them. Whether it was a conscious movement or a planned conspiracy, the effect was no less decisive. Because of the peculiar, if somehow admirable, flaw in Breckinridge's makeup which made him return loyalty for loyalty, friendship for friendship, no matter the deeds of the recipients—in the eyes of the nation he *was* one of them. He needed take but one step more to make that vision a reality.[27]

On March 26 the debate continued over the resolution on forts and arms in the seceding states, and Douglas attempted to answer Breckinridge's charges that the Republicans had not retreated from a single one of the adamant planks on their Chicago platform. He maintained that they actually were recognizing the rights of property in the territories by allowing Nevada, Colorado, and the Dakota territories to decide the slave question for themselves. To this, Senator Breckinridge answered that Douglas' argument was meaningless since Lincoln had appointed all the judges and other officials of these new territories from among those who agreed with the president's views against slavery. The men in control were abolitionists, and when those territories came to apply for statehood, these men would

27. Joseph Holt to Buchanan, March 20, 1861, in Buchanan MSS; *O.R.*, LIII, 136.

naturally write slavery out of their state constitutions. The argument was well taken, but curious. In defending Lecompton, Breckinridge had approached the question, not through the subtle implications of the act, but by the plain fact that the constitution had been approved in a manner in strict accordance with the laws. Douglas had gone much closer to the heart of the matter. Now, however, with Douglas behaving in strict compliance with the regulations, it was Breckinridge who sought subtleties, and found them. As always, his argument and logic were keener when on the offensive.[28]

The remainder of the special session went rapidly, with Breckinridge making one or two firm reavowals of his great preference for union, and introducing his own resolution to instruct Lincoln to remove all Federal troops from within the confines of the Confederacy. Douglas and the Republican Lyman Trumbull tried to bring the resolution to a vote, but they were unsuccessful, and on March 28, the Senate finally adjourned.[29]

Breckinridge returned immediately to Kentucky, speaking to the legislature on April 2 for two hours or more urging the same plan he had decided upon when he took his senatorial oath. Once again he suggested a border state convention in order to present the North and South with a compromise based upon Crittenden's resolutions. The slave states, and particularly Kentucky, must have guarantees. To remain in the Union without them would mean that the state would be the "little end" of a northern confederacy and would be forced to give assistance to the "subjugation" of the other states of the South. He declared that a state was empowered to leave the Union upon sufficient provocation, and that it might set itself up as independent, or affiliate itself with other states of a like mind. As a last resort, he regarded casting Kentucky's lot with the Confederacy as an acceptable solution. But first, and most important, the legislature should call a state convention to determine the state's course.[30]

The best the legislature could do was call another border state convention for May 27, 1861, and invite the other border slave states to send delegates. The rival factions in Kentucky—the Union Democrats, which included Crittenden, and the Southern Rights men, Breckinridge among them—immediately put candidates in the field for the state delegation to the

28. *Congressional Globe*, 36th Cong., 2nd Sess., Pt. 2, pp. 1506–11; Nichols, *Disruption*, 507–508.

29. *Congressional Globe*, 36th Cong., 2nd Sess., Pt. 2, pp. 1513–19.

30. Lexington *Kentucky Statesman*, March 29, April 2, 5, 1861; Frankfort *Tri-Weekly Yeoman*, April 1, 1861; Heck, "Breckinridge in the Crisis," 336–37.

convention. Breckinridge, who quipped that it "non-plussed" him to see the old Whig and American Crittenden now under a "Democratic" ticket, took the stump at once to advocate the election of General Butler and James B. Clay. He spoke and made appointments for other speeches almost daily as April wore on, urging his hopes for the proposed convention, but declaring that he would not support any proposal at that meeting which was not submitted for approval to the people of Kentucky. Then, on April 12, the secessionists fired on Fort Sumter.[31]

With this outbreak of open hostilities, a greatly dismayed Breckinridge decided that the Union of old was no more and could not likely be reunited. Lincoln immediately issued a call for four regiments of volunteers from Kentucky to help in putting down the rebellion. Virginia seceded immediately, the first of the border states to go over to the Confederacy, while Governor Magoffin steadfastly refused to supply Kentucky troops for the president's "wicked purpose." In this emergency, Breckinridge called even more urgently for a sovereign state convention, not merely to reunite the Union, but to prevent war. He proposed that the convention include Kentucky's congressional representatives in order that they might take a peace plan to present at the coming special session of the new Congress in July. He declared himself in favor of a united South and common cause with the people of the South. Lincoln must be shown that "his unholy war is to be waged against thirteen millions of free men and fifteen sovereign states." [32]

Breckinridge continued to speak once and twice daily, and his power was felt to the extent that Crittenden was called on for rebuttal. Breckinridge often spoke from the same stand with Clay, an unquestionable secessionist. It is doubtful that he felt any hesitation about appearing with Clay, though in fact his associations were hurting him. His old friend Combs—who should have known better—now actually believed that Breckinridge was manipulating Magoffin and working actively for disunion. It mattered little, for in the face of Fort Sumter, the secession of Virginia, the imminent withdrawal of Arkansas, and a general feeling of futility over the planned border state convention, the senator's party withdrew their candidates for the delegation on April 25.[33]

31. Coulter, *Civil War*, 37; Frankfort *Tri-Weekly Yeoman*, April 1, 1861; Lexington *Kentucky Statesman*, April 8, 12, 19, 1861.

32. Coulter, *Civil War*, 38–39; Lexington *Kentucky Statesman*, April 10, 1861.

33. Andrews to Crittenden, April 16, 1861, in Crittenden MSS, LC; Frankfort *Tri-weekly Yeoman*, April 30, 1861; Coulter, *Civil War*, 52; O.R., LII, Pt. 1, p. 136.

Even with the Union falling apart and the state being split, many Kentuckians thought they saw a solution in neutrality. The state's staunch Unionists could not countenance coercion to reunite the nation, and armed neutrality—a posture whereby Kentucky would arm herself on all borders to fight only in defense of her own soil from any invader, North or South—seemed to be the answer. The idea swept the state. Though it would require legislation, the assumption seemed general that this was the course that Kentucky would adopt.[34]

Breckinridge did not heartily approve of neutrality. He did feel that the state should be armed in any event, particularly for the defense of those counties bordering on the Mississippi. Late in April he actually wrote to an agent from that part of the state asking that something be done to borrow or purchase five thousand stands of arms in Tennessee. It seems not to have been his intent that these weapons should be used to aid the Confederacy, and he did not himself enter into any discussion of them with Confederate officials, but his name was used in other attempts to obtain weapons. As for armed neutrality, Breckinridge did not believe that it could long exist. While most secessionists opposed it, some did see in it a transitional state which could lead Kentucky eventually into the Confederacy, but Breckinridge rejected this. First of all, he would not put his head in the sand, nor did he wish for Kentuckians to sit idly by as spectators. A stand must be taken. It was clear that he preferred to stand with the South, for to remain in the Union, even though neutral, would make it impossible to avoid furnishing arms and money for the Federal war effort. Besides, if Kentucky endorsed Magoffin's refusal to Lincoln, then the state was already in rebellion. There could be no middle way. "Our proud old Commonwealth must play a manly part as she [has] ever done," Breckinridge declared.[35]

On May 4 the legislature met for another special session, and Magoffin once more advanced Breckinridge's urgent suggestion of a sovereign convention. Instead on May 10, undecided on what to do, the body's two factions, Union Democrats and Southern Rights men, each decided to appoint three commissioners to consult and recommend a plan to the state. The Unionists chose Crittenden, Archibald Dixon, and Judge Samuel S. Nicholas; the Breckinridge wing appointed Magoffin, and Richard Hawes and the senator himself. They met almost immediately and conferred no more

34. Coulter, *Civil War*, 44–46.
35. Frankfort *Tri-Weekly Yeoman*, April 23, 1861; *O.R.*, LII, Pt. 2, pp. 78, 94–95; Louisville *Daily Democrat*, April 23, 1861; Lexington *Kentucky Statesman*, April 26, 1861.

than two or three days. The southern men, probably through Breckinridge, made the first proposal, advancing the old idea of calling a state convention. This was unacceptable to the Crittenden men. Instead, Breckinridge and his associates gave in to a plan of neutrality which would deny both North and South entrance into or succor in Kentucky. The conference agreed unanimously on this course and then proceeded to the consideration of raising arms and men for defense. The Union men, not trusting the matter to Magoffin's management, obtained instead a five-man board headed by Simon B. Buckner. They even refused, after caucus deliberation, to allow Magoffin a seat on this board. It is to Breckinridge's credit that he gave in on these points in order to place Kentucky on a united course of action, even though he had little hope for neutrality and doubted that it was the manful thing to do. By May 24 the legislature had adopted the recommendation, and most Kentuckians approved of it.[36]

Breckinridge's exertions on the stump, aggravated by his emotional tension, left him quite ill and weak through most of May. The week before he met with Crittenden and the others, he received a call from an old friend, the Lexington banker David Sayre, who urged him not to continue on his present course. It would ruin him and the nation. Breckinridge replied that he was a good Union man. A few days later he told Sayre that, if his health would permit, he would journey throughout the nation addressing the people, for his heart bled for his country. Sayre took him at his word, but Breckinridge was unable to live up to his wish. His illness lasted on into June, forcing him to cancel a number of engagements at which he would have promoted moderation and neutrality. Only willpower allowed him to attend the all-important conference with Crittenden. His enemies, seizing the opportunity, charged that Breckinridge was "broken, demoralized, drunken half the time and is failing continually to meet his appointments." He was not broken yet, but he was sick in body and heart for his beloved Union which was falling apart.[37]

36. Coulter, *Civil War*, 52–56.
37. Lexington *Kentucky Statesman*, May 24, June 4, 14, 1861; Edward McMurdy to Samuel Chase, June 14, 1861, in Albert Bushnell Hart (ed.), "Letters to Secretary Chase from the South, 1861," *American Historical Review*, IV (January, 1899), 345.

CHAPTER 14

I Intend to Resist

By late June Senator Breckinridge was recovered enough to journey back to Washington for the extra session. He left under ominous circumstances so far as his own future was concerned. Although still intimate friends, he and Beck had terminated their partnership. Three more states, Arkansas, North Carolina, and Tennessee, had seceded, leaving Kentucky isolated below the Ohio. The opposition had swept the state in the special June congressional election, and it was more evident than ever that Kentucky no longer stood strongly behind him. Most symbolically, even as he was settling down at his desk in the Capitol, one of his namesakes from the vice-presidential days, Fort Breckinridge, New Mexico Territory, was living out its last six days of life before the War Department ordered it permanently abandoned. None of the signs were good.[1]

With all of the changes that had taken place since the adjournment in March, there was curiosity about the position Breckinridge would take now that the country was at war. Neutrality seemed the most likely course for him, though it had actually been rumored that he would accept a Federal command in Kentucky under Major Robert Anderson, formerly of Fort Sumter. Of course, many saw allegiance to the Confederacy in his future. Indeed, the session had barely begun when he was taken off his seat on the Committee on Military Affairs. "He is not to be trusted," wrote the Treasury man Chittenden.[2]

The senator did not wait long to take his stand. Of the old Democratic leaders, few remained. Douglas, spent from his exertions for the Union and

1. *O.R.*, Ser. I, Vol. XIV, Pt. 1, pp. 456–57, IV, p. 1; Heck, "Breckinridge in the Crisis," 339.
2. *O.R.*, Ser. I, Vol. LI, Pt. 2, p. 96; Lucius E. Chittenden, *Invisible Siege: The Journal of Lucius E. Chittenden April 15, 1861–July 14, 1861* (San Diego, 1969), 130.

from his own disappointment, had died on June 3. Now Breckinridge and Bayard of Delaware were the only anti-Lincoln Democrats of real power and force left, and leadership of the opposition fell on them, though Bayard feared he would bear the burden alone. Other senators like Powell had lost their impact; some like Pearce of Maryland would simply shirk responsibility and stay quiet; and Bayard expected Breckinridge to be feeble. He believed that the senator would not go beyond a mere vote, a poor token in such times. A few days after the opening of the session, when Breckinridge told him that he would make a speech on July 16, Bayard predicted that it would be "too tame." He must have been pleasantly surprised when Breckinridge took the floor.[3]

The subject which brought Breckinridge to the floor was a resolution which proposed to grant congressional approval to those extraordinary acts conducted by Lincoln since his inauguration, among them denial of the writ of *habeas corpus*, raising of arms and men without legislative sanction, the imposition of a blockade of the southern ports, unlawful searches and seizures, and other necessities of wartime which, nevertheless, violated the Bill of Rights. Others had spoken out against it already, but, as the most prestigious remaining member of his party, it befitted Breckinridge to comment on it.

Moving to the attack at once, he asserted that the fact that the Republicans sought to pass such a resolution was a bald admission that Lincoln had been operating in violation of the Constitution and the laws. He denied emphatically the right or power of one branch of the government to indemnify illegal actions of another branch, for, if such could be done, then it meant that Congress could set aside the Constitution at will, from which it followed that Congress might as well alter that document, though that power was solely reserved to the states.[4]

Breckinridge asked rhetorically, what the justification was for the president taking these extralegal steps, and answered, "Necessity." He rejected the excuse. It was not necessary for Lincoln to raise an army and a navy, to blockade ports, to launch a campaign in Missouri, or to imprison numbers of men from loyal states whose only crime was disagreement with him and his policies. In doing this, Lincoln had drawn to himself the powers of his own branch of the government; that of Congress, which alone was empowered to grant him such authority; and that of the Supreme Court,

3. Nichols, *Disruption*, 511; James A. Bayard to Thomas F. Bayard, July 8, 12, 15, 1861, in Bayard MSS.
4. Riddle, *Recollections*, 34.

which was responsible for deciding the guilt or innocence of those arrested. Breckinridge felt this concentration of power was an act "which, in every age of the world, has been the very definition of despotism."

He worked around to the war itself, and its prosecution. He believed that if its purpose was to preserve the Union under the Constitution, then it should be conducted in a constitutional manner. Breckinridge thought he saw in the present mode of operation among Republicans an inclination to use the war to change the character of the government. He charged Lincoln's good friend—and his own—Senator Edward Baker of Oregon with advocating the extinction of state divisions, leaving no more Virginians or Pennsylvanians, but making everyone simply American. At the same time, he asserted that Baker actually spoke in favor of a dictatorship for the prosecution of the war, and that if the southern states, once subjugated, refused to cooperate with the Federal government, then they should be turned into territories and governed by appointees. There was nothing constitutional in any of this. Not only was the dominant party bent on an unlawful war, but they would also have it conducted contrary to the Constitution. He did not deny that Congress possessed the power to make war against the seceded states, if it was conceded that they were no longer states as such, but there was no authority anywhere for an attempt to return them to a territorial condition.

From this, Breckinridge went into a discussion of slavery's influence in creating the crisis. He believed that the institution and the rights to practice in it had, at one time, a great influence on the southern men who led secession. However, he pointed out that although the proportion of slaveholders to nonslaveholders was quite small, he believed the general population was nevertheless overwhelmingly in favor of that form of property. This made all the more odious another resolution before the Senate entitled "A bill to suppress the slaveholders' rebellion." It proposed to emancipate all slaves within the seceded states, and to accept the services of those who offered to help in the war effort. It was not actually stated that the Negroes might be enlisted as troops, but the implication was unmistakable, and Breckinridge did not miss it. He damned the entire resolution as but a congressional act of emancipation which also intended to promote war between masters and slaves. He used the old argument that if Congress could legislate and deny this particular right, then it might overthrow all rights, personal and political. Like so many before him, Breckinridge failed to see, or admit, that although the majority of the people of the North felt a moral repugnance for slavery, they did not care a whit how a southern state constituted its schools, levied taxes, or elected its legislature. In decrying the eventual outcome of a policy beginning with the abolition of slavery, he and others like him were carrying their arguments out to an absurdity that did not exist.

Through the entire speech, it had been obvious from Breckinridge's words that he did not really expect to influence any of the senators present. "I am quite aware that nothing which the few of us who are here, who take the same views as I do, can utter, will have the slightest effect." After Fort Sumter, it is doubtful that he ever seriously believed that his words would have any effect, but he felt it his duty to speak out. And he had spoken out, in one of the most eloquent addresses of his career. Indeed, throughout this session, his speeches were particularly able. He spoke clearly, logically and, in a strict sense, correctly. He was constitutionally right on almost every question. If the issue before the Senate had been a treaty or an appropriation, he might well have won acclaim from all sides. But the issue was war, a war entirely different in nature and scope from even the Mexican War of little more than a decade before, a war involving populations as well as armies. In a conflict between nations such as this, the blood of the soldier was not enough for a victory; the parchments of his freedoms must, for the duration of the war, bleed their share as well. This, Breckinridge simply could not, and perhaps never would, understand.[5]

The reactions to the senator's speech were predictable. In Lexington, the *Statesman* termed it a "terrible Phillipic," while Cincinnati papers believed it "Bold, clear and logical." Even the Republican Representative Riddle thought the senator "was at his strongest." Breckinridge's opposition had apparently expected him to speak in defense of the Confederacy, but he surprised them.

After his speech he denied that he had, as rumored, written with Magoffin to Jefferson Davis promising seven thousand Kentuckians for the southern cause. Of course, this did not deter his more outspoken enemies from damning him nevertheless, and *Harper's Weekly* accused him of "peurile folly," contrasting his address with a strongly pro-Lincoln speech by another Kentuckian, Joseph Holt. The New York *Tribune* thought it "treasonable sophistry." As for the administration, in a perfect example of those violations of freedom that Breckinridge had attacked, it would not allow the Associated Press to telegraph his speech over the wires.[6]

5. *Speech of Hon. John C. Breckinridge, of Kentucky, on Executive Usurpation; Delivered in the Senate of the United States, July 16, 1861* (Washington, 1861), *passim*.
6. Lexington *Kentucky Statesman*, July 19, 1861; Riddle, *Recollections*, 34; Samuel F.

Thereafter, Breckinridge was seldom quiet. Two days later he moved an unsuccessful amendment to an amendment on an army and navy bill, seeking to bring about an enactment that those services should not be used for the subjugation of any state. On July 25, four days after the first great battle at Manassas Junction, Virginia, he rose again, this time to oppose the new Crittenden resolution introduced in the House on July 19. Since the resolution asserted that the South had brought on the war, Breckinridge argued against it; although the resolution stated that the war was not to be prosecuted for conquest or oppression, Breckinridge cited the statement of John Sherman of Ohio just a few days before, which declared that if the southern states did not willingly yield, he was for depopulating them; although the resolution denied any purpose to interfere with established institutions in the southern states, Breckinridge argued that by an amendment previously passed, which allowed confiscation of any slaves being used to promote the rebellion, Congress actually was interfering with a domestic institution.

Sherman shot back at him, accusing him of not representing the true will of Kentucky, and rhetorically linking his name with the disunionists. Breckinridge denied the charge that he was not a true representative, but answered, "To that tribunal, however, I will submit the question; and if, indeed, it be true that the people of Kentucky shall believe that the prosperity and peace of this country can be best promoted by an unnatural, fratricidal, and horrible war ... I will acquiesce, in sadness and in tears, in her decision; but I will no longer be her representative on the floor of the American Senate." [7]

In truth, Breckinridge could hardly have failed to sense that he no longer held the loyalty of Kentucky. This very resolution that he was speaking against had already been passed by the House and, when it was put to a vote in the Senate, only Breckinridge and four others stood against it. The next day, in response to a resolution pledging the full resources of the Union to the war to suppress the rebellion, he declared that even though he agreed with that portion of the resolution which upheld the Constitution and the Union, he could not countenance pledging the nation to force. Of thirty-five members voting on it, he alone said "nay." This, combined

---

duPont to Henry W. Davis, July 18, 1861, in John D. Hayes (ed.), *Samuel Francis duPont: A Selection from His Civil War Letters, Volume I, The Mission 1860–1862* (New York, 1969), 106; *Congressional Globe*, 37th Cong., 1st Sess., 143; New York *Harper's Weekly*, August 3, 1861, pp. 482–83; New York *Tribune*, July 17, 1861.

7. *Congressional Globe*, 37th Cong., 1st Sess., 194, 261–62, 265.

with his continued attacks on the Lincoln administration and, a few days before, his visit to Old Capitol Prison to see Confederate prisoners from Manassas, made Breckinridge more suspect than ever. A few, like Republican pamphleteer Anna Ella Carroll, still admired Breckinridge's courage in standing alone in the Senate. Others did not. "Can anyone doubt," wrote one critic, "that the U.S. Senator, 'who does not conceal his sympathy with the wounded' of the army that are trying to destroy the Government he has sworn to protect—will communicate to that Army any information he may acquire in the secret sessions of the Senate?" The same feeling surely prevailed among many in the Senate. Late that month, when Prince Napoleon of France visited the United States, Seward presented him and his retinue to numerous members of the Congress, Breckinridge among them. Napoleon's aide, Lieutenant Colonel Ferri Pisani, saw the senator the day after the defeat at Bull Run, and Pisani, expecting that Breckinridge would shortly go over to the Confederacy, sensed the resentment against the Kentuckian. "One realizes easily," wrote the Frenchman, "what silent angers his presence . . . must arouse in the hearts of the opposite party!" Yet Breckinridge himself had not lost his sense of balance, his ability to detach his view of politics from his view of the men who espoused them. Despite his opposition to the Crittenden resolution on a variety of grounds, he regarded it as a manly attempt, the crowning title to fame of old Crittenden.[8]

In fact, Breckinridge's contacts with the Confederates were very few, and wholly nonpolitical or military. Even his letters regarding purchase of arms for Kentucky—while those arms would come from the Confederacy—were not addressed to Confederates. So far his only correspondence with those in the seceded states seems mainly to have been in the nature of introductions for travelers, while his personal associations in Washington were almost as much involved with Republicans as with suspected Rebel sympathizers. Indeed, he was not an infrequent visitor at the White House, where he and his cousin Mary Lincoln reportedly joked about the Confederacy. Speaking to Mary's guest Elizabeth Grimsley, Breckinridge quipped: "Cousin Lizzie, I would not like you to be disappointed in your expected stay at the White House, so I will now invite you to remain here as a guest,

---

8. New York *Harper's Weekly*, August 3, 1861, p. 483, August 10, 1861, p. 511; *Congressional Globe*, 37th Cong., 1st Sess., 275; R. Mussey to O. Barrett, July 26, 1861, in Abraham Lincoln Collection, UC; Margaret Leach, *Reveille in Washington* (New York, 1941), 106; Georges J. Joyaux (ed.), "The Tour of Prince Napoleon," *American Heritage*, VIII (August, 1957), 69; Breckinridge to Mrs. Coleman Chapman, April 16, 1869, in John J. Crittenden MSS, DU; Winifred E. Wise, *Lincoln's Secret Weapon* (New York, 1961), 108.

when the Confederacy takes possession." Mary Lincoln quickly shot back that "We will be only too happy to entertain her until that time, Senator." Adding to the evidence that Breckinridge still had no intention of aiding or abetting the Confederacy are one or two curious votes during the session. One, regarding the relative pay of chaplains in the regular and volunteer service, showed that he felt a particular concern that the regular army not be slighted in favor of the new volunteers, a sympathy hardly commensurate with a traitor. Even more convincing is his argument, late in July, in favor of an appropriation for experimentation and construction of an ironclad warship that could resist solid shot. Surely he knew that such a ship would be used against the Confederacy, yet he voted for it nevertheless, helping to pass the enactment that laid the groundwork for the great Union ironclad navy.[9]

The votes notwithstanding, Breckinridge was giving moral aid to the South. Whether he realized it or not, he no longer represented his constituency. He was committed to neutrality, to embrace neither side, and while he did not embrace the South, his wholly one-sided attacks on the northern regime constituted an unbalanced representation based upon ignoring the Confederacy, and assaulting the North. As the session wore on it became clear that the primary constituency for which he now spoke was himself.

His position, the arguments against him, the accusations, the acrimony, everything, crystallized on August 1, 1861, in one of the most memorable scenes in Senate history. Under consideration was a bill to use martial law to suppress the rebellion, and Breckinridge, as usual, met it with drawn sword. He first traced the history of the unconstitutional legislation that had been passed during the session; a confiscation act embracing all property that was used against the Union, which he interpreted to mean everything in the South, since there was nothing that was not, in one way or another, used to help the Confederate war effort; the act of "general emancipation" which he had already attacked previously; the suspension of the writ of habeas corpus; unlawful searches, seizures and arrests, approved, or

9. Breckinridge and Lazarus Powell to Francis Pickens, March 26, 1861, Miscellaneous American Autograph Collection, Pierpont Morgan Library, New York; Mary Lincoln to "Miss Shearer," March 28, 1861, in Justin G. and Linda Turner, *Mary Todd Lincoln, Her Life and Letters* (New York, 1972), 82; Elizabeth Todd Grimsley, "Six Months in the White House," *Journal of the Illinois Historical Society*, XIX (April, 1926), 57; *Congressional Globe*, 37th Cong., 1st Sess., 81, 347; Robert MacBride, *Civil War Ironclads* (Philadelphia, 1962), 11; Allan Nevins, *The War for the Union: War Becomes Revolution 1862–1863* (New York, 1960), 51.

at least not condemned, by Congress; and now this bill, which would empower every departmental military commander to declare martial law and suspend the writ himself. All of this was for the sake of the Union.

> Mr. President, gentlemen talk about the Union as if it was an end instead of a means. They talk about it as if it was the Union of these States which alone had brought into life the principles of public and of personal liberty. Sir, they existed before, and they may survive it. Take care that in pursuing one idea you do not destroy not only the Constitution of your country, but sever what remains of the Federal Union. These eternal and sacred principles of public and of personal liberty, which lived before the Union and will live forever and ever somewhere, must be respected; they cannot with impunity be overthrown; and if you force the people to the issue between any form of government and these priceless principles, that form of government will perish; they will tear it asunder as the irrepressible forces of nature rend whatever opposes them.[10]

This war was being conducted counter to the Constitution, and according only to the laws of warfare. Well then, why not admit it, he asked, instead of trying to pass bill after bill to excuse or indemnify that which was unlawful. If an unjust war was to be prosecuted illegally, at least let Congress admit the fact manfully, and then go ahead, as he knew it would go ahead. In any event, he deplored the conflict. If it did not come to a halt, and soon, it would be the ruination of both North and South. There were already two confederacies; let the war go on another year and there would be three, another year and there would be four, such was the internal excitement and animosity generated by this crisis. In an expression indicative of his wish that there still might be a reconciliation, he quoted Calhoun: "War is separation . . . it is disunion, eternal and final disunion." If it went on, those remaining common interests and sympathies that still bound the peoples of North and South would be extinguished and with them the last hopes of reunion. Breckinridge knew, of course, that his words were having little or no effect, but still he spoke. "We are making our record here; I, my humble one, amid the sneers and aversion of nearly all who surround me, giving my votes, and uttering my utterances according to my convictions, but with few approving voices, and surrounded by scowls."

During the latter part of his speech, Senator Edward Baker of Oregon, who had been absent for several days at Fort Monroe, Virginia, drilling the

10. Blaine, *Twenty Years*, I, 344–45; Forney, *Anecdotes*, I, 42; Dawes, "Two Vice-Presidents," 464; Allan Nevins, *The War for the Union: Improvised War 1861–1862* (New York, 1959), 186. Breckinridge's speech is in *Congressional Globe*, 37th Cong., 1st Sess., 376–77.

regiment of which he was now colonel, strode into the chamber in full uniform, kepi and riding crop in hand. He obtained the floor at Breckinridge's conclusion. Rising and laying his sword on his desk, he began coolly to question the Kentuckian, asking him to point out a particular provision in the bill before them which violated the Constitution. Breckinridge would not cooperate; since Baker now had the floor, he would be able to criticize at length any answer made, whereas Breckinridge would not have the parliamentary right to rebut such criticism. Despairing of this line of attack, Baker went on in a defense of this bill, admitting that he, too, was wary of giving the military too much power. Shortly, however, he moved on to the subject of what Breckinridge would have the government do, and then he gave vent to a flurry of heated eloquence that sent a spark through his hearers. Would Breckinridge have them yield to rebellion? Would he shrink from such insurrection? Would Kentucky justify it? Should they send in a flag of truce? What would he have? "These speeches of his, sown broadcast over the land, what clear distinct meaning have they? Are they not intended for disorganization in our very midst? Are they not intended to dull our weapons? Are they not intended to destroy our zeal? Are they not intended to animate our enemies? Sir, are they not words of brilliant, polished treason, even in the very Capitol of the Confederacy?"

Baker went on to ask, rhetorically, what would have happened to a senator such as Breckinridge in the days of ancient Rome. Fessenden of Maine, perhaps sensing the need for a little humor to ease passions, said in an audible whisper, "He would have been hurled from the Tarpeian Rock." When Baker had finished, Breckinridge obtained the floor for a reply. It was anticlimactic after the colonel's effort. He reiterated his theory of the nature of the Union. To the question "what would you have us do," Breckinridge replied:

> I would have us stop this war. We can do it. I have tried to show that there is none of that inexorable necessity to continue this war which the Senator seems to suppose. I do not hold that constitutional liberty on this continent is bound up in this fratricidal, devastating, horrible contest. Upon the contrary, I fear it will find its grave in it. . . . Sir, I would prefer to see these States all reunited upon true constitutional principles to any other object that could be offered me in life. . . . But I infinitely prefer to see a peaceful separation of these States, than to see endless, aimless, devastating war, at the end of which I see the grave of public liberty and of personal freedom.

If he was speaking treason, Breckinridge continued, he was not aware of it, and as for the remark by Fessenden—which he thought had been uttered by Sumner of Massachusetts—he did not hold contempt enough for the man and motives that spawned it. "He [Sumner], and men like him, have brought the country to its present condition." Then, after repeating his promise to resign if Kentucky did not approve of his course, he concluded. With the exception of a brief speech in opposition to a bill tampering with the Federal district courts in Kentucky and Missouri, on August 3, this was the last time he would address the Senate, dignified, gentlemanly, conservative to the end.

Baker's speech had captured the essence of the charges against Breckinridge throughout this session. From the very beginning he had been accused of misrepresenting Kentucky, of seeking to aid the Confederacy. More often than not, the charges were couched in offensive tone and language that he must have resented but to which he seldom replied in kind. His friends, those who knew him well, always felt that Breckinridge forgave his enemies too readily. From his own point of view, however, and with the possible exception of Sumner, he had no enemies, only political opponents. What happened on the floor of the Senate had no influence on his relations with those opponents outside the Capitol. When his friend, Republican Orville H. Browning, made his maiden speech against a bill of Powell's that the war should not be for subjugaton of any state or abolition of slavery, Breckinridge later paid him hearty compliments on the compactness, logic, and fervor, of a speech which he fully opposed, yet just as fully admired. This feeling was in large part returned by his opponents, for even those who attacked him did so in accompaniment with expressions of regard and esteem for him personally. Sherman, Lyman Trumbull, Browning, and others all spoke favorably of Breckinridge as a man. Even Baker in his Phillipic paid Breckinridge numerous compliments.[11]

A good example of this feeling is the relationship between Breckinridge and Baker. The very evening of the day that the Oregon senator assailed Breckinridge—or not more than a day or two later—the two came walking out of the Capitol together, and then went to Bladensburg, where the Kentuckian was to be the colonel's guest for a visit with his regiment. Upon seeing Breckinridge, the men did not conceal a general groan, and Baker sprang forward—"almost 10 feet at a bound," thought one observer—to cut them off saying, "I hope you will remember the courtesy due your Commander's guest." Baker then apologized to Senator Breckinridge in front of the regiment.[12]

Yet it was obvious that being the object of so much censure was affect-

11. *Congressional Globe*, 37th Cong., 1st Sess., 143–219; New Orleans *Times*, May 18, 1875; Pease and Randall, *Diary of . . . Browning*, I, 483.

12. Francis Young to Breckinridge, March 30, 1867, in JCB Papers; Henry C. Blair and Rebecca Tarshis, *Colonel Edward D. Baker, Lincoln's Constant Ally* (Portland, Ore., 1960), 138.

ing Breckinridge; the frustration and the feeling of helplessness in the crisis plagued him. There were threats against his life. A woman in Columbus, Ohio, heard such threats against him and actually suggested that he wear a coat of chain mail to protect himself. The combination of all this for doing what he thought was his duty, shortened his temper noticeably, making him quicker to burn. Of course, the day after the confrontation with Baker, when he discovered that it was Fessenden who muttered the Tarpeian Rock jibe, and that it was done in jest, Breckinridge apologized to the Senator from Maine. However, Sumner would get no such apology. Clearly Breckinridge was feeling the same internal unbalance and turmoil that was felt throughout the troubled nation. Breckinridge's distress was increased when, against his expressed wishes, his sixteen-year-old son Cabell, after two unsuccessful attempts to run away, had gone into Tennessee, lied about his age, and, on July 13, enlisted in the Second Kentucky Infantry, then being raised for the Confederate service.

Now Breckinridge was even more undecided which way to turn. With the Confederacy lay friends, family, and the better portion of his sympathies, but to join them would cost him a terrible price; the remnant of a great political career and, more important, forfeiture of his allegiance to the Constitution, which he loved above all else. Remaining with the Union, where he would find an almost equal number of family and friends, would alleviate his conscience, but he would still be crying in vain against the Republicans, and he would have to accept being part and parcel to the unholy war. It was a terrible decision to face, and he was still reluctant, thought his good friend Albert Pike, "to believe in the necessity of a separation of the States." [13]

There were those, however, who believed that Breckinridge had already made his decision, whether he knew it or not, and that his destiny lay with the Confederacy. On the evening of August 6, just after the adjournment of the session, Breckinridge said an affectionate goodbye to Forney.

"No, not Good bye, Breckinridge," replied the Pennsylvanian, "but farewell. You will never again take your seat in the United States Senate."

Surprised, the major asked, "What do you mean? I will undoubtedly return to my post in December."

"No, my dear sir, you will follow your doctrine into the Confederate

13. O.R., Ser. II, Vol. II, 1524; J. L. Shannon to Breckinridge, December 25, 1869, in B. MSS; Congressional Globe, 37th Cong., 1st Sess., 397; Telephone interview with Mrs. Kenneth B. Kirkland, New York, April 21, 1969; Joseph Cabell Breckinridge, Compiled Service Record, NA; Louisville Courier-Journal, June 18, 1875.

army; you will go there to show that you are with the enemies of your country."

"If I go over the lines," said Breckinridge, "it will be to bring back with me my runaway son, Cabell, who has gone into the other army wholly against my will; but we shall meet, if we live, in the winter."

"I wish it could be so, my friend," replied the sad Forney, "but still I feel that your good-bye will be a long farewell." [14]

The trip home to Lexington was nearly as frustrating as the past month in Washington. Apparently Breckinridge had planned to make one or two speeches at Baltimore and, perhaps, New York, no doubt to reaffirm his stand for the Union. However, in Baltimore, where he and Vallandigham were entertained with a dinner at the Eutaw House given by Henry May and other prominent southern sympathizers, a near-riot ensued when he attempted to respond to a serenade. As though by signal, fist fights broke out immediately. Union men began crying out "Union," "Crittenden," "Scott," and the general shouting reached such a pitch that Breckinridge could not be heard and was forced to retire. There is some evidence that the Mozart Hall Democrats of New York had also extended an invitation to him but that, upon hearing of the row at Baltimore, they telegraphed a representative to beseech him not to come. Reportedly a scene ensued at which Breckinridge charged the invitation committee with deliberately insulting him, denounced the New York Democrats as no better than Black Republicans, and declared that a "terrible retribution" was in store for it when they would find the armies of the South in New York City's marble palaces and the rebel flag flying over city hall and the Merchant's Exchange. Since this report came in a Radical newspaper that had been attacking Breckinridge repeatedly for the past five years, it is not unlikely that much of the story—especially the threats—was either fabrication or rumor heavily embellished. Nevertheless, it undoubtedly mirrored some of his frustration and resentment at the repeated and increasingly hostile acts against him by those who could not understand the simple truths that he spoke, truths that seemed to him so plainly obvious. [15]

14. Wilson, *History of Kentucky*, II, 356. John R. O'Connor, "John Cabell Breckinridge's Personal Secession: A Rhetorical Insight," *Filson Club History Quarterly*, XLIII (October, 1969), 345–51, argues that Breckinridge talked himself out of the Union by way of his embittered Senate speeches. This is rather a simplistic view, overlooking many other far more significant factors, but does add weight to the argument that his public image—formed, in part, by the fact that his views of the Constitution coincided with those of the secessionists'—is what drove him South.

15. Frank L. Klement, *The Limits of Dissent, Clement L. Vallandigham & the Civil*

Traveling west with friends like Browning and the Union Democrats John McClernand and David Voorhees, Breckinridge reached Lexington on August 15, unheralded, and was received by a gathering of friends that seemed small in comparison to the crowds of former days. He met a gloomy prospect. Sensing that the legislature and the general Union sentiment in the state would condone—or at least not condemn—their actions, Federal authorities were now openly recruiting in Kentucky at Camp Dick Robinson only thirty miles south of Lexington. The commander at the camp had been an old friend of Breckinridge's, Lieutenant William Nelson of Maysville, but the same day that the senator reached Lexington, Colonel George H. Thomas took over the command. Also, Breckinridge's party had been resoundingly defeated in the state legislature elections just a few days before, and the representation at Frankfort would now be 103 to 38 against him.[16]

Breckinridge's first concern was with Camp Dick Robinson and, three days after his arrival, he met with Magoffin and twenty-six other Southern Rights men at the home of Romulus Paine in Scott County. They decided that the governor should demand that Lincoln abandon the camp and disband the regiments being formed there. On their own part, they should set about organizing a series of "anti-Lincoln" picnics for the next several weeks. No proposals had been made for violence or armed resistance, but Magoffin had barely had the chance to dispatch two commissioners to see Lincoln before an armed confrontation seemed imminent in Lexington.[17]

A shipment of guns for the Dick Robinson recruits was expected to arrive in the city before daylight on August 20. Although Union men in the town were resolved to see that the weapons reached the soldiers, southern sympathizers led by John Hunt Morgan and his Lexington Rifles designed to capture all or part of the shipment. Word of the plot reached Camp Dick Robinson, and a detachment of two hundred cavalry was sent out immediately. As planned, the guns arrived before dawn, and shortly afterward signals were sounded for the gathering of the Union and southern

War (Lexington, 1970), 78–79; Baltimore *American*, August 9, 1861; New York *Harper's Weekly*, August 24, 1861; Cleveland *Leader*, August 15, 1861.

16. Pease and Randall, *Diary of . . . Browning*, I, 495, August 13, 1861; Lexington *Kentucky Statesman*, August 16, 1861; Thomas B. Van Horne, *History of the Army of the Cumberland* (Cincinnati, 1876), I, 26; Dean Sprague, *Freedom Under Lincoln* (Boston, 1965), 258.

17. J. Stoddard Johnston, *Kentucky* (2nd ed.; New York, 1962), 27–28, Vol. IX of Clement A. Evans (ed.), *Confederate Military History*; Lorine Letcher Butler, *John Morgan and His Men* (Philadelphia, 1960), 38.

men. At the same time the cavalry reached Lexington and a conflict seemed certain. However, at this moment, Breckinridge stepped in. He was living at the Phoenix again, and now, in company with his friend, Unionist Madison C. Johnson, he went to the Rifles' armory and persuaded Morgan to give up his plan, thereby preserving peace. The prospect of Kentuckians fighting Kentuckians made him sick at heart, and committed him more than ever to neutrality.[18]

With this emergency past, and even though Lincoln rebuffed Magoffin's request, Breckinridge went forward with plans for the picnics. At least four were scheduled, in addition to other smaller meetings, and Breckinridge intended to be present at all of them. He appeared at the first, in Lexington, on August 29, and spoke along with Preston and others. The next day he spoke at Richmond, in Madison County, this time surrounded by an impressive array of his friends, including Clay, Vallandigham, Charles Morehead, Powell, Stevenson, Woolley, Magoffin, R. H. Stanton, Beck, and Roger Hanson; he spoke again at Newport shortly afterward. The meetings went off with no incident, though some thought that their sole purpose was to sound out prospective recruits for the Confederacy, Then things began to happen too fast for anyone to grasp fully what was going on.[19]

On August 29, the same day as the Lexington picnic, a considerable group of Union men met at Dick Robinson, among them Nelson, soon to be a brigadier, Colonel Thomas Bramlette of the Third Kentucky Infantry, and several others. It was Nelson's belief that these picnics were military in nature, designed to promote enlistments with the South, and too dangerous to be allowed to continue. His fears were exaggerated, but understandable, thanks to the known sympathies of most of the men leading the meetings. Their protestations for neutrality did not convince him, and his particular concern now was a gathering to be held in Owen County on September 5. He proposed to capture its leaders and disperse everyone else; reluctantly observing protocol he would warn Governor Magoffin of his intentions first. On September 2, however, a Confederate force under Brigadier Gen-

18. Frankfort *Yeoman*, August 30, 1861; Butler, *Morgan*, 40–41; Daniel Stevenson, "General Nelson, Kentucky, and Lincoln Guns," *Magazine of American History*, X (August, 1883), 137. The author's account of this affair is based on an eyewitness version by Hiram Shaw, given in Stevenson's article. Van Horne, *Army of the Cumberland*, I, 22, provides a very fanciful account in which Morgan and Breckinridge scheme together to disrupt the arms delivery.

19. Lexington *Kentucky Statesman*, August 27, 30, 1861; Cincinnati *Commercial*, November 15, 1887; Cincinnati *Daily Enquirer*, September 3, 1861.

eral Leonidas Polk entered Kentucky in protest to the raising of Union troops there, and four days later Brigadier General U. S. Grant led his Federal command into the state to occupy Paducah and oppose Polk. Both felt justified in their actions and, strictly speaking, both were. Under a rigid interpretation of neutrality, both North and South had made several violations in past months, but that all mattered very little now. Neutrality was at an end, and since the legislature was strongly pro-Union, it almost immediately demanded the withdrawal of the Confederate forces, and asked the Federal authorities for aid. Meanwhile at the Owen meeting, which took place unmolested, a "Peace Convention" was called for Frankfort on September 10. It was the last hope of the southern sympathizers to maintain the neutrality that all feared the legislature would officially renounce.[20]

During these confusing and troubled days, Breckinridge continued in the course he had set for himself when he arrived back at home. He did not regard the actions of either Polk or Grant as sufficient reason to abandon neutrality, and he preached his doctrine ably at a meeting on September 9 in Mason County, near May's Lick. He, William Simms, and George B. Hodge were entertained at a dinner, after which each spoke. Breckinridge, of course, was the chief object of attention, especially since the southern men in the audience of some 10,000 were anxiously awaiting his declaration that they might follow his lead. It had been rumored that there would be trouble, many were armed, feeling ran high, and the senator sensed it all when he arose and exclaimed: "What a scene! And hard upon it all is crowding grim war, with death and devastation in train, with ruin for every interest, and sable for many a hearthstone! The thought of it makes my heart ache." He spoke for nearly three hours, reviewing once more the efforts at compromise that had been rejected by the dominant party of the North, Lincoln's executive usurpation of power, the violation of every right of person by unlawful arrests and imprisonment, and the subversion of all civil authority to the military. He pleaded that Kentucky should maintain a strict neutrality between the warring sections and strive without regard to party or faction for peace, peace at any price. At his conclusion, Breckinridge cried: "In God's name, my countrymen, what more can I say to you!"[21]

20. Robert J. Breckinridge, The Secession Conspiracy in Kentucky and its Overthrow, in B. MSS; Coulter, Civil War, 107–14.
21. Maysville (Ky.) Bulletin, July 16, 1906, clipping in John C. Breckinridge MSS in possession of the late Mrs. Jeter Horton, New York, N.Y.; Frankfort Weekly Kentucky Yeoman, September 13, 30, 1861.

The senator had planned to go on to Maysville as Stanton's guest and speak at the courthouse that evening. However, a friend, A. G. Browning, who was to have gone with him, happened to overhear a conversation in the audience which changed their plans. He passed three men who were talking, and distinctly heard one of them say: "I tell you, men, 'twill never do to make the attempt on the grounds. John Breckinridge has more fanatical fool friends than any man alive. Everyone here today is armed to the teeth and will fight to the death. The slaughter would be awful. And think of the women and children. Wait till we get him in the courthouse tonight, when seizing our opportunity, we can land him in prison without firing a gun." Browning, fearing that the conspirators knew he had overheard them, hurried to Breckinridge with the news, urging him not to go to Maysville, and to leave immediately. As they discussed what to do, Stanton came up and exclaimed, "John, it will never do for you to go to Maysville tonight! I have reason to believe there's a plot to arrest you there; you must take the back track at once, or a dire calamity may befall you and all your friends." There was some difficulty in making Breckinridge realize the gravity of the situation, but he finally assented to follow their advice so far as Maysville was concerned. Just who was responsible for the plot to arrest him is uncertain. There is no indication that the military was involved, though Nelson, who was now in command at Maysville, may have had something to do with it.[22]

Breckinridge, Hodge, Simms, and perhaps others, went on to Frankfort. Now the precariousness of his position became clear to Breckinridge. Although the military may not have been involved in this arrest attempt, surely it was only a matter of time before official orders went out for his capture. Rumors were now abroad in Washington that he was a member of the Knights of the Golden Circle, a supposedly subversive society whose motives and numbers were grossly exaggerated. Many in the capital feared that his "malign influence" would force Kentucky out of the Union. It was only in the face of this, and perhaps for the first time since his Frankfort speech nearly two years before, that Breckinridge made a truly realistic judgment of his situation. He spoke with a number of friends that night in Frankfort, most of them good Union men. They would later report that he stated his conviction that, ultimately, the Confederacy was bound to be overthrown. At the same time he knew that if he, like his friend McClernand, remained in the Union loyally supporting Lincoln, he could secure

22. Maysville *Bulletin*, July 16, 1906.

high command in the army, become a trusted counselor of the Federal administration and, with these feathers in his cap, probably get back on the track to the White House. Nevertheless, his loyalty to those who had loved and supported him—and perhaps his proud refusal to retract that "wrong step" taken in this city in December, 1859—won out. He loved the South and its people and was resolved to cast his lot with them, regardless of the consequences to himself. He still hoped for neutrality and did not yet plan to take up arms for the South, but it was clear that he would do so if the decision was forced upon him. When his friends made a final appeal for him to take his stand with the Union, he could only reply that he was "already over the dam." [23]

The next day, despite the danger, Breckinridge took his seat as a Fayette representative in the Frankfort Peace Convention. He and his friends wished to avoid any demonstration or attention to himself, however, and his was a totally passive part in the proceedings. No doubt they feared that any attention just now could result in his arrest or, perhaps, violence. The convention sat all day, adopting resolutions reaffirming neutrality, and refusing to allow either side to recruit on Kentucky soil. They denounced Major General John C. Frémont's premature act of emancipation in Missouri and called for the appointment of a peace commission to work for a negotiated settlement.[24]

Breckinridge spent the next nine days peacefully and unmolested in and about Lexington, even running a horse in the races. Nevertheless, the knowledge that his arrest was imminent, hinging only on the state's tenuous stance on neutrality, stood foremost in his mind. Thanks to one of the bills that he had opposed in the Senate, as soon as Kentucky embraced the Union, Federal commanders would be free to arrest whomever they chose without warrant or writ.

On September 11 some letters to or from Breckinridge were found in the possession of William Winder of Philadelphia, brother of a Confederate present at Fort Sumter, and the government in Washington chose to regard this as proof that Breckinridge, Vallandigham, and Winder's other correspondents were traitors. Knowing that confiscation of property of suspected traitors would soon follow their arrests, Breckinridge on September

23. *Ibid.*; David Donald (ed.), *Inside Lincoln's Cabinet, The Civil War Diaries of Salmon P. Chase* (New York, 1954), 126; Blaine, *Twenty Years*, I, 330–31. The account of Breckinridge's conversation with friends in Frankfort is pieced together from the Cincinnati *Commercial*, November 15, 1887, and the Louisville *Courier-Journal*, May 30, 1900.
24. Frankfort *Weekly Kentucky Yeoman*, September 13, 1861.

13 transferred by deed of trust the title to all of his landholdings to Madison C. Johnson. He still had committed no overt act nor, but for one innocuous character reference written to Jefferson Davis, had he even been in correspondence with the rebels. His only crime so far had been to speak out against the Lincoln administration, and even that had been in terms much less harsh than those used by Bayard of Delaware or Vallandigham of Ohio, and they were not in immediate danger of arrest. What made his case different was the crucial role that Kentucky would have to play in the contest. To Lincoln it was the key, and in its present precarious position, the state's Union men could not afford to stand on the letter of the law in silencing what was, or might be, disloyal opposition.[25]

Matters came to a head rapidly. On September 18 the Kentucky legislature formally ended neutrality and took the side of the Union. The arrests began the same night, and among the first to be taken was former governor Morehead of Louisville. At the same time, the prosouthern Louisville *Courier* was suppressed. That same day several men throughout the nation advised Washington authorities that Breckinridge should be arrested. Some like Captain Samuel F. duPont believed that he should have been incarcerated following his appearance in Baltimore, and others thought that he had actually been taking notes on the armament of Fort McHenry for the enemy. When the heads of the two houses of the legislature at Frankfort recommended the senator's arrest to General Thomas, the die was cast. Thomas ordered Bramlette to go to Lexington on September 19 with a detachment from Camp Robinson. They were to break up, or at least closely observe, the peace meeting scheduled for the twentieth and take Breckinridge into custody.[26]

Records of Breckinridge's movements during these last days are obscure, no doubt because he preferred to stay quiet. He spent them in Lexington, waiting for the peace meeting. When the legislature ended neutrality he was probably not surprised, nor is it likely that the arrest of Morehead—which he surely knew of by midday of the nineteenth—alarmed him for his own safety. He remained in town all day and planned to attend a wedding that night. However, shortly before sundown that evening, a man named Smith hurried in to Lexington to tell Breckinridge that he had just come

25. Lexington *Kentucky Statesman*, September 7, 1860; *O.R.*, Ser. II, Vol. II, 275; Cloutier, "Superior City Speculator," 17.

26. Coulter, *Civil War*, 114; Sprague, *Freedom Under Lincoln*, 265–67; *O.R.*, Ser. II, Vol. I, 614, 684, Ser. II, Vol. II, 65–66, 71, Ser. I, Vol. IV, 262–63, 267; duPont to Matthew Maury, August 30, 1861, in Hayes, *The Mission*, 140; Van Horne, *Army of the Cumberland*, I, 30–31.

from Nicholasville, where he had seen Bramlette headed for Lexington. It was believed that he was coming up to arrest the senator and some of his friends before the meeting on the next day. Immediately, Breckinridge took a pencil and hastily scribbled *"Hawks are about"* on a crumpled piece of paper. He gave it to a little boy and sent him running to Preston who knew the sender of the unsigned note and heeded the boy's urging that the gentleman wanted to see him.[27]

Preston found the senator in his rooms at the Phoenix. Quickly Breckinridge told him what he had heard. It was now sunset, and he proposed to leave the city as soon as it became dark, for it was either escape to freedom, or suffer arrest and indefinite imprisonment without warrant or a writ of habeas corpus. He consulted briefly with Preston, after which his mother came in to bid him farewell. She was calm, but obviously anguished, and said little. After a few whispered words and a long embrace, she left, perhaps sensing that she and her only son would never see each other again.[28]

Preston left shortly afterward, probably after agreeing to meet Breckinridge at or near Winton, a mansion house seven miles north of Lexington. The senator then packed a few belongings in a valise, while the family stood quietly around him, each deep in his own thoughts. Little Mary carried the memory of that last hour with her for over forty years, even though she had no idea of what was happening. Her mother's sorrow was obvious; her brother Clifton was boyishly eager as he helped his father prepare his things. And through it all, her father himself wore a sad smile that bravely concealed untold anguish. It was expected that there might be someone watching the hotel, so, to allay any suspicion, Breckinridge's valise went out before him, carried by the Phoenix's housekeeper, a favorite with the family, Ann E. "Mammy" West. Shortly, Breckinridge left the room, followed by his family. Behind them, spread out on the bed, lay the dress Mary was to have worn to the wedding that night.

Breckinridge rode off through the dark toward Winton. There he was joined by a noted horse breeder, A. Keene Richards, and perhaps Preston. Apparently unable to retain the horse he had ridden thus far, Breckinridge was forced to search for a mount with Richards, and the best they could come up with was a broken-down old gray mare. After hastily savoring a long drink of Jesse Wood's fine Old Crow bourbon, they mounted up and set out, presenting the humorous—and ironic—aspect of perhaps the finest horseman in Kentucky and one of the state's best breeders, bouncing along

27. *O.R.*, Ser. I, Vol. IV, 263, 267; Louisville *Courier-Journal*, June 18, 1875.
28. Louisville *Courier-Journal*, June 18, 1875.

on a weary plug through Clark County, toward the mountains to the east, Virginia, and the Confederacy.[29]

No matter what the Federal authorities thought, Breckinridge's friends knew that he was loyal to the last. The Republican Cassius Clay, who believed that "John C. Breckinridge was foremost wherever fortune led him," would later declare, "He never was at heart a Secessionist." Henry Watterson, a friend and reporter for the Washington *Daily States*, regarded Breckinridge as "One of the least confident of those who looked on and afterward fell in line" with secession. Forney, Blaine, and other personal friends and political opponents, would agree. Even a bearded little Union general, U. S. Grant, sympathized with the senator in some degree. "He was among the last to go over to the South," Grant would say, "and was rather dragged into the position." And everyone seemed to see that, secessionist or not, Breckinridge would suffer more than his share of obloquy on another account. He could not offer the poor excuse that he was following his state into the Confederacy. He, Trusten Polk, and Waldo Johnson of Missouri, were the only senators to leave Washington for the South who did not do so in obedience to the instructions of their states through ordinances of secession. "He followed the logic of the doctrines he had preached," read one editorial, "and fought for his friends." [30]

And so Breckinridge was riding toward the mountains. Through it all he had been largely a victim; the victim of his own narrow conservatism, the victim of an erroneous but persuasive national image and, most of all, the victim of a chain of circumstances that left him saying the wrong things in the wrong place and at the wrong time. He had fought for compromise and failed; he had sought peace and moderation and found only bitterness; he had proclaimed his devotion to the Union to the best of his ability and found, after all, that he had only convinced himself.

John C. Breckinridge had much to ponder as he jogged along to Owingsville. As his closest friends would later testify, to the very day of his flight he had never intended to "go South." He did so now only because his arrest had been ordered by the government. He was an innocent man, but he

29. Mary Breckinridge Maltby, "Recollections of Civil War Times In Kentucky," *Register of the Kentucky Historical Society*, XLV (July, 1947), 227; Ann West to Mary C. Breckinridge, May 16, 1875, in JCB Papers; A. Keene Richards to Breckinridge, July 8, 1868, in B. MSS; Robert D. Meade to the author, February 16, 1071.

30. Clay, *Memoirs*, I, 220; Watterson, "*Marse Henry*," I, 151–52; John Russell Young, *Around the World with General Grant* (New York, 1870), II, 461–62; Cincinnati *Commercial*, May 18, 1875. The quotation of Beck's is from the Louisville *Courier-Journal*, November 17, 1887.

would be taken, denied his rights, and, like Morehead, spirited away to a prison deep in the North to sit for months without hope. Then, too, it cannot be doubted that his pride was deeply wounded that for doing his duty as he saw it, he would be arrested. Even those of his friends who remained firmly attached to the Union throughout the war, approved his leaving. Indeed, in later years Beck would seek Breckinridge's permission to defend his flight and present the full story behind it, on the floor of the United States Senate. As for Breckinridge himself, he never ceased to regret this day.[31]

Since he had decided not to accept unlawful arrest, he saw only two alternatives before him; he could continue to remain neutral in the conflict and go into exile somewhere, or he could take arms with his fellow southerners in resistance to the tyranny that had driven him from his home. Since he had never been able to play a passive part in any conflict, he chose the latter course. It was a decision made out of anger and frustration, and he would live to regret it as perhaps the greatest mistake of his life. For now it appeared to be all that he could manfully do, and he committed his allegiance to the Confederacy.[32]

From Owingsville, Breckinridge turned southeast, passed through Morgan County, and into Prestonburg. There he met Preston and others, made a speech, and otherwise helped in raising some three hundred men, along with blankets and rifles. Many of those who joined him did so for the same reasons that had caused him to flee—fear of arrest because of their political sympathies—when actually they had done no disloyal acts. From Prestonburg, Breckinridge went on to Piketon, remained there three days, and then crossed into Virginia. By October 2 or 3 he was at Tazewell Court House.[33]

His movements were of no small interest to Kentuckians, and rumor put him in several places at once. It was even stated in the Cincinnati press

---

31. McClure, *Recollections*, 159; James B. Beck to Breckinridge, April 19, 27, 1874, in JCB Papers; J. Stoddard Johnston Diary, August 14, 1862, in J. Stoddard Johnston MSS, FC.

32. Jonathan T. Dorris, interviewing J. W. Cammack, circuit judge in Kentucky and member of the board of regents of Eastern Kentucky State College, was told that "older men, who knew Breckinridge intimately, expressed opinions that the distinguished Kentuckian regretted toward the end of his life that he had ever espoused the cause of the Confederate States of America." Dorris, "Pardoning John Cabell Breckinridge," *Register of the Kentucky Historical Society*, LVI (October, 1958), 323; J. Paul Jones to Breckinridge, October 13, 1871, in JCB Papers.

33. Louisville *Daily Democrat*, September 29, October 11, 1861; *O.R.*, Ser. II, Vol. II, 814; Richmond *Daily Dispatch*, October 1, 1861.

that he had been shot and killed, while R. H. Stanton supposedly received a message from him stating that he was in Richmond, Virginia, and would soon be back with a general's commission to take command of the secession companies at Hazel Green. In fact, he went south through Cumberland Gap to Knoxville. He spoke to a crowd there in response to an enthusiastic greeting, promising his audience that Kentucky would soon drive the "Lincoln invaders" from her soil. Then he went back into Kentucky to join Buckner's Confederate forces occupying Bowling Green. As he approached Bowling Green, Breckinridge encountered an Alabama regiment that Buckner had sent out to meet and escort him into town. One of the Alabamians, rather well filled with "applejack," injudiciously quipped of the Kentuckian's flight from the Union that "as they wouldn't give you what you wanted over there, you can come now to us." Breckinridge looked at him for a moment, quietly, then smiled as the soldiers cheered him. Indeed, he had now come to them, back to his native state, and it was time to live up to the promises he had made in the Senate. On October 8, 1861, from Bowling Green, he issued his last address as a statesman, and his first as a Confederate. It was in the form of an open letter which would be widely published throughout the Union and the Confederacy.[34]

He returned the trust given him to represent Kentucky in the Senate, he said. He could no longer keep it. He had tried to stand for the state's wishes in Washington, he had opposed Lincoln's war policy at every step, even to refusing Kentucky's men and money, for "I would have blushed to meet you with the confession that I had purchased for you exemption from the perils of the battlefield and the shame of waging war against your Southern brethren by hiring others to do the work you shrank from performing." He denied that he had committed any crimes or that he had misrepresented his fellow Kentuckians. "I resign," he said, "because there is no place left where a Southern Senator may sit in council with the Senators of the North. In truth, there is no longer a Senate of the United States within the meaning and spirit of the Constitution."

The Union no longer existed, he continued. Lincoln had assumed dictatorial powers. The rights of person and property were being flagrantly violated every day. Unlawful arrests were the rule. The subjugation and con-

34. Louisville *Daily Democrat*, October 11, 1861; *O.R.*, Ser. I, Vol. IV, 293, Ser. II, Vol. II, 916; Frankfort *Kentucky Yeoman*, October 4, 1861; Oliver R. Temple, *East Tennessee and the Civil War* (Cincinnati, 1899), 374; Richmond *Daily Dispatch*, October 7, 1861; L. B. Ulmer, "A Glimpse of Johnstone [*sic*] Through the Smoke of Shiloh," 1901, Choctaw County Public Library, Butler, Ala.

quest of the South were the rallying cries in the Federal Congress. As for Kentucky, her neutrality had been violated repeatedly, arms secretly supplied to Federal sympathizers, troops unlawfully raised within her borders, the legislature intimidated and packed with the minions of Washington, freedoms of speech, press, and assembly, restricted, and hundreds forced to flee their homes for safety. He explained his own flight to avoid arrest, saying he would have welcomed it if he had any assurance that it would have been followed by a trial by judge and jury, but he knew that would not be. Witness the case of Morehead, he said, and by now he might have added Clay and others as well.

Would Kentucky stand by while all of this went on? Would she consent to the usurpations of Lincoln and his hirelings; would she suffer her children to be imprisoned and exiled by the "German mercenaries" that the Union was enlisting to fight its war? Never, he said. "Never, while Kentucky remains the Kentucky of old—never, while thousands of her gallant sons have the will and the nerve to make the State sing to the music of their rifles." Whatever might be the future relations of the two nations, the old Union could never again be reunited as it once was. He wanted peace between them lest one conquer the other and the result be military despotism. He was casting his lot with his eyes wide open, he said. He, like the Indian chiefs, had seen the North; he knew what an "almighty big country" they would have to fight but, nevertheless, he had made his choice. To defend his own birthright and that of his fellow Kentuckians who had been denied the protection due them, and were forced to choose between arrest, exile, or resistance, he now exchanged "with proud satisfaction, a term of six years in the Senate of the United States for the musket of a soldier." As one of those forced to make that choice, he said, "I intend to resist." [35]

35. "Address of John C. Breckinridge to the People of Kentucky," October 8, 1861, in Frank Moore (comp.), *The Rebellion Record* (New York, 1864), III, Documents, 254–59.

Book II
Soldier

CHAPTER **1**

The Musket of a Soldier

The hard road from Lexington to Virginia and back to Bowling Green, wrought many changes upon John C. Breckinridge. Suddenly the old life was a memory. The man who had never shown any particular interest in the military life other than, perhaps, the possibilities it held for advancing the beginnings of his political career, had now forsaken the statesman's podium for "the musket of a soldier." The Kentuckian, as a lawyer too sensitive to accept cases which would require him to act as prosecutor, was now embarked on the business of killing. Breckinridge, the conservative who had never entertained a disruptive thought nor uttered a revolutionary word, joined hands with rebellion. Of course, from his point of view, he was acting only in self-defense, not revolution, and in his particular case this attitude might seem justified. Indeed, if there had been any loyal man in the Union whom the civil and military authorities truly forced to "go South," that man was Breckinridge. Now that the act was done, the semantic differences between defense and disunion ceased to be important. Breckinridge was born into a strange new world this October in Bowling Green, a world wholly different from anything he had known. As he went out to discover it, the experience would reveal in him a curious paradox— a character and intellect naturally adapted for leadership in the profession of arms, but a heart and soul whose revulsion for war's bloody work would leave him wandering down another path, toward great sadness and slow death.

Breckinridge delivered his resignation address almost immediately upon his arrival at Bowling Green, having left Nashville only the day before. He paid his first call on Brigadier General Simon B. Buckner, who was in command of the Central Division of Kentucky—about four thousand Confederates at Bowling Green, and several thousand elsewhere in the state.

293

Together they discussed the most obvious subject at hand, the course of Kentucky now that neutrality was at an end. Both wanted their state to join the Confederacy. Breckinridge still hoped that a united block of slave states, Kentucky included, would force Lincoln to negotiation, with one of two goals: either congressional and constitutional guarantees or a peaceful separation of the South. But first Kentucky must be drawn to the South, and toward that end Breckinridge tendered Buckner his services, to be used in whatever position was offered—as a private if necessary.[1]

Naturally, no one in the Confederacy would have been foolish enough to let a man of Breckinridge's stature enlist in the ranks, nor is it likely that he thought he would have to. Buckner almost immediately wrote to General Samuel Cooper at Richmond, the adjutant and inspector general of the army, suggesting that the former major be commissioned a brigadier general and given command of the First Kentucky Brigade or a similar unit. It required no persuasion to see that, if anyone could bring the Southern Rights element in Kentucky under the Confederate banner, it was Breckinridge. Even as he wrote to Cooper, Buckner already envisioned sending him through the eastern counties of the state for this very purpose, and his conversations with the former senator made him confident that the exile approved the plan.[2]

Breckinridge and his former political foe Humphrey Marshall, Preston, William Simms, and others left for Richmond only a few days after his arrival in Bowling Green. Going by way of Nashville, they reached the Confederate capital on October 21, taking rooms at the Spotswood Hotel. That evening Marshall spoke briefly to a welcoming crowd outside the hotel, and the citizens were disappointed to hear that Breckinridge would not appear, having gone to call on old friends.[3]

Immediately after Breckinridge reached Richmond his potential position as a Confederate became a subject for rumor. A brigadier's commission at the very least seemed assured, but hints went abroad of a higher station. The first Confederate secretary of war, Leroy Pope Walker, had resigned in ill health on September 14, and Attorney-General Judah P. Benjamin had been acting in his place pending a permanent appointment. Now there was speculation that Breckinridge would assume this portfolio. Indeed, it would have been a wise appointment, and surely President Davis consid-

1. *O.R.,* Ser. II, Vol. II, 1503, Ser. I, Vol. IV, 445.
2. *Ibid.,* Ser. I, Vol. IV, 445.
3. Frankfort *Commonwealth,* October 30, 1861; James G. Leach to Breckinridge, November 5, 1874, in JCB Papers; Richmond *Daily Dispatch,* October 22, 1861.

ered it, perhaps even discussed the matter with Breckinridge. The Kentuckian would have brought stature to an otherwise—save for Benjamin—lackluster cabinet, and his four years as vice-president had equipped him with more than sufficient administrative skills. However, the turn of events, common sense, and perhaps Breckinridge's own preference, led Davis back to Buckner's original proposal.[4]

Kentucky was the great question in the last months of 1861, and it was generally agreed that a mere army of invasion could not wrest it from the Union. "Kentucky cannot be rallied by Confederate generals or anything else," wrote the Richmond *Daily Dispatch*. "It can only be rallied by its own native citizens to whom they have a habit of looking up in the past contest of the parties. Breckinridge . . . and others can bring Kentucky into line with the South." The press believed that this was the real reason for Breckinridge's visit to Richmond. Davis decided that, statesmen though they were, Breckinridge, Marshall, and certain others could best serve the cause by returning to their native state. Consequently, on November 2 the president appointed Breckinridge a brigadier general in the Provisional Army of the Confederate States, and the Kentuckian accepted his commission the next day, pending its confirmation by the Senate. At the same time, he received orders from Benjamin to report back to Buckner to assume command of a brigade of Kentucky troops, and on November 6 he left once more for Bowling Green. Since he had remained in the United States Senate for several months after the actual outbreak of war, Humphrey Marshall thought that at the least he had been "hesitating and over cautious." There were Confederates who distrusted his sincerity in coming south, but with his appointment, wrote a clerk in the War Department, "no one doubts that he is now with us, and will do good service." [5]

Three days put Breckinridge back in Nashville, and from there he went on to Bowling Green to report to Buckner. The new general's movements had not gone unnoticed in what was left of the old Union, and already the villification had begun. "Judas Cataline Breckinridge," the Frankfort *Commonwealth* called him, one of "those wily politicians . . . who caused all this misery for purposes looking to their own personal aggrandizement." Since

4. Richmond *Daily Dispatch*, October 28, 1861.

5. *Ibid.*, October 22, November 7, 1861; Statement of Appointment, Breckinridge, Service Record, NA; *O.R.*, Ser. I, Vol. IV, 504. Unless otherwise cited, all citations from NA are from RG 109. John B. Jones, *A Rebel War Clerk's Diary at the Confederate States Capital* (Philadelphia, 1866), I, 95; *Journal of the Congress of the Confederate States of America* (Washington, 1904–1905), I, 474; Humphrey Marshall to Edward O. Guerrant, June 20, 1867, in Edward O. Guerrant MSS, FC.

the Federal authorities had not been able to capture him, they took full advantage of the incontrovertible grounds now furnished by his formal enlistment with the Confederacy, to bring constitutional charges against him. Kentucky's legislature began even while Breckinridge was fleeing into Virginia. On October 2 both houses declared that he and Powell no longer represented the will of the people and instructed them to resign, though Magoffin's refusal to endorse the resolution kept it from being enforced. Soon a movement began to confiscate his landholdings in the North. While Breckinridge was in Richmond, a Federal grand jury and district court at Frankfort indicted him and thirty-two other Kentuckians for treason, and on December 2, 1861, the United States Senate passed a resolution expelling "the traitor Breckinridge." The loyal friend Powell raised the sole objection to the act, asserting that Breckinridge had already resigned his seat on October 8, and that expulsion was unnecessary. Powell's son would later tell the general, "My father esteemed & loved you with a deep devotion." Despite the war that separated the two old friends, Powell never ceased to speak of Breckinridge "in more than affectionate terms," and brought up his children to respect and esteem his Confederate friend. But nothing the senator could do would sway his colleagues, and the expulsion resolution passed unanimously with Powell wisely refraining from voting in order not to jeopardize his own uncertain tenure in office. One Federal, at least, Captain duPont, discovered a new found respect for Breckinridge now that he had committed himself to fight for the doctrines he had preached in the Senate.[6]

On November 14 the general was officially assigned to Buckner's Second Division, Western Department, of what was now called the Central Army of Kentucky. A few days before the assignment Breckinridge briefly returned to politics to aid in promoting the organization of the provisional government of Kentucky, perhaps serving on a committee to organize the sovereign convention that met at Russellville on November 18. It adopted a constitution, an ordinance of secession, and elected officers, among them a governor, Mary Breckinridge's cousin, George W. Johnson. At that very moment Mary and the children were staying with Johnson's wife Ann at their home near Georgetown. Breckinridge was a general, now, however,

6. Frankfort Weekly Kentucky Yeoman. November 22, 1861; Frankfort Commonwealth, October 30, 1861; Coulter, Civil War and Readjustment, 140–41; Baltimore American. November 13, 1861; Moore. Rebellion Record. III, 102: J. Henry Powell to Breckinridge, October 7. 1869, in JCB Papers; Samuel duPont to Charles duPont, February 20, 1862, in Hayes, The Mission, I, 339.

and his role at Russellville, if any, was a minor one. He did make a number of speeches before large crowds in and around Bowling Green, sometimes speaking as often as three times a day advocating secession. Still, so long as the state remained in the Union, he did not approve entirely of showing the Confederate flag. After a speech in Hopkinsville he walked up and removed a miniature banner from the bridle of a carriage horse. "Wait, my boy," he told the enthusiastic young driver, "til Kentucky adopts that flag and then we'll do our best to keep it flying." Then, two days before the convention, on November 16, 1861, Breckinridge assumed his first command, the First Kentucky Brigade.[7]

The brigade was already unique and would become more so as the war went on. Organized on October 28 from regiments that had begun their formation back in July, it was composed entirely of volunteers from a state still in the Union. There had been no duress imposed on the men, either legal or moral, to enlist; they did so because they believed in the southern cause. Most of the men volunteered "for the war," rather than for the standard twelve months common among most such organizations in 1861, and they would give full service. For the next two years they would be intimately associated with their new general; their story would be his, and the ever-increasing attachment and affection between him and his men would stand unexcelled in the Confederate service.[8]

Breckinridge had about five thousand in his brigade, divided among the Second, Third, Fourth, Fifth, and Sixth Kentucky Infantry regiments, and artillery batteries under Captains Rice Graves and Robert Cobb. There was also a cavalry squadron under Captain John H. Morgan officially attached to the brigade, but it was usually off on detached service. Among the regimental commanders was Breckinridge's friend and old stump foe Roger W. Hanson, colonel of the Second. The captain of Company B of Hanson's regiment was the general's cousin, Robert J. Breckinridge, Jr., and one of the privates in the captain's company was the general's son, Cabell. There were Breckinridges in the other regiments as well, and it is doubtful if any other brigade commander in the army had so many relatives in his command. Thanks to this, and the fact that most of the officers and enlisted men in the brigade had been his political supporters in times past, the gen-

7. O.R., Ser. I, Vol. IV, 552, 556; Coulter, Civil War and Readjustment, 135–39; Maltby, "Civil War Times," 228; H. E. Horde, "Recollections of Gen. J. C. Breckinridge," Confederate Veteran, XVII (December, 1909), 594.

8. Albert D. Kirwan, "The Orphan Brigade," Louisville Courier-Journal, November 20, 1960, special supplement, 95–96; Thompson, First Kentucky Brigade, 51–55.

eral almost immediately became the darling of the brigade, and their pride in him was fierce and unwavering.[9]

Breckinridge's position at Bowling Green was one of great strategic importance to the overall line of the army's new commander, Kentuckian General Albert Sidney Johnston. Hundreds of miles long, the line was thinly manned and, in some spots, not well chosen. Anchored on the east at Cumberland Gap, it ran gradually southwesterly to Nashville, and back up to Columbus, Kentucky. Nashville had been its midpoint but, at almost the same time that Breckinridge arrived, Johnston had pushed Buckner up to Bowling Green. From this advanced position he hoped to be able to protect the fertile crop-yielding fields north of Nashville, as well as the valuable recruiting stations throughout central Tennessee. Because Buckner's line was so thinly spread, Johnston's center—Nashville—provided a target of enhanced temptation to Federal advance. For this reason, an advanced center at Bowling Green was a protective buffer.

Other factors made Bowling Green—and Breckinridge's position there—important. The abandonment of neutrality had been a major catastrophe to Confederate hopes for Kentucky. All through the summer of 1861 the Bluegrass State had served as an effective, neutral buffer, protecting Tennessee from overland invasion. Now it was open to the enemy as a natural path to the Confederate heartland. For the rest of the war, the South would entertain the elusive vision of regaining Kentucky. Now, with untold resources in manpower yet untapped in the states' rights counties of the southern central portion of the state, Johnston's occupation of Bowling Green could serve both to swell his ranks and as a rallying point from which Confederate sympathy in the state might yet swell to claim it for the Stars and Bars. It was for this reason that Breckinridge was assigned to this portion of Johnston's line. By far the most important and influential Kentuckian to don the gray uniform, he embodied the best opportunity of stirring the sentiment necessary to carry the state out of the Union. Some Confederates hailed his conversion to the cause as equivalent to the addition of a new division or more to their strength, and great hopes lay with the new general's future course.

His first and most immediate concern upon assuming command was to arm his men. Breckinridge took over a brigade that carried a staggering array of weapons. United States Harpers Ferry rifles, Belgian smoothbores, Allen and Mississippi rifles, buck-and-ball muskets, squirrel rifles, flintlocks,

9. Thompson, *First Kentucky Brigade*, 57; Statement of Appointment, J. Cabell Breckinridge, Service Record, NA.

converted flintlocks, shotguns, bowie knives, and all manner of worn and obsolete arms made up its arsenal. With help from an old friend, Virginia's Governor John Letcher, he standardized the Kentuckians' weaponry. Then began a rigorous training program. Daily drill, schools for officers, and discipline of his sometimes unruly men, required his every attention.[10]

Although he worked them, and punished them if necessary, the general was uniformly courteous and respectful to the men of his command. He did not abuse them, and he allowed no one else to do so, which surely accounts for much of the affection they felt for him. And when someone did attempt to mistreat the men, he took the matter seriously. While in camp at Bowling Green, a captain ordered a private to sweep out his tent. The soldier's reply was, "Go to hell," an answer that put him in the guardhouse. When news of this reached Breckinridge, he mounted up immediately and, "whipping his horse with his slouch hat," raced down to the captain's tent. After the captain admitted to his part in the incident, the general told him: "I want you to understand that when a private refuses to voluntarily sweep out my tent I will do it myself." Privates were not menials in the Kentucky Brigade, he went on. "They are all gentlemen, and you have no right to command one of them to do a menial service. Now you go to the guard house and apologize to the soldier you have insulted and sweep about your own tent, or you will take his place." [11]

Most of the training, organization, and discipline of the brigade had to be done on the move, for the army's new commander, General Albert Sidney Johnston, kept Breckinridge busy going back and forth holding points along part of the line established to keep Tennessee safe from Federal incursion. His movements did good service in keeping the enemy confused and on guard. Breckinridge was rumored to be advancing on Owensboro, seventy miles northwest of Bowling Green on the Ohio River, while Union authorities were on guard for him south of Elizabethtown, ninety miles east

10. Thompson, *First Kentucky Brigade*, 58–60; George B. Hodge to H. Allen, December 19, 1861, Special Order No. 30, December 19, 1861, Special Orders Received, First Kentucky Brigade, November 1861–October 1862, all in Chap. 2, CCCXVI, RG 109, NA; Hodge to George Cosby, December 5, 1861, January 2, 1862, Breckinridge to his regimental commanders, December 11, 1861, Hodge to N. R. Chambliss, January 2, 1862, Hodge to the regimental commanders, January 27, 1862, Hodge to John Morgan, December 16, 1861, Telegrams Received & Sent by Gen. Breckinridge's Command, December 1861–November 1863, all in Chap. 2, CCCXI, RG 109, NA; Breckinridge to Charles Dimmock, November 30, 1861, in "Governor Letcher's Official Correspondence," *SHSP*, I (June, 1876), 461.

11. Hodge to John A. Buckner, January 2, 1862, Chap. 2, CCCXI, NA; U.S. Congress, *Congressional Record*, 67th Cong., 1st Sess., Pt. 7, p. 7393.

of the river city. Meanwhile, the general busied himself sending out scouting parties and pickets, establishing courier lines between his headquarters and outlying detachments, and digging trenches and felling trees across roads to obstruct any Federal advance toward Bowling Green. When he could free himself from his duties, Breckinridge occasionally rode back to Bowling Green to visit friends. He called often on Reuben Davis, a friend from the vice-presidential days, and now a major general of Mississippi state troops in charge of the fortifications of the city. The Mississippian, who enjoyed the general's company, wrote, "He was a goodly sight, sitting on stool or table, with a glass of old shuck in his hand, and that grand voice of his vibrating through the tent like a deep-toned bell. . . . He was not only a most elegant gentleman, but genial and full of spirit, and ready to meet the worst of days with a sort of gay courage that sat well upon his stalwart manhood." Whenever Breckinridge left Davis' tent, he usually produced "a small demijohn, artfully concealed somewhere," and, as the Kentuckian put it, "loaded up for emergencies." [12]

The real emergency appeared in February, 1862, when Johnston's impractical line of defense began crumbling. It actually started on January 19 when the right flank under Generals Felix Zollicoffer and George Crittenden suffered defeat at Mill Springs, ninety miles east of Breckinridge's position at Oakland Station. Hard on this came the surrender of Fort Henry, Tennessee, on the Tennessee River, which isolated Johnston from his extreme left at Columbus, Kentucky, under Major General Leonidas Polk. Six days later the victor at Fort Henry, Federal Brigadier General U. S. Grant, laid siege to Fort Donelson, on the Cumberland River, the last bastion of the Confederate line. Johnston was left with no choice but to withdraw from Kentucky. The orders for the movement went out on February 11.

The news was particularly bitter to Breckinridge and his brigade. As he drew them up on the Nashville Pike for the move south the next morning, there was a gloom over the whole command. They were not just leaving their state and homes; they were abandoning them to the unrestrained wh'm of the enemy. All that day as they marched to Bowling Green, and the next as they went on towards Franklin, just five miles from the border,

12. Frankfort *Weekly Kentucky Yeoman*, November 29, 1861; Breckinridge to Roger W. Hanson, December 22, 1861, Chap. 2, CCCXI, NA; *O.R.*, Ser. I, Vol. VII, 549; Charles E. Hooker, *Mississippi* (2nd ed.; New York, 1962), 250–51, Vol. VII of Clement A. Evans (ed.), *Confederate Military History*; Reuben Davis, *Recollections of Mississippi and Mississippians* (Boston, 1889), 423–24.

they held out hope that something would develop to turn their march around. It snowed the night of February 13, and the next morning, disheartened, cold and hungry, the Kentuckians got temporarily out of hand, straggling in and around Franklin, appropriating local livestock and liquor, and tearing up fences along the pike for fires. It was afternoon before Breckinridge had them under control again, to continue the agonizing march. That same day, forming the rear guard infantry of the army, they passed out of Kentucky, silently, steeped in anger and melancholy. It was one of the saddest moments of Breckinridge's life, and it would grow sadder still. He could not have guessed that it would be seven long years before again he set foot in his native state.[13]

Two days later came the news of the capture of Fort Donelson, including Hanson's Second Kentucky and Graves's battery which Buckner had taken there as reinforcements some weeks before. Johnston notified Breckinridge of the disaster immediately and urged him to hurry his column. Finally, after considerable delay, Breckinridge led his command into Burnsville, Mississippi, near Corinth. Here Johnston was consolidating his army with the troops newly brought by the hero of Bull Run, General P. G. T. Beauregard. Breckinridge resumed the drilling of his brigade and sent a cavalry screen out to observe the movements of Grant's army encamped at Pittsburg Landing. One of the Federals out there, the colonel of a Kentucky cavalry regiment, was James M. Shackleford, the same weary Private Shackleford of the Fourth Kentucky who rode Breckinridge's horse on the march to Mexico City fourteen years before, while the major walked beside him.

While the general was on the march toward Burnsville, Albert Sidney Johnston had merged his army into the command structure of Beauregard's column, three corps under Major Generals William Hardee and Leonidas Polk, and Braxton Bragg, and a reserve corps, which included Breckinridge and the Kentucky Brigade, to be commanded by Crittenden. Then, only nine days after the general's arrival in Burnsville, Crittenden—whose conduct at the Mill Springs defeat brought severe criticism—and one of his generals were relieved of command and placed under arrest for alleged drunkenness. As a result, being senior brigadier, Breckinridge suddenly found himself, on March 31, in command of the Reserve Corps, Army of Mississippi.[14]

13. Thompson, *First Kentucky Brigade*, 77–80.
14. D. J. Noblitt, "Forty-Fourth Tennessee Infantry," in John B. Lindsley (ed.), *The Military Annals of Tennessee. Confederate* (Nashville, 1886), 529; Thompson,

Johnston and Beauregard may have felt some trepidation in giving the general this assignment. In the entire high command of the western army—Johnston, Beauregard, Bragg, Hardee, and Polk—Breckinridge stood out as the only one not a graduate of the Military Academy at West Point, the only one with no formal military training, and the only one with no real combat experience. The other brigadier in the Reserve Corps, John S. Bowen, had seen little or no fighting, but he was a graduate of West Point. However, since Breckinridge's commission antedated Bowen's by several months, seniority demanded that the Kentuckian be given the command. Despite Breckinridge's lack of experience, Johnston set a high store by his talents and, more important, prestige. The commander wanted Kentucky back, and the leader of the Reserve Corps could be a key figure in taking and holding the state. Johnston needed Kentucky for his own prestige, for the events of the last two months had seriously jeopardized his position, and raised a clamor for his replacement. He probably did not know, however, that among those suggested to command in his place was John C. Breckinridge. Indeed, Breckinridge's friends in Congress had been scheming for several weeks to get him a promotion, and on March 14, 1862, Jilson Johnson wrote that his name would probably be presented for major general shortly. A. S. Johnston was in danger of losing favor, and they wanted another high-ranking Kentuckian available to fill the possible gap. Breckinridge himself did not countenance their machinations. "I will not move in the matter," he decided.[15]

From the moment he took command, if not before, Breckinridge knew that a battle was imminent. On his first day he ordered a report on the amount of ammunition available in the different commands and how many rounds there were per man. Then, late on April 2, the general received notification to come to the telegraph office at Burnsville to await orders.

First Kentucky Brigade, 82–83, 85; *O.R.*, Ser. I, Vol. VII, 261, 905, 911, 916–17, Ser. I, Vol. X, Pt. 2, p. 363; William G. Stevenson, *Thirteen Months in the Rebel Army* (New York, 1864), 124; Breckinridge to W. W. Mackall, March 13, 1862, Breckinridge to Thomas Jordan, April 13, 1862, in Breckinridge, Service Record; Breckinridge to H. T. Brewster, March 27, 1862, in Chap. 2, CCCXI, NA; Brewster to Breckinridge, n.d., in Breckinridge MSS, CHS; Thomas L. Connelly, *Army of the Heartland: The Army of Tennessee, 1861–1862* (Baton Rouge, 1967), 146, 151.

15. *O.R.*, Ser. I, Vol. X, Pt. 1, p. 384, Pt. 2, pp. 314, 377; "Albert Sidney Johnston," *Confederate Veteran*, III (March, 1895), 82; William Preston Johnston, "Albert Sidney Johnston at Shiloh," in Robert U. Johnson and Clarence C. Buel (eds.), *Battles and Leaders of the Civil War* (New York, 1887), I, 564; endorsement on Johnson to Breckinridge, March 14, 1862, Jilson P. Johnson Service Record, NA.

Sometime after midnight the news came; Johnston was going to move on Grant at Pittsburg Landing.[16]

The delays that followed seemed endless. It was April 5 before the army was in position, and Breckinridge did not reach the battle line until late afternoon. As he rode up toward the front, he found Johnston, Bragg, Beauregard, and Polk in conference at a crossroad. Joining them a little after 4 P.M., Breckinridge, who was not feeling well, spread his blanket out on the wet ground and lay down on it near their small fire. The attack had already been delayed again, till the next morning, but now Beauregard and Bragg had lost their confidence. Arguing that the delays and some chance encounters with enemy pickets had ruined any chance for surprise, they advised that the army retire to Corinth and wait for another day. Johnston and Polk still favored an attack, and Breckinridge agreed with them, occasionally sitting upright on his blanket and adding a few words of counsel, knowing that Grant's defeat here would be the first step on the road back to Kentucky. His enthusiasm probably sprang more from inexperience than thoughtful reflection. In the end, of course, the decision rested with Johnston, and he decided to attack. The generals all met again later that night for further discussion, and Johnston's determination remained the same.[17]

The position the Confederates were to assault the next morning offered a glowing opportunity for victory. Despite the brushes their pickets had with Hardee, no one in the Federal high command seemed to fear an attack, nor were they prepared for it. Five divisions of infantry lay spread out in their camps between the supply base at Pittsburg Landing, on the Tennessee River, and the little Shiloh Church. The area was heavily wooded, cut by ravines, bordered on the Federal right by Owl and Snake creeks and on the left by Lick Creek, all of which fed into the river. With these creeks forming natural barriers for containing the Federals, Johnston could form his line between the creeks and push the enemy back against the river, then by a flanking movement on his right drive them back into a convex bend in

16. Hodge to Winfield S. Statham, March 31, 1862, in Chap. 2, CCCXI, NA; Thompson, *First Kentucky Brigade*, 87; Ed. Porter Thompson, *History of the Orphan Brigade* (Louisville, 1898), 630; Thomas Jordan, "Notes of a Confederate Staff Officer at Shiloh," in Johnson and Buel (eds.), *Battles and Leaders*, I, 594–95.

17. Breckinridge to Jordan, April 21, 1862, in Chap. 2, CCCXI, NA; William Preston to Leonidas Polk, December 1, 1874, in Leonidas Polk MSS, SHC; Stevenson, *Thirteen Months*, 138, 147; Grady C. McWhiney, *Braxton Bragg and Confederate Defeat, Volume I: Field Command* (New York, 1969), 226–27; Charles P. Roland, *Albert Sidney Johnston, Soldier of Three Republics* (Austin, Tex., 1964), 323–24.

the Snake. This would cut them off from the landing, leaving no escape route, and no choice but surrender or destruction. But Johnston and Beauregard devised an impractical scheme for achieving this. Instead of assigning each corps a place in the line, they ordered a three-mile front from Hardee's corps alone, to be followed by Bragg in the same formation. Polk and Breckinridge were to be held in reserve, and this may have been the only sound feature of the plan, especially where the Reserve Corps was concerned. Johnston would state that he held back Breckinridge because his Kentuckians, well used to hard and rapid marches, would best be able to move quickly to any endangered point on the long line. The real reason was probably apprehension over Breckinridge's inexperience.[18]

Sunday, April 6, dawned sunny and peaceful. The Reserve Corps, camped on a ridge on the Corinth road, woke early, and the men were eating breakfast when the first sound of Hardee's guns signaled the opening of the Battle of Shiloh. Breckinridge, charged with holding the Corinth road and the one immediately north of it, had to wait until Polk moved up to the battle line before he could advance. By now, his corps had grown to number 6,439, a sizable reserve for an army of 40,000, but it did not last. Following Polk, Breckinridge advanced as far as the Bark Road, just over three miles back from the front, keeping a cavalry screen out to guard his right flank. The surprised Federals were being pushed back steadily but Johnston was apprehensive about his left. As a result, Beauregard sent Breckinridge an order to take two of his brigades to that flank, but just as the general was advancing them in line of battle, Johnston changed his mind and wanted them on the right, where he planned for the flank attack that would drive the Federals away from the landing. Consequently, shortly before 8 A.M., Breckinridge moved Bowen and W. S. Statham's brigades off to the right, while R. P. Trabue continued toward Bragg where he was needed. With both portions of his command being ordered into battle, the general's corps was no longer a reserve.[19]

At 10:20, as Breckinridge was still moving toward the right, Johnston sent an order to him to feel his way to the Tennessee, then turn and press the left flank of the enemy. Forty minutes later, since the general had not

18. Alfred Roman, *The Military Operations of General Beauregard in the War Between the States* (New York, 1884), I, 329.

19. Thompson, *First Kentucky Brigade*, 89–91; William Preston, Memoranda of A. S. Johnston's Death; Battle of Shiloh, April 6, 1862, Box 2, Special File, RG 94, NA; Report, April 21, 1862, in Chap. 2, CCCXI, NA; *O.R.*, Ser. I, Vol. X, Pt. 1, pp. 386, 401; Pierre G. T. Beauregard, "The Campaign of Shiloh," in Johnson and Buel (eds.), *Battles and Leaders*, I, 586.

yet appeared, Johnston sent another staff officer to find Breckinridge and lead him into position. Breckinridge, like his fellow corps commanders, had little or no knowledge of the terrain of the field, no maps, and may well have been lost or blindly groping his way toward the river when Johnston's officer found him. They reached the right sometime before noon only to find that the enemy, Colonel David Stuart's brigade of Brigadier General William T. Sherman's division, had withdrawn somewhat, forming a line with the divisions on its right under Brigadiers Stephen Hurlbut and Benjamin Prentiss, and a brigade under Colonel John McArthur. They were posted in a heavy wood in and about the foremost of two campsites, leaving Breckinridge a front of over a mile to cover.[20]

Fortunately, Johnston appropriated the brigade of Brigadier General John R. Chalmers to extend the right of Breckinridge's line, placing it near the river, Bowen on its left, and Statham to the left of Bowen, in echelon, each 800 yards behind the other, with Chalmers in the lead. Johnston, perhaps not quite content to trust the attack entirely to the untested Breckinridge, especially in this crucial portion of the field, joined Bowen for the advance, while the Kentuckian himself went over to Statham. There, awaiting the order forward, the general and his staff gathered under a great spreading oak.

Breckinridge presented quite a sight. The uniforms of Confederate general officers were notoriously individual, and the general's was no exception. Instead of the more or less standard gray, he wore a uniform coat of dark blue "Kentucky jeans." And he may already have grown, or started to grow, his long flowing moustache. Always clean-shaven when a lawyer and statesman, Breckinridge probably did not realize that his new whiskers well symbolized his almost complete break with the past. He would wear them for the rest of his life. Thomas Jordan, Johnston's adjutant, was standing nearby and, looking over at Breckinridge, was struck by what he saw. "His dark eyes seemed to illuminate his swarthy, regular features," thought Jordan, "and as he sat in his saddle he seemed to me altogether the most impressive-looking man I had ever seen." Just then a Federal shell struck the oak and, exploding inside it, sent Breckinridge and staff dashing out in a storm of splinters. It was time to advance.[21]

Breckinridge led his men slowly forward, crossed a ravine, and by ten

---

20. Preston, Memoranda, April 6, 1862, RG 94, NA; Samuel H. Lockett, "Surprise and Withdrawal at Shiloh," in Johnson and Buel (eds.), *Battles and Leaders*, I, 604–605.
21. *O.R.*, Ser. I, Vol. X, Pt. 1, p. 404; Jordan, "Notes," 601; John Cunningham, "Reminiscences of Shiloh," *Confederate Veteran*, XVI (November, 1908), 577.

minutes past noon was on the hill occupied by the first Federal camp. He saw nothing until a sudden volley halted him momentarily. Jordan, who had taken upon himself much of Johnston's responsibility for directing the battle, ordered the brigade forward again, and Breckinridge complied. A Federal battery to his left was giving the line a heavy fire now, and the men had their first sight of their own dead on the field. "Never mind this, boys," he told them, "press on!" Riding hurriedly to the left to Brigadier General J. K. Jackson, who was commanding one of Bragg's brigades, Breckinridge asked for help against the Federal cannon, but Jackson was himself too heavily engaged. Rushing back to his brigade, the general was in the act of rallying the men to take the battery when it withdrew. By 12:30 Breckinridge was in possession of the enemy camp.[22]

The general continued the advance toward the second Federal camp, three-quarters of a mile behind the first, and drove the foe out of it a few minutes after one. Here he was stopped. Just beyond the camp lay a sunken wagon trail running parallel with Breckinridge's line, and here Prentiss and Hurlbut were making their stand, pouring out a volume of shot and shell that earned their position a nickname, the Hornets' Nest. Since McArthur and Stuart had now withdrawn all the way back to the landing, Johnston could have bypassed this trouble spot and taken Grant's base with minimal opposition. He chose instead to assault the Hornets' Nest, and brought up Bowen's brigade to support Breckinridge and Statham in the attack. For the next hour, the general made repeated advances against the enemy and just as many times was repulsed. The nature of the ground, heavily wooded, dictated that his men advance with the bayonet, and his attacks were directed toward a low elevation from which they would be able to fire. He finally determined upon an all-out charge, but finding, to his dismay, that one of his Tennessee regiments was badly demoralized, he had to ride to Johnston for help. Isham Harris happened to be with Johnston at the time, and Johnston sent the former Volunteer governor to rally the Tennesseeans. Harris got them back in line, but it was not long before Breckinridge rode back to Johnston to report that, after two hours of heavy fighting and casualties, he feared that he could not get Statham's brigade to charge. "Oh, yes, general, I think you can," replied the commander, but Breckinridge, his frustration apparently overcoming his customary reserve, shot back

22. Lockett, "Surprise and Withdrawal," 605; Preston, Memoranda, April 6, 1862, RG 94, NA; O.R., Ser. I, Vol. X, Pt. 1, pp. 404, 554; Stevenson, Thirteen Months, 151.

with some feeling that he had tried and failed. Johnston decided to aid in the charge.[23]

Breckinridge and Johnston rode together to the front of the troublesome Tennessee regiment, probably the Forty-fifth, and went along the brigade's line encouraging the men. Johnston placed himself in front of Statham's center, on the left of the Forty-fifth, while Breckinridge, "whom he loved and admired," rode his bay over to the right of the regiment. Taking his own place, the general spurred his horse as the line moved forward with a wild shout. They had not gone far when a clerk in his adjutant's office, Charles Ivey, suddenly rode forward in front of Breckinridge, between him and the enemy. Ivey had been a page for the general during his vice-presidency, and now in his enthusiasm sought to protect his commander from the shot and shell falling all about. Breckinridge saw what the boy was doing and, as Ivey put it, "roasted me," ordering the mortified clerk back to the rear.[24]

The Confederates swept down a slope, across a ravine, and up against the troublesome hill. The Federal line broke under the attack and pulled back to the cover of Prentiss' batteries in the sunken road, pursued by Breckinridge crying "Charge them, Tennesseeans! Charge them!" along the line. The general was the only one of his staff not wounded. George Hodge and Cabell, riding by his side, both had their horses shot from under them, Cabell riding one belonging to his father. T. T. Hawkins took a bullet in the face, while another had his leg torn to pieces by a shell fragment. Still, they held the hill, and the general was in the act of ordering the men to lie down just behind its crest to avoid the Federal artillery fire when, shortly after 2:30, a message came from Colonel William Preston in the ravine they had recently passed. General Johnston was dead; he had bled to death from an otherwise minor wound in the leg.[25]

23. Preston, Memoranda, April 6, 1862, RG 94, NA; *O.R.*, Ser. I, Vol. X, Pt. 1, p. 404; Thompson, *First Kentucky Brigade*, 103; W. B. Pipper, "Concerning Battle of Shiloh," *Confederate Veteran*, XVI (July, 1908), 344; W. P. Johnston, *Johnston*, 611.
24. W. P. Johnston, *Johnston*, 611–12; W. P. Johnston, "Johnston at Shiloh," 564; W. J. McMurray, *History of the Twentieth Tennessee Regiment Volunteer Infantry, CSA* (Nashville, 1904), 209; Thompson, *First Kentucky Brigade*, 104; Lexington *Morning Herald*, November 1, 1897.
25. Thompson, *First Kentucky Brigade*, 104–105; Breckinridge to Jordan, April 15, 1862, in Chap. 2, CCCXI, NA; Breckinridge to Samuel Cooper, May 1, 1863, Breckinridge, Service Record, NA; T. B. Anderson, "A Boy's Impression of Shiloh," *Confederate Veteran*, XIX (February, 1911), 72; Preston, Memoranda, April 6, 1862, RG 94, NA.

Soon afterward there came an order from Beauregard, now in command of the army, to keep Johnston's death a secret. The battle had hardly gone according to plan thus far. Largely it was Johnston's fault, for he allowed the conflict to rage for several hours before beginning in earnest the advance of his right which was the real object of his battle plan. The attack had bogged down on the left in the morning, and now three hours had been devoted to trying to dislodge Prentiss and Hurlbut from a near-impregnable position. Meanwhile, no one in the army's high command except Beauregard had acted his part. Johnston had spent most of the day personally leading brigades and regiments into action, and otherwise engaging in activities which he should have left to his subordinates. At the same time, Bragg, Polk, and Hardee hardly functioned as corps commanders, devoting themselves to directing individual brigades and divisions rather than exercising a unified control over their corps. Breckinridge was guilty of the same thing, having spent nearly the entire battle thus far with Statham's brigade. He can be excused in some measure because of his inexperience, and because so far Johnston had been directing his corps, but still the general's showing as a commander left something to be desired. Part of his command became mixed up with one of Brigadier General Charles Clark's brigades, Polk's corps, and he had actually lost the Nineteenth Tennessee of Statham's brigade, which spent the afternoon fighting with another of Polk's brigades in Brigadier General Benjamin F. Cheatham's division. In one thing, however, Breckinridge excelled. He showed remarkable courage, and with the possible exception of his momentary frustration before this last charge, resolute determination. In a war where the performance of the troops often depended upon the inspiration they could derive from their commander's manner in battle, the general's bravery was, and would continue to be, a major asset. Still, he had much to learn.[26]

A temporary lull in the battle followed Johnston's death, and Breckinridge managed to retrieve the Nineteenth Tennessee. All the corps had become irretrievably intermixed, and the commanders were now directing portions of the line without particular regard to corps organization. As a result, Breckinridge had attached the Crescent Regiment of New Orleans from Bragg's corps, now on his left, to Statham's brigade. A Federal battery, set up during the lull, was giving Bragg serious trouble, and, perhaps at Bragg's request, or on his own, Jordan rode to Breckinridge and ordered him to advance and take the enemy guns. Again Jordan was struck with

26. O.R., Ser. I, Vol. X, Pt. 1, pp. 422, 455; Connelly, *Army of the Heartland*, 162–67.

the general's appearance. "As I gave the order," he noted, "General Breck-enridge clad in a dark jeans blouse, and surrounded by his staff, close to the rear of Statham's brigade, sat on his horse more like an equestrian statue than a living man, except the fiery gleam that shot from his eyes." [27]

Breckinridge sent forward the Crescent Regiment. Battle smoke filled the ravine, and it was difficult to make out the regiment's progress until, through the rifting cloud, the Confederate line could be seen to waver and fall back. A soldier standing near the general looked over to see "those large blue eyes of Breckinridge filled with tears," a sight that would be-come common on the South's battlefields. In the midst of fighting and dying, it was impossible to restrain all feeling, all sensitivity. He probably did not try. Despite the tears, he ordered up the Nineteenth Tennessee to support the Crescent Regiment, and together they took the battery.[28]

By now it was nearly 4:00, and the Confederate right had been without unified leadership for an hour and a half, engaged mostly in a series of un-coordinated attacks. Breckinridge should have resumed command of his corps—more particularly, those forces on the right of the line—and operated it as a unit, but he stuck to Statham, and at this juncture Bragg came over to take charge. One of his divisions under Jones M. Withers was already there, and when he arrived he found that the line under Withers, Cheat-ham, and Breckinridge was holding back, undecided what to do. Following the example set by Johnston, Bragg did nothing but order them forward against the left flank of Prentiss' now nearly enveloped position. It was about 4:30 when he gave the order forward, and he saw a beam in Breckin-ridge's eyes as they advanced. During the attack, the general went over to Bowen's brigade for the first time that afternoon, wheeling it to the left against Prentiss' flank. Then they began battering the Federals with sledge-hammer blows. By this time, the remainder of the enemy army had with-drawn nearly a mile, leaving Prentiss as a sacrifice to buy time while re-inforcements were hurried toward the battlefield. The decoy did his work well until sometime after 5:00 when, almost completely surrounded, he finally surrendered.[29]

Breckinridge, Polk, Bragg, and Hardee all came into the captured Fed-

27. Thomas Jordan, "The Campaign and Battle of Shiloh," *United Service Magazine*, XII (April, 1885), 303–94.

28. *Ibid.*; D. Sullins, "Heroic Deed at Shiloh," *Confederate Veteran*. V (January, 1897), 10; James Dinkins, "The Battle of Shiloh, April 6, 1862," *SHSP*, XXXI (January–December, 1903), 307.

29. Braxton Bragg to Elise Bragg, April 8, 1862, in Braxton Bragg Photostats, LC; *O.R.*, Ser. I, Vol. X, Pt. 1, pp. 466, 622, Vol. XVI, Pt. 2, p. 995.

eral stronghold at about the same time, while some 2,200 prisoners were being taken to the rear. As the general rode in from the right, the Kentucky Brigade entered from the left, and they met for the first time since early that morning, both now bloodied, now veterans. Many of the Kentuckians exchanged their antiquated guns for the captured Federal issue, but shortly they regrouped, now under their own general, to continue the attack on the enemy in his last line right in front of the landing. Breckinridge, Polk, Cheatham, and others sat their horses in a small glade on the general's left, until Bragg's order to attack came. A. P. Stewart's brigade of Polk's corps was placed under Breckinridge for the advance, and he moved forward around 5:30. Pursuing the Federals down the main road to Pittsburg Landing, the general reached a point only three-fourths of a mile from the river, the most advanced position held by any Confederate command that day. Four or five hundred yards down the road he could see enemy flags. The Federals were posted behind a hastily assembled mass of artillery that was pouring a terrific shelling on Bragg, now leading the right of the line. Breckinridge, leading the right center, was less affected by the barrage, and, as Captain Francis A. Shoup started to unlimber a part of his artillery battalion to return their fire, the general told him: "Hold on, I am going to charge." "If you are going to charge," replied Shoup, "now is your time." Breckinridge moved his line up a few paces beyond Shoup's guns and had halted them to prepare for the attack when a courier rode up with an order from Beauregard. It was 6:00 now, and in the fading light of evening, the general read instructions to break off the engagement and retire to shelter and safety. He obeyed the order, but it was a disappointment to leave when victory, complete and devastating, seemed so surely within sight. To those around him he confided, "It is clearly a mistake." [30]

Actually, Breckinridge himself was mistaken, and it appears that he later realized it. The Confederate army was staggering from its losses of the day. It was disorganized, on the brink of exhaustion, and suffering from desertions and men breaking ranks to loot the captured Federal camps. Continued assaults on a new enemy position nearly as formidable as the Hornets' Nest might well have disintegrated what remained. Johnston's son, William Preston Johnston, would years later devote himself to proving that his father had won the battle by 2:30, only to have Beauregard throw

---

30. *O.R.*, Ser. I, Vol. X, Pt. 1, pp. 428, 616; Thompson, *First Kentucky Brigade*, 105; William Polk, *Leonidas Polk, Bishop and General* (New York, 1893), II, 278–79; F. A. Shoup, "How We Went to Shiloh," *Confederate Veteran*, II (May, 1894), 139; Alex. W. Campbell, "Thirty-Third Tennessee Infantry," in Lindsley (ed.), *Annals*, 487.

away the victory with his withdrawal order at 6:00. The younger Johnston earnestly solicited corroborating opinions from the commanders in the battle, and got them from Bragg and others, but Breckinridge would persistently avoid committing himself. From this it would appear that, after reflection on the course of the battle, the condition of his men, and all those things that he could not know from his limited vision of the field on April 6, the general revised his opinion of Beauregard's order. He may still have had some reservations about it, but he ceased to regard it as so clearly mistaken.[31]

After dark, the general rode back to Beauregard's headquarters to receive orders for renewing the fight in the morning. The commanding general switched the positions of some of the commands, and now assigned Hardee to the right, with Breckinridge on his left flank, in position somewhat in advance of the Hornets' Nest. There they passed the night while, from across the river, Grant was being reinforced heavily from the Army of the Ohio. This, plus the hasty and none-too-thorough job of reorganization done by the Confederate high command, left Beauregard in poor shape to receive the stunning blow delivered by the Federals the next morning.[32]

This morning attack brought home to Breckinridge, in later reflection, the first and most stark realization of the horror of civil war, and how it affected Kentuckians in particular. The first enemy unit to contact his command in the gray predawn light was the division of his friend Brigadier General William Nelson of Maysville, and in his division were four regiments of Kentucky Federal infantry. Nelson barely engaged Breckinridge, however, before he turned toward Hardee, giving his place in line to another division that contained another four Kentucky regiments, and this one slammed into the general's command with stunning force, slowly driving him back. Here Federals from the Bluegrass fought Confederates who had been friends, townsmen, even kin. "Wherever Kentucky met Kentucky, it was horrible," wrote a rebel gunner. Perhaps the greatest horror belonged to Breckinridge, however, for the man in command of this enemy division was one who had been as close to him, perhaps, as anyone in his youth and young manhood, his own former commander and now a brigadier himself, Thomas L. Crittenden.[33]

31. Connelly, *Army of the Heartland*, 168–71; W. P. Johnston to Jefferson Davis, December 8, 1874, in Rowland, *Jefferson Davis*, VII, 413.

32. Jordan, "Notes," 602.

33. Barnes F. Lathrop, "A Confederate Artilleryman at Shiloh," *Civil War History*, VIII (December, 1962), 378.

There was more tragedy in store for the general this morning. George W. Johnson, now without a state to govern, had taken a place as volunteer aide to Breckinridge the day before, then served with Trabue. Having his horse shot from under him, Johnson took the oath as a private in the Fourth Kentucky, and this morning was serving as a simple soldier in the ranks. He was sworn in within sight of his friend Breckinridge, and then took a place in the lines as the general was about to launch his first counterattack to retake his lost position and a battery captured by the enemy. The general had been ordered to make the attack earlier but the absence of Cheatham's division to support his left made the assault too dangerous. Beauregard sent him Trabue from another part of the line, and now Breckinridge advanced. In the face of stubborn resistance, he managed to recapture the battery before being forced back once more, but it cost him dearly, and Johnson lay among the mortally wounded left on the field. His last words were instructions leaving his personal effects to Breckinridge. Afterwards carried behind the Federal lines, the governor would be mistaken by some, Grant included, for Breckinridge, and there was much disappointment when the error was corrected.[34]

It was about noon when the general retook his guns, leading the fight in person, and for the next hour he was hard pressed on his left, even though Cheatham finally appeared and took his position. By 1:00 in the afternoon the Federals had retaken the Hornets' Nest. By 2:00 the sudden change in affairs, the fresh Federals on the field, and the exhaustion and loss of heart of his own men, decided Beauregard to withdraw the army. A staff officer rode up to Breckinridge with the news, informing him at the same time that he would cover the withdrawal. It took about two hours to pull the corps off the field and put them on the road back to Corinth, while the remnant of the Reserve Corps was left behind as a rear guard. Bragg ordered Breckinridge to hold on until pressed, while bringing off all the wounded possible, and seeing to the burial of the terrible number of dead. That night, the enemy seemingly content to hold what it had taken that day without pursuing, the general went into bivouac a mile and a half from the battlefield, near the headquarters where, just two nights before, an optimistic Johnston and a troubled Beauregard awaited the morrow's surprise attack

34. Thompson, *Orphan Brigade*, 103; Lot D. Young, *Reminiscences of a Soldier of the Orphan Brigade* (Louisville, 1912), 24–25; Roman, *Beauregard*, I, 314; *O.R.*, Ser. I, Vol. X, Pt. 1, p. 436; Scrapbook No. 2, J. S. Johnston MSS, FC.

on which so much of the hope of the Confederacy in the West depended.[35]

The losses in Breckinridge's corps attested to the brutal fighting in which it had engaged. Officially, his casualties numbered 386 killed, 1,682 wounded, and 165 missing, a total of 2,233, or 34.7 percent of the 6,439 who went into battle on April 6. Bowen had suffered 38.3 percent, one of the highest brigade losses in the battle, and the Richmond *Enquirer* speculated that, on the whole, the general's was "the heaviest loss sustained by any one brigade [corps] since the war began." However, this official report does not take into account his losses from other sources—desertions, most of them temporary, and walking wounded who would not go on the casualty list until after the battle was over. In fact, his morning reports of April 8 revealed only 3,505 effectives present for duty, a loss of 45.6 percent; and poor Statham's brigade, which Breckinridge led personally through all of April 6 and much of the 7th, showed only 868 effectives out of 2,423, a staggering 64.2 percent reduction.[36]

Some of the blame for such high casualties must surely be Breckinridge's. Had he exercised a unified command over his corps on April 6, wielding it as a unit in the heavy attacks of the afternoon, its weight would have been felt much sooner, and the enemy forced to retire or surrender the Hornets' Nest before the losses mounted so greatly. This was a common failing in everyone that day, however, and the general could not be faulted any more than his fellow commanders. On the positive side, his men had captured 1,393 weapons to replace their own battered arms, 4 cannon, and a number of prized but rather useless enemy flags. Breckinridge sent all of the latter to Richmond except one, captured by the Ninth Kentucky from an imaginative outfit calling itself the Chickasaha Desperadoes, emblazoned with the motto "Victory or Death." This one he would keep to hang outside his headquarters tent. As for Breckinridge's own performance, he disappointed no one. His courage stood proven by his continuous presence on the front, often in the hottest part of the field. He was twice struck by spent bullets—painful but not serious—and found several holes in his clothing, evidence of a number of near misses. Beauregard expressed his pleasure with Breckin-

35. Manning Force, *From Fort Henry to Corinth* (New York, 1881), 169; *O.R.*, Ser. I, Vol. X, Pt. 1, pp. 441, 507–508, 514, 583, Pt. 2, p. 398; Connelly, *Army of the Heartland*, 173–75; T. Harry Williams, *P. G. T. Beauregard: Napoleon in Gray* (Baton Rouge, 1954), 184–85; Roman, *Beauregard*, I, 322.

36. *O.R.*, Ser. I, Vol. X, Pt. 1, p. 305; Richmond *Enquirer*, April 25, 1862; Breckinridge, report, April 21, 1862, Chap. 2, CCCXI, NA.

ridge, "than whom there is not a nobler soul," he said. He reportedly declared that the Kentuckian "displayed great aptitude and sagacity, and handled his brigade with skill and judgment." [37]

Clearly, Breckinridge proved himself at Shiloh. He showed that in battle, as on the stump, he was a born leader. On the basis of this alone, in a war where personal leadership was such a basic requisite, he appeared destined to rise to a great career.

37. *O.R.*, Ser. I, Vol. X, Pt. 1, pp. 389, 613, Vol. LI, Pt. 2, p. 689; J. Stoddard Johnston, "Sam Laurence," *Confederate Veteran*, X (May, 1902), 200; Thompson, *Orphan Brigade*, 101; Thomas Bragg, Diary, April 8, 1862, in Bragg MSS, SHC; Richmond *Enquirer*, April 22, 1862.

CHAPTER 2

I Will Lead You on to Victory

Late that night, after the army had retired, Breckinridge posted his command on high ground around Mickey's and waited for morning. The dawn revealed no Federal intentions to pursue, and the general was able to turn his attention to his shambles of a command. Rations were so scarce that Breckinridge's own breakfast this morning was to have been two biscuits, one of which he shared with an aide while he gave the other to two hungry privates. There were stragglers everywhere, and his men lay exhausted. "My troops are worn-out," he told Bragg, "and I don't think can be relied on after the first volley." [1]

Still Breckinridge covered the retreat admirably, bringing off nearly all the wounded and much abandoned equipment. Finally, the order to retire to Corinth came on April 10. It had been "hard duty," wrote Trabue, but "the general was equal to the great undertaking." He and his men "suffered heavily," wrote a diarist, "but won imperishable glory by the successful cover of the retreat." It also won him the respect and gratitude of his fellow officers, and of the Confederacy. One week after his arrival in Corinth on April 11, Breckinridge was nominated by Jefferson Davis for promotion to major general. The Senate confirmed the commission, to date from April 14. While the ever-present Kentucky lobby in Richmond no doubt pressured for such a promotion, it came clearly as a reward for good service. When notice of Breckinridge's new commission came to Bragg, he endorsed the document, "Nobly won upon the field, with . . . hearty congratulations." [2] He was the only politician Davis would so promote.

1. *O.R.*, Ser. I, Vol. X, Pt. 1, p. 924, Pt. 2, pp. 398–400; Joseph T. Derry, "The Battle of Shiloh," *SHSP*, XXIX (January–December, 1901), 359; P. L. Smithson and J. L. Gee, "Comments of Comrades," *Confederate Veteran*, II (February, 1894), 40.

2. *O.R.*, Ser. I, Vol. X, Pt. 1, pp. 111, 619–20, Pt. 2, pp. 403–405, Ser. II, Vol. III, 450–51, 502–504, 863; J. Stoddard Johnston Diary, July 13, 1862, in J. Stoddard John-

Reorganization faced the new major general on reaching Corinth. New officers were needed, particularly staff. Breckinridge still had much to learn in the proper use of his staff during a battle. They should have carried the messages and orders which he took in person, and Shiloh taught him his lesson. He increased his staff to ten officers carefully chosen, replacing Hodge with Captain John A. Buckner when his adjutant went to Richmond to take a Kentucky seat in Congress. His corps now consisted of four brigades under Statham and three new brigadiers, James M. Hawes, William Preston, and Lincoln's brother-in-law Benjamin H. Helm. The corps numbered 5,780 effectives in time, and throughout April, Breckinridge acted as the army's reserve at Corinth. The following month, with the threat of a Federal advance, he stayed constantly in motion protecting point after point. Then, with an enemy attack imminent, he joined Bragg, Hardee, Polk, Sterling Price, and Major General Earl Van Dorn, in advising Beauregard to withdraw.[3]

The movement was carried out by May 29, Beauregard evacuating his troops in such a manner that the enemy actually thought he was being reinforced. Once again Breckinridge covered the retreat, marching his corps uneventfully south to Tupelo, Mississippi. The Kentuckian was suffering from recurring illness as the summer came on and, once in Tupelo, he applied for and received a four-week leave of absence. He used it to visit Brokenburn plantation in Madison Parish, Louisiana, just across the Mississippi from Vicksburg. Here he visited with friends whose daughter, Katherine Carson, would one day marry his son Clifton. Meanwhile, on June 19 his corps was transferred to Van Dorn's command at Vicksburg. The Federals had begun their bombardment of this river bastion with a Union fleet under David Farragut. At the same time, infantry led by Brigadier General Thomas Williams marched up from New Orleans to assist the gunboats. In the face of this threat, Bragg—having replaced Beauregard—sent Breckinridge's brigades south under Preston, and ordered their major general to meet them in Vicksburg. On June 28 the Kentuckian left Brokenburn

---

ston MSS, FC: Statement of Promotion, Breckinridge, Service Record, NA; George W. Randolph to Breckinridge, April 18, 1862, in "Confederate Rag-Bag," *Historical Magazine*, 3rd ser., II (August, 1873), 92.

3. Breckinridge to Thomas Jordan, April 13, 15, 1862, Chap. 2, CCCXI, NA; Breckinridge to Jordan, April 12, 15, 1862, in Breckinridge, Service Record, NA; *O.R.*, Ser. I, Vol. LII, Pt. 2. pp. 302, 300–10, Vol. X, Pt. 2, pp. 433, 458, 487, 494, 496–97. 521, 525, 527, 532, 550; Thompson, *Orphan Brigade*, 111–15; *Southern Bivouac*, o.s., III (April, 1885). 333; Robert G. Hartie, *Van Dorn: The Life and Times of a Confederate General* (Nashville, 1967), 181; Roman, *Beauregard*, I, 388.

in a carriage and braved a Union picket line to get across the river to Van Dorn.[4]

Once in the city, Breckinridge placed his men on picket north of the town. His command was changed from a corps to a division in Van Dorn's organization, and, when another Federal shelling began on July 2, the Kentuckian's division was moved closer to the river. On July 4 he directed in person the repulse of an attempted gunboat landing below Vicksburg and narrowly missed capturing one mortarboat which came too close to shore. It is not likely that the irony of the occasion escaped him. After years of observing the Fourth of July as a national holiday in the old Union, here he was battling against ships that flew the flag he had loved so dearly.[5]

When not in action, Breckinridge's men suffered terribly from the heat, and, though he tried every remedy, his camp hospitals gradually filled. Besides this unhappy note there was Van Dorn. Initially the two generals got along well, even playing together somewhat foolishly. One day early in July as the Federals shelled the city, Breckinridge and Van Dorn joined another general at one of the river batteries and personally manned its guns against an enemy gunboat "to amuse themselves." When the Federals detected the gold embroidery on their generals' collars, they sent a hail of bursting shells against the Confederates. Escaping, Breckinridge may have been amused to reflect on the fact that these gunboats were the very ones which his vote in the Senate a year ago had helped create.

The situation with Van Dorn, however, soon ceased to be amusing. Breckinridge found his commander's blatant egotism repulsive. Although it did not interfere with their official dealings, it caused the Kentuckian to become increasingly formal with Van Dorn in private. His Kentucky soldiers felt much the same. "Coxcomb, dandy, fop, ball-room beau," one of them thought of Van Dorn, "and such a thing of paint, perfume, and feathers to command our Breckinridge—and us!" For some the contrast was too much. They could not accept "the incongruity of having the finest-looking man

4. Thompson, *Orphan Brigade*, 116–19; *O.R.*, Ser. I, Vol. X, Pt. 2, pp. 563, 574, 583, 587, Pt. 1, p. 777, Ser. I, Vol. XV, 761, 1120; Leave of Absence, June 8, 1862, Breckinridge, Service Record, NA; Preston, Memoranda, June 9–10, 1862, RG 94, NA; John Q. Anderson (ed.), *Brokenburn: The Journal of Kate Stone, 1861–1868* (Baton Rouge, 1955), 120, 126, 286; John D. Winters, *The Civil War in Louisiana* (Baton Rouge, 1963), 105–107.

5. *O.R.*, Ser. I, Vol. XV, 7–9, 11; Thompson, *Orphan Brigade*, 118–21; Breckinridge to Manning Kimmel, July 12, 1862, Chap. 2, CCCXI, Special Orders No. 243, July 3, 1862, Chap. 2, CCCXVI, NA; C. W. Heiskell, "The Nineteenth Tennessee Infantry," in Lindsley (ed.), *Annals*, 375; McMurray, *Twentieth Tennessee*, 215.

in the Confederacy, and that man a Kentuckian, subordinate to one so apparently inferior in every way." [6]

The highlight of the month in Vicksburg came on July 15 when the new Confederate ironclad *Arkansas* came out of the Yazoo River to run the gauntlet of Farragut's fleet to Vicksburg. Breckinridge sent Helm to the Yazoo to help cover the vessel, and, when the ship reached the Federal fleet, the Kentuckian, Van Dorn, and others climbed to the dome of Vicksburg's courthouse to watch the action. The *Arkansas* came through safely, thanks in part to cover provided by Breckinridge, and thereafter he provided a number of volunteers to man the formidable ironclad. On July 24, thanks largely to the *Arkansas*, the Federals gave up the siege and retired to Memphis and New Orleans. [7]

Anxious not to allow the enemy time to plan another campaign, Van Dorn decided on an ill-advised offensive against Baton Rouge and Port Hudson, Louisiana. This would open up the Red River to Confederate transportation, giving Van Dorn a supply route to the West, but it was the worst time of the year for campaigning. Heat, malaria, and "camp fever," would claim hundreds on such a march. Nevertheless, on July 25 he ordered Breckinridge to have four thousand men of his division ready to move the next morning. At his own request, Breckinridge would lead them. [8]

The division barely had four thousand fit for duty. He had over twelve hundred men sick in their camps, and the number increased daily. Nevertheless, Breckinridge got what remained of his brigades together and boarded a train for Jackson, where they would switch to another bound for Camp Moore, Louisiana. There they were to meet a small command under Brigadier General Daniel Ruggles and then attack Baton Rouge. Breckinridge was to hold the city if possible, or else destroy anything of

6. John D. Pickett to B. H. Helm, William Preston, W. S. Statham, July 9, 1862, Chap. 2, CCCXI, NA; Thompson, *Orphan Brigade*, 117–21; John S. Jackman, "Vicksburg in 1862," *Southern Bivouac*, o. s., III (September, 1884), 3; Hartje, *Van Dorn*, 200–201, 216, 240, 325.

7. Breckinridge to Helm, July 14, 15, 1862, Simon Buckner to Breckinridge, July 18, 1862, Breckinridge to Earl Van Dorn, July 22, 1862, in Chap. 2, CCCXI, NA; George W. Gift, "The Story of the Arkansas," *SHSP*, XII (March, 1884), 116; L. S. Flateau, "A Great Naval Battle," *Confederate Veteran*, XXV (October, 1917), 459; *O.R.*, Ser. I, Vol. XV, 1122–23; Thompson, *Orphan Brigade*, 122.

8. Hartje, *Van Dorn*, 205–207; Van Dorn to Breckinridge, July 25, 1862, Breckinridge to Van Dorn, July 26, 1862, in Chap. 2, CCCXI, NA.

use to the enemy and retire.[9] It was late on July 28 when, finally, his hot, tired command bivouacked near Camp Moore. Problems immediately confronted the general. Ruggles' men boosted his numbers to slightly over four thousand, but there was another brigadier present, Charles Clark. Reorganization was needed to give each a proper command, and Breckinridge divided his force into two small divisions of two brigades each. Meanwhile, two days of camp sickness cost him four hundred men. "The climate and exposure are reducing regiments to companies," he lamented, but when he received a definite order from Van Dorn to advance on Baton Rouge, Breckinridge obeyed.[10]

The fifty-mile march became a nightmare. The white, sandy road reflected the heat, and water was so scarce that men flocked even to the most filthy, stagnant little pools to drink polluted water. Bad water and sunstroke forced them out of ranks by the score. "Almost every farm-house on the roadside was converted into a hospital," wrote the Chattanooga *Rebel*'s correspondent Charles D. Kirk. With his men collapsing at every step, Breckinridge was hardly encouraged to learn that the enemy in Baton Rouge numbered five thousand or more, with three gunboats to back them. Immediately he wired to Van Dorn requesting the *Arkansas* to be sent to divert the Federal ships. It was a novel idea, the first time a Confederate commander in the West proposed a combined land and water attack. The principal difficulties were the *Arkansas*' incomplete state of repair, and the precision it would require to bring her down two hundred miles of river to attack at the same time Breckinridge did.[11]

Late on August 3 the command reached the Comite River, ten miles from Baton Rouge. Breckinridge would attack the next morning, he told Van Dorn, but the slowness of the *Arkansas* caused a one-day delay. Meanwhile the men rested. The march had cost him six hundred men, dwindling

9. B. W. Avent to Breckinridge, July 22, 1862, in Chap. 2, CCCXI, NA; *O.R.*, Ser. I, Vol. XV, 786.

10. *O.R.*, Ser. I, Vol. XV, 76, 1124; John B. Pirtle, "Defense of Vicksburg in 1862— The Battle of Baton Rouge," *SHSP*, VIII (June–July, 1880), 328; General Order No. 2, July 29, 1862, Special Orders No. 15, July 30, 1862, in William Yerger MSS, Mississippi Department of Archives and History, Jackson.

11. J. S. Johnston Diary, August 14, 1862, in Johnston MSS; G. T. Shaw to John Buckner, July 31, 1862, in Yerger MSS; Pirtle, "Defense of Vicksburg," 328; *O.R.*, Ser. I, Vol. XV, 76–77; Eliza McHatton Ripley, *From Flag to Flag: A Woman's Adventures and Experiences in the South During the War, in Mexico and in Cuba* (New York, 1889), 30–31. The correspondent Kirk's narrative is in Moore, *Rebellion Record*, V, 309–12.

the little army to barely three thousand, and they continued to fall out ill. To cheer the men, Breckinridge spoke to them, promising to lead them personally in the coming fight. He also sent word into Baton Rouge by a slave named Willie who belonged to his old friend James McHatton. He needed men and arms, and most of all hospital supplies. Then, having received confirmation that the *Arkansas* would be ready to attack at daylight, August 5, Breckinridge began the march to Baton Rouge. The night movement was pleasant by comparison to the march to the Comite, but still the men fell out. By the time they reached the city's outskirts just after 4 A.M., the command was down to twenty-five hundred. The Thirty-first Alabama Infantry could count only ninety-seven men and officers present. Before them lay an enemy of twice their number.[12]

There was some confusion in the early morning, and a crisis in the Kentuckian's command. Malaria had put Preston out of action, and Statham was dying in Vicksburg. Now an accident injured Ben Hardin Helm, Breckinridge's only battle experienced brigade leader. The same accident also put two of Cobb's three cannon out of action, and killed Helm's aide Alexander Todd, brother of Mary Todd Lincoln. Order was restored but now all of the general's brigade commanders were amateurs. It would have comforted him at least to know that the enemy in Baton Rouge was little better off. The garrison was itself severely reduced by sickness, and most of the men, including their commander, Williams, were inexperienced. But they knew Breckinridge was coming. They had eighteen guns to his eleven, five gunboats instead of the anticipated three, and good food and equipment. And at the prospect of a battle, many of the Federal sick heroically came out of their hospitals to take up arms. While Williams' numbers did not much exceed the Confederates' in effectives, he held a decided advantage.[13]

At ten minutes before 5 A.M., Breckinridge made contact with Federal skirmishers, driving them in. Ruggles opened the battle with his two brigades under Colonels A. P. Thompson and Henry Watkins Allen supported by a four-gun battery and a little cavalry. Behind Ruggles, Breckinridge kept one tiny regiment as a reserve. As Ruggles slowly pushed the enemy back into the suburbs of Baton Rouge, Breckinridge accompanied Clark's division to the right near the river, where he expected to see the

12. Moore, *Rebellion Record*, V, 309–11; Pirtle, "Defense of Vicksburg," 328–29; *O.R.*, Ser. I, Vol. XV, 77, 85; Ripley, *From Flag to Flag*, 31; Heiskell, "Nineteenth Tennessee," 376.

13. Moore, *Rebellion Record*, V, 310–11; *O.R.*, Ser. I, Vol. XV, 11, 33–34, 52, 54, 77; Butler, *Butler's Book*, 481.

Arkansas' approach. Some hours earlier he had sent a small command far around the Federal left with two field pieces, their mission to open fire on Williams' flank when the battle began. Now they did so, only to find the enemy had withdrawn before them. As the little battalion pursued, it passed across the front of Clark's advance and accidentally received the fire of its own troops.[14]

Breckinridge and Clark encountered little opposition at first. Clark's Second Brigade, led by Lieutenant Colonel Thomas Hunt, and the Fourth Brigade under Colonel Thomas Smith, pushed the Federals out of their camps before them. Driving them through a second camp, the Confederates pushed them into a ravine near the Louisiana State Penitentiary. Here Hunt was seriously wounded. Not knowing where Hunt's second-in-command could be found in the confusion, Breckinridge ordered his adjutant Captain Buckner to take over the brigade.[15]

Now an order from some unknown source—probably Clark—came to fall back even though the enemy was obviously in trouble. Grudgingly Buckner withdrew. Over on the left Thompson's brigade of Ruggles' division, seeing this, began to fall back as well, being told by an unidentified officer that the army was retiring. The enemy pursued, and now Thompson fell. At the same time Allen, trying to take a Yankee battery, fell with both legs shattered by canister. Ruggles lost two of his staff officers; two of Thompson's staff fell as well; the colonel of the Sixth Kentucky fell ill in the middle of the fight; the colonel of the Thirty-fifth Alabama collapsed of sunstroke; and one of Allen's regimental commanders fell with a mangled arm. With the command structure in his division disintegrated, only Ruggles' cool head and his four cannon prevented disaster.[16]

During the fighting thus far Breckinridge was where he should have been, behind the lines watching. Learning from his mistakes at Shiloh, he gave his division commanders their orders before the battle, then let them have their head. Indeed, from the commencement of the fight, his only order had been for Buckner to take over from Hunt. Meanwhile, he stayed where he expected the turning point of the battle to come, on his right near the river, waiting for the *Arkansas*. Now, however, with his command stripped of its officers and his men weakened by disease—men of the Nine-

14. *O.R.*, Ser. I, Vol. XV, 77–78, 90–91, 104–105; Winters, *Civil War in Louisiana*, 116.

15. *O.R.*, Ser. I, Vol. XV, 78, 83; J. S. Johnston Diary, August 14, 1862, in Johnston MSS; Pirtle, "Defense of Vicksburg," 331.

16. Moore, *Rebellion Record*, V, 310–11; *O.R.*, Ser. I, Vol. XV, 78, 94; Sarah A. Dorsey, *Recollections of Henry Watkins Allen* (New York, 1866), 138–39.

teenth Tennessee shook from chills even as they fought—he had to step in to prevent the unauthorized withdrawal. He sent Buckner back into the fight, and then personally led Smith's brigade forward. Then, while the Kentuckian helped Buckner reform his scattered regiments, Clark fell seriously wounded. The situation on his right was now as critical as that of Ruggles on the left.[17]

Breckinridge rode to the front. "His presence had a magical effect upon the men," wrote Kirk, who witnessed the battle. "There was no danger he did not share with them. His tall form seemed ubiquitous—here, there, and every where in peril, where there was an enemy to drive or a position to gain." Fulfilling his pledge to lead the men personally, Breckinridge reportedly exclaimed, "Come, my brave boys, and follow me—I will lead you on to victory!" Buckner's brigade followed him to smash into the Federal center. There, supported by Smith, he battered the enemy until Ruggles pushed forward once more. The fight raged for an hour on this line, Breckinridge's only relief being the fact that his command was now too close to Williams' for the Federal gunboats to continue the shelling which had bothered him since the beginning of the fight.[18]

Soon the Confederates' ammunition ran so low that Breckinridge ordered them to use the bayonet. He personally led repeated assaults, sword drawn, and yelling—as Kirk heard it—"My men, charge!" Finally he won the Federal position, in part because Williams fell dead on the field with a bullet in his chest, leaving his troops leaderless. The Union center crumbled under another charge, and by 10 A.M. Breckinridge had forced the enemy all the way through Baton Rouge to the river, where the Federals halted under cover of resumed fire from the gunboats.[19]

All morning Breckinridge listened for the guns of the *Arkansas*. Still there was no sign of her, and without something to distract the Union gunboat fire, there was no way he could hold his position in the town. Reluctantly, he withdrew temporarily to await the ironclad, leaving Buckner's brigade to guard against a Federal attack. While the men looked for water to combat the sun's heat, Breckinridge began caring for the wounded. Clark's wound proved not to be mortal as originally thought, and he was sent to a nearby house. Meanwhile, the Kentuckian found a surgeon and

17. Heiskell, "Nineteenth Tennessee," 376.

18. Moore, *Rebellion Record*, V, 311; "Personne" [Felix G. De Fontaine], *Marginalia: or Gleanings from an Army Note-Book* (Columbia, S.C., 1864), 34; *O.R.*, Ser. I, Vol. XV, 78, 91–92; Dorsey, *Allen*, 141.

19. *O.R.*, Ser. I, Vol. XV, 78–79, 87, 99, 546; Moore, *Rebellion Record*, V, 311; McMurray, *Twentieth Tennessee*, 201.

ordered him to find and tend to Allen. *"Find Allen,"* he said, *"save him—stay with him, Doctor! he is as brave a man as God ever made."* Allen's wounds were desperate, but Breckinridge directed the doctor to stay with him for the next three weeks, and eventually the colonel recovered.[20]

Still the *Arkansas* did not appear. The ironclad had gotten very close to the battle, within four miles, when engine trouble forced her to stop. Breckinridge tried to urge her on, saying the Federals could still be decisively beaten, but to no avail. The *Arkansas* could not move, and when two Federal gunboats approached, the crew fired the ship and cast her adrift to explode when the fire reached her magazine. Word of the disaster reached Breckinridge at 4 P.M. Unable to hold the town without river support, he immediately ordered a withdrawal to the Comite.[21]

It had been an uncertain battle. Breckinridge out-generaled and out-fought the Federals everywhere on the field, but he could not hold the town. Thus, both sides claimed the victory. The day after the battle the Kentuckian issued a congratulatory order to his troops, ascribing their failure only to the *Arkansas.* Two days later his old friend and former supporter Major General Benjamin F. Butler, commanding in New Orleans, issued his own order. The Federals exaggerated Breckinridge's numbers to be as high as 15,000, and some reported that the Kentuckian had lost an arm in the fight. Breckinridge overestimated his opponents' numbers at about 4,500, the actual number of Federals present but many more than actually fought.[22]

The persistence of Breckinridge's attacks showed up in the number of his killed and wounded. A few days after the battle, before all reports were in, he estimated his loss at 450. Subsequent reports put it at 453, though Breckinridge later believed 467 to be a more correct figure. The Federals lost 383 killed and wounded. As soon as the battle was over, of course, sickness and heat resumed their deadly work, and Breckinridge's medical director warned that the little army might soon be destroyed by malaria, dysentery, and diarrhea.[23]

Even though the attack on Baton Rouge had not proved successful, the

20. *O.R.,* Ser. I, Vol. XV, 79; Moore, *Rebellion Record,* V, 311–12; Dorsey, *Allen* 144.

21. C. W. Reed, "Reminiscences of the Confederate States Navy," *SHSP,* I (May, 1876), 360; Moore, *Rebellion Record,* V, 312; Butler, *Butler's Book,* 483.

22. Breckinridge to "Officers and Soldiers Under My Command," August 6, 1862, in Moore, *Rebellion Record,* V, 308; *O.R.,* Ser. I, Vol. XV, 40, 42, 52, 54, 79.

23. J. S. Johnston Diary, August 14, 1862, in Johnston MSS; *O.R.,* Ser. I, Vol. XV, 51, 55, 80, 82, 93, 1225; Moore, *Rebellion Record,* V, 312.

general made his campaign bear fruit on August 12 when he sent Ruggles to occupy Port Hudson. The next day an order from Van Dorn arrived proposing this very move. Ruggles took the place unopposed, and immediately Breckinridge set him to work fortifying it. Its high bluffs commanded the Mississippi in a way Baton Rouge did not, and the Kentuckian believed it a better position even than Vicksburg. It secured for the Confederacy the navigation of the Red River, and would stand as a bastion in the South's river defense for more than a year.[24]

Breckinridge's performance in the campaign was excellent. He organized his army well, made good use of his staff in battle, and had the good sense to keep himself out of the fight until needed. The only serious fault to be found is in his brigade's commanders not being instructed to obey only his written orders or those conveyed by recognized members of his staff. This would have allayed the confusion created by the mysterious officer giving withdrawal orders. Once the battle was over, Breckinridge did what he failed to do after Shiloh. He wrote and submitted a complete report of his operations. It was short, clear, concise, and unadorned. Van Dorn was much pleased with the "skill and intrepidity" of his subordinate, and willingly gave praise despite their strained relations. The Confederate Congress went further. On August 23, 1862, Congressman James W. Moore of Kentucky introduced a resolution bestowing on Breckinridge and his command the thanks of Congress for their conduct in the Battle of Baton Rouge. The resolution passed unanimously.[25]

While Breckinridge dug in at Port Hudson, the Federals from Baton Rouge began confiscating slaves, looting homes, and harassing Confederate sympathizers. Breckinridge protested this conduct in a letter to Williams' successor, Colonel Halbert Paine, adding that Van Dorn had authorized him to regard this conduct as a violation of the rules of civilized war, and that further such outrages would force him to "raise the black flag, and neither give nor ask quarter." Paine denied the charges and, indeed, the threat of retaliation mattered little since Baton Rouge would be evacuated on August 21. But there was a barb in Paine's reply. "I shall never raise that flag which all civilized nations abhor," he wrote to Breckinridge, "but

24. O.R., Ser. I, Vol. XV, 80, 85, 795, 797–800, 1124–25, Ser. I, Vol. LII, Pt. 2, p. 340; Breckinridge to Daniel Ruggles, August 13, 1862, in Daniel Ruggles MSS, DU; M. Jeff Thompson to Breckinridge, August 19, 1862, in Samuel Griswold Flagg Collection, Yale University Library, New Haven, Conn.

25. Roman, Beauregard, I, 377; O.R., Ser. I, Vol. XV, 12; "Proceedings of the First Confederate Congress, Second Session," SHSP, XLV (May, 1925), 210; House of Representatives to Breckinridge, August 23, 1862, Breckinridge, Service Record, NA.

I shall try to maintain the flag which you have too often promised to defend." [26]

If the general chafed at Paine's insult, his discomfort was relieved greatly at 10 P.M. on August 14 when Colonel J. Stoddard Johnston unexpectedly stepped into his tent. Johnston found Breckinridge well but restive under orders that kept his command in this sickly climate, and the colonel brought good news. He had seen Mary and the children. They were well. Then he gave the general a letter from Bragg, written just a week before. The Confederates were moving north again; Breckinridge was needed in Kentucky. [27]

Since the abandonment of Bowling Green the year before, the Confederates in the West had dreamed of returning to the Bluegrass, of retaking Tennessee and moving north to the Ohio. Just as Breckinridge had overestimated the Southern Rights sympathy in the state in 1861, so now did other high-ranking Confederates misjudge the sympathy there for their cause. The state merely needed the presence of a southern army, they felt, and its sons would flock to their banners. Kentucky was a gigantic strategic asset as well, controlling as it did several hundred miles of the Ohio from Virginia to the Mississippi. Its redemption would become a Confederate mania, especially to expatriate Kentuckians like Breckinridge, Buckner, Marshall, Preston, and others.

Largely in response to repeated urgings to invade the state, Bragg decided early this summer to mount a campaign. He shifted his army from Tupelo to Chattanooga in a complex and brilliant maneuver, and there met another small army under Major General Edmund Kirby Smith. Together they would make the invasion. Needing reinforcements, they called in detachments from far and wide. Kirby Smith brought in Humphrey Marshall from Virginia, and on August 8, 1862, Bragg called J. Stoddard Johnston in to take a letter to Breckinridge. [28]

Bragg and Breckinridge had gotten along well up until now. Bragg had been pleased with the Kentuckian's performance at Shiloh, and he entertained great expectations of what Breckinridge could do in Kentucky. "I should be much better satisfied were you with me on the impending cam-

26. O.R., Ser. I, Vol. XV, 130, 550–51; Winters, Civil War in Louisiana, 122–23.
27. J. S. Johnston Diary, July 27, August 8, 13, 14, 1862, in Johnston MSS; J. Stoddard Johnston, Kentucky, 77; Charles H. Morgan Letter to Breckinridge, August 5, 1862, in CHS.
28. Connelly, Army of the Heartland, 195–200, 207–208; Coulter, Civil War and Readjustment, 135–39; McWhiney, Bragg, 268; J. S. Johnston Diary, August 14, 1862, in Johnston Papers.

paign," he wrote. "Your influence in Kentucky would be equal to an extra division in my army. . . . A command is ready for you, and I hope to see your eyes beam again at the command 'Forward,' as they did at Shiloh, in the midst of our greatest success." [29]

Breckinridge was considerably ahead of Bragg. As early as July he had heard of the proposed Kentucky movement, and had written a letter to President Davis asking to go along. His aide Jilson P. Johnson personally delivered the letter to Davis, and the chief magistrate received calls from Kentucky congressmen at about the same time. Davis was "moved" by the letter, he told Johnson, but could do nothing since Van Dorn was hard pressed for troops, too. All he could do would be to write to Bragg and leave the matter up to him.[30]

"I would make any sacrifice to join you," Breckinridge replied to Bragg through Johnston, but he could not leave his men behind. Yet that seemed to be the only way he would be able to leave Van Dorn. "My heart goes with you." Meanwhile, Van Dorn had his own plans. He and Sterling Price envisioned a campaign into western Tennessee and Kentucky, and they wanted the Kentuckian with them. A great deal of seesawing ensued, with Breckinridge caught in the middle. For three weeks and more he seemed to be going to Bragg, and then not. Disappointed with the indecision of a matter meaning so much to him, he could only lament, "I groan and obey." [31]

Finally Bragg gave Van Dorn a peremptory order to release Breckinridge. Still there was no action. Only when Secretary of War George W. Randolph was persuaded that Van Dorn was obstructing the order did action ensue. On Randolph's order, Breckinridge was freed, and even here Van Dorn continued to interfere by holding up some of the troops the Kentuckian was to have taken with him. In all, Breckinridge would have only twenty-five hundred men of his own division, and about eighteen hundred exchanged prisoners who would shortly follow. Still, elated to be rid of Van Dorn, he put his little command in motion by rail on September 19, hopeful for what lay ahead.[32]

29. O.R., Ser. I, Vol. VII, Pt. 2, p. 628, Vol. XVI, Pt. 2, p. 995.

30. Robert M. Johnson to Breckinridge, August 10, 29, 1862, H. C. Burnett to Breckinridge, August 5, 1862, in B. MSS.

31. O.R., Ser. I, Vol. LII, Pt. 2, p. 340, 350, Vol. XVI, Pt. 2, pp. 771–72, 809, 995, Vol. XV, pp. 81, 800–801, Vol. XVII, Pt. 2, pp. 692, 701, 897–900; J. S. Johnston Diary, August 14, 1862, in Johnston MSS; J. Stoddard Johnston. Kentucky, 78–80; Burnett to Randolph, August 22, 1862, Secretary of War, Register of Letters Received September 1862–April 1863, A–L, Chap. 9, XXVI, NA; Hartje, Van Dorn, 209–11; Committee of Invitation to Breckinridge, August 24, 1862, D. Adams to Breckinridge, September 9, 1862, in B. MSS.

32. O.R., Ser. I, Vol. XVI, Pt. 1, p. 1010, Pt. 2, pp. 775, 798, 805–806, 815, 822, 852,

There followed a troop movement whose brilliance matched that of Bragg the previous July. Organizing his trip from his saddle, with little equipment and no warning for advance planning, Breckinridge moved with remarkable speed. Embarking his scattered units at Jackson, Mississippi, he followed the best available rail lines south to Mobile, then east to Montgomery, Alabama, on to Atlanta, through Chattanooga, and into Knoxville on October 3. In only fourteen days, hampered by official interference, hasty planning, and poor supply, the Kentuckian had moved his men over eleven hundred miles on seven different railroads. "I hope you are satisfied with my energy since I was allowed to leave," Breckinridge wired Bragg on his arrival in Knoxville. "I have encountered every difficulty a man could meet." [33]

But Bragg was not impressed. After two weeks in Kentucky during which the expected recruits were not forthcoming, he was disillusioned about the state and its people. Needed supplies could not be obtained either, and it soon became evident that Bragg, Breckinridge, and all the others had been sadly misguided as to Confederate sympathy in the Bluegrass State. Bragg, however, could not accept this. His psychological instability made him mortally afraid of error, and of blame for error. Consequently, with a failing campaign on his hands, he began to seek scapegoats. Breckinridge was a natural for the role. As early as September 17 he complained that some fifteen thousand arms which the Kentuckian was supposed to have brought from Knoxville were desperately needed, though in fact he had no recruits to shoulder them. A week later Bragg had amplified the general's sins. "The failure of Genl Breckinridge to carry out his part of my program has seriously embarrassed me, and moreover the whole campaign," he cried to the president. Then he went on to declare that the poor recruiting was the Kentuckian's fault, since men would have enlisted in droves with Breck-

996–98, Vol. XVII, Pt. 2, p. 703, Ser. II, Vol. IV, 800, 903; Johnson to Breckinridge, August 29, 1862, in B. MSS; Johnson and Burnett to Breckinridge, September 16, 1862, in Breckinridge MSS, CHS.

33. Thompson, *Orphan Brigade*, 146, 148–49; Breckinridge to J. Sullivan, September 18, 1862, Breckinridge to Commanding Officer at Chattanooga, September 19, 1862, Buckner to A. Evans, September 19, 1862, John A. Buckner to Lucius Walker, September 20, 1862, Breckinridge to Sullivan, September 26, 1862, Breckinridge to E. Pollard, September 22, 1862, Breckinridge to O. Fleming, September 23, 1862, Breckinridge to Walker, September 23, 1862, Breckinridge to Robert Trabue, September 25, 1862, all in Chap. 2, CCCXI, NA; McWhiney, *Bragg*, 268–71; Special Orders No. 17, September 9, 1862, No. 18, September 10, 1862, No. 20, September 12, 1862, No. 21, September 15, 1862, No. 22, September 16, 1862, No. 23, September 18, 1862, all in Chap. 2, CCCXVI, NA; *O.R.*, Ser. I, Vol. XVI, Pt. 2, pp. 996–97, 999; Breckinridge to Sullivan, n.d., in Eldridge Collection, HL.

inridge there to incite them. It seemed not to matter to Bragg that Breckinridge lost his own state in 1860, and those who would not vote for him
could hardly be expected to come out and fight for him. Yet by the end of
September the notion was firmly rooted in Bragg's mind. "Breckinridge has
failed," he told Polk. Well aware of the obstacles Van Dorn and others had
used to delay Breckinridge, Bragg still chose to ignore them. Hereafter the
Kentuckian as well as several others would take from their commander the
calumny for a responsibility he would not accept to himself.[34]

Despite the failure of recruiting, Bragg and Kirby Smith remained in
Kentucky in hopes of capturing the state permanently for the Confederacy. Consequently, on arriving at Knoxville, Breckinridge was anxious to
continue. He found here some four thousand troops under Brigadier General Samuel B. Maxey, and within two or three days he was joined by the
recently exchanged Second Kentucky Infantry under Colonel Roger W.
Hanson. With this the Kentuckian's command numbered eight thousand
or more, and he was ready to move out when more obstacles cropped up.
There was no transportation for supplies. Then Tennessee authorities, fearful of a Federal advance, tried desperately to keep him in Knoxville. Once
again, only the intercession of the powers in Richmond got Breckinridge
out of a mess. When finally he was freed, it was too late. On October 8
Bragg was severely defeated at the Battle of Perryville and immediately
commenced a retreat toward Tennessee. Now, more than ever, he needed
whipping boys. He would find them among his corps and division commanders, and at the same time the animosity he felt for Kentuckians—who
had failed him—reached a new height. The misunderstandings and hatreds
generated in him by this disastrous campaign would before long have his
army's command in chaos. It was a tragic situation in which his rapidly deteriorating relationship with Breckinridge would figure prominently.[35]

It was October 15 before the Kentuckian finally marched out of Knoxville. For two days the command moved under beautiful skies. By the night

34. McWhiney, *Bragg,* 295–99; *O.R.,* Ser. I, Vol. XVI, Pt. 2, p. 846; Connelly, *Army
of the Heartland,* 206; Grady C. McWhiney, "Controversy in Kentucky; Braxton
Bragg's Campaign of 1862," *Civil War History,* VI (March, 1960), 41.

35. *O.R.,* Ser. I, Vol. XVI, Pt. 2, pp. 819, 888–89, 891, 929–30, 933–35, 997–98, Vol. LII,
Pt. 2, p. 369; Roger Hanson to Breckinridge, October 2, 3, 4, 5, 1862, E. Briggs to Breck-
inridge, October 5, 1862, Samuel Cooper to Breckinridge, October 12, 1862, all in
Breckinridge MSS, CHS; Thompson, *Orphan Brigade,* 148; Buckner to Samuel B.
Maxey, October 5, 1862, Breckinridge to S. Noble, October 10, 1862, Breckinridge to
B. Miers, October 10, 1862, Breckinridge to J. Caldwell, October 10, 1862, all in Chap. 2,
CCCII, NA.

of the sixteenth, they were just thirty miles from Cumberland Gap, and Kentucky. The next morning they set out again, but the column was not entirely out of its camps when a courier delivered an order from Bragg. Breckinridge was to halt. All that day and the next he awaited further orders. Finally it came. Fall back to Knoxville, it said; the campaign was over. After over a month of terrible struggle to get himself and his men back to their native state, Breckinridge was to turn away when almost in sight of his beloved Kentucky. He could not know that it was as close as he would get for years to come.[36]

With one campaign a failure, Bragg immediately commenced another. He ordered Breckinridge to go back to Chattanooga and, from there, to proceed to Murfreesboro, Tennessee. Here he was to defend the middle of the state with an eye toward threatening enemy-held Nashville. Once again the general had to execute a difficult movement with uncertain transportation. Still he conducted the transfer smoothly and, on October 28, 1862, rode into Murfreesboro. The town was not the most ideal spot to concentrate an army. While it did control two prime invasion routes, there were several others open to the Federals which ran right past it. The city could easily be flanked, leaving the Confederates in a difficult position.[37]

Once in his new location, Breckinridge faced yet another reorganization of his command. He had three brigades: the Kentucky Brigade now led by Hanson; the Tennesseeans and a North Carolina regiment soon to be led by William Preston; and several other Tennessee and Alabama troops commanded by Colonel Joseph B. Palmer. In his front at Nashville, Major General William S. Rosecrans was massing an entire army, the same army that defeated Bragg at Perryville, and now Breckinridge feared that the Federals might advance before Bragg brought up the remainder of his army.[38]

Fortunately, Rosecrans threatened but did little else. Consequently, to buy further time, Breckinridge took the initiative, sending the cavalry commands of Brigadier Generals John H. Morgan and Nathan B. Forrest on a raid against the Federal supply line at Edgefield. Although only partially successful in destroying enemy supply and transport, the raid did

36. O.R., Ser. I, Vol. XVI, Pt. 2, pp. 951, 962, 966, 969, 999–1002; George Brent to Breckinridge, October 12, 1862, Chap. 2, CCCII, NA; Thompson, Orphan Brigade, 148–49.
37. O.R., Ser. I, Vol. XVI, Pt. 2, pp. 1000, 1002–1003, Pt. 1, pp. 463, 465; Thomas L. Connelly, Autumn of Glory: The Army of Tennessee, 1862–1865 (Baton Rouge, 1971), 17, 23–24; Stapleton Crutchfield to Breckinridge, October 27, 1862, in Breckinridge MSS, CHS; Thompson, Orphan Brigade, 150.
38. O.R., Ser. I, Vol. XVI, Pt. 2, pp. 980–81.

put Rosecrans on his guard. He began overestimating Breckinridge's meager eight-thousand-man command, inflating it to twenty-five thousand and more. As a result, the Federal commander delayed making an advance, and the time thus bought gave Bragg the chance he needed to reach Murfreesboro.[39]

Throughout November, Breckinridge sent intelligence back to Bragg—now in Tullahoma marshaling his forces—constructed defensive works, and skirmished almost constantly. Still these were weeks of general inactivity; they were restful weeks. Bragg reorganized his command again, dividing it into two corps under Polk and William Hardee, transferring Breckinridge's division from the former to the latter. Snow fell, no one seemed to think that Rosecrans would advance before spring, and officers' wives began filtering into the encampments to winter with their husbands.[40]

The general had not seen Mary since his flight from Lexington over a year before. In October, however, through the efforts of friends, she was able to meet him in Knoxville as he was moving to meet Bragg. She had been living with relatives in Kentucky when a message arrived from her husband advising her of his approach. Beck took her to Richmond where Breckinridge hoped to meet her but, thwarted in this, she came on to Knoxville to join him. It was a joyful reunion. "I had been separated so long," she told him, "that when I did see you I was in a *transport* of joy." Their daughter Mary would later recall, "I never knew any human love more devoted and loyal than that of my Mother for my Father. To be near him was all she asked, and to secure that end she would face any peril, or endure any hardship with the utmost cheerfulness, and I do not believe anyone ever heard her complain of her lot during the years of War . . . although she literally 'suffered the loss of all things' for his sake, and did it gladly." Mary Breckinridge herself would say of her husband: "I never saw him come without being glad, or leave without being sorry." For the rest of the war she would stay as close to him as possible. They were together now, and

39. W. T. Gunter to Nathan B. Forrest, October 29, 1862, Johnston to Forrest, October 29, 1862, Morgan to Forrest, October 29, 1862, Lewis Cann to Forrest, October 29, 1862, Forrest to Breckinridge, November 1, 1862, all in Breckinridge MSS, CHS; Forrest to Breckinridge, November 4, 1862, Roger Hanson to Breckinridge, November 4, 1862, Breckinridge to Hanson, November 4, 1862, Breckinridge to Bragg, November 8, 1862, all in Chap. 2, CCCXI, NA; O.R., Ser. I, Vol. XVI, Pt. 1, pp. 464, 468, Vol. XX, Pt. 1, pp. 3–7, Pt. 2, p. 388; Basil W. Duke, *A History of Morgan's Cavalry* (Reprint; Bloomington, Ind., 1960), 296–97.

40. O.R., Ser. I, Vol. XX, Pt. 2, pp. 393, 398, 402, 411, 415, 432; Connelly, *Autumn of Glory*, 32–42.

she would tell him in days to come that "my stay in Murfreesboro will always be remembered as the happiest period of my life." [41]

The Breckinridges camped with other generals and their wives on the spacious grounds of a local plantation, and enjoyed a pleasant society which included a visit from President Davis and the Kentuckian's service as an usher at the colorful marriage of General Morgan. Underneath the calm, however, the entire army quaked with discontent from the very time that Bragg brought up his troops and took command on November 30. The Kentuckians in particular were angry. They objected to Bragg's having conscripted in Kentucky to fill his ranks, and objected further to his order to draft into the army all male refugees from the state. When the enlistments of some of Breckinridge's Kentucky regiments ran out, he spoke to them, appealed to their belief in the cause, and won their voluntary re-enlistment for the duration. To see other Kentuckians forced into the army when their state still was not a part of the Confederacy rankled men like Breckinridge, Buckner, Preston, and others. It was rumored that they threatened to resign in protest. Whatever the case, their outcry hardly served to make Bragg love Kentuckians any more than he did when retreating from Perryville. The men of that state were cowards, he said; they were not worth liberating. As for its generals, he regarded them with contempt as mere politicians playing at war. All this, combined with Bragg's great discomfort under the hail of newspaper criticism over his recent failure, made him all the more unfriendly. The growing feud, hot but reasonably controlled, boiled over in December, its catalyst a deserter.[42]

Corporal Asa Lewis, Company E, Sixth Kentucky, had not personally re-enlisted when his regiment was reorganized for the duration of the war. Still he stayed on for months until December, 1862, when his family back in Kentucky fell into desperate straits and asked him to come home. He left on December 4, promising to return. He was caught, court-martialed and,

41. Clifton R. Breckinridge, Service Record, NA; *O.R.*, Ser. I, Vol. XVI, Pt. 1, pp. 455, 460; Mary C. Breckinridge to Breckinridge, October 31, 1862, February 8, 1863, in Breckinridge, Service Record; Maltby, "Civil War Times," 225–26; Maltby, *Mary Cyrene Breckinridge*, 2, 10.

42. Rowe C. Webster, "Some Reminiscences," *Confederate Veteran*, VII (July, 1899), 324; Polk, *Leonidas Polk*, II, 177; Officers of the Fifth Kentucky to Breckinridge, September 16, 1862, in Simon B. Buckner MSS, HL; Breckinridge to Officers of the Fifth Kentucky, September 18, 1862, Breckinridge to Cooper, October 3, 1862, Breckinridge to Bragg, November 19, 1862, Randolph to Bragg, November 6, 1862, all in Chap. 2, CCCXI, NA; *O.R.*, Ser. I, Vol. XX, Pt. 2, pp. 179, 456; Connelly, *Autumn of Glory*, 19–20; McWhiney, *Bragg*, 331–33; Allan Nevins, *The War for the Union: Volume II, War Becomes Revolution 1862–1863* (New York, 1960), 407.

despite his good record and intentions, condemned to death. On December, 20 Bragg approved the court's findings and directed its sentence be carried out in the presence of the Kentucky Brigade on December 26.

For the next five days the Kentucky officers pleaded with Bragg to reconsider, to take into account the questionable aspect of Lewis' reenlistment. On Christmas day they all signed a petition requesting that the matter be referred to the president for final decision. Bragg refused all, saying that there were too many desertions, and that an example was needed. On the morning of the assigned day, Breckinridge and others made another call on the commanding general to appeal the case. He turned them down, allegedly stating that Kentuckians were too independent for the good of the army and that he would shoot every one of them if he had to. Incensed, Breckinridge shouted back that his men would not be treated like animals and that this execution would be murder. Hearing the result of the appeal, several companies of Kentuckians ran to their arms, dangerously close to mutiny. Only the strenuous efforts of Breckinridge and the others controlled them.

With some difficulty the brigade was formed into a three-sided hollow square, with Lewis standing, bound, facing it from the open side. A firing squad stood ready, though only after a succession of officers had refused to command it. At 11 A.M. everything was ready. Breckinridge, sitting his horse with his staff, dismounted and walked to Lewis. He had visited him repeatedly during the past days, going to his cell just the night before to comfort him. To the general Lewis had given his only possession, a pocketbook, asking that it be given to his mother. Now Breckinridge said a few last words, bade him goodbye, and returned to his horse. As a heavy rain began to fall, the squad fired and killed Lewis instantly. Men of the brigade saw that "when the young man fell Gen. Breckinridge was seized with a deathly sickness, dropped forward on the neck of his horse, and had to be caught by some of his staff." Mindful of his promise to the dead boy, the general would carry Lewis' pocketbook with him for seven long years, through the greatest hardships of his life, until finally he could redeem his pledge and give it to the boy's mother.[43]

If there had been any remaining chance of repairing the estrangement be-

43. Thompson, *Orphan Brigade*, 201–202, 774; B. L. Ridley, "Camp Scenes Around Dalton," *Confederate Veteran*. X (February, 1902), 68; Nevins, *War Becomes Revolution*, 407–408; Sallie Lewis to Breckinridge, September 21, 1869, A. Ward to Breckinridge, July 22, 1874, in JCB Papers; Interview with Mrs. Kenneth Kirkland, New York, September 17, 1968.

tween Bragg and Breckinridge, the death of Asa Lewis destroyed it forever. The execution may have seemed justified under existing circumstances but in view of the animosities already existing between the commanding general and the Kentuckians, how unfortunate it was that the example had to come from among their number. The breach it made between Bragg and Breckinridge created in each, for the other, a potent enemy. And how much more unfortunate that it all culminated when the army stood on the very brink of a major battle that could decide the fate of middle Tennessee.

CHAPTER 3

When a Man Is Right

Finally Rosecrans had moved. Having massed some 47,000 troops in Nashville, he began an advance on Murfreesboro the very morning that Corporal Lewis was shot, moving over two of the three roads that Breckinridge had for so long been watching. Bragg, his troops numbering in all about 38,000, decided to stay in position and fight. Early on December 28 he called Breckinridge and his other corps and division commanders together to assign them their positions. He put Polk's corps on the left, or west, side of Stones River, and Hardee's on the right. Hardee in turn placed Breckinridge's division in the front line, backed up by the division of Major General Patrick Cleburne some distance in the rear. Now numbering 7,698, Breckinridge's command contained a new brigade, under Brigadier General Daniel W. Adams, of Alabama and Louisiana troops. Hanson, appointed a brigadier just the week before, still led the Kentuckians, but there had been some reorganization in the other two brigades. Preston had some Florida regiments added to his North Carolina and Tennessee men, while some of his other Volunteer State men had been taken out to make an all-Tennessee brigade now commanded by Colonel J. B. Palmer. In addition, the brigade of Brigadier General John K. Jackson—Mississippi, Georgia, and Alabama men—was temporarily assigned to Breckinridge. The result was that he commanded the most diversified division in the army, with men from eight different states.[1]

Following the conference, Breckinridge placed his brigades in position, Adams on the right next to the Lebanon Pike, Preston to his left, Palmer to his left, and Hanson on the right, by the river. Jackson was later that day sent east of the Lebanon Pike, in prolongation of Adams' line, while about 500 cavalry under Brigadier General John Pegram were sent out on the

---

1. *O.R.*, Ser. I, Vol. XX, Pt. 1, p. 659.

flank for observation. Bragg and Hardee inspected the general's dispositions and gave their approval. Facing him was a variety of routes available
to Rosecrans, west, north, and east, by which the enemy could gain Bragg's
flank or rear. The Nashville Pike came in from the northwest; stretching
down from the north—a direct threat to the general's flank—was the Lebanon Pike; from the east came the Lascasas Pike. All were open to the Federals. These roads dictated the line Breckinridge held, his placement, and
his part in the coming battle.[2]

For two days Bragg had been worried about a reported force advancing
down the Lebanon Pike, one of the reasons why Breckinridge's line had to
be stretched to cover that road. Now, with this in mind, the Kentuckian
found that he could not move his whole command forward to occupy
Wayne's Hill, a commanding eminence six hundred yards in his front because, thanks to a convex bend in the river around the base of the hill, it
would require a line more than a mile in width to hold the road and still
keep his left flank on the river. Consequently, Breckinridge sent Hanson's
brigade forward to Wayne's Hill, moved Adams in to Hanson's old position, and pulled Jackson over from the east side of the pike to form in line
on Adams' left. He then had a line of skirmishers thrown forward to impede any enemy progress until the general could push the balance of his
command up to repel an assault.[3]

Meanwhile, Bragg had received new intelligence that there was no
threat on the Lebanon Pike after all. Toward late afternoon on December 30 he ordered Hardee to remove Cleburne's division from the east to
the west side of the river. This left Breckinridge all alone at Wayne's,
occupying the most strategically important portion of the battlefield. He
probably did not know it yet, but the Federal corps facing him across
Stones River was commanded by the same friend he had fought at Shiloh,
Thomas L. Crittenden.[4]

The morning of December 31, 1862, dawned fog-bound and cold. During the night, Bragg had decided to attack Rosecrans' right, which left
Breckinridge almost entirely out of his plan of battle. However, the Federals planned an identical assault, which meant that Crittenden would be

2. Theodore O'Hara to Breckinridge, January 16, 1863, Rice E. Graves to Breckinridge, January 25, 1863, in Breckinridge MSS, NYHS; Special Orders No. 59, December 29, 1862, in Breckinridge MSS, CHS; O.R., Ser. I, Vol. XX, Pt. 1, p. 782.

3. O.R., Ser. I, Vol. XX, Pt. 1, p. 782; Special Orders No. 60, December 30, 1862, in
Breckinridge MSS, CHS.

4. Thomas Roy to Breckinridge, 3:30 P.M., December 30, 1862, in Breckinridge MSS,
CHS; Connelly, Autumn of Glory, 50–51.

sending his divisions against his old friend. Whichever of the two armies began the attack would have the advantage, and Bragg took it at 6 A.M. that morning. The Battle of Stones River began. With the exception of providing support with his artillery on Wayne's Hill, Breckinridge took no part in the morning's fighting. He had been assigned no part in the battle, perhaps because of Bragg's earlier worries for the Lebanon Pike, and reports came in from Pegram that morning which seemed to confirm that worry. Shortly after 7 A.M., the Federal division of Brigadier General Horatio Van Cleve began crossing Stones River about a mile down from Wayne's Hill, as part of Rosecrans' offensive. However, when a crisis developed in front of Polk and Hardee, Van Cleve was ordered back across the river. Pegram failed to report the recrossing, leaving Breckinridge under the impression that there was still an enemy in his front.[5]

At about 10 A.M., Bragg's aide Major William Clare rode up to Breckinridge with an order from the commanding general to advance his division. Suspecting that Bragg was unaware of the supposed presence of the enemy in his front, he sent Clare back with a message that Van Cleve was probably advancing against him, and that the Lebanon Pike was unprotected. By 10:30 he received Bragg's reply. He was first to make sure whether there were Federals in his front, and then, when certain, attack them before they advanced. Breckinridge told Clare that he could be sure of nothing—perhaps a criticism of Pegram's intelligence—but just then J. Stoddard Johnston rode up with another message from Bragg. Probably only moments after dispatching Clare, Bragg received what he regarded as reliable information from Pegram that infantry were crossing the river in his front. Now he ordered the Kentuckian to attack.[6]

Breckinridge moved forward immediately, wheeling his division to the left, pivoting on Hanson's brigade. He advanced one-half mile, perhaps more, when his left became engaged with skirmishers from Van Cleve's brigade guarding the ford.[7]

5. Connelly, *Autumn of Glory*, 52–58; O'Hara to Breckinridge, January 16, 1862, in Breckinridge MSS, NYHS; Polk, *Leonidas Polk*, II, 193.

6. William Clare to Braxton Bragg, June 2, 1863, John Pegram to Bragg, 10 A.M., December 31, 1862, in William Palmer Collection of Braxton Bragg Papers, WRHS; *O.R.*, Ser. I, Vol. XX, Pt. 1, pp. 666, 783, 789.

7. Bragg charged from Clare's report of Breckinridge's reluctance to advance when first ordered—a report written six months after the fact—plus the statement in Breckinridge's 11:30 A.M. December 31 message that "I am obeying your order," that the Kentuckian did not begin his advance until that hour, one hour after he was ordered to do so. However, O'Hara's January 16, 1863, letter, written just two weeks after the fight, says, "You promptly put your line in motion" upon receiving Bragg's order. It is also

At 11:30, Breckinridge sent John Buckner to Bragg with a note reporting that he was advancing, engaged with the enemy. He could go no farther, he said, without giving up the Lebanon Pike. Buckner returned in a few minutes with an order for Breckinridge to fall back and send "at least one" brigade, and two if possible, over to support Polk. The Kentuckian began the movement right away, getting orders to Jackson's and Adams' brigades, and putting Jackson in motion by noon. Then he sent scouts out to check on Pegram's intelligence.[8]

Now Bragg suddenly changed his mind and canceled his order for a brigade(s) for Polk, instead ordering two other brigades to cross and reinforce Breckinridge. But by 12:50 the Kentuckian, now in doubt that there was an enemy in front of him, suggested that Bragg place the two brigades at the river ford, so that they could go to Polk easily if Pegram's reports turned out false. Pegram was proved wrong almost immediately, no enemy force of any size was found on this side of the river, and about 1 P.M. Bragg ordered Breckinridge to follow Adams and Jackson over to Polk. It had been a costly three hours of confusion, and Pegram, Breckinridge, and Bragg all must share the guilt. Although Pegram's was the greater error, all were culpable.[9]

Leaving Hanson to hold Wayne's Hill, Breckinridge rode ahead of Palmer and Preston, across Stones River to Polk. He arrived to find that Jackson and Adams had already been sent in against the enemy without waiting for his other two brigades, and now he saw them falling back, nearly shattered by the resistance in a wooded stronghold called the Round Forest. He rode forward to rally Adams, only to find the general wounded, and Colonel Randall L. Gibson now in command. Jackson had fallen back much

---

clear from the Kentuckian's 11:30 note that he had already covered much ground. In it he says his left is engaged with the enemy, yet the only Federals on his side of the river at this time were a brigade of Van Cleve's stationed a mile and a quarter from Breckinridge's starting position. Thus, by 11:30 when he sent his message, Breckinridge had already advanced at least a mile. Jackson, Palmer, Preston, and several regimental commanders all mention a good deal of skirmishing and maneuvering this morning before going over to Polk (*O.R.*, Ser. I, Vol. XX, Pt. 1, pp. 804, 821, 835, 838).

8. *O.R.*, Ser. I, Vol. XX, Pt. 1, pp. 694, 702–703, 783, 789; John Buckner to Breckinridge, May 20, 1863, James Wilson to Breckinridge, January 20, 1863, Leonidas Polk to Breckinridge, March 31, 1863, O'Hara to Breckinridge, January 16, 1863, all in Breckinridge MSS, NYHS; marginal note by Clifton R. Breckinridge on p. 184 of his father's copy of Thompson, *First Kentucky Brigade*, in JCB Papers. There is some conflict over whether Bragg ordered over one or two brigades at first. Breckinridge believed that it was just one, and most of those present agree.

9. *O.R.*, Ser. I, Vol. XX, Pt. 1, pp. 666, 789–90. None of Breckinridge's brigade commanders reported being called back once set in motion for Polk.

farther to the left. Meanwhile, the general's two fresh brigades went into line, Preston with his right on the river, and Palmer to his left. Polk ordered Breckinridge to assault the Round Forest, and the general led his men in person.[10]

His attack was more successful than those before it. By the time he made contact with the enemy, he discovered that they were in line at an acute angle to his line of advance, Preston meeting them first along the river. The Federals, partly covered in a cedar forest—the Round Forest—handled Preston severely with shells and musketry, but finally he rallied and, along with Palmer, did drive them from the forest. Breckinridge stopped his advance in the cedars, and shortly afterward Hardee came up to observe the situation, bringing much of what remained of his corps with him. Hardee joined the Kentuckian in a ride along the edge of wood to reconnoiter the enemy position. They then rode along their line, saw that it was too weak to stand making another assault, and ordered the men to go into bivouac. At 9 P.M. that night Polk called Breckinridge up to Bragg's headquarters. Two hours later the Kentuckian sent an order to his staff to return to the other side of the river, and for Palmer to follow and form on Hanson's right. Bragg expected an attack on Hanson's position in the morning. It had been a costly day. The three brigades of Breckinridge's division that were engaged lost 730 casualties, a staggering 544 of them from Adams' command. Jackson's brigade lost an additional 305. When he found time, the Kentuckian sent his son Clifton—now serving in a cavalry battalion attached to his father's headquarters—into Murfreesboro to see Mary and tell her that her husband and sons had come through the battle unharmed. Breckinridge wanted to go and see her himself, but felt it best that he remain on the ground with his men.[11]

Contrary to widespread expectations, Rosecrans did not abandon the field that night. He remained and strengthened his position, taking new

10. *O.R.*, Ser. I, Vol. XX, Pt. 1, pp. 783, 818; J. S. Johnston Diary, December 31, 1862, in Johnston MSS; Connelly, *Autumn of Glory*, 60–61; O'Hara to Breckinridge, January 16, 1863, in Breckinridge MSS, NYHS.

11. *O.R.*, Ser. I, Vol. XX, Pt. 1, pp. 678–81, 722, 784; O'Hara to Breckinridge, January 16, 1863, Buckner to Breckinridge, May 20, 1863, in Breckinridge MSS, NYHS; Lindsley (ed.), *Annals*, 816; Connelly, *Autumn of Glory*, 61; William Preston to Breckinridge, n.d., quoted in Charles S. Hamilton's Auction Catalog No. 16, 1966, p. 9; unnumbered special order, January 1, 1863, Breckinridge MSS, CHS; Thompson, *Orphan Brigade*, 175–77; "Conversational Remarks by C. R. Breckinridge," September 27, 1932, in Prewitt Collection; Mary Breckinridge to Breckinridge, January 1, 1863, in Breckinridge, Service Record, NA.

ground. About two miles in Breckinridge's front, part of Crittenden's corps once again crossed the river at McFadden's Ford, setting out skirmishers and artillery on a high ridge some distance in advance of Wayne's Hill. In fact, Van Cleve's division crossed over to the east bank, but the Confederates seemed unaware that they faced anything other than a skirmish line. Again his cavalry did not serve Breckinridge well, and again he failed to take adequate steps to secure better, more reliable, information. Bragg, hearing of the enemy skirmishers, asked the general early on January 1 to watch closely for any crossing of the river. The Kentuckian complied, but his scouts failed him. Breckinridge still did not know the true state of affairs on the ridge as late as the next morning.[12]

Early on January 2, before daylight, the general came into his field headquarters to find Clifton warming coffee sent out by Mary. Still uncertain of the Federal force before him, Breckinridge had sent an officer of the Fourth Kentucky forward to make a reconnaissance of the enemy position. Now that officer came to headquarters to report that the placement of Federal artillery across the river indicated that Rosecrans was setting a trap for Breckinridge, probably hoping that he would attack Van Cleve and thereby come under flank fire from the guns. In company with his son Cabell, Theodore O'Hara, and Major James Wilson, his assistant inspector general, Breckinridge rode down toward the river and came upon Polk, Hardee, and Colonel William D. Pickett. They all rode along the river toward the right to make a reconnaissance. Shortly, staff officers came to call both Polk and Hardee back to their own lines, but Pickett remained and went on with Breckinridge.

The general was particularly interested in Hanson's left resting on the river. He moved forward to Hanson's skirmish line about five hundred yards in advance of the main position, and once there ordered the enemy skirmishers driven in so that he might see what was behind them. This done, Breckinridge discovered that a sizable Federal force occupied the crest of the slope before him. Van Cleve was in a line almost at right angles to Hanson, sixteen hundred yards distant, and partly sheltered by a wood on his left. The ground in between lay open for about five hundred yards back from the river, and rose gently to the Federal position. Breckinridge was

12. George Brent to Breckinridge, 10:15 A.M., January 1, 1863, Roy to Breckinridge, January 1, 1863, Buckner to John Palmer, January 1, 1863, all in Breckinridge MSS, CHS; Special Order No. 2, n.d. [January 1, 1863], in Eldridge Collection, HL; O.R., Ser. I, Vol. XX, Pt. 1, p. 784.

about to seek out the size of the enemy force, and its position relative to the Federals on the other side of the river, when he received a summons to join Bragg.[13]

During the night and morning Bragg had sent several cavalry patrols of varying size around Rosecrans' rear. At first they reported that the enemy was withdrawing, but later dispatches revealed that the Federal army was still in position, and had taken the ridge in front of Wayne's Hill. It was Bragg's opinion that enemy artillery on this eminence would be able to enfilade Polk's position, while Confederate guns placed there could do the same to Crittenden. Without consulting Breckinridge, Bragg sent his adjutant, Colonel George W. Brent, and a personal favorite, Captain Felix H. Robertson, over to the right to find a suitable place for artillery to enfilade the Federals. Their report that Van Cleve's hill was the ideal spot decided the matter. Bragg resolved to attack.[14]

It was between noon and 1 P.M. when Breckinridge and Pickett rode up to Bragg's headquarters along the Nashville Pike, near the bank of Stones River. The Kentuckian found the commanding general already committed to an assault, though unfamiliar with the ground and troop positions involved. Worse yet, Bragg had not even consulted Breckinridge, beforehand, nor had he bothered to discuss it with either of his corps commanders, even Breckinridge's superior Hardee. None of the three approved of the plan, and Polk did not even think Van Cleve's hill presented a threat to his line.[15]

The Kentuckian met Bragg under a large sycamore near the river. Bragg opened his remarks by noting that Breckinridge's division had suffered little in the fighting of December 31, and that this was the reason he had selected

13. Marginal note by Clifton R. Breckinridge on p. 187 of his father's copy of Thompson, *First Kentucky Brigade*, in JCB Papers; Mary Breckinridge to Breckinridge, January 1, 1863, in Breckinridge, Service Record, NA; Young, *Reminiscences*, 46–47; *O.R.*, Ser. I, Vol. XX, Pt. 1, pp. 784–85; William D. Pickett, "A Reminiscence of Murfreesboro," Nashville *American*, November 10, 1907; O'Hara to Breckinridge, January 16, 1863, in Breckinridge MSS, NYHS. A member of the Ninth (Federal) Kentucky Cavalry serving on Rosecrans' left, also thought that the guns were being concealed on the height across the river; John Worley to his mother, January 10, 1863, in Worley Family Letters in possession of Stanley R. Levitt, New York, N.Y.

14. George W. Brent Diary, January 2, 1863, in Palmer Collection; *O.R.*, Ser. I, Vol. XX, Pt. 1, pp. 667–68; Alexander F. Stevenson, *The Battle of Stones River near Murfreesboro, Tenn.* (Boston, 1884), 128–29. For establishment of the authorship of the Brent Diary, see, June I. Gow, "The Johnston and Brent Diaries: A Problem of Authorship," *Civil War History*, XIV (March, 1968), 46–50.

15. Polk, *Leonidas Polk*, II, 194; Nathaniel Cheairs Hughes, Jr., *General William J. Hardee, Old Reliable* (Baton Rouge, 1965), 145; *O.R.*, Ser. I, Vol. XX, Pt. 1, p. 778.

it for the attack now contemplated. Others would later disagree, maintaining that Bragg resented the manner in which the general had stood up to him over the accused cowardice of Kentuckians and the Asa Lewis execution, and chose Breckinridge for the assault in the hope that he would be killed. Now again Breckinridge argued. Backed up by his own personal reconnaissance as well as that of others, he was certain Rosecrans was heavily placed on the bluff on the side of the river opposite the proposed line of attack. Their ground was higher than his, and artillery well placed could hit him in front and flank, turning the attack into disaster. Picking up a stick, Breckinridge sketched his position and Crittenden's on the ground, trying to dissuade his commander. Bragg was adamant. "Sir," he replied, "my information is different. I have given the order to attack the enemy in your front and expect it to be obeyed." Shocked but helpless, Breckinridge listened on. Bragg wanted Van Cleve's position taken so that batteries could be placed to enfilade the enemy. For the attack, the Kentuckian was to form his division in two lines—Adams and Preston being returned to him—while the artillery would come up once the hill was taken. Cavalry under Pegram and John Wharton were somewhere off to Breckinridge's right and had been instructed by Bragg to protect the general's flank and cooperate in the attack. In addition, Felix Robertson's six-gun battery and four more guns under Captain Henry C. Semple were ordered to Breckinridge. Polk would be ordered to open an artillery barrage at 3:45 that afternoon to soften the enemy on the west side of the river, while the main attack was to begin fifteen minutes later when signaled by a single shot from the center of Bragg's line.[16]

The general raced back to his position to ready the attack, temporarily attaching Pickett to his staff for the day. None of his brigade commanders approved of the order, and Hanson was incensed. Clifton Breckinridge years later recalled that this hot tempered Kentuckian "denounced the order as absolutely murderous and felt so infuriated at the men being ordered to do an impossible thing that he wanted to go at once to headquarters and kill Bragg." Breckinridge and Preston managed to talk him out of it. Meanwhile, the general himself was vocal in his opposition. Taking Preston aside, he confided: "General Preston, this attack is made against

16. Stevenson, *Stone's River*, 131; Pickett, "Reminiscences"; Young, *Reminiscences*, 47–48; Cincinnati *Commercial*, May 18, 1875; New York *Turf, Field and Farm*, May 21, 1875; *O.R.*, Ser. I, Vol. XX, Pt. 1, pp. 785, 790; H. B. Clay, "On the Right at Murfreesboro," *Confederate Veteran*, XXI (December, 1913), 588; O'Hara to Breckinridge, January 16, 1863, in Breckinridge MSS, NYHS.

my judgment, and by the special orders of General Bragg. Of course we all must try to do our duty, and fight the best we can. If it should result in disaster, and I be among the slain, I want you to do justice to my memory, and tell the people that I believed this attack to be very unwise, and tried to prevent it." It was the only time during the war that Breckinridge spoke of the possibility of death before a battle.[17]

Now Bragg visited another misfortune upon him. Brigadier General Gideon J. Pillow, on the battlefield without a command, appealed to Bragg for an assignment, and the commanding general ordered him to take Palmer's brigade. A liar, intriguer, and almost wholly incompetent, Pillow could only claim high connections in Richmond. Breckinridge did not attempt to conceal his displeasure at this change in his command. It is unfortunate that Breckinridge could not know that the commanding general had sent him not one, but two, of the army's most corruptible officers, for everything that Pillow was, the handsome and ambitious young Captain Robertson would soon become.[18]

Breckinridge ordered Pickett to put in place the two brigades that would be on the right in each of his two lines, Pillow in front and Preston behind, while O'Hara led Hanson to his place on the left of the front rank, and Gibson to the left of the second. An interval of 150–200 yards separated the two lines as they formed under cover of the wood alongside Wayne's Hill. Meanwhile, the general determined to place his division artillery in the rear of the second line and have it advance with the infantry, in order that it might be put into action as soon as possible after the crest of the hill was taken from Van Cleve. When Robertson came up with his own and Semple's batteries, Breckinridge directed that, once the hill was taken, Semple would immediately place his four guns on the right of the division's line while Robertson's six would go to the left and protect that flank from the Federal artillery fire that he anticipated from across the river. There may have been some disagreement between Breckinridge and Robertson over just how his batteries were to advance, but they were finally placed in the rear of the division artillery, with orders to move forward behind the troops.[19]

Breckinridge left reserves from Hanson's and Gibson's commands on

17. "Conversational Remarks by C. R. Breckinridge," September 27, 1932, in Prewitt Collection; Stevenson, *Stone's River*, 132.

18. G. H. Baskette, "Eighteenth Tennessee Infantry," in Lindsley (ed.), *Annals*, 363; *O.R.*, Ser. I, Vol. XX, Pt. 1, p. 785.

19. Pickett, "Reminiscence"; *O.R.*, Ser. I, Vol. XX, Pt. 1, pp. 758–61, 796, 798; O'Hara to Breckinridge, January 16, 1863, Graves to Breckinridge, January 25, 1863, in Breck-

Wayne's Hill and in the woods, and finally had ready for the attack about 5,000–5,300 infantry and artillery of his own division. Robertson's and Semple's batteries added to his numbers somewhat, and Pegram and Wharton with their cavalry made even more. However, the general seriously misused—or failed to use—the cavalrymen. Bragg had vaguely ordered Pegram, at least, to be ready to cooperate with Breckinridge in the attack. It appears that he did not so inform Wharton. What is important is that Bragg told Breckinridge that they were to work with him, yet there is no evidence that Breckinridge made any attempt to communicate with them, as he should have, to perfect a mutual plan of attack. By 3:30 that afternoon, after all his dispositions had been made, the general apparently still had not tried to communicate with the cavalrymen. Now Pillow rode up and asked about the supports on the right. Being told that nothing had been heard from them, and that no communication had been sent to them, he remarked to Breckinridge that they should be contacted. The general finally sent a staff officer over to the right, but nothing was heard of either Pegram or Wharton up to the moment the attack began.[20]

Breckinridge heard the signal at precisely 4 P.M., and ordered his lines forward. It was one of the greatest Confederate infantry assaults of the war in the West. The day was clear, the scene spectacular. Then the steady tread of thousands of marching feet was drowned in the yelling and din of the charge. The enemy could hear the Confederates cheering fifteen minutes before a shot was fired. Hanson and Pillow moved out of their wooded cover and into the open field, bayonets fixed. Breckinridge rode behind the center of the second line and, when he emerged from the trees, he saw his first line about halfway across the field. The men moved at the "double quick" in the face of a heavy fire. Glancing to the left, Breckinridge could see plainly the Kentucky Brigade charging smartly up the slope toward Van Cleve. "Look at old Hanson!" he exclaimed to his staff. Then he saw something less pleasing. Pillow, instead of going forward with his brigade, had remained in the woods and was hiding behind a large tree when the second line passed him. He stayed there until Breckinridge personally ordered him away.[21]

---

inridge MSS, NYHS. For reasons which will later become evident, Felix Robertson's perjured report was not used in preparing this account.

20. *O.R.*, Ser. I, Vol. XX, Pt. 1, pp. 785–86, 790, 969; Brent to Bragg, March 15, 1863, in Palmer Collection; Clay, "On the Right at Murfreesboro," 588–89.

21. *O.R.*, Ser. I, Vol. XX, Pt. 1, p. 786; Pickett, "Reminiscence"; Rice E. Graves, Charges and Specifications of charges against Brig Genl G. J. Pillow, n.d., in Breckinridge MSS, CHS; Worley to his mother, January 10, 1863, in Worley Family Letters.

A crisis arose on the right. Pegram and Wharton were not there, thanks to the general's oversight, and a Federal brigade was overlapping Pillow. The Tennesseean later blamed this on Breckinridge, though the major general's line simply could not stretch far enough without opening his left flank. To meet this emergency, Breckinridge ordered Captain Rice Graves to move a battery to support Pillow, and this temporarily checked the Federals. The advance continued.[22]

Almost immediately, still only two thirds of the way across the field, Hanson's men halted. Breckinridge rode over at once to find the cause. To his dismay, he saw Hanson on the ground, mortally wounded, bleeding profusely from an artery severed above the knee by a piece of shell. Breckinridge himself bent over his friend and firmly grasped Hanson's leg, attempting without success to stop the flow of blood. An ambulance came up, Breckinridge uttered a few brief words to Hanson, and the wounded general was carried back to Murfreesboro.[23]

While one old friend lay dying, another one in blue was across the river arranging to send even more destruction into Breckinridge's division. Massed on a hill directly across the river sat Crittenden's artillery, the same guns that Breckinridge had feared when protesting Bragg's attack order. Within a few minutes there would be fifty-one pieces of artillery aimed at the Kentuckian's division, though not more than forty-seven were firing at any one time, and these would soon be joined by another six-gun battery. For the time being, Breckinridge would have only Robert Cobb's six guns to answer them. The rest of his artillery was limbered and in motion, except for the battery supporting Pillow, and Polk's guns back on the other side of the river provided only a nominal distraction to the Federals. For perhaps ten or fifteen minutes, Crittenden delivered round after round into the Confederate advance virtually unopposed.[24]

Again the advance resumed, and all observers testified to the magnificent sight of its still uniform ranks, its flying battleflags. The alignment of the brigades was perfect, but soon the ever-increasing artillery fire took effect. By the time the front line reached the crest to battle hand-to-hand with the

22. *O.R.*, Ser. I, Vol. XX, Pt. 1, pp. 786, 808–809.
23. Pickett, "Reminiscence"; Thompson, *Orphan Brigade*, 200.
24. Various claims have put the number of Mendenhall's guns at from fifty-two to sixty and more. However, Edwin C. Bearss, "Stone's River: The Artillery at 4:45 P.M., January 2, 1863," *Civil War Times Illustrated*, II (February, 1964), 38–39, conclusively places the number at fifty-seven. The fact that only fifty-three were firing at any one time is explained by Batteries H and M, Fourth U.S. Light Artillery, alternating fire with each other.

Federals, Pillow's brigade and Hanson's, now led by Trabue of the Fourth Kentucky, were overlapping each other in the center. As a result, their line did not hit the enemy as hard as it could have. It mattered little at this point. After a brief fight, the Federals began streaming down the back side of the hill to McFadden's Ford. Unfortunately, many men of Trabue's command, carried away in their enthusiasm, actually followed the enemy across the river while the rest of the line went down the back slope some distance. Here the men came under the full force of the Yankee guns, firing at short range, and it took but a few minutes to send Trabue and Pillow back up the hill.[25]

Breckinridge was almost frantic over his artillery. The crest of the hill had been taken according to plan, and now he desperately needed Semple on the right side of the crest to hold off the Federals still on that flank. Robertson's presence was even more imperative on the left to distract and, if possible, neutralize the fire from across the river. Despite the explicit orders he had given, he looked in vain for Robertson's guns. Graves set up the division artillery as soon as possible, but it was not nearly enough, and Breckinridge sent one staff officer after another to look for Robertson. Meanwhile, Graves himself rode back to Semple and asked him to advance. Semple moved forward, claiming that he had received no orders at all from Robertson regarding his part in the attack. Buckner looked unsuccessfully all over the field for Robertson and his command. The reason that he did not find him was that—in Robertson's own words—"I decided to alter the plan," a plan made by a major general, his superior. Mistakenly believing that Breckinridge's infantry had failed to take the left side of the hill, Robertson never moved his battery beyond the wood during the attack.[26]

Robertson's presence at the appointed place would not have saved the attack. Breckinridge had taken the hill, but he could not hold it. When the first line rushed the crest, the second, led by Preston and Gibson, laid down on the field. The fire from Crittenden soon fell heavier on them, however, than it did on Pillow and Trabue, and forced them up to their feet and forward to the crest, only to run into the front line retreating from the river. The resulting confusion was heightened by the Federal artillery now at its peak, firing an estimated one hundred shells per minute. At the same time

25. Brent Diary, January 2, 1863, in Palmer Collection; Clay, "On the Right at Murfreesboro," 589; O.R., Ser. I, Vol. XX, Pt. 1, p. 827; Breckinridge to George B. Hodge, March 9, 1863, in Breckinridge, Service Record, NA.

26. O'Hara to Breckinridge, January 16, 1863, Buckner to Breckinridge, May 20, 1863, Graves to Breckinridge, January 25, 1863, in Breckinridge MSS, NYHS; O.R., Ser. I, Vol. XX, Pt. 1, p. 759.

the Federals re-formed and began to recross the river in Breckinridge's front. Assailed from all sides, the Kentuckian had no choice but to retire. They fell back in considerable disorder, with little semblance of organization. The whole command retired to the wood from which it began the advance, assisted, at last, by covering fire from Robertson's guns. It did not help that Pegram's men finally took part in the battle, firing into Breckinridge's retreating brigades by mistake.[27]

It had cost Breckinridge a shattered division to prove to Bragg that the attack was a mistake. Behind him on the field lay over fifteen hundred casualties, 30 percent of the attacking force. The whole affair lasted about three quarters of an hour; the greatest destruction took barely fifteen minutes.[28]

Observing the attack for Bragg, Brent saw the troops begin to retire and raced to the commanding general with the news. Bragg immediately ordered him to lead Brigadier General J. Patton Anderson's brigade over to support the retreating division. Meanwhile, thanks in very large measure to fine work by Robertson's guns, the Federals were held back while Breckinridge re-formed his brigades on their original line at the edge of the woods. He pulled them back two hundred to three hundred yards more to prolong the line on Wayne's Hill. Robertson remained forward to hold off the Federals and was still there at twilight when Anderson came on the field. Buckner was there to meet Anderson, and he told him that the main line had been pulled back from the wood. Accordingly, Anderson put his brigade in line immediately where he was, being the only body of infantry to face the enemy, and had skirmishers out when Breckinridge himself rode up and told him to pull back to the main line. What the general did not yet know was that, thanks to the darkness and confusion, he had moved his center and right brigades back farther than he intended. Consequently, Anderson was moving toward a position that was still in advance of the division, with no support on the right, and an eight-hundred-yard interval between Wayne's Hill and his left.[29]

27. O.R., Ser. I, Vol. XX, Pt. 1, pp. 785, 798, 806, 808, 813, 817, 827; Pickett, "Reminiscence"; Brent Diary, January 2, 1863, in Palmer Collection; Clay, "On the Right at Murfreesboro," 589.

28. Breckinridge gave various estimates of the time elapsed from beginning to end in the charge. In his report he said one hour and twenty minutes (O.R., Ser. I, Vol. XX, Pt. 1, p. 787), but later put it at forty-five minutes (Clay, "On the Right at Murfreesboro," 589). The latter figure is the more accurate, and roughly agrees with Anderson's stated arrival at twilight, which would have been about 4:45 on January 2.

29. O.R., Ser. I, Vol. XX, Pt. 1, pp. 759, 765-66; O'Hara to Breckinridge, January 16, 1863, in Breckinridge MSS, NYHS; E. T. Sykes, "Singular Things Done Just Before the War," Confederate Veteran, XIX (June, 1911), 306.

Leaving Anderson, Breckinridge rode back to his line to inspect the remnant of the division. He grew increasingly angry as he witnessed the results of Bragg's attack order. "I never, at any time, saw him more visibly moved," wrote one of the Kentucky officers. "He was raging like a wounded lion, as he passed the different commands . . . but tears broke from his eyes when he beheld the little remnant of his own brigade." Over five hundred of the Kentuckians had been lost in the attack, including their commander. Unable to contain his sorrow, Breckinridge exclaimed: "My poor Orphan brigade! They have cut it to pieces!" Just why he called it the "Orphan brigade" is conjecturable. It may have been because its commander, Hanson, was dying back in Murfreesboro; he may also have said it in reference to the fact that the men had not seen their native state for nearly a year; or it could be that he was thinking of the brigade fighting for a cause which its home state had officially denounced. Whatever the reason, the general's unwitting sobriquet caught on. To posterity the men in the command would always be known as the Orphan Brigade.[30]

Sometime before 10 P.M. that night Breckinridge and the other generals were called to a council. Bragg expressed no displeasure with Breckinridge's conduct of the assault that day, and the only real topic of discussion was what to do now. It was decided to move heavy reinforcements over to the right side of the river but, beyond that, the army would remain in position with no further plan of attack. Meanwhile, Anderson had made a reconnaissance on both sides of his position, and discovered that he was seriously exposed. He sent a message to his own division commander, Major General Jones M. Withers, who apparently did not attend Bragg's council. Withers forwarded the report to Bragg, and shortly an order arrived for Anderson's adjutant, Captain E. T. Sykes, to come to headquarters.

Sykes came into the conference room muddied from his ride, and took a seat to answer a variety of questions from Bragg. Breckinridge also questioned Sykes and stated to Polk that supports had been ordered up for Anderson, and that they were then in position. He was wrong, however, and repeated questioning revealed the error, which Breckinridge finally acknowledged. Bragg had already come to the same conclusion, and so stated to the Kentuckian. As for Sykes, he later wrote that "I do not conceive that General Breckinridge was censurable for this mistake." The division had

30. For a full discussion of the controversy over the origin of the name Orphan Brigade, and for the author's reasons in accepting this version, see the author's introduction in Ed. Porter Thompson, *History of the Orphan Brigade* (2nd ed.; Dayton, Ohio, 1973), vii–ix.

fallen back in disorder, and did not rally on the line he had designated for it because of the darkness and heavy forest. "The darkness of the night and the density of the undergrowth having prevented General Breckinridge from accurately discerning and forming his troops on the line where directed," Sykes and many others felt inclined to excuse the general this error. The situation of Anderson remained unremedied, however, for some hours yet, the only plausible explanation being that Breckinridge's brigades were still too tired or disorganized to be pushed through the dark and brush to support him.[31]

Breckinridge left the conference at about 10:30 and went to a nearby home for dinner, soon to be joined by Hardee. As they waited for their food, at about 12:30 or 1 A.M., January 3, a courier arrived from Bragg bringing a message from cavalry outposts. They believed that the Federals were advancing on Breckinridge's part of the field. The report was erroneous, but Bragg ordered Hardee out to take personal command in that portion of the field just the same. Breckinridge returned immediately as well, and it was shortly after this that his brigades finally came up on Anderson's right and left. Meanwhile, Bragg received another message indicating a crisis on his army's left. A retreat from the field was imperative. At about noon Hardee notified Breckinridge of the movement and assigned his division to cover the retreat of the corps. Breckinridge had everything in order by 6 P.M. He fully believed that the retreat was necessary, and at 7 P.M., called to a conference with Bragg, Hardee, Polk, and Cleburne, he urged that the retreat be made that night, rather than wait an additional twenty-four hours to gather all of the wounded. The others agreed.[32]

Breckinridge covered the retreat with the same skill he had shown at Shiloh. Despite constant threats, the Federals showed no disposition to follow up on the Confederate withdrawal, and Bragg's army moved leisurely southward as he looked for a new place to establish his line. He settled on the area around the Duck River, some thirty miles south of Murfreesboro, and on Tullahoma in particular. Here the army would sit in inactivity for the next six months, but not so the high command. The wounded from

31. E. T. Sykes, "A Cursory Sketch of General Bragg's Campaigns," *SHSP*, XI (October, 1883), 473–74; E. T. Sykes, "Walthall's Brigade," *Publications of the Mississippi Historical Society* (Jackson, 1916), 503–504; *O.R.*, Ser. I, Vol. XX, Pt. 2, p. 477.
32. Statement of Lt. Col. Urquhart, June 12, 1863, in Palmer Collection; *O.R.*, Ser. I, Vol. XX, Pt. 1, pp. 682, 700; Connelly, *Autumn of Glory*, 66–67; unnumbered Special Order, January 3, 1863, Military Departments, Orders Received and Orders Issued by the First Kentucky Brigade, 1862–1863, in Chap. 2, CCCVIII, NA.

Murfreesboro had barely stopped bleeding before a new, and potentially more destructive, battle began within Bragg's own corps of generals.[33]

The fight opened almost immediately. Several newspapers attacked Bragg's conduct of the battle, and one, the Chattanooga *Daily Rebel*, charged that he ordered the retreat from Murfreesboro against the advice of his generals. On January 11 he drafted a letter to his corps and division commanders in which, at first, he asked their written testimony that they had advised the retreat, as well as their opinion on whether or not the army still had confidence in him. Later he wrote a second draft that omitted this last interrogatory, not at all sanguine about the answers he was likely to receive, but including the statement that he would resign if his subordinates no longer believed in him.

The replies were uniformly displeasing to Bragg. Hardee and Breckinridge wrote back to Bragg the very next day, and Cleburne the day after. Hardee admitted agreeing to a retreat, but denied advising one, while both Breckinridge and Cleburne reminded the commanding general that they had not been consulted in council until the evening of January 3, when retreat had already been agreed upon. However, the Kentuckian went on to add that if he had been consulted in the morning of that day when retreat was under consideration, he would have advised in its favor.

Despite the support which this last implied—and, in saying it, Breckinridge went farther in Bragg's favor than any of the others who replied to his letter—the commanding general was hardly pleased by the remainder of his reply. Like Hardee and Cleburne, Breckinridge interpreted Bragg's statement that "I shall retire without a regret if I find I have lost the good opinion of my generals," as both a solicitation of that opinion, and a promise to act upon it. Accordingly, he discussed the matter with his brigade commanders, and they replied unanimously that "it is their opinion that you do not possess the confidence of this army to an extent which will enable you to be useful as its commander." "In this opinion," added Breckinridge, "I feel bound to state that I concur." Hardee and Cleburne both agreed.[34]

33. Luke Blackburn to Breckinridge, January 4, 1863, Roy to Breckinridge, January 4, 1863, Joseph Wheeler to Breckinridge, January 4, 6, 1863, Wheeler to Roy, January 4, 1863, Wheeler to O'Hara, January 4, 1863, all in Breckinridge MSS. CHS.
34. *O.R.*, Ser. I, Vol. XX, Pt. 1, pp. 682–84, 699. A copy of the original of Breckinridge's reply to Bragg is in the Jefferson Davis Collection, LHAC. For a good assessment of Bragg's character, see Connelly, *Autumn of Glory*, 70–73, and McWhiney, *Bragg*, 28ff.

To a mind like Bragg's, this could only connote a conspiracy in Hardee's high command, and it was equally clear, to him at least, that Breckinridge was at its center. It did not help that some of the most vicious newspaper attacks against Bragg came as a result of information furnished by O'Hara, whose hatred for the commanding general went back more than a year and a half. Despite Breckinridge's denial that any members of his staff had taken part in the criticisms of Bragg's retreat, it was easy for Bragg to assume that O'Hara was really operating with his master's tacit approval, if not at his bidding. Ten days after Breckinridge replied to Bragg's circular letter, it was assumed at army headquarters that he was behind the disaffection in Hardee's corps, and that he had actually been responsible for turning Hardee himself against Bragg. The passage of another three weeks would reveal a Bragg who had convinced himself that Breckinridge was the chief malcontent in the army.[35]

While Breckinridge did discuss army affairs with friends, he had not written to officials in Richmond, nor had he made any statements to the press. The bad feeling between him and Bragg was no secret, but there is no evidence that he did anything to promote dissatisfaction with the commanding general. Instead, he devoted most of January to getting reports of the battle from his brigade, regiment, and battery commanders, as well as from members of his staff. Several were tardy, particularly Palmer and Colonel W. L. L. Bowen of the Fourth Florida, and it was February 12 before he had all of the reports together to submit them to Hardee, who would not then complete his own report until February 28, 1863. Meanwhile, late in January, Breckinridge began his own report, using those that his subordinates had so far submitted.[36]

By and large it was a well-reasoned report, totally lacking in that venom which Bragg probably expected it would contain, particularly with reference to the suicidal attack order of January 2. Breckinridge's almost violent opposition to that order was well known in the army, even by the public as far away as Richmond, but he made no mention of it at all in the report. Bragg, however, took no chances. Ignoring the usual procedure of army commanders in making out battle reports, he wrote his own without having seen Breckinridge's or Hardee's and sent it off to Richmond nearly a week

35. *O.R.*, Ser. I, Vol. XX, Pt. 1, p. 701; Connelly, *Autumn of Glory*, 73–74, 76; Brent Diary, January 22, 1863, in Palmer Collection; Bragg to W. W. Mackall, February 14, 1863, in William W. Mackall MSS, SHC.
36. Breckinridge to Hodge, March 9, 1863, in Breckinridge, Service Record, NA; *O.R.*, Ser. I, Vol. XX, Pt. 1, pp. 771, 804–805, 815. Breckinridge dated his report January, 1863.

before Hardee submitted the reports from his corps. The replies from Hardee, Breckinridge, and Cleburne, relative to the army's lack of confidence in him had put Bragg in a tight spot. His promise to resign in this event had backfired on him, and the only way out of the situation was to show that the failure at Murfreesboro was not his fault. To accomplish this, he had to get his version of the battle's conduct in to Richmond well ahead of the others.[37]

He implied that it was only the delay in the arrival of Breckinridge's brigades on December 31 that prevented him from destroying Rosecrans. The Kentuckian arrived too late to support Hardee's movement on the left, he said, though in fact Breckinridge had his four brigades across the river shortly after 1 P.M., with still four hours of daylight left, more than enough time to move around to Hardee to join in another assault. At the same time, said Bragg, Breckinridge's brigades arrived too late to make a successful attack in Polk's front, though they were severely bloodied in the attempt. The reason, said Bragg, was that the delay in getting Adams, Jackson, and Preston—in his report Bragg totally forgot that Palmer was ordered over as well—had allowed the Federals to repair their broken lines. There was some truth in this, but the real reason for the failure on this front was that Bragg simply sent the brigades to the wrong place. Once Polk had them, he misused them terribly.

The heaviest censure was applied to the January 2 assault. Since it had been the final and decisive action of the battle, and since he had ordered it without consulting either of his corps commanders and in direct opposition to the counsel of the general commanding in that part of the field, it was imperative that he pass the blame for failure to Breckinridge, or else accept it himself.

Bragg laid the groundwork well, and it was here that Robertson came to be useful. The artilleryman submitted a report of his part in the January 2 fiasco to Breckinridge on January 12, and in it said nothing in any way disparaging of Breckinridge or his conduct of the assault. Bragg was not at all satisfied. Since Robertson had held a "special command" that day, under orders from Bragg but commanded by Breckinridge, the commanding general ordered him to make another report, this one to come directly to his headquarters and not, as usual, through Breckinridge. Further, Bragg re-

37. Richmond *Examiner*, February 25, 1863. Connelly. *Autumn of Glory*. 82, asserts that Breckinridge wrote his report as a rejoinder to Bragg's, though in fact Bragg wrote his nearly a month or more after the Kentuckian had completed and submitted his to Hardee.

minded Robertson, who was well attuned to his temperament, that "As artillery is always dependent on the support of infantry, you are expected to refer to that support in such a manner as will do full justice to both arms, and to all commanders and corps engaged." Obviously, Bragg wanted more than a simple report of a battery's operations; he was asking for a commentary on the management of the whole movement, and Robertson read well enough between the lines to know how that report should be written.[38]

On February 18, 1863, the captain sent in an insidious document whose every paragraph criticized Breckinridge's conduct of the assault. First of all, he implied that the Kentuckian disobeyed Bragg's orders by moving artillery up with the attacking columns instead of keeping them back until the enemy position was taken. He charged that Breckinridge's disposition of the artillery was calculated to crowd the narrow field. Robertson painted a picture in which he resisted a series of impractical suggestions by the general, at the end of which Breckinridge ignored his advice and formed his division guns to advance with the infantry. Beyond this, the captain declared that the general alerted the enemy to the point to be attacked by injudiciously sending two guns to open fire on their skirmishers, and that it was this fire which prompted Crittenden to mass his guns. Once the assault was under way, Robertson asserted, Breckinridge's artillery acted in thorough confusion and, after the repulse, he could find no organized body of troops. "I am clearly of the opinion," he wrote, "that if there had been no artillery on that field the enemy would have gone into Murfreesboro easily that evening. . . . I have never seen troops so completely broken in my military experience," he said. The report was a "tissue of lies" from beginning to end. When Breckinridge later saw it he would find it entirely at odds with his recollection, and Robertson himself eventually admitted that he knowingly wrote an incorrect report at Bragg's suggestion. Now, however, he was rewarded with a soft position as one of Bragg's lobbyists at Richmond.[39]

Armed with Robertson's report, one of the few items that he appended to his own report, Bragg proceeded to present an account of the January 2 action which blamed the accidental crossing of the river by some of Han-

38. O.R., Ser. I, Vol. XX, Pt. 1, pp. 665–66, 758–59; Bragg to Felix Robertson, February 16, 1863, in Breckinridge MSS, NYHS.
39. O.R., Ser. I, Vol. XX, Pt. 1, pp. 759–61; Breckinridge to Henry Dawson, January 20, 1873, Breckinridge MSS, NYHS; Stevenson, Stone's River, 143n; Connelly, Autumn of Glory, 91.

son's men on Breckinridge. The only accurate statement regarding the attack was a comment on the lack of participation by Pegram and Wharton, and even here the censure, though implied, fell solely on Breckinridge. Finally, Anderson was given sole credit for saving Breckinridge's division and preventing a rout, a remark which Anderson himself later regarded as much more than he was entitled to.[40]

Bragg went beyond this with another enclosure. Appended to this report was a tabular statement of the numbers present, and losses, of the various corps, divisions, and brigades. However, out of the five infantry divisions in the army, Breckinridge's alone was singled out for an additional, separate, tabular statement. Bragg let unqualified statistics do his talking. In figuring the statistics for December 31, Bragg added Hanson's brigade into the force sent across the river to Polk, when it had been by Bragg's very order that Hanson was left behind that day on Wayne's Hill. The result was that Breckinridge's division showed only 10 2/5 percent losses for the battle instead of the correct 14 1/7 percent arrived at by leaving out Hanson. The correction was later made, prior to submission of the statement to Richmond, though who made it is unknown.

Ostensibly, the reason for showing Breckinridge's losses broken down by day was that his was the only division heavily engaged on January 2, whereas the losses from other units were all, or almost all, incurred on December 31. The trouble was, however, that this method made his losses look deceptively small when compared with the rest of the army. Cheatham lost 36 percent, Withers 28 1/4 percent, Cleburne 29 1/2 percent, and McCown 21 4/5 percent. Alongside these, Breckinridge's 10 2/5 percent—corrected to 14 1/7—looked puny, indeed. What the statement failed to say was that the other units had been engaged almost all day December 31, while the Kentuckian's brigades were only in the fight for three or four hours. In fact, Adams' brigade on that day suffered the highest percentage loss of any brigade in Hardee's corps, with the exception of Jackson's small command, which fought alongside it. Both lost over 33 percent.[41]

It is clear that Bragg's report got his message across. When it was re-

40. O.R., Ser. I, Vol. XX, Pt. 1, p. 668; "Autobiography of General Patton Anderson," SHSP, XXIV (January–December, 1896), 67.

41. O.R., Ser. I, Vol. XX, Pt. 1, pp. 674–81. The tabular statement is printed in O.R., Ser. I, Vol. XX, Pt. 1, p. 675, showing the correction by Hanson's absence on December 31 as a footnote, giving no indication of when the note was added. However, the original "Tabular Statement of the Present for duty on 31st Dec: 1862 ... of Breckinridge's Division," in the Eldridge Collection, HL, clearly shows that the note is an interlineation, in a different ink, and obviously a later addition.

ceived at the War Department in Richmond, Robert Kean, head of the Bureau of War, immediately commented on the severity of its censure of Breckinridge. However, even before the report reached the capital sometime in the first week of March, the dissension between Bragg and Breckinridge was well known. As part of his attempt to avoid guilt for Murfreesboro's mistakes, Bragg had been writing letters to many throughout the Confederacy, complaining of a conspiracy against him among his generals, and naming Breckinridge in particular. The Kentuckian had "failed most *signally* at Murfreesboro," he said. Breckinridge was anxious to lay the blame on Bragg, he claimed, "but will be beautifully shown up." Meanwhile, the Kentuckian's friends were active in his defense. One way or another, the Kentucky members of the Confederate Congress became apprised of the growing controversy, particularly the January 2 affair, and the feud became public record. On February 24, bypassing standard channels, Hodge introduced in the House a call on the adjutant general for the general's Murfreesboro report. Since that report had been written and submitted to Bragg at least a month before, and still had not shown up in Richmond, Hodge and others grew suspicious. Two days later, commenting on a pending resolution of thanks to Bragg, Hodge refused to vote until he received a full explanation of why the January 2 attack was ordered, and why no supports were sent to Breckinridge's division—the rest of the army being largely idle—until after the repulse. It was even rumored in Richmond that Breckinridge and Bragg had agreed to meet on the dueling ground.[42]

So far in the growing difficulty, Breckinridge himself had remained idle, just as he had when under attack during the campaign of 1860. Shortly after the battle, in response both to the suicidal January 2 attack order as well as to early criticism from Bragg, several Kentucky officers reportedly begged Breckinridge to resent the insult, resign his commission, and challenge Bragg. The Kentuckian would have nothing to do with this. From the first he had maintained a policy of official silence. As late as March, 1863, he still had written to no one in Richmond on the subject. He had not engaged a friendly press or otherwise made public statements. As when he was a statesman, the general felt disdain for intrigue and personal poli-

42. Edward Younger (ed.), *Inside the Confederate Government: The Diary of Robert Garlick Hill Kean* (New York, 1957), 42; Jilson P. Johnson to Breckinridge, March 18, 1863, in Jilson P. Johnson Service Record, NA; Bragg to Mackall, February 14, 1863, in Mackall MSS; *O.R.*, Ser. I, Vol. XXIII, Pt. 2, pp. 652–53, Vol. LII, Pt. 2, p. 407; Connelly, *Autumn of Glory*. 82: "Proceedings of the First Confederate Congress, Third Session in Part," *SHSP*, XLVIII (1941), 193, 211.

ticking. "It is a great mistake to suppose that there is a 'controversy' between Gen. Bragg and myself," he told Hodge on March 9. "In a word, [I] *have done nothing* in conflict with strict military propriety. You knew what my opinions were on this subject when you served with me. They remain unchanged. Since I entered the service I have been simply a soldier trying to serve a cause which every true Southern man is willing every day to die for." He well knew that Bragg had powerful friends in Congress. "Strange influences seem to have been at work," he told Hodge, "but I do not know what they are." Apparently the general did not know about Bragg's substantial lobby in Richmond, headed by the efficient Colonel John Sale, and manned by, among others, the accommodating Robertson. Breckinridge wanted nothing to do with anything that smacked of political intrigue now that he was a soldier. Indeed, he told Jilson Johnson to be quiet, and even scolded Hodge for introducing the resolution calling for his Murfreesboro report. "If anything is said to my discredit," he charged the congressman, "I hope my friends will be silent unless it touches my honour or that of my command. When a man is right there are no remedies equal to silence and time. It is only when he is wrong that it is necessary to preoccupy the public mind by clamor." [43]

Meanwhile, reports reached Bragg that Hodge and others were getting anxious for the Kentuckian's report. Since his own report had already been sent to Richmond, Bragg could not just send Breckinridge's bare report on now without, in a manner, giving the Kentuckian the last word. Consequently he held on to the report until March 11, carefully compiling an appendix of documents and his own observations which, in effect, amounted to a commentary on the report. "Some errors and misapprehensions of Maj. Genl. Breckinridge incorporated in his report, will be corrected," said Bragg in a letter transmitting the documents. "To these papers appended to General *Breckinridge*'s report, I invite special attention." [44]

The "Appendix" contained the several notes passed back and forth between Bragg and Breckinridge on December 31 as they worried through the confusion caused by Pegram's poor reconnaissance and the Kentuckian's neglect. Here Bragg was in part correct. However, not content with this, Bragg went on to try to show by the notes that Breckinridge had

43. Albert D. Kirwan (ed.), *Johnny Green of the Orphan Brigade* (Lexington, 1956), 77; John B. Gordon, *Reminiscences of the Civil War* (New York, 1903), 192–94; Breckinridge to Hodge, March 9, 1863, in Breckinridge, Service Record, NA; Connelly, *Autumn of Glory*, 91; Johnson to Breckinridge, March 1, 4, 1863, in Jilson P. Johnson Service Record, NA.

44. Bragg to Samuel Cooper, March 11, 1863, in Breckinridge MSS, NYHS.

waited an hour before obeying his 10:30 order to advance on December 31 and that, at 12:50, after nearly an hour and a half in motion by Bragg's reckoning, the Kentuckian's division had covered only one-half mile. Nowhere did the commanding general mention that, part way through that advance, he had himself ordered Breckinridge to halt. In fact, however, it is clear from the reports of the general's brigade, regimental, and staff officers that Breckinridge advanced without delay when ordered, and was engaged with the enemy skirmishers throughout the morning.[45]

It was in his comments on the January 2 assault, however, that Bragg pressed the attack. He included a copy of a note sent to Pegram at 1:00 that afternoon, which said that "The General"—no mention of which general, Bragg, Breckinridge, or someone else—was going to attack on the right, and that Pegram was to cooperate. It also stated that Wharton would be there to help as well. What Bragg did not mention—probably because he did not know it—was that Pegram had apparently been further informed of the exact time and place of the attack, and what troops were making it, by a scout who had been told this by Bragg. This lifts a little of the guilt from Breckinridge's shoulders, but only a little. However, the report of the battle by Wharton revealed that this officer had "no intimation" of the advance from anyone, Breckinridge or Bragg. Thus, the commanding general was himself apparently remiss in not notifying Wharton that he was to cooperate, as he had Pegram.[46]

The portion of this appendix which does the least harm to Breckinridge, and the most discredit to Bragg, is the latter's criticism of the Kentuckian's estimation of his numbers and losses on January 2. In his report Breckinridge said: "The division, after deducting the losses of Wednesday, the troops left on the hill [Wayne's Hill], and companies on special service, consisted of some 4,500 men." He believed that his casualties in the assault numbered about 1,700. Both figures were wrong, but the discrepancies were barely objectionable.[47]

Bragg set about with deliberation to distort these figures to the general's disparagement. First of all he called attention to Breckinridge's mistake in his losses of December 31. The Kentuckian reported 440, when subsequent reports showed it to be 730, but then Bragg turned right around and used

45. "Appendix by General Bragg to Report of Major General Breckinridge," in Palmer Collection. See above, note 8, for evidence that Breckinridge moved immediately when ordered.

46. "Appendix," in Palmer Collection; Clay, "On the Right at Murfreesboro," 588; O.R., Ser. I, Vol. XX, Pt. 1, p. 969.

47. "Appendix," in Palmer Collection; O.R., Ser. I, Vol. XX, Pt. 1, pp. 785, 787.

the incorrect figure in his computations. Citing a tabular return of the morning of December 31 which showed Breckinridge's strength at 7,053, Bragg subtracted the *440* losses of that day, subtracted also the Ninth Kentucky and Cobb's battery left in reserve on January 2, and then *added* the men of the two batteries under Robertson. Since, in his view, the discrepancy between the December 31 estimate of 440 and the true 730, nearly canceled out the difference between the 1,700 losses that Breckinridge estimated and the 1,338 that Bragg stated, the commanding general was content to say that the Kentuckian actually had over 6,000 men for the attack, and accused him thereby of underrating his force by more than 25 percent.[48]

Bragg had played a canny game with numbers. The addition of Robertson's batteries was wholly specious, since in his report Breckinridge's 4,500 estimate applied only to "the division," his division, and not any special attachments. Even if Robertson were to be counted, only Semple and his 45 men actually took part in the assault. Then too, while Bragg did subtract the 498 men of the Ninth Kentucky and Cobb's battery who were left behind, he ignored completely the fact that the Thirty-second Alabama Infantry and the Fourteenth Louisiana Battalion of Adams' brigade—409 men at the least—were also left as a reserve. Thus, the number of reserves, 907, combined with the 730 losses of December 31, require a deduction of 1,637 from the 7,053 original strength of the division. This leaves a maximum of 5,416 men of the division available for the assault, and this does not take into account any of those "companies on special service" that Breckinridge mentioned, and for which no enumeration has been found. The fact that the Thirty-second Alabama and the Fourteenth Louisiana were left out was included in Gibson's report which Bragg forwarded along with Breckinridge's. Surely he read it, and yet he ignored it. Also ignored was a correction of the morning reports of December 31, sent in by Hardee on January 17, which showed that the Kentuckian's division strength was actually 6,824 instead of 7,053. While this report appears questionable, it would, if true, reduce Breckinridge's maximum numbers on January 2 even more, to 5,187. Discounting this statement by Hardee, and making conservative allowance for those unknown numbers on "special service," it is reasonable to assume that Breckinridge actually carried into the assault not less than 5,000, nor more than 5,300, of his division. This agrees with a later estimate by Preston of 5,000 engaged. Instead of the Kentuckian underestimating

---

48. "Appendix," in Palmer Collection. It should be noted that this item is published in *O.R.*, Ser. I, Vol. XX, Pt. 1, pp. 788–90, but with many errors.

his numbers by over 25 percent as charged, Bragg deliberately overestimated those numbers by 20 percent.[49]

Of course, what Bragg was doing was attempting to discount any excuse for the failure of the January 2 attack on account of insufficient strength. He chose, instead, to present the case that the attack failed because Breckinridge bungled it, and to do this it was necessary to show that the Kentuckian's troops really had not fought well. The most visible measure of the severity of a fight is the number lost, so here, again, Bragg presented false figures, though he may have done so unwittingly. A return of casualties which he submitted covering the entire army credited Hanson's brigade with 372 casualties on January 2, the only day it was engaged. However, the brigade's own record of morning reports, which he probably did not see or ask to see, shows the number lost at Murfreesboro to be—exclusive of Cobb and the Ninth Kentucky—532, some 160 more than Bragg accounted for. This difference, added to the 1,338 shown in the casualty report, raises Breckinridge's losses to at least 1,498. Since the losses in some of his brigades were computed by subtracting those present for morning roll calls taken one and two weeks after the battle from those present on December 31, this figure also doubtless includes the number of very minor casualties—walking wounded—who returned to their regiments before the roll calls were taken. Thus, Breckinridge's losses in the charge of January 2 were at least 1,500, less than the Kentuckian reported, but more than Bragg's estimate by nearly an equal amount. While the commanding general may have been innocent of this error in his appendix, he still did not let the casualty figure go untampered with. Interestingly enough, where he saw fit to add Robertson and Semple's numbers where they did not belong, he here neglected to include their losses in his accounting.[50]

At no other time in the life of the Confederacy did a commanding officer forward a subordinate's report accompanied by such a damning commentary, and with so much of that comment based upon misuse of the evidence, much of it conscious. If there had been any doubt, even after his own report went to Richmond, there could be none now; Bragg was at war with Breckinridge. In that war, he would do few other things as pernicious, as indicative of his imbalance, as this attack on Breckinridge's report.[51]

It is uncertain how much time passed before the Kentuckian saw or

49. *O.R.*, Ser. I, Vol. XX, Pt. 1, pp. 780, 798–99, 802, 807, 826, 909; Louisville *Courier-Journal*, June 18, 1875.

50. "Appendix," in Palmer Collection; *O.R.*, Ser. I, Vol. XX, Pt. 1, p. 679.

51. See McWhiney, *Bragg*, 384.

heard of Bragg's appendix to his report, but Johnson and others in Richmond gave him the gist of it in mid-March. It was March 29, however, when he first read Bragg's report, with its accompanying documents. Indignant, Breckinridge reflected for two days on what to do about it, and then wrote to General Samuel Cooper in Richmond. "I cannot conceal from myself the fact that so much of the report as refers to my conduct and that of my command . . . is in tone and spirit a thorough disparagement of both." He charged that Bragg was guilty of omission of pertinent facts, while distorting others, and remarked that, since the report was written before his subordinates' reports were in, some investigation should be made into the sources that he did use, an obvious reference to Robertson's "special report." Since Bragg was particularly critical of the January 2 affair, Breckinridge here showed the greatest indignation. He told Cooper that "the failure of my troops to hold the position which they carried on that occasion was due to no fault of theirs or of mine, but to the fact that we were commanded to do an impossible thing." This was the general's first and only official criticism of Bragg's attack order. Now, in view of all this, he asked Cooper to convene a court of inquiry when convenient in order to investigate Bragg's charges.[52]

The day after writing to Cooper, the general sent a request for an official copy of Bragg's report to army headquarters, but Bragg refused it on a technicality. Meanwhile, he also requested from Robertson a copy of his "special report," and that officer, perhaps hoping to redeem himself in some measure, sent not only the report, but a copy of Bragg's letter ordering it as well. As for testimony supporting his own version of the battle in his report, the Kentuckian already had a number of statements from Polk and his staff officers written before the feud with Bragg broke out. They had all been critical of Robertson's conduct on January 2, but the general chose to ignore their strictures in his report. Having felt the artilleryman's perfidy, Breckinridge was happy to have these accounts to use at the anticipated court of inquiry. By May 1, 1863, knowledge of Robertson's actions and conflicting reports reached Richmond, and Burnett of Kentucky introduced in the Senate that day a resolution calling for copies of both. Just what he had in mind is unknown since, unfortunately, the Senate adjourned before the copies could be transmitted.[53]

52. *O.R.*, Ser. I, Vol. XX, Pt. 1, pp. 790–91; Johnson to Breckinridge, March 18, 1863, in Jilson P. Johnson Service Record, NA.
53. Polk to Breckinridge, March 31, 1863, Brent to Breckinridge, April 2, 6, 1863, Robertson to Breckinridge, April 2, 1863, Wilson to Breckinridge, January 20, 1863,

This was all the testimony that Breckinridge gathered, and he did nothing with it, assuming that a court would examine it and make conclusions of its own. Bragg, however, was much more diligent in collecting his evidence. From his adjutant, Brent, a fine officer, he got a trustworthy account of Pillow asking if any communication had been made with Pegram and Wharton on January 2. Soon thereafter Bragg solicited Pillow's testimony on the same event. Besides the fact that Pillow was unprincipled, he now had some reason to dislike Breckinridge. After all, the Kentuckian had caught him behind a tree shielding himself from the battle, and Major Graves, assisted by two other witnesses, had actually submitted charges and specifications against Pillow for conduct unbecoming an officer and soldier. Breckinridge held on to the charges without forwarding them to Bragg or Cooper, but still Pillow did have the Kentuckian's knowledge of the affair hanging over his head. Consequently, in conversation with Bragg and in a written statement describing that conversation, he gave the commanding general a report of January 2 almost as condemnatory as Robertson's. Breckinridge's alignment for the battle was wrong, and was responsible for the left going into and over the river, and for the right being enfiladed. As he went on, Pillow began speaking as though only he should have been in charge of the attack that day, and actually criticized Breckinridge for not putting the second line under his command. Worst of all, however, he stated that he had no prior knowledge that Pegram and Wharton were ordered to support Breckinridge until Bragg mentioned it in this conversation. This was in direct conflict with the statement of Brent, a much more reliable officer, and makes the whole even more questionable than Pillow's character would have otherwise.[54]

Bragg's gathering of testimony would go on for months, but meantime his friends in Richmond did something much more damaging to Breckinridge; they got Bragg's report published. When the Kentuckian found this out, he immediately wrote again to Cooper, on May 6, complaining that the publication of Bragg's report, with nothing in print to present his own side of the story, could be very detrimental to his reputation and that of his command. Consequently, while awaiting the hoped for court of inquiry, Breckinridge asked that his letter of March 31 requesting that court be pub-

Graves to Breckinridge, January 25, 1863, O'Hara to Breckinridge, January 16, 1863, Buckner to Breckinridge, May 20, 1863, all in Breckinridge MSS, NYHS; *O.R.*, Ser. I, Vol. XX, Pt. 1, pp. 694, 703–704; *Journal of the Congress*, III, 424.

54. Brent to Bragg, March 15, 1863, in Breckinridge MSS, NYHS; Charges and Specifications of charges against Brig Genl G. J. Pillow, Breckinridge MSS, CHS; *O.R.*, Ser. I, Vol. XX, Pt. 2, pp. 498–99.

lished "as an act of simple justice to myself and my division." As always, Bragg added his own rebuttal to the general's request before forwarding it, stating that Breckinridge's original application for a court contained errors, insinuating that it should not be published. However, a friend of the Kentuckian's, perhaps one of the Bluegrass delegates to Congress, called on Cooper before long and managed to secure both a copy of Breckinridge's letter, and Cooper's permission for its publication. Shortly, the letter appeared in the press, and Bragg was furious. Complaining to Cooper, he was told that the adjutant general had not completely understood that there was a controversy between the two generals, or else he would not have consented to publication of the letter. Both Cooper and Bragg assumed that Breckinridge's friend was acting in the Kentuckian's behalf in getting and publishing the letter, but, in fact, it was done without either his knowledge or his consent. Indeed, ten years later he still did not know exactly how his friend had secured a copy of the letter. As always, the general wanted his affairs conducted properly, according to regulation, or not at all.[55]

The controversy would continue to smolder on, kept alive by Bragg's hatred, as well as the unconcealed discontent of the Kentucky officers in the army, but after late May, Breckinridge ceased any active part in it, content to await a court that never came. So far as he was concerned, he was right. Silence and time would vindicate him. As it happened, the controversy between him and Bragg worked to his advantage. Since the Perryville failure had already disposed much of the Confederacy against Bragg, a critical state of mind prevailed toward him, one which was ready made to continue after Murfreesboro and his feud with Breckinridge. As a consequence, it was easy to regard Breckinridge as what, in large part, he really was in this quarrel, an innocent victim. Indeed, this view of the affair existed even within Bragg's own staff, and turned at least one of his former partisans against him. J. Stoddard Johnston, long a friend of Breckinridge's, served in Bragg's official family for nearly a year. He was close to the commanding general, and felt so keenly the obloquy heaped on Bragg after Perryville that he wrote a lengthy vindication of him and sent it to Richmond. Immediately after Murfreesboro, when Breckinridge asked Johnston to be his chief of staff, the colonel declined to leave Bragg because of the kindness he felt for him. By July of 1863, however, after witnessing

55. Clare to Bragg, June 2, 1863, Statement of Lt. Col. Urquhart, June 12, 1863, Bragg's endorsement on Breckinridge to Cooper, May 6, 1863, Cooper to Bragg, May 31, 1863, in Palmer Collection; Breckinridge to Dawson, January 20, 1873, in Breckinridge MSS, NYHS; O.R., Ser. I, Vol. XX, Pt. 1, p. 792, Pt. 2, p. 477.

from the inside for six months the way that Bragg conducted his war on the Kentuckian, Johnston abruptly resigned. Bragg begged him to remain on his staff but, said Johnston, "My relations were too intimate with Breckinridge & my sympathies were with him." Nothing better symbolizes the discord Bragg had sown in his own army, but, unfortunately, Breckinridge was not there to see it. He was back in Mississippi.[56]

56. J. S. Johnston Diary, July 19, 1863, in Johnston MSS.

Senator John C. Breckinridge, summer, 1861. The strain of defeat, disunion, and insult and accusation had wrought a grimness in his face. Before the year was out he donned the gray of the Confederacy. (Library of Congress)

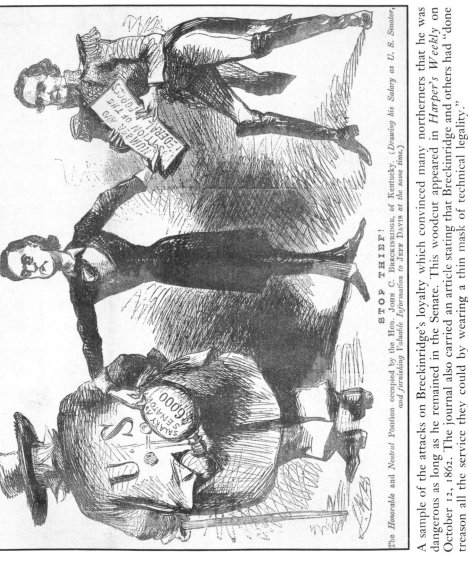

STOP THIEF!

The *Honorable and Neutral* Position occupied by the Hon. JOHN C. BRECKINRIDGE, of Kentucky. (*Drawing his Salary as U. S. Senator, and furnishing Valuable Information to JEFF DAVIS at the same time.*)

A sample of the attacks on Breckinridge's loyalty which convinced many northerners that he was dangerous as long as he remained in the Senate. This woodcut appeared in *Harper's Weekly* on October 12, 1862. The journal also carried an article stating that Breckinridge and others had "done treason all the service they could by wearing a thin mask of technical legality."

CHAPTER 4

Well, Gentlemen, This Is What Is Left of Me

The months following the Battle of Stones River had been peaceful, even monotonous, but they provided relief for Breckinridge in spite of the feud with Bragg. Rosecrans showed no disposition to advance, and the army lay at rest, in stark contrast to the almost continual traveling of his division in June–December, 1862.

Having Mary with him made the months most pleasant for the general. Back on January 2, when Hanson was brought to her room in Murfreesboro, she stayed up all night assisting the surgeons that vainly tried to save his life, herself cutting the boot off his wounded leg and tearing up her clothing for bandages. The general joined her for a time, keeping a vigil over his mangled friend. When Hanson's wife came to look after her dying husband, Mary ceased her ministrations there and went to care for the wounded Graves. At the request of Breckinridge—who felt fatherly toward the twenty-four-year-old major—she took him on a harrowing trip to Chattanooga to convalesce under her care. While away, she wrote to the general every other day, though his responses were as infrequent as usual. "I think you might answer at least every other one of mine," she implored, "I will be willing to take short ones, much space taken up in writing my name and yours and my place of residence &c, &c." Though the chiding came partially in fun, she was deadly earnest when she said: "Remember my darling if there is any prospect of a battle be sure and send for me. I must be accessible then as close as I can." Her greatest fear was that he would be hurt or killed when she was not nearby to tend him.[1]

Further cause for joy was a letter from his mother. He had not heard

1. Bullock, "John C. Breckinridge," in Prewitt Collection; Maltby, *Mary Cyrene Breckinridge*, 2–3; Mary C. Breckinridge to Breckinridge, January 8, February 5, 15, 1863, in Breckinridge, Service Record, NA; J. S. Johnston Diary, March 7, 1863, in Johnston MSS; Thompson, *Orphan Brigade*, 378–79.

from her since he left Lexington. What she had to say reflected not a little the high southern feeling in Maryland, where she now lived. "You have no idea how gratifying it is to me to know your standing here. I am constantly called on by Baltimorians strangers and prisoners paroled—on your account. I am lionized, not for any merit in me but because I am your mother. The cry is I want to see the woman that is mother to John Breckinridge—even on the streets I can sometimes hear as I pass that is John C. Breckinridge's mother!" [2]

A highlight this spring came on March 19, 1863, when Hardee asked Breckinridge to manage a grand review of the corps. The general placed his own division in front, Cleburne's behind it, and put them through the drill for an hour or more in the afternoon. Breckinridge rode with Polk during the affair, after which the divisions enjoyed horse racing. It was a special moment for one of the general's regiments. For the first time it displayed a handsome new banner. Mary had made a Confederate battleflag out of the dress she wore on her wedding day and, giving it to Breckinridge, charged him to present it to his most gallant regiment. In February he drew his division up in a hollow square with the Twentieth Tennessee in the center. Delegating O'Hara to make the presentation speech, Breckinridge had chosen the Twentieth in honor of its outstanding performance on December 31 at Stones River. He would have given it to one of the Kentucky regiments but found that he could not, or dared not, distinguish between them. For its part, the Twentieth was elated. "If a regiment ever worshipped a division commander," recalled one of those honored, "the Twentieth Tennessee idolized Gen. John C. Breckinridge." [3]

On May 23 the pleasant interlude came abruptly to an end. Out in Mississippi, Grant and Sherman had moved down the great river to besiege Vicksburg. Faced with this, General Joseph E. Johnston and President Davis sent out appeals to Bragg for reinforcements with which to relieve Lieutenant General John C. Pemberton and break the siege. This was an opportunity Bragg must have welcomed, for it gave him a means to get Breckinridge and the troublesome officers of his division out of the army. On May 23, therefore, orders went to Breckinridge to be ready to move immediately. He was ordered to leave all of his Tennessee regiments be-

2. Mary C. Breckinridge to Breckinridge, n.d., in Clifton R. Breckinridge Service Record, NA.

3. J. S. Johnston Diary, March 19, 1863, in Johnston MSS; Polk, *Leonidas Polk*, II, 212; McMurray, *Twentieth Tennessee*, 250, 375; Mary C. Breckinridge to Breckinridge, February 15–16, 1863, in Breckinridge, Service Record, NA.

hind, which served the dual purpose of keeping these men in their home state, while also removing in a block some of the most loyal supporters the Kentuckian had in the army.[4]

Breckinridge had his men ready well in time, but found himself faced with a dilemma. He knew that his Kentuckians did not relish going back to Mississippi to suffer once more from its fever and heat. As a result, he asked Bragg for permission to take a brigade of Mississippians in their stead, men who would be glad to return to their state. Bragg assented, though leaving the matter entirely up to Breckinridge, and the Kentuckian, loath to make this sort of decision on his own, appealed to the Kentucky Brigade for their views. The Kentuckians interpreted the matter as a choice between Bragg and Breckinridge in which their remaining with the army would be a move in favor of the former. Viewing it thus, they unanimously chose to go with their general. "They said where thou goest," wrote a soldier in the Ninth Kentucky, "there we will go also." Still there was a sadness before the departure, for Breckinridge had to leave behind the Twentieth Tennessee, which was as dear to him as his Kentucky regiments. Before leaving he rode to where they were assembled, remained on his horse and tried to speak. "It was a sad parting," wrote a captain of the Twentieth; "the boys crowded around him as if he were some dear relative about leaving. We had been with him a long time and had become attached to him and he to us. I felt as if I had lost some dear friend and the whole Reg't. looked quite dissatisfied for several days. We are willing and ready to follow him anywhere in the world." Breckinridge only got out a half dozen tearful words before he wheeled his mount abruptly and rode off out of sight.[5] A month later the officers of the Twentieth sent him a new horse "as a simple expression of the feelings cherished by soldiers for their favorite chieftan."

With the brigades of Adams, Helm, and Preston, the latter now commanded by Brigadier General Marcellus A. Stovall of Georgia, Breckinridge retraced his route of the previous September, back to Jackson. His fifty-two hundred men filled three trains, one behind another, and bystanders along their way were impressed that "all seemed in the highest spirits, cheering and yelling like demons." His arrival at Jackson on June 1

4. O.R., Ser. I, Vol. XXIII, Pt. 2, pp. 849, 851; J. S. Johnston Diary, May 24, 1863, in Johnston MSS.

5. Thompson, Orphan Brigade, 206–207; Kirwan, Johnny Green, 78; Deering J. Roberts, "Service with Twentieth Tennessee Reg't.," Confederate Veteran, XXIII (March, 1925), 100; J. S. Johnston Diary, May 5, 1863, in Johnston MSS; W. G. Erwin to "My darling Sisters," June 7, 1863, in possession of Ray Marshall, Clarksville, Tenn.; Erwin and others to Breckinridge, July 15, 1863, in Breckinridge Service Record, NA.

was a welcome relief, and Joseph Johnston ordered him to take command there immediately, attaching to his division all forces in the area. At once, Breckinridge began sending out reconnaissances in force toward the Federals near the Big Black River. He impressed local slaves to act as hospital stewards and called on Governor John J. Pettus for an additional two hundred Negroes to work on Jackson's defenses as well as five hundred militiamen for post duty to relieve his experienced troops for the field. With the fall of Vicksburg imminent, he worked feverishly to put Jackson in shape for a defense, as well as to serve as a base for an attack on Grant. "Time is blood now," he said.[6]

Johnston, gathering troops at Canton twenty-five miles north, had about twenty-three thousand by late June. Grant had over seventy thousand at Vicksburg, and half of them were on their guard for Johnston. Though the situation seemed hopeless for relieving Pemberton, Johnston resolved to try, and by July 1 had his whole army, twenty-eight thousand including Breckinridge, at Jackson ready to advance. On that day, he moved out toward the Big Black, Breckinridge advancing along the Vicksburg and Jackson Railroad to Clinton. Three days later the Kentuckian reached a position by Champion's Hill, six miles from the Big Black, and still twenty miles from Vicksburg. The weather had been so hot that men died of sunstroke on the march, and he found straggling a severe problem despite the fact that his was considered the best division in Johnston's army. This march cut his number considerably, and Breckinridge was seriously worried over the depletion when a new disaster presented itself. At 11 P.M. on July 4 a Federal prisoner was brought in. The general's advance pickets had captured him earlier that evening, and he had news. Vicksburg had fallen.[7]

Johnston faced an emergency. Now Grant's entire army was free to turn on him, and he was miles from his defenses at Jackson. Consequently, early on July 5, he ordered Breckinridge and the others to retreat with all possible speed. Two days later the general and his division were in camp again on the Pearl River, two miles below Jackson, and on the ninth he put them in position to meet the announced advance of the Federals.

6. Walter Lord (ed.), *The Fremantle Diary* (Boston, 1954), 107; *O.R.*, Ser. I, Vol. XXIV, Pt. 3, pp. 942, 945–46, 964, 980; Joseph E. Johnston, "Jefferson Davis and the Mississippi Campaign," in Johnson and Buel (eds.), *Battles and Leaders*, III, 480; John Buckner to ?, June 6, 1863, Buckner to Lyon, June 6, 1863, Breckinridge to John Pettus, June 8, 1863, Buckner to J. M. Smylie, June 18, 1863, all in Chap. 2, CCCXI. NA.
7. *O.R.*, Ser. I, Vol. XXII, Pt. 2, p. 992, Vol. XXIV, Pt. 2, pp. 228, 540, Vol. XXIV, Pt. 3, pp. 945, 978–88; Thompson, *Orphan Brigade*, 208–209; S. A. R. Swan, "Perilous Service of Joseph R. Mason," *Confederate Veteran*, XIV (December, 1906), 553.

His preparation paid off. On July 10 the enemy approached Jackson with three corps and part of a fourth, commanded by Sherman. The Thirteenth Corps under Major General Edward O. C. Ord, with the Fourth Division of the Sixteenth Corps attached, drew up opposite Breckinridge's division, but did nothing until dawn on July 12. That morning Ord sent the three brigades of the Sixteenth Corps out on a reconnaissance in force against Stovall in Breckinridge's center. Stovall kept his men hidden behind their works, allowing the Federals to advance within two hundred yards before opening fire. By about 11 A.M., the enemy broke in the face of flank fire from the well-placed guns of Cobb and Slocomb, leaving behind two hundred prisoners and several stands of colors. The Federals had not made a vigorous attack, but, after the debacle at Vicksburg, any little victory helped to cheer Johnston. To Breckinridge he expressed his pleasure and confidence "in your fine division," while the Kentuckian was fulsome in his praise of Stovall and, in particular, Cobb and Slocomb. Out of five thousand men of the division present, Breckinridge lost seven killed and thirty-eight wounded.[8]

As Sherman extended his lines around Jackson, it became evident that Johnston could not hold the place. On July 16 he ordered his army to withdraw across the Pearl. Breckinridge, as usual, covered the retreat, then marched east to the vicinity of Morton, Mississippi, and put his division in bivouac at a place subsequently dubbed Camp Hurricane. Just this thirty-five mile march in the summer heat cost him 500 men, and the general must have been happy to have over a month to spend in his new camp, rebuilding the health of his command.[9]

Indeed, Breckinridge had been quite content throughout his stay in Mississippi, thanks largely to his relationship with Johnston. Each found the other congenial, a striking contrast to the situation both had found with Bragg, and Breckinridge wrote several times to Mary expressing his pleasure at serving under a commander whom he could respect, and who re-

8. O.R., Ser. I, Vol. XXIV, Pt. 1, pp. 201, 245, Pt. 2, pp. 521, 652, 654–55, 992–93, Pt. 3, pp. 994, 1001–1003; Thompson, *Orphan Brigade*, 208; Breckinridge to Daniel Adams, July 9, 1863, Breckinridge to Marcellus Stovall, July 9, 1863, Breckinridge to Benjamin H. Helm, July 9, 1863, Breckinridge to Adams, Stovall, and Helm, July 9, 10, 1863, all in Chap. 2, CCCXI, NA; Bell I. Wiley (ed.), *Confederate Letters of John W. Hagan* (Athens, Ga., 1954), 23–24; Joseph E. Johnston, *Narrative of Military Operations* (New York, 1874), 207; "Diary of W. J. Davidson," *Annals of the Army of Tennessee*, I (August, 1878), 218; Richmond *Daily Dispatch*, July 25, 1863; Louisville *Evening Post*, May 31, 1900.

9. O.R., Ser. I, Vol. XXIV, Pt. 3, pp. 1006, 1008, 1039; Unnumbered General Order, July 17, 1863, Chap. 2, CCCXI, NA; Thompson, *Orphan Brigade*, 209.

spected subordinates. The only unhappy note of his stay in Mississippi was his separation from Mary. Still in Chattanooga staying with his friend Eli Bruce, she kept trunks packed always, ready to leave any time word should come. She sent him rose leaves in an envelope—"as you open it the perfume will rise like incense, emblematic of my love for you." "I love you better than my own life," she wrote, "and would freely give it to save yours. . . . May the God of Battles watch over you all." She did not feel the separation any more than he did and, seeking to take advantage of this period of inactivity in the army, Breckinridge applied for twenty days' leave on August 23. His timing could not have been worse. Just two days later, orders came to pack up his division and take it once again over the now familiar route to Tennessee. As part of a large interdepartmental shift of troops to Tennessee, he was going back to his old enemy. Bragg was in trouble.[10]

In a brilliant, and bloodless, campaign, Rosecrans had feinted Bragg out of his position and sent him flying back to Chattanooga. The movement had been intended to prevent Bragg from sending any relief to Vicksburg and, once completed early in July, it was suspended until August 16. Then, however, Rosecrans advanced again, this time to make battle. Faced with this threat, Bragg called out for help, and was not particular as to who brought it. When Breckinridge arrived at Tyner's Station, eight miles east of Chattanooga, on September 2, he was a welcome addition. With him he brought forty-five hundred effectives, and he had moved them in only eight days, despite the lack of planning and unexpected changes in the route forced by Federal threats along the line.[11]

Bragg placed Breckinridge's division in the corps of a new man from the eastern theater of the war, Lieutenant General Daniel H. Hill, who had taken Hardee's old command when that officer went to Mississippi in July. The Kentuckian was favorably impressed by his new corps commander from the beginning and, for his part, Hill found in Breckinridge an able subordinate. Hill's adjutant, J. W. Ratchford, was singularly impressed. "Prominent in my memory of great men," he wrote, "there stands John C. Breckinridge, whose physique, I believe, was the most perfect I have ever seen." Brief though they would be, the general's relations with Hill proved

10. Mary C. Breckinridge to Breckinridge, June 11, 13, 26, August 11, 25, 1863, Breckinridge to Benjamin Ewell, August 23, 1863, in Breckinridge Service Record, NA; Kirwan, *Johnny Green*, 84.

11. Thompson, *Orphan Brigade*, 209; *O.R.*, Ser. I, Vol. XXX, Pt. 4, pp. 502, 547; Johnston, *Narrative*, 254.

to be the best that he would enjoy with any of the corps commanders under whom he served in the West.[12]

The ground over which the armies would fight stretched for seven miles along the west side of the Chickamauga, from Glass's Mill on the south, to Dyer's Bridge to the north, and roughly formed the shape of a triangle. The Chickamauga formed the long side, or base, while the other two sides met at a point some four and one-half miles north of Glass's and three miles southwest of Dyer's, near Snodgrass Hill. The creek—actually a river—was fordable in a number of places, among them Lee and Gordon's Mill, a mile and a half up from Glass's, and bridges allowed crossings at other points, most particularly at Alexander's Bridge, halfway up the creek. Running straight north from Lee and Gordon's was the Rossville road, which passed in front of Snodgrass Hill, and it was generally along this road that Rosecrans began placing his three corps under Thomas Crittenden, George Thomas, and A. M. McCook.

Since Bragg planned to fight the battle on the west side of the creek, he was rightly concerned about preventing a Federal crossing above or below his army, a movement that would endanger his rear. Cavalry went out on both wings even as he moved his divisions north along the creek, and Breckinridge, bringing up the rear, guarded a succession of mountain passes and fords. By the evening of September 17, he was at Catlett's Gap, about twenty miles south of the scene of the coming battle. The next morning, he moved up to the east side of the creek opposite Glass's. He now occupied the extreme left of Bragg's line, but did not make any contact with enemy skirmishers across the water until nightfall.[13]

The next morning, while the Battle of Chickamauga began to rage off to the north, Breckinridge moved Helm across the stream with six guns to reveal the enemy position, while opening an artillery duel from the east bank. Helm remained engaged for some time before Federal artillery reserves began to tell against the Confederates. At about this time Hill, at last ordered by Bragg to hurry his corps up to the field where the battle had developed, sent Breckinridge an order to move up to Lee and Gordon's. Leaving two regiments and a section of guns to guard the ford, the Kentuckian pulled Helm back and headed north. By late afternoon he had the

12. Breckinridge to D. H. Hill, October 15, 1863, in Daniel H. Hill MSS, NCDAH; D. H. Hill, "Chickamauga—The Great Battle of the West," in Johnson and Buel (eds.), *Battles and Leaders*, III, 653; J. W. Ratchford, *Some Reminiscences of Persons and Incidents of the Civil War* (2nd ed.; Austin, Tex., 1971), 53.
13. O.R., Ser. I, Vol. XXX, Pt. 2, pp. 139–40, 197.

division in position, only to receive another order, this time from Bragg, to move to the extreme right of the army. Breckinridge's and Cleburne's commands had been selected to make the main attack on the morrow, though neither knew it yet.[14]

The general moved his men again immediately, this time toward Alexander's Bridge, where he would cross the Chickamauga. It was late, probably shortly after 10 P.M., by the time he got the division across and met a staff officer sent by Hill to guide him into position. However, shortly before meeting Hill's envoy, Breckinridge encountered Polk. Informed that Hill was now placed under Polk, who would command the right wing of the army, Breckinridge got permission from the one-time bishop to bivouac his men on the other side of the bridge. They were tired, needed rest, and could be off soon enough to reach their assigned position on the right if they took up the march again before daybreak. Polk did not tell Breckinridge that there was to be an attack at daylight the next morning, nor that, since his division would form the extreme right of the army, the Kentuckian was supposed to attack first, followed by progressive assaults of the divisions on his left. Thus, even though the morning advance depended on Breckinridge being in place in time, Polk not only did not tell him of the ordered movement, but had allowed him to stop for rest a mile and a half from the assigned position. When Hill's staff officer came up with orders for Breckinridge to follow him to the right, Polk, now senior to Hill, disregarded the communication and allowed the Kentuckian's division to remain in bivouac. Worse yet, Polk had not yet informed Hill that an attack was to be made the next morning.[15]

Polk invited Breckinridge to accompany him to his headquarters near the bridge for dinner and some rest, and, as they rode, they were joined by another of Hill's officers. The Kentuckian heard the conversation that ensued. Polk did ask the officer to tell Hill to come to his headquarters, but he said nothing about the attack. Only upon reaching his tents at 11:30 did Polk sit down to draft an attack order to Hill, an order which he could have sent previously by either of Hill's two staff officers he had met in the last hour. Instead, the dispatch was taken into the night by one of Polk's men, not even a staff officer, who would never find Hill. Even though he probably wrote the order in Breckinridge's presence, still he said nothing to the general about what was expected of him in the morning. Instead, the

14. *Ibid.*, pp. 140, 197–98, 202, 233, 329, Pt. 4, p. 671; Hill, "Chickamauga," 642.
15. *O.R.*, Ser. I, Vol. XXX, Pt. 2, pp. 198, 203, 215, 233; Polk, *Leonidas Polk*, II, 256; Connelly, *Autumn of Glory*, 215.

two ate a quiet supper, talking over prospects for the outcome of the battle, and then Breckinridge went off to Polk's private tent to sleep for about three hours. All Polk had told him so far was that he was to take a position in line of battle at that place where Hill's first officer was supposed to have taken him. When Breckinridge awoke at about 3:30 A.M., September 20, and left to take his division to the right, Polk finally hinted that some sort of assault was expected when he told the departing Kentuckian that he hoped that "the attack" would be made as soon as possible. He did not say precisely what attack, and Breckinridge did not pursue the matter. Perhaps he assumed that Polk was speaking in a general way of the fighting of the coming day, and not of any specific movement. In any event, the general rode off to his division in the clear, frosty dark, wholly ignorant that Bragg and Polk expected him to move his men a mile and a half and open an attack in barely two hours.[16]

Guided by the officer that Hill had sent the night before to take him to his place in the line, Breckinridge moved his command slowly toward the right. It took nearly two hours to reach the new position, and the division finally arrived to take its place on Cleburne's right a few minutes before 6 A.M. Placing Adams on his right, Stovall in the middle, and Helm on the left of his line, Breckinridge sent skirmishers out a few hundred yards to annoy the enemy, and then went to his left to see Cleburne.[17]

While Breckinridge talked with Cleburne, Hill rode up sometime before 7 A.M. and dismounted to confer with them. In the discussion over positions —all of them ignorant of the ordered attack—the three generals agreed that their slender line was no match for Thomas' four divisions facing them. During the night, the Federals had time to erect log breastworks and rudely emplace cannon while, for their part, the Confederates would be hampered in an attack by the irregular woods that broke up the ground before them, and which would make artillery support in an attack almost impossible. Obviously, all expected that an attack would be ordered sometime that day, and Hill actually reassigned two of Breckinridge's brigades farther to the right, to a point from which they could take Thomas' works in flank. At

16. Polk, *Leonidas Polk*, II, 256–58; Breckinridge to Hill, October 16, 1863, in Hill MSS; Connelly, *Autumn of Glory*, 212–13; *O.R.*, Ser. I, Vol. XXX, Pt. 2, pp. 47, 52, 198; W. D. Gale to Hill, December 28, 1872, in Polk MSS; Joseph H. Parks, *General Leonidas Polk, C.S.A.* (Baton Rouge, 1962), 333–34. In his report Breckinridge says that he left Polk's headquarters two hours before dawn, and repeats the same statement in his October 16 letter to Hill. According to Polk, *Leonidas Polk*, II, 264, daylight on September 20, 1863, came at 5:47 A.M.

17. *O.R.*, Ser. I, Vol. XXX, Pt. 2, pp. 52–53, 57, 198, 203.

the same time, it was obvious that none of them expected the attack to be early that morning, for Hill allowed Breckinridge and Cleburne to have their men bring up rations and cook their breakfast.[18]

While the rations were being brought up, the three sat down around a campfire. As they conversed a staff officer rode up with orders from Polk. Despairing of finding Hill, Polk had sent out the order at 5:30 directly to Breckinridge and Cleburne. Even now, however, there was no urgency in the dispatch, nor any indication that an attack was to be made at daylight, now more than an hour past. Instead, Polk merely told the generals to attack Thomas as soon as they were in position. After reading his copy of the order, the Kentuckian handed it to Hill, as did Cleburne, commenting that the men would not be in shape to fight until they had eaten. Hill agreed, and sent back a reply that his divisions would not be ready for the attack for at least another hour, and probably more. There had been no immediacy in the order, and none of these three generals read any into it. Breckinridge's division went ahead with its breakfast. Indeed, he would not have been in much shape to make an attack at daylight even if he had known about it. Not only were his men tired and hungry, but also half of Stovall's brigade, the Glass's Mill guard, still had not come up. It marched all night, and reached Breckinridge at 8 A.M. as the command was eating.[19]

Only when Bragg finally rode up did Hill discover that a dawn attack had been ordered. After directing some epithets at the absent Polk, Bragg gave Hill peremptory orders to attack as soon as possible. Breckinridge may not have been present at the Bragg-Hill interview, for he spent much of the morning after leaving Hill and Cleburne in riding among his regiments while they ate their breakfasts. The night before, the men in some regiments, the Sixtieth North Carolina for one, grew strangely silent and introspective, sensing that there was a bloody day ahead. Breckinridge himself may have felt somewhat the somber atmosphere. Late on the nineteenth, while putting his division in bivouac at Alexander's Bridge, he met Major General John B. Hood, who arrived with men from Robert E. Lee's Army of Northern Virginia. Hood's men thought Breckinridge "a game-looking, handsome man," but their commander found him somewhat gloomy and tried to cheer him with the opinion that the morrow would bring victory. Hood thought that his expression of confidence produced the desired effect, and perhaps it did, but Breckinridge certainly had good reason for apprehension. Once again he was to hold the right of a line com-

18. *Ibid.,* Vol. LIII, 198; Connelly, *Autumn of Glory,* 218–21.
19. *O.R.,* Ser. I, Vol. XXX, Pt. 2, pp. 52–53, 61, 233.

manded by Braxton Bragg, and the memory of Murfreesboro would not die easily.[20]

At 9:30, after a four-hour delay for which neither Breckinridge nor Cleburne was at fault, the Kentuckian moved his brigades forward toward the enemy breastworks. Not only was he still without any reserve, but he did not have any sort of cavalry protection on his right flank. Nathan B. Forrest's horsemen were dismounted and placed on that flank, but they would hardly be enough if the Federals decided to launch a spirited counterattack. Polk was at fault for this, as he was for so much of the badly managed affairs on this wing of the army, despite the fact that Hill had asked for a reserve, and that such a force under W. H. T. Walker was nearby and available. Meanwhile Cleburne, who was to attack shortly after Breckinridge moved into battle, was not in proper position and had to hurry to dress on the Kentuckian's advancing left. The result of it all was that Breckinridge was going into battle virtually unsupported, in a line only one brigade in depth, with no available fresh troops to exploit an advantage, and none to help prevent rout in case of repulse.[21]

The division moved forward rapidly. Thanks to Hill's shifting of Adams and Stovall that morning, they encountered light initial resistance and enjoyed the added blessing of confronting the enemy in a position that was unfortified. Consequently, they had little trouble in passing beyond Thomas' left flank. Stovall stopped on the Rossville road, and Adams passed over the road, which put both brigades actually in the left rear of Thomas' line of defense. The only obstacle so far had been two lines of skirmishers and a light artillery fire. Their part of the attack had gone far better than expected.[22]

Helm, however, met more than his match. Two of his regiments on the left ran into the left end of Thomas' breastworks and were checked immediately. Meanwhile, the rest of the brigade on the right, hitting a line of Federals unprotected by works, moved along with Adams and Stovall,

20. *Ibid.*, Vol. LIII, 198, Vol. XXX, Pt. 2, p. 198; Connelly, *Autumn of Glory*, 218–20; William Polk to Breckinridge, September 22, 1874, Breckinridge to Polk, November 12, 1874 (copy), in JCB Papers; Fred Joyce, "The Orphan Brigade at Chickamauga," *Southern Bivouac*, o. s., III (September, 1884), 31; Bullock, "John C. Breckinridge," in Prewitt Collection; James M. Ray, "Sixtieth Regiment," in Walter Clark (ed.), *Histories of the Several Regiments and Battalions from North Carolina in the Great War, 1861–1865* (Raleigh, 1901), III, 487–88; John C. West, *A Texan in Search of a Fight* (Waco, 1969), 115; John B. Hood, *Advance and Retreat: Personal Experiences in the United States and Confederate States Armies* (Reprint; Bloomington, Ind., 1959), 62.

21. O.R., Ser. I, Vol. XXX, Pt. 2, pp. 154, 198–99.

22. *Ibid.*, pp. 217, 220–21, 231.

driving the enemy back, and halting with Stovall on the Rossville road. What prevented them from going any farther was the stymie met by the regiments battling along the barricade. The two regiments, the Second and Ninth Kentucky, with seven companies of the Forty-first Alabama, rallied and attacked three successive times, only to meet failure. Thomas' strong position accounted for much of their failure, but equally distressing was the enfilading fire on their left, coming from a part of the Federal line that Cleburne was supposed to be attacking. The works in that place angled out from the general line, and the result was that Helm's regiments were caught in a crossfire. Its effect was deadly. In a few minutes the colonel and three captains of the Second Kentucky were killed, the senior colonel, Caldwell of the Ninth, was wounded and several of his officers killed, and a number of company officers from the Forty-first Alabama died also. A bullet struck Helm in his right side, mortally wounding him. Of the 1,404 men of the Kentucky Brigade who went in to the attack, nearly 30 percent were lost in less than an hour, and more would fall.[23]

The news of Helm's fate shook Breckinridge. "Helm has been killed," he told his staff with unconcealed emotion. He hurriedly drafted an order for Colonel Joseph Lewis of the Sixth Kentucky to take command, sending Cabell riding off through the murderous fire to deliver it. Then the general himself rode over to see about Adams and Stovall. Upon arriving, he quickly saw that they had almost bloodlessly gained an advantage which might be decisive. Sending off a suggestion to Hill that he wheel the brigades to the left, on a line perpendicular to the Rossville road and Thomas' breastworks, Breckinridge may not have waited for permission to do so, but formed them on a line astride the road and sent them forward.[24]

By this move, Breckinridge cut off one Federal line of retreat, threatened two more within range of his brigades, and began a perfect flanking attack that might have proved decisive if there had been troops there to support him. Despite Hill's entreaties, however, Polk neglected to send Walker forward in time. Meanwhile, the Federals had been reinforced just before Adams and Stovall advanced, first by their old adversary from Murfreesboro, John Beatty and his brigade, and then by two more brigades.

23. *Ibid.*, pp. 108, 204, 206–207; Glenn Tucker, *Chickamauga: Bloody Battle of the West* (Indianapolis, 1961), 230. Tucker says that Helm was killed by a Kentucky bullet, but this is rather fanciful since the only Federal Kentucky unit, the Fifteenth, was facing the right of the Kentucky Brigade, whereas Helm was on its extreme left when killed.

24. Castleman, *Active Service*, 46; Hill, "Chickamauga," 655; Tucker, *Chickamauga*, 233; *O.R.*, Ser. I, Vol. XXX, Pt. 2, pp. 142, 199.

Hitting the Federals full force, Breckinridge's initial flank attack made "quite a sensation," thought Hill, but not so much as might have been desired. Stovall was stopped and repulsed when he hit the end of Thomas' breastworks. Adams, on the right, was more successful, driving back a first line under Beatty, but he too was stopped when he struck a second line. Here Adams was seriously wounded and captured.[25]

During the attack, Breckinridge sat his bay at a vantage point slightly behind the battle line, stroking his moustaches, and apparently oblivious of the enemy shells whistling through the trees above him. His attitude may have been more studied than unconscious, for this was a crucial time when the men needed an example of courage and indifference to the danger around them. If so, then his posture worked, for the soldiers fought with unusual fury, many of them inspired by the sight of the general. "I never saw a more god-like hero than Breckinridge at that moment," one recalled, and the impression even reached across the battle line to the enemy. There Beatty could look across the raging battle and see the Kentuckian. Years later, when someone complimented the Ohio-born general on being the handsomest mounted figure he had even seen, Beatty thought back to Chickamauga and replied: "You certainly never saw the Confed. Gen. John C. Breckinridge on a horse."[26]

The general spread this same confidence to the Kentucky Brigade. After seeing Adams and Stovall off into another in a series of assaults, he rode over to where the Orphans were regrouping from their first repulse and the loss of so many officers. "I shall never forget his stately presence," one of the Kentuckians later recalled. "He sat erect on his horse, his whole body seeming to indicate attention to the business on hand." The repulse of the brigade had driven it back and away from the end of Cleburne's line, leaving that officer's flank exposed. Fortunately, Cleburne had finally moved in to attack shortly afterward and managed to push the Federals back from their first line of log breastworks. Breckinridge viewed part of Cleburne's action from a little grassy opening in the forest. With him were Cheatham and Polk, who had finally come forward to view the fighting. Cleburne's success was reported to the group of generals, and, at almost the same time,

25. Connelly, *Autumn of Glory*, 221; Hill, "Chickamauga," 656; Tucker, *Chickamauga*, 233–37, 248–50; O.R., Ser. I, Vol. XXX, Pt. 2, pp. 199–200.

26. Mercer Otey, "Story of Our Late War," *Confederate Veteran*, VIII (August, 1900), 342; Clark, *My Quarter Century*, I, 47. Since Beatty and Breckinridge only faced each other at Stones River and Chickamauga during the war and were not acquaintances, the latter battle, where their lines were much closer together, is most likely the place where Beatty saw the Kentuckian.

they began hearing the sounds of harsh battle off to their left, near the center of the line. At this, Polk ordered the generals to attack Thomas once more—Breckinridge may have received the order from Hill—opening almost two hours of continuous brigade assaults. It was 11 A.M., and that sound off toward the center heralded the approaching fruits of Breckinridge's finest performance as a division commander, and the only occasion of the war when his action would exert a decisive influence on a major battle.[27]

Almost from the moment that the general's brigades first hit the Federals that morning, Thomas repeatedly called on Rosecrans for reinforcements. This had brought Beatty's and four other brigades to Thomas within the first hour, and left Breckinridge's three brigades, numbering some 3,769, battling six brigades that totaled over 8,500, and two of those units were behind breastworks. Despite this, Thomas continued to ask for more, especially when the Kentuckian turned Adams and Stovall and sent them against the Federal flank from a position 400 yards behind the breastworks. By 10:45 Rosecrans had dispatched an additional four brigades to Thomas and, as they were en route, another message came from Thomas asking for yet more. The result was confusion in the Union line from the movement of so many units to Thomas, confusion which culminated in the opening of a quarter-mile wide gap in Rosecrans' center just as Lieutenant General James Longstreet began an assault. The open space was almost directly in his line of advance, and Longstreet's troops poured through the hole, sending two divisions, Rosecrans, Crittenden, and McCook with their staffs, flying back to Rossville. By 1 P.M. the battle was already a great victory, the most complete defeat suffered by any Federal army during the war.[28]

Breckinridge's friends were wont to give him almost sole credit for causing that hole to be opened in the Federal line, placing him second only to Longstreet as the architect of the Confederate victory. "It was [the] urgent demand for troops to drive back the division of Breckinridge which led to a gap being left in the Federal line," wrote one of the Orphans. Hill agreed. "Surely there were never nobler leaders than Breckinridge and Cleburne," he would say, and to the former in particular he gave credit for the

27. Joyce, "Orphan Brigade at Chickamauga," 31; Tucker, *Chickamauga*, 243–44; Polk, *Leonidas Polk*, II, 307.

28. Tucker, *Chickamauga*, 233, 242, 253–55, 258–59; *O.R.*, Ser. I, Vol. XXX, Pt. 1, pp. 253, 310, 312, 367–69, 371, 378–79, 427, 429, 555–56, 781, 785, 823, 827, Pt. 2, p. 197. An additional brigade under Ferdinand Gross came to Thomas' aid but saw little fighting.

gap. Ratchford said of the Kentuckian: "I saw him in the fight at Chickamauga, where his bearing was all my admiration could desire. I cannot speak of his behavior in higher terms than to say he suffered none in comparison with the gallant Cleburne." The Kentuckian himself made no such claim, content to note that the attacks on Thomas had "compelled him to weaken other parts of his line to hold his vital point." John C. Breckinridge did not win the Battle of Chickamauga, but it would not have been won in the way it was nor could the victory have been as complete, without him.[29]

The battle was not yet over. While Longstreet was breaking through the enemy center, the Kentuckian's assaults on Thomas continued until about 1 P.M. As the brigades battered each other, he received word that Daniel Adams' brigade, now led by Colonel Gibson, was being driven back along the Rossville road. Breckinridge rode over to his right to inspect the situation, and found the brigade re-forming behind a company of the Washington Artillery, one of the best batteries in the army. They were holding their position under heavy attack, but it could hardly have cheered the general, for lying among the guns, he saw the prostrate form of his young chief of artillery, Rice Graves, dying. Breckinridge dismounted and bent over the wounded major, whispering a few soft words. Graves, perhaps thinking back to his Murfreesboro wound, said he thought he might recover if Mary were to be his nurse again. As the enemy was pressing the brigade back again, Breckinridge ordered Graves removed to the field hospital in the rear, while he rode off to try and bring up support from Walker's reserve corps, which Polk still had lying idle.[30]

Around noon, Polk finally sent Walker's men into the lines, though by this time Breckinridge had been forced back from the Rossville road, and Thomas once more commanded it. When the fresh divisions went into battle, Hill ordered the Kentuckian to withdraw his men to rest and regroup. Breckinridge joined Hill and Polk, and shortly afterward they were startled by a new threat. A Federal corps under Major General Gordon Granger was moving down the Rossville road to Thomas' relief, heading straight for the Kentuckian's right flank. Polk counseled Hill to fall back

29. Bullock, "Breckinridge," in Prewitt Collection; John A. Wyeth, *That Devil Forrest* (Reprint; New York, 1959), 229; Hill, "Chickamauga," 656; Ratchford, *Reminiscences*, 35; *O.R.*, Ser. I, Vol. XXX, Pt. 2, pp. 144, 200.

30. *O.R.*, Ser. I, Vol. XXX, Pt. 2, pp. 200–201, 229; J. A. Chalaron, "Vivid Experiences at Chickamauga," *Confederate Veteran*, III (September, 1895), 278–79; J. A. Chalaron, "The Washington Artillery in the Army of Tennessee," *SHSP*, XI (April–May, 1883), 220; Maltby, *Mary Cyrene Breckinridge*, 13.

in the face of Granger's threat, advice which Breckinridge believed would have thrown away what victory had been gained so far, and which Hill ignored.[31]

By this time Thomas, fighting an enemy on three sides, was putting up a heroic defense around Snodgrass Hill. Most of the battle was brought to him by Longstreet, while Polk contented himself with making sporadic and disjointed brigade assaults here and there until about 3:30. Then Polk decided to act on Bragg's orders and conduct a major assault on Thomas. The order was relayed to Hill. Knowing that Breckinridge's division was shattered by the day's fighting, he asked Cheatham, whose division Polk had sent up in reserve, to make the attack with Cleburne. Cheatham declined, and Hill had no choice but to ask Breckinridge if his division was able to make the assault. "Yes, I think they are," came the reply, and Hill ordered him forward. The Kentuckian rode to his division, had them formed, and then moved along the weary line encouraging the men. They were to attack with the bayonet, he said, "we have got them in a bad fix and must finish them this time." [32]

By 4 P.M. the divisions were under way. Cleburne shortly broke through Thomas' line near its center, while Breckinridge and units from Walker's corps pushed the enemy left back across the road, and took portions of the breastworks. It was already growing dark when the attack began, and nightfall ended it soon afterward. Hill ordered Breckinridge and the others back, but not before their attack had convinced Thomas that he too must leave the field.[33]

The cost of victory had been terrible for Breckinridge. Of the 3,769 men and officers of his division who went into the battle, 1,240, almost one third, were casualties. The loss of Helm was a terrible blow, Adams' capture no less a loss, and the mortal wound of Graves may have been the worst of all. Throughout the war Breckinridge tended to attach young men, often minors, to his staff. He felt fatherly toward many of them, and to none more than Graves. This evening, once his division was in bivouac on the field, the general rode to the field hospital to say his last farewell to

31. O.R., Ser. I, Vol. XXX, Pt. 2, pp. 200, 252–53; Charles W. Anderson, "Gracey-Chickamauga-Whitaker," *Confederate Veteran*, III (Auguist, 1895), 251; Breckinridge to Hill, October 16, 1863, in Hill MSS; Connelly, *Autumn of Glory*, 222.

32. Endorsement by D. H. Hill on Breckinridge's Chickamauga Report, *SHSP*, VII (April, 1879), 167–68; Vieux Seconde, "The Second Tennessee Regiment at Chickamauga," *Annals of the Army of Tennessee*, I (May, 1878), 58; Lexington *Morning Herald*, November 1, 1897; Kirwan, *Johnny Green*, 98.

33. O.R., Ser. I, Vol. XXX, Pt. 2, pp. 144–45, 200.

the dying artilleryman. "Breckinridge's tones were as tender as if he were talking to his own son," recalled one of the Orphans.[34]

That evening he rode over the field, counting the enemy dead as well as his own. It was a horrible night, the moon shining down on the white faces of the dead and dying as they stared sightlessly into the sky, the bloated bodies and pitiable screams and groans of thousands making it a nightmare. The memory of that night ride would haunt him for years.[35]

Some release came when he went back to the rear, having received word that a number of Federal prisoners had asked if they might see him. He presented himself, saying: "Well, gentlemen, this is what is left of me." "Yes," one of them shot back, "and a damn fine specimen of humanity you are, too! There is not another such a hunk of humanity in our land! I voted for you once, and I want this cursed war over with so that I may vote for you again for president." The presidency, 1860, and Washington City, must all have seemed very far away to the general this night.[36]

34. *Ibid.*, p. 201; Bullock, "Breckinridge," in Prewitt Collection.
35. Hill, "Chickamauga," 651.
36. John L. McKinnon, *The History of Walton County* (Atlanta, 1911), 289.

CHAPTER 5

I Never Felt More Like Fighting

Rosecrans had retreated to Chattanooga, and early on September 23 Bragg sluggishly put his corps in motion. He would besiege the Federals in the city. He would starve the enemy into giving up Chattanooga without a fight, or Rosecrans would have no choice but to make battle against his formidable line along those slopes.[1]

Almost as soon as the battle was over, the controversy began, and now Bragg made war in earnest. By this time his army's high command, and with it much of the rest of the Confederacy's leadership, stood crystallized into what recent historians have called the "western concentration bloc." It was a number of separate but intersecting power blocs formed on the basis of: family ties among officers; opposition to Bragg; partisanship toward the out-of-favor Beauregard and his strategy; and the dream of returning to Kentucky. Breckinridge was a member of each in varying degrees, though he never recognized them as such. His ties to the Beauregard group were most slender, consisting mainly of occasional correspondence on strategic matters. Family links—often distant—tied him with men like Floyd, Preston, J. E. Johnston, Wade Hampton, and others. The chief effect was a chain of loyalties based largely on kinship. As for the anti-Bragg bloc, Breckinridge has always been undeservedly recognized as one of its leaders. In all the controversy with Bragg, both past and future, the Kentuckian's actions were motivated solely in self-defense. He never attacked Bragg, and never would. His old resolution against scheming and politicking, as expressed to Hodge, remained unchanged through the war.

However, as a member of the Kentucky bloc, Breckinridge assumed a natural, though reserved, leadership. Formed of men like Preston, Buckner,

1. See Connelly, *Autumn of Glory*, 231–34, for background on the decision to resort to siege.

Morgan, Marshall, Hodge, and others, it sought to influence the Confederacy to retake Kentucky, their recurring argument being that the people of the state needed only to be freed of the Federal yoke before they would flock to Confederate banners. It was a delusion, proven so in Bragg's Perryville Campaign, but Breckinridge thought otherwise. From his Bowling Green speech in October, 1861, down to the present he vainly tried to help bring the state into the Confederacy. In July, 1862, he sent Adam R. Johnson into the Bluegrass to issue a proclamation calling on Kentuckians to rally to the South. Telling the people that others thought the state lost, Johnson declared that "there is one man who has never despaired; that man is John C. Breckinridge." Then came the hope and disappointment of Perryville. Still, Breckinridge and others continued to hope and plan for another, successful, invasion.[2]

All of this posed a threat to Bragg, and knowing it, he determined to break up what he could. He would combine his attacks with his usual retribution against those who had failed him in the campaign just past. The commanding general moved first on Polk for his delay of the attack on September 20, and on Thomas Hindman for an earlier failure, the result being that both were suspended from command. Breckinridge had no significant part in this though he sympathized with Bragg's charges against Polk, especially since a minor clash broke out between Polk and Hill in the former's attempt to shift the blame. The Kentuckian was by this time an earnest friend of Hill.[3]

The army's chief malcontents were Longstreet, Hill, and Buckner, and their object was the removal of Bragg. There were a number of secret meetings among the three, which culminated on October 4 in a letter to Davis asking Bragg's removal ostensibly because of "the condition of his health." Cleburne, Preston, and Gibson, and others signed it, but interestingly enough Breckinridge refused. Since he already had application for a court of inquiry involving the commanding general—nearly a year after Murfreesboro he still hoped for that court—he felt that his motives might be misunderstood if he signed the petition. Breckinridge was present at the meeting which drafted the petition and stated his reasons.[4]

2. Thomas L. Connelly and Archer Jones, *The Politics of Command* (Baton Rouge, 1973), 54–55, 73–75, 77–78; Richmond *Daily Dispatch*, September 28, 1863; Younger, *Inside the Confederate Government*, 114–15; James M. Goggin, "Chickamauga—A Reply to Major Sykes," SHSP, XII (May, 1884), 223; Adam R. Johnson, *The Partisan Rangers of the Confederate States Army* (Louisville, 1904), Chap. 2 *passim*.
3. Breckinridge to D. H. Hill, October 15, 16, 1863, in Hill MSS.
4. *O.R.*, Ser. I, Vol. XXX, Pt. 2, pp. 65–66; Connelly, *Autumn of Glory*, 238–40;

Even before Davis could receive the letter, the agent he had sent to the West, Colonel James Chesnut, reported the near–civil war within the army's high command, and the president hurried out to Atlanta to see for himself. He arrived on October 8 and was met by a number of the anti-Bragg men, including Breckinridge, Longstreet, and Governor Joseph Brown of Georgia. The next day they rode with him to Bragg's head-quarters at Marietta, and along the way each probably presented the case against Bragg. Breckinridge, though, appears to have demurred, or at least he spoke fairly, chastely. "There is nothing narrow, nothing self-seeking about Breckenridge," Chesnut's wife, Mary, wrote. "He has not mounted a pair of green spectacles made of prejudices so that he sees no good except in his own red-hot partizans." [5]

If Breckinridge said nothing during the ride to Marietta, he certainly presented his views during the president's five-day stay. He was with Davis for some time on October 10 when the president rode along the lines. Al-though he may have commented on Bragg, Breckinridge's principal re-marks were in endorsement of Hill. Already, Bragg had turned much of his ire toward the North Carolina officer. Polk had nearly convinced Davis, and the commanding general as well, that Hill was actually responsible for the September 20 delay, and Bragg had ample reason to dislike him because of the October 4 petition. Bragg hoped to replace Hill with Pemberton, now out of a command, but Breckinridge and Cleburne expressed them-selves "adverse" to such an appointment, and that ended the matter. Still, the removal of Hill had been decided on by the time Davis arrived, and Breckinridge's words in his behalf had no effect other than to further en-dear him to his corps commander.[6]

Davis left to return to Richmond on October 14, and the next day Bragg relieved Hill of his command. Upon receiving Bragg's order, Hill turned

---

A. C. Avery, "The Life and Character of Lieutenant General D. H. Hill," *SHSP*, XXI (January–December, 1893), 143; Conversational remarks by C. R. Breckinridge, Sep-tember 27, 1932, in Prewitt Collection. Clifton Breckinridge stated that his father was present at the meeting of October 4.

5. Rowland, *Jefferson Davis*, VI, 58; Ben Ames Williams (ed.), *A Diary from Dixie* (Boston, 1949), 317; Isabella D. Martin and Myrta Lockett Avary (eds.), *A Diary from Dixie, as Written by Mary Boykin Chesnut* (New York, 1905), 249.

6. Richmond *Daily Dispatch*, October 24, 1863; William Polk to Breckinridge, Sep-tember 22, 1874, in JCB Papers; Breckinridge to Polk, November 12, 1874, in Polk MSS; Hill to William A. Graham, January 30, 1865, in William A. Graham MSS, SHC; Connelly, *Autumn of Glory*, 247–49; Moxley Sorrell, *Recollections of a Confederate Staff Officer* (Reprint; Jackson, Tenn., 1958), 197–98; Hill to Breckinridge, October 26, 1863, in "Notes," *Historical Magazine*, 3rd ser., I (February, 1872), 119–20; Fitzgerald Ross, *Cities and Camps of the Confederate States* (Reprint; Urbana, Ill., 1958), 137.

the corps over to his senior major general, John C. Breckinridge. The Kentuckian, too, was dismayed, and wrote Hill a brief testimonial of his own regard for him. The next day he would also furnish Hill with his own recollections of the events of September 19–20, but they did not help the North Carolinian. Before long, Hill left the army, telling his successor: "I hope that you may remain permanently in charge of the Corps." Bragg shortly thereafter so reorganized the corps, however, that it bore little resemblance to what Hill relinquished. To break up the troublesome Kentucky and Tennessee factions, whole divisions were shifted and dispersed, including Breckinridge's.[7]

The rumors soon went out that Breckinridge had been recommended for promotion to lieutenant general, and some of the eastern press actually announced it. The fact was that there were no other lieutenant generals available who were in favor, and regulations directed that Breckinridge, as senior officer, command until Hill was replaced. Meanwhile, Davis told Bragg, "my confidence in the patriotism and manliness of General Breckinridge assures me that as commander of the corps, during the absence of Gen. Hood, he will give the general commanding in chief the support which is his due, and in a manner most conductive to the public interest."[8]

The impression was widespread that Breckinridge was not only ready for, but deserved, the promotion and the command. "Breckinridge is regarded as a fine soldier," noted a diarist in the Washington Artillery, while a British observer with the army found that "Breckinridge, although not a soldier by profession, has established a very good reputation as a general during this war." From South Carolina, Beauregard wrote to assure Breckinridge that "it would give me unfeigned gratification to know that you had actually been promoted to the command of a Corps." Even the war correspondents were pleased with him. One who encountered the Kentuckian shortly after Hill's relief was fulsome in his praise. "Breckinridge is a model of manly beauty, knightly bearing and noble dignity—tall, strongly knit in bone and sinew, with a graceful carriage, an open, unreserved expression of countenance, written all over mind and courage, he reminds one, as he rides along in his Kentucky hunting suit, of *beau chevalier*, belonging to another era—a hero who has accidentally stepped out of one of Sir

7. *O.R.*, Ser. I, Vol. XXX, Pt. 4, p. 752; Breckinridge to Hill, October 15, 16, 1863, in Hill MSS; Hill to Breckinridge, October 26, 1863, in "Notes." 119–20.

8. Cincinnati *Commercial*, November 15, 1887; P. G. T. Beauregard to Breckinridge, November 25, 1863, in Breckinridge MSS, FC; *O.R.*, Ser. I, Vol. XXVIII. Pt. 2, pp. 523–24; Jefferson Davis to Braxton Bragg, October 29, 1863, in Rowland, *Jefferson Davis*, VI, 71.

Walter Scott's poems, to lend a helping hand to the young Confederacy." [9]

Breckinridge was ready for corps command. He had worked well with all of his superiors except Bragg, shown more ability at organization and logistical planning than many professionals of equal rank, and displayed aptitude for independent command. No division commander in the army had moved as many men, as many times, over as much distance, as the Kentuckian had in his three treks from the Mississippi to Chattanooga and back. Each had been conducted with little or no prior notice or planning, and yet each trip took less time than the one before it. Breckinridge had proved to be one of those rare men who could work efficiently with superiors of almost any temperament, from the egotism of Beauregard or the pettiness of Van Dorn, to the sometime irascibility of Hill. Even Bragg had found him an excellent subordinate until the failures of the Kentucky Campaign and Murfreesboro gave him need of a scapegoat. On the battlefield Breckinridge proved himself time and again a fighter and a leader who could get the best from his men. Beauregard, Hardee, J. E. Johnston, and Hill, had all paid compliment to his handling of his command under fire. The general's one independent battle, Baton Rouge, showed not only competent planning for a small action, but also a sense of innovation in his plans for the *Arkansas*. Best of all, from Shiloh through Chickamauga, he exhibited an ability to learn and develop, to profit from his mistakes. He seldom made the same error twice. In all, by the time Bragg invested Rosecrans in Chattanooga, Breckinridge stood as an all-round general without peer among the division commanders of the Army of Tennessee, not excluding Cleburne, whose surpassing battlefield brilliance would not emerge for some months yet. If any major general in the army was ready for promotion and/or corps command, it was John C. Breckinridge.[10]

He would have a chance to prove himself. There was a battle coming. Thomas had replaced the tarnished Rosecrans in command of the Army of the Cumberland, Sherman's Army of the Tennessee was on its way to Chattanooga, part of a corps under Major General Joseph Hooker had been sent from the East, and Grant had arrived to take overall command and lift the siege. Bragg saw his only opportunity for success now in an immediate attack. On October 31 he sent Breckinridge, Longstreet, and the newly ar-

9. William M. Owen, *In Camp and Battle with the Washington Artillery* (Boston, 1885), 274; Ross, *Cities and Camps*, 127; Beauregard to Breckinridge, November 25, 1863, in Breckinridge MSS, FC; Richmond *Daily Dispatch*, November 12, 1863.

10. See Book Three, Chapter 5 herein for a full discussion of Breckinridge *vis-à-vis* the other major generals of the Army of Tennessee.

rived Hardee—who now commanded the third of the army's three corps—
to the summit of Lookout Mountain to reconnoiter and decide on the prac-
ticability of bringing on a general battle against Hooker's troops around
Wauhatchie. The generals were unanimous in rejecting the idea of such an
attack, and faced with this, Bragg decided instead to move on a plan suggested by Davis. He would send two divisions north to attack a small Federal army under Ambrose Burnside at Knoxville, hoping that it would force
Grant to weaken Chattanooga. At the same time, Bragg saw in the plan an
opportunity to rid himself of a few more of the dissidents. He later claimed
that Breckinridge was actually his choice for the mission—and he would no
doubt have been happy to be rid of him—but Davis preferred Longstreet.
A token council of war was held on November 3, at which the corps commanders proposed and discussed various courses of action, but Bragg had
already decided the matter beforehand, and Longstreet left two days later.
This left Bragg barely thirty-six thousand men to face a Federal mass of
sixty thousand, and he would shortly order more to Longstreet. It would
seem that the commanding general had made all the mistakes he could.[11]

Unfortunately, he had not. After weakening his army by nearly one-
fourth, Bragg was still determined to hold his entire line around Chattanooga. This meant that Breckinridge had only sixteen thousand troops to
defend over six miles of terrain, from rugged Lookout Mountain on his
left, across Chattanooga Valley, to equally precipitous Missionary Ridge
on his right. Bragg probably ordered the actual placement of the divisions,
but, although Breckinridge had confidence in the strength of the line, the
Kentuckian was not entirely sanguine. On November 19, with some sort
of fighting obviously in the offing, he ordered his division commanders to
be prepared for a withdrawal. Stragglers were to be collected, and William B. Bate was ordered to take charge of Breckinridge's division.[12]

Breckinridge had not long to wait. On the evening of November 22,
fearing that his right was in danger, Bragg detached Cleburne from the
corps and sent him north to join Longstreet. Hindman's division of Hardee's corps, led by Brigadier General J. Patton Anderson, was informally
included in the Kentuckian's corps to make up for the loss. That night,
Breckinridge had fires burned on the line vacated by Cleburne to mask his

---

11. O.R., Ser. I. Vol. XXXI, Pt. 1, pp. 218, 455; Bragg to E. T. Sykes, February 8,
1873, in Polk MSS; Connelly, *Autumn of Glory*, 262–64; James Longstreet, *From
Manassas to Appomattox* (Reprint; Bloomington, Ind., 1960), 481.

12. O.R., Ser. I, Vol. XXXI, Pt. 2, p. 656, Pt. 3, pp. 717–18; Connelly, *Autumn of
Glory*, 270–71; Circular, November 19, 1863, in Chap. 2, CCCXI, NA.

absence, and began putting his meager reserves into his line to fill it. The next day he put Stewart to work organizing a mobile reserve to be used at any point in the line on a moment's notice, and meanwhile ordered his divisions on Missionary Ridge into the trenches and earthworks that had been dug. On the twenty-fourth, Grant made his first move, sending Hooker against Carter L. Stevenson's division on Lookout Mountain. Stevenson, part of the Kentuckian's corps, put up a stiff resistance, assisted by a brigade of Cheatham's, but the fog that shrouded the heights was too thick to allow use of his artillery, and he was steadily pushed back, off of the west slope, to the eastern slope leading to the Chattanooga Valley. Breckinridge regarded the mountain as essential to the maintenance of his line—which it was—and sent an order that it must be held at all hazards. However, Stevenson was pressed too hard. Both Bragg and Breckinridge had promised reinforcements if necessary, and that evening the Kentuckian led in person a brigade for Stevenson's relief. Because of the distance he had to move, the general did not reach the base of Lookout until 7:30 in the evening, too late to do anything but cover a partial withdrawal. He met with Stevenson and Cheatham briefly, assisted them in driving back Hooker a few hundred yards, and then left the withdrawal from the summit in their hands while he went back to Bragg's headquarters on the ridge for a council of war.[13]

Clearly, with Lookout lost, the whole army was threatened, especially since Sherman had arrived, crossed the Tennessee, and was now menacing Tunnel Hill. With both flanks in peril, Bragg asked Hardee and Breckinridge for their views. The former favored withdrawing the army at once to Chickamauga Station, about four miles east of the ridge. Breckinridge, however, in agreement with Bragg, doubted that there was sufficient time for such a move, and that the attempt to remove his troops from the east slope of Lookout would give away their plan. Besides, the Kentuckian argued, if the army could not make a stand on such favorable ground as it then held, it could not do so anywhere. Bragg agreed, and Hardee also felt that the position was a good one. They would stay on Missionary Ridge. As he left the meeting sometime around 10:00, Breckinridge confided another reason for remaining to one of Cleburne's officers. "I never felt more

13. *O.R.*, Ser. I, Vol. XXXI, Pt. 2, pp. 673, 676, 721, 739; S. R. Watkins and J. S. Jackman, "Battle of Missionary Ridge," *Southern Bivouac*, o. s., II (October, 1883), 50–51; "Report of Carter L. Stevenson, Jan. 2, 1863 [1864]," *SHSP*, VIII (June–July, 1880), 274; Moore, *Rebellion Record*, VIII, Documents, 237; Richmond *Daily Dispatch*, November 30, December 15, 1863.

like fighting than when I saw those people shelling my troops off of Lookout today," he said, "and I mean to get even with them." [14]

While the general's enthusiasm may be excused, his estimate of his position is open to severe criticism. To reinforce the right, where he expected the heaviest attack, Bragg that evening ordered Cheatham and Stevenson to Hardee. This left Breckinridge with only Stewart, Anderson, and Bate to defend the lion's share of the ridge, four miles of it from Rossville Gap to Hardee's left a mile or so below Tunnel Hill. Worse yet, Bragg had ordered half of each regiment in Breckinridge's corps to hold rifle pits at the foot of the ridge, while the other half held the crest. The result was that the men were over three feet apart in the line—seven and eight feet in places—and when the first line had to withdraw up the slope, the second line would be unable to fire for fear of hitting their own men. The works at the top had only been begun two days before, were badly planned, and even more badly constructed, thanks largely to an inept Confederate engineer. And Bragg had given the officers of the force at the base secret orders to fire only one volley when attacked, and then retreat up the ridge. The danger was that the men in the ranks, in both lines, not knowing that such a withdrawal was part of the plan, might mistake it for a rout. Yet despite all this, Breckinridge favored making a stand. As with Bragg, Missionary Ridge had him fooled. Neither he nor Bragg, nor the Army of Tennessee, had ever fought a defensive battle, and none of the three was experienced in selecting positions from which to receive attacks of the magnitude which characterized this war. As a result, to their unaccustomed eyes, Missionary Ridge's commanding eminence seemed formidable indeed.[15]

After midnight, while Stevenson and Cheatham were on their way to the right, Breckinridge ordered Stewart up out of the valley and onto the ridge, to form the left of his line. Fearing for his left flank at Rossville Gap, the general had Stewart place a battery and two regiments of Brigadier General Henry D. Clayton's Alabama brigade on the ridge above the gap. This put his entire corps on the ridge, Stewart on the left, Bate in the center, a lone returned brigade from Buckner's division next to Bate, and Patton Anderson on the right resting against Cheatham of Hardee's corps.

14. Irving A. Buck, *Cleburne and His Command* (Reprint; Jackson, Tenn., 1959), 166–67; "W.N.M.," "The Battle of Missionary Ridge," *Southern Bivouac*, o.s., II (January, 1884), 195; Brent Diary, November 24, 1863, in Palmer Collection.
15. Hughes, *Hardee*, 172; *O.R.*, Ser. I, Vol. XXXI, Pt. 2, pp. 679, 739; Anderson, "Autobiography," 69; "W.N.M.," "Missionary Ridge," 197; G. W. Gordon, "Eleventh Tennessee Infantry," in Lindsley (ed.), *Annals*, 297–98; E. P. Alexander, *Military Memoirs of a Confederate* (Reprint; Bloomington, Ind., 1962), 475–80.

Bragg's fears for the army's right at Tunnel Hill left Breckinridge defending two-thirds of the Confederate line with considerably less than one-half of the army. It did not help when, before daylight, Bragg ordered Lewis' brigade over to the right as well. There was already a considerable gap between Bate and Anderson, and this made it worse. That morning the line on the crest was further weakened when reports of a gap in the picket lines at the foot of the ridge reached the general. Consulting with Bate, he had part of Finley's brigade sent down. It was not long before Breckinridge and his corps, from their vantage point on Missionary Ridge, could see in the morning light Hooker's three divisions moving toward their left at the gap. At the same time, Thomas' Army of the Cumberland, four divisions strong, lay spread out behind its fortifications to their front. The unusual activity in the Federal works made it obvious that something was going to happen. Picket firing had been going on since sunup along most of the line, and before long the sound of heavy gunfire from the right indicated that Sherman had moved on Hardee.[16]

By 1 P.M. the activity in their front made it obvious that there would be an attack on the center of the line, and Breckinridge accordingly ordered Bate to close up with Anderson on his right. At the same time, however, he directed that men at the base of the ridge stay in position, an error in judgment as subsequent events would disclose. While Bate was in motion, the Kentuckian received word through Bragg that the left at Rossville Gap was now being threatened by Hooker. As corps commander, it was his duty to be where the greatest danger to the security of his line might lie, and nothing shows more vividly his mistaken confidence in the strength of the position atop the ridge than the fact that he now decided to go and manage his left at Rossville in person. The decision to do so came on short notice, but probably after a brief conversation with Bragg, for, when Bate came up to report just as Breckinridge was getting ready to leave for the left, he was directed to Bragg, who gave him his orders during the remainder of the afternoon. Breckinridge and Bragg arrived at an understanding whereby the latter took immediate command of the center on the ridge while the Kentuckian was on the left. Discounting their misapprehensions over the invulnerability of the line, it was a logical arrangement.[17]

Breckinridge moved off toward the left sometime before 2 P.M., accom-

16. *O.R.*, Ser. I, Vol. XXXI, Pt. 2, pp. 679, 740; Young, *Reminiscences*, 70.
17. *Ibid.*, pp. 665, 740–41.

panied by Cabell, his adjutant, Major James Wilson, and a number of his
headquarters escort. It was nearly three miles to the gap, and along the
way the general showed some sign of irritability. He had probably slept
little, if at all, that night or the night before, as was his wont during critical times, and tiredness, poor food, and tension, had begun to tell. He sent
one of his escort back to deliver a verbal order for the movement of part
of Jesse J. Finley's command, and, when the courier returned and the general had him repeat what he had said, he suddenly turned angry even
though the courier had repeated the order exactly as given. Calling for another courier, the general gave him the order to carry, this time in a different variation, probably that which he intended in the first place. It was
wholly unlike Breckinridge to vent anger on a soldier. It was only the beginning of a bad day.[18]

The general reached the left flank on the end of the ridge above the gap
shortly after 3 P.M., to find that Hooker had already begun his attacks. A
two-brigade division had driven two of Clayton's regiments back and out
of the gap itself, one of the brigades then taking a position to his left rear.
At the same time, the Federal division of Brigadier General Charles Cruft
seized a lodgment on the base of the ridge north of the gap. Breckinridge
barely had time to take command of the remaining two regiments of Clayton's brigade before the Federals attacked at 3:30. In the first assault,
Cruft's two brigades drove the Confederates to the top of the ridge, and
thereafter continued with a series of attacks that steadily drove Breckinridge back. He exerted himself conspicuously in trying to maintain his defense, so much so that Federals would later comment on his handling of
those regiments. Falling back, he took advantage of fortifications constructed precisely for this purpose, as well as other works left over from
a time when the enemy had kept a line on Missionary. The nearest troops
that might have provided support were men of Stovall's brigade, a mile up
the ridge, and another Union division led by Breckinridge's old political
friend John W. Geary was keeping them occupied. With no hope of help,
the general repeatedly fell back. In the noise and confusion, he probably
did not know at first that at the height of Cruft's first charge Cabell had
been captured by two men of the Ninth Iowa Infantry when he accidentally rode into them looking for his father. Shortly afterward, Major Wil-

18. Troop Movement Map—Chattanooga—November 25, 1863, Chickamauga-Chatta-
nooga Military Park Library, Chattanooga, Tenn.; J. N. Carpenter, "Courtesy of the
Truly Great," *Confederate Veteran*, XXIX (November–December, 1921), 424.

son, too, was taken prisoner, and Breckinridge himself narrowly escaped capture repeatedly.[19]

It was not long before the general and the remnants of his two regiments, outnumbered more than six-to-one, had been driven back to within a quarter-mile of Bragg's headquarters. Testimony to the steadfastness of his resistance is the fact that losses in Clayton's brigade more than doubled those in any of Stewart's other brigades, and were nearly ten times that of Stovall's. Well over three hundred were captured alone out of the two regiments he led.[20]

Breckinridge found chaos when he neared the center of the ridge. While the Kentuckian was being pushed back by Cruft, Thomas had marched his army out of their fortifications with great display and advanced against the main line on the ridge. Only then did the error in remaining and dividing the troops between the crest and the base become evident. Men in the first line, withdrawing up the slope, threw into confusion some units at the top, among them Finley, while the premature explosion of shells from the heights caused more damage to friend than foe. The Federals, without orders, pursued the retiring Confederates up the slope, and here found natural cover which Bragg and his generals overlooked. Moving up under this, they were able to approach within a few yards of the summit in places without coming under fire, especially in front of Anderson. Then a sudden charge broke through the line at the position of Zachariah Deas's brigade, and soon the rest of Anderson's division was in confusion, giving way in several places. Almost simultaneously there was a breakthrough in Stewart's division between Otto F. Strahl and Marcellus Stovall, just as Breckinridge arrived with the remnant of his two regiments. Joining Bragg, he tried to stop the rout, but they soon found that the impact of the Federal attack had been too great. Faced with the reality of the situation, the general cried to the men: "Boys, get away the best you can!" It did not exactly comport with proper military diction, but the order seemed to fit the occasion.[21]

19. Van Horne, *Army of the Cumberland*, I, 429, 432; *O.R.*, Ser. I, Vol. XXXI, Pt. 2, pp. 615, Pt. 3, p. 801; Richmond *Daily Dispatch*, December 1, 1863; Gordon, *Reminiscences*, 225.

20. *O.R.*, Ser. I, Vol. XXXI, Pt. 2, pp. 684, 745.

21. *Ibid.*, pp. 741–42; Ray, "Sixtieth Regiment," in Clark (ed.), *North Carolina Regiments*, III, 491; G. F. W. Harper, "Fifty-Eighth Regiment," in Clark (ed.), *North Carolina Regiments*, III, 436; Alexander, *Military Memoirs*, 476–79; John T. Irion, "Fifth Tennessee Infantry," 198, Lewis R. Clark, "Tenth Tennessee Infantry," 288, J. P. McGuire, "Thirty-Second Tennessee Infantry," 477 in Lindsley (ed.), *Annals*;

Bragg and Breckinridge barely escaped capture themselves. Bate, with his own and Finley's brigades making the only division not put to precipitate flight, fell back about one thousand yards and established a line of resistance to cover the retreat of Stewart and the brigade from Buckner. Bragg had determined to fall back to Chickamauga Station, and ordered Bate to hold this position as long as possible. Bate put this line in good order, sent out skirmishers, and then withdrew a regiment to form the nucleus of another line a few hundred yards farther back, leaving Finley in command of the advanced line. While Bate was gone, Breckinridge heard the firing from Finley's rearguard, and rode toward it, arriving an hour after dark. Where he had been in the past two hours since the rout from the ridge is a mystery, but it is likely that he was off trying to make some order out of the retreat of Stewart's division, which had been hit from front, rear, and both sides in the battle, and was thrown into terrible confusion. Then too, the Federal penetrations may have cut him off from his command, necessitating a wide detour to rejoin it. And it is possible that, disoriented like thousands of others in the wake of this terrible rout, he just wandered.[22]

When he reached Finley's line, which had held off attacks from the Federal division of Philip H. Sheridan for over an hour, the general asked some men of Bate's brigade what command this was and why it was there. He told Finley that the entire corps had been broken and was retreating, that Finley himself was surrounded on three sides, and ordered him to withdraw. Tipping his hat to some of the brave regiments that had held on so tenaciously, Breckinridge rode to the head of the column in time to meet Bate, coming up from the second line. Bate relayed Bragg's order to fall back on Chickamauga Station, and the Kentuckian directed him to proceed as ordered. After giving Bate a few additional instructions, Breckinridge rode off to join Bragg. Crossing the Chickamauga on a pontoon bridge at Bird's Mill, he met Captain C. H. Slocomb of the Washington Artillery. Although most of the command's guns were lost, Breckinridge ordered Slocomb to keep the men of the unit together.[23]

It was nearly midnight when the general reached Chickamauga Station and reported to Bragg. Here he received orders to move his corps out for Ringgold, Georgia, at 2 A.M., on a road to the east of one that Hardee

Smith Powell, "A Boy Soldier of Alabama," *Confederate Veteran*, XXIX (January, 1921), 22.

22. *O.R.*, Ser. I, Vol. XXXI, Pt. 2, pp. 69, 742–43; Young, *Reminiscences*, 71.

23. J. J. Turner, "Thirtieth Tennessee Infantry," in Lindsley (ed.), *Annals*, 453; Harper, "Fifty-Eighth Regiment," in Clark (ed.), *North Carolina Regiments*, III, 437; *O.R.*, Ser. I, Vol. XXXI, Pt. 2, p. 743, Vol. LII, Pt. 1, p. 98.

would use. His rearguard would be the brigade of Brigadier General States Rights Gist, of Walker's division. Immediately, Breckinridge set up his own headquarters at Chickamauga Station in the Watkins house, and issued orders for the anticipated movement of his corps, Bate to take the lead, and Stewart following. Cleburne and Stevenson would remain with Hardee's corps for the time being, as would the remnant of Anderson's. The corps moved out on time that morning, and none too soon, for the Federals who had battled Hardee around Tunnel Hill, after halting their pursuit, commenced it once again, moving to within one and a half miles north of Chickamauga Station by about 2:30 A.M. Breckinridge moved out with Gist to stop them and personally directed a fight shortly after sunrise that halted men of Brigadier General James D. Morgan's brigade, among them the Twenty-first Kentucky.[24]

Breckinridge stayed with the rearguard all day, following behind Cleburne and the army's wagon train. Mud and bad roads stalled the march several times, leaving the general and his small command dangerously exposed to attack from an overwhelming enemy. Still, they fell back, mile after mile, toward Ringgold. By nightfall he had crossed Pigeon Mountain's northernmost summit, closely pursued. A message came from Gist that the enemy had gotten in his front, closing off that line of retreat, and Breckinridge promptly turned around and went back up the mountain. Sending out pickets, he rested the men of the rearguard, and let them build fires to fight the night chill. The general walked over to one of the fires and sat talking for some time with a few privates from his escort. One of them he recognized as the courier he had been cross with the day before. After inquiring to make sure, he told the boy that, after thinking over the matter, he had decided that he was wrong to scold him, and apologized. Surely there were few, if any, other occasions in this war when a major general commanding half an army took out time to apologize to a private. Then, after a few minutes more of conversation, Breckinridge mounted up and rode, by a different route, around the Federals to join Bragg, spending the night at his headquarters two miles beyond Ringgold near Catoosa.[25]

The next morning, November 27, Breckinridge put his corps on the road for Dalton, ten miles off to the southeast, and then joined Cleburne, apparently bringing Gist on with him. The Federals were in their front, and Cle-

24. Bragg to Sykes, February 8, 1873, in Polk MSS; O.R., Ser. I, Vol. XXXI, Pt. 2, pp. 499, 679–80.
25. Buck, *Cleburne*, 175; Carpenter, "Courtesy," 424–25; Brent Diary, November 26, 1863, in Palmer Collection; O.R., Ser. I, Vol. XXXI, Pt. 2, p. 47.

burne had orders to hold them back until the army's wagon train was safely out of the way. Consequently, Cleburne put his division on Taylor's Ridge, an eminence looking down on Ringgold Gap, through which the Chickamauga flowed, and through which the Federals would have to pass to pursue Bragg. By 8 A.M. the enemy moved against the Confederate position. Breckinridge and Major General Joseph Wheeler, commanding the army's cavalry, stayed with Cleburne through the ensuing five hours of battle, lending their assistance by directing portions of the line in the defense. The Federals were repulsed repeatedly, in some instances by having rocks and boulders thrown and rolled off the ridge upon them. By 1 P.M., with the wagon train at a safe distance, Cleburne began to withdraw his men across the ridge and over the Chickamauga, burning the bridges behind them. Once over, he and Breckinridge put them in a new line on Dick's Ridge, about a mile behind the gap, to await any further attack. By now the enemy had artillery on the field and began shelling the position, but no assault was forthcoming. The two generals walked along the line to steady the men under the fire of the big guns, as well as to observe enemy dispositions on the other side of the Chickamauga. To their dismay, they discovered that a number of stragglers had been left on the other side. Breckinridge and Cleburne rode down to one of the burning bridges and yelled across to them to go down the stream to a ford. Shortly afterward, Cleburne withdrew several miles east to Tunnel Hill, where he remained without further molestation. The pursuit of Bragg's army was over.[26]

Breckinridge rejoined his corps at Dalton, Georgia, late on the 27th, or sometime the next day. Some surprises awaited him. Bragg, finally convinced that it was fruitless to retain command of the army any longer, had telegraphed to Richmond asking to be relieved. However, characteristically, he did not regard this disastrous conclusion to his term of command of the Army of Tennessee as growing out of his own failings. Rather, it was the culmination of the year-long conspiracy of his subordinates against him and, before he left the army under Hardee's temporary command on December 2, he made one final assault on an old enemy, Breckinridge. In the long history of their feud, it would be the one most damaging to the Kentuckian, and the one reflecting least honorably upon Bragg. The opening rounds came on November 30, when Bragg issued an order transferring Cleburne and Stevenson to Hardee's corps, while moving Anderson officially to Breckinridge. He did this in response to news just received

26. W. W. Gibson, "Reminiscences of Ringgold Gap," *Confederate Veteran*, XII (November, 1904), 526; *O.R.*, Ser. I, Vol. XXXI, Pt. 2, pp. 666, 755–57.

that Hindman, former commander of Anderson's division, had been released from arrest by the War Department, an arrest that had come about at Bragg's urging after Chickamauga. Hindman's commission as major general predated Breckinridge's. Putting his division in the Kentuckian's corps would make him the senior officer present, thereby replacing Breckinridge in the corps command. Then, on December 1, Bragg opened with his big guns. In a dispatch to Davis he stated that Breckinridge had been useless, unfit for command, from November 23–27, during the army's trials; the reason—drunkenness.[27]

In all of Breckinridge's lifetime as a moderate drinker, Bragg was the only person ever to claim having seen him intoxicated. Two years before, when the general was in command of the Kentucky Brigade in and about Russellville, Kentucky, the Louisville *Journal*, a long-time enemy of Breckinridge's, claimed that he had become a common drunkard, an object regarded with "mingled disgust and contempt" by fellow officers. The source belies the veracity of the report, and is further put to the lie by Breckinridge's performance during his early months as a general, as well as by the regard felt for him by his superiors. The only sure proof that Breckinridge had any liquor at all during the war exists in a few diary notations, and in the fact that Mary sent him an occasional bottle of brandy or porter. This last is particularly significant. If Breckinridge really had a drinking problem, Mary would know of it if anyone would, and she would hardly feed the illness by sending him the drink.[28]

Nevertheless, Bragg made the charge. In his first dispatch to Davis, he did not refer to Breckinridge by name, speaking only of the commander of his second corps. Davis, curious as to the identity of the culprit, telegraphed back and was told that it was the Kentuckian, and that measures had been taken to replace him with Hindman. Bragg's allegation against Breckinridge contained two charges: the first that he was intoxicated November 23–27; and the second that he was unfit for duty during those four days. Bragg would elaborate on these accusations some nine years later when speaking of the influence of whiskey in the failures of his army.

> At Missionary Ridge, Breckenridge, as gallant and true a man as ever lived, was overcome in the same way, whilst in the active command of a corps, and was really unfit for duty, one of the many causes of our disaster. At night

27. Brent Diary, November 28–30, 1863, in Palmer Collection; *O.R.*, Ser. I, Vol. XXXI, Pt. 3, p. 767, Vol. LII, Pt. 2, pp. 745–46.
28. Moore, *Rebellion Record*, IV, Rumors & Incidents, 88; Mary C. Breckinridge to Breckinridge, December 5, 1863, in Breckinridge Service Record, NA.

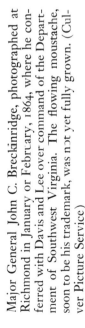

Major General John C. Breckinridge, photographed at Richmond in January or February, 1864, where he conferred with Davis and Lee over command of the Department of Southwest Virginia. The flowing moustache, soon to be his trademark, was not yet fully grown. (Culver Picture Service)

An unpublished photograph taken in Cuba within days after Breckinridge arrived from the South in 1865. Although heavily retouched, the picture shows the effects of his journey, including his trimmed-down moustache. Breckinridge was forty-four at the time. (Courtesy Peter H. Ten Eyck)

John C. Breckinridge, the exile, photographed in Paris, August 15, 1867. While in Europe he toured the Continent and the Holy Land. (Author's collection)

[November 25] he came into my office, a little depot hut at Chickamauga station, where I sat up all night giving orders, soon sank down on the floor, *dead drunk,* and was so in the morning. I sent for the Commander of the Rear Guard, Brig. General Gist, of S.C., and told him not to leave General B—— and if necessary, to put him in a wagon and haul him off. But under no circumstances to allow him to give an order. At Dalton I relieved General B of his command and he acknowledged the justice of it, but said it was the deepest mortification of his life.[29]

A few things speak circumstantially in Bragg's favor. Breckinridge had shown an uncharacteristic irritability in dealing with the courier from his escort on November 25. His failure to take an initial part in Bate's rearguard action after the rout, and the two hours preceding his order to Finley to withdraw during which his movements are unknown, could be evidence of some disorientation. The closest thing to corroborative testimony, however, comes from a reporter with the army, Peter W. Alexander, the "Sallust" of the Richmond *Daily Dispatch.* Writing from Dalton on December 2, he told his readers, "You will be surprised and mortified to learn that this army is not free from the vice of intemperance. I am referring to the painful subject here merely to warn those officers who are guilty of this abominable offense that if I forbear for the present to publish their names it is only to give them an opportunity to reform their habits and do their duty." He did not mention Breckinridge in connection with this intemperance, but the proximity of this paragraph to another telling of the Kentuckian's anticipated relief by Hindman caused some to fear that Breckinridge had been on Sallust's mind as he wrote. However, Bragg's claim still remains the only concrete accusation of drunkenness.[30]

In Breckinridge's favor, all of the above can be explained away, though with an equal lack of conclusiveness. His irritability could be accounted for by his lack of sleep during the past one or two nights, a factor which would also explain his supposedly sinking down on the floor of Bragg's hut at Chickamauga Station, unconscious. His failure to assist Bate in setting up the line of resistance and his two-hour absence might well have been due to the fact that portions of Sheridan's attacking division breached the ridge line between Breckinridge and Bate, driving the general back with the rout. And as for the report of Sallust, it was no secret at the time that he was a

29. *O.R.,* Ser. I, Vol. LII, Pt. 2, pp. 568, 573, 745–46; Bragg to Sykes, February 8, 1873, in Polk MSS. This Bragg letter has been published several times, including Polk, *Leonidas Polk,* II, 308–13.

30. Richmond *Daily Dispatch,* December 11, 1863; Willis Jones to William C. P. Breckinridge, December 12, 1863, in B. MSS.

mild partisan of Bragg. Even more important is the fact that on December 2, having heard that the commanding general had been relieved, he went to Bragg's headquarters and heard the general's own version of the recent disaster and its causes. Bragg spoke freely, the reporter believed, and it was that night that Sallust wrote the letter to his paper. Thus his statement about intemperance in the army and the implication that he knew the names of the offenders may well have been based on what Bragg told him, rather than first-hand observation. Most persuasive in Breckinridge's behalf, however, is the fact that Bragg took no overt action against him. Just before Shiloh, he had shown no hesitation about relieving George Crittenden and Brigadier General William Carroll from command for drunkenness, and having them court-martialed, with Breckinridge sitting on the court. After Murfreesboro, hearing that Cheatham had been intoxicated on the field during the battle, he called it to the attention of Polk, suggesting a reprimand. Now, even though he was leaving the army, there was no reason why Bragg could not have dealt similarly with Breckinridge. Yet Bragg did nothing except transfer Hindman's division into Breckinridge's corps, a move which, in reality, merely made official a reorganization that had been an accomplished fact since the night of November 24. This strongly suggests that Bragg's accusation in his letter to Davis was simply a blow in the dark, a last hit at an old enemy to whom he could attach nothing more conclusive. This view takes on added weight when an additional allegation in Bragg's letter to the president is considered, one in which he charges that Breckinridge's drunkenness had also prevented complete success at Murfreesboro. Why did Bragg wait a year to mention this? He showed no compunction about censuring Cheatham for intemperance at Stones River, so why would he not do the same to the Kentuckian? In view of the campaign Bragg waged against him following the battle, it hardly seems likely that the commanding general would withhold this most damning piece of evidence.[31]

The sum of this is that while it cannot positively be denied that Breckinridge was drunk during those four days, Bragg's charge is hardly sufficient to warrant the assumption that the Kentuckian was under such influence. And the commanding general's accusation is made all the more suspect when the second portion of his allegation against Breckinridge is examined.

Supposedly, the Kentuckian had been unfit for command from November 23–27, from the day before Lookout Mountain until the Battle of Ring-

31. J. Cutler Andrews, *The South Reports the Civil War* (Princeton, 1970), 376–77; McWhiney, *Bragg*, 217; Bragg to Sykes, February 8, 1873, in Polk MSS.

gold. However, on November 23, Breckinridge actually was creating a reserve for his line, had his men working on their defenses, and was positioning his brigades to make up for the loss of Cleburne from the line. The next day he was not so unfit that he could not assist Stevenson with the resistance on Lookout, first by orders, and later by personally leading a brigade to the mountain and giving instructions for the successful withdrawal. That night he had not been so drunk that Bragg did not listen to his counsel to remain on Missionary Ridge, nor was he unable to oversee bringing Stewart up out of the valley or the reinforcement of the ridge above Rossville. On the twenty-fifth he managed dispositions in the lines on the ridge and at its base, again led troops in person against Hooker's attack at Rossville, and was fit enough to meet two or more brigades with just two regiments. After the rout he oversaw withdrawing Bate and Finley.

That evening came his supposed collapse in Bragg's hut at Chickamauga Station, where, said Bragg, he remained until morning. While times are indefinite, it was well after nightfall—but before midnight—that Breckinridge arrived at the station and reported to Bragg. Certainly he seemed other than his normal self. The rout had shaken everyone, even the commanding general, who one soldier thought looked "so scared . . . hacked and whipped and mortified and chagrined at defeat." Then too, Breckinridge was suffering from bewilderment over Cabell, who might have been dead for all he knew then. All of this on top of his ill-advised habit of going two or more days without sleep in critical times might well have caused him to sink down on Bragg's floor. If Breckinridge had taken a few drinks that day, even just enough to scent his breath, it would have been enough for Bragg who, thanks largely to his wife, had become hypersensitive to drinking by his officers and men. But even if the Kentuckian did collapse on the floor, it was not for the entire night as Bragg alleges for, at midnight, he had taken headquarters of his own and was giving orders for the next day's movement to his divisions. This could not have been more than an hour or so after he first reported to Bragg. Also, Bragg said that he was still asleep on the floor in the morning, but in fact Breckinridge was out north of the station covering the retreat by battling Morgan's Federal brigade.[32]

Just as the above portions of Bragg's charge are incorrect or groundless, so is his statement that Gist had to watch over the Kentuckian demon-

32. Bragg to Sykes, February 8, 1873, in Polk MSS; Sam Watkins, Co. "Aytch," Maury's Grays, First Tennessee Regiment (Nashville, 1882), 126; McWhiney, Bragg, 161–62, 217; O.R., Ser. I, Vol. XXXI, Pt. 2, p. 690.

strated to be false. Indeed, during the remainder of the retreat, Breckinridge spent most of his time with Cleburne. Gist was not watching over him when he crossed Pigeon Mountain and then redirected the course of the rearguard, nor is he mentioned when Breckinridge assisted Cleburne for five hours in repelling the enemy at Ringgold. Indeed, there is no record anywhere that Breckinridge and Gist were even seen together at any time during the retreat, much less that the general was being kept from giving orders by his subordinate. And where Bragg charged him with unfitness throughout the retreat, Breckinridge actually took an active part in protecting the army's withdrawal, including his assistance at Ringgold, an action for which Cleburne would receive the thanks of Congress.

Finally, Bragg's statement that he relieved Breckinridge at Dalton, and that the Kentuckian acknowledged the justice of the act, is quite false. All Bragg did was to clear the way for Hindman to replace Breckinridge whenever he reached the army. Indeed, instead of being relieved, Breckinridge continued to exercise command of his corps for nearly two weeks after Bragg left for Richmond, not relinquishing it until December 15 upon Hindman's arrival.[33]

Thus Bragg's charges, both those made to Davis and those made after the war, are shot with holes through and through. They were one more example of his inability to accept the responsibility for his defeat. "We must mark the men," he said of his enemies in the army's command shortly after he was relieved. "They will bear watching." His charges against Breckinridge were his own last attempt to mark one of them. It would be charitable to presume that the errors and untruths in his accusations were the result of a temporary imbalance, rather than intentional misrepresentation, but the extent and number of those false accusations, coupled with Bragg's past record regarding Breckinridge, makes inescapable the conclusion that they were not.[34]

Breckinridge himself may never have known of Bragg's charges against him, for the documents containing them were not made public until after his death. However, it is likely that he did know of them, though he never made any answer or reply. It is sure, though, that he shared with Bragg the mortification over the collapse of his corps on November 25. It could not

33. O.R., Ser. I, Vol. XXXI, Pt. 3, p. 833; General Order No. 17, December 4, 1863, General Order No. 59, December 15, 1863, Military Departments, Orders and Circulars Received, First Kentucky Brigade, August 1863–January 1865, in Chap. 2, CCCXIV, NA.
34. Bragg to "Dear General," March 6, 1864, in Marcus J. Wright MSS, SHC.

be blamed on any failing of his, for he simply had too few men in too vulnerable a position, but that could hardly ease his embarrassment. Reputations in this war were made and maintained by success, whatever the circumstances; not by defeat with valid excuses. The rout of his corps was one of the most shameful days of the Confederacy, and it did not help that it could be compared with the successful stand of Hardee's corps on the right, regardless of the fact that Hardee had four divisions to Breckinridge's three and was fighting fewer Federals. Just as Bragg could not retain command after such a defeat, neither could Breckinridge. Guilty or not, such a disaster required a change in command. The general felt keenly both the justice and the injustice of thus having to share in the responsibility and the consequences for Missionary Ridge. A month after he was relieved by Hindman, when a civilian unwisely goaded him, "Well sir! How came we to lose Chattanooga?" Breckinridge replied with chilling coldness, "It is a long story," and turned away.[35]

35. Williams, *Diary from Dixie*, 362.

CHAPTER 6

A Worthy Successor of Jackson

Great as Breckinridge's dismay must have been after the disasters at Chattanooga, it was nothing compared to what many in the old Union believed that he suffered. If somehow the general obtained a copy of the December 7, 1863, issue of the New York *Times*, then he had the mixed pleasure of reading about his own death. At the same time, nothing could have brought home to him more the increased hatred felt for the man who stepped from the vice-presidential chair and the floor of the Senate, into Confederate gray. "If it be true, as is now positively declared," said the *Times*, "that a loyal bullet has sent this traitor to eternity, every loyal heart feels satisfaction and will not scruple to express it." Ordinarily the death of a worthy foe would evoke sympathy, but not in the case of Breckinridge, said the editorial. Such an event, if noticed at all, should be met with welcome. He was as bad as Davis, or worse. "Of all the accursed traitors of the land there has been none more heinously false than he—none whose memory will live in darker ignominy. God grant the country a speedy deliverance of all such parricides."

Even if the general did see the *Times* editorial, he had more urgent personal matters to worry him. It is uncertain whether or not he knew that Cabell was alive when he was captured, but Breckinridge did receive certain information that his son was a prisoner within a week after the rout. Taken first to Louisville, Cabell was sent to the prison camp at Johnson's Island on Lake Erie on December 5. The general, working through the War Department's Bureau of Exchange, found the location of the boy and was shortly able to get a letter off to him, while beginning the preliminary procedures for getting him exchanged. Meanwhile, as soon as he knew Cabell was safe, Breckinridge sent a dispatch to Mary at Tuskegee, Alabama, where she was slowly recovering from a near-fatal fight with malaria. Her health had been another worry, his constant companion, during the days at Chattanooga. While he sent some medicines to her, he did not at the time know how really serious her illness had been. When she appeared on the verge of death, her attendants urged her to send for the general, but Mary refused. "Not yet," she said, "if he left the army at this time General Bragg might use it as an occasion to injure him." Now, however, convalescent, she was rejoiced to hear that Cabell was safe. "I just made a promise that if I could hear he was not wounded I would never shed another tear," she wrote her husband on receiving the good news, "but sometimes in the silent hours of the night unbidden tears will steal down my cheek." [1]

With affairs of his widely scattered family somewhat in order, Breckinridge settled down to camp life with the army. His standing with his soldiers, always high, was evidently enhanced as shown by the kindnesses shown them here in Dalton, while his relations with his fellow generals were most cordial after Bragg left. Johnston liked him, as did Hardee and, when Hindman relieved him on December 15, he still remained a valued member of the army's chief councils. It was in these meetings that, after a two-year hiatus, he dabbled briefly in politics.

By this time, it was obvious to almost everyone that the Confederacy's chief military deficiency was manpower; there simply were not enough men in uniform. Substitutions, draft exemptions, age limits, and the interference of state and local officials, were keeping thousands of men out of the army, where they were sorely needed, especially in the Western Department. Breckinridge, Hardee, Hindman, Cleburne, and a number of chief officers of the army discussed this need on more than one occasion, and the result was a memorial to Congress drafted by one of them and signed by all on December 17. It was their opinion, they said, that all troops now in service should be held for the remainder of the war. At the same time, all white males between eighteen and fifty should be put in the service, pending physical fitness of course, and at the same time they recommended drafting other eligible men between the ages of fifteen and eighteen, and fifty and sixty. They urged the prohibition of substitutions, in which one man paid another to take his place for him in the army. Breckinridge was particularly adamant over this point during the discussions.

The generals also asked that exemptions be abolished, except in necessary

1. Mary C. Breckinridge to Breckinridge, December 5, 1863, in Breckinridge Service Record, NA; Robert Ould to Breckinridge, December 18, 1864, in Confederate Collection of Stanley E. Butcher; J. Cabell Breckinridge, Service Record, NA; Maltby, *Mary Cyrene Breckinridge*, 2–3.

cases for civil officers, that discharges, furloughs, and details of able-bodied men to noncombatant jobs, be curtailed as much as possible. Toward this end, they suggested that Negroes, free and slave, be enlisted as cooks, hospital stewards, teamsters, and workmen. At the same time, to increase the morale of the men then in arms, they recommended a raise in pay and a subsistence allowance when rations themselves were not available. And all of this must be done quickly, they emphasized, before the opening of the spring campaign. Even the lapse of thirty days would make the situation much worse. It was a hopeful effort, this memorial, and it set a precedent in communications between the army and Congress, where it was well received. The officers signing it were so impressed with its urgent importance that they tried to persuade Breckinridge to go to Richmond and present it personally, "in such manner as may suggest itself to you." The general had already obtained a leave of absence to go to the capital, and Hardee suggested that he could extend it should Breckinridge accept this "semi-official mission." The Kentuckian declined, however, wishing to avoid all semblance of playing in politics. Besides, as he could have predicted, the letter was lost in committee in both houses of Congress and was never acted upon.[2]

Cleburne signed the memorial with some reservations. During the discussions of the high command he had been formulating a solution of his own to the manpower problem, and on January 2, 1864, he put it in writing. He would arm the slaves in grand numbers, bring them to the battlefields to fight with their masters, and promise as reward for their blood, freedom. It was a radical proposal that could shake the foundations of a confederacy begun largely in the interest of preserving slavery. At the same time, foreign opposition to slavery had been a stumbling block in Confederate diplomacy since the beginning, and a significant factor in British reluctance to grant recognition. Thus, Cleburne's proposal, radical though it was, deserved the most serious consideration. His division commanders approved the idea and, on January 8, in a meeting at Hardee's headquarters, Cleburne presented the paper to the rest of the army's general officers.

Breckinridge was in agreement with Cleburne and, indeed, had been for a week or more prior to the presentation of the memorial. On December

2. James H. McNeilly, "In Winter Quarters at Dalton, Ga." *Confederate Veteran*, XXVIII (April, 1920), 131; Frank E. Vandiver (ed.), "Proceedings of the First Confederate Congress, Fourth Session," *SHSP*, L (1953), 140–42; Richmond *Daily Dispatch*, December 30, 1863; Williams, *Diary from Dixie*, 367; J. S. Johnston to Breckinridge, December 24, 1863, in J. Stoddard Johnston Service Record, NA.

28, 1863, Breckinridge expressed himself in favor of the idea of raising 300,000 Negroes for the service and beginning them in drill. His only reservation was an uncertainty that the proper time to do so had yet arrived. Hardee and Johnston agreed with Cleburne, but the commanding general, thinking the paper more political than military in nature, decided not to send it on to the War Department.

Nevertheless, thanks to the hostility of Walker to the idea, as well as his jealousy of Cleburne, a copy of the document did reach Richmond in January, but only Davis, his cabinet, and a very few others knew of it. Although Breckinridge had not signed the paper, it was apparently thought that he and Hindman had some part in its origins along with Cleburne, the result of a secret meeting Postmaster General John H. Reagan recalled. Whatever the case, Davis and his cabinet disapproved of the proposal, suppressed knowledge of it from the public, and directed that Cleburne not pursue the subject any farther. Nevertheless, barely two weeks after the meeting at Hardee's, Breckinridge was more convinced than ever of the necessity of arming the slaves, and was not reluctant to say so.[3]

He was not present at the meeting at Hardee's. A day or two before, he went to Richmond on leave. Despite the unfavorable attitude with which many looked on the general after the Chattanooga fiasco, both houses of the Confederate Congress passed unanimous resolutions on his arrival, inviting him to privileged seats on their floors, a rare honor for any general. An even better welcome awaited Breckinridge with the number of Kentuckians then in Richmond. Preston, Morgan, the convalescing Hood, and a number of others had already formed one of the most memorable contingents the capital had seen. They were here to lobby for another Kentucky campaign. The general found equally good company at the Ballard House when he checked in. Besides Morgan, his fellow boarders included Lee's renowned cavalryman J. E. B. Stuart, and the leader of the Army of Northern Virginia's famed Third Corps, Lieutenant General A. P. Hill. Besides the men of Longstreet's corps, these were the first of Lee's officers that Breckinridge had the opportunity to meet and talk with, and he met Lee himself sometime during his stay. They had met once or twice before the war, but still knew each other only by reputation.[4]

3. Buck, *Cleburne and His Command*, 189, 191; *O.R.*, Ser. I, Vol. LII, Pt. 1, pp. 586–93; Wirt A. Cade (ed.), *Two Soldiers: Campaign Diaries of Thomas J. Key & Robert J. Campbell* (Chapel Hill, N.C., 1938), 16; Connelly, *Autumn of Glory*, 318–21; Williams, *Diary from Dixie*, 362; John H. Reagan, *Memoirs: With Special Reference to Secession and the Civil War* (New York, 1906), 148.

4. Williams, *Diary from Dixie*, 353; Vandiver, "First Confederate Congress, Fourth

Breckinridge did have some business to conduct in Richmond and, characteristically, much of it dealt with his men of the Kentucky Brigade. For some weeks he had been attempting to get the Orphans mounted. The proposition was originally put to Secretary of War James Seddon back in December, and he had directed the general to confer with J. E. Johnston on the matter. Johnston was not enthusiastic because the brigade, "though small, is an excellent one," one of the very finest in the army. On January 15, Breckinridge and the other Kentucky generals addressed a letter to Davis proposing that all of the Kentucky troops in the service—and they were widely scattered—be consolidated into one special state organization. This would raise their morale and *espirit*, while providing an inducement to those Kentuckians not in the service to enlist, that they might serve in such a special unit. Mounting the Kentuckians would do further service by giving them a change, and at the same time make them a natural organization for raids into their native state. Nothing came of it, but this proposal was an excellent example of the ever-recurrent interest in Kentucky. Richmond was packed with Bluegrass men who fed the government's mania for the lost Kentucky. Indeed, Longstreet, Beauregard, and even Lee, were making proposals for invasion. Bragg, always deluded by the fantasy of a Confederate conquest of Kentucky, was now in a policy making position, and helped influence Davis' receptiveness to such proposals. Breckinridge, always anxious to return to the Bluegrass, was a natural participant in the perennial movement.[5]

The general's other business here was to seek an appointment for Clifton to a cadetship with the army or the navy. Speaking to J. M. Elliott, Congressman from Kentucky, he expressed his son's wishes, and soon had him appointed to the Confederate Naval Academy as a midshipman.[6]

Session," 216; *Journal of Congress*, III, 608; Invitation of House of Representatives, January 11, 1864, in Breckinridge Service Record, NA; Betsy Fleet and John D. P. Fuller (eds.), *Green Mount: A Virginia Plantation Family During the Civil War* (Lexington, Ky., 1962), 305; W. C. P. Breckinridge to Issa Breckinridge, January 14, 20, 1864, in B. MSS; W. G. Bean (ed.), "Memoranda of Conversations Between General Robert E. Lee and William Preston Johnston, May 7, 1868, and March 18, 1870," *Virginia Magazine of History and Biography*, LXXIII (October, 1965), 479.

5. *O.R.*, Ser. I, Vol. XXXI, Pt. 3, p. 878, Vol. XXXII, Pt. 2, p. 520; Breckinridge, Simon Buckner, John Morgan and Joseph Lewis to James A. Seddon, January 15, 1864, in Davis MSS, LHAC; Thompson, *Orphan Brigade*, 28; Morning Report, December 1, 1863, in Chap. 2, CCCXIV, NA; Connelly and Jones, *Politics of Command*, 54–55, 73–75, 77–78.

6. R. G. H. Kean to R. E. Lee, February 26, 1864, John M. Elliott to Stephen Mallory, February 5, 1864, Elliott to Seddon, February 6, 1864, in Clifton R. Breckinridge Service Record, NA.

The balance of Breckinridge's stay in the Confederate capital was given over to society with old friends, and to a much needed rest. He kept company with Mrs. Chesnut much of the time, attending plays, presidential receptions, the popular taffy parties, and made a good show of being his usual cheerful self. He observed Congress in session, and sadly informed J. S. Johnston that "there is a good deal of antagonism and bad feeling here. Congress seems, however to be making up, yet its action, knowing as we do the urgent need, is distressingly slow." But beneath all this, Breckinridge was tired, troubled. Many in the city held him responsible for the loss of Chattanooga, and some did not hesitate to say so to his face. At the same time, the situation of the Army of Tennessee, as well as that of the Confederacy at large, had him troubled, thinking more and more of the need for men and Cleburne's proposal, and anxious for the future. At one of the taffy parties at Mrs. Chesnut's, he paced up and down her drawing room "like a caged lion," talking about the military situation while the others played. His own problems with Bragg, his relief by Hindman, and his memories of the terrible days in the summer and fall of 1861, harassed him as well. While visiting Hood in his room at the Spottswood, Breckinridge remarked almost enviously: "My dear Hood, here you are beloved by your fellow-soldiers, and, although badly shattered, with the comfort of having done a noble service, and without trouble or difficulty with any man." Worst of all, however, was what two years of the occupation of killing was doing to his sensitive nature. Death had taken a score of friends— Hanson, Helm, Graves, A. S. Johnston, George Johnson—left men like Hood with brilliant glory and mangled bodies, pitted Kentuckian against Kentuckian, and sent his son Cabell to a northern prison camp. The memories of battlefields after the fight hurt him the most. He was haunted by the moonlit hell of the night after Chickamauga.

Walking home with Mrs. Chesnut after *The Rivals*, he pondered it all in the 3 A.M. moonlight. "You have spent a jolly evening," she said. "I do not know," came Breckinridge's reply. "I have asked myself more than once tonight: 'Are you the same man who stood gazing down on the faces of the dead on that awful battlefield; the soldiers lying there, they stare at you with their eyes wide open. Is this the same world? Here and there?' " [7]

The general left Richmond to return to the army on February 5, teasing Hood a last time by giving a farewell kiss to his cousin Sally Preston, with

7. Breckinridge to J. S. Johnston, January 19, 1864, in J. S. Johnston MSS, FC; Williams, *Diary from Dixie*, 353, 355, 362, 366, 368–69, 370–71, 374–75; Hood, *Advance and Retreat*, 68; Martin and Avary (eds.), *Diary from Dixie*, 286.

whom Hood was in love, while he enviously looked on. An order had gone out the day before for him to report to Cooper for assignment, though, whether the general received the order before he left, or not until his arrival back in Dalton, is unknown. Just the day after he left, the rumor was out in Richmond that Breckinridge was going to be given command of the Department of Western Virginia. It is most likely that this subject had been under discussion between the general and the president or Seddon during his visit, so neither the order nor the rumor must have come as a surprise. On February 15 Breckinridge was officially relieved from duty with the Army of Tennessee, and ordered to report to Richmond.[8]

Many were truly grieved to see him leave. Hardee had been counting on him to command his old division in a newly organized corps, and J. E. Johnston lamented losing one of the few subordinates with whom he could get along without jealousies or rivalries. Saddest of all, of course, were the men of the general's division, and the Kentuckians in particular. When they found out that they were not to accompany him, they gathered outside the Anderson house in Dalton, his headquarters, and called on him to come out. He was met by a wave of cheers and applause such as he had not heard since 1861, but declined to make "a set speech," thinking that Kentuckians had heard enough of that from him and others in 1860. He spoke simply to testify his love for his old comrades, to explain that he had tried his best there and in Richmond to have them accompany him, and that their outstanding service in the past had been their own undoing. Indeed, he still had not given up hope and promised to keep trying, a declaration that was answered by shouts of "We will go with you anywhere." Meanwhile, he reassured their faith in the ultimate success of the Confederacy—a subject upon which he was himself uncertain—then retired amid the shouts and cheers of his loving fellow Kentuckians. The other two brigades of his division said their own farewell to him with the presentation of a handsome dress sword, inscribed in gold as "A mark of esteem and admiration for their much loved Commander." In view of the sentiment it conveyed, Breckinridge probably overlooked the misspelling of his name on the inscription.[9]

The general was reunited with Mary briefly at Dalton, where she was so

8. Williams, *Diary from Dixie*, 374–75; *O.R.*, Ser. I, Vol. XXXII, Pt. 2, pp. 669, 743; Jones, *War Clerk's Diary*, II, 144.

9. Hughes, *Hardee*, 193; *O.R.*, Ser. I, Vol. XXXII, Pt. 2, pp. 714, 727; Lewis to Breckinridge, May 2, 1864, in B. MSS; Young, *Reminiscences*, 90; Thompson, *Orphan Brigade*, 234; New York *Times*, February 28, 1864. The sword is in the possession of Mrs. J. C. Breckinridge.

busy nursing wounded soldiers and sewing for them that she feared she would be unable to join him for the trip back to Richmond. However, she soon found herself able to go after all, as did J. Stoddard Johnston. With the capture of Major Wilson at Missionary Ridge, Breckinridge had finally made Johnston his adjutant, and the three left around February 18, putting the Army of Tennessee and all the memories it held for the general behind them, and heading for a new assignment, a new theater of war.[10]

The Breckinridges spent about two weeks in the capital while he consulted with Davis and Seddon over the pending assignment. On February 25, Cooper made the rumor official by ordering the general to relieve Major General Samuel Jones, the present commander of the Trans-Alleghany or Western Department of Virginia. For the next week, Breckinridge was engaged in briefings and meetings with Lee and others to prepare himself for his new command, and then, early in March, leaving Mary behind temporarily, he set out for Dublin, his headquarters. Arriving on the evening of March 4, he relieved Jones the next day, and began at once the most important military service he would render the Confederacy.[11]

The department was no plum. Few such geographical commands in the South covered more ground with so few available resources and men, and it had been the burial ground of more than one reputation. Originally it had been a part of the Department of Northwestern Virginia, a mammoth command that went through a succession of generals, including Lee, before the lower portion of it was incorporated into a separate area, the Department of Southwestern Virginia. In November, 1862, it was reorganized once more into the present shape, and Jones was assigned to the command. Since then the department's territorial limits had been expanded, though never precisely defined, and Breckinridge was confronted by a staggering amount of country to defend. Roughly, the command included all of Virginia west of the Blue Ridge Mountains and south of Staunton, in the Shenandoah Valley; the southern portion of the new Union state of West Virginia, from Greenbrier County on the east, to the Kentucky border, and as much of Kentucky as was "necessary," meaning as much as could be held. In all, it comprised portions of three states, two of which never left

10. W. C. P. Breckinridge to Issa Breckinridge, February 10, 1864, in B. MSS; Mary C. Breckinridge to Breckinridge, February 15, 1864, in Breckinridge Service Record, NA; Mary C. Breckinridge to Ann Johnson, February 16, 1864, in Mary C. Breckinridge MSS.
11. Williams, Diary from Dixie, 385; J. Stoddard Johnston, "Sketches of Operations of General John C. Breckinridge, No. 1," SHSP, VII (June, 1879), 257; O.R., Ser. I, Vol. XXXIII, 1198, 1210–11.

the Union. From northeast to southwest it ran almost two hundred miles, and was ninety miles deep; eighteen thousand square miles of the most rugged, mountainous, and in many places impenetrable, wilderness in the Confederacy. Just its exposed front, that subject to enemy attack, formed three sides of its rectangular shape, and gave Breckinridge a line over four hundred miles long to watch over.[12]

It was important territory. In Wythe County were located the chief lead mines of the Confederacy, the major source of supply for both Lee and Johnston. East of the mines, in Smyth County, lay Saltville, where almost all of the salt for that part of the South east of Mississippi was mined and processed. In the southern, or "upper," part of the Shenandoah grew crops that helped feed Lee's Army of Northern Virginia, while the rest of the department in general had been used as a source of supply for foodstuffs and forage for some time, often to its own neglect. And through it all ran the Virginia and Tennessee Railroad, once the principal lifeline of communication between Virginia and the Deep South, and still a major objective of Federal raids even though it was effectively cut by Burnside's presence at Knoxville. Too, within its mountainous reaches lived one of the greatest concentrations of tories, Union sympathizers, in the Confederacy. They formed secret societies, engaged in minor espionage, and actively encouraged and protected deserters from the army. They had to be suppressed before they could present a serious threat to the security of the army. Most important of all, however, were the roads into the department. Through a score of mountain passes and gaps lay more invasion routes than a full army could adequately guard, and each one presented a potential back door to Lee and Richmond east of the Blue Ridge. Holding this part of Virginia was vital. Indeed, Lee told Davis six weeks before, when a new commander was being sought, "so important do I consider the maintenance of Western Virginia to the successful conduct of the war," that he was willing to give up any one of his best officers—excluding only A. P. Hill—to take over its defense.[13]

Thus Breckinridge came on the scene. A variety of reasons for his appointment present themselves. One possibility, though unsupported except by the feelings of some of the Orphans, is that it was Bragg's work. The department was notorious—Breckinridge was its ninth commander—and Bragg, now in Richmond and with free access to the president's ear, might

12. William P. Amann, *Personnel of the Civil War* (New York, 1961), I, 198, 202–203; *O.R.*, General Index, xlvi.

13. *O.R.*, Ser. I, Vol. XXXIII, 1124.

have seen in such a move a final blow at his old enemy. However, the most likely explanation for his assignment was the one given by Seddon when he told Jones of his pending relief. Jones had lost the trust of the people in the department, Seddon wrote, and considerations had pointed out to him and Davis that Breckinridge, "an officer of distinction in the Western army, who has political as well as military influences to aid his administration," was better adapted for the command.[14]

On taking over the department, Breckinridge found his new command in terrible shape—disorganized, lax, with few of its vital services operating efficiently—and the men themselves scattered all over in the vain hope of covering all points at once. There were two small infantry brigades under Colonel John McCausland and Brigadier General John Echols, totaling 1,268 and 1,143 respectively, a total of 1,769 cavalry divided into two brigades—one of them scattered and unorganized—and a battalion of couriers, and a few batteries mustering only fourteen guns. In all, his total effectives numbered 5,175. There were a number of other troops belonging to the department who were absent on detached service to Buckner, commanding the Department of East Tennessee, including a brigade under Brigadier General Gabriel C. Wharton, the Forty-fifth Virginia doing post duty at Saltville—it would not be attached to Breckinridge's department until March 19—and an additional cavalry brigade led by one of Stuart's finest pupils, Brigadier General William E. "Grumble" Jones.[15]

Breckinridge's troops were so widely spread that, barring staff and escort, there were few to meet him in Dublin except Cabell, now exchanged, and immediately appointed aide-de-camp. The general's first action was well advised, one that Jones should have performed some time before; he set out on a four-hundred-mile ride of his entire line to inspect troops, get the feel of his generals, become acquainted with the territory he must defend, and select suitable places for fortifications. The ride took over three weeks, used up two horses, and thoroughly wore him out. "Everybody is favorably impressed by the new commander," wrote a correspondent at Monroe Draught. Breckinridge now knew his department, its strengths and its weaknesses. After a good sleep he would be ready to meet them both.[16]

14. *Ibid.*, Vol. LI, Pt. 2, p. 820.
15. *Ibid.*, Vol. XXXIII, 1107, 1203.
16. *Ibid.*, 716, 1211; J. Stoddard Johnston, "Sketches of Operations, No. 1," p. 258; John McDaniel to Breckinridge, March 9, 1864, D. M. Hayden to Breckinridge, March 27, 1864, in B. MSS; Breckinridge to Braxton Bragg, April 27, 1864, in Dearborn Collection; Breckinridge to Hayden, March 30, 1864, in Palmer MSS, WRHS; Staunton (Va.) *Spectator*, March 22, 1864.

Indeed, the general began working on his command while he was still in the saddle. On March 17 he officially appointed Stoddard Johnston his adjutant, and started a stream of orders through the department. His first concern was his limited manpower. He reduced details, canceled furloughs, and called in shirkers. By March 30, when he reached Dublin once more, he had already increased the number of effectives in the department by 10 percent, to 5,667. Thanks to his measures, among them the organization of his loose cavalry regiments into an additional brigade under Brigadier General Albert Jenkins, Breckinridge could look with satisfaction on his report for the end of April, which showed a total effective force of 6,538, an increase of 1,363—over 26 percent—above the department's strength just two months before.[17]

Solving this problem of manpower, however, only contributed to another, supply. Not only did he not have enough food and forage for his own men, but the commissary general, Lucius B. Northrop, was ordering what he did have out of the department for Lee's use. Breckinridge had tangled with Northrop before when he commanded Middle Tennessee during Bragg's retreat from Perryville, and, like most other officers in the service, he harbored a growing resentment of Northrop's mismanagement. Nevertheless, all through March, Breckinridge tried to get along on what was left him. Soon impressment—offering the farmer government price in Confederate paper, then confiscating if he refused—seemed to be the only answer. "This odious recourse was only resorted to under extreme necessity," said Breckinridge.

Even at this he was thwarted by Northrop who, besides ordering his own supplies out of the department and ignoring Breckinridge's requisitions, sent orders to the general's quartermasters to cease the impressment. The orders were not even sent through Breckinridge, as they should have been. In this state of affairs, Breckinridge decided by the end of March to take drastic measures. Northrop had ignored his requisitions; very well, then, henceforth Breckinridge would ignore Northrop's supply demands. From now on the supplies raised in the Department of Western Virginia would be used in that department, and Breckinridge so notified Cooper, adding that this policy would be pursued until such a time as he received orders to stop, not from Northrop, but directly from the adjutant general.

17. General Orders No.'s 16–29, March 13–April 24, 1864, Military Departments, General Orders and Circulars, Department of West Virginia, 1862–1864, in Chap. 2, LXII, Special Order No. 110, April 23, 1864, Chap. 2, LXIII, NA; *O.R.*, Ser. I, Vol. XXXIII, 1250, 1292, 1298–99, 1334.

When complaint of the hardship this might bring on the army in eastern Virginia was raised by a citizen, Breckinridge frankly replied, "I would say 'Peccavi' but for . . . the highly respectable declaration that who so provideth not for his own household is worse than an infidel." By the end of April, thanks to these and other measures, Breckinridge finally had the collection and disbursement of meat and other rations regularized. The spring grass was late in coming this year but, by the beginning of May, the horses, too, were eating regularly.[18]

All the while that he was putting his department in shape, Breckinridge's own defenses were constantly on his mind. On his arrival in western Virginia, he received from Echols a few maps of the territory he would command and, a few days later, Lee sent down a map of the Valley which showed the various roads leading through the mountain passes into West Virginia. Along with it he sent a diagram of a defensive line chosen for the area some time before by Major General Jubal A. Early, including directions for earthworks and abatis at proper places. The chosen line had been used with some effectiveness in the past, and Lee now recommended that Breckinridge exercise himself to see the works completed, including sending seven hundred men to aid in their construction. In this he was to cooperate with Brigadier General John Imboden, commanding the Valley District, or the Shenandoah.[19]

Breckinridge had his own ideas about defending the department, and chose his own line. Its right rested at Colonel William L. Jackson's position near Warm Springs, then moved southwest, including all of Allegheny, much of Greenbrier, all of Monroe, as well as portions of several other West Virginia counties. Generally it ran fifty miles in advance of Early's line. Breckinridge placed his forces in such a way that they covered all of the main roads leading into the department. Echols, at Monroe Draught, protected the routes from Lewisburg and White Sulphur Springs, while McCausland, now at New River Narrows, would be moved a few miles west to Princeton, Mercer County. Breckinridge regarded this place as the

18. *O.R.*, Ser. I, Vol. XXXII, Pt. 3, p. 749, Vol. XXXIII, 1254, 1289–90; Special Order No. 64, March 5, 1864, Special Order No. 71, March 12, 1864, Special Order No. 99, April 10, 1864, in Chap. 2, LXIII, NA; H. King to Breckinridge, April 11, 1864, F. M. Mullin to Breckinridge, April 24, 1864, in B. MSS; Breckinridge to John Miller, April 16, 1864, in F. L. Pleadwell MSS, Smithsonian Institution, Washington, D.C.; General Order No. 32, May 1, 1864, Chap. 2, LXII, NA.

19. *O.R.*, Ser. I, Vol. XXXIII, 1211; Lee to Breckinridge, March 9, 1864, Military Departments, Letters and Telegrams Sent Army of Northern Virginia, March 1863–March 1864, Chap. 2, LXXXIV, NA.

key to the southern half of the department, since it covered every principal road leading to the railroad, the lead mines, and the salt works.[20]

The line showed excellent planning, and Breckinridge wasted no time in putting it into effect. Echols went to work immediately constructing his defenses for his brigade, while Jackson's men were put to work at Warm Springs, and along the Cow Pasture River. When Wharton arrived late in April, Breckinridge stationed him at the Narrows and sent McCausland to Princeton. The Kentuckian wished to close every possible avenue of invasion, and he admitted that it would be difficult. "It is hard work with the troops we have to defend the salt-works, the lead mines, the railroad, the iron-works, &c., dotted over an extended country accessible to attack from many quarters," he told Echols. "Yet I will do all I can short of entire and fatal separation of the troops." [21]

Thus, at the end of six weeks in command of the department, Breckinridge had accomplished much in the organization and building of his command, increasing its efficiency and morale, providing rations, constructing works and laying out a well-conceived defensive line, and distributing his men according to a viable, though hopeful, defensive plan of action. And he had improved relations with the citizens, too, despite impressment. He was feeding destitute families out of his own meagerly stocked warehouses, letting men off duty to help with the crops, and keeping a tighter rein on the conduct of his soldiers. On April 27, 1864, when he reported on the work of his first six weeks, he gave evidence of considerable progress toward those goals. Though he did not say so, he might have boasted that in less than two months he had put the department in better all-round shape—save only in the ever-troublesome area of supply—than it had enjoyed at any time since the beginning of the war. But this was not the time for speaking or reflecting on such things. Indeed, as he told the men of Echols' command at Monroe two weeks before, this "was no time to dwell on the past"; "the time for speeches has passed," he said, "and ... the hour for action has arrived." [22]

Almost from the day he assumed command, Breckinridge received a

20. *O.R.*, Ser. I, Vol. XXXIII, 1231.
21. *Ibid.*, 1231, 1239, 1323; Marshall to Breckinridge, March 21, 1864, Chap. 2, LXXXIV, NA; Special Order No. 92, April 3, 1864, Special Order No. 104, April 16, 1864, Special Order No. 117, April 30, 1864, in Chap. 2, LXIII, NA.
22. Breckinridge to Bragg, April 27, 1864, in Davis MSS, LHAC; McDaniel to Breckinridge, March 9, 1864, Robert M. Johnson to Breckinridge, April 11, 1864, Thomas Hunt to Breckinridge, April 12, 1864, all in B. MSS; *O.R.*, Ser. I, Vol. XXXIII, 1211; James Z. McChesney to Lucy Johnson, April 12, 1864, in James Z. McChesney MSS, Confederate Collection of Stanley E. Butcher.

steady flow of reports on anticipated or threatened Federal raids into the department. Events took on more urgency late in April when reports came from Richmond that a raid was pending. On April 27 definite word came that Brigadier General William Averell was advancing with his division. Breckinridge already had Echols and McCausland under orders to be ready to move at a moment's notice, but now he was faced with the dilemma of anticipating the route that the enemy would choose. He was prudently fearful of separating his forces too much, and consequently ordered Echols and McCausland to be ready to support each other, one falling back from the enemy while the other advanced to its aid in case of attack. Scouts were to be kept out well in advance. This was especially important since Breckinridge was unsure whether Averell would advance east or west of New River. Up to this time, he had actually toyed with the idea of advancing himself and was particularly interested in raiding the Baltimore and Ohio as it passed through northern West Virginia, but now this would have to wait. "Matters look too imminent for delay," he told Echols.[23]

Grant, whose victory at Chattanooga had won him command of all the Union armies, was now in Virginia overseeing the Army of the Potomac. Brilliant strategist that he was, he conceived the first coordinated offensive for all fronts combined that the North had yet experienced. With the opening of the spring campaign, Mobile, Alabama, would be attacked, Sherman would commence a drive against J. E. Johnston in Georgia, and Grant would move on Lee from three directions. The Army of the Potomac, under his direct command, would advance through a wooded tangle called the Wilderness; a separate force led by Breckinridge's old Democratic ally Benjamin Butler, would move up the James River peninsula on Richmond; and yet another army was to take the Valley and Breckinridge's department, thereby turning Lee's vulnerable left flank and rear. If the plan were successful, Lee would have no choice but to abandon almost all of Virginia, or else be caught simultaneously from three sides.[24]

The man selected for command of the operations in the Valley was Major General Franz Sigel, a German immigrant, and a veteran of campaigns in Missouri, Arkansas, and Virginia. At his disposal were between twenty-two to twenty-five thousand troops aligned between his headquarters at Martinsburg, and the Kanawah. The commander of the force in West Virginia was Sigel's capable subordinate, Brigadier General George

23. *O.R.*, Ser. I, Vol. XXXIII, 1236, 1287, 1295–97, 1301, 1305, 1310–11, 1318–19, 1322–25; Breckinridge to Lee, April 28, 1864, in James W. Eldridge Collection, HL.
24. *O.R.*, Ser. I, Vol. XXXIII, 1295.

Crook, who had some six thousand infantry, and about twenty-five hundred cavalry under Averell. His part in the plan was to move against the railroad, destroy as much of it as possible and anything else that presented itself, and then capture Lynchburg. While he was doing this, Sigel was to march on and threaten or capture Staunton, distracting Breckinridge. This would give the Federals control of the Valley, a back door to Lee's rear, and disrupt severely communications and supply. The Shenandoah's grain crop, vital for feeding Lee's army, could thus be denied to him. The operation, if conducted well, would be disastrous for the Confederacy.[25]

The importance that Lee attached to western Virginia is evident in the hurried reinforcements ordered to Breckinridge in the first days of May. On the second, Richmond ordered Morgan's cavalry out of East Tennessee and officially placed it under Breckinridge's command. At the same time, Lee arranged with the governor and adjutant general of Virginia for the Corps of Cadets of the Virginia Military Institute at Lexington to report to the Kentuckian for orders, 291 strong. This put at Breckinridge's disposal a total force of approximately 9,000 infantry and cavalry. With still no definite information of an enemy advance, he continued construction on his defenses. But on May 3 came information from Imboden that Sigel had moved out of Martinsburg and occupied Winchester, some twenty miles south. Although Imboden reported only 3,000 Federals, there were, in fact, nearly 9,000. At the same time reports came in from Echols and Jones which gave definite information that Averell was on the move with 2,000 cavalry. By the next day Breckinridge also knew of the advance of Crook's infantry. Thus, there was a definite threat from over 8,000 Federals moving on his front, while more were coming down from the north to meet Imboden, who had barely 1,600 to resist them.[26]

Now the general was faced with a real dilemma. He could not move to meet either of the advancing foes with a sufficient force, without leaving the way clear for the other. If he divided his command to meet both of them, then neither half would be strong enough to expect success. Lee made the decision a little easier for him by directing that he take command of Imboden, but still left direction of the Valley and the department up to

25. *Ibid.*, 765, 874, Vol. XXXVII, Pt. 1, pp. 9–10, 368–69.
26. *Ibid.*, Vol. XXXVII, Pt. 1, pp. 707–12, Vol. LI, Pt. 2, p. 887; John D. Imboden, "The Battle of New Market," in Johnson and Buel (eds.), *Battles and Leaders*, IV, 480. These figures, and all those stated in this chapter, are based on intensive research into some three hundred different sources used in preparing a history of the Battle of New Market now awaiting publication. They are too numerous to cite here.

Breckinridge, saying only that he wanted Sigel to be engaged in battle, or at least drawn away from his threatening position on Lee's left.[27]

With Lee's vague instructions, Breckinridge lost no time in making up his mind what to do. He would take the infantry from the department, four thousand strong, and join Imboden, who had called out some reserves to augment his own command. Their strength, combined with the Corps of Cadets, would give Breckinridge about six thousand of all arms. This would leave only the six hundred infantry of the Forty-fifth Virginia, and about four thousand cavalry under Jenkins and Jones in the department. Then, when Jenkins reported a sudden threat in his front, Breckinridge had no choice but to detach McCausland to him temporarily. Originally he had planned to take Jackson's cavalry with him, but this, too, he was forced to leave behind. As a result, he would have not more than twenty-eight hundred infantry and artillerymen going with him. Immediately he put Echols and Wharton en route for Jackson River Depot, where they would board cars for the trip north.[28]

The logistics of the movement were complex. Echols was thirty-six miles from the depot, and Wharton sixty. They would be arriving at different times, and so, in order to get as many men on their way as possible, he arranged for cars to leave the depot on the morning of May 7, that evening, and the next morning. Also rations would be needed, and while ordering out three days' allotment of meat for forty-five hundred men, he also directed that an equal amount be waiting for him at Staunton. When the railroad failed him, elements of Wharton's command had to march over one hundred miles to reach Staunton. After seeing to these arrangements, Breckinridge himself, with his staff, put their essentials on a pack mule and started out ahead of the command for Staunton, arriving on the evening of May 8.[29]

When he reached Staunton Breckinridge immediately went to work. He called out the Augusta County reserves and awaited the arrival of Echols and Wharton. They came in on May 10–11, and meanwhile he sent out an

27. O.R., Ser. I, Vol. XXXVII, Pt. 1, pp. 712–16.

28. Special Order No. 121, May 5, 1864, Breckinridge to King, May 5, 1864, Chap. 2, LXIII, NA; O.R., Ser. I, Vol. XXXVII, Pt. 1, pp. 713, 721, 723.

29. Special Order No. 121, May 5, 1864, Chap. 2, LXIII, NA; O.R., Ser. I, Vol. XXXVII, Pt. 1, pp. 712, 716–19; Johnston, "Sketches of Operations, No. 1," p. 258; John C. Breckinridge, Report of the Battle of New Market, New Market File, Alumni File Room, Virginia Military Institute, Lexington, hereinafter cited as Breckinridge, Report, New Market File, V.M.I.

order for the Corps of Cadets to come up. Breckinridge spent the next two days organizing a defense. During that time, disheartening news came in daily. Crook had advanced toward Princeton, sending a single regiment as a diversion by way of the road to Lewisburg. McCausland had all but abandoned Princeton as he hastened to Dublin to join Breckinridge on the march and, as a result, Crook took the place with barely a struggle. This was on May 6. The next two days Crook employed in moving toward Dublin and, on May 9, Jenkins and McCausland met him in battle on Cloyd's Mountain, shortly in advance of the depot. Jenkins was killed and the rest of the force driven back. Crook took Dublin, destroying some quantity of stores and equipment. He remained in the vicinity for three more days before retiring back into West Virginia. Meanwhile, Averell had ridden through Tazewell, met determined resistance in an attempt to take Wytheville, and then moved on to Dublin and Christianburg, where he destroyed railroad shops, some rolling stock, and about four miles of track. Then fearful of Confederate reinforcements believed coming into the area, he too retired into West Virginia. Richmond, anxious for the security of the territory, and apparently unaware as yet that the Federals were retiring, sent out an order that Breckinridge detach a brigade and send it back if possible. Lee had earlier suggested the same thing, however, and left the decision up to Breckinridge. "You must judge," he said, and the Kentuckian decided to keep all of his infantry with him to meet Sigel. At the moment, Lee's flank was more important than Western Virginia. "If I meet the enemy," he wired Richmond, "I will engage him." [30]

Meanwhile, Imboden enjoyed some success. He had sent a party of rangers on a diversionary raid on the Baltimore and Ohio. They struck, burning shops and machinery, destroying property worth millions, and drew away 500 of Sigel's 3,000 cavalry from the movement up the Valley. A few days later, while Breckinridge marshaled his forces in Staunton, Imboden met and defeated 300 more cavalry that Sigel had sent out to guard his flanks. Consequently, the Federal army was moving blind until May 11, when Sigel took Woodstock and there captured copies of Breckinridge's telegraphic messages to Imboden, giving his numbers and destination. The information decided Sigel not to move forward any farther, though he

30. Johnston, "Sketches of Operations, No. 1," p. 259; *O.R.*, Ser. I, Vol. XXXVII, Pt. 1, pp. 10, 12, 41–42, 44–48, 89, 724–37, Vol. LI, Pt. 1, p. 932; John McCausland to Samuel Cooper, May 9, 1864, Seddon to Bragg, May 12, 1864, in Breckinridge MSS, CHS.

would send out skirmishing parties. If the Confederates wanted battle, they would have to come to him.[31]

This was exactly what Breckinridge had in mind. His advance under Imboden had pulled back to Mount Jackson, twelve miles south of Woodstock. They were now sending back regular and reliable information on Sigel's numbers, underestimated at six thousand of all arms, with twenty-eight guns. It was also good to hear from scouts that none of the Federals had crossed the Blue Ridge, thus ensuring that Lee's left was still secure as he battled Grant at Spotsylvania.[32]

The Corps of Cadets, now numbering 261, arrived with some reserves in Staunton on May 12, and most assumed that with all his forces now gathered Breckinridge would fortify the city and await Sigel's attack. Instead, he sent out that evening orders for a march the next morning at 6 A.M. Breckinridge was unaware that his correspondence with Imboden had been captured and still believed that Sigel did not know of his coming. "Being convinced that the enemy was advancing in comparative confidence," he would report, "I determined not to await his coming, but to march to meet him and give him battle wherever found." [33]

On May 13, Breckinridge marched out of Staunton and moved twenty miles down the Valley pike to Mount Crawford. That day, contrary to his determination not to advance further, Sigel sent part of one of his two infantry brigades out of Woodstock, accompanied by cavalry and artillery, to move on Mount Jackson. Breckinridge was kept well apprised of the enemy advance during the march, and heard that evening that Imboden had taken position on Rude's Hill, north of New Market, and was determined to stand and fight unless enemy infantry or artillery joined the cavalry in his front. He also added that the next best place for a defense against attack was Lacey Springs.[34]

The next day, Breckinridge marched to Lacey Springs, ten miles from New Market, through a heavy rain that turned the roads into a mire. More news from the department arrived, none of it encouraging, and Lee sent a

31. O.R., Ser. I, Vol. XXXVII, Pt. 1, pp. 427–28, 446–47, 725–26.

32. Ibid., pp. 729–32.

33. O.R., Ser. I, Vol. XXXVII, Pt. 1, p. 730; Preston Cocke, The Battle of New Market and the Cadets of the Virginia Military Institute, May 15, 1864 (N.p., 1914), 5; J. Stoddard Johnston, The Battle of New Market, ca. 1911, Breckinridge Report, New Market File, V.M.I.; John S. Wise, Battle of New Market (N.p., 1882), 38; Johnston, "Sketches of Operations, No. 1," p. 259.

34. O.R., Ser. I, Vol. XXXVII, Pt. 1, pp. 732–33; Johnston, "Sketches of Operations, No. 1," p. 259.

dispatch that the general's troops were now much needed with his army if possible. Imboden, at least, sent cheering word that morning. The enemy had made no demonstrations against him so far this day, and he was of the opinion that they were falling back. Consequently, when the cavalryman learned at 10 o'clock that morning that Breckinridge would reach Lacey by noon, he rode back to meet with him. The two sat down over a meal to discuss their situation, and as they talked a message arrived from New Market saying that Sigel's cavalry had suddenly moved against Rude's Hill in force, and that the Confederates were retiring through the town. Immediately, Imboden mounted to return to his command, but not before Breckinridge gave him explicit orders to hold New Market "at all hazards," until nightfall. Then he was to fall back to a position about two miles south of the town which they had just been discussing, there to await the general's arrival with the rest of the army. Breckinridge decided to attack Sigel the next morning, still under the impression that his presence was unknown to the enemy. At 1 A.M., May 15, he put the army in motion again.[35]

The town of New Market lay on the macadamized turnpike which ran the length of the Valley, a lazy village of less than one thousand, with only a few rows of houses, a church or two, and a country store. New Market was neatly encased between two streams, the north fork of the Shenandoah River on the left, and Smith's Creek on the right, both of them running roughly parallel with the pike, and bordered north and south by two hills, Rude's and Shirley's. The Shenandoah was a natural barrier on the left of the town, because the rains had swollen it too much for fording, and high bluffs on its eastern bank denied access. From the crest of the bluffs, the ground sloped gently east toward the pike, to Smith's Creek. On the other side of the creek sat Massanutten Mountain and, cutting through it, New Market Gap. The gap gave access to the other side of the mountain—the only access—and a small force placed there could prevent a much larger one from passing through. If Sigel were to do this, Breckinridge would be forced to make a march of two days or more around the mountain to Luray on the other side of the gap. By that time, Sigel could have crossed the Blue Ridge to move, with a two-day head start, on Lee's left.

As Breckinridge marched his column toward New Market, he formulated his initial plan for the coming battle. He would have Imboden go in and attack Sigel, and then withdraw, bringing a pursuing enemy with him,

35. O.R., Ser. I, Vol. XXXVII, Pt. 1, pp. 734–36; Johnston, "Sketches of Operations, No. 1," p. 259; Imboden, "Battle of New Market," 482; Johnston, Battle of New Market, New Market File, V.M.I.

right into the position that had already been discussed. If the plan worked, it might very well put the Federals to rout.[36]

The general himself reached Imboden's position about two hours before daylight. It had rained all night, and was still pouring when the general's troops came into view at daybreak, tired, muddy, and hungry. Breckinridge halted them for breakfast and a rest, and then laid out his line, while sending Imboden's skirmishers in an unsuccessful attempt at drawing Sigel out of the town. Standing with Imboden and his staff on the top of Shirley's Hill, Breckinridge now looked at the country spread out before him from a new point of view. Imboden, familiar with the area, sketched for him those details of the terrain not readily visible, and later believed that the general had mastered the landscape and made his battle plans within five minutes. A Confederate standing nearby looked at Breckinridge as he surveyed the ground, and said later, "I think he was the handsomest man I ever saw." The general took out his watch, saw that it was now 11 A.M., and made his decision. "Well, I have offered him battle and he declines to advance on us," he said to those around him, "I shall advance on him." Then to Imboden he added: "We can attack and whip them here, and I'll do it." [37]

Ordering the cavalry skirmishers called in, Breckinridge rode back to oversee the preparations for the attack. As he approached the cadet's position, they began cheering him. Cadets in the rear were at first puzzled by the shouts, but, "We soon learned its import as General John C. Breckinridge and staff approached, and we joined heartily in the cheering as that soldierly man, mounted magnificently, galloped past, uncovered, bowing, and riding like a Cid." Raising a gloved hand, he explained to them his earnest hope that he would not have to use them, but warned that he would do so freely if the absolute necessity arose.[38]

The general's first move was an old but artful deception, and it worked

36. E. Raymond Turner, *The New Market Campaign, May, 1864* (Richmond, 1912), 24–25.

37. Imboden, "Battle of New Market," 482–83; John D. Imboden to Henry Wise, February 18, 1896, John D. Imboden Alumni File, George H. Smith to Wise, March 7, 1896, George H. Smith Alumni File, George M. Edgar to Wise, February 18, 1896, George M. Edgar, Alumni File, V.M.I.; J. W. Parsons, "Capture of Battery at New Market," *Confederate Veteran*, XVII (March, 1909), 119.

38. Parsons, "Capture of Battery," 119; T. H. Highwater, "Speech of Col. Francis Lee Smith before the Constitutional Convention of Virginia," *Confederate Veteran*, XXVI (February, 1918), 84; John Clark Howard, "Recollections of Battle of New Market," *Confederate Veteran*, XXXIV (February, 1926), 57; John S. Wise, *End of an Era* (Boston, 1902), 294.

admirably. He set his regiments to marching and countermarching on and around Shirley's Hill, hoping to create the illusion of greater numbers than he really possessed. Going beyond this, he then arranged them in three lines, roughly overlapping one another. The first, and longest, line consisted of Wharton's brigade—the Fifty-first Virginia and the Thirtieth Virginia Battalion—and a dismounted regiment from Imboden's command, the Sixty-second Virginia, on its right. About two hundred yards to its right rear, in echelon, Breckinridge placed the second line, two of Echols' three units, the Twenty-second Virginia and the Twenty-third Virginia Battalion. Finally, the cadets, and Echols' other battalion, the Twenty-sixth Virginia, made up the third line, on the left rear of Echols' line, in echelon. The intent of this formation, as Breckinridge sent it forward out of the woods on the top of the hill, was to create the impression that all three lines were of the same length as the first, and it worked. Sigel, despite the fact that the captured telegrams gave a precise accounting of Breckinridge's infantry at four thousand—before the detachment of McCausland—now believed that the Confederates had seven thousand infantry alone, and an army of eight to nine thousand all together. Some Federals claimed he had twenty thousand. In fact, Breckinridge's little army numbered barely fifty-three hundred.[39]

It was noon when the Confederates moved out, their right resting on the pike. Breckinridge had sent ten of his now eighteen guns over to the right of the road, placed the others on the crest of the hill, and rushed Imboden's cavalry over to hold the extreme right between the pike and Smith's Creek. Under cover of their fire, Breckinridge advanced his three lines. Enemy artillery in town was soon driven back down the pike and Sigel, riding into New Market to inspect the situation, decided to withdraw, ordering those in the town to fall back a half mile to a line already selected on the southern slope of Bushong's Hill.[40]

Breckinridge moved his army through the rain that had been falling all morning, and occupied New Market, while the artillery firing between the opponents continued. The general and his staff rode forward to the north side of town and stopped in a group to reconnoiter near the cemetery which had recently been the position of Sigel's guns. Breckinridge and the others were standing a few yards away from St. Matthew's Lutheran

39. George M. Edgar, Notes on the Battle of New Market, 1911–12, Edgar Alumni File, V.M.I.; O.R., Ser. I, Vol. XXXVII, Pt. 1, pp. 76, 446.

40. Imboden, "Battle of New Market," 483; Turner, New Market, 28; Cecil D. Eby, Jr. (ed.), "With Sigel at New Market: The Diary of Colonel D. H. Strother," Civil War History, VI (March, 1960), 79.

Church, beside the graveyard, where a sharp-eyed Federal gunner sighted them and, surmising the importance of the group of officers, sent a three-inch shell at them. It lodged in a post in the churchyard, only a few feet from Breckinridge. Showering him with splinters, it failed to explode.[41]

Shifting the troops again, he laid out two lines, one made up of one of Wharton's regiments—the other being used as skirmishers—and the Sixty-second Virginia from Imboden. The other line, slightly to the right rear of Wharton, in echelon, was Echols' brigade. To Echols' left rear he sent the cadets. Breckinridge had not wanted to use them, but now he had to have a reserve, however small, for his thin line. He hoped they could still be kept out of the fight. Imboden was still on the right with two guns, while the remainder of the general's cannon were on the pike, ready to move on it when the lines advanced. Breckinridge had seen a number of good positions for artillery on the right of the road north of town, and he would move with the guns in the advance to oversee their placement.[42]

Then came a message from Imboden. A dense wood lay in the cavalry-man's front, behind which, on Sigel's left, were concealed the Federal cavalry under Major General Julius Stahel. Imboden had been unaware of their presence until, shortly after noon, he rode through the trees and came upon the enemy horse, drawn up with their extreme left resting on Smith's Creek. He thought he saw here an opportunity to turn Sigel's flank, for by crossing the stream he could actually move his command down it and against Stahel's left rear without fear of counterattack. Rains had made the creek almost unfordable. Imboden would cross at the bridge on the road to Luray, take his guns with him, and surprise the enemy. He sent a messenger to Breckinridge asking permission to take his command across the creek. The general not only consented to the movement, but also augmented it with the keenest tactical command he would give during the war, one which he may have given at the outset of the battle as well. Smith's Creek flowed into the north fork of the Shenandoah a few miles north of New Market, just short of Mount Jackson. Neither was fordable, and there was only one bridge, the one crossing the Shenandoah by which the valley pike proceeded northward. By burning that bridge, Breckinridge would have Sigel trapped, unable to cross anywhere, and faced with the choice of drowning, fighting, or surrendering. Consequently, the general ordered

41. Johnston, "Sketches of Operations, No. 1," p. 260; note in JCB Papers on the shell-struck post.
42. Turner, *New Market*, 34–35, Johnston, Battle of New Market, New Market File, V.M.I.

Imboden to cross the creek "and to use every effort to destroy the bridge across the river in rear of the enemy with a view to cut off his retreat in case of a reverse to his arms." It is indicative of Breckinridge's confidence that this plan hinged entirely upon his forcing Sigel to retire.[43]

Sigel had made an error two days before in sending a portion of his command forward toward New Market, while holding the bulk of it behind at Woodstock. The result was that his command was divided by nineteen miles of muddy road, and on the morning of May 15 several units still had not joined the army. He now compounded the error by dividing his remaining forces into two lines, a good deceptive deployment for an advance as Breckinridge was showing, but a poor alignment for a defense, especially since Sigel put the weaker line in front. About four hundred yards below the Bushong House on the hill, he placed two regiments of his First Infantry Brigade, the other two being still en route. They took up a line starting on the pike, and extending toward, but not quite reaching, the bluff overlooking the Shenandoah. Guarding its left, on the pike, stood the six-gun battery of Captain Albert von Kleiser. The second line, by far the stronger, formed nearly one-half mile behind the first, its right resting on the very highest part of the hill, directly overlooking the river. There Sigel placed twelve more guns. Then, on their left, he aligned the Second Brigade of his infantry, with three regiments on the line, and one in reserve. This force stretched to the pike and a little beyond, its left protected by yet another battery. On the extreme left, of course, sat Stahel's cavalry. Another battery was on the road coming up but, like the other two regiments of the First Brigade, it would not reach the battlefield in time.[44]

Sigel had set up his lines well before Breckinridge ordered his command forward, around 2 P.M. The general himself moved first with his artillery on the valley pike. He oversaw the firing, limbering up, advancing, unlimbering, and firing again, of the guns as they moved, making what Stoddard Johnston called "a skirmish line of artillery." The Confederates suffered heavy casualties at the hands of excellent enemy gunnery during this advance, but finally Breckinridge had the guns where he wanted them, on a slight rise to the right of the road. The Federals in Sigel's front line put up, by all accounts, a feeble defense, falling back in disorder after only token

43. Imboden, "Battle of New Market," 483; Imboden to Wise, June 6, 1895, in Imboden Alumni File, Breckinridge Report, New Market File, V.M.I.; Harry Gilmor, *Four Years in the Saddle* (New York, 1866), 156.

44. Turner, *New Market*, 6–7, 35–38; Eby, "With Sigel at New Market," 79, 83; *O.R.*, Ser. I, Vol. XXXVII, Pt. 1, p. 80; Franz Sigel, "Sigel in the Shenadoah Valley," in Johnson and Buel (eds.), *Battles and Leaders*, IV, 489.

resistance. Most of them ran back to and through the second line, throwing it into some confusion, while a few withdrew to Stahel's position.[45]

One of Stahel's cavalrymen, Lieutenant F. Wyneken of the First New York (Lincoln) Cavalry, was mortified by what he saw happen in the Federal front line. A few months after the war ended, he would write Breckinridge, "It was the misconduct of our army and not less the bravery of your soldiers, which turned my mind first in favor of the confederate cause. I never shall forget the magnificent aspect of your infantry attacking our left and centre, the triumphant yell and—my cowardly comrades running back for their miserable life!—I was ashamed to be in such an army, and repented bitterly what I had done." Indeed, Wyneken's repentance was such that he resigned his commission as soon as possible, and in this letter tendered his services to Breckinridge in the event that the conflict should ever be renewed![46]

Now was the time for the final blow, it seemed, with the Federal line in an uproar. Breckinridge, sensed that the Federal right, the position of Sigel's guns on the highest point of Bushong's Hill, was the point of primary importance. He supported Wharton's line with the Twenty-sixth Battalion and brought in his skirmishers. This done, he moved the line forward just after 2 P.M.[47]

As they moved forward, a bend in the river made it impossible for the two regiments to advance in line, so the Twenty-sixth Battalion dropped behind the Fifty-first and continued the charge. Federal skirmishers, the twelve guns on the hill, and some flank fire from one of Sigel's regiments, soon began to flood the Fifty-first, which had already done most of the fighting on this side of the pike. The fire became intolerable before long, and company by company, the men of the Fifty-first began first lying down, and then running back to the rear, disrupting somewhat the line of the Twenty-sixth.[48]

This was a critical juncture. With his right weakened, and now his left threatening to fall apart, Breckinridge was in danger of trading places with Sigel, and being the one to fall back. Fortunately, the men of the Twenty-sixth were resolute, held many of those falling back in place—some of them at gunpoint—and kept their ground. Then Breckinridge came riding along

45. Johnston, "Sketches of Operations, No. 1," p. 261; *O.R.*, Ser. I, Vol. XXXVII, Pt. 1, pp. 80, 82; Turner, *New Market*, 43–45.

46. Francis Wyneken to Breckinridge, August 2, 1865, in B. MSS.

47. Turner, *New Market*, 46–47.

48. D. H. Bruce, "The Battle of New Market," *Confederate Veteran*, XV (December, 1907), 554.

the rear of their line shouting "Charge! charge! charge!" Responding to his order and to that of their most competent colonel, George Edgar, the men of the Twenty-sixth rushed forward and up the slope with the rest of the Fifty-first. The ensuing battle may have lasted as long as an hour and a half. They drove in the Federal skirmishers, and then trudged slowly up the hill amid the ever-present rain and a low hanging cloud of smoke from the enemy guns. In a last charge they drove Sigel's batteries from the hill, capturing three of the guns, and a number of prisoners. The Federal right had been taken.[49]

Just as Wharton had been moving forward, so had the Confederate right. Conscious of their weakness, they had no choice but to hope as the men of the Twenty-third Virginia Battalion, under Lieutenant Colonel Clarence Derrick, and a portion of the Twenty-second Virginia, led by Colonel George S. Patton, advanced toward Sigel's entire cavalry command. The portion of the field Derrick had to cover stretched nearly one-half mile from the pike to Smith's Creek, and his command could barely make a skirmish line over that distance. The only strength to his command was the concentration of fourteen of Breckinridge's guns behind his line. Some aid might have been expected from Imboden, who now had his cavalry and four guns across the creek and on Stahel's flank, but all that happened was that the Federal cavalryman moved his command away from the river, out of range of the artillery. This left Imboden's whole command absolutely useless, when its numbers were sorely needed behind Derrick. Worse yet, there is no evidence that Imboden made a concerted effort to carry out the remainder of his orders—to ride back toward Mount Jackson, recross the creek, and destroy the bridge over the Shenandoah—and, as a result, his whole command was of no help at all.[50]

Because Stahel withdrew a little to avoid Imboden's fire, the rest of the Confederate line had become engaged before Derrick, with part of Patton's regiment, came up to them. Immediately the Federals opened a hot fire, which the Confederates withstood well despite their inferior numbers. Nevertheless, the situation looked critical, for Stahel began massing his horsemen for a charge. Derrick's men gathered in little clusters behind trees in a sparse wood, while Breckinridge, seeing the impending attack, ordered his cannon double-shotted with canister. Then, as the enemy horse began its charge, Patton wheeled his regiment to the right, taking Stahel in flank,

49. Richmond *Times-Dispatch*, October 15, 1905; Edgar to Wise, February 18, 1896, in Edgar Alumni File, V.M.I.; Turner, *New Market*, 49–50.
50. Turner, *New Market*, 61–62; Imboden, "Battle of New Market," 483–84.

and began shooting down his horses, as did Derrick. The result was a terrible repulse. Only three of Stahel's nearly two thousand cavalry made it to Derrick's line. While there was some sporadic skirmishing and artillery firing after this, the Confederate right held secure.[51]

While the left and right of the Confederate line were engaged, the crucial part of the battle was being acted out in the center. Between Wharton on the left and Derrick on the right, stood the Thirtieth Battalion, the Sixty-second Virginia, most of Patton's Twenty-second Virginia and, in the rear as reserve, the Corps of Cadets. They advanced with the rest of the army, meeting little difficulty until they came to the Bushong House, about halfway to the Federal line. Here the Sixty-second began to suffer the fire from its front, as well as a galling hail of bullets from the left by Federals who had just halted the Fifty-first Virginia in its advance. In only a few minutes, the Sixty-second suffered 243 casualties out of about 500 present on the field. Its colonel, George Smith, moved the regiment forward nevertheless, but was soon compelled to fall back into a slight hollow to the right of an orchard fronting the Bushong House. Here the fire from Kleiser's battery, posted in the middle of Sigel's line, mauled Smith severely.[52]

Had Sigel chosen to launch a counterattack at this moment, the battle might have been his. It was this danger, in part, which forced Breckinridge to make a crucial, agonizing decision. His left under Wharton was faltering, the right was too weak for him to expect it to do anything but hold its ground if possible, and now there was a gap in his center thanks to the near-rout of the Fifty-first and Thirtieth Virginia from the Sixty-second's left. The general's young aide, James B. Clay, Jr., regarded the Confederate center at that juncture as "nothing more than a skirmish line." There seemed to be no remedy, for Breckinridge did not have enough men to cover both flanks *and* the center, yet it was obvious that Sigel would direct his attack precisely at this vulnerable point. Breckinridge told Major Charles Semple of his staff to contract the lines to strengthen the center, but Semple complained that this would expose the flanks. "General," he said, "why don't you put the cadets in line? They will fight as well as our men."

Breckinridge, still determined not to expose the cadets, refused. "No, Charley, this will not do," he said, "they are only children and I cannot

51. Turner, *New Market*, 62; Johnston, "Sketches of Operations, No. 1," p. 261; J. N. Upshur and others, "New Market at V.M.I.," *SHSP*, XXXI (January–December 1903), 180.

52. Smith to Edgar, March 16, 1906, in Smith File, V.M.I.; George H. Smith, "More of the Battle of New Market," *Confederate Veteran*, XVI (November, 1908), 570; Turner, *New Market*, 53–55.

expose them to such a fire as our center will receive." Semple rode off to attempt contracting the line, but returned in a few minutes, saying "General, it is too late. The Federals are right on us. If the cadets are ordered up we can close the gap in our center."

There was no choice. "Major, order them up," said the general, "and God forgive me for the order." Most of Breckinridge's staff were impressed with the agony that decision caused the general, and at least one of those around him at the time he gave the order believed that he turned his head away as the cadets moved into the battle.[53]

The cadets obliqued to the left and moved into the orchard in front of the Bushong House, filling the gap. Already they had suffered a few casualties from the Federal artillery fire, but here they really began to feel the sting. They held, however, firing from behind a fence while the Fifty-first rallied on their left and Patton brought his regiment up on the right of the Sixty-second. This stabilized the center, and just in time, for now Sigel launched his belated counterattack. Three regiments sallied down from their plateau against the Confederates, but met a withering fire from the cadets behind their fence, as well as the commands on either side of the corps. As a result, they were hurled back.

Immediately, Breckinridge countercharged the disorganized center of Sigel's line. The men had to move across rain-soaked ground so sticky that it sucked the shoes and stockings from the feet of many, but still they moved on. At the same time, the Fifty-first was moving forward again, while Derrick had repulsed Stahel on the right. Almost the entire army was in forward motion, and Sigel could not resist it. His center gave way, Wharton was taking the position of his artillery on his extreme right, and his left was beginning to fall back. The cadets took a cannon in his center. Stahel was retreating up the pike in disorder. The Federal commander was forced to withdraw from the field. To Sigel's good fortune, portions of two of his regiments which had not been in the battle, now came up to cover the withdrawal, along with a fresh battery.[54]

Breckinridge, unaware that Imboden had been unsuccessful in burning the bridge near Mount Jackson, showed that he had learned well the lesson to be derived from Bragg's failure to pursue and press Rosecrans after the

53. "Henry Clay and John C. Breckinridge. Selection of Capt. J. B. Clay for Places in Hall of Fame, of Whom He Writes Interestingly," April 1905, in Prewitt Collection; Walter A. Clark, "The Boy Cadets at New Market, Va." *Confederate Veteran*, XX (February, 1912), 86; J. S. Johnston, *Kentucky*, 186–87.

54. Turner, *New Market*, 82–89.

rout at Chickamauga. Not content with victory, he rushed after the retreating Federals, even though his own army was nearly worn out. Breckinridge himself, covered with mud up to his waist, had been on foot much of the day, cheering the men, and must have been exhausted. Yet he rode with the lead elements in the pursuit, mounted once again. Passing Edgar of the Twenty-sixth Battalion, he called out, "Colonel, we are mightily scattered, but we are driving them." Even when the men with him ran out of ammunition, he did not call a halt, but kept them moving forward while sending back to the rear for the supply wagons to come up. Meanwhile, Imboden returned from across Smith's Creek, and at last Breckinridge knew that the bridge had not been destroyed, all the more reason to press his pursuit. Imboden came up to him just as the ammunition wagons arrived and, while the men replenished their cartridge boxes, Breckinridge rested briefly in an orchard that was in the line of fire of Federal guns that were still trying to cover Sigel's retreat. When the shells passed perilously close and exploded nearby, Imboden chided the general for being in such an exposed and dangerous position. Breckinridge laughed, said that this orchard was the only place in the vicinity with ground still firm, and that he preferred to risk a stray shell than brave that infernal mud again.[55]

Sigel posted his command on Rude's Hill, five miles north of the battlefield, overlooking the Shenandoah bridge. When his men had finished supplying themselves from the wagons, Breckinridge sent Imboden to move his cavalry off toward the Federal left, still, perhaps, hoping to get someone around behind the enemy to destroy the bridge. At the same time, he sent his artillery racing up the pike. Moving his whole line forward, now somewhat reorganized, Breckinridge pressed forward. The armies traded artillery fire for a while, Imboden was unsuccessful in the attempt to turn Sigel's right, and soon Sigel saw that this position, too, was untenable. When Breckinridge's batteries reached Rude's Hill, they topped the crest to see the rear guard of the Federal army crossing the Shenandoah bridge. In the fading light, they sent a few shells toward the fleeing enemy, but to no effect, and soon flames illuminated the swollen river, signaling the burning of the bridge, and the end of further pursuit. Breckinridge, coming up, saw the situation, and ordered his exhausted army to bivouac on the hill.[56]

In truth, it might be said that any one of two or three score Confederate generals could have beaten Sigel at New Market. The German was a brave

55. Edgar to Wise, February 18, 1896, in Edgar Alumni File, V.M.I.; Imboden, "Battle of New Market," 484–85.
56. Imboden, "Battle of New Market," 485.

man, but an almost wholly incompetent commander. However, the same was true of the men Jackson had defeated in the Valley two years before. Now, as Sigel raced down the Valley, Union Chief of Staff Major General Henry W. Halleck wired Grant that he was "already in full retreat on Strasburg. If you expect anything from him you will be mistaken. He will do nothing but run. He never did anything else." On May 19 Sigel was relieved of his command.[57]

Even the German's ineptitude cannot dull the brilliance of Breckinridge's victory, for Sigel possessed advantages which even the most bumbling of commanders should have been able to marshal for success. His army was better supplied, better fed, and well rested after a march from Martinsburg that can only be termed leisurely. It had taken Sigel two weeks to cover the 65 miles to New Market. Breckinridge took one week to reach the same place, traveling over 160 miles, and most or all of it without the benefit of the rail transportation that he had counted on. His men were worn out before going into the battle, as Imboden's cavalry must have been also, from its vigorous work in harassing Sigel's flanks.

Sigel came to the battlefield in command of 8,000 of all arms. Two of his regiments, however, numbering 1,500, did not reach the field in time to participate, another battery arrived too late as well, and so he had only about 6,300 men and 22 guns actually available for the battle. Breckinridge, on the other hand, after having to leave McCausland behind, arrived at Staunton with no more than 2,250 infantry, and about 350 artillerymen.[58] In Staunton he was joined by the 261 cadets of V.M.I., and the Augusta and Rockingham reserves, numbering perhaps 500, though they took no part in the battle. Imboden's command, about 1,400 strong, contributed only the 500 men of the Sixty-second Virginia to the battle, the rest being as much out of it on the east side of Smith's Creek as if they had not been present at all. The result is that Breckinridge had barely over 3,400 infantry, and certainly not more than 4,000 of all arms, including odd companies and artillerymen, available on the battlefield.[59] Thus, Sigel outnumbered him in available forces by over 2,000. Yet, with three-to-two odds against him, Breckinridge so skillfully managed and concentrated his troops

57. O.R., Ser. I, Vol. XXXIII, Pt. 2, pp. 840–41.

58. Reports of numbers engaged and casualties vary wildly. These figures are the best conclusion based on extensive research in sources too numerous to cite. See the author's history of the Battle of New Market to be published in the near future.

59. William Couper, The V.M.I. New Market Cadets (Charlottesville, Va., 1933), 253; Sigel, "Sigel in the Shenandoah," 491; Turner, New Market, 114–15. The author's figures vary from these sources somewhat.

in the fight that when his line west of the pike made its final decisive charge on Bushong's Hill, its numbers were equal or slightly superior to the Federal line facing it.

Breckinridge took and maintained the initiative throughout the entire day, surrendering it only briefly when the Federals half-heartedly charged his center, then seizing it once again to countercharge to victory. The secret of the Kentuckian's success lay in his gamble in committing almost his entire force at one time, all along the line, and in his confidence from the outset that he would win. Sigel kept at least one full regiment in reserve, as well as part of his artillery, and allowed Stahel's cavalry, his entire left wing, to sit idle through much of the day. Here alone, Breckinridge made up for some of his disadvantage by a far superior use of the troops at hand.

The general outfought Sigel as well. His handling of his artillery was one of the outstanding features of the battle. He used it not just in the conventional manner as a means of softening the enemy before an attack, but actually made it the most mobile arm of his offense. Under his personal direction, his guns first drove the enemy out of New Market, then played a large part in driving in Sigel's first line on Bushong's Hill, hopped from one position to another along the pike as a skirmish line, a moving, frontline support for his advance, made a shambles of Stahel's attack on the right, and spearheaded the pursuit of the fleeing enemy. But by far the most brilliant action of the day was Breckinridge's order to Imboden to move around behind Sigel and destroy the Shenandoah bridge. Before the battle had fairly begun, Breckinridge was not only confident of victory, but looked ahead as well to making that victory utterly complete. Stoddard Johnston would later write that, "Had Imboden succeeded in carrying out his instructions, the whole of Sigel's command would have been captured." [60]

The casualties on both sides were severe. Sigel lost 842 killed, wounded, and captured, and Breckinridge suffered nearly 550. Particularly painful to the general were the casualties among the Corps of Cadets, for 5 were killed on the field, 5 more would die of wounds in the following days, and another 47 were wounded. Before the battle his veterans had ridiculed the corps of boys, singing nursery songs as they passed, but they had proven themselves men this day. They filled a crucial gap in the line, and played a significant part in the Confederate victory. Breckinridge had not wanted to use them, and the memory of that agonizing decision to put them in the

60. Johnston, "Sketches of Operations, No. 1," pp. 261–62.

line never left him. Years later his aide Clay recalled that "Invariably, irresistibly, a tear would start in his eye and sadness overspread his face when he recalled the scenes of that memorable day in May 1864." Nevertheless, now he was proud of them and gave the corps his thanks and a personal commendation. From now on, and in later years, they would remain always in his memory as "my cadets." [61]

That evening at 7 P.M., just as the action had closed for the night, Breckinridge sent a wire to Lee, informing him of the day's victory. The next day would bring Lee's brief reply: "I offer you the thanks of this army for your victory over Genl Siegel." Indeed, Lee was overjoyed at Breckinridge's success. This one stroke had eliminated a dangerous threat to his flank at a critical time, and fully justified the wide discretion he had wisely allowed Breckinridge in the conduct of affairs in the Valley. The wheat crop, so essential for feeding Lee's army, had been saved, staving off hunger a little longer. The portion of the railroad that ran through the upper Valley was still safe. And the morale boost that a victory, any victory, over the Federals gave to the tired soldiers in Virginia, was beyond computation. Clearly, at last the Confederacy had found the right man to command in western Virginia.[62]

Just as clearly, the South wanted another hero, another "Stonewall" to replace the Jackson who had died so tragically almost exactly a year before. For a time, New Market made Breckinridge their man. Scouts present at the battle spread the word that " 'Old Breck' was most gallant in his conduct of the battle." Johnston found that "everybody hailed Breckinridge as the new Jackson, who had been sent to guard the Valley and redeem it from the occupation of the enemy," and the men serving with the general did nothing to halt the comparison. Indeed, Edgar of the Twenty-sixth Battalion, decided that "General Breckinridge had few if any superiors on the field of battle. Besides being a man of wonderful courage, he had a keen eye to discern the strong and weak points of the enemy's position, skill in using his forces to the best advantage, and a celerity of movement which reminded me of Jackson." Only three days after the battle, with most of

---

61. New York *Tribune*, May 27, 1864; Richmond *Whig*, May 18, 1864; Bennett H. Young, "John Cabell Breckinridge," *Confederate Veteran*, XIII (June, 1905), 259.

62. Breckinridge to Lee, May 15, 1864, in Charles S. Venable MSS; Lee to Breckinridge, May 16, 1864, photocopy in JCB Papers; *O.R.*, Ser. I, Vol. XXXVII, Pt. 1, pp. 87, 737. Douglas S. Freeman, Lee's biographer and perhaps the most perceptive student of the Virginia campaigns, wrote of New Market: "How admirably Breckinridge discharged his duties and cooperated with the Army of Northern Virginia." (*Lee's Lieutenants*, III, 325).

its details still unknown, the Richmond press took up the cry. The *Daily Dispatch* declared that "Gen. Breckinridge, in celerity of movement, has proved himself a worthy successor of Jackson." "General Breckinridge seems to be following the example of our great Jackson," said the *Whig*. "He marches rapidly and whips the enemy in detail." In the War Department, Colonel Josiah Gorgas, chief of ordnance, shortly found that "General Breckinridge appears to be rising in favor as a dashing commander." The comparison with Jackson was made complete by the fact that, in the battle, Breckinridge rode a bay given to him by Cheatham, a horse which bore the same name as the mighty Stonewall's mount, "Old Sorrel." [63]

Indeed, there was much truth in the comparison with Jackson. Not since Stonewall's death, and never again after New Market, did a Confederate commander in the Valley display such versatility, innovation, or resolution. The movement of Wharton and Echols from the department to New Market even surpassed those brilliant marches of 1862 which made Jackson famous and won his infantry the sobriquet "foot cavalry." In his great campaign he averaged 14.1 miles per marching day. But Echols averaged slightly over seventeen, and those elements of Wharton's brigade who could not get rail transportation achieved better than 21 miles per day on the march. Like Stonewall, Breckinridge had fought his battle on a Sunday. Like Jackson, he went into the campaign heavily outnumbered, yet so maneuvered against his opponent that, at the critical time, he concentrated a greater force on the crucial line than the enemy. The constant advance, seizing and holding the initiative in spite of poor odds, and the all-out attack, were characteristics of Stonewall's campaigns, and Breckinridge used them well at New Market. Indeed, the Kentuckian's handling of his artillery was a chapter that even Jackson had not written, and his masterful reading of the ground and the way he turned its lie and the streams' fullness to his advantage, smacked mightily of his predecessor's brilliant use of the Massanutten in 1862. The dispatch of Imboden around Sigel's left flank toward his unsuspecting rear was a direct quote from Jackson's decisive flank marches at Second Bull Run and Chancellorsville.

Those who wished could see great portent in this victory. Not only was it won in the classic fashion of Stonewall by a general who called his horse

---

63. McChesney to Johnson, May 31, 1864, in McChesney MSS; Johnston, "Sketches of Operations, No. 1," p. 262; Edgar to Wise, February 18, 1896, in Edgar Alumni File, V.M.I.; Richmond *Daily Dispatch*, May 19, 1864; Richmond *Whig*, May 19, 1864; Frank E. Vandiver (ed.), *Civil War Diary of General Josiah Gorgas* (Tuscaloosa, Ala., 1947), 110–11; F. M. Imboden, "Gen. G. C. Wharton," *Confederate Veteran*, XIV (September, 1906), 392; Bruce to Breckinridge, June 7, 1864, in B. MSS.

Old Sorrel, but also it was fought on the anniversary of the great general's burial. Breckinridge's final charge put the Federals to rout one year to the very hour from those sad moments when Jackson was lowered to his grave. The omens were strong, but regardless of whether Breckinridge would prove to be Stonewall reincarnate, his performance here at New Market was brilliant. He won the most important secondary victory of the war in the East. This battle represented the finest display of all the abilities, physical and mental, that he had developed in the Confederate service; it was the fruition of two and one-half years of education in war. The question that remained after Shiloh here found its answer. John C. Breckinridge *was* a general, and a fine one.

CHAPTER 7

We Will Soon Drive the Enemy Out

The Valley did not keep its new Stonewall for long. Lee was still hard pressed in his front, and was calling to his army all available reinforcements. Consequently, upon hearing the extent of Breckinridge's success, he directed that Sigel be pursued into Maryland if possible, but added that, should it prove otherwise, the Kentuckian was sorely needed east of the Blue Ridge. Breckinridge felt solicitous over affairs in his own department, but when Lee reported that Averell and Crook had retired, his fears were allayed. Since Sigel had too much the head start on him, the general decided to join Lee. He set Imboden to work rebuilding the burned bridge, organized a guard for the Valley, rested the men one day, and then marched Wharton and Echols back to Staunton, forty miles south, on May 17. There he entrained the command for Hanover Junction, over one hundred miles east, and some thirty-five miles behind Lee's lines at Spotsylvania. He brought about twenty-six hundred infantry and artillery, and by May 20 had the entire command at Hanover, another example of his now well-developed talent for moving men quickly over long distance. Regrettably, he had to leave all his cavalry behind as a guard with Imboden, but he took with him their best wishes. "May new honors crown you in all the future," wrote Imboden, "is the sincere hope of myself and little command, whose hearts you have so completely won." [1]

Lee had a double reason for ordering Breckinridge to Hanover Junction. For one thing, it was the most convenient place from which to send him

---

1. *O.R.*, Ser. I, Vol. XXXVII, Pt. 1, pp. 738–40, 743; J. S. Johnston, "Sketches of Operations, No. 1," p. 262; Breckinridge to R. E. Lee, in Charles S. Venable MSS, SHC; J. Stoddard Johnston, Statement of Total Effectives, May 21, 1864, in New Market File, V.M.I. Breckinridge later stated that his forces brought to Hanover Junction totaled "less than 3,000 muskets." Breckinridge to Jubal A. Early, April 11, 1866, in Jubal A. Early MSS, LC.

back to the Valley, in case another threat appeared. More important, however, was the fact that, near Hanover, lay railroad bridges crossing the North and South Anna rivers, the most vulnerable links in his rail communications between Spotsylvania Courthouse and Richmond. The Federal general Sheridan who, like Breckinridge, had been transferred to the eastern theater, had begun a raid several days earlier designed to disrupt this line. He had met and defeated J. E. B. Stuart at Yellow Tavern on May 11, and left Lee's dashing cavalryman dying. Indeed, it was rumored that Breckinridge was slated to take Stuart's command. Now Lee needed Breckinridge at Hanover to guard the bridge. Immediately, the Kentuckian began the construction of works to guard the bridge, as well as the vital intersection of the Hanover and Haw's Shop roads, putting pickets out well in advance to prevent surprise by Sheridan. Meanwhile, he stood under orders from Lee to be ready to move at any time.[2]

By the time Breckinridge reached Hanover Junction, detraining under fire, the danger from Sheridan was past. However, the general had barely taken his position before Grant began a movement around Lee's right which forced the Army of Northern Virginia to fall back to Hanover Junction on May 22, where it took up a line just below the North Anna. Here Lee met Breckinridge for the first time since the previous February, and the Kentuckian received his warm personal thanks for the victory at New Market. "I thank you for the relief it has afforded me, as well as for the ability and zeal you have displayed in the management of the affairs of your department and of the Valley District," Lee had said. The compliments did not stop with just the commander. "The veterans of Lee and Jackson greeted him with cheers whenever he came within sight," Stoddard Johnston wrote of Breckinridge's reception by the men of the army, "and wherever he moved among them, in camp or in line of battle, it was a perfect ovation." The Maryland troops treated him to a serenade on his arrival.[3]

There was little time for applause, however, for Grant did not let Lee

2. J. S. Johnston, "Sketches of Operations, No. 2," *SHSP*, VII (August, 1879), 317; *O.R.*, Ser. I, Vol. XXXVI, Pt. 3, pp. 815, 826, Vol. LI, Pt. 2, p. 998; Douglas S. Freeman and Grady C. McWhiney (eds.), *Lee's Dispatches: Unpublished Letters of General Robert E. Lee, C.S.A., to Jefferson Davis and the War Department of the Confederate States of America, 1862–1865* (New York, 1957), 189; Charles Halpine to James Gordon Bennett, May 27, 1864, in James Gordon Bennett MSS, LC.

3. A. S. Johnston, *Captain Bierne Chapman and Chapman's Battery: An Historical Sketch* (Union, W. Va., 1903), 20; J. S. Johnston, "Sketches of Operations, No. 2," p. 317; J. Stoddard Johnston, *Kentucky*, 188; *O.R.*, Ser. I, Vol. XXXVII, Pt. 1, pp. 744–45; J. Grayson to Breckinridge, October 4, 1871, in B. MSS.

out of his sight. Lee formed his line with its right at Hanover Junction, and then instructed Breckinridge to place his small division between the corps of Richard H. Anderson and Richard S. Ewell. He remained in this line for several days while Lee waited hopefully for Grant to attack him in this strong position, but the Federal demurred, and instead moved once again around Lee's right. Left with no choice but to fall back once more in the attempt to stay between Grant and Richmond, Lee sent Breckinridge off with Anderson's First Corps down the Richmond, Fredericksburg and Petersburg Railroad to Atlee's Station, only three miles from the outer defenses of the Confederate capital. The next day, May 28, he shifted the Kentuckian toward Haw's Shop, on the right center of the line laid out just below Totopotomoy Creek. Here Breckinridge was once again on Anderson's right. To his own right was an impenetrable jungle, so dense that Lee left it barely guarded, and beyond was Ewell's corps, soon to be under a new commander, Major General Jubal A. Early. Here near the Totopotomoy, Early and Breckinridge met for the first time, the genesis of a lifelong friendship.[4]

On May 30 Breckinridge found enemy skirmishers building rifle pits and throwing up works in his front, and later that day he engaged them in a desultory artillery duel. Grant was moving to Lee's right again, and most of the Army of Northern Virginia had shifted to the right to counter the move. As a result, Breckinridge found himself on June 1 on the left center of the line, to the right of the brigade of Brigadier General William Mahone. Together they drove back the only concerted attack on their front during the Totopotomoy operations, an attack, incidentally, led by Breckinridge's childhood playmate, Major General David Birney. Only when Birney had been driven back could Breckinridge obey an order just received from Lee. He was to move to the southeast, to join the main part of the army now in line at Cold Harbor.[5]

In the capital a new rumor had sprouted that Breckinridge was soon to have a corps, and probably a promotion. Where the rumor started is a mystery, and it appears not to have had any official origins. Most likely it arose from the fact that two of Lee's three corps were led by temporary commanders, Anderson and Early, and that, in fact, Breckinridge was senior to

4. O.R., Ser. I, Vol. XXXVI, Pt. 1, p. 1058, Pt. 3, pp. 832, 839–40, Vol. LI, Pt. 2, p. 957; Jedediah Hotchkiss Diary, May 27, 1864, in Jedediah Hotchkiss MSS, LC.
5. O.R., Ser. I, Vol. XXXVI, Pt. 1, pp. 1031–32, Pt. 3, pp. 378–79, 863, Vol. LI, Pt. 2, p. 969; Breckinridge to Walter Taylor, May 30, 1864, in Edward Porter Alexander MSS, SHC; Breckinridge to Taylor, June 1, 1864, in Charles S. Venable MSS; Breckinridge to Early, January 25, 1873, in Early MSS.

every major general in the Army of Northern Virginia, including these two. Had he been officially attached to this army, there is no doubt that he would have succeeded one or the other of them. However, his little division was still a separate organization, reporting directly to Lee and, consequently, he was not in line for a succession. Meanwhile, Breckinridge made yet another attempt to stir interest for Kentucky. He asked Lee if a move into Kentucky might not offer the dual advantage of drawing troops away from Grant while encouraging southern recruiting in the contested state. Lee agreed, and proposed that such a move might be made if conditions in Kentucky were as favorable as Breckinridge thought they were. Of course, they were not, and nothing came of the proposal.[6]

For Breckinridge himself, activity did not cease. Shortly after 10 P.M., June 1, he put his division in motion for Cold Harbor, with the assistance of a guide sent by Lee. It was a march of better than seven miles, at night, with men weary from constant movement over the past three weeks, and now tired from battle. It did not help that Lee's guide got them lost, taking the wrong road. As a result, the men had to be rested every half hour; in the morning, when Breckinridge should have been at Cold Harbor going into the line, he was at Mechanicsville, five miles east; and when Lee rode out to meet him, his anger at the guide stood second only to the urgency of getting Breckinridge's division up to the main line.[7]

Lee sent Breckinridge to the right wing of the army, just south of Cold Harbor, where he went into line between the divisions of Cadmus Wilcox—the extreme right—and Robert Hoke. That same day he saw his first real action since leaving the Valley. Lee had ordered that a commanding height, Turkey Hill, be occupied so that artillery might be placed there to stabilize his right, but Hoke apparently neglected to do so. As a result, the Federals put troops on most of it, and Lee was anxious to retake the hill as soon as fresh units arrived. Thus, when Breckinridge pulled into the line, supported by two of Wilcox's brigades, Lee sent him against the enemy. The Kentuckian cleared the hill, captured several hundred prisoners, and thereby secured Lee's right, though at some cost. Then, as dark settled over the field, accompanied by a heavy rain, he settled back into the Confederate line, with Mahone behind him in support.[8]

6. Eli M. Bruce and John T. Pickett to Breckinridge, June 1, 1864, John Echols to Breckinridge, June 1, 1864, Allen T. Caperton to Breckinridge, June 2, 1864, all in B. MSS.

7. Circular, June 2, 1864, in B. MSS; Freeman, *R. E. Lee*, III, 381–82; Hotchkiss Diary, June 2, 1864, in Hotchkiss MSS.

8. Hotchkiss Diary, June 2, 1864, in Hotchkiss MSS; Richmond *Daily Dispatch*, June 3–4, 1864; Reagan, *Memoirs*, 193; Freeman, *R. E. Lee*, III, 383.

No one expected what came the next morning at 4:30 A.M. Grant launched one of the bloodiest frontal assaults in the history of warfare against the right half of Lee's army. Nowhere was the fighting heavier than in Breckinridge's front. He repulsed the first charge and perhaps a second or third, when, under cover of the morning fog, a portion of Winfield Scott Hancock's Federal corps penetrated a salient on his left and broke through the front of a battalion. Immediately Mahone sent over the Florida brigade of Brigadier General Joseph Finegan, while Breckinridge called forward a unit Lee had attached to his division sometime before, and of which he had become quite fond, the Second Maryland Battalion. With the Marylanders and Finegan, he retook the salient, with an enemy loss estimated at two hundred killed. There followed more assaults and more repulses, until, by 5:30, it was over. Immediately, Breckinridge reported the results to Lee. In later years he would be most proud of the conduct of his division this day. It had held one of the most important positions in the line against the heaviest concentration of the assault. "I have been in many battles," he said after the war, "but there was one to which I turn always with especial pleasure, and that is the second Cold Harbor." He could not know now, and perhaps never knew, that one of the hundreds of dead in front of his position was his own cousin and boyhood friend, Colonel Peter Porter of the Eighth New York Heavy Artillery, whose body was riddled with bullets just twenty yards from Breckinridge's salient as he led his regiment in Hancock's attack.[9]

Lee sent his compliments to the Kentuckian on the "gallant manner" in which he withstood the repeated attacks, adding the warning that some of his breastworks were too high for effectiveness, and ordering that this be corrected. Breckinridge spent a busy day, and that evening, shortly after 8:45, he and Mahone began reestablishing the skirmish line in front of his position. Suddenly, the Federals launched another attack, though a weak one, and it was easily repulsed. Breckinridge led his men personally in the fight—"I have told them that I would head them, and I will do it." During the engagement a solid shot from an enemy gun struck "Old Sorrel" full in the chest, killing him almost instantly. In falling, the horse rolled on top of

9. *O.R.*, Ser. I, Vol. XXXVI, Pt. 1, p. 1052, Pt. 3, p. 870, Vol. LI, Pt. 2, p. 983; "J.F.T.," "Some Florida Heroes," *Confederate Veteran*, XI (August, 1903), 363; Richmond *Daily Dispatch*, June 4, 6, 1864; Breckinridge to J. Thomas Scharf, January 6, 1874, in Lamar Hollyday, "Maryland Troops in the Confederate Service," *SHSP*, III (March, 1877), 134; Breckinridge to Taylor, 5:20 A.M., 9 A.M., June 3, 1864, in Charles S. Venable MSS; undated clipping *ca.* May–June, 1875, from an unidentified Baltimore newspaper, in JCB Papers; Henry R. Swan to Abbie Swan, June 4, 7, 1864, in Swan Papers in possession of Commander Paul W. Williamson, Arlington, Va.

Breckinridge, pinning him to the ground. In the darkness and confusion the immediate impression among those nearby was that the general had been killed, but this fear was quickly allayed. The horse had his right leg pinned. It took several men to pull the dead animal off Breckinridge. "How are you wounded?" they asked, "Where? How?" Breckinridge reassured them. "No, no, not seriously," he said, "all will be right with me, but . . . ." He looked at his quivering horse. "My horse! My noble horse; poor old Sorrel, he had carried me so gallantly through so many battles and through such dangers, that I had even fancied he bore a charmed life, and would survive the war; but he is gone." Though his leg was so badly bruised that he could not ride for several weeks, the general did not have to be hospitalized. As a precaution, however, General Wharton was given command of the division for a few days while he went to Richmond to recuperate.[10]

While Breckinridge rested, alarming news came of a disaster in the Valley. Following Sigel's removal, Major General David Hunter had received command of the Federal army in that field of action, and almost immediately began another raid up the Shenandoah. On Sunday, June 5, he met a hastily assembled force under Jones at Piedmont, soundly defeated it, and left old "Grumble" dead. As a result, Staunton and the whole of the upper Valley lay open, with only Imboden and a weak infantry brigade put together in Breckinridge's department and brought up by Brigadier General John C. Vaughn, to impede Hunter.[11]

News of the disaster reached Richmond early June 6, followed by more disheartening news of another advance by Crook and Averell in West Virginia. The problem was referred to Lee, and he saw no reasonable alternative but to return Breckinridge. "He can do a great deal personally in rallying the troops & People," Lee told Davis. The order went out that same day, and at 11:30 that night Breckinridge, still unable to ride, put the 2,100 men of Wharton and Echols' brigades on the march for Richmond. Echols, seriously ill, had turned his command over to Patton. At 8 A.M. the next morning they boarded the Virginia Central for Rockfish Gap, ten miles east of Staunton, by a circuitous route through Lynchburg and Charlottesville. The general reached Lynchburg on June 8, picked up a battery, and

10. *O.R.*, Ser. I, Vol. XXXVI, Pt. 1, pp. 1032–33, Pt. 3, p. 870, Vol. LI, Pt. 2, pp. 982–84; Richmond *Daily Dispatch*, June 6, 1864; New York *Turf, Field and Farm*, May 21, 1875; J. S. Johnston, "Sketches of Operations, No. 2," p. 317; Vandiver, *Diary . . . of Gorgas*, 113; Bruce to Breckinridge, June 7, 1864, in B. MSS; Lynchburg *Daily Virginian*, June 8, 1864; Richmond *Enquirer*, June 7, 1864.

11. The best available source on Piedmont is Marshall M. Brice, *Conquest of a Valley* (Charlottesville, 1965).

then started north for Charlottesville. Well aware that the cavalry in the Valley was probably thoroughly disorganized, he requested that Morgan be sent to him from Western Virginia, while he also needed two brigade commanders for Vaughn's infantry. Unfortunately Morgan, on a raid into Kentucky, would not be available.[12]

Breckinridge sent his brigades ahead of him to Blue Ridge Tunnel, near Rockfish, and his intention was obvious. He would concentrate all of his forces at the gap, and then move through it and attack Hunter at Staunton. Toward that end, he no sooner reached Lynchburg than he ordered Vaughn to send cavalry out to harass the Federal flanks. "We will soon drive the enemy out," he said, "or destroy him." Once again Breckinridge would trust to initiative and determination to clear out the Valley. He would have seemed foolhardy, though, if anyone then knew that Crook and Averell had joined Hunter this same day, and that they counted over 18,000 effectives, while Breckinridge was sure of only 5,000.[13]

The next morning, June 9, the general followed his brigades to Charlottesville, and then he learned that Crook was at Staunton as well. Immediately he asked Lee to send him another battery, as well as for the return of the reserves from that region, temporarily in Richmond. Even if he could not defeat Hunter, he could protect Charlottesville and perhaps hold Rockfish Gap, thus protecting Lee's flank from any threat from the Valley. Now that his forces were concentrated, he organized them into two divisions of infantry under Wharton and Vaughn, while Imboden was assigned all the cavalry. This gave him a force of 5,023 infantry, and 4,000 mounted troops, but he hardly concealed his lack of faith in Imboden's cavalry. It was what his adjutant Johnston called "wild cavalry—of the inefficiency of which there was constant complaint and almost daily exhibition."[14]

On June 10 Breckinridge waited at Rockfish for his trains to come up, and received the first intelligence of a Federal move south from Staunton. He ordered Imboden to follow and attack, or at least to send back information. The general estimated Hunter's numbers at 13,500, more than twice what he regarded as his effective force, but he remained determined to at-

12. *O.R.*, Ser. I, Vol. XXXVII, Pt. 1, pp. 50, 753, Vol. LI, Pt. 2, p. 993; Freeman and McWhiney (eds.), *Lee's Dispatches*, 215–19; J. Stoddard Johnston, Notes of movement of Breckinridge's command from 6th June on leaving Cold Harbor to June 19th, June 6, 1864, in Breckinridge MSS, NYHS.

13. *O.R.*, Ser. I, Vol. XXXVII, Pt. 1, pp. 754–55.

14. *O.R.*, Ser. I, Vol. LI, Pt. 2, pp. 1000, 1002; Johnston, Notes of movement, June 9, 1864, in Breckinridge MSS, NYHS; Breckinridge to Bragg, June 10, 1864, in Davis MSS, LHAC; Johnston, "Sketches of Operations, No. 2," pp. 318–19.

tack. Two days later at daylight, his men now supplied from their wagons, he marched out toward Staunton on the other side of the Blue Ridge. He had moved only twelve miles, however, when definite information came that Hunter had gone to Lexington, taken the town, and burned V.M.I. This gave the Federals a head start of over forty miles on him, and obviously Hunter would keep moving south. Breckinridge guessed that his objective was Lynchburg. Immediately he turned the command around, moved them to the top of the Blue Ridge, and marched them south, while he ordered the train which had supplied him to reverse engines and drive to Lynchburg. Despite this new turn of events, he remained confident of success. When a telegraph operater asked permission to go to Staunton and reestablish communications, claiming that the city was now behind the lines, Hunter having passed south, Breckinridge, his mind on driving the enemy back down and out of the Valley, replied that "it may very soon be in the front again." [15]

Two more days of marching, with one day out to rest the exhausted men, put the command within twenty miles of Lynchburg. Meanwhile, Breckinridge had gone ahead, arriving to take command in the city on June 15. Its defense was vital, for it controlled the vital James and Kanawha Canal, a water supply route linking Richmond with western Virginia, as well as being one of the principal supply bases in the state. As soon as he arrived, Breckinridge sent three scouts to bring back more accurate information on Hunter's numbers and his intentions. While his intuition told him that this city was the Federal objective, the enemy might very well be planning a raid through his old department instead. As he waited definite intelligence, he went to work on Lynchburg's fortifications. At the same time, fed up with Imboden's inefficiency, he requested another general to command his cavalry. Imboden was an energetic and devoted officer, but he could not control his men. They had done, as Breckinridge put it, "less than nothing," and he warned that they would go to ruin if not under a more capable hand. As a result, Richmond dispatched Major General Robert Ransom to take over. [16]

15. Johnston, "Sketches of Operations, No. 2," p. 318; Johnston, Notes of movements, June 10–12, 1864, in Breckinridge MSS, NYHS; O.R., Ser. I, Vol. XXXVII, Pt. 1, p. 759, Vol. LI, Pt. 2, pp. 1002, 1007; "XYZ," "Hunter's Raid," SHSP, XXXVI (January–December, 1908), 102.

16. Johnston, Notes of movements, June 13–16, 1864, in Breckinridge MSS, NYHS; O.R., Ser. I, Vol. XXXVII, Pt. 1, pp. 760–61; Bushrod C. Washington, "Henry D. Beally," Confederate Veteran, XII (August, 1904), 400; Breckinridge to Braxton Bragg, June 15, 1864, in Charles S. Venable MSS.

Ransom was not the only relief sent to Breckinridge. Hunter's raid had Lee and Davis worried. Bragg had already recommended that the Kentuckian be reinforced with six thousand men to clear the Valley. Lee hardly had them to spare, the threat from Hunter had to be met, and no one thought that Breckinridge could do it with his limited numbers. Then too, if a reinforcement was sent to Lynchburg, it might destroy Hunter and move down the Valley and into Maryland on a raid, a diversion that might relieve some of the pressure from Grant. Consequently, in a daring gamble, Lee detached Early's corps on June 13 with orders to join Breckinridge and clear the Shenandoah.[17]

Just when Breckinridge first learned that Early was coming is a mystery, but certainly he knew about it by the time he reached Lynchburg, for at the same time that he reported Hunter's movements to Richmond he also sent Early word of his situation. The next day, June 16, Breckinridge's divisions marched into Lynchburg, "a reassuring sight," wrote one citizen, "and never were a lot of bronzed and dirty looking veterans, many of them barefooted, more heartily welcomed." The people lined the streets and waved hats and handkerchiefs as the general's men passed by. Breckinridge's forced march had been a success. He left Rockfish Gap on the same day that Hunter was in Lexington, and marched sixty miles to Lynchburg in the same time that it took the Federals to move about thirty-five miles, to a point still ten miles west of the city.[18]

It was another example of his ability at covering distance in a hurry, but it came at a cost. His men were dirty and exhausted, and Breckinridge himself lay near collapse, bedridden. The injury from Cold Harbor had never been given time to heal, and now it kept him immobile, unable even to inspect or attend his defensive lines. However, Breckinridge hit on a piece of luck, for in the city at this time was his former commander and friend, Daniel H. Hill. Consequently, late in the afternoon he asked Hill to oversee the placement of troops and artillery on the hills immediately around town in positions that Breckinridge had hastily selected. Hill gladly agreed. Vaughn, however, with that characteristic lack of attentiveness to orders which had caused Breckinridge to lose faith in him as well as Imboden,

17. *O.R.*, Ser. I, Vol. XXXVI, Pt. 3, p. 897; Jones, *War Clerk's Diary*, II, 230; Frank E. Vandiver, *Jubal's Raid: General Early's Famous Attack on Washington* (New York, 1960), 19–26.

18. Jubal A. Early, *Autobiographical Sketch and Narrative of the War Between the States* (Philadelphia, 1912), 372–73; J. S. Johnston, Notes of movements, June 16–17, 1864, in Breckinridge MSS, NYHS; Susan Blackford, *Letters from Lee's Army* (New York, 1942), 262–63.

made no attempt to comply, and as late as 10:30 that night his troops still were not in line, which brought a sharp note from the general.[19]

Breckinridge had sent every bit of rolling stock available in Lynchburg up to Charlottesville to facilitate Early's advance. Both were well pleased when "Old Jube" pulled into the city at 1 P.M., June 17 with one division under Stephen Ramseur, and two others on the way. Early found Breckinridge in his sickbed. Upon seeing Early's confidential instructions for the impending campaign, Breckinridge immediately offered to cooperate with him and serve under his command. In fact, since Breckinridge had been given command of all forces in the Valley, he could have maintained his separate status had he wished, but such arrangements had doomed campaigns before, and he recognized clearly the need for unified command if they were to succeed. In his present infirmity, he asked Early to allow Hill to take temporary charge of his own troops, and at the same time asked for a replacement for his senior brigadier, Vaughn. Both requests were granted, and Major General Arnold Elzey was dispatched immediately to relieve Vaughn.[20]

On leaving Breckinridge, Early rode around the lines with Hill, and then a few miles west of town to where Imboden was harassing Hunter's advance. Bringing up some of Ramseur's men, Early repulsed the Federals in an evening battle, and engaged them in some skirmishing the next day while waiting for his other divisions to arrive. Elzey came in that day and took command of Breckinridge's infantry, and then Early awaited the coming dawn of June 19 to launch an attack. When dawn came, however, it was discovered that the Federals had withdrawn, and Early determined to follow. Lynchburg had been saved.[21]

From the time of Early's arrival until this morning, Breckinridge remained in bed, unable to walk. Now, however, as his troops were put on the road at 9 A.M., he found he could ride, and Early asked him to stay with him and give counsel on the country they would pass through. The next day the Kentuckian was sufficiently recovered to resume command of his men, the two small divisions under Wharton and Elzey—barely two thousand strong now—and the cavalry led by Ransom. With them he helped in the pursuit for two days before it became obvious that Hunter would outdistance their tired troops. There was a momentary fear that the enemy

19. Early, *Narrative*, 373–74; *O.R.*, Ser. I, Vol. XXXVII, Pt. 1, pp. 764–65.
20. *O.R.*, Ser. I, Vol. XXXVII, Pt. 1, pp. 762–63, 765, Vol. LI, Pt. 2, p. 1020; Hotchkiss Diary, June 17, 1864, in Hotchkiss MSS; Early, *Narrative*, 373.
21. Early, *Narrative*, 374–75.

would head for Wytheville or Saltville, but soon it became obvious that Hunter's only object was to get out of Virginia entirely, and as quickly as possible.[22]

The men were rested for a day, and many of them sorely needed it. Breckinridge's dismounted cavalry, unused to marching, developed some severely blistered feet. Meanwhile, the general himself was closeted with Early in discussion over the course of action they would take. "Old Jube" had been given discretion to decide whether or not to undertake the proposed raid down the Valley into the North, and he sought Breckinridge's advice. Just what the Kentuckian said is unknown, but the decision rested with Early, and he elected to gamble. The next morning his little Army of the Valley marched north for the Shenandoah.[23]

In the following five days, Breckinridge marched his men an average of sixteen miles per day, to reach Staunton on the morning of June 27. Here Early reorganized his little army, and gave Breckinridge a command more in keeping—at least in name—with his position and seniority. Since his own infantry divisions numbered no more than a good sized brigade, the Kentuckian was assigned also the division of Brigadier General John B. Gordon, forming an organization to be known as Breckinridge's Corps. Elzey's ill health forced him to ask to be relieved, and Early took this opportunity to consolidate Wharton and Vaughn's commands, which unfortunately put the senior Vaughn once again in command of a division. Ransom's cavalry was removed from Breckinridge's management, and put directly under Early. The result was what Breckinridge originally suggested—a unified command structure. This left the Kentuckian second in command of the army.[24]

The corps, numbering 6,881 effectives, moved north again on June 29, Gordon in the lead.[25] During that day and the next three, he covered

22. Vandiver, *Jubal's Raid*, 54; J. Stoddard Johnston, Notes of march of Breckinridge's Corps from Lynchburg June 19th to Leesburg July 15th, dated July 15, 1864, entry for June 19, in Breckinridge MSS, NYHS; *O.R.*, Ser. I, Vol. XXXVII, Pt. 1, p. 766.

23. J. S. Johnston, Notes of march, June 22–23, 1864, in Breckinridge MSS, NYHS; Vandiver, *Jubal's Raid*, 60.

24. Johnston, Notes of march, June 23–28, 1864, in Breckinridge MSS, NYHS; *O.R.*, Ser. I, Vol. XXXVII, Pt. 1, p. 768; Early, *Narrative*, 381.

25. This figure, somewhat at variance with previous estimates, is as precise as a thorough study of the sources can make it. It is compiled from Field Report of 2d Division Breckinridges Corps, June 28, 1864, Field Return of the Regiments and Battalions composing the different Brigades of the 1st Div Breckinridges Corps, n.d. [June 24–26, 1864], Field Return of Troops Commanded by Major Genl Breckinridge July 15, 1864, in Eldridge MSS, HL, and the Staunton *Vindicator*, July 8, 1864. Intri-

seventy-six miles through intense heat alleviated only a little by brief afternoon summer showers. Many of the men were barefoot, blistered, and
bleeding, but still the march went on. By July 2 Gordon was in Winchester, and Vaughn nine miles south of him. Martinsburg, Maryland, base
of Sigel's ill-fated campaign, and still his headquarters, lay only twenty
miles ahead. Sigel had been demoted to command of the Reserve Division
of the army he once led, and was in charge of a considerable store of supplies in this city, supplies which Early's army needed sorely. The next day
Breckinridge sent Sigel scurrying in a panic for the second time. Harry
Gilmor was here acting as the Kentuckian's advance, and watched the general in the desultory fighting before the rout. "General Breckinridge is certainly as perfectly fearless under fire as any man I ever saw," he declared.[26]

Breckinridge remained in Martinsburg until 3 P.M. the next day gathering
stores to send back to the rear, and then moved off toward Harpers Ferry,
burning the Baltimore and Ohio bridges behind him. Early hoped to take
Harpers Ferry, and its garrison with it, but the Federals evacuated the town
and took position on the commanding heights above, making it impossible
for Early to occupy the city without coming under a terrible fire from
enemy artillery. Consequently, "Old Jube" ordered Breckinridge to cross
the Potomac at Boteler's Ford and move on the heights from the rear. In
so doing, the Kentuckian became the vanguard of the third, and last, Confederate invasion of the North.[27]

Breckinridge crossed on July 5, camped near Sharpsburg, and the next
morning sent Gordon against the positions on Maryland Heights overlooking Harpers Ferry. While the opponents skirmished through much of the
day, the general joined Gordon, Ramseur, and Early, in a visit to the
nearby battlefield at Antietam, which had been the scene of the war's
bloodiest single day, and probably the first of the great eastern battlefields
that Breckinridge had seen. Some might have seen a paradox in these generals, who any day now might turn some new piece of farmland into a
battleground, wanting to visit the scene of an old conflict.[28]

cate comparison of the figures in these returns, as well as some marginal notations by
Breckinridge, establish convincingly that the consolidated divisions of Wharton and
Vaughn, commanded by Vaughn (later Echols), numbered 3,290 on June 28. Gordon's
division numbers are established at 3,591, thus putting the total for Breckinridge's Corps
on June 28, 1864, at 6,881.

26. J. S. Johnston, Notes of march, June 29, July 2, 1864, in Breckinridge MSS,
NYHS; Early, Narrative, 393; Gilmor, Four Years, 184–85.

27. J. S. Johnston, Notes of march, July 4–5, 1864, in Breckinridge MSS, NYHS;
O.R., Ser. I, Vol. XXXVII, Pt. 2, pp. 591–92.

28. J. S. Johnston, Notes of march, July 5–6, 1864, in Breckinridge MSS, NYHS;
Henry Kyd Douglas, I Rode with Stonewall (Chapel Hill, N.C., 1940), 293.

The next day little happened, but skirmishing continued until a stroke of good fortune finally got Vaughn out of the general's way. Echols, at last recovered from his illness, reported to Breckinridge and was promptly put in command of the Second Division, reducing Vaughn to charge of a brigade. That night Early ordered the corps to withdraw and march east, and the next day it linked up with the other corps, under Robert Rodes, the two having marched independently up to this time. They camped at Middletown, six miles from Frederick, Maryland, where a Federal garrison awaited, supported by a hastily assembled force three miles south guarding the Baltimore and Ohio bridges at Monocacy Junction. The troops at Monocacy were commanded by a man Breckinridge had met before on the fields of Shiloh, Major General Lew Wallace.[29]

The army marched the six miles to Frederick early on July 9, Gordon in the lead, only to find the city evacuated, its garrison gone south to join Wallace. Enemy skirmishers remaining behind gave Ramseur some action, while Early directed his infantry to move south of the town toward Monocacy. Wallace had taken a position on the south side of the Monocacy River, commanding each of the three routes open to Early for an advance on Washington. The only hope of opening a way for a crossing was to drive Wallace out of the way with an attack on his flank and, as soon as he found a ford somewhat below the left of the Federal line, Early sent orders back to Breckinridge to cross the Monocacy and attack.[30]

Immediately Breckinridge ordered Gordon forward. At 2:30 his division was in motion; it crossed over the Monocacy and hit the Federals in flank. Wallace had his left change front to face Gordon, having some brief warning of the attack, and the Confederates met a stubborn resistance. Three lines of Federal infantry would have to be beaten back. Another attack in conjunction with a move by Ramseur against Wallace's center, beat back this last line, and an hour after the battle began the Federals were in full retreat toward Baltimore.[31]

Breckinridge oversaw the entire movement, the crossing of the river, and Gordon's attack, though the latter officer probably made all the dispositions for battle himself. The Kentuckian preceded Gordon's division across the Monocacy, and rode to the home of John T. Worthington, on a slight

29. J. S. Johnston, Notes of march, July 7, 1864, in Breckinridge MSS, NYHS; Early, *Narrative*, 384–86.

30. J. S. Johnston, Notes of march, July 9, 1864, in Breckinridge MSS, NYHS; Early, *Narrative*, 387–88.

31. *O.R.*, Ser. I, Vol. XXXVII, Pt. 1, pp. 350–52; Early, *Narrative*, 387–88; J. S. Johnston, "Sketches of Operations, No. 2," p. 319; J. S. Johnston, Notes of march, July 9, 1864, in Breckinridge MSS, NYHS.

rise very close to the scene of the coming battle. There he could watch the whole affair and be near enough to give rapid orders. When Worthington chided him about the danger, Breckinridge replied simply, "It is my duty to be here." [32]

What Breckinridge saw left him well pleased with Gordon. "Gordon," he said, "if you had never made a fight before, this ought to immortalize you." This Georgian, eleven years Breckinridge's junior, was one of the Confederate Army's three most outstanding general officers of infantry from the volunteer service—that is, from among those generals who had not had professional training at a formal military school such as West Point or V.M.I. The other two were Breckinridge and Cleburne. Breckinridge thought highly of him, and the feeling was returned. "The Kentucky Game-Cock," Gordon called his commander. He said of Breckinridge: "Tall, erect, and commanding in physique, he would have been selected in any martial group as a typical leader. In the campaign in the Valley of Virginia, where I . . . saw much of him, he exhibited in a marked degree the characteristics of a great commander. He was fertile in resource, and enlisted and held the confidence and affection of his men, while he inspired them with enthusiasm and ardor. Under fire and in extreme peril he was strikingly courageous, alert, and self-poised." [33]

Gordon was not the only one at Monocacy who found the general impressive. A prisoner captured from the Ninth New York Heavy Artillery, being moved back to the rear sometime after the battle ceased, saw Breckinridge riding along the line, and remarked that he was "one of the finest looking men I ever saw." "His face was so classically cut," he wrote, "and his eyes so piercing." Such notice of Breckinridge's physical magnificence had become commonplace by now, but Early, Gordon, and others thought they had a fitting way to display it. When they took Washington City in a few days, they would install the Kentuckian in his old chair as president of the Senate.[34]

Breckinridge camped at Monocacy that night, and then set out for the Federal capital at 5 A.M. on July 10. His corps covered nineteen miles that day, within a day's march of Washington, and set out just as early the next morning, bringing up the army's rear. He marched his men thirteen miles to Silver Spring, five miles from the greatest prize any Confederate could

32. Early, *Narrative*, 388; Glenn H. Worthington, *Fighting for Time, or the Battle that Saved Washington and Mayhap the Union* (Baltimore, 1932), 166–67.

33. John H. Worsham, *One of Jackson's Foot Cavalry* (Reprint; Jackson, Tenn., 1964), 155; Gordon, *Reminiscences*, 192, 320.

34. Alfred S. Roe, *The Ninth New York Heavy Artillery* (Worcester, Mass., 1899), 318; Gordon, *Reminiscences*, 314–15; Freeman, *Lee's Lieutenants*, III, 497, 558.

capture. Federal cavalry had been at his rear through much of the day, but they stayed out of harm's way, and the general's corps came into line this afternoon unmolested. Early that afternoon the sound of heavy guns from the front indicated that the Confederates had at last come within sight and range of Washington.[35]

When he was able to ride forward to the front, he stopped along the way to perform an act of kindness. Near Silver Spring stood the home of his friend and cousin, Montgomery Blair, now Federal postmaster general. Having seen the disposition of some of his more unruly privates toward looting during their performance at Martinsburg, as well as being under the influence of an order from Early strictly forbidding plunder or destruction in enemy country, Breckinridge ordered a guard placed around Blair's house, and forbade anyone to enter it or in any way disturb the property. The estate, called Silver Spring, was a scant one hundred yards from the position of the Twelfth Alabama, one of whose officers witnessed the general's action, and commented that "Breckinridge is the very soul of honor."[36]

That evening the general went to the nearby home of another Blair, Francis Preston, for a conference with Early, Gordon, Rodes and Ramseur. Early had made the house his headquarters which, considering Breckinridge's concern for the sanctity of Montgomery's home, may not have been much to the Kentuckian's liking. Nevertheless, when a few bottles of wine were found in the cellar, he joined with the others in toasts over their future. The house, the wine, the proximity to Washington, all brought back a host of memories for Breckinridge, and some mixed feelings. As he told the generals of old times at the Blair house, the irony of his situation could not have escaped him. He had served his state and his country in the city before him. His greatest achievements, and those most dear to him, occurred here. Washington represented the symbol of the authority and sanctity of the Union and the Constitution, an authority which he had felt and respected instinctively for as long as he could remember. Yet here he was now, on the verge of attacking this almost sacred city. But it was also fitting that he should be here, for it was in this place, almost three years before, that he made his decision between conscience and authority, and chose the path of duty as he saw it. That duty led him out of Washington just as, now, it had led him back.[37]

35. J. S. Johnston. Notes of march, July 10–11, 1864, in Breckinridge MSS, NYHS; O.R., Ser. I, Vol. XXXVII, Pt. 2, p. 594; Vandiver, *Jubal's Raid*, 151.

36. Robert E. Park, "Diary," *SHSP*, I (May, 1876), 379–80.

37. Douglas, *I Rode with Stonewall*, 294–95; J. Stoddard Johnston, *Kentucky*, 180.

The generals discussed their situation at length, considering the prospects for success. Early had seen reinforcements from Grant's army marching into the Federal defenses that afternoon, and he faced the possibility of losing heavily in an attack. On the other hand, it would be terrible to have come this far only to turn around without a fight. Consequently, they would attack in the morning. Breckinridge concurred in this decision, proposing a plan wherein he would penetrate the enemy works at Rock Creek, then move up their flank. The morrow's assault would bring him the unenviable distinction of being the only member of the United States executive branch in the nation's history to lead hostile troops against the city where once he sat as vice-president. Perhaps during the warm hours of the night, waiting for the dawn, his thoughts turned back to his childhood, and his Aunt Frances Prevost's stories of her step-grandfather, Aaron Burr, another vice-president whom fortune had turned from the road to the White House to the path of an outcast.[38]

Early the next morning, however, it was clear that Washington had been even further reinforced, and "Old Jube" was left no choice but to call off the ordered attack and wait until nightfall to withdraw. Skirmishing went on all day as Breckinridge sent out Gordon's pickets to harass the enemy in Fort Stevens, the main Federal work in their front. If Breckinridge, standing within range of the fort's guns, scanned it with his field glasses, he may well have seen a familiar figure peering over the parapet, the long, lank, stovepipe-hatted figure of an old friend, Abraham Lincoln. Curious about the aspect of war, the president stood for some time in the works observing the scene before him, thus sharing with Breckinridge another unhappy first; the only occasion in United States history when two former opponents in a presidential election faced each other across battlelines.[39]

After sundown, having beaten back a single, stiff, enemy assault late in the day, Early called Breckinridge and Gordon for a meeting. It was time to make arrangements for their withdrawal, and they sat up in Blair's house until past midnight. Breckinridge received orders to take the lead, bringing off the wagon train, laden with captured stores. As he put the command in motion, a final note of dismay closed the scene around Washington for him.

38. Early, *Narrative*, 391–92; Freeman, *Lee's Lieutenants*, III, 566; William V. Cox, "The Defense of Washington—General Early's Advance on the Capitol and the Battle of Fort Stevens, July 11 and 12, 1864," *Records of the Columbia Historical Society, Washington, D.C.*, IV (1901), 145n.

39. J. S. Johnston, Notes of march, July 12, 1864, in Breckinridge MSS, NYHS; J. S. Johnston, "Sketches of Operations, No. 2," p. 319; Leach, *Reveille in Washington*, 343; New York *Times*, July 22, 1864.

Stragglers, men of the Forty-fifth North Carolina, looted and set ablaze Montgomery Blair's home. Breckinridge was incensed, his anger only soothed by his saving Francis P. Blair's home and papers from a similar fate.[40]

The raid on Washington was over. The costs had been high, but the results justified the expense. Breckinridge had lost a total of 1,021 killed, wounded, and missing, 15 percent of his corps. This figure is deceptive, however, for of that total, Echols' division suffered only 281 missing, and none were reported killed or wounded. Breckinridge had Gordon do all the fighting, and it told on the Georgian. His losses ran 21 percent, a high figure for a campaign lasting less than three weeks and involving but one small-scale battle. However, on the positive side, Early had scared the North, the capital, and perhaps even Lincoln, as they had never been frightened before. He drew almost two full army corps away from Grant's army facing Lee, captured a considerable store of supplies and, perhaps best of all, showed the North and the world that the Confederacy could still mount a major threat to its antagonist.[41]

With what force he had, Breckinridge moved to Leesburg, near Big Spring, then across the Shenandoah to Berryville. Already another Federal force, the Sixth Corps from the Washington defenses and Crook's small army from the Federal Department of West Virginia, stood right behind the Confederates, pursuing. On July 18, Sunday, a deserter showed Crook a crossing on the Shenandoah unprotected by Breckinridge's pickets, and soon three brigades were sent over. Meanwhile, the Kentuckian was taking a rare opportunity to attend services at Grace Episcopal Church in Berryville. In the middle of the proceedings, a courier rushed into the church with the news that the enemy was crossing the river. Immediately, Breckinridge ordered Echols and Gordon out to meet the threat, while the danger was communicated to Early. Breckinridge engaged Crook through much of the afternoon, buying time for Rodes to be brought down on the Federal flank from a position several miles north, and the result was a most successful repulse, sending Crook back across the river, sad over his losses, and not a little unhappy with the failure of others to support him.[42]

40. J. S. Johnston, "Sketches of Operations, No. 2," pp. 319–20; Douglas, *I Rode with Stonewall*, 296; J. S. Johnston, Notes of march, July 12, 1864, in Breckinridge MSS, NYHS; C. F. Swain, "Burning of the Blair House," *Confederate Veteran*, XIX (July, 1911), 336; Cyrus B. Watson, "Forty-Fifth Regiment," in Clark (ed.), *North Carolina Regiments*, III, 55; Petersburg *Daily Register*, July 19, 1864.

41. Field Return, July 15, 1864, in Eldridge MSS, HL.

42. *O.R.*, Ser. I, Vol. XXXVII, Pt. 1, p. 346, Pt. 2, pp. 596–97; Winchester *Evening*

Despite this modest victory, the number of Federals converging on Early's little army convinced him of the necessity of withdrawing up the Valley. He pulled his corps back to Fisher's Hill, twenty-four miles south of Winchester. Now Breckinridge once again assumed the role of a Jackson. Word came that Crook's force had advanced to Kernstown, the scene of one of Jackson's 1862 engagements, some six miles in advance of Winchester. Breckinridge now proposed to Early that, on the morning of July 24, the army take the offensive once again. The infantry should advance straight up the pike to the attack, while Ransom's cavalry moved on a parallel road, two miles to the right, to get around Crook's flank, move on his rear, and cut off retreat in case of a Federal rout. It was New Market all over again, another plan worthy of Stonewall which, appropriately enough, would be enacted on his old ground. Early adopted the plan, and put it in motion on the morning of July 24. As Breckinridge rode along his lines he was surrounded by cries for bread. "Never mind, boys," he told them, "we will have plenty to eat to-night. Those fellows in front of us have got our mills, and they have the biggest droves of fat cattle you ever saw; we are going now to capture them." [43]

The second battle of Kernstown was a fine Confederate victory, but once again, as at New Market, the cavalry failed to make it complete. Breckinridge led the army toward Crook's position, and then conducted a thorough reconnaissance in person in which he went as far forward as his furthermost skirmishers, a habit formed after the embarrassing failure of Pegram's scouts at Murfreesboro. In so doing, he saw a wooded ridge on Crook's left flank, which he could reach by way of covered ravines without the Federals' knowledge. Breckinridge conducted this flank movement himself, and it was "handsomely executed," thought Early. As Crook's line advanced to attack Echols' skirmishers, the general, in a linen duster, led the bulk of the division down the hill at a charge and doubled back the Federal flank. Then Gordon and the other divisions moved forward and in a half hour Crook was in full retreat. Here is where the cavalry let Breckinridge down. It was not in its place when the rout began, and missed the opportunity to capture all of Crook's trains, as well as, perhaps, his army. The battle did not have the repercussions for the Confederacy as a whole that New Market had, but for Early's Army of the Valley, it was the most im-

Star, July 15, 1964; Marti F. Schmitt (ed.), *General George Crook: His Autobiography* (Norman, Okla., 1960), 122; Early, *Narrative*, 396.

43. Early, *Narrative*, 398–99; J. S. Johnston, "Sketches of Operations, No. 2," pp. 320–21.

portant victory of the summer. It gave the soldiers food, renewed their spirits, cleared the Valley once more for a brief time, and served as yet further incentive for the hope that there was another Stonewall in the Shenandoah. The general's young aide Clay was already sure of it after Kernstown. "Gen Breckinridge is the bravest man I ever saw," he wrote home. "He is not afraid to go anywhere in the world."[44]

The ensuing weeks were ones of almost constant movement, occasional skirmishing, and little or no rest for Breckinridge and his corps. From Kernstown the army moved north again, crossing the Potomac to Sharpsburg in the first week of August, as Early sent McCausland on a raid to Chambersburg, Pennsylvania. Breckinridge was charged with the duty of destroying Baltimore and Ohio equipment and track in Martinsburg, and then took possession of Sharpsburg to cover McCausland's raid. Cabell was accidentally wounded by his own men, during these operations, but not seriously enough to take him off active duty. After a day in Maryland, Breckinridge recrossed the Potomac, going into camp at Bunker Hill, a few miles south of Martinsburg. Then on August 9 Early learned that the Federals had been reinforced, and that now he faced the Sixth, Eighth, and Ninth corps, as well as three divisions of enemy cavalry, a total of 37,300 men to his own force of barely half that number. With this intelligence also came word that there was a new commander facing him, Philip H. Sheridan, and that he was advancing on the Confederates.[45]

Left with almost no alternative, Early moved his army south, charging Breckinridge with most of the work of covering the withdrawal, and keeping his corps constantly at the ready. It was a sad march toward Fisher's Hill, and both Breckinridge and Early were feeling low over their situation, as well as that of the Confederacy at this moment. Then old Early broke the silence. "Well, Breckinridge, what do you think of our rights in the territories now?" Stoddard Johnston, who overheard the comment, remarked later that "The inquiry was so humorous and in a vein so much in

44. O.R., Ser. I, Vol. XXXVII, Pt. 1, p. 286; Schmitt (ed.), George Crook, 123; Worsham, One of Jackson's Foot Cavalry, 158–59; W. W. Stringfield, "Sixty-Ninth Regiment," in Clark (ed.), North Carolina Regiments, III, 751; James B. Clay, Jr., to Susan M. Clay, July 26, 1864, in Thomas J. Clay MSS, LC. Johnston is the chief source for this. Although his "Sketches" differs in some details from Early's Narrative, Johnston's is written from his own diary and, due to his intimate association with Breckinridge, it is deemed the more accurate.

45. O.R., Ser. I, Vol. XXXVII, Pt. 2, pp. 600–606, Vol. XLIII, Pt. 1, pp. 992–93, 1000–1001; Diary of Captain W. W. Ould, July 31–August 10, 1864, Early MSS; Early, Narrative, 402–403; James B. Clay, Jr., to Susan M. Clay, July 31, 1864, in Clay MSS; Park, "Diary," 385.

contrast with the gloomy feelings of the company, that General Breckinridge and all present were thrown into good spirits at once."[46]

The remark typified the friendship that had grown up between Breckinridge and Early. Once the Kentuckian joined the Confederate service in 1861, he rarely afterward spoke of his old political career. It seemed generally understood that, in his presence, such subjects were not to be discussed. Only once did the subject come up among his staff, and that was when one of them quipped that two-thirds of his military family was composed of men who, in former times, had been his political foes. This may have been true on occasion—since his staff was always changing in some degree—and it is indicative of the total separation that Breckinridge made with all his past partisan feelings, though even before the war he never allowed views to interfere with his social relations. Now that he was in the war, he was also never heard to utter a word of reproach against his former friends and associates who chose to wear the blue.[47]

Yet Early could make such a remark, one which Gordon thought was in the worst possible taste, and Breckinridge would laugh. The clue to this incongruity lies in the genuine bond between Early and the Kentuckian. Even their friendship seemed incongruous to some, with Breckinridge the graceful, elegant, and above all gentlemanly epitome of the old southern aristocracy, and Early the exact opposite, profane, careless, irascible in a greater degree than any general could well afford. Yet beneath the surface, the two were surprisingly alike, for Breckinridge, though a romantic in manner and inclination, was always in heart and thought a realist. He was in large part within, what Early was without, and their similarities were cemented into friendship by their mutual regard, and by the perverse sense of humor shared by both. Just as Early was the only person who would think of making a remark to Breckinridge such as the one that he let out on this retreat, so was the Kentuckian one of the very few people, before or after the war, who could criticize "Old Jube" to his face and leave him smiling. Early made a number of enemies among the Confederate officer corps by his annoying habit of strongly rebuking what to his sometimes jaundiced eye appeared to be their mistakes or shortcomings. When he tried this on Breckinridge, however, he got the reply that "you are at your old habit of keeping your weapon on edge by sharpening it upon your friends." The

46. Early, *Narrative*, 406–407; O.R., Ser. I, Vol. XLIII, Pt. 1, pp. 991–93, 1000–1001; J. S. Johnston, "Sketches of Operations, No. 2," p. 322. Gordon, *Reminiscences*, 325, gives a slightly different account of Early's remark. However, since Johnston's account was written at least twenty-four years before Gordon's, it is adjudged the more accurate.

47. Thompson, *First Kentucky*, 306.

Kentuckian would make only three lasting friendships with generals he met in the Confederate service. Two were with Lee and Echols, the former based primarily upon mutual respect and admiration rather than enjoyable companionship, and the latter largely the result of postwar business interests. But in Early, Breckinridge found a true friend, one whose company was a joy, and with whom he would pass many a dark day ahead.[48]

By September 19, Breckinridge's divisions were down the Valley again, encamped at Stephenson's Depot with Rodes, just over four miles north of Winchester, while Ramseur was several miles south of them, just outside the city. For the past few days Early had some hints that Sheridan would advance on him, yet he split his forces in spite of it, and only saw the folly of his action when the Federal advance struck Ramseur early that morning. When Early viewed the situation, he immediately sent off a courier to bring the three divisions at Stephenson's Depot down to him. Because of some miscarriage in the order, only Gordon and Rodes began the movement, and Breckinridge did not receive it. This did not matter much at the moment, for he had already taken Echols' division—now under Wharton—east to Ridgway's Ford, where part of Sheridan's cavalry was attempting to make a crossing of the Opequon to get on Ramseur's flank. The general met them at the ford, and repulsed a series of attacks which kept him occupied through the rest of the morning while the main battle developed at Winchester. Early sent another urgent order to bring his division to the main army just before noon, but it was nearly 1 P.M. before the Kentuckian was able to pull away from the force in his front. He fell back just in time. As the Federal cavalry crossed in front of him, another division under Averell was moving down on his flank from the north. By 2 o'clock he had the division back to Early's line which, until now, had run from north to south, parallel to the main line of Sheridan's infantry. But Breckinridge brought word of the advancing cavalry from the north, and Early felt compelled to extend his line at right angles to his left to cover the advancing threat. During a brief lull in the battle, as Sheridan prepared another attack, Breckinridge, Gordon, and Early rode along north of town to lay out this new line. Early then put George Patton's small brigade in this position, and ordered the Kentuckian's other two toward his center, somewhat behind Gordon, as a mobile reserve.[49]

These arrangements had scarcely been made when the Federal cavalry

48. Gordon, *Reminiscences*, 325; Breckinridge to Early, August 10, 1873, in Early MSS. As yet there is no good biography of Early.

49. O.R., Ser. I, Vol. XLIII, Pt. 1, p. 555, Pt. 2, pp. 875–76; Early, *Narrative*, 424; Worsham, *One of Jackson's Foot Cavalry*, 169.

swooped down on the left, driving back the Confederate horsemen. Early sent Breckinridge back with his other two brigades and the attack was halted briefly. However, the sound of the firing in Breckinridge's front made the men in Gordon's and Rodes's lines believe that the enemy had somehow gotten in their rear, and they began to break from their posts and fall back despite the pleadings of their generals. Then another, more powerful cavalry attack hit Breckinridge's front. He held it off until Crook's command got its revenge for Kernstown and turned his left flank. Then his men began retreating in confusion back through Winchester, mingling with the disorganized regiments of the rest of the army as they fought to make a last defense on the city's perimeter. In the confusion, Breckinridge rode over to Gordon as they tried to rally their beaten troops. "His Apollo-like face was begrimed with sweat and smoke," the Georgian recalled. "He was desperately reckless—the impersonation of despair. He literally seemed to court death. Indeed, to my protest against his unnecessary exposure by riding at my side, he said: 'Well, general, there is little left for me if our cause is to fail.' " [50]

Even the general's desperate show of courage could not stem the rout of his men. Soon the whole army was in retreat towards Fisher's Hill. Mary had been with him for some time now, and she and Mrs. Gordon, as well as other wives, stood in the city streets pleading with the men to stand and fight, but to no avail. Only Wharton's division retained some semblance of organization, under Breckinridge's personal management, and the next day they arrived at Fisher's Hill and went into bivouac. Behind them lay terrible losses, including the mortally wounded Patton. The enemy captured a white pacer belonging to the Kentuckian. Sheridan himself appropriated the horse and named him Breckinridge.[51]

Winchester was to be the general's last major battle, and the end of his service with Early. The day after arriving at Fisher's Hill he received an order from the War Department. His old department had been hard pressed in the months of his absence, and had run through a series of commanders, Jones, George Crittenden, and Morgan. None had been successful in turning back the continual raiding, or in adequately controlling a host of internal problems that the area presented. By mid-September, Lee was looking for another commander. The number of Kentucky Confeder-

50. *O.R.*, Ser. I, Vol. XLIII, Pt. 1, p. 555; Gordon, *Reminiscences*, 322; Robert E. Park, "Diary," *SHSP*, II (July, 1876), 27–28.

51. Early, *Narrative*, 425–27; Horace Porter, *Campaigning with Grant* (Reprint; Bloomington, Ind., 1961), 428.

ate cavalry then in the department led him to believe that "the presence of General Breckinridge in that department would be attended with good results," and Richmond agreed. Orders for him to go there and resume command went out just before the Battle of Winchester. With some sadness he mounted his horse, taking Johnston with him, but leaving behind all of the troops he had brought out of the department. He did not know it, but his departure could not have been better timed, for yet another Federal raid, bigger than any before it, was even then on its way.[52]

52. *O.R.*, Ser. I, Vol. XLIII, Pt. 2, pp. 873–76; J. S. Johnston, "Sketches of Operations, No. 2," p. 323.

CHAPTER 8

It Does Seem Incredible

The department sorely needed its general. Since his departure in May, it had suffered under the raid by Averell and Crook in May, Hunter in June, and a host of minor forays against its outposts during July and August. Albert Jenkins had been killed at Cloyd's Mountain, "Grumble" Jones at Piedmont, and on September 4 at Greeneville, Tennessee, Morgan had been shot down in his nightshirt. Temporarily in command again was Echols, whose health forced him to be relieved from Early's army several weeks before. He had no reliable infantry, only scattered cavalry commands, many of them indifferent, and a host of civil problems confronting him. It was hardly a desirable situation to be in with another powerful Federal raid on the way.

The general had taken a steady hand in managing affairs in the Department even while away. Now as he rode south, once again in command, the War Department added to his responsibilities by appending to his territory the Department of East Tennessee, creating a new command, the Department of Western Virginia and East Tennessee. It included all of Virginia south of Staunton and east of the Blue Ridge, all of West Virginia that he could hold, an equal amount of Kentucky, the western part of North Carolina from Ashville onward, and all of eastern Tennessee as far west as Knoxville. With Sheridan to the north, Sherman in Atlanta to the south, Grant slowly working his way around to the west of Lee at Petersburg, and a wide frontier in Federal control across West Virginia and Kentucky, Breckinridge's department was vulnerable to attack from every side but North Carolina, and there other troubles would unexpectedly spring up to cause as much worry as any enemy raid. The total number of men with which he must defend this wide expanse was 1,551 cavalrymen, many of them without arms. In addition, there were eighteen guns, but only four of them had sufficient teams and equipment for service. Against this, the Federals were advancing with over 7,600 men.[1]

This new raid was the brainchild of Brigadier General Stephen G. Burbridge, next to Hunter, one of the most despised officers in the Federal service. With 5,200 men, including 600 soldiers of the Fifth United States Colored Cavalry, he was moving out from Mt. Sterling, Kentucky, toward the mountain passes northeast of Saltville, while 800 men under Brigadier General Jacob Ammen and 1,650 led by Brigadier General Alvan C. Gillem moved as a diversion from Tennessee across the southern border of Virginia. Saltville, Wytheville, and the rail depot at Abingdon were to be caught between them and destroyed.[2]

Even as he rode toward the department, Breckinridge went to work on supplementing his meager forces. He appealed, without success, to Early for the loan of one infantry brigade, but did receive temporary loan of a 1,700-man cavalry command under his old friend John S. Williams. However, the enemy had a start on him, and there was doubt that either Williams or Breckinridge would arrive in time. Burbridge's advance was moving with little opposition, and he would reach Saltville by the first of October. Fortunately Breckinridge had in Echols one of the most capable subordinates a commander could wish for, and the Virginian worked wonders in assembling a force to meet Burbridge. There were about 600 cavalry under Vaughn in East Tennessee, and Echols sent them to meet Ammen and Gillem. Outnumbered four-to-one, Vaughn surpassed himself in holding the Federals back, until, by October 1, they were still over forty miles from Saltville, and effectively out of the way so far as the coming battle was concerned.[3]

There was battle coming. By that date, Burbridge had crossed the Alleghenies and reached Laurel Gap, barely four miles from Saltville. He could have pushed on that evening and taken the town, then defended by less than 400 reserves. Instead he waited for morning, and that was time

1. O.R., Ser. I, Vol. XXXIX, Pt. 1, pp. 72, 84, 555, 557, Pt. 2, pp. 638–39, 877, Vol. XLV, Pt. 2, p. 864.

2. The only complete account of the Battle of Saltville and its aftermath is the author's "Massacre at Saltville," Civil War Times Illustrated, IX (February, 1971), 4–11, 43–48.

3. O.R., Ser. I, Vol. XXXIX, Pt. 1, pp. 558–59, 561, Pt. 2, pp. 476, 879, 887, XLIII, Pt. 2, pp. 871, 881; J. Stoddard Johnston, "Sketches of Operations, No. 3," SHSP, VII (October, 1879), 385; Unnumbered Special Order, September 28, 1864, Military Departments, Letters Sent, Orders, and Circulars, Department of East Tennessee and Department of Western Virginia and East Tennessee April 1863–October 1864, Chap. 2, CCXXXIV, NA.

enough for Echols. By the addition of Williams, who arrived just as the battle of October 2 was opening, a regiment of reserves, and a few other scattered, and not entirely trustworthy, commands, Echols began the fight with about 2,800. Echols himself directed all of this from his headquarters at Abingdon, twenty miles southwest of Saltville, where he remained to await Breckinridge's arrival. When the Kentuckian came in on October 1, the two set out for the front.

They did not arrive until the early evening of the next day. The better portion of the battle had already been fought and, like the hairbreadth assembly of the Confederate troops, it had been a close, last-minute, fight, a Confederate victory.

The next morning, when Breckinridge rode through the thick fog to the front and asked where the enemy was, no one knew. He sent parties out to scout and pursue, but was greatly relieved that Burbridge was gone. Another Federal raid was repulsed, and the department was still safe. But any elation Breckinridge may have felt was soon dispelled. In the wake of victory came one of the most disgraceful episodes of the war.[4]

The morning after the battle, men in the center and left of the line began hearing sporadic firing over on the right. At first they thought that Burbridge had renewed the fight, but, on finding that the Federals had retired, they soon discovered the real source; Williams' men were roaming over the field murdering every wounded Negro they could find. Men of now Brigadier General Felix Robertson's brigade and that of George G. Dibrell went out early to find the wounded Burbridge had left on the field. "Our men took no prisoners," a Confederate lieutenant recorded in his diary. Near a make-shift field hospital, one sixteen-year-old Confederate, pistols in his hands, shot down eight wounded Negroes huddled against a wall. Another rebel, a Texan from Robertson's brigade, later boasted that he killed nineteen of them with his Colt. A wounded white Federal saw the Tennessee guerilla chief, Champ Ferguson, take the unfortunate blacks out of a small hut by twos down to the thicket where pistol shots signaled their deaths. "We surely slew negroes that day," recalled one who was still a boy, and even Breckinridge's aide Clay, wandering over the field after the carnage, would write to his mother, "I assure you it was a great pleasure . . . to go over the field & see so many . . . of the African descent lying mangled & bleeding on the hills around our salt works." In about one hour's time, one

4. Davis, "Saltville," 7–10; Edward Owings Guerrant Diary, October 2–3, 1864, in SHC; George D. Mosgrove, *Kentucky Cavaliers in Dixie; or, the Reminiscences of a Confederate Cavalryman* (Louisville, 1895), 205; O.R., Ser. I, Vol. XXXIX, Pt. 1, p. 552.

hundred or more men of the Fifth United States Colored Cavalry were murdered and, by all accounts, without either provocation or defense.[5]

Equally as reprehensible as the murders themselves, was the failure of Robertson or Dibrell, or their subordinate officers, to put a stop to the massacre. There is no evidence that anyone did anything until Breckinridge, hearing the firing, rode up to the scene with Brigadier General Basil Duke and, "with blazing eyes and thunderous tones, ordered that the massacre should be stopped." When he rode away, however, the firing began again and did not stop until every Negro who had not escaped or hidden was dead. The killing did not end here, for on October 7 Ferguson and others marched into the Confederate hospital on the grounds of Emory and Henry College, near Abingdon, and murdered two more Negroes who had escaped the massacre. The next night they shot down a wounded white officer.[6]

Of course, there had been other so-called massacres in this war, barbarities committed on black Union soldiers, at places like Poison Springs, Arkansas, and Olustee, Florida, and most notable of all, Fort Pillow, Tennessee. At the last place, some 120 blacks were supposedly murdered after they had surrendered to Forrest. Controversy would surround the story for decades, though it appears that a massacre was perpetrated. In these cases, the Confederates involved had the weak excuse that they had just finished a battle and were still flushed with the fight. The Tennesseans and Texans at Saltville had no excuse. They had passed a peaceful night before their bloody work of October 3 and awoke the next morning to find no enemy threat confronting them. There can be no explanaton other than they went out that morning with the sole purpose of killing the Negroes.[7]

At first, Breckinridge did not realize the magnitude of the crime com-

5. T. L. Burnett, "Battle of Saltville," *Southern Bivouac*, o.s., II (September, 1883), 21; Lee Smith, "Experiences of a Kentucky Boy Soldier," *Confederate Veteran*, XX (September, 1912), 440; Guerrant Diary, October 3, 1864, in SHC; Mosgrove, *Kentucky Cavaliers*, 207; Marion W. Mitchell to the author, July 7, 1971; James B. Clay, Jr., to Susan M. Clay, October 16, 1864, in Clay MSS; Thurman Sensing. *Champ Ferguson, Confederate Guerilla* (Nashville, 1942), 181, 183, 185; Davis, "Saltville," 45–46; O.R., Ser. I, Vol. XXXIX, Pt. 1, pp. 553, 557, 560–61. The figure of 100 for the number murdered is an approximation based on all the sources available, and is in some wise borne out by the Richmond *Daily Dispatch*, October 12, 30, 1864, which reports that 150 Negroes were buried on the field. It is obviously an exaggeration.

6. Mosgrove, *Kentucky Cavaliers*, 207; O.R., Ser. I, Vol. XXXIX, Pt. 1, p. 555, Vol. XLIX, Pt. 1, p. 765.

7. For a full examination of the Fort Pillow question, see Albert Castel, "The Fort Pillow Massacre: A Fresh Examination of the Evidence," *Civil War History*, IV (March, 1958), 37–50.

mitted, for, late on October 3, he wired Lee of the victory, calling it a "bloody repulse" of the enemy, but making no mention of the murders. Two days later, however, he knew more, and instantly telegraphed details to Lee along with his own condemnation of the atrocity. Indeed, not only was he now aware more fully of the extent of the murder, but also he discovered that one of the general officers present at Saltville actually took some hand in the killing, either by pulling a trigger himself or by encouraging his men. Recalling the events in the wake of Murfreesboro, Breckinridge was probably not surprised to learn that the guilty officer was Felix Robertson.[8]

Just what Robertson did may never be known, but Lee joined Breckinridge in condemning it and ordered that he be arrested and brought to trial. By the time the Kentuckian heard this from Lee, however, Robertson had already gone back to join Wheeler's cavalry in Georgia, and no further action was taken. From the day of the massacre Robertson had been surly, insubordinate, even rude, and had refused to take orders. Instead, he went to report to the Army of Tennessee to serve out the remainder of the war, often a thorn in the side of other commanders as well. Significantly, the Confederate Senate consistently voted against confirmation of his commission in any of the officer grades from major to brigadier, Robertson having been appointed the latter on July 26, 1864. It seems probable that his activities as a lobbyist for Bragg in 1863 made him a number of enemies in the Senate.[9]

With Robertson out of his grasp, Breckinridge did what he could for the few survivors of the massacre, parolling their surgeon immediately, and sending him to Emory and Henry to help his wounded. The disgrace at Saltville which greeted the general on his arrival in the department was only the beginning of a host or troubles, difficulties so numerous, complex, and important to the Confederacy, that Davis sent his aide, Colonel William Preston Johnston, to southwest Virginia to confer with Breckinridge

8. Jones, *War Clerk's Diary*, II, 299–300; Freeman and McWhiney, *Lee's Dispatches*, 300; *O.R.*, Ser. II, Vol. VII, 1020. Selection of Robertson as the guilty general was first made by a process of elimination (see Davis, "Saltville," 47). However, John Echols to Samuel Cooper, February 22, 1865, Felix H. Robertson Compiled Service Record, NA, confirms it, ordering Robertson to appear before a court of inquiry to answer charges against his conduct at Saltville on October 3, the day after the battle and the date of the massacre.

9. In James H. Colgin (ed.), "The Life Story of Brig. Gen Felix Robertson," *Texana*, VIII (Spring, 1970), 154–82, an interview between Robertson and Helen P. Baldwin, the general makes no mention of his part in either the battle or the massacre at Saltville.

on confidential matters. As a result, the general began his second tour of duty in the department faced with a task of awesome dimensions. He must forge an efficient military and civil command out of a virtual shambles.[10]

Despite the mess that faced him, Breckinridge lost no time in tearing into the department's ills. His first concern before all others was bringing to justice the Saltville criminals. He set an investigation on its way to look into the massacre and name the guilty parties with a view toward bringing them to trial. No charges appear to have been forthcoming for the October 3 murders, but Ferguson and others were named as offenders in the Emory and Henry killings, and their arrest urged. Since they had left the department, it would actually be four months before Ferguson was brought back and placed under arrest, and the war would be over for two months before he finally met justice on the scaffold from a Federal hangman, surrounded, fittingly, by a regiment of Negro troops.[11]

Breckinridge met with better success in dealing with a Unionist band called the Heroes of America. Echols had been working on the Heroes for a month before Breckinridge arrived, and Richmond had sent in spies to infiltrate the organization and gather information on key members for arrests. Breckinridge had consultations with the spies, heard their information, and made his arrests when he could. On one foray, Morgan's successor Basil Duke managed to catch the "lieutenant governor" of the Heroes' "New State," along with some 200 of the membership. One of Duke's detachments pursued another 125 of the tories into North Carolina, engaged them in battle, killed 25, and put the rest to flight. Breckinridge would find it a fruitless battle in the coming months. The tories and other disloyal elements were too numerous for his limited force to control. Though he would succeed in driving them underground in a few places, in general the attempt to curtail their activities proved a failure. With fewer than 2,000 troops to defend a 35,000-square-mile expanse from enemies in uniform, Breckinridge simply could not fight effectively a civilian enemy as well.[12]

It did not help that other departments laid claim to what few troops he

---

10. *O.R.*, Ser. I, Vol. XXXIX, Pt. 1, p. 554; Jefferson Davis to William Preston Johnston, September 20, 1864, in Rowland, *Jefferson Davis*, VI, 340; William Preston Johnston to Breckinridge, September 21, 1864, in Breckinridge MSS, DU.

11. Surgeon J. H. Morton, October 18, 1864, Milton P. Jarrigan, November 8, 1864, MIAC. Endorsements on Letters Department of East Tennessee, 1862–1864, in Chap. 8, CCCLVII, NA; Sensing, *Ferguson*, 189, 251–52.

12. *O.R.*, Ser. IV, Vol. III, 804–12, Ser. I, Vol. XLIII, Pt. 2, pp. 906–907; Duke, *Morgan's Cavalry*, 549–50; Wise, *End of an Era*, 384–91; D. Thurm, October 25, 1864, in Chap. 8, CCCLVII, NA.

possessed. Early in particular cried for assistance in his hopeless bout with Sheridan in the Shenandoah, and Breckinridge could not deny him. Barely more than two weeks after his arrival in the department, the general dispatched portions of Henry Giltner's and George Cosby's brigades to Early's aid, a precious 500 men who were sorely needed where they were. To fill the gap they left, however, he worked with energy to make full use of the available manpower at his disposal. He took a realistic look at the failure of conscription in his backwoods command and applied tailored measures for recruiting in the mountain reaches.[13]

Among the regular troops Breckinridge would have some difficulties. With the death of Morgan, command of his cavalry devolved on the senior colonel, Mary's none-too-reliable cousin D. Howard Smith. Under his leadership the command became completely demoralized, in danger of falling apart. Echols had arbitrarily replaced Smith with the capable and energetic Basil Duke. Breckinridge fully approved the move and carried it on to his artillery when he arrived. Finding it in deplorable condition, he had Lee assign him a capable officer, Major R. C. M. Page, as chief of artillery. Breckinridge oversaw the testing of the guns in person near his headquarters at Wytheville and sadly saw nine of the guns condemned. This left him with seventeen of all calibers, while drill and inspection reduced the total artillery command to 344. This was a heavy attrition in the name of efficiency, but what remained was a useful, effective, and organized arm of service.[14]

The condition of his cavalry, and most of all their state of discipline, would remain a constant headache. One of the first problems that Breckinridge met on returning to the department was investigation of charges of robbery made against some of Morgan's men on their disastrous raid into Kentucky. Colonel Vinson Witcher led a cavalry raid through western Virginia, and on the way the discipline of his command fell apart. The men plundered farmers' graneries; cattle and oxen were taken and slaughtered for meat; and even private citizens were robbed. Maintaining discipline would have been much easier if the department had not been so stripped.

13. R. E. Lee to Jubal A. Early, October 12, 1864, in Early MSS; *O.R.*, Ser. I, Vol. XLIII, Pt. 2, pp. 898–99, Ser. IV, Vol. III, 863–64.

14. John Echols to Breckinridge, September 8, 1864, in Breckinridge MSS, CHS; Sydney K. Smith, *Life, Army Record and Public Services of D. Howard Smith* (Louisville, 1890), 151; R. C. M. Page, "Diary," *SHSP*, XVI (January–December, 1888), 58–61. Smith later claimed that Seddon offered him command of Morgan's cavalry, but that he declined, proposing Duke instead.

"I can hardly express to you the destitution of this department," Breckinridge would say.[15]

Personal loss added to the general's burden as he took over his department. In Baltimore, on October 8, Mary Clay Smith Breckinridge died at the home of the Reverend J. J. Bullock. Like Grandma Black Cap before her, she had survived over forty years of widowhood before going to join her husband Cabell. In her last hours her chief concern was for her only son, whom she had not seen for almost exactly three years. On his part, he may have received no more than one letter from her through the lines in that time, and it is uncertain when the news of her death reached him. However, it is good that he had Mary and Cabell with him when it arrived. Along with Stoddard Johnston and young Clay, they all "messed" together, and lived almost as a family. "Gen. Breckinridge . . . is as kind as a father," Clay wrote to his mother, "& Mrs. Breckinridge is like a mother to me."[16]

The general had little time for personal grief. Besides the myriad problems of organization and command that he faced, an enemy hovered on his borders. Over one thousand were reported encamped along the Kanawha, though later estimates lowered the figure, and soon he found that the Federals had no infantry to face him in West Virginia. This was something of a relief, but the general would have been even more relieved if he had known that throughout the month of October the enemy in that state actually feared that he was going to launch an attack against them. The result was that little or no threat posed itself from the northwest, though two Federal regiments did occupy Lewisburg briefly on October 28. By that time it was plain that the real scene of activity, for the immediate present, would be east Tennessee.[17]

Breckinridge had Vaughn patrolling that portion of the department, and it soon became evident that he could expect action there. Vaughn met and defeated an enemy force at Greeneville, Tennessee, on October 12, and four

15. *O.R.*, Ser. I, Vol. XXXIX, Pt. 1, pp. 80–84, Vol. XLIII, Pt. 2, pp. 900, 904, 906; John "Owen" Breckinridge to Breckinridge, October 12, 1864, in Breckinridge MSS, CHS.

16. "In Memorium," n.d. [October, 1864], obituary of Mary Clay Smith Breckinridge, in Prewitt Collection; James B. Clay, Jr., to Susan M. Clay, October 16, 1864, in Clay MSS; Mary C. Breckinridge to Ann Johnson, September 13, 1864, in Mary Breckinridge MSS, UK; John "Owen" Breckinridge to Breckinridge, October 12, 1864, in Breckinridge MSS, CHS.

17. *O.R.*, Ser. I, Vol. XLIII, Pt. 2, pp. 429, 450, 461, 467, 887, 900, 908.

days later several of Breckinridge's scouts managed to burn the Virginia and East Tennessee bridge over Mossy Creek in Jefferson County. This bridge was a key link with Knoxville essential for communications from that place to Federal outposts at Bull's Gap and beyond, a vital line for launching any raid into Virginia. By ordering the bridge burned, Breckinridge forced the Federals to evacuate Bull's Gap, twenty-five miles northeast of Mossy Creek, thereby denying them a position of strategic importance and opening to his own use the railroad from Abingdon down as far as the burned bridge. This meant access for transportation of supplies from a territory previously denied him, but his hold was perilous, and depended on Vaughn. That hold was lost when the cavalryman met disaster at Russellville on October 29, and had his command stampeded back to Carter's Station, near the North Carolina line. At the same time, the Federals advanced, retook Bull's Gap, and moved dangerously close to Bristol, Virginia.[18]

The general decided that the enemy must not move any closer to the heart of the department. He resolved to take the offensive away from the Federals and rode down to Carter's Station to organize his campaign. Duke was called down from the vicinity of Bristol; D. Howard Smith was ordered to send a company from Washington County, and Breckinridge directed his adjutant, Johnston, at Wytheville to send down a number of unmounted men from Duke's, Cosby's, and Giltner's brigades, along with his company of engineers, and Major Page with a section of guns. As a diversion, he sent Witcher on a scout toward the Baltimore and Ohio. The addition of some Tennessee reserves and a few miners brought his command up to nearly eighteen hundred men, to which another six hundred would be added when Lee ordered the Fifty-eighth North Carolina to cooperate with Breckinridge. From Richmond he obtained authority to make prisoner exchanges in East Tennessee. This would allow him to add to his own command by trading for Federals taken.[19]

Breckinridge moved his small army out on November 9, and by the next evening had reached Greeneville, less than twenty miles southeast of Bull's Gap. The enemy, three Tennessee cavalry regiments and two batteries under Brigadier General Alvan Gillem, had retreated to Lick Creek on

18. *Ibid.*, Vol. XXXIX, Pt. 1, pp. 559, 565–66; Freeman and McWhiney (eds.), *Lee's Dispatches*, 301.

19. J. S. Johnston, "Sketches of Operations, No. 3," p. 385; *O.R.*, Ser. I, Vol. XXXIX, Pt. 1, pp. 852, 892, Ser. II, Vol. VII, 1046, 1114, 1125; Breckinridge to Basil W. Duke, November 6, 1864, Breckinridge to F. G. Terry, November 6, 8, 1864, Breckinridge to J. Stoddard Johnston, November 6, 1864, in Eldridge MSS, HL; Page, "Diary," 61–62.

Breckinridge's approach. The general estimated their numbers at twenty-five hundred, though this figure may have been a little high. The number of effectives in both armies was roughly equal, and, on arriving in Greeneville, Breckinridge promptly reported to Lee that he had resolved to keep the offensive and attack.[20]

On the evening of the next day, Breckinridge sent Duke to engage Gillem's rear guard at Lick Creek, and Duke drove his entire force in to Bull's Gap. The Federals made three attempts to attack out of their works at the foot of the gap, but Duke held them back, and passed the night in line before the enemy. That evening Breckinridge decided that he would attack Gillem the next morning, despite the fact that the expected infantry from North Carolina had not yet arrived. "It was a resolution audacious almost to rashness," Duke thought, "for the position was very strong and the enemy outnumbered us by at least five hundred men." The general's plan was to send about three hundred men under George Crittenden in a demonstration against Gillem's front while Vaughn and about one thousand cavalry moved through an adjacent gap and took the enemy in the rear. At the same time, another demonstration would be made on Gillem's left, while Breckinridge personally led Duke and Cosby around for a surprise attack on his right. A signal gun fired at dawn would begin the battle.[21]

Breckinridge had to make a wide detour and climb a steep ridge to reach his position for the attack. Consequently, guided by a civilian, he set out with Duke in command of five hundred cavalry while it was still dark. The trip was a difficult one, but they reached their destination just after dawn, and just as a shot from one of Page's guns signaled the opening of the attack. Before Breckinridge, lay earthworks running perpendicular to the ridge he had ascended and, at each end of the works, an earthen fort. As a result, the Federals had a crossfire on the ground in their front. Despite this, Breckinridge ordered the men forward, leading the charge himself. He was able to take most of the line of works but found it impossible to withstand the fire from the forts. He led assault after assault, Duke observing that "General Breckinridge exposed himself in a manner that called forth the almost indignant remonstrance of the men, and it is a matter of wonder that

20. Breckinridge to R. H. Sanford, November 8, 1864, Breckinridge to M. Wood, November 10, 1864, in Eldridge MSS, HL; Breckinridge to Lee, November 10, 1864, in Abraham Lincoln MSS, Brown University Library, Providence, R.I.; O.R., Ser. I, Vol. XXXIX, Pt. 1, pp. 888–92.

21. Breckinridge to Lee, November 12, 1864, in Eldridge MSS, HL; O.R., Ser. I, Vol. XXXIX, Pt. 1, pp. 592–93; Duke, Morgan's Cavalry, 552; Duke, Reminiscences, 186; Page, "Diary," 62.

he escaped unhurt." The men on the other side of those works, the Thirteenth Tennessee Cavalry, were just as impressed, regarding Breckinridge "as one of the bravest and ablest Generals in the Confederate service." But neither the respect of his own men, nor that of the enemy, enabled the general to hold the works.[22]

Yet he did not give up. The next afternoon the North Carolina troops arrived led by his old brigade commander at Murfreesboro, Colonel John Palmer, and Breckinridge resolved to take by strategy what he could not win by force. Gillem had carelessly left Taylor's Gap, two miles below Bull's Gap, unguarded, and after dark the general led Duke and Vaughn through the gap toward Gillem's command. An unusual number of campfires illuminated the enemy's works that night, and they gave Breckinridge reason to suspect that they were a cover for withdrawal. Thus, his situation might be even better. Instead of attacking Gillem's fortifications again from the rear and cutting off his communications, he might be able to catch the Federal column spread out on the road leading toward Knoxville.

It was midnight by the time Breckinridge passed through Taylor's Gap and sent scouts ahead. The news they brought back could not have pleased him more. Gillem was moving on the road to Knoxville, having evacuated his works, and he was strung out in the open, his whole flank exposed to Breckinridge. Immediately, the general ordered Duke and Vaughn forward, the former to move ahead of Gillem to cut off his retreat, while Vaughn struck him on the road. Always Breckinridge thought not just of defeating the enemy, but of destroying him.

The Confederates hit Gillem at 1 A.M., November 14, in the vicinity of Russellville, setting him off down the road in confusion. The rear regiment was completely cut off from the rest of the command and most of it captured. Duke, unable to get in front of the Federals, began hitting them in flank with Vaughn's forces, and then followed a pattern of repeated assaults on parts of the retreating column, driving portions off in confusion into the woods. In this fashion Breckinridge pursued Gillem about twelve miles to Morristown. Here the Federals, joined by a fresh regiment, halted to put up a resistance. The entire fight so far had been conducted by moonlight, the fire of the guns adding further illumination to a scene beautiful despite its circumstances. As Gillem re-formed under cover of the fresh

22. Page, "Diary," 62; Duke, *Morgan's Cavalry*, 553; Duke, *Reminiscences*, 186–87; Breckinridge to Lee, November 12, 1864, in Eldridge MSS, HL; Samuel W. Scott and Samuel P. Angel, *History of the Thirteenth Regiment, Tennessee Volunteer Cavalry* (Philadelphia, 1903), 202.

troops and fire from a single gun placed on the crest of a steep hill, the Confederates could see by the moonlight that Breckinridge was leading a small squad up the slope against the troublesome piece. They captured it; Duke and Vaughn broke the Federal line once more; and the race began anew. It did not end until 5 A.M., after a chase of twenty-five miles, when Gillem rushed the remainder of his command through New Market to Strawberry Plains, across the Holston, just fifteen miles from Knoxville.[23]

Breckinridge was elated over his success, and he had good reason. Even Gillem was forced to admit that it was a "terrible reverse." Writing that morning from his headquarters at Morristown, Breckinridge reported the capture of several hundred prisoners, ten flags, six 10-pounder Parrott rifles complete with teams and caissons—Gillem's entire artillery command—ambulances with medical supplies, and at least fifty commissary wagons loaded with rations. The number of prisoners would rise above three hundred.[24]

The general did not rest after his victory, but continued to work on Gillem. Advancing to Strawberry Plains himself, he faced the Federals across the river for several days, trading artillery and rifle fire with the reinforced enemy, and then sent Vaughn across the stream some distance above Gillem's flank, forcing him to withdraw to the safety of the fortifications at Knoxville. By this time, he had duped the Federals into thinking that he had three to eight thousand men instead of barely two thousand effectives. "It does seem incredible that Breckinridge should be able to come in with so large a force," they said.[25]

During the skirmishing across the Holston occurred one of those scenes that made Breckinridge's sensitivities revolt at the cost of war. He and Duke sat conferring in his headquarters one evening when a woman came in bearing her three-year-old daughter. The little girl had been struck in the leg by a Federal bullet that partially shattered the bone. Immediately Dr. B. C. Duke, the general's acting medical officer, took over, and Breckinridge and General Basil W. Duke offered to do whatever they could. As they watched, probably helping to hold the child down, the doctor began

---

23. *O.R.*, Ser. I, Vol. XXXIX, Pt. 1, p. 893; Duke, *Morgan's Cavalry*, 555–57; Duke, *Reminiscences*, 188–89; Richmond *Daily Dispatch*, November 16, 25, 1864; Breckinridge to Lee, November 14, 1864, in Eldridge MSS, HL; T. H. Hightower, "Lynch's Battery at Bull's Gap," *Confederate Veteran*, XXV (August, 1017), 315.

24. James B. Clay, Jr., to Susan M. Clay, November 14, 1864, in Clay MSS; *O.R.*, Ser. I, Vol. XXXIX, Pt. 1, pp. 885–86, Vol. XLV, Pt. 1, p. 1208; Breckinridge to Lee, November 14, 1864, in Eldridge MSS, HL; Richmond *Daily Dispatch*, November 25, 1864.

25. *O.R.*, Ser. I, Vol. XXXIX, Pt. 1, p. 893, Vol. XLV, Pt. 1, p. 97, Pt. 2, p. 77; Duke, *Reminiscences*, 189–90; Duke, *Morgan's Cavalry*, 557–58.

probing to find and extract the bullet. He maintained his composure when the little girl began screaming in pain, but not so the two generals. Duke later recalled that "that child's demonstration of suffering completely unnerved me. I became sick at the stomach and hurriedly left the room and the house." It was not long before Duke found that he had company. "In a moment I heard some one else rush out of the house, and turning around discovered that it was General Breckinridge. He was affected just as I had been, and like me was seeking relief in flight and fresh air." [26]

Even while Breckinridge faced Gillem across the Holston, he began to have fears for the Virginia end of his department. He expected a raid from Kentucky sometime around the first of December and, on November 21, set out by a diversionary route to return to Wytheville and prepare his forces there. Leaving Duke, Vaughn, and Palmer at Strawberry Plains, he took four guns and the dismounted men and moved due north toward Cumberland Gap. This led Burbridge to fear that the general's raid would be extended to Kentucky, and he moved out of Lexington with part of his division to protect his southern border. Breckinridge, however, passed through Powell's Gap some six miles from Cumberland, and moved on east to Wytheville.[27]

The results of his November campaign more than repaid him for the risks taken. Most important, east Tennessee had been cleared of the enemy for over 130 miles from Knoxville east to North Carolina. Gillem had been routed and his command demoralized. Valuable stores were captured, and lines of supply and communication were reestablished from Virginia into Tennessee. Since there was little likelihood of another Federal offensive in that territory during the winter, this portion of his department was relatively secure. At the same time, the general's bold raid gave the enemy an inflated idea of his forces, and his intentions. In Virginia, Grant now believed that Breckinridge would strike next somewhere on the Ohio River, while Federal authorities in Tennessee and Kentucky believed that he was leading an expedition against Murfreesboro. Indeed, one of the best side products of his expedition was that this fear of invasion so upset Burbridge that he felt forced to neglect his recruiting program in Kentucky to devote himself to defense against an attack that never came. "Breckinridge seems to infuse energy and confidence wherever he goes," the press said in Rich-

26. Duke, *Reminiscences*, 247–48.
27. *Ibid.*, 190; *O.R.*, Ser. I, Vol. XXXIX, Pt. 1, pp. 892–93, Vol. XLV, Pt. 1, p. 1237; Duke, *Morgan's Cavalry*, 557–58; Breckinridge to R. C. M. Page, November 21, 1864, in Eldridge MSS, HL.

mond, "General Breckinridge is doing everything well in Southwestern Virginia and East Tennessee." [28]

In the brief time that he had delayed a Federal advance into southwestern Virginia, Breckinridge faced anew all of the old problems. Desertion still plagued the command. There were roaming squads of bushwhackers, stragglers, and absentees terrorizing the hills, and these he decided to wage war against, sending a company through several counties to capture or disperse the renegades, some of whom rode under a black flag. More strict penalties than he preferred had to be used. Officers who, as had previously been customary in these informal mountain commands, strayed from their units when under orders, were arrested and brought before court-martial, and at least one deserter was hanged at Breckinridge's order. [29]

As well as being military commander of the department, Breckinridge found that—perhaps in part because of his former political prominence—he was looked upon as the chief civil authority as well, a peculiarity made possible by the breakdown of the regular civil courts and justice system in the tory-ridden territory, as well as the fact that the war had completely absorbed both the endeavor as well as the thought of the mountain people loyal to the Confederacy. Every manner of complaint came to him, and "if history shall accord to him praise for his military administration," Johnston would say, "it should give him no less credit for the wisdom, prudence and firmness with which he guarded the civil interests of the people. Even a tory agreed. "I received kindness and protection from Genl Breckinridge," he wrote; "when he had power ... he did not abuse it; when he might have imprisoned he liberated; when he might have persecuted and oppressed Union men (including myself) he protected them."

Of course, with all his other duties, Breckinridge also held the unique responsibility for keeping the Confederacy supplied with salt, lead, and other necessities. Although the salt works was absorbed by the state of Virginia, he was charged with seeing that the trains to carry its produce to Richmond and other points ran regularly despite the myriad other demands on his limited rail facilities. The same was true of the lead from Wytheville, and regular shipments had to leave the department. Iron fur-

28. *O.R.*, Ser. I, Vol. XXXIX, Pt. 1, p. 893, Vol. XLV, Pt. 1, pp. 1164, 1223, Pt. 2, pp. 96, 224–25, 244; Richmond *Whig*, October 19, 1864; Richmond *Daily Dispatch*, November 28, 1864.

29. *O.R.*, Ser. I, Vol. XLV, Pt. 1, p. 1236; Breckinridge to ?, n.d., in Eldridge MSS, HL; Mosgrove, *Kentucky Cavaliers*, 231; Guerrant Diary, December 9, 1864, in SHC; Breckinridge to James A. Seddon, November 27, 29, 1864, Secretary of War Register of Letters Received, February 1864–April 1865, Chap. 9, XXXI, NA.

naces and forges in his command formed the chief supply of horseshoes;
Lee's army depended on the grain and beef shipped sometimes daily; and
all of this came under his administrative umbrella. That he was successful
is attested by the fact that during his tenure in the department, nearly
100,000 bushels of salt were shipped to Richmond. As for the lead, Breckinridge shipped out higher quarterly tonnages of it during 1864 than at any
time during the war, excepting only the July–September quarter of 1862.
Meanwhile, under orders from the War Department, he had his men recovering spent lead from battlefields.[30]

One thing he could not replenish from the battlefield, however, was his
dwindling manpower. In a department large enough to require an army
corps for its defense, his command was now reduced to less than a medium-
sized brigade, one thousand to fifteen hundred. As November drew to a
close, he confided to a Richmond friend that if the situation got much
worse, he would not have even enough men to meet the deserters and bushwhackers in battle, much less the enemy, and at precisely this time, in
Knoxville, a new Federal offensive with over six thousand troops was being
planned by General George Stoneman. "I will have him out of Tennessee,"
the Federal said of Breckinridge, "in less than a week."[31]

Breckinridge received his first news of Stoneman's opening campaign on
December 1, with the report that Burbridge with four thousand had moved
out of Cumberland Gap toward Bean's Station, Tennessee. It caught him
with his available forces spread out over quite a bit of territory. The reserves were out arresting deserters in several counties, with one battalion
of about four hundred of them at Saltville. Witcher was fifty miles away
near Princeton guarding the approaches from the Kanawha. The portions
of Cosby's and Giltner's brigades that were sent to Early had returned, the
former at Saltville shoeing his horses, and the latter in nearby Russell
County. Fortunately, at the first news of Burbridge's advance, Vaughn
pulled back to Greeneville, and Duke to Rogersville, establishing a line of
couriers between their commands. Breckinridge sent them instructions to
unite near Carter's Station at the first news of a heavy advance. Even then,

30. J. S. Johnston, "Sketches of Operation, No. 3," p. 386; N. Harrison to Andrew
Johnson, January 6, 1868, Records of the Adjutant General's Office, Amnesty Papers,
1865, Kentucky, John C. Breckinridge, RG 94, NA; Ella Lonn, *Salt as a Factor in the
Confederacy* (University, Ala., 1965), 212–13; Ralph W. Donnelly, "The Confederate
Lead Mines of Wytheville, Va.," *Civil War History*, V (December, 1959), 405–406.

31. Edward O. Guerrant, "Operations in East Tennessee and Southwest Virginia,"
in Johnson and Buel (eds.), *Battles and Leaders*, IV, 479; O.R., Ser. I, Vol. XLV, Pt. 1,
p. 1164, Vol. XLVI, Pt. 2, p. 1201.

there was still a chance that the Federals might separate them from him.[32]

Breckinridge knew that Burbridge had not gone back into Kentucky, but he did not suspect an advance, an opinion that was fortified by reports from citizens who had seen the Federal camps. Thus, he must have been surprised on December 12 to receive a dispatch from Vaughn or Duke announcing that Stoneman's entire army was on the move towards Kingsport, Tennessee, barely twenty miles from Bristol. After reporting this to Lee, he ordered the cavalrymen to fight and delay the enemy if possible, but by the time the telegram arrived it was much too late. On the morning of December 13, Stoneman's fifteen-hundred-man advance under Gillem met Duke at Kingsport and beat him soundly. That same evening, Burbridge marched into Bristol almost unopposed, and began destroying the railroad buildings and government sheds. At the same time, he took over the telegraph office and, forcing the operator to cooperate, was able to monitor all of Breckinridge's dispatches for several hours, learning valuable information on the general's numbers and positions.[33]

That evening Vaughn notified Breckinridge of Duke's reverse. The general had already ordered Echols to assemble all of the department reserves, called Witcher toward Saltville, and ordered Cosby and Giltner to head for Abingdon. Now he directed Vaughn to speed to Bristol in advance of Burbridge if possible, or to harass his rear, but Vaughn did not receive the message. Fortunately, he began to move north on his own judgment. Meanwhile, Duke had brought the remnant of his command to Saltville, as had Cosby and Giltner when Stoneman took Abingdon on the fourteenth, and Breckinridge and Echols arrived by train early the next day. Witcher would arrive soon, giving Breckinridge about sixteen hundred men. Vaughn was expected, but Gillem, advancing from Abingdon, caught him at Marion, about ten miles southeast of Saltville, and drove him back toward Wytheville on the morning of December 16. Gillem pursued and, by that evening, was on the outskirts of the town, Vaughn having been driven through it and beyond. Breckinridge had been cut off from all communication with Wytheville during the day, and had sent young Clay on a hair-raising ride to attempt to get through to Stoddard Johnston, in command at the lead town. To avoid the enemy, Clay had to ride sixty-eight

32. *O.R.*, Ser. I, Vol. XLV, Pt. 2, pp. 632, 649, 663, 669; Report of Breckinridge to Walter Taylor, January 3, 1865, in Breckinridge MSS, CHS, hereinafter cited as Breckinridge Report.

33. Breckinridge Report, in CHS; Richmond *Whig*, January 7, 1865; *O.R.*, Ser. I, Vol. XLV, Pt. 1, p. 835, Ser. III, Vol. V, 372.

miles at a gallop, only to find that he was too late. When Vaughn passed on, Johnston was left to hold the town with less than a dozen pickets, at least one of them drunk. He used his little command to good advantage, showing them as conspicuously as possible, while he stalled Gillem for an hour and one half by parleying for the surrender of the place. During that time, he managed to get fourteen carloads of government supplies on their way to safety before being forced out. Then Gillem marched in and began the destruction.[34]

Stoneman had threatened Saltville with a brigade, but was content for the time being to leave Breckinridge isolated there while he worked on Wytheville, the lead mines, and the railroad above and below Marion. Besides, Saltville had strong fortifications which the Federals, remembering Burbridge's fiasco in October, were not anxious to attempt again.

Breckinridge was uneasy sitting at Saltville, cut off from outside communication. Not knowing Vaughn's fate, he still hoped that he might unite with him and move on Stoneman's rear while the Federals were occupied along the railroad. Too, he felt concerned over the lead mines and Wytheville, and probably did not know their fate until December 18. W. A. Stuart, one of the managers of the salt works, assured Breckinridge that any damage the Federals might do to the wells could be only minimal should the general have to leave the town. These influences, added to Breckinridge's belief that "it would not be creditable to remain there and surrender the whole Dept to the Enemy," decided him. He would advance on Stoneman's rear without Vaughn. At moonrise, December 16, he ordered Giltner to lead the way toward Marion.[35]

Breckinridge was exhausted. He had not slept for several nights during the emergency, but now, on the eve of battle, he tried to take some rest at the home of a hospitable citizen. Strict orders were left not to awaken him, and, when an officer called during the night, the master of the house refused to disturb the general. "We must be careful of the health of our General," he said. "Much depends upon him, for I regard him as one of the pillars of the Confederacy." The gentleman's daughter shot back, "You had better call him one of its sleepers, father." The pun delighted Breckin-

34. Breckinridge Report, in CHS; Mosgrove, *Kentucky Cavaliers*, 231–32; *O.R.*, Ser. I, Vol. XLV, Pt. 1, pp. 825, 827–28, Pt. 2, pp. 695, 711–13, 930; Guerrant Diary, December 15, 1864, in SHC; James B. Clay, Jr., to Susan M. Clay, December 29, 1864, in Clay MSS.

35. *O.R.*, Ser. I, Vol. XLV, Pt. 1, pp. 811–12; James B. Clay, Jr., to Susan M. Clay, December 29, 1864, in Clay MSS; Breckinridge Report, in CHS; Guerrant Diary, December 16, 1864, in SHC; Mosgrove, *Kentucky Cavaliers*, 233.

ridge when he awoke, but the men outside shivering in the cold might not have seen the humor in it. At least a few of them resented their lot as they had to "wait for *Gen Breckinridge to come up*, or get through his nap." The general was not as popular with Giltner's Kentuckians as with Duke's, probably because the former felt that the latter received preferential treatment. They had not fought under him before, but their opinion would change once they had. Indeed, he began softening their feelings toward him that very morning when he rode out along Giltner's line. "What a handsome and imposing appearance he made!" one recalled. "Tall, straight, dignified, he was the ideal Kentuckian among Kentuckians." As the general rode toward the front, cries went up of "Boys, he'll do," "W-h-e-w! ain't he grand?" and "Boys, that man has been Vice-President of the United States." [36]

There was a report that morning that the enemy had left Marion before dawn, and Breckinridge moved his command rapidly forward. He left four hundred reserves at Saltville, and now had no more than one thousand to face almost all of Stoneman's combined force, still well over five thousand. Shortly after leaving, Breckinridge received a report that the Federals had turned and were on their way back toward Marion, Witcher putting up a courageous but inadequate, resistance to their advance. Rapidly the general moved on to Marion, just reaching the town when a more urgent message came from Witcher. Finally the two armies collided about a mile east of Marion, two brigades under Burbridge in the Federal vanguard. They met at a covered bridge over the Holston. Duke crossed the low stream at a nearby ford and managed to push Burbridge's left back some distance before dark halted his movements, whereupon Duke took position on a ridge, forming the right of Breckinridge's little army, and the only portion of it across the river. Meanwhile, Giltner on the left, and Cosby in the center, repulsed a series of light assaults that were finally halted by nightfall. Still, the brief battle thus far had so disorganized Burbridge's command that Stoneman, coming up ahead of the balance of his force, had to devote much of the evening to straightening it out. A trooper of the Eleventh Michigan Cavalry could see Breckinridge across the lines during the fight. "I saw you riding up and down your line of battle," he wrote, "encouraging your men by your own acts of daring." [37]

36. J. S. Johnston, "Sketches of Operations, No. 3," pp. 387–88; Guerrant Diary, December 17, 1864, in SHC; Mosgrove, *Kentucky Cavaliers*, 234.
37. *O.R.*, Ser. I, Vol. XLIII, Pt. 2, p. 941, Vol. XLV, Pt. 1, p. 812; Mosgrove, *Kentucky Cavaliers*, 235–36; Guerrant Diary, December 18, 1864, in SHC; Breckinridge

That night, while Duke was being pressed on the right, Breckinridge ordered a regiment across the river to his support, and then himself rode over to see Giltner. Along the way he had to run a gauntlet of fire from Burbridge's black troopers. After looking over his command, the general ordered the line advanced but soon found that it could not be done in the darkness. Burbridge, meantime, sent a detachment of Negro soldiers to a position on the covered bridge from which he hoped to use them as sharpshooters.[38]

The coming of dawn showed Burbridge's error. Far from being effective sharpshooters, the cavalrymen were themselves caught by the fire of the Kentuckians, unable to go forward, and unable to retreat. This was the only action in the forepart of the morning, for Stoneman consumed a good deal of time in positioning his troops. Gillem had arrived during the night, and now he sent him off around Breckinridge to move against the salt works, eighteen miles distant. However, sometime before noon, when Stoneman sent in his first attack, the strength of the resistance convinced him that Breckinridge had pulled together his full force. Immediately, Stoneman ordered Gillem back, even though the flank march had put the latter within eight miles of Saltville. Gillem would not arrive until dark, too late to take further part in the battle, but as subsequent events would show, his bloodless march gave Stoneman the battle.[39]

After feeling the Kentuckian's line from left to right, the Federals determined to concentrate their attack on Duke. This was largely because they felt their own left threatened as Breckinridge kept trying to push Duke around that flank. The first attack pushed Duke back, but he held, and then withstood a second assault. That afternoon Breckinridge sent Witcher over with about sixty men as a reinforcement, and together Witcher and Duke made a move around Stoneman's left flank. By this time, ammunition was running very low. Breckinridge began the campaign with one hundred rounds per man but, thanks to the loss of several wagons at Kingsport, as well as the rapid firing of the cavalrymen, the little army now stood reduced to about fifteen per soldier, with no reserve supply.

By evening, after withstanding odds of nearly four-to-one for an entire day and holding Stoneman at bay, Breckinridge and his men were ex-

Report, in CHS; Duke, *Morgan's Cavalry*, 561; James Lion to Breckinridge, April 13, 1875, in JCB Papers.

38. Guerrant Diary, December 18, 1864, in SHC; Mosgrove, *Kentucky Cavaliers*, 236–37; T. H. Hightower, "Mixin' with the Yankees," *Confederate Veteran*, XXXV (December, 1927), 455.

39. Mosgrove, *Kentucky Cavaliers*, 237–38; *O.R.*, Ser. I, Vol. XLV, Pt. 1, p. 821.

hausted. He ordered them to hold their fire except at close range in order
to preserve ammunition, and then began weighing disturbing reports of
Federal columns moving around his flanks. He was told that nine to twelve
hundred men had passed around his right and were camped six miles in his
rear at Seven Mile Ford, while another, Gillem, had moved beyond and
behind his left. Most of his men believed that they had won the battle, even
those few who knew that the enemy was now at their rear, but they did
not know, as Breckinridge did, that the command's ammunition was so low
that it would be lucky to withstand an attack on one side, let alone assaults
from front and rear. This left Breckinridge forced to make the most frustrating decision of his tenure in the department. Never before in southwestern Virginia had he ever withdrawn his army from the fight, or left an
enemy army victorious. Now, however, he found no choice but to retreat
quickly to save what remained of his command from being surrounded and
captured or destroyed. On important decisions, Breckinridge generally kept
his own counsel, and at 11 P.M. he ordered the army to withdraw by the
right flank, south over Glade Mountain.[40]

Amid a heavy rain that turned the road to mud and chilled the men, the
order went out, and the troops did not like it any more than the general.
Cosby, Giltner, and Witcher led the retreat back to Marion, followed by
Page, with Duke covering the rear. Moving along a creek which led around
Stoneman's right, to the east, Breckinridge, "somewhat excited," thought
one of his officers, pushed the men as Duke fought a brief rearguard picket
action. Before long they came to a fork in the road, and the general, showing visibly the frustraton he felt at retreat, stood before a fire for nearly
half an hour to decide which road to take. When the army reached the top
of the mountain Breckinridge halted at the summit amidst a dense wood.
The brush and branches were too wet to burn, and the Confederates passed
the rest of the night there in the chill rain. Breckinridge, thoroughly disgusted, sat down on a stump, "looking mad, dreary and forlorn." On a
stump next to him sat a corporal alternately nodding and swearing.[41]

The next morning Breckinridge set off down into the Rye Valley and
marched north through it to Mount Airy on the road between Wytheville
and Marion, twelve miles from the latter. Now part of the reason for his

40. Breckinridge Report, in CHS; F. H. Mason, *The Twelfth Ohio Cavalry* (Cleveland, 1871), 89; Duke, *Reminiscences*, 190–91; Duke, *Morgan's Cavalry*, 562–63; Guerrant Diary, December 18, 1864, in SHC; Mosgrove, *Kentucky Cavaliers*, 240–41; Page,
"Diary," 64.
41. Guerrant Diary, December 18, 1864, in SHC; Mosgrove, *Kentucky Cavaliers*,
240–41.

depression over the night's delays became evident. While there was no doubt that he was forced to retire from Stoneman's front, he did so in a manner that took him completely around the rear of the enemy army and put him, at morning, some distance in rear of where the Federal flank had been the night before. Wytheville was at his back, thus protected from further destruction, and he ordered Johnston, who had returned to the town, to have ammunition sent down at once. If Stoneman was still in his position, Breckinridge could move swiftly down on his unsuspecting flank and rear, and it would be an entirely new battle. The general planned his retreat with the offensive uppermost in his mind. Duke marveled at his audacity. "I have never, I think, witnessed an indifference to danger so absolutely calm and imperturbable as I have seen him display under very extraordinary exposure to personal peril," the brigadier wrote of Breckinridge. "Nature seemed to have formed him to deal with emergencies. He rose to his full stature only in the midst of danger and disaster, and was at his best when the occasion seemed desperate." [42]

So completely did the general fool Stoneman as to his whereabouts that the Federal believed he had gone into North Carolina, many miles south. Breckinridge duped him too well, for Stoneman moved his command toward Glade Spring that same night, and prepared to attack Saltville, which was taken the next day with little difficulty. Breckinridge already had Duke moving down the road toward Saltville to relieve the garrison if possible, for he felt great fears for its safety, but, on December 20, as he was moving behind Duke, he received a report that Saltville had fallen. Arriving the next morning, Breckinridge pressed Stoneman's rearguard, but inconclusively, as the Federal army, its work of destruction done, moved off west toward Kentucky and home. [43]

The damage done by Stoneman on his raid was significant, though not as great as he believed. Most serious to the department immediately was the loss of the quartermaster stores at Bristol and Abingdon, both of which saw the torch liberally applied. Wytheville also suffered terribly. Some estimated that the mines would be out of production only eight days as a result of this, but the superintendent set the limit at two months at least, and it turned out to be three before they resumed operation. As for Saltville, much machinery and many buildings were destroyed, railroad iron was dumped down the salt wells, and most of the Negroes who worked the op-

42. Breckinridge Report, in CHS; O.R., Ser. I, Vol. XLV, Pt. 2, pp. 713–14, 716; Duke, Reminiscences, 193.
43. O.R., Ser. I, Vol. XLV, Pt. 1, pp. 812–13; Breckinridge Report, in CHS; Duke, Morgan's Cavalry, 564.

eration were taken away to Kentucky. Nevertheless, one of the proprietors, estimated that the damage done would not keep him out of production for long. The chief loss was some 50,000–100,000 bushels of salt destroyed as it awaited shipment. And it would take two months to get the department's rail line back in operation.[44]

Breckinridge's gains from the campaign were few. Four usable guns were abandoned by Stoneman, as well as eight hundred cavalry horses that were much needed. He left at least two hundred prisoners and lost more on the retreat, while his killed numbered the same or more. As for the Kentuckian, his losses are unknown. Whatever they were, he could ill afford them. Meanwhile, criticism of the campaign began in Richmond. His old friend Simms had earlier suggested that Breckinridge would do himself no harm by keeping a correspondent for one of the capital papers with him to carry his side of affairs, and it would have helped in the face of the disappointment felt over Stoneman's raid. Nevertheless, Breckinridge had his champions in the press, and they seemed to understand his problem. "It is impossible for General Breckinridge to defend such an extensive frontier with a mere handful of men," said the Richmond *Whig*. "But few seem to appreciate the position occupied by the Department Commander, and some would appear to demand of him impossibilities. His military history, and that of his subordinates, should be sufficient evidences of the interest felt for the defenses of the country. Let the exempted fraternity and officers in easy positions be cautious in their denunciations." [45]

The most immediate concern now facing Breckinridge was the rebuilding of his department. He set out to reorganize the command, and bad weather notwithstanding, saltmaking resumed, work began on the lead works, and his engineers showed unexpectedly rapid results in repairing the burned bridges. In a few weeks they were serviceable. Although much of what needed doing did not get done, Breckinridge's energy in reorganizing the area brought from Lee several expressions of thanks and gratitude for his efficiency. His respect for the Kentuckian, already high after the New Market Campaign, continued to grow despite the reverses of De-

44. Guerrant Diary, December 20, 24, 1864, in SHC; Duke, *Reminiscences*, 192; Mosgrove, *Kentucky Cavaliers*, 242; *O.R.*, Ser. I, Vol. XLIII, Pt. 2, pp. 945–46, Vol. XLV, Pt. 1, pp. 830, 834; Mason, *Twelfth Ohio*, 82–83; Donnelly, "Confederate Lead Mines," 412; Richmond *Whig*, January 7, 1865; Lonn, *Salt*, 201–202; Breckinridge Report, in CHS; Lee to Seddon, December 24, 1864, in Richmond *Daily Dispatch*, December 27, 1864.

45. Breckinridge Report, in CHS; *O.R.*, Ser. I, Vol. XLV, Pt. 1, pp. 808, 824–27; Duke, *Reminiscences*, 191; William Simms to Breckinridge, November 4, 1864, in Breckinridge MSS, DU; Richmond *Whig*, January 7, 1865; Carter Harrison to W. C. P. Breckinridge, December 22, 1864, in B. MSS.

cember. But, as everywhere in the Confederacy, the breakdown of civilian and military morale in southwest Virginia and east Tennessee lay almost complete by the opening of 1865. The soldiers and the people were simply worn out by war.[46]

There were those in Richmond who found the war tiring as well, and one of them was Secretary of War James Seddon. Sick of his job and of the calumny heaped upon him for Confederate failures, Seddon offered his resignation on January 19, just as Congress was making a movement toward directing a general reorganization of the president's cabinet. Davis foresaw this several days in advance. Sometime during the second week of January, Breckinridge received a mysterious summons to Richmond, its purpose a secret from everyone, perhaps from himself. The general called his staff around him for what he seemed to know was a last farewell, presented one of them with the sword taken from Federal General Abel D. Streight by Forrest, a gift to Breckinridge from the cavalryman, and then took his leave. By January 17 he was in Richmond, staying inconspicuously at the home of Gustavus A. Myers, influential capital lawyer.[47]

Of all of those who had commanded in the department, Breckinridge stood as the only one to leave that command with a reputation enhanced for having served there. His management of affairs during the past year won for him the love and esteem of the men serving under him, of the civilians who looked to him for their protection, and of those like Lee whose armies depended on sound management in southwestern Virginia and east Tennessee. Breckinridge handled one of the most difficult and most important departments in the Confederacy, saved its productivity for the country against an enemy more numerous than he, and still managed to save the Valley in May, destroy Sigel as an effective force, help beat back Grant's terrible assaults at Cold Harbor, save Lynchburg and drive Hunter out of the valley, lead a corps in the Confederacy's most spectacular penetration of the enemy's country, and aid in Early's futile defense against Sheridan. Here, more than anywhere else in his service as a general in the field, Breckinridge significantly contributed to keeping the Confederacy alive a while longer.[48]

46. Richmond *Whig*, January 12, 1865; J. S. Johnston, "Sketches of Operations, No. 3," p. 387; Page, "Diary," 65; *O.R.*, Ser. I, Vol. XLV, Pt. 2, pp. 750–51, 763, 768, 782, 797–98, Vol. XLVI, Pt. 2, p. 1035, Vol. XLIX, Pt. 1, p. 764, Ser. II, Vol. VIII, 57–58, 222–23; Guerrant Diary, January 17, 1865, in SHC.

47. Jones, *War Clerk's Diary*, II, 389; New Orleans *Times-Democrat*; "Capt. Charles J. Mastin," *Confederate Veteran*, III (April, 1895), 117.

48. *O.R.*, Ser. I, Vol. XLIX, Pt. 1, pp. 964–65.

CHAPTER 9

This Has Been a Magnificent Epic

Breckinridge was not entirely sure why he was summoned to Richmond. If he had listened to gossip, he would not have learned much. Governor William "Extra Billy" Smith had been clamoring for Early's removal in the Valley and told Lee that, to replace him, "General Breckinridge is of all men the man." The Kentuckian, however, helped in large measure to quell this movement by his own testimony to Lee of his confidence in the soundness of Early's judgment. Talk had been heard of late that Breckinridge would be the natural choice to succeed Davis in the presidency when his term expired in 1868, but that was three years away yet. Most likely of all was the rumor that he had been offered Seddon's portfolio as secretary of war. The speculation began immediately on his arrival in the Confederate capital, and did not cease for several days.[1]

For once, a rumor about Breckinridge was correct. Although the exact time of the offer is uncertain, Davis definitely offered the general the cabinet post sometime during the third of fourth week of January, giving him a few days to make up his mind. The president's reasons were numerous. His administration bowed under the weight of vicious attacks from Congress and the state legislatures. It was axiomatic that when the war went well, the generals received the credit—when it went badly, the fault was all at Richmond. Seddon, despite honest and earnest efforts, stood so discredited that his usefulness was exhausted. In his place Davis needed not only an able administrator, but someone who commanded a large share of the public's respect and esteem, someone whose personal popularity could outweigh disappointment over defeats and renew enthusiasm for the cause. With this in mind, Breckinridge was a logical choice. Of all of the statesmen who joined the southern ranks, he stood at once the most illustrious and the most

1. *O.R.*, Ser. I, Vol. XLIII, Pt. 2, pp. 894, 897; Jones, *War Clerk's Diary*, II, 426.

popular. Indeed, Davis himself had been accused of being jealous of the Kentuckian's popularity and talents. Envious or not, he respected and esteemed Breckinridge. In fact, Davis regarded the general as "the best representative of the interests and avowed policy of the South" during the 1860 campaign, and since Breckinridge had followed that policy into the Confederacy, Davis' opinion of him could not have undergone much change. Add to this the general's wide experience in the several theaters of the war, his proven ability at departmental administration, and the prestige that he brought as a former vice-president, and his selection as secretary of war was natural.[2]

Some drawbacks accompanied the offer, and the general made his decision conditional. Congressmen from Kentucky supposedly opposed his acceptance, but Lee wrote to him confidentially urging that he take the post. The chief stumbling block seems to have been Northrop. Davis still remained adamant about retaining the man, probably the most unpopular single official in the Confederacy. As long as the commissary general remained in office, thought one employee in the War Department, the position of war secretary "cannot be desirable." Breckinridge had experienced his share of trouble with Northrop, beginning with the occupation of Murfreesboro back in November, 1862, through his tenure in southwestern Virginia, where his own men went hungry because this official took the department's supplies for use elsewhere. Breckinridge defied Northrop then, and would do so now, for the bulk of the testimony indicates that the general made Northrop's dismissal the condition upon which he would accept the portfolio as secretary of war. Davis gave in. On January 30 Eli M. Bruce, Breckinridge's old friend, was temporarily named commissary general by the outgoing Seddon. The next day, it was general knowledge that the Kentuckian had notified Davis of his acceptance. On February 6, 1865, the president sent Breckinridge's nomination to the Senate, and that body did unanimously advise and consent to the appointment, making the general, at forty-four, the youngest cabinet minister of the war.[3]

2. Jones, War Clerk's Diary, II, 390, 394–95; O.R., Ser. I, Vol. XLVI, Pt. 2, p. 287, Vol. XLVIII, Pt. 1, pp. 737, 1341; Richmond Whig, January 22, 1865; New York Turf, Field and Farm, May 21, 1875; John H. Reagan, "Flight and Capture of Jefferson Davis," Annals of the War Written by Leading Participants, North and South (Philadelphia, 1879), 152; Robert McElroy, Jefferson Davis: The Unreal and the Real (New York, 1937), I, 221; Archer Jones, Confederate Strategy from Shiloh to Vicksburg (Baton Rouge, 1961), 36.
3. Jones, War Clerk's Diary, II, 390, 394–95, 403; J. S. Johnston, "Sketches of Operations, No. 3," p. 388; Augusta (Ga.) Tri-Weekly Constitutionalist, February 8, 1865;

Reactions to the new secretary stood mixed, even among his own most fervid partisans. J. Stoddard Johnston, whom he had been forced to leave behind with Echols in the old department, was not sanguine about his chief's prospects. Writing of Breckinridge in later years, he would say:

> He had not the elements of a bureau officer. He was good at the organization of an army, but his success in this, where he had the opportunity to practice it, arose from his thorough knowledge of the officers and men under him. Abstractly, he had not a taste for that plodding attention to details, that methodical measuring of every point, without reference to its importance, which is essential to the administration of such an office. His faculty was more of the executive turn. Phrenologically, his organs of perception were better developed than those of reflection. The same qualities which made him more an orator than a writer, more the leader of a congress than a cabinet officer, a better advocate before a jury than solicitor in chancery, fitted him also more for the success he won early and maintained as a General in the field, than for the less active and more confining duties of a secretaryship.

Others agreed with Johnston, among them the assistant secretary of war, John A. Campbell. He thought Breckinridge not a good appointment, "as he is not a man of small *details*." John B. Jones, a clerk in the War Department and an intimate, though often quite prejudiced observer, disagreed with Campbell, expressing the hope that Breckinridge "is not going to indulge in so many of them as the judge [Campbell] and Mr. Seddon have done, else all is lost." [4]

The majority of those in the War Department, as well as the Richmond public, saw cause for hope with the new appointment. Jones was most pleased, as was Robert Tyler, register of the Treasury. Josiah Gorgas, chief of the Bureau of Ordnance, found news of Breckinridge's promotion most gratifying. Robert G. H. Kean, head of the Bureau of War, though generally in sympathy with Campbell, kept an open mind toward the Kentuckian. Meanwhile, Mrs. Chesnut was elated. "If we had had Breckinridge in [Leroy Pope] Walker's place at the beginning, what a difference it might have made," she wrote. Sallie Putnam, who ran in circles less exalted than Mary Chesnut's, felt much the same. "This appointment was popular," she later recalled, "and from the character of the new secretary, the people

Thomas R. Hay, "Lucius B. Northrop: Commissary General of the Confederacy," *Civil War History*, IX (March, 1963), 19; Foote, *Casket of Reminiscences*, 297; Guerrant Diary, January 31, 1865, in SHC; *Journal of Congress*, IV, 525; Jefferson Davis to the Congress, February 6, 1865, copy in JCB Papers; Richmond *Sentinel*, January 28, 1865.

4. J. S. Johnston, "Sketches of Operations, No. 3," pp. 388–89; Jones, *War Clerk's Diary*, II, 401; Younger, *Inside the Confederate Government*, 199.

were induced to hope for and expect a more judicious management of the War Department than had been exercised by his predecessor." Wrote Jones: "Every effort will be made to popularize the cause again." [5]

Although Breckinridge accepted the appointment around January 28, he did not take office for more than a week; he had to wait for Senate confirmation, and he had to see to the affairs of his old department. Then, on February 7, with final arrangements completed, the secretary rode through four inches of snow down to Ninth and Franklin streets to a large brick building leased by the government from the Virginia Mechanics Institute. Here was the War Department. Stepping inside, Breckinridge took the oath of office from notary public H. A. Claiborne, said farewell to Seddon, and entered as secretary of war upon the task of trying to save a nation that was doomed.[6]

There was not a more difficult post in all the government, excepting only, perhaps, the presidency. The weight and sphere of responsibility of the secretary of war were staggering. By the time Breckinridge took the helm, the War Department consisted of no less than fourteen official branches; his own office, that of the adjutant and inspector general, the quartermaster general, the commissary general, the surgeon general, Engineer Bureau, Bureau of Indian Affairs, Bureau of Ordnance, Army Intell'gence Office, Bureau of Exchange, Bureau of Conscription, Niter and Mining Bureau, Bureau of Foreign Supplies, and the Office of the Commissary General of Prisoners. In addition, his jurisdiction extended technically over every army, corps, division, brigade, and regiment in the Confederate service, as well as state commands. It was a chore just keeping straight and remembering the different branches, much less overseeing their work. The secretary's job was not, as former occupant, Judah P. Benjamin remarked facetiously, "a bed of roses." [7]

It is a singular fact that the position had been occupied consistently by men who possessed neither the experience, talent, nor prestige to meet their tasks. The first secretary, Leroy Pope Walker of Alabama, brought as his

5. Frank E. Vandiver, *Ploughshares into Swords: Josiah Gorgas and Confederate Ordnance* (Austin, Tex., 1952), 261; Jones, *War Clerk's Diary*, II, 435; Williams, *Diary from Dixie*, 473; Sallie B. Putnam, *In Richmond During the Confederacy* (Reprint; New York, 1961), 365.

6. Younger, *Inside the Confederate Government*, xxiii, 193, 190; Breckinridge to R. E. Lee, March 30, 1865, in Chap. 9, XXXI, NA; Jones, *War Clerk's Diary*, II, 411; Henry Putney Beers, *Guide to the Archives of the Confederate States of America* (Washington, 1969), 138.

7. Beers, *Guide*, viii; Meade, *Benjamin*, 185.

only credentials the fact that Davis needed an Alabamian to balance the state representation in his cabinet. He devoted more energy to the pomp and show of office than to setting up his department. Next, with the characteristic bad judgment that Davis would show for some time in his war appointments, he then turned the portfolio over to a proven statesman, but one who was rising in unpopularity throughout the Confederacy, Benjamin. Formerly attorney general, Benjamin actually admitted that he knew nothing of war and armies, and proceeded to prove it. Then Davis finally made what, on the surface, looked like a promising appointment, George Wythe Randolph.[8]

Randolph, a grandson of Thomas Jefferson, bore a surname known and respected throughout the South. Better still, he had some army experience, though limited. The organizer of the Richmond Howitzers, his service in 1861 won for him a brigadier's commission. Almost as soon as he took office, however, Randolph ran afoul of Davis, and resigned in a huff in November, to be followed briefly by Gustavus Smith, who served only three days as interim secretary. Then came Seddon. A true plantation aristocrat, Seddon lived almost a monastic life, immersed in his books, and perpetually plagued with one minor illness after another. He made himself inaccessible, ignored callers, and alienated many of those who did see him, thanks to his humorlessness and aloof manner. In two years and two months as secretary of war, he showed himself to be almost wholly spineless. He would not stand up to Davis and, as a result, like Walker, Benjamin, and Randolph before him, acted more as a clerk than a cabinet minister.[9]

In some measure, these men could not help but fail, for each faced one of the most formidable obstacles any minister could encounter, Jefferson Davis. Once he took over the presidency, Davis made no attempt to conceal the fact that his primary concern would be management of the war. He did so out of interest and selfish desire rather than firm conviction that he knew better than anyone else how to run the Confederacy's armies, though his choice of war ministers certainly insured that he was more capable than the man in the War Office. Davis used each of his secretaries in turn with shameful discourtesy and disregard. He gave orders, moved armies, made appointments, and dictated War Department policy, sometimes without

8. "An Act to Establish the War Department," February 21, 1861, *Statutes at Large of the Provisional Congress of the Confederate States of America* (Richmond, 1864), 32; Burton J. Hendrick, *Statesmen of the Lost Cause* (Boston, 1935), 178–82, 324–29; Meade, *Benjamin*, 180.

9. See Roy W. Curry, "James A. Seddon, A Southern Prototype," *Virginia Magazine of History and Biography*, LXIII (April, 1955), 123–50.

even consulting his secretaries. Randolph in particular fumed at discovering that new promotions and major decisions had been made by "his" department, by reading about them in the capital press. Davis purposely appointed subservient men to the cabinet post, men who would bend to his will without trouble or question. When Randolph broke this rule and made a major decision on his own without consulting the president, Davis was furious, demanded that Randolph's order be recalled, and soon afterward accepted the Virginian's resignation. There would be no policy made that did not originate in the Confederate White House on Clay Street, or which did not meet the complete approval of the president. Most of all, however, he would take no opposition or dissension. His secretaries must agree or leave.[10]

All of this made Breckinridge's appointment one of broad significance. He possessed in a high degree every qualification which his predecessors so sadly lacked. He fitted the mold of the ideal war minister in a civil state—one who, though a civilian by profession, possessed extensive military experience. Breckinridge, as one of the outstanding major generals from the volunteer service, had served in every major theater of the war except the Gulf states, was intimately acquainted with all of the major commanders with whom he would work—Lee, Johnston, Beauregard, Hood, Hardee, Forrest—and he knew, and was known and respected by, the rank and file of the Confederacy's two major armies. The only principal generals with whom he was not on personal terms were Richard Taylor and Edmund Kirby Smith, but their relations would still be most cordial. Indeed, Breckinridge had no enemies in the Confederate Army except Bragg, and that officer had left his position as military advisor to Davis and returned to North Carolina. Breckinridge had fought and planned campaigns, suffered the administrative torture of departmental and army command, and experienced in significant degree all of the varied problems which, magnified many times, confronted a war minister. From the standpoint of understanding of the army, its workings, and its needs, he was an excellent choice.

Breckinridge was also an excellent choice politically. Finally Davis had appointed someone who could bring the weight of a vast personal popularity and prestige to the War Department, one whose esteem in the public eye could survive disaster in the field. Breckinridge's administration would

10. Meade, *Benjamin*, 181; Hendrick, *Statesmen*, 325. As yet there has not been a good, thorough biography of Davis, or a complete study of his relations with the War Department, but see William J. Cooper, "A Reassessment of Jefferson Davis as War Leader: The Case from Atlanta to Nashville," *Journal of Southern History*, XXXVI (May, 1970).

see the greatest defeat of all, the fall of the Confederacy. Yet he would emerge with a reputation that, far from being diminished, was enhanced by his service.[11]

The Kentuckian's appointment represented the surrender by Davis of some of his jealously guarded independence of congressional and public opinion. Congress had been giving him so much trouble over his cabinet that he was forced to appoint someone popular to fill Seddon's place, and Breckinridge enjoyed wide favor among Confederate politicians, most of whom had supported him in 1860. It also revealed an admission by the president that his own power over the War Department and its minister would have to be curtailed somewhat. John C. Breckinridge was as well known in the Confederate states as any public man and was personally more popular than Davis by this stage of the war. The president could not impose upon or neglect a man of this stature. Even if he did not realize this from his own long friendship and political experience with Breckinridge, it stood evident from the fact that the Kentuckian, as the highest ranking living official of the old Union to join the South, was simply too eminent a man to be treated with less than absolute respect. What ensured a change in Davis' attitude, however, was Breckinridge's own personality. Of all of the secretaries, he was the only one—save, perhaps, Randolph—who neither feared, nor stood in awe of the president. He would be the first secretary of war to disagree with or criticize Davis' policy to his face. He would be the only one to whom the president not only listened, but with whom he discussed war policy as an equal. Not infrequently the general's opinion won out. A new era appeared to be coming to the Confederate War Department with a new secretary who was decidedly his own man.[12]

Breckinridge's first act as secretary of war was to call Campbell into his office for a long private interview. Their principal topic of discussion was the current state of the Confederacy. Just the day before, Campbell had turned in to Congress his report of a peace conference held at Hampton Roads on February 3. It had failed completely, and Campbell now regarded the southern cause as hopeless. He told this to Breckinridge, backing it up with his conviction that the nation did not have enough money or resources to continue the war to a successful conclusion. Breckinridge resolved in that meeting to send a circular letter to the heads of all the bureaus, order-

11. For evidence of the esteem in which Breckinridge was held by former Confederates, one need only look through the issues of the *Confederate Veteran*, where he is consistently placed in the pantheon with Davis, Lee, and Jackson.

12. The testimony on Davis' regard for Breckinridge is legion. Specific references will be found throughout this chapter.

ing them to send him "a succinct but clear statement of the means and resources you have on hand for carrying on the business of your Bureau and
your ability for carrying it on, and what impediments exist and what is
necessary for that purpose." This was the first time that any secretary displayed the imagination to conceive such an idea.[13]

Beyond this, Breckinridge and Campbell discussed the management of
the department, and Campbell was confirmed in his opinion that the Kentuckian was a poor choice for the position. He feared that the secretary did
not wish to oversee personally the entire department, but rather would concentrate his energies only in certain areas, exercising a much more loose rein
than Seddon had. They spoke of Campbell remaining as assistant secretary,
for a number of hungry applicants wanted the post. Campbell suggested in
a note later that day that he be retained, and Breckinridge agreed.[14]

There was much to do while awaiting the answers to his circular, and
Breckinridge started at the bottom. The day after he took office he called
Northrop in. No action had been taken on Bruce's replacing the commissary general as yet, and Breckinridge wanted to hear the whole story from
Northrop, as well as confront him with the deficiencies in his administration. His timing could not have been more perfect. While they talked a
letter came from Lee which showed that his men had no meat at all, that
the Commissary Department was sadly deficient, and that unless something
were done, there would be dire consequences. Lee's letter stated Breckinridge's case against Northrop as well or better than he could have himself,
and he confronted the commissary general with the dispatch. Northrop said
it was no surprise. He had predicted this long ago, and if only everyone had
listened to him earlier, this would not have happened. Breckinridge, more
interested in solutions than excuses, interrupted Northrop's narrative to
come to the point. "But Colonel," he said, "what shall we do?" Northrop
did not know.

While the commissary general was still present, Breckinridge sent the
letter to Davis' office for immediate perusal, and soon it came back with a
telling endorsement. This situation was too sad for words, said the president, "and cannot have occurred without criminal neglect or gross incom-
petency." A few minutes later another note arrived from the president
directing Breckinridge to borrow or impress supplies if necessary, and that

13. Younger, *Inside the Confederate Government*, 190; Jones, *War Clerk's Diary*, II,
411–12, 416; *O.R.*, Ser. I, Vol. XLVI, Pt. 2, p. 466, Ser. IV, Vol. III, 1064. Breckinridge
never claimed the idea of the circular as entirely his own, but the evidence in favor of
Campbell's authorship is too inconclusive to credit the idea exclusively to him either.
14. Jones, *War Clerk's Diary*, II, 412; Younger, *Inside the Confederate Government*,
199; John A. Campbell to Breckinridge, February 7, 1865, in Chap. 9, XXXI, NA.

they should be sent to the army before the next dawn. When Breckinridge showed this to Northrop, the commissary general was nonplussed, said it was exaggerated, that he could not borrow or impress, and then blamed the situation on Lee and Seddon. If Breckinridge went into this conversation with any doubts about dismissing Northrop, they dissolved here. The secretary took the matter into his own hands. Seeing that Colonel Isaac M. St. John, presently in charge of the Niter and Mining Bureau, had proved to be an excellent man at both administration and innovation, he recommended his promotion to brigadier on February 14. Davis agreed, and a day later appointed him to succeed Northrop. Breckinridge later stated that on taking office he found the Commissary branch "in very deplorable condition," and its revitalization obviously stood at the top of his list of priorities. An army unfed could not fight.[15]

Shortly afterward the secretary moved to correct another injustice. On or before February 22, he sent Echols an order directing that Felix H. Robertson be brought before a court of inquiry to meet charges against his conduct at Saltville. As the Confederacy rushed on toward its fate in these last months, Robertson would never face the court, but a measure of justice was meted out. The same day that Echols received Breckinridge's order, the Confederate Senate rejected for the last time Robertson's nomination as brigadier.[16]

Already Breckinridge showed his influence in the War Department, though it would not be one of change for its own sake. With the exception of St. John's replacement in Niter and Mining by Colonel Richard Morton, only one other bureau head would be dismissed. The secretary's bureau chiefs apparently understood and approved his course. While Campbell might lament that Breckinridge was not monarchical enough, and Kean would fester over the difficulty in getting the secretary to answer his correspondence, Josiah Gorgas of the Ordnance Bureau, the most capable administrator in any branch of the department, saw immediately the wisdom of the Kentuckian's course. "Gen. B. carries his duties cheerfully," he thought, "and will I hope make a good Sec. because he evidently intends to push work off upon others & not involve himself in details, which is right."[17]

Two days after Breckinridge sent out his circular to the heads of bu-

15. Younger, *Inside the Confederate Government*, 200; *O.R.*, Ser. I, Vol. XLVI. Pt. 1, pp. 381–82. For an evaluation of Northrop, see Hay, "Northrop," 5–23. See also Breckinridge to I. M. St. John, May 16, 1871, in Rowland, *Jefferson Davis*, VII, 356; *Journal of Congress*, IV, 557; Jones, *War Clerk's Diary*, II, 423.

16. John Echols to Samuel Cooper, February 22, 1865, in Robertson, Service Record.

17. Vandiver, *Diary of Gorgas*, 169; Younger, *Inside the Confederate Government*, 200; Vandiver, *Ploughshares into Swords*, 261.

reaus, their reports began coming in. Despite their general optimism, the bureau chiefs all expressed two major complaints in unison: lack of sufficient funds, and interference with their personnel by military authorities.[18] Pay problems had been with the Confederacy since its birth, and were never met effectively. In this field of endeavor, Breckinridge would follow largely in the footsteps of his predecessors, failing to see or heed the need for radical reformation of pay procedures and sources. However, for the troops in the westernmost reaches of the Confederacy, those who received pay most seldom, he did begin work with General Richard Taylor for the sale of cotton to raise funds for payrolls. Though certainly solicitous of the plight of the soldiers in this matter, he would show little more imagination in coping with the problem than his predecessors. It was a problem whose magnitude and urgency justified a separate bureau of the department, but none of the secretaries seem to have thought this practical.[19]

As for the manpower needed to carry on the operations of his bureaus, Breckinridge had little reason to expect better success than with the pay problem. All told, his chiefs estimated that they needed 15,622 white and 37,749 Negro workers to carry on their work, and even this did not include some unaccountable needs. With most of the able-bodied men in the country in the army, there were few prospects for filling these needs except where invalids or cripples could perform light duties. This glaring insufficiency of manpower, coupled with the extremity of the department's financial situation, gave Breckinridge his first truly graphic picture of the desperate condition of the Confederacy. Indeed, he regarded the reports from his bureau chiefs as so important that instead of putting them in the War Office files as usual he gave them directly to Kean with instructions that they be kept in his personal charge.[20]

Despite the discouraging condition of things, Breckinridge went ahead with what reforms he could effect, his chief concern being the commissary general's department. St. John had been reluctant to take Northrop's job,

18. *O.R.*, Ser. I, Vol. XLVI, Pt. 2, pp. 1211–14, Ser. IV, Vol. III, 1071–76.

19. *O.R.*, Ser. I, Vol. XLIX, Pt. 1, pp. 978–79, 987, Ser. IV, Vol. III, 1094; Breckinridge to Davis, February 15, 18, 22, 1865, in Chap. 9, XL, NA; Breckinridge to Davis, February 15, 1865, "Communication from the Secretary of War," University of Texas Library, Austin; Harry N. Scheiber, "The Pay of Confederate Troops and Problems of Demoralization: A Case of Administrative Failure," *Civil War History*, XV (September, 1969), 234–36; Breckinridge to Walter Taylor, February 28, 1865, Breckinridge to the Treasury, February 10, 1865, in Chap. 9, XXXI, NA.

20. *O.R.*, Ser. IV, Vol. III, 1095–96; R. G. H. Kean to Jubal A. Early, November 15, 1873, in "Resources of the Confederacy in February, 1865," *SHSP*, II (July, 1876), pp. 56–57.

but soon justified the secretary's confidence in him. With cooperation from the other bureaus as well, St. John soon had a flow of foodstuffs and meat coming in beyond his expectations. Breckinridge and St. John worked closely in this endeavor and, as a result, three weeks after the new commissary general took office, Lee sent Breckinridge a letter of compliment stating that his army had not been so well supplied for months. By April 1, they would have collected for the army in depots at Richmond, Danville, Lynchburg, and Greensboro, North Carolina, over 2,980,000 rations of bread and 2,480,000 rations of meat. Furthermore, St. John and Breckinridge devised a system of collecting the supplies from farmers and getting them directly to the army without going by way of the central depots that Northrop had set up, and which delayed their transmission. By March they would have supplies coming in in quantities which outstripped the transportation facilities and available troops to guard shipments.[21]

While the secretary directed most of his physical energies to supply in the first month of his tenure, his main thought was on the military situation. From his vantage point in the War Office, he could see the overall picture of war as nowhere else, and he could see as well the deteriorating condition of the Confederate armies, especially the Army of Tennessee. Always plagued by internal dissension, only the players in its drama changed. Where before Bragg, Polk, and Breckinridge had been the chief actors, now they were replaced by Hood, J. E. Johnston, Hardee, and others. Hood, in disgrace after his disastrous Franklin and Nashville Campaign of December, 1864, turned in a report to Breckinridge in which he tried to pass blame for his failure on to Johnston and Hardee. Some time later Hardee would submit his own report, asking the secretary to have it published in rebuttal to Hood. It took little military acumen to see that an army which fought so viciously within itself, held little hope of defeating an enemy at the same time.[22]

During February, Breckinridge's chief suggestions in the line of strategy were directed toward beating back the advancing horde under Sherman. To Lee, now general in chief of the entire Confederate Army, he proposed a plan whereby uncovering or abandoning points of secondary importance would free a significant number of men to be combined against the Fed-

21. St. John to Davis, July 14, 1873, Breckinridge to St. John, May 16, 1871, in Rowland, *Jefferson Davis*, VII, 349–52; Hay, "Northrop," 20; Clement A. Evans, *The Civil History of the Confederate States* (2nd ed.; New York, 1962), Vol. I of Clement A. Evans (ed.), *Confederate Military History*, 622; O.R., Ser. I, Vol. LI, Pt. 2, pp. 1063–64.
22. O.R., Ser. I, Vol. XXXVIII, Pt. 3, p. 697; Hudson Strode, *Jefferson Davis, Tragic Hero* (New York, 1964), 149.

erals. Furthermore, he suggested that Lee should put himself at their head, adding that "something of this sort must be done at once or the situation is lost." While Lee agreed with the necessity of holding back Sherman, he thought the plan impractical, and there the matter rested. Although Breckinridge technically held authority over Lee, he would always defer to the Virginian's greater military knowledge and instinct.[23]

In contrast to the unsettled condition of the armies in the lower South, Lee's Army of Northern Virginia showed a satisfying stability, the result of notable élan and a reverential love of the men for its general. Breckinridge too knew this feeling for Lee, and saw it in operation. He met Lee exactly a week after taking office as secretary of war and had an interview with him again two days later. On February 24 the secretary and Davis rode out to visit the army and saw a number of returned prisoners. Both spoke to them, and then conferred with Lee. Lee and Breckinridge met frequently now, and carried on an active correspondence, and their relations convinced the great general that at last the Confederacy had found the right man for the premier cabinet post. Lee had gotten along well enough with all of Breckinridge's predecessors, with the possible exception of Benjamin, but in the Kentuckian he found a particularly capable and congenial minister. William Preston later recalled that when Breckinridge took over the War Department, and Lee was informed of the change, he said with warmth that "from his experience of the abilities and character of Breckinridge he was the ablest general in the Confederacy to command a great army." He said, "If I had an army I would at once put it under his command." After a few weeks of working with the new secretary, the general would feel this even more strongly. After the war he told William Preston Johnston that he deeply regretted that Breckinridge had not been made secretary of war at the beginning. "He is a great man," said Lee. "I was acquainted with him as Congressman and Vice-President and as one of our Generals, but I did not *know* him until he was secretary of war, and he is a lofty, pure strong man." Clearly, of all the war ministers with whom Lee worked during the war, he believed that John C. Breckinridge was the best.[24]

At Breckinridge's request, Lee kept him constantly informed on the military situation around Petersburg, while the secretary forwarded to him

23. *O.R.*, Ser. I, Vol. XLVI, Pt. 2, pp. 1245, 1247, Vol. XLVII, Pt. 2, p. 1208, Vol. LIII, 1049–50.

24. Jones, *War Clerk's Diary*, II, 430–32; Louisville *Courier-Journal*, May 18, June 18, 1875; Bean, "Memoranda," 479.

information from other points in the Confederacy. Not forgetting his recent service in southwestern Virginia, Breckinridge advised Lee on matters and policy there, and the general welcomed his counsel. Despite his refusal to take details out of the hands of his subordinates, the secretary obviously took a deep interest in everything that occurred within the province of his department. "Gen. Breckenridge seems to have his heart in the cause," thought clerk Jones, "not his soul in his pocket, like most of his predecessors." [25]

Anyone with his heart in the cause was most dismayed at the rate of desertion from the armies, and Breckinridge was no exception. On February 24 Lee reported to him that in less than two weeks four hundred had absented themselves in just two divisions, and asked if Breckinridge could not devise some remedy. He could not, beyond making an appeal to Governor Zebulon Vance, since the bulk of the deserters were North Carolinians. The chief method now employed to fill the ranks thus depleted by desertion was conscription, a policy which failed for the most part. In the absence of an effective draft, Breckinridge saw the chief source of manpower for the armies in exchanged prisoners. Very soon after taking the War portfolio, he had a conversation with Secretary of the Treasury Christopher Memminger and Colonel Robert Ould, agent for prisoner exchange, in the parlor of a Richmond club. At the Hampton Roads peace conference, Ould had spoken with Lincoln briefly on the subjects of supplies for Confederate prisoners in the North, as well as renewing the exchange. While nothing came of it then, Union authorities did agree to resume the exchanges which they had discontinued almost two years before. By February 20 there were several thousand Federal prisoners on hand at Wilmington ready for freedom, and, after a brief delay, the transactions began. Soon thereafter an agreement was made for the exchange of civilian prisoners as well. Breckinridge found himself so busy with other matters that he had to turn most of this prisoner business over to Campbell's attention, but when he saw an inequity, he took it up personally. Once the exchanges began, he discovered that in many cases men who had been in Federal prisons only a few months were being exchanged, while others who had been there for two or three years remained behind bars. The secretary told Ould that he wanted the prisoners with the longer terms to be exchanged first. This coincided with Ould's views, though the Federals had been reluctant to cooperate. Finally they gave in late in March, and the in-

25. O.R., Ser. I, Vol. XLVI, Pt. 1, pp. 382–83, Vol. XLIX, Pt. 1, p. 970; Jones, War Clerk's Diary, II, 438–40.

equity stood corrected. Breckinridge also did what he could to curtail the policy of holding Federal prisoners liable for death in retaliation for Confederates tried and so convicted in the North. In one case, where a Federal had been captured, tried as a spy, and sentenced to be hanged—and the enemy had selected a prisoner of similar rank to die in kind—Breckinridge battled even Davis' adherence to the practice, finally turning the president's mind and getting the spy's sentence commuted.[26]

Breckinridge's attention also took in the care of Federal prisoners in the Confederacy, a subject properly in the province of the office of Commissary General of Prisoners. On his first day as secretary of war, Breckinridge heard from Vance that conditions at Salisbury prison were terrible, and immediately he ordered an investigation. The result was the dismissal of the prison quartermaster and the reduction in rank and responsibility of a number of prison officials. Meanwhile, hearing of bad conditions at other prisons at Columbia and Florence, South Carolina, Breckinridge ordered the prisoners there removed to a new camp to be constructed in more healthful surroundings. Beyond these personal dealings with the prisoners of war, however, the secretary generally left such matters in the hands of the proper subordinates.[27]

The real desperation of Lee's situation during all of this time remained the secretary's chief concern. Faced by Grant with an army more than twice the size of his own, and infinitely better equipped, Lee had little hope of being able to hold his line at Petersburg indefinitely. Sooner or later he would be forced to evacuate it and Richmond, or be bottled up at the capital, with his route of escape or junction with Johnston cut off. By February 19, viewing the situation in South Carolina as Sherman advanced, he knew that time was short; he told Breckinridge that it might be necessary to abandon all of the Confederacy's major cities including Richmond and advised the secretary to make preparations accordingly. Immediately Breckinridge ordered officers to begin collecting supplies, while asking Lee what

26. *O.R.*, Ser. I, Vol. XLVI, Pt. 2, pp. 1254, 1257, 1265, Vol. XLVII, Pt. 2, p. 1296, Ser. IV, Vol. III, 1119–22, Ser. II, Vol. VIII, 286, 293, 297–98, 304, 335, 356–57, 426, 443, Ser. III, Vol. V, 700–10; Breckinridge to Zebulon Vance, March 1, 1865, in Breckinridge Service Record, NA; Jones, *War Clerk's Diary*, II, 395; A. L. DeRosset, "Interesting Statement of Judge Robert Ould," *Confederate Veteran*, XV (October, 1907), 455; Frank Battle, "An Old Reb' at Richmond," *Confederate Veteran*, XV (August, 1907), 347; Breckinridge to Robert Ould, March 8, 1865, Chap. 9, XXXI, NA.

27. *O.R.*, Ser. I, Vol. XLVI, Pt. 2, p. 1279, Ser. II, Vol. VIII, 167, 205, 211, 213, 224, 251; Patricia Bell, "Gideon Pillow," *Civil War Times Illustrated*, VI (October, 1967), 19.

route of withdrawal he would probably take. Upon being advised that Lynchburg would be the probable advantageous site for a supply center, the secretary began the process of directing stores in the capital to be shipped there. A few days later, Campbell also advised the secretary that thought should be given to what would be done about the War Department and its functions should Richmond be evacuated. The subject had been on Breckinridge's mind since he first took office, and on February 24 he asked Lee for a direct answer: Should Richmond only prepare for an evacuation, or did the situation warrant that the actual removal of public stores and archives should begin immediately?[28]

Without waiting for Lee's reply, Breckinridge called all of his bureau chiefs in for private interviews on February 25, apprised them of the possible evacuation, and later issued a circular directing that whatever they did not deem indispensable to the operation of their bureaus should be sent to Danville without delay. That which they thought they could not do without, in the line of archives and stores, must be retained until the last minute. At the same time, he asked Lee if he could count on having ten or twelve days to effect the removal, since it would enable him to have it better organized and more thorough. Breckinridge introduced the subject at a cabinet meeting that day, but nothing came of it since such meetings had long since ceased to produce practical policy. Whatever would be accomplished in preparation for an evacuation would have to be done by Breckinridge and Lee. Although they gave no public utterances on the subject, word of the preparations soon leaked out to a few in the capital. Lee had sent Lieutenant General Richard S. Ewell, commanding the defenses and reserves of Richmond, an order to remove cotton and tobacco from the city, burning what could not be taken away. Shortly afterward, the secretary received a call from a committee of the Virginia Assembly. Somehow they knew of the order before Breckinridge did and now spoke with him for some time on the possible evacuation. The secretary, not pleased that the information had thus leaked out, immediately ordered Ewell not to put Lee's directive into action until further notified, and sent the order directly to Ewell rather than through the adjutant general's office, which indicates that he may have suspected a leak there. Joseph Mayo, mayor of Richmond, also obtained a copy of Lee's order, and brought it before the city council,

28. Lee to Breckinridge, February 19, 1865, in Clifford Dowdey and Louis Manarin (eds.), *The Wartime Papers of R. E. Lee* (Boston, 1961), 905; *O.R.*, Ser. I, Vol. XLVI, Pt. 2, pp. 1242, 1244–45, 1252–53.

which directed a committee to cooperate with the government in the removal of the stores.[29]

The secretary plainly saw that he needed to speak with Lee directly to establish a plan of action. Fortunately, Davis had called the commanding general to Richmond. On February 26 or 27 he met with Lee and Longstreet at the Executive Mansion, with the Kentuckian present. In the course of their conversation Lee said that Breckinridge could probably count on having the ten or twelve days necessary to effect the removal of archives and other necessities, and reaffirmed his conviction that the city would have to be abandoned. Then the discussion turned to a new subject, another proposal to effect a peace. Longstreet and Federal Major General E. O. C. Ord had engaged in some communication, including a conference on February 21, at which they spoke of the fear of northern politicians to touch the peace-without-victory question. Ord suggested that a cease fire should be called, that Grant and Lee should meet, and that while they sought some arrangement, the wives of the ranking officers in both armies should pay calls, escorted by officers, on the wives of generals in the other army. This would ease tensions between the belligerents wh'le the ranking generals sought some agreement. Several hours were devoted to the subject, and Breckinridge gave his approval, being especially pleased by the imaginative use of the wives. As with the other hopeful peace proposals of this winter, however, nothing came of Longstreet's plan.[30]

While Breckinridge's subordinates worked on removing the'r bureaus' less essential materials, the secretary began looking into the local defense troops. If Lee had to leave Petersburg, he could not have his troops oversee an orderly evacuation. Consequently, Breckinridge relied on Ewell's locals, numbering about 3,000 on February 25, including walking wounded and Negroes. Another month would see that figure rise to 4,529, a sufficient force for the need. Ewell would also oversee some of the removal of government supplies, and the destruction of the rest. This destruction worried others besides the tobacco and cotton people, especially the owners of the Tredegar Iron Works, the Confederacy's principal such installation. Arguing that the North had so many iron furnaces at their disposal that leav-

29. *O.R.*, Ser. I, Vol. XLVI, Pt. 2, p. 1257; Breckinridge to Richard S. Ewell, February 25, 1865, in New York *Times*, July 0, 1865; Louis H. Manarin, *Richmond at War: The Minutes of the City Council, 1861–1865* (Chapel Hill, N.C., 1966), 570–71.

30. *O.R.*, Ser. I, Vol. XLVI, Pt. 2, pp. 1264–65; Longstreet, *Manassas to Appomattox*, 584.

ing Tredegar behind intact would not aid them, its owners begged that it be spared. Breckinridge consulted Navy Secretary Stephen Mallory and Gorgas on the subject, the former favoring destruction and the latter opposing, and then decided to let Tredegar stand. Besides the logic of its owners' argument, he also saw by now that the Confederacy had little chance of survival, and that the South would need all of its existing industry for the task of rebuilding under the Union.[31]

And it is certain that by the first or second week of March, and probably some time before, Breckinridge was convinced that the cause of the Confederacy was hopeless. On March 4 he spent several hours in private conversation with Lee, Quartermaster General A. R. Lawton, and St. John, and the result of their talk was not hopeful. Then the next day he read a private letter from Campbell. Convinced that the South stood doomed, Campbell cited the department's staggering debt and the consequent paralysis of all its bureaus, the deflation of Confederate notes, the terrible condition of what remained of the armies, and the slim hope, as he saw it, of any of the schemes for raising fresh troops. Arms and accouterments stood in short supply, with access to foreign markets almost cut off, desertions were mounting, and the country was barren after four years of war. At the same time, some states of the Confederacy, and particularly Georgia, were what he called "insurrectionary." Governor Joseph E. Brown of Georgia had been interfering for years with the conscription laws, impressment and procurement, and hampering and criticizing Davis at every turn. From his vantage point in the War Office, Breckinridge felt this long before he read Campbell's letter, and it probably planted in him the first seeds of doubt over the propriety of the states' rights precedent that the Confederate experience sought to set, though it would be some time before those doubts crystallized into conviction.

Campbell concluded with the statement, "The South may succumb, but it is not necessary that she should be destroyed." He favored negotiating for power on the basis of reunion and emancipation, before the war degenerated into a partisan mode that would debase the heroic struggle thus far waged. He suggested that Lee be asked for his candid views, and that Davis ask the Senate to act on his recommendation. To add weight to his plea, Campbell also included with his letter a copy of memoranda of the

31. *O.R.*, Ser. I, Vol. XLVI, Pt. 2, pp. 1259–60, 1287–89, Pt. 3, p. 1331; Charles B. Dew, *Ironmaker to the Confederacy: Joseph R. Anderson and the Tredegar Iron Works* (New Haven, 1966), 285–86.

Hampton Roads failure, and a statement from Secretary George A. Trenholm on the plight of the Treasury.[32]

Breckinridge found much in the letter with which he agreed, spoke to Campbell on it, and then took action. On March 8 he wrote to Lee asking for his candid view of the military situation. "Since I assumed the control of the War Department," he told the general, "a more extended knowledge has convinced me that our condition is full of peril, and that it demands united counsels and prompt action." He proposed to give Lee's letter, with his own remarks appended, to the president, with the hope that they would be laid before Congress. Breckinridge spoke of that body enacting some measure of rescue for the Confederacy, but, more likely, he did not wish to expose his mounting pessimism to Lee. If so, he need not have worried, for Lee's reply used Breckinridge's own words to describe the situation as "full of peril." He could not supply his army adequately since a breakdown in transportation facilities had almost nullified St. John's work of collection, and in such straits the evacuation of his position was imminent.[33]

On March 10 Breckinridge sent another confidential circular around to his bureau chiefs. The replies were still optimistic, but tempered by a reserve not evident in the circular replies from these same officers a month before. Breckinridge put these reports, together with his letter to Lee and the general's reply, in an envelope and gave it to Davis on March 13. With it went a covering letter explaining his own concurrence in what Lee said. This prompted the president to ask Congress to postpone its adjournment in order to consider new proposals, including the arming of the slaves, which the secretary favored more than ever. Congress remained in session, but it was too late. Breckinridge's and Lee's efforts came to nothing.[34]

By submitting these papers to Davis and Congress, the secretary actually

---

32. Jones, *War Clerk's Diary*, II, 440; St. John to Davis, July 14, 1873, in Rowland, *Jefferson Davis*, VII, 352–53; *O.R.*, Ser. I, Vol. LI, Pt. 2, pp. 1064–67; John A. Campbell, *Reminiscences and Documents Relating to the Civil War During the Year 1865* (Baltimore, 1887), 22, 32–34; Campbell to B. R. Curtis, July 20, 1865, in "Open Letters," *Century Magazine*, XXXVIII (October, 1889), 952. The original of Campbell to Breckinridge, March 5, 1865, is in the John A. Campbell MSS, SHC.

33. Campbell, *Reminiscences*, 32; Breckinridge to Lee, March 8, 1865, in Davis MSS, LHAC.

34. *O.R.*, Ser. I, Vol. LII, Pt. 2, pp. 1067–68, Ser. IV, Vol. III, 1136–37; Richard Morton to Breckinridge, March 10, 1865, A. R. Lawton to Breckinridge, March 10, 1865, Josiah Gorgas to Breckinridge, March 11, 1865, in Louis T. Wigfall MSS, LC; Breckinridge to Davis, March 13, 1865, in Dearborn Collection; Campbell, *Reminiscences*, 32; Jones, *War Clerk's Diary*, II, 447.

hoped that some movement toward general and honorable surrender would be initiated. Breckinridge even called on Senator R. M. T. Hunter of Virginia to discuss Lee's advice, but he couldn't get the subject on the Senate floor. However, a day or two after submitting the reports to Davis, but before Congress adjourned, he called a number of congressmen to the hotel room of his friend Senator Henry Burnett of Kentucky. Present were Wigfall of Texas, Hunter and Allen Caperton of Virginia, and Waldo Johnston and George G. Vest of Missouri. As Vest remembered the meeting ten years later, Breckinridge opened the discussion with a frank statement of his conviction that the cause was hopeless and lost, that but a few days of life were left. In this situation, he was anxious to consult with the congressmen from Missouri and Kentucky over the fate of Confederate soldiers from those states, states which were represented in the capitals of both North and South. "If the Confederacy goes to pieces," he said, "and our armies are disbanded without any formal action on the part of the Confederate Government, the soldiers from the cotton States and from that portion of our territory not occupied by the enemy will go to their homes and probably remain there unmolested." However, he feared for the Missourians and Kentuckians who, far from their states, would be stranded when the armies disbanded, and might not meet a friendly reception at home. To what extent they might be proscribed if the Confederacy fell apart piece by piece, he feared to speculate.

> Our first duty, gentlemen, is to the soldiers who have been influenced by our arguments and example, and we should make any and every sacrifice to protect them. What I propose ... is this: That the Confederacy should not be captured in fragments, that we should not disband like banditti, but that we should surrender as a government, and we will thus maintain the dignity of our cause, and secure the respect of our enemies, and the best terms for our soldiers. As for myself ... I may be, for reasons known to us all, more obnoxious to the North than many others, but I am willing to assume the risk, and to surrender as Secretary of War.

His chief fear, said Breckinridge, was that Davis would not agree to escape the country. He was probably the most hated of all and might find himself facing trial for treason. Breckinridge knew the president well, he said, and believed that he would not consent to any arrangement that would save him from facing the possible retribution others would meet. Nothing was settled on this point, and if Breckinridge had hoped to influence the congressmen to take some action toward formal surrender before adjournment, they disappointed him. However, before leaving the meeting, he bade them farewell with a firm injunction. "This has been a magnificent epic," he said. "In God's name let it not terminate in a farce." [35]

Curiously enough, while the Confederacy underwent the upheaval of its last few months, Breckinridge's domestic life was more stabilized than any time during the war. Mary, ill again, stayed with him at the Richmond home of their friend Bruce. Clifton, now a midshipman fourth class in the Confederate Navy, was stationed on the training ship *Patrick Henry* on the James River below Richmond, and Cabell was in and out of the capital, spending much of his time with Fitzhugh Lee's cavalry, and acquiring some unfortunate drinking habits which caused strained relations with his father. Despite this, the secretary seems to have enjoyed himself as much as possible in Richmond. Capital social life, no longer glittering, remained studiously active, and Breckinridge took what pleasure he could. He was a particular favorite with Mrs. Davis, and the wife of her husband's private secretary found that "the splendid General Breckinridge" was one most frequently to be seen at drawing room parties.[36]

Breckinridge worked hard for his $10,000 salary. Though he might not keep up his correspondence to suit Kean and Campbell, a steady stream of communications went out from his office. He generally arrived at the War Department early in the morning, and held meetings with congressmen and other cabinet members. Hunter was conspicuous by his absence from these meetings, seldom paying a call on the secretary. Clerk Jones ascribed this to Hunter's jealousy of Breckinridge as a potential rival for Davis' succession, which may also in part explain the failure of Breckinridge's formal surrender proposal to reach the floor of Congress. Following these meetings came a daily interview with St. John over the accumulation of supplies and handling and filling requisitions, as well as setting up and maintaining the supply depots along Lee's proposed line of withdrawal from Petersburg. Then came conversations with other bureau heads, occasional cabinet meetings, a trip to the front to see Lee or an afternoon at the Executive

35. R. M. T. Hunter to William Jones, October 1877, in Rowland, *Jefferson Davis*, VII, 577; George G. Vest, "John C. Breckinridge: Recollections of One Who Knew Him in the Prime of His Manhood," Louisville *Courier-Journal*, June 8, 1875.

36. Breckinridge to J. S. Johnston, February 23, 1865, in Breckinridge MSS, FC; "Children of the Confederacy in Kentucky," *Confederate Veteran*, IX (May, 1901), 227; Clifton R. Breckinridge Service Record, NA; Breckinridge to Clifton R. Breckinridge, June 17, 1866, in JCB Papers; Ishbel Ross, *First Lady of the South* (New York, 1958), 186; Constance Harrison, *Recollections Grave and Gay* (New York, 1912), 178; "Journal of Congress," *SHSP*, LII (July, 1959), 285.

Mansion on Clay Street. Every day there were scores of reports and communications to read and answer, decisions to make, and policy to decide.

Often that policy conflicted interestingly with his old political beliefs. As a statesman he would never have accepted censorship of the news in the public press, but now he was forced to practice it himself, declaring a sort of embargo on military information in the capital press. He was particularly guarded about letting out reports on affairs with Johnston's army. However, where any of his predecessors would have been cut to pieces in the prints for this, the secretary was treated kindly throughout. They trusted him to notify them if something really important happened, and, as the *Whig* confidently stated, "if anything of interest transpires which can be published, we are confident that the intelligent Secretary of War will cause the news to be promptly communicated to the press." Breckinridge also stood not above interfering with the treasured rights of the states, even the imperious Zebulon Vance's North Carolina. To make uniform the rail gauge of the Confederacy's railroads appeared to him a necessity, since the losses of rolling stock made it imperative that cars from anywhere in the country be able to go to any point that the army's movements required. When Vance objected to changing the gauge on a road in North Carolina, the secretary told him bluntly that he would take possession of the road if necessary, and impress all its rolling stock into government service.

With all of this, the secretary was managing the planned evacuation of Richmond, dealing with civic and official leaders over removal and destruction of property, and overseeing the preparations of his own department for the move. At noon on March 6 the emergency came home to the War Department when he had boxes brought in and put the clerks to work packing them with the department archives, telling them to be quiet about it to avoid alarming the people. Almost two months before, when Seddon's successor was as yet unchosen, the Richmond *Whig* declared, "We want generally in supreme command of the army, some man of large capacity, of controlling will, and of great aptness for practical affairs, at the head of the War Office." Clearly, in Breckinridge they got that man, and a man of industry as well. During the first three weeks of his secretaryship, he did not get to bed once before 2 o'clock in the morning. Hopefully he wrote to Stoddard Johnston, "I will get some relief after a while." [37]

37. Jones, *War Clerk's Diary*, II, 425–26, 434, 441, 454; Breckinridge to I. M. St. John, May 16, 1871, in Rowland, *Jefferson Davis*, VII, 357; *O.R.*, Ser. I, Vol. XLVII, Pt. 3, p. 712; Richmond *Whig*, January 16, March 7, 1865; Breckinridge to Vance, March 23, 1865, in Chap. 9, XXXI, NA; Breckinridge to J. S. Johnston, February 23, 1865, in Breckinridge MSS, FC.

Naturally, the most absorbing subject in the War Office was the news from the various fronts, and as March wore on it got progressively worse. The men in Kirby Smith's and Johnston's armies were clamoring for their pay, news came of Early's plight in the Valley and, on March 2, of his smashing defeat by Sheridan at Waynesboro. Thereafter, Early stayed barely out of reach of the Federals, sending one disheartening telegram after another, all of them indicating that Sheridan was moving to join Grant and that, together, they would cut off retreat from Petersburg. Equally disheartening was a communication from Lee that Thomas' army was moving again in Tennessee, that Dabney Maury at Mobile was threatened, that Burbridge and the east Tennessee Federals were on the move to an unknown destination, and that Sherman was advancing against Johnston. News of the Army of Tennessee's defeats at Averasboro and Bentonville, North Carolina, on March 16 and 19 came almost immediately afterward, and obviously only the question remained of how long Grant would wait to move against Lee.[38]

Then, on March 25, came the word. With no choice but to attempt to break through Grant's line in the hope of causing the Federals to call back their advancing left flank, the commanding general sent Gordon in a surprise predawn attack against Fort Stedman. It went well, but unexpected resistance forced Gordon back to his own lines, and Lee reported its failure to the War Department at 11 A.M. The last act had begun. "Something must be done," Breckinridge told Gorgas.[39]

All he could do was wait, and read the dispatches as they came off the telegraph. On March 29 the enemy was moving around Lee's right at Hatcher's Run; March 30, the enemy now is west of Hatcher's Run; March 31, Lee's right, under Pickett and Fitzhugh Lee, has withdrawn to the vital crossroads at Five Forks; April 1, Five Forks is lost, Pickett's whereabouts is unknown, and the avenue of escape for the Army of Northern Virginia is nearly cut—Lee wants to confer with Davis and Breckinridge, but cannot leave the front. The topic he wishes to speak on is obvious.[40]

Throughout the previous week, officials had been departing Richmond daily. Only Davis and the cabinet remained, and of their number only

38. O.R., Ser. I, Vol. XLVI, Pt. 2, p. 1285, Pt. 3, pp. 1318–19, Vol. XLVII, Pt. 2, p. 1290, Vol. XLVIII, Pt. 1, pp. 1424–25; Jubal A. Early to Breckinridge, March 15, 1865, in Breckinridge MSS, CHS.

39. Jones, War Clerk's Diary, II, 460; Lee to Breckinridge, March 25, 1865, in Dowdey and Manarin (eds.), Wartime Papers, 916; Vandiver, Diary of Gorgas, 178.

40. Lee to Breckinridge, March 29, 30, 31, April 1, 1865, Lee to Davis, April 1, 1865, in Dowdey and Manarin (eds.), Wartime Papers, 920–24.

Breckinridge and Secretary of the Navy Stephen Mallory continued to function as department chiefs. The secretary of war stayed in the Mechanics Institute building all day April 1, managing as much as possible the arrangements for the imminent evacuation. When Longstreet's troops had to be withdrawn that evening from their position protecting the South Side Railroad, the only line out of the capital toward Danville, Breckinridge had to order out Ewell's reserves to take their place. Then, with little else to do but wait as the Confederacy crumbled, he joined Rear Admiral Raphael Semmes, commander of the James River squadron, and a private from the defense troops. Together, the unlikely trio stayed long into the night packing department records into wooden cases, nailing on the tops, and marking them for shipment to Charlotte, North Carolina. Then came morning, Sunday, April 2, 1865.[41]

41. W. H. Swallow, "Retreat of the Confederate Government from Richmond to the Gulf," *Magazine of American History*, XV (June, 1886), 596; *O.R.*, Ser. I, Vol. XLVI, Pt. 3, pp. 1370, 1375.

CHAPTER 10

Nothing Can Be Done

Breckinridge spent the night at the War Department. Dawn found him nervously pacing back and forth in his office, awaiting news from Lee. As the hours slowly dragged on, Postmaster General John H. Reagan and Benjamin joined him in the vigil, while Davis and the other cabinet members attended Sunday services. Campbell was there too, with Jones, Kean, Colonel F. R. Lubbock of Texas, and a few others. At 10:40 A.M. the telegraph started clicking out an urgent message from Petersburg. Lee's lines had been broken. He could do no more than hold out until night-fall, and then withdraw. Richmond must be abandoned that evening.[1]

The news did not surprise the secretary of war. He took it calmly. While Kean went to work packing more books, Breckinridge sent a copy of the telegram to Davis at St. Paul's Episcopal Church, one block up from the War Office, on Ninth Street. Immediately the president came to the department, spoke briefly with Breckinridge and the others, and called a cabinet meeting. As the ministers gathered in his office in the Customs Building, everyone remained quiet. This had been anticipated. Breckinridge walked over with Reagan and found the others there, including Mayor Joseph Mayo. Here Davis read Lee's dispatch again, explained the situation in a few words, and then charged the ministers to see to final packing for the departure.[2]

Breckinridge's chief role in the meeting was the arrangement of trans-

1. Rembert W. Patrick, *The Fall of Richmond* (Baton Rouge, 1960), 7–8; Jones, *War Clerk's Diary*, II, 465; Reagan, *Memoirs*, 198; John A. Campbell, *Recollections of the Evacuation of Richmond, April 2, 1865* (Baltimore, 1880), 4; Younger, *Inside the Confederate Government*, 205; O.R., Ser. I, Vol. XLVI, Pt. 3, p. 1378.

2. Younger, *Inside the Confederate Government*, 205; Strode, *Tragic Hero*, 167; Patrick, *Fall*, 19–20; Stephen R. Mallory Diary, April 2, 1865, in Stephen R. Mallory MSS, SHC, used by kind permission of Mr. T. S. Kennedy, Pensacola, Fla.

portation to get the cabinet out of the city before the enemy cut the road to Danville, their anticipated destination. He had wired to Lee to determine if the railroad was still open, which it was, and told the cabinet that a train would be awaiting them at the Danville station at 8 P.M. After the meeting was over, Breckinridge returned to the War Department where he engaged in a hurried afternoon of giving orders, and making further arrangements for the train to carry the president and cabinet away. Just before 5 o'clock he received assurance from Lee that the Danville road would probably be safe for the rest of the day. Two hours later came further confirmation from Lee. He would have to abandon his lines before morning. In the hustle, Breckinridge did not see this last message, for when it arrived at 7 P.M. he was at the Danville station walking with Davis to his seat in the cabinet coach. Thus neither he nor the president knew that Lee planned to withdraw upon Amelia Courthouse, where he would desperately need supplies.[3]

Other matters commanded attention that day before Breckinridge left for the depot. The most pressing problem remaining was what to do with the stores that could not be removed. The day before, he and Ewell met with Gilmer and Gorgas to discuss the proposed destruction of tobacco by fire. The two bureau chiefs protested the order. Both feared that the fire might spread to the city, and Gorgas suggested pouring turpentine on the stores, which would destroy them just as effectively. That same day Mayo met with the secretary and Ewell to argue against the same order. Ewell remained adamant in favor of the torch, while Breckinridge disagreed, saying that "it would be a disgrace to the Confederate government to endanger the destruction of the entire city." However, he did order that the bridges across the James should be burned once the city was evacuated, an act which Gorgas feared might send flames too close to the government arsenal. Unfortunately, even though the secretary had the power to overrule Ewell and forbid the burning of the tobacco warehouses, he did not[4]

Last details presented themselves. By 6 P.M. the department archives were

3. Mallory Diary, April 2, 1865, in Mallory MSS; *O.R.*, Ser. I, Vol. XLVI, Pt. 3, pp. 1378–79; Patrick, *Fall*, 21, 33; Lewis Harvie to I. M. St. John, January 1, 1876, in "Resources of the Confederacy in 1865," *SHSP*, III (March, 1877), 110–11; Jones, *War Clerk's Diary*, II, 466; Younger, *Inside the Confederate Government*, 205; Breckinridge to St. John, May 16, 1871, in Rowland, *Jefferson Davis*, VII, 356–57.

4. Vandiver, *Ploughshares Into Swords*, 266; Richmond *Whig*, April 14, 1865; Patrick, *Fall*, 42–43, 43n; Charles C. Coffin, *The Boys of '61* (Boston, 1886), 541. Sources vary widely on how Breckinridge felt about burning the stores, though his well-known feelings about other destruction in the war make it likely that he opposed this waste as well.

packed and at the Danville station. St. John had 350,000 rations in the city as a reserve, had wired Lee earlier in the day asking what should be done with them, and that evening received the reply that they should be sent on to Danville if possible. By this time, the train at the station, the last one to leave a Confederate Richmond, stood filled, unable to take out any supplies. Consequently, St. John began collecting a wagon train to move what it could, and put men to work distributing what remained among the city's people. Then, sometime after six o'clock, Breckinridge left the department and rode to the station.[5]

He arrived before Davis and found Clifton awaiting him. Some $500,000 in gold and silver, the remnant of the Confederate Treasury as well as the money from Richmond's banks, had been loaded on the train that would carry Davis and the cabinet to Danville. To guard the specie, the midshipmen from the *Patrick Henry* had been brought up. If Clifton and his father had time to speak, it could not have been for long, for soon Davis appeared, followed shortly by the cabinet. The secretary of war led the president to his car, spoke to his fellow ministers briefly, and then mounted his horse to ride along the standing train inspecting it. He alone of the high officials would remain in the city to oversee what remained of the evacuation. As the secretary rode along the cars, Captain William H. Parker, commandant of the Naval Academy, saw that he "was as cool and gallant as ever, but the others had the air of wishing to be off." [6]

Until about 10 P.M., the secretary of war passed the time in talking with Davis, riding around the train, and speaking with Parker. The captain brought to his attention several bales of clothing and blankets lying in the station that had come in for Petersburg that morning. News of Lee's impending withdrawal left them stranded here, and Parker wanted to let his cadets equip themselves with what they could carry. Dismayed that Lee would not now have these articles—for there was no more room in the train or any wagons—the Kentuckian assented.[7]

By ten o'clock, the train was two hours late in departing. Some felt that Davis and Breckinridge were holding it up, hoping that favorable news would yet come from Lee. In fact, however, they were in the office in the Danville station, speaking with Lewis E. Harvie, president of the Rich-

5. Younger, *Inside the Confederate Government*, 205; St. John to Davis, July 14, 1873, in Rowland, *Jefferson Davis*, VII, 353; John Leyburn, "The Fall of Richmond," *Harper's New Monthly Magazine*, XXXIII (June, 1866), 93.

6. Alfred J. Hanna, *Flight into Oblivion* (Richmond, 1938), 5–6; William H. Parker, *Recollections of a Naval Officer, 1841–1865* (New York, 1883), 350–52; Patrick, *Fall*, 33.

7. Patrick, *Fall*, 34.

mond, Danville and Piedmont. The three spoke for an hour or more on the route that the wagon supply train should take, still ignorant of Lee's intentions to move through Amelia. At 11 P.M. Davis returned to the train, Breckinridge mounted his horse, stood outside Davis' window for a few final words, and then the engine slowly steamed off towards the west. The secretary's last act, being repeatedly beseeched by a number of people for passage aboard the already overcrowded train, was to allow an invalided artillery captain to sit atop one of the cars and ride to Danville.[9]

Breckinridge had final matters to attend to as the cabinet moved toward Danville. Another sad parting from Mary may have been the last duty. She would have to remain in Richmond, being too sick and too tired to undergo the trip west with other cabinet wives. "We sat in darkness that night," she later recalled, for no one had the heart to light a lamp. Then came the time to destroy the remaining munitions. While sailors placed powder in the ships of the river fleet, the main magazine was primed, and two of the James River bridges fired. Sensing what was happening, a mob gathered in the streets, moving toward the warehouses where St. John's men were removing stores. Then he turned them over to the people, while other of his agents began dumping government supplies of whiskey into gutters. Soon, explosions from the river signaled the end of the squadron, followed shortly by the thunderous roar of the magazine going up in flames. Next the tobacco warehouses were fired, despite the order not to burn them. The city still seemed safe, since there was no wind to spread the flames, but the mob within promised to do as much damage as any fire. With the few men at hand, there was no controlling them.

There was little time. Dawn approached, and when the sun appeared, Breckinridge and a few others were still in the city. One bridge now remained for their escape, the Mayo Bridge across the James to Manchester. The Seventh South Carolina Cavalry, held behind to collect stragglers, made a final run through the city, and then raced across the bridge, throwing firebrands on it as they went. Secretary of War Breckinridge may have been the last to cross it. Dressed in the civilian black that he wore in lieu of a uniform during his cabinet service, he rode alongside Ewell, a cape over his shoulders, alternately talking with the general and looking back over his shoulder at the city. Reaching Manchester, he joined Lieutenant Colonel Walter Taylor, of Lee's staff, and Peter Helms Mayo of the Danville line.

8. *Ibid.*, 34, 40; Harvie to St. John, January 1, 1876, in "Resources, 1865," 110–11; Mallory Diary, April 2, 1865, in Mallory MSS; J. Milledge to Breckinridge, November 10, 1869, in JCB Papers.

The three turned their horses around to view the capital, and were shocked to see the fire and smoke spread toward the heart of the city. Despite the fact that there was no wind, the flames at the warehouses created their own drafts, and sent hot coals floating into the city's rooftops. Now, however, there was nothing to be done. When the smoke completely hid Richmond from view, Breckinridge and the others rode off toward Lee's retreating army. In less than half an hour, the Federals would take possession of the Confederate capital.[9]

Lawton and St. John rode with Breckinridge now, as did his friend and former adjutant, the recently exchanged Colonel James Wilson. Breckinridge seems to have seen or heard at last of Lee's order for supplies to be sent to Amelia Courthouse. As Breckinridge rode west toward Powhatan, he encountered a number of wagon trains of army supplies sent out of the capital. With St. John he began gathering them together with directions to press on toward Amelia Springs, where he believed Lee might be. He passed through Powhatan that day and, on April 4, moved on to the Genito Bridge over the Appomattox River. Finding it burned, Breckinridge took the train along the north bank of the river toward Clementon. By now a few stragglers had attached themselves to the column, as well as Generals Bushrod Johnson, Joseph Davis, and Walter H. Stevens.[10]

A telegram which probably did not reach Breckinridge would have informed him somewhat of the army's movements, but by April 5 he knew as much as was necessary without it. By that morning the train had crossed Clementon's bridge, where it halted while the generals discussed recent intelligence that Federal cavalry was moving toward it from Jetersville, about fifteen miles south. Breckinridge called for three volunteers to scout ahead and find the truth, while he rode to the head of the wagon train to be ready when they returned. A ride of two miles disclosed the enemy cavalry in some force driving back yet another wagon column. The scouts reported back to the secretary, while a panic-stricken quartermaster began riding

9. Maltby, *Mary Cyrene Breckinridge*, 8; Patrick, *Fall*, 44–52; Coffin, *Boys of '61*, 506; *O.R.*, Ser. I, Vol. XLVI, Pt. 3, p. 594. Campbell was surprised to see the warehouses burning, which strengthens the contention that their firing was by accident rather than by order. Campbell, *Recollections*, 5.

10. St. John, in 1873 (St. John to Jefferson Davis, July 14, 1873, in Rowland, *Jefferson Davis*, VII, 354) says that on April 3 he and Breckinridge headed for Amelia Springs, knowing that Lee would be there. However, in Festus P. Summers (ed.), *A Borderland Confederate* (Pittsburgh, 1962), William L. Wilson's diary for April 4 (p. 95) says that Breckinridge had no clear idea of Lee's whereabouts. Wilson traveled with the secretary that day, and says that Breckinridge was directing a wagon train which "was ordered from Richmond direct to Amelia C.H."

down the wagon train shouting that the enemy was upon them. With no guard to protect them, the teamsters and many others present abandoned almost everything in a shameful fright, and ran back across the bridge, leaving Breckinridge nearly alone on the southern bank. An hour passed, during which, with some effort, he managed to collect about twenty horsemen and one hundred infantrymen, and then, accompanied by nearly as many generals as privates, he led the little command down the road to find the enemy.

As it turned out, the only action they saw was a drunken captain in command of the mounted men, leading his troops in a wild charge against an empty wood. Meanwhile, a Federal scouting party got behind them briefly and succeeded in capturing a small part of the wagon train. Breckinridge, riding back, was able to drive them away. The brief escapade gave him the distinction of being the only cabinet minister in American history to lead and fight troops in battle. At this point he sent the remainder of the train off to the southwest toward Farmville, twenty-five miles distant, while he and the generals and staff forced their way through Union patrols and roads jammed with the flotsam of Lee's retreat, to Amelia Springs.[11]

Late that night or early the next morning, Breckinridge and party rode the twenty-five miles west to Longstreet's temporary headquarters near Farmville. Here, at last, he found Lee, and they spent a few hours of the morning in private conversation. The meeting concluded, Breckinridge, St. John, Lawton, and now Gilmer, rode on into Farmville. Analyzing the commanding general's plans in a dispatch to Davis, Breckinridge surmised that it was still Lee's intention to make a junction with Johnston in North Carolina, but he could not help giving the impression that chances were slim. The Kentuckian was no fool. His now trained military eye could see that Lee and the Army of Northern Virginia were nearly run out. As he said his farewell to the general that morning, he undoubtedly suspected that it would be a long time before they met again. "The situation is not favorable," Breckinridge told the president, and this belief was punctuated by bad reports and the lack of news from other points.[12]

11. O.R., Ser. I, Vol. XLVI, Pt. 3, pp. 1383–84; Summers, Borderland Confederate, pp. 96–97; M. W. Venable, "On the Way to Appomattox—War Memories," Confederate Veteran, XXXII (August, 1924), 303; St. John to Davis, July 14, 1873, in Rowland, Jefferson Davis, VII, 354.

12. Breckinridge to St. John, May 16, 1871, St. John to Davis, July 14, 1873, in Rowland, Jefferson Davis, VII, 354–55, 357; Joseph Packard, "Ordnance Matters at the Close," Confederate Veteran, XVI (May, 1908), 228; O.R., Ser. I, Vol. XLVI, Pt. 3, p. 1389.

The secretary did not leave Farmville until the enemy was reported to be approaching the outskirts of town. Although he surely did not know it, just a few miles south of Farmville marched the approaching columns of Major General E. O. C. Ord's Twenty-fourth Corps and, moving with it on detached service, one division of the Twenty-fifth Corps. Its commander, now a major general, was Breckinridge's childhood playmate and closest friend, William Birney. Meanwhile, the secretary of war rode on toward Pamphlin's Station, twenty miles west of Farmville, and just ten miles south of Appomattox Courthouse. A soldier who joined the party for part of the trip watched Breckinridge during the day, and found that "his calm, buoyant manner was very impressive." The next night, April 8, he stayed at Red House, a few miles west of Pamphlin's, and the same distance south of Appomattox where, that same night, Grant finally encircled Lee. The next day, the Army of Northern Virginia would be no more.[13]

In the week that Davis and the cabinet had been in Danville the government had been put back in limited operation, but now the place stood clearly untenable, and before the secretary of war could arrive, Davis packed up and steamed south towards Greensboro, North Carolina. Thus, when Breckinridge reached Danville sometime on April 11, he found Kean, who had opened the War Department and been left behind. Here, too, he found Clifton, who had four days earlier been discharged from the navy. "I saw that the time had come for those who loved our leaders to gather around them," the midshipman later recalled, "& I resigned that I might join my father—which I did." [14]

Recognizing that the Confederacy was dying, Breckinridge regarded the welfare of the surrendered and paroled soldiers returning home as second only to that of the men still under arms, and he seemed never to be too busy to give a few minutes to a weary and confused private. Here, at Danville, three such tired Confederates trudged into his office, one of them with feet bleeding from fifty miles of walking in soleless boots. One of the privates, Leeland Hathaway, had met Breckinridge briefly more than six years before, and now he was astonished to see the secretary rise from his desk and, "with that immaculate grace & charm which never left him," walk over and greet him by name. "His memory of faces & names was phenomenal," stated the soldier.[15]

13. Packard, "Ordnance Matters," 229; St. John to Davis, July 14, 1873, in Rowland, *Jefferson Davis*, VII, 355.

14. *O.R.*, Ser. I, Vol. XLVI, Pt. 3, p. 1390; Younger, *Inside the Confederate Government*, 206; Sidney S. Lee to Clifton R. Breckinridge, April 6, 1865, in JCB Papers.

15. St. John to Davis, July 14, 1873, in Rowland, *Jefferson Davis*, VII, 355; *O.R.*,

Breckinridge left Danville early April 12 and reached Greensboro that evening, expecting Kean to bring off the remainder of the department files. On his arrival, the secretary of war found that Davis was staying at the home of Captain John Taylor Wood. Immediately he reported to the president, bringing final confirmation of Lee's surrender. Johnston and Beauregard were in Greensboro this day, and each had delivered an unfavorable report in a cabinet meeting earlier that morning. Davis now called another meeting for 10 A.M., April 13, to decide what should be done. That night Johnston and Beauregard spoke privately, concluding that all was lost, that there was no hope. Johnston went to his friend Breckinridge, repeated his conversation with the Creole, and declared that any further resistance would only bring needless suffering. Breckinridge promised to give Johnston an opportunity to air his views in the morning's cabinet meeting.[16]

The cabinet gathered the next morning in a small second-story room at Wood's. After about two hours of discussion, Johnston and Beauregard were called in, as Breckinridge fulfilled his promise to get Johnston a hearing. The general spoke for some time in advocacy of suing for terms while the ministers listened in silence. When he had finished, Davis asked Beauregard for his views, and heard his agreement with Johnston, the proposal being that he should contact Sherman and ask for a suspension of hostilities pending a conference to agree on peace terms. Davis did not approve, but put the question to his cabinet members. Breckinridge, Mallory, and Reagan all gave their assent to the plan, while only Benjamin advocated further resistance. Outvoted, Davis agreed to let Johnston proceed with his attempt at negotiation. Reagan proposed some possible terms of agreement, one of them being that Confederate soldiers should be granted an amnesty, though there was general agreement among the conferees that they and Davis might have to be excluded in order to gain this provision.[17]

With Johnston's surrender imminent—and no doubt fearful that the high officials would be excluded from any amnesty—Davis led his government out of Greensboro on April 15, bound for Charlotte near the South Caro-

---

Ser. I, Vol. XLIX, Pt. 2, p. 1220; Hotchkiss, April 12, 1865, in Hotchkiss MSS; Leeland Hathaway, "Recollections," VII, 36–38, SHC.

16. O.R., Ser. I, Vol. XLVII, Pt. 3, pp. 795–96; Younger, *Inside the Confederate Government*, 206; H. V. Boynton, *Sherman's Historical Raid: The Memoirs in the Light of the Record* (Cincinnati, 1875), 223–24; John H. Reagan to Davis, December 12, 1880, in Rowland, *Jefferson Davis*, VIII, 536; Joseph E. Johnston, *Narrative*, 396–98; Mallory Diary, n.d., in Mallory MSS.

17. Reagan to Davis, December 12, 1880, in Rowland, *Jefferson Davis*, VIII, 536–37; Reagan, *Memoirs*, 200; Boynton, *Sherman's Historical Raid*, 224–25; Mallory Diary, n.d., in Mallory MSS.

lina border. From this point on, Breckinridge personally took over command of the troops with the column. He, Dibrell, and Colonel W. C. P. Breckinridge, had arranged the daily order of march and picketing before leaving, and now Davis, Mallory, Reagan, and Breckinridge, rode out on horseback, while the others took ambulances. The ride was slow and tedious, made more so by the cumbersome wagon train carrying the government archives and cabinet baggage, and by the incessant rain. The first night out of Greensboro saw the party only ten miles south, at Jamestown, and the next day took them even less distance, to Lexington.[18]

Governor Vance had been following them for some time, wishing to confer with Davis over the future course of North Carolina. Here in Lexington he caught up with the cabinet, and the president invited him to attend its meeting. To Vance he spoke hopefully of the retreat beyond the Mississippi, where the Confederacy would rally around the army of Kirby Smith. Vance saw immediately that the president wanted him to come with him to the West, bringing the North Carolina troops to help continue the fight. Silence met Davis' propositions for a time, and then one by one his ministers spoke, Benjamin in favor heartily, Mallory and Reagan probably agreeing with reluctance, if at all. When they had finished, the secretary of war put an end to the business by taking a stand against the president *and* a significant portion of the cabinet in his determination to end the war peacefully. "I shall never forget either the language or the manner of that splendid Kentuckian," Vance would recall. Breckinridge spoke bluntly and to the point. They were not being candid with Vance. All hope of accomplishing what Davis proposed was so remote that he refused to advise the governor to comply. Vance was needed in North Carolina. He should stay there, said the secretary, see to his people, and share their fate. Vance agreed completely with Breckinridge. Davis, with a patience and deference that he had seldom shown to any cabinet officer, sighed and said, "Well, perhaps, General, you are right." That ended the matter, and they said farewell to Vance that same night.[19]

Sometime that evening urgent word came from Johnston to Breckinridge. He apparently had been trying to reach the secretary since the day before, and now a message finally got through: "Your immediate presence

---

18. W. C. P. Breckinridge to William Walthall, April 3, 1878, in Rowland, *Jefferson Davis*, VIII, 153; James M. Morgan, *Recollections of a Rebel Reefer* (Boston, 1917), 235; Hanna, *Flight*, 40–41; Breckinridge to Joseph E. Johnston, 1865, in Basil W. Duke MSS, SHC.

19. Clement Dowd, *Life of Zebulon B. Vance* (Charlotte, N.C., 1897), 485–87. There are several errors in Vance's account, including the placing of this meeting at Charlotte.

is necessary, in order that I should be able to confer with you." Davis called
Breckinridge and Reagan to his quarters as soon as the message was received, about 10 P.M. Johnston had made arrangements to meet with Sherman on the morrow, April 17, and he wanted some representative of the
government there to advise with him, since the contemplated surrender
might go beyond the Army of Tennessee. Less obvious was Johnston's belief that Breckinridge's relations with Davis might aid in overcoming the
president's objections to whatever surrender arrangements were made.[20]

Breckinridge and Reagan rode out of Lexington minutes after meeting
with Davis, to reach Greensboro the next morning at 9:30. Here the secretary spoke with Beauregard, found that Johnston had received a favorable
reply to his request for an interview, and immediately wired the general
to see if his presence was still needed. At 5:30 P.M. the word came. Johnston wanted him.[21]

The cabinet officers, accompanied now by Vance, reached Hillsborough
during the morning of April 18 and immediately went to confer with Johnston at Wade Hampton's headquarters. Johnston filled them in on what
had transpired at the meeting the day before. He and Sherman, wishing to
go beyond the terms given to Lee by Grant, hoped to extend the surrender
to all the remaining troops of the Confederacy. The trouble was that Johnston did not have authority over any but those in the Army of Tennessee.
However, Breckinridge did, and in talking with Johnston that morning he
authorized the general to treat for all armies of the South. Meanwhile, Reagan began putting on paper an elaboration of the surrender terms he had
proposed several days before in cabinet session, but Johnston had to leave
to meet Sherman before the postmaster general was through.[22]

Shortly a staff officer came from Johnston. Sherman had agreed to let
Breckinridge attend the conference, though only in his capacity as a major
general, and at once the Kentuckian left for the James Bennett home, near
Durham Station. When he arrived, he strode through the circle of staff officers and onlookers surrounding the little house, where Johnston introduced
him to William Tecumseh Sherman. The conflict was coming full circle
for Breckinridge, for this was the man he first met in battle three years be-

20. O.R., Ser. I. Vol. XLVII. Pt. 3, pp. 801, 803; Reagan to Davis, December 12, 1880,
in Rowland, *Jefferson Davis*, VIII, 537; Johnston. *Narrative*, 404–405.

21. Reagan, *Memoirs*, 201; Reagan to Davis, December 12, 1880, in Rowland, *Jefferson Davis*, VIII, 537; O.R., Ser. I, Vol. XLVII, Pt. 3, p. 806; Swallow. "Retreat," 601;
Breckinridge to Vance, April 17, 1865, in Zebulon B. Vance MSS, NCDAH.

22. Johnston, *Narrative*, 404–405; Alfred H. Guernsey, *Harper's Pictorial History of
the Great Rebellion* (New York, 1866–68), 773.

fore. Now, with Shiloh, Jackson, and Chattanooga behind them, they were meeting again to try to end that war.[23]

When the presentations were done, Sherman postponed opening the discussion for a few minutes by bringing out a bottle of whiskey and passing it around among those present. Johnston, looking on, later reminisced that the expression on Breckinridge's face at sight of that bottle was "beautific." [24] The generals then settled down to the business at hand. Johnston and Sherman went over once more the ground they covered the day before. Breckinridge listened quietly until they came to one of the points of uncertainty, the political rights of Confederate officers and men in case of surrender. Johnston expressed worry over this the day before, and now the secretary of war spoke up to confirm the uneasiness felt by many. They were in the midst of discussing this when a messenger finally brought in Reagan's proposal. Breckinridge and Johnston retired for private conversation for a few minutes. Reagan suggested six points: Surrender of all Confederate armies, recognition of the authority of the United States and its Constitution, the preservation of the existing southern state governments, no interference with the political and property rights of former Confederates as guaranteed by that Constitution, no reprisals against southerners for participation in the conflict, and a suspension of hostilities pending an agreement.[25]

One of them handed the paper to Sherman, and though he would later claim that he rejected it out of hand, he obviously read it carefully, thoughtfully. When he had finished it, Breckinridge then rose and spoke for several minutes in advocacy of Reagan's terms. He did not waste time on the "property rights" of the South—both he and Johnston frankly admitted to Sherman that slavery was "as dead as anything can be." Breckinridge did speak eloquently on the civil provisions. When he finished, Sherman, perhaps after some additional discussion, began writing out his own terms. They revealed that, though he may have disdained Reagan's ar-

23. William T. Sherman, *Memoirs* (New York, 1875), II, 352–53; Johnston, *Narrative*, 404–405; Guernsey, *Great Rebellion*, 773–74.

24. Wise, *End of an Era*, 451–53. Wise here gives quite an account of Breckinridge, Sherman, and the bottle, a widely republished anecdote. Sherman himself never recalled it, and Wise only got it second-hand from Johnston after the passage of fifteen years. Yet this single, unsubstantiated story—augmented by Bragg's allegations—is the sole basis for the widely held and repeated notion that Breckinridge was a heavy, constant, drinker during the war, an image perpetuated by a number of recent "popular" historians.

25. Joseph E. Johnston, *Narrative*, 405; Sherman, *Memoirs*, II, 352–53; *O.R.*, Ser. I, Vol. XLVII, Pt. 3, pp. 806–807.

ticles, Sherman surely felt their influence. All Confederate armies were to be disbanded, their officers and men accepting Federal authority. The state governments were to be recognized upon their members taking an oath of allegiance. Federal courts should be reestablished. Southerners were to be guaranteed their Constitutional rights of person and property, and were not to be molested so long as they respected the laws and remained in peace. Finally, a general amnesty was to take effect when the foregoing conditions had been met by the Confederate military and civil authorities. A cease fire should be in effect until these terms were accepted or rejected.[26]

Precisely what influence Breckinridge exerted on Sherman's terms is difficult to determine. The provision for reestablishment of Federal courts had not been mentioned previously by anyone, and it was a subject that would have occurred to Breckinridge's legal mind. The stress on guarantees to the legal rights of former Confederates, and their protection from recriminations, must have been in some measure due to the secretary's emphasis on the subject during the opening of the meeting. Breckinridge's friends, particularly J. Stoddard Johnston, later claimed that his "concise and statesmanlike mind" impressed itself especially upon those civil and constitutional points embraced in Sherman's articles.[27]

Breckinridge and Johnston read Sherman's terms, and both gave their approval. The Kentuckian assured the Federal that Johnston was empowered to carry out the military provisions of the settlement, but that there were portions of it, beyond Davis' sphere of authority, which would have to be submitted to the various state governments for ratification. Consequently, Sherman added a clause to the document, stating that, because he and Johnston did not have control over all of the subjects embraced in the basis of agreement, both would pledge themselves to secure that authority from the proper sources.[28]

Before going outside to await the making of several copies of the agreement, Sherman and Johnston told Breckinridge of Lincoln's assassination. They told him how the president had been shot in Ford's Theater on April 14. Bleeding and dying, he had been carried across the street to the Peter-

26. Sherman, Memoirs, II, 353, 355–57; Joseph E. Johnston, Narrative, 405; Wise, End of an Era, 451–52; Guernsey, Great Rebellion, 773; Stanley Horn, The Army of Tennessee (Norman, Okla., 1952), 427.

27. Sherman, Memoirs, II, 351; J. S. Johnston, "Sketches of Operations, No. 3," p. 389; Frankfort Tri-Weekly Yeoman, May 18, 1875; Wise, End of an Era, 451; Horn, Army of Tennessee, 427.

28. O.R., Ser. I, Vol. XLVII, Pt. 3, p. 243; John J. Craven, Prison Life of Jefferson Davis (New York, 1866), 132–33; Sherman, Memoirs, II, 357.

son boarding house, the same house where Breckinridge had lived when a congressman. Perhaps even in the same room that the Kentuckian had rented, his old friend and opponent died. The news stunned Breckinridge. Whatever their differences over politics, Lincoln and Breckinridge had remained on friendly personal terms up to the Kentuckian's flight south. On Lincoln's part, that regard was not diminished by the war. When a nephew of the secretary's visited the president in Washington, he was asked: "Do you ever hear from your uncle John C. Breckinridge?" On being told that word did occasionally come through, Lincoln continued. "Well," he said, "I was fond of John, and I was sorry to see him take the course he did. Yes, I was fond of John, and regret that he sided with the South. It was a mistake." Breckinridge had retained kind feelings toward Lincoln and now visibly showed his sorrow over the assassination. Several witnesses later reported his expressions at the time he heard the news, and they all agreed with one who recalled him saying: "Gentlemen, the South has lost its best friend." [29]

The generals adjourned to the yard where Breckinridge and Johnston were presented to the members of Sherman's staff. Taking Breckinridge aside, Sherman advised the Kentuckian that it would be well for him to leave the country as soon as possible, "as the feeling of our people was utterly hostile to the political element of the South, and to him especially, because he was the Vice-President of the United States . . . and yet that he had afterward openly rebelled and taken up arms against the Government." Breckinridge told Sherman that he intended to leave as soon as possible, despite the fact that in March he had assured Vest, Burnett, and others that he would take his chances by surrendering as secretary of war. What changed his mind in the interim was not Sherman's warning—though knowledge of the attitude toward him in the North surely influenced his decision—but rather Davis's situation. Even if no one else escaped, the president must be gotten out of the country, and Breckinridge regarded it as his duty to get it done. Already he and Reagan had discussed means to accomplish the escape.[30]

It was nearly dark when Sherman and Johnston signed their agreement, and then Breckinridge immediately wired the result to Davis. The president directed that he join the rest of the cabinet at Charlotte as soon as

29. Rufus R. Wilson, *Lincoln Among His Friends* (Caldwell, Idaho, 1942), 361; Swallow, "Retreat," 602; Eliza McHatton Ripley, *Social Life in Old New Orleans, Being Recollections of My Girlhood* (New York, 1912), 288.

30. Sherman, *Memoirs*, II, 353; Reagan, "Flight," 151.

possible. On arriving in Charlotte, Breckinridge's first concern was to see Davis, whom he found sitting in the doorway of the house serving as his temporary quarters. After shaking hands, the president asked if the report of Lincoln's death were really true, and Breckinridge sadly confirmed it. Then the two went inside where the secretary handed Davis a copy of the Sherman–Johnston agreement. As they discussed it, a crowd gathered outside, calling loudly for Breckinridge to appear and speak. He came to the door, gracefully excused himself, and returned to the conversation with Davis. A cabinet meeting was called for that evening, and there the president presented the agreement for his ministers' inspection. Still not satisfied that all was lost, he asked each of them to give him his views in writing on whether or not to accept the terms, and what to do if they were accepted.[31]

Breckinridge replied the next day with his customary frankness. At no point east of the Mississippi could the Confederacy assemble, equip, and maintain an army of even thirty thousand. And if the government should reject the Sherman proposal and continue the fight, the contest "will be likely to lose entirely the dignity of regular warfare. Many of the States will make such terms as they may; in others, separate and ineffective hostilities may be prosecuted, while war, wherever waged, will probably degenerate into that irregular and secondary stage out of which greater evils will flow to the South than to the enemy." Clearly, the war could no longer be waged with hope, and the time had come to end it. Sherman's terms were not ungenerous, and although Davis did not have authority to decide on some of the stipulations, he could go far toward bringing peace by them. Breckinridge advised the president to do all he could toward disbanding the remaining Confederate organized bodies. Next, he should recommend to the states acceptance of those portions of the agreement within their authority. Finally, he suggested that "Having maintained, with faithful and intrepid purpose, the cause of the Confederate States while the means of organized resistance remained, that you return to the States and the people the trust which you are no longer able to defend." Then, with words well capsulating his own action in embracing the South, he concluded: "Whatever course you pursue, opinions will be divided. Permit me to give mine.

31. *O.R.*. Ser. I, Vol. XLVII, Pt. 3, pp. 809–20, 828–29, Ser. I. Vol. LIII, p. 418; W. C. P. Breckinridge to Issa Breckinridge, April 22, 1865, in B. MSS; Beverly R. Wellford Diary, April 19–20, 1865, in White, Wellford, Taliaferro and Marshall Family Papers, SHC; Varina Davis, *Jefferson Davis*, II, 629; Davis to Joseph E. Johnston, April 24, 1865, in Rowland, *Jefferson Davis*, VI, 563; Joseph T. Durkin, *John Dooley, Confederate Soldier, His War Journal* (Georgetown, 1945), 197–98; Hanna, *Flight*, 49–50.

Should these or similar views accord with your own, I think the better judgment will be that you can have no higher title to the gratitude of your countrymen and the respect of mankind than will spring from the wisdom to see the path of duty at this time, and the courage to follow it, regardless alike of praise or blame." [32]

Breckinridge spoke with Basil Duke, who had brought the remnant of his brigade to Charlotte, soon after arriving, and the cavalryman found his old commander "in cheerful spirits," and expressing the belief that the terms he helped form would take away some of the sting of defeat. The day after arriving, Breckinridge rode with Duke to his camp, received a warm welcome from his old comrades, and made a brief speech on the proposed agreement. When finished, he sat beneath a large tree and spoke to the swarm of soldiers who gathered round. For an hour he met their questions on the surrender with absolute frankness, until one who had not heard his speech rode up.

"General Breckinridge," he said, "is it true that you have concluded negotiations which contemplate the surrender of all Confederate soldiers on this side of the Mississippi river?"

"It is true," responded the secretary of war, "and I think the terms are such as all should accept."

"Do you think, general, that any terms of surrender are honorable and should be accepted?"

"I do, or I certainly should not have endorsed them."

"Well I do not," said the ardent rebel, "and shall accept no terms."

"I regret that," Breckinridge replied, "and your comrades here, who are all good soldiers, do not agree with you." Then, thanking Duke's men once again for their loyalty in following their commander all the way to Charlotte, the secretary of war returned to town and his business. [33]

Breckinridge must have been greatly relieved when Davis wired Johnston on April 24 that he approved of the terms. That elation was quickly dampened, however, by word from Johnston that Washington had disapproved the agreement, and would allow Sherman to receive Johnston's surrender only on the same terms given to Lee. Sherman, thought Attorney

32. Breckinridge to Davis, April 23, 1865, "Last Letters and Telegrams of the Confederacy—Correspondence of General John C. Breckinridge," *SHSP*, XII (March, 1884), 100–102.

33. *O.R.*, Ser. I, Vol. XLVII, Pt. 3, p. 834; Duke, *Reminiscences*, 383–84; Basil W. Duke, "Last Days of the Confederacy," in Johnson and Buel (eds.), *Battles and Leaders*, IV, 764; Durkin, *John Dooley*, 198; H. C. Binkley, "Shared in the Confederate Treasure," *Confederate Veteran*, XXXVIII (March, 1930), 88.

General James Speed, "had been seduced by Breckinridge." [34] This changed the situation entirely. Even if Johnston went ahead and surrendered, there would now still be two armies left in the field, Richard Taylor's and Edmund Kirby Smith's. Davis and the cabinet could hardly leave the country while they still had armies, small though they were, and they would have to change their plans accordingly. Now the column would try to reach the West, if for no other reason than to be present to advise with those generals on their own surrender terms. Meanwhile, despite orders from Davis to move his whole army away from Sherman, Johnston informed the secretary of war that he would meet Sherman on Grant's terms. [35]

Immediately, plans for the movement of the column were laid, while Breckinridge undertook a special mission of his own. He now made an immeasurable contribution to American historiography and one of his greatest contributions to his nation. For over three weeks Kean had been dragging the War Department archives along in trains and wagons, following, and sometimes preceding, Davis and the column. On April 21 he reached Charlotte, and there, two days later, Breckinridge had instructed him to go on ahead as soon as ferries had been completed to cross the Catawba River. They were not done by April 25, however, and at noon that day the secretary informed Kean that the April 18 agreement had been rejected. He then ordered the head of the Bureau of War to store the archives in some safe place in Charlotte, and to stay with them until the Federals occupied the town, at which time he was to turn over the records to the officer in charge. At all odds, the archives were to be protected against destruction. Only the small bundle of reports in reply to Breckinridge's February 7 circular was to be taken out, and this the secretary charged to Kean's personal care, to take with him when he went back to Virginia. Perhaps the secretary felt that, in case the bulk of the archives met a sorry fate, at least these would survive as testimony of the conditions that signaled the end of the Confederacy, and as evidence of his concerned service. It was decided between Breckinridge and Davis that Cooper would remain behind at Charlotte as well, and the secretary gave him instructions to guard carefully the records and give them to the enemy if necessary. They impressed the adjutant general that these archives were "essential to the history of the

34. Micajah H. Clark, "Confederate Treasure," Louisville Courier-Journal, January 16, 1882; N. E. B. Lawson to Susan M. Clay, May 4, 1865, in Clay MSS; Breckinridge to Post Commandant, April 22, 1865, in Breckinridge MSS, DU; O.R., Ser. I, Vol. XLVII, Pt. 3, pp. 820, 828–29; Welles Diary, April 25, 1865, in Welles MSS.
35. O.R., Ser. I, Vol. XLVII, Pt. 3, pp. 834–37, 841.

struggle." This was Breckinridge at his best. His family always had a keen sense of their own history, and diligently preserved over a span of two centuries every scrap of correspondence, receipts, and records that they received. What he and his ancestors had done for the Breckinridges, now John C. Breckinridge did for the Confederacy, thereby incurring the indebtedness of countless future scholars who would seek to reconstruct the four-year story of the Confederate States of America.[36]

Shortly after Breckinridge made these arrangements with Kean, the fifty-two officers from Virginia in the column held a meeting and selected a committee to wait upon the secretary of war and find out exactly what he expected them to do in the present circumstances. He told them bluntly that there was nothing further that they could accomplish by proceeding with Davis, and had Cooper issue an order allowing them to go home. After their departure, however, Davis still had a sizable escort. Duke was there, as well as cavalry "brigades" under Vaughn, Dibrell, General Samuel W. Ferguson, and the secretary's cousin, Colonel W. C. P. Breckinridge; in all two to three thousand men. Around noon, April 26, they all mounted up and followed Davis and the cabinet out of Charlotte to the south, Breckinridge at their head. As the ranking officer present, he continued to act both as a major general and secretary of war. Before they left, the final dissolution of the cabinet began. Attorney General George Davis turned in his resignation and, the next day, the ailing secretary of the treasury George A. Trenholm followed suit.[37]

With the Catawba ferries finally completed, the party pressed forward to Fort Mill, South Carolina, where they passed the night and left Trenholm. The next morning Davis assembled his ministers on the lawn in front of their temporary quarters, and held a brief discussion concerning the best route to take. It was decided that, for the time being, they could continue to move in a southwesterly direction, through Georgia, toward Taylor's army near Mobile, Alabama. They crossed the Catawba and moved on to Yorkville, South Carolina, where a cavalry company under Captain Given Campbell met them. Breckinridge assigned Campbell as special escort to Davis and the cabinet, and then the column moved on toward Scaife's Ferry on the Broad River. There they halted at a house some distance back from the river to spend the night. Davis and Breckinridge passed the evening in

36. Younger, *Inside the Confederate Government*, 206–207; R. G. H. Kean to Jubal A. Early, November 15, 1873, *SHSP*, II, 57; *O.R.*, Ser. I, Vol. XLVII, Pt. 3, p. 842.
37. Younger, *Inside the Confederate Government*, 207.

conversation on the porch while Reagan and Mallory pitched coins in the garden.[38]

Crossing the Broad the next day at sunrise, the column moved on toward Unionville. Davis and Breckinridge frequently took their breakfast with the soldiers, and all of the cabinet members mingled freely with them, contributing to morale. From this association, the men in the ranks received the distinct impression that Davis could escape the country if he would, that Breckinridge and Reagan could do so without difficulty, and that Benjamin just as surely could not. Passing through Unionville, they crossed the Saluda River and, by the evening of May 1, had reached Cokesbury, just a few miles from Abbeville. Here General Braxton Bragg joined the party, having been until now in command of a scattering of troops in North Carolina. Upon arriving, he went to Davis immediately, taking off his hat and, after a brief conversation, moving over to Breckinridge. As he spoke with the secretary, Bragg stood before him, cap in hand. Captain Campbell looked on and thought to himself on how different was Bragg's deference to Breckinridge compared to "his treatment of the same man at and after the Battle of Murphysborough." [39]

Early the next morning Breckinridge rode into Abbeville at the head of the fleeing column, taking quarters along with the other cabinet members at the home of a hospitable Mr. Perrin. Davis went to the spacious mansion of Mr. Armistead Burt. The secretary of war at once took over measures for continuing the flight, stationing Ferguson on the road ahead of Abbeville, near the pontoon bridge over the Savannah River. Then at 4 P.M., after resting for several hours, Davis called a "council of war" to meet at Burt's mansion. They sat around a table, Breckinridge on the president's left, Bragg on his right, and Duke, Ferguson, Dibrell, Vaughn, and Colonel Breckinridge, before them. Significantly, Davis was turning now to the generals rather than his remaining cabinet members. The reason was plain, for Davis could see that his ministers had no stomach for what he wished to discuss. Captain Parker observed them in Abbeville, and thought that all but the secretary of war had the air of wishing to be gone. "General Breckinridge presented his usual bold cavalier manner," he noticed. Indeed, Duke

38. Given Campbell, "Memorandum of a Journal Kept Daily During the Last March of Jefferson Davis," April 28, 1865, LC; Hanna, *Flight*, 58; *O.R.*, Ser. I, Vol. XLVII, Pt. 3, p. 851.

39. Campbell, Memorandum, April 17, 29, May 1, 1865, LC; Duke, "Last Days," 764; Duke, *Reminiscences*, 385.

was now convinced after several days' observation that of all the cabinet members, only Breckinridge "knew what was going on, what was going to be done, and what ought to be done."[40]

Davis began with small talk as was his custom, but soon came to the point. He wanted to decide how to continue the war. He was confident that, with only three thousand soldiers about him, he could rally the people to the cause. Each of the brigade commanders stated his belief that further resistance was futile. They would ask their men to help him escape, but nothing more. Davis disdained fleeing the country, once more appealed to them, and finally saw that they would not be persuaded. Crying that all was indeed lost, he arose, pale, to leave the room. When he faltered and nearly fell, Breckinridge arose to help him out. While the tired president slept, the secretary of war returned to the council room, where he and Bragg approved the stand taken by the generals. They promised to see that Davis would escape and agreed that Campbell would continue to be his escort, while Breckinridge would reassume command of the cavalry which Bragg had taken the day before.[41]

At 10 P.M. Duke received a summons from Breckinridge. What remained of the Confederate treasury, as well as money from some Richmond banks, was on a train at the Abbeville depot. The secretary wanted Duke to take charge of its removal to wagons, to act as escort. Breckinridge was unsure of the amount of the treasure, but trusted Duke to guard it well. It was not long before word came that Federal troops were approaching. It had already been agreed that the command would move out again at 11 P.M., and while the brigades readied themselves, the secretary went to the president's room to awaken him. Davis arose and soon they were on their way to the Savannah. Breckinridge had authorized the brigade commanders to allow those of their men who wished to go no farther to leave, and about half availed themselves of the opportunity. The rest rode behind him. Along the way, the secretary rode for a time with Davis, reaffirming the reluctance of the brigadiers for further hostile service, and finally persuaded the president that he must flee. Then Breckinridge dropped back and joined Ferguson, bringing up the rear. He would never see Davis again.[42]

40. Campbell, Memorandum, May 2, 1865, LC; "Extracts From Gen. Ferguson's Diary, 1865," May 2, 1865, in Rowland, *Jefferson Davis*, VIII, 250–51; Parker, *Recollections*, 366; Basil Duke to Walthall, April 6, 1878, in B. MSS.

41. Duke, "Last Days," 764–65; Davis to William Preston Johnston, April 5, 1878, in B. MSS.

42. Duke, *Reminiscences*, 387–88; John W. Headley, *Confederate Operations in Canada and New York* (New York, 1906), 433–34; "Ferguson's Diary," May 2, 31,

Davis with his escort rode considerably ahead of the main column, and did not see what was happening behind him during this night march. The remaining cavalrymen were in deplorable condition, grumbling, throwing away their arms, and already casting covetous glances at the wagons carrying the treasure. At every halt, most of those in the column congregated around the wagon train and Duke's nervous guards. Soon they were saying that they would take the money rather than let the Federals get it. Finally Breckinridge, riding up from Ferguson's brigade in the rear, found the train stopped, the cavalry surrounding it. They might never get the wagons to Washington, Georgia, their destination, they claimed. The train contained specie while their own paper money would soon be worthless. Why should not they take the gold and silver now? In this tense situation, the secretary moved to the center of the mob, impressing at least one of those present that "Breckinridge in his native manhood was equal to the occasion." Here again, almost ready to explode into reality, was the "farce" he so dreaded.

Wearing the hunting jacket that was a staple of his wardrobe, Breckinridge made a brief speech to the crowd. They were still Confederate soldiers, he said, and they had a responsibility to act the part. They were all southern gentlemen, not highway robbers. On a hundred battlefields they had shown that they knew how to die bravely. Now, in these dark hours, they must also show that they could live honorably. As soon as they reached Washington, he said, they would be paid from the treasure train. This did not quiet the men, however, for most doubted that they would reach Washington. They wanted their pay now. Breckinridge told them that, if they wanted him to fulfill his promise immediately, he would, and promptly he ordered the wagons drawn up at a house just across the Savannah.

Paying the escort took almost all day. Breckinridge chafed at the delay and wanted to go forward to see Davis, but was too ill to ride. He drew twenty-six dollars just as everyone else did, and then looked after the command. Even paying the men did not ease the situation in several companies, and he told Davis sadly, "Nothing can be done with the bulk of this command." Vaughn and Dibrell with their brigades were resolved to remain where they were unless absolutely ordered to go on. Consequently, Breckinridge told them to stay, while Duke, Ferguson, and Breckinridge made it plain that they would follow the secretary into Mexico if he wished.[43]

1865, in Rowland, *Jefferson Davis*, VIII, 251; Duke to Walthall, April 6, 1878, Davis to William Preston Johnston, April 5, 1878, in B. MSS; Reagan, *Memoirs*, 212.

43. *O.R.*, Ser. I, Vol. XLIX, Pt. 2, pp. 1277–78; "Ferguson's Diary," May 3, 1865, in

When the payment was completed late that night, the remainder of the specie was loaded back on the wagon. By then it was past dawn, May 4, and Breckinridge ordered Ferguson to move out towards Washington. After saying his farewells to Vaughn and Dibrell, the secretary followed with the rest of the command. They arrived within a mile of Washington only after Davis and a small company set out deeper into Georgia. Mallory had resigned and left, and Benjamin set out to make his own escape the day before. As a result, only Reagan and Breckinridge remained of the Confederate government.[44]

The secretary had Duke set up camp with the treasure wagons outside of the town, and there Micajah Clark, now acting treasurer, began the disbursement of the remainder of the specie. Breckinridge was given $1,000 to transfer to the Trans-Mississippi when and if he reached it, and Bragg received twice that amount for the same purpose. The secretary also drew funds from Clark in two capacities. As secretary of war he requisitioned $5,000 for the Quartermaster Department's operation at Washington, and as major general, he drew an additional $4,000 for the support of the troops remaining with him. Breckinridge gave Clark the use of his own ambulance and team for the several trips between camp and the town that were required, particularly for placing the $200,000 from Richmond's banks in a local vault. Other small amounts were placed in trustworthy hands, and Breckinridge himself took a meal sack with $6,000 and gave it to his host Robert Toombs, Washington's most notable resident. Then he set about the final business of his own department. In a circular to the chiefs of bureaus—Lawton and St. John were still with him—the secretary, in effect, disbanded the War Department. In the present posture of affairs, he said, their services were not needed. They were to remain where they pleased and join the department when their services were needed, or when they should be ordered to report. Meanwhile, they would dispose of the public property as they felt best. Then, in an act somehow curiously fitting in this war that no one wanted, Breckinridge authorized the last official resignation of the Confederate War Department. Resigning his commission as second lieutenant was James B. Clay, Jr., the grandson of Henry Clay, the man

---

Rowland, *Jefferson Davis*, VIII, 251; Duke, "Last Days," 765; Clark, "Confederate Treasure," Louisville *Courier-Journal*, January 16, 1882; Joseph A. Brown, "The Confederate Treasure Train," *Confederate Veteran*, XXV (June, 1917), 258; "Notes," *Civil War History*, VII (June, 1961), 202.

44. W. C. P. Breckinridge to Walthall, April 3, 1878, "Ferguson's Diary," May 4, 1865, Dibrell to Johnston, April 9, 1878, all in Rowland, *Jefferson Davis*, VIII, 153, 163, 251.

who strove so long and hard to avert the calamity that was now entering its final act.[45]

Breckinridge spoke with Reagan briefly before the latter left to catch up with Davis. Reports still came in sporadically from Richard Taylor, and the Kentuckian was giving some thought to trying to take the remnant of the command west to join him, probably wishing to be present to give counsel when Taylor, too, was forced to surrender. Reagan disapproved the idea, thinking that the troops would not follow, and this may have convinced the secretary that it would be wiser to make his escape with a small escort through Florida, and from there to the Trans-Mississippi by way of some Caribbean port. That night Reagan left with Clark and a few others, and what remained of the Confederate government was now in Breckinridge's hands, with but one final duty to perform.[46]

The next morning, May 5, the secretary discharged most of Ferguson's men, complimenting their general on his loyal service. Then he called upon Colonel Breckinridge for a party of volunteers to accompany himself and staff on a diversion that he planned to aid in drawing the enemy away from Davis' route of escape. While Duke and the remaining three hundred of his brigade marched east toward Woodstock, Breckinridge and this volunteer escort would take a different route to the same place, meeting Duke there and, they hoped, attracting to themselves the Federal patrols then searching for the president. Between forty-five and fifty of the Kentuckians volunteered. With these arrangements made, the secretary prepared to leave Washington. The remnants of Ferguson's command, as they topped a hill marching off to take their paroles, looked back to see Breckinridge quietly unpacking his valise and dividing his shirts, tobacco, and other effects, among the couriers who had attended him during the march. Then he packed what was left in his saddle-bags, mounted up and rode off into the woods.[47]

Duke had no difficulty in reaching Woodstock by the appointed hour, but Breckinridge and his escort took their time. On May 6 they were only

45. Clark, "Confederate Treasure," Louisville *Courier-Journal*, January 16, 1882; *O.R.*, Ser. I, Vol. XLIX, Pt. 2, p. 955; "Federal Veterans at Shiloh," *Confederate Veteran*, III (April, 1895), 104; Breckinridge, circular, May 4, 1865, in Jeremy F. Gilmer MSS, Museum of the Confederacy, Richmond, Va.; General Order No. –, May 4, 1865, in JCB Papers. Clay's resignation is endorsed by Clifton Breckinridge as being the last one accepted, and he was in a position to know.

46. Reagan, *Memoirs*, 213; *O.R.*, Ser. I, Vol. XLIX, Pt. 2, pp. 1255, 1267.

47. F. E. Richardson to Walthall, August 26, 1878, in Rowland, *Jefferson Davis*, VIII, 252, 266; "Ferguson's Diary," May 5, 1865, Duke, "Last Days," 766.

about seven miles outside Washington on the Woodstock road, and the secretary had taken up quarters in a farmhouse, while his cousin camped his men in an adjacent orchard. Early that morning Breckinridge sent young Clay off with an order for Duke, and then entered into consultation with Colonel Breckinridge. Suddenly Clay hurried in with the news that a Federal company was in sight and approaching. They were the 250 men of Major Andrew Campbell. The secretary gave Breckinridge his permission to mount the escort and confront the Federals on the road, though saying that battle and bloodshed should be avoided if at all possible. The colonel led his command down the road, encountered Campbell, and both stopped for parley. While they talked, Breckinridge, Cabell, Clifton, Clay, Wilson, the secretary's long-time body servant Tom Ferguson, and a few others made ready to ride off into the woods. When Colonel Breckinridge sent back word that his surrender had been demanded, and he had refused, the secretary knew that the time had come at last. The colonel was resolved to charge if the Federals did not let him pass unmolested and, knowing this, Breckinridge sent a last message forward. He had reason to believe, he said, that Taylor had probably surrendered by now and that, even if the small command could press on beyond the Mississippi, it would find little but another army on the verge of capitulation. Consequently, he advised the colonel—and Duke if the word could reach him—to surrender immediately, "urging that it was folly to think of holding out longer and criminal to risk the lives of the men when no good could possibly be accomplished." Go home to your families, your friends, he told them; go home to Kentucky. When it was suggested that part of the command might accompany him on his escape, he refused. "I will not have one of these young men to encounter one hazard more for my sake," he said, and then turned his horse to the south.[48]

48. Lexington *Morning Herald*, May 28, 1900; W. C. P. Breckinridge to W. R. Bringhurst, September 1892, "Unwritten History Worth Preserving," *Confederate Veteran*, VIII (December, 1900), 534; W. R. Bringhurst, "Survivor of President Davis's Escort," *Confederate Veteran*, XXXIV (October, 1926), 368–69; H. G. Damon, "The Eyes of General Breckinridge," *Confederate Veteran*, XVII (August, 1909), 380; Duke, *Morgan's Cavalry*, 576–77.

CHAPTER 11

Should My Friends Ever Know My Part

Breckinridge's object now was to make a junction with Davis' retreating party to add his small numbers to the president's guard. After leaving Colonel Breckinridge, he rode south toward Sandersville on the Oconee River, still uncomfortable from his recent illness. As he moved on, he encountered a number of Confederate soldiers on the road returning home. Although no one seemed to know who he was, Breckinridge determined to affect some modest disguise. No doubt with some sadness, he cut off the long, flowing moustaches that had been his distinctive trademark among the general officers of the Confederacy, and assumed the name Colonel Cabell for the remainder of the journey.[1]

Their horses in good condition and their hopes high, the fleeing Confederates made over forty miles that day, camping near Sandersville. The next morning, after sending forward a few scouts, Breckinridge announced that henceforth the party would move in a direct line toward Madison, Florida, a haven for Confederate refugees about 175 miles away. Then, before leaving, the secretary decided that it was time to send Clifton and young Clay back to safety. The parting from his son must have been painful, for the bond of affection and mutual respect between them was the greatest that the general felt for any of his sons. As for Cliff, he later told his father that, at that moment, "I would gladly have died for you." Breckinridge entrusted the boy with the sword given him by Finley and Bate, and a letter to a friend back in Kentucky. In it he expressed his own final judgment on his service as secretary of war and his fight to see the Confederacy meet its end with dignity. "Should my friends ever know my part in the occurrences of the last three months," he said, "I venture to think it will give me

1. Swallow, "Retreat," 606; John Taylor Wood, "Escape of the Confederate Secretary of War," *Century Magazine*, XLVII (November, 1893), 111.

an increased claim on their confidence and regard." Three days later the boys were captured near Macon, the sword appropriated from Clifton by a soldier who later named his own son Breckinridge, and the letter prevented from reaching its destination. On May 17 Cliff took his parole and headed for home.[2]

The general moved only a short distance that day before incessant rains forced him to take shelter at a nearby farmhouse. When the rain let up, he continued the march down the east bank of the Oconee, making camp that night just outside Dublin. Around 9 P.M. that evening he sent one of his scouts into the village for some provisions. Reaching a store just as it was closing, the scout made the necessary purchases, seemingly without arousing suspicion. However, at midnight Breckinridge and his companions were startled and nearly captured by a company of Federals that passed down the road near their camp, coming within one hundred yards of the fugitives, and near enough for the Kentuckian to distinguish the horsemen's uniforms. This close call caused him some anxiety, and the next morning, breakfasting and feeding the horses before sunrise, Breckinridge determined to reach the Ocmulgee River, sixty miles south, by nightfall. All that day his progress was deterred by heavy rains, which, though they slowed his movement, fortunately washed away all trace of his passing.

It was long after midnight when he called a halt near Jacksonville, still a few miles short of the river. Suffering from chills and fever, his men needed rest, and they camped that night in a dense thicket. The next morning found them all in bad condition, their horses broken down, tired and hungry. Still, they were temporarily out of reach of the enemy, or so they thought. The next day, May 10, less than forty miles west of their camp, at Irwinville, Jefferson Davis was captured by Federal cavalry.[3]

Breckinridge resolved to spend part of that day resting at some suitable farmhouse, and soon found one not too far from the Ocmulgee. The lady of the house was most accommodating, served the men a noonday meal, and then let the general use a bedroom to lie down and rest. While he slept, however, word spread rapidly that important visitors had come, and Breckinridge awoke that evening to find most of his host's neighbors congregated in the house to see what many believed to be officers from Lee's army. A

2. Swallow, "Retreat," 606–607; O.R.. Ser. I, Vol. XLIX, Pt. 2, p. 719; R. Neuman to Breckinridge, May 6, 1869, in B. MSS; Clifton R. Breckinridge to Breckinridge, May 13, 1874, Parole of Clifton R. Breckinridge, May 17, 1865, in JCB Papers.

3. Swallow, "Retreat," 606–607; New York Herald, June 22, 1865.

few, however, were more sharp, especially the ladies, and they felt that someone important was here. Occasionally they glanced back and forth between Breckinridge and a photograph of President Davis hanging on a parlor wall. When that failed to bring a match, one of the ladies asked a member of the escort for a detailed description of each member of the cabinet, staring all the while at Breckinridge. Only his hosts knew his real identity, but that did not prevent him from enjoying himself with the visitors. "I had known Breckinridge for years as a member of Congress, and while he was Vice President of the United States," recalled one of the escort, "had been in his company often, but never saw him appear to the advantage that he did this night." The general remained here until the next morning, when he set out for the Ocmulgee. After he left, his hostess remarked that "he was a very pert gentleman." [4]

A guide led the party to the river crossing where he expected to find a boat. Discovering that it was gone, he directed the travelers to rest while he searched for it. Breckinridge and the others unsaddled their horses, and then Ferguson spread a blanket on the ground in the shade of a great tree. The secretary laid down on it for some time, pulling out a copy of Plutarch's *The Rise and Fall of Athens*, a subject whose peculiar relevance to his present situation struck his companions. For five hours he waited and read until the boat was found. Slowly it made several trips across the three-hundred-yard wide Ocmulgee, carrying over the escort, until finally only Breckinridge remained on the north bank. Wilson brought the boat back over to get him, and found the general standing on the bank as if waiting, his eyes turned west, and lost in deep thought. Wilson called to him repeatedly but Breckinridge did not answer. Finally, brought back to the present, he motioned the colonel to wait a bit, and then broke into the melodic verses of a long popular poem, "Oh! Come to the South." Its last stanza seemed especially meaningful as he stood here ready to ride ever farther from his home and native soil.

> Oh! here would thy beauty most brilliantly beam,
> And life pass away like some delicate dream;
> Each wish of thy heart should realized be,
> And this beautiful land seem an Eden to thee.

Wilson and the other two men waiting in the boat were speechless. "We remained almost spell-bound by the grandeur of the occasion," one of them

4. Cincinnati *Enquirer*, April 10, 1868; Swallow, "Retreat," 607.

said, "and not a word was spoken until after we had crossed, when Breckinridge, springing to his saddled horse, called for us to 'mount and away.'"[5]

Now Breckinridge moved deep into southern Georgia, crossed the Saltilla and, on May 11, crossed over the Allapaha to Milltown, only a few miles short of the Florida border. Here he resolved to remain waiting for the president, even though the next day word came that Federal patrols were about. As long as there was any chance of contacting and aiding Davis, however, Breckinridge felt bound by duty to put off any personal considerations, even if he must risk capture. Consequently, he waited at Milltown until the afternoon of May 14, when finally word came of the president's capture. At the same time he found out that an enemy party was just fifteen miles away at Nashville. With nothing now to detain him any further, Breckinridge dismissed the faithful men who had escorted him this far and, accompanied by Tom Ferguson, Wilson, and Cabell, rode out early the next morning, crossing the line and reaching Madison that evening.[6]

Arriving at the home of Judge Benjamin Wardlaw, where he would pass the night, the secretary rode on into Madison after dark to see General Joseph J. Finegan, for three years commander of Confederate forces in Florida. If anyone would know an escape route through the state, it would be he. While there, the secretary found that Captain John Taylor Wood, one of Davis' aides, had escaped the Federals at Irwinville, and was nearby. A message went out to him to come to Finegan's the next morning, and he was quite pleased to discover Breckinridge there to meet him. Together they discussed the best mode of escape, for Wood needed to flee the country almost as much as the secretary. As commander of the dread commerce raider *Tallahassee*, he stood second only to Admiral Semmes in the number of Federal merchantmen captured during the war. He was a seaman of nineteen years' experience, and would be valuable in the attempt to reach the Bahamas, which he and Breckinridge now decided should be their destination for the immediate present, Wood favoring a passage down Florida's eastern coast. Wood and Wilson then rode ahead to Moseley's Ferry on the Suwannee River, while Breckinridge remained behind for several hours. A sympathizer traded a fresh mount for the general's spent animal, and then he and Cabell rode into Madison, risking the daylight to procure some supplies for the escape. There he met a number of other Confederates returned from their surrender, and one of them later claimed that the general was recognized by a Federal lieutenant in town, who followed

5. Cincinnati *Enquirer*, April 10, 1868.   6. Swallow, "Retreat," 607.

Breckinridge everywhere he went. "Finally he confronted us," the soldier recalled, "and then Breckinridge showed what stuff he was made of. He turned, drew himself up to his full height, [and] without a word gave him a look. The effect was magical. The man turned and went away, and we did not see him again." [7]

Now it was time to part from Cabell. Like several members of the Breckinridge family, the general's oldest son bore a terrible allergy to mosquito bites. Because that insect swarmed on the trails and rivers ahead, he told his son to go to Tallahassee and take his parole. This done, Breckinridge, too, rode off for Moseley's Ferry. [8]

The general joined Wilson and Wood that evening, learning then that Benjamin had passed through on his own escape just two days before. Moving on south, they arrived at Gainesville on May 18, shortly after a Federal patrol had been through, and just in advance of another. Quickly he made his arrangements. Colonel J. J. Dickison was paroling his men just a few miles north of the town. Known as the Swamp Fox of the Confederacy, he knew the country intimately. Breckinridge sent him a summons signed "Confederate officer." Dickison arrived the next morning and was most pleased to meet Breckinridge. The secretary said he must join Smith before he could surrender and told the colonel that he wanted to get to the Trans-Mississippi by boat from the west coast of the state. Dickison convinced him that this avenue was too closely guarded. Then it was decided that, instead, he would have to go Wood's route down the east coast, along the St. John's River. Dickison said he had a lifeboat taken from the Federal gunboat *Columbine* at his disposal, and that it was Breckinridge's if he wanted it. The general accepted, and Dickison then detailed his son as an escort to Millwood Plantation some twenty miles south, while he set about having the boat raised from its hiding place in a shallow lake. [9]

7. John Taylor Wood Diary, May 15–16, 1865, in John Taylor Wood MSS, SHC; Hanna, *Flight*, 29–30, 152–53; Damon, "The Eyes of General Breckinridge," 380.

8. Telephone interview with Mrs. Kenneth Kirkland, July 4, 1971; Breckinridge to John "Owen" Breckinridge, July, 1865, in Prewitt Collection. This letter, in the form of a diary, is hereinafter cited as Breckinridge, Escape Diary. It was published, with some errors in transcription, in Alfred J. Hanna (ed.), "The Escape of Confederate Secretary of War John Cabell Breckinridge as Revealed by His Diary," *Register of the Kentucky Historical Society*, XXXVII (October, 1939), 323–33. All quotations here are from the original.

9. J. J. Dickison to ?, October 1884, Mary E. Dickison, *Dickison and His Men* (Reprint; Gainesville, Fla., 1962), 224–25; Wood Diary, May 18–19, 1865, in Wood MSS; Breckinridge, Escape Diary, May 18, 1865, in Prewitt Collection; Dickison to Breckinridge, August 9, 1872, in B. MSS.

Breckinridge spent the nineteenth and twentieth at Millwood, while Wood rode off to try to find Benjamin. While there, Dickison came up again, and told the general that the boat would be ready for him at Fort Butler on the St. John's, with three of his men to man it. At the same time, he left as a guide Lieutenant William McCardell. From this point, the party moved on at a leisurely pace to allow time for the boat to be readied and brought to the appointed place. On May 22 they reached Wauchula, the plantation home of Colonel A. G. Summer, former Confederate quartermaster general of Florida. Here Breckinridge decided to rest for a day and, the next afternoon, went with his host on a hunt. The summer heat was already growing intolerable, Wood was ill from it, and all were plagued by countless mosquitoes. To add to his discomfort, Breckinridge, while waiting for a deer, sat on a log and was immediately covered with red bugs, or small ticks, that buried themselves in his skin. The irritation from them caused him to scratch his ankles "and other parts of the person" almost raw.[10]

Breckinridge left Colonel Summer's on May 24, traveled around the western shore of Lake Weir, and spent the night along its banks, bathing in its cool water to soothe his sore body after a day's ride that must have severely aggravated his mosquito bites. The next day, the party moved on around the southern shore, unaware that at that same time, back in Washington, the grand jury of the District of Columbia was finding a bill of indictment against the general and Davis for high treason. He and Davis were indicted separately, Breckinridge being charged with leading troops in Early's 1864 raid, "the killing of citizens and the destroying of property." In fact, this was only the most recent of a number of such acts. Back in January the General Assembly in Federally occupied Tennessee declared by a joint resolution that Breckinridge, Davis, Benjamin, and others should be executed for their treason. Throughout his flight south thus far, Breckinridge had been denounced as a traitor in the northern press, and a trial date had actually been set for him and Davis. "The Davises, the Benjamins and the Breckinridges," said the New York *Times*, "should die the most disgraceful death known to our civilization—death on the Gallows." [11]

The mosquitoes now became worse than ever, making the ride a torment, and the nights almost sleepless. But by the evening of May 25, they were

10. Wood Diary, May 21–23, 1865, in Wood MSS; Breckinridge, Escape Diary, May 22–23, 1865, in Prewitt Collection.
11. New York *Times*, May 1, 27, 1865; J. L. M. Curry, *Civil History of the Government of the Confederate States* (Richmond, 1901), 106; New Orleans *Daily Picayune*, June 9, 1865; Lynchburg *Daily Virginian*, June 9, 1865.

only a day's ride from Fort Butler. Breckinridge spent the night gathering two weeks' supplies, getting directions on his future course, and acquiring a map of Florida. Appropriately enough, the map was one prepared and published by order of Jefferson Davis when he was Pierce's secretary of war. It, with the general's pocket compass, would be his guide. The next morning his party set out to cover the thirty-two miles to Fort Butler, and arrived at midday to find their boat waiting.[12]

"It was a small, open craft, only 17 or 18 feet long," noted Breckinridge, "with a place in front to 'step' a very small mast, so as to use a sail when there was wind, by holding the end of the rope in the hand." In addition, there were four oars for rowing. To help man them, Breckinridge found three of Dickison's paroled men with the craft, Sergeant Joseph O'Toole, Corporal Richard Russell, and Private P. Murphy. They had raised the boat, repaired its seams, and brought it down the St. John's. Breckinridge was exceedingly grateful to all of those who helped him procure the craft, and to one of them—probably Lieutenant McCardell—he immediately showed his gratitude. "I will have but few more hours of authority," he said, "but such services as you have rendered your country deserve reward. You shall be a major; I will make out your commission now."

The recipient was thankful enough, but stood thoughtfully scratching his head.

"Well, my friend," said Breckinridge.

"Well, you see, gineral, thar's a feller in our regiment what hain't done nothin', and he is a major and a quartermaster; and if its all the same to you, I would just like to rank him for onst."

On the spot, Breckinridge wrote out a commission as lieutenant colonel and presented it to his friend. It was the last official act of the Confederate War Department, and of the Confederate States of America. The secretary did not know it, but Taylor had surrendered back on May 4, and most of the Trans-Mississippi was being turned over to the Federals just as Breckinridge wrote out the commission. Only a skeleton army under Kirby Smith remained, and it had been disintegrating for weeks, having ceased long since to be an organized force. Curiously enough, then, the Confederate government was terminated here on the swampy banks of the St. John's by a secretary of war who in times past had done his best to prevent the birth of that Confederacy, his final act a promotion given half in jest to a man

12. Wood Diary, May 25–26, 1865, in Wood MSS; Breckinridge, Escape Diary, May 26, 1865, in Prewitt Collection. The map which Breckinridge used is in the Museum of the Confederacy, Richmond.

who had already taken his parole from the enemy. The "magnificent epic," as Breckinridge termed it, could not have suffered a less dramatic demise.[13]

The general's party boarded immediately, now seven in number, and they soon discovered that the water was almost up to the gunwales. Looking upon this, Breckinridge reflected that "it might do for the river, but it seemed a very frail thing to go on the ocean in." It was four o'clock in the afternoon, and they rowed off up the river without further delay.[14]

A severe storm came up that evening, forcing them to anchor in midstream, and now they found out how truly uncomfortable the craft could be. Loaded as it was with seven men, two weeks' supplies, arms and ammunition, there was no room to lie down. Thoroughly drenched by the rain, they passed a wretched night, only to discover the next morning that the water had ruined much of their gunpowder and a considerable portion of their supplies. Nevertheless, after a meager breakfast of corn mush washed down with rum and water, they set out again, rowing all that day and the next, and anchoring in the middle of the river at night to avoid the swarms of mosquitoes along the banks. The stream fascinated Breckinridge. "St. John's river is the most crooked and bewildering stream I ever saw. Its general course is almost due north, but frequently the boat's head pointed to every point of the compass, and we were often led astray by false channels that ended in nothing." As they rowed south he saw all along its banks cranes and pelicans. Deer frequented the banks, but more numerous were the alligators, and their ominous presence seldom left the travelers' minds. "Sometimes they would swim across our bow with their black scaly backs just visible, like a gun boat low in the water," wrote the general. "I shot one with my pistol, and after we got him ashore it required three more balls through the place where his brains should have been to finish him." Along these same banks they found sour oranges in a deserted orchard, and with them and some dirty brown sugar they made "a very miserable lemonade." Fortunately for their weak larder, the fish in the river bit well.[15]

13. Breckinridge, Escape Diary, May 26, 1865, in Prewitt Collection; Wood Diary, May 26, 1865, in Wood MSS; "Breckinridge's Last Official Act," letter of Thomas P. Ochiltree to ?, n.d. [August 20, 1867], in clipping from an unidentified newspaper in the JCB Papers. The story is told as related to Ochiltree "at a *dejeuner* yesterday," in Paris. Breckinridge Diary, August 19, 1867, in Prewitt Collection, mentions seeing "Col. Ochiltree of Texas" that day, which therefore dates Ochiltree's letter. This story is verified by Clifton R. Breckinridge in an endorsement on General Order No. –, May 4, 1865, in the JCB Papers. Surely he knew this from being told the story by his father.
14. Breckinridge, Escape Diary, May 26, 1865, in Prewitt Collection.
15. *Ibid.*, May 27-29, 1865; Wood, "Escape," 111; Wood Diary, May 27-28, 1865, in Wood MSS.

On the morning of May 29, Murphy left the party to go home, taking with him one hundred dollars that Breckinridge paid the soldier for the life-boat, which he claimed as his own. Then the rest of them rowed on the twenty miles to Cooke's Ferry. The night before, Wood and O'Toole had gone a few miles inland to arrange for a wagon and team to meet them here, in order to haul the boat the twenty-eight miles overland to the Indian River, down which they would continue their journey. George Sauls, the man engaged, met them here at Cooke's Ferry, and it was arranged to start out the next morning. The party spent the night indoors for the first time in several days, at the Cooke home. Two of the girls there were old friends of Sergeant O'Toole's, and Breckinridge and Wood noted wryly that the swelling abdomen of one of them gave evidence of more than casual acquaintance.[16]

At daybreak the men started off on foot for the Indian River. From the very beginning the boat gave them trouble, for it could not be fastened securely to the wagon frame. As they passed over the bumpy, rutted road, the front wheels often "ran away from the hind ones," dropping the craft to the ground. They made only eighteen miles that day, camping amidst a plague of mosquitoes so thick that they had to build a fire and sit up most of the night in the protection of its smoke. The next day's travels proved as arduous and frustrating. The driver Sauls, whom Wood described as having "the shrewdness of the white, the good temper of the negro, and the indolence of the red man," apparently thought his part of the bargain stood fulfilled when he provided the team. He loitered behind most of the way, giving no assistance with the oxen, but always on hand at mealtime. Finally he was told, "No work, no grub; no drive bulls, no tobacco." This encouraged him to expend more effort, though Wood still believed that "It would have been less labor to have tied the beasts, put them into the boat, and hauled it across." [17]

Finally they reached Carlisle's Landing, opposite Cape Canaveral, on May 31, and lowered their boat into the waters of the Indian River. Actually it was no river at all, but an inland arm of the Atlantic Ocean running three hundred miles along Florida's eastern coast, separated from that body by a long strip of land only a few hundred yards wide. On launching the boat, it was found to be seaworthy in spite of its rough journey. The real

16. Wood Diary, May 29, 1865, in Wood MSS; Breckinridge, Escape Diary, May 29, 1865, in Prewitt Collection.

17. Wood Diary, May 29–31, 1865, in Wood MSS; Breckinridge, Escape Diary, May 29–31, 1865, in Prewitt Collection; Wood, "Escape," 112.

sufferers, however, were Sauls's oxen, terribly bitten and bloodied by mosquitoes and flies. He claimed that one of them would die—which the general doubted—and got an extra five dollars on its account. "He was very ignorant," Breckinridge thought, "but keener and more provident in all parts of a contract than any Yankee I ever saw." He feared that Sauls had recognized him, but the driver claimed to know nothing, and soon departed. Immediately the fugitives set off down Indian River to cover a few miles before nightfall. It was so brackish that they were forced to dig in the sand on shore to find fresh water.[18]

They covered fifty miles the next day, June 1, the same day that Mary Breckinridge was arriving back at home in Lexington through the permission of the new president, the general's old acquaintance Andrew Johnson of Tennessee. She had left Richmond a few days after the evacuation with General Lee's help, and now had not seen or heard of her husband for nearly two months. That night, as she was being welcomed by old friends in Kentucky, she could scarcely imagine that he was battling for his life against the ever-present mosquitoes. "I cannot give you any adequate idea of these insects," he wrote. "They attacked us, not two or three at a time, but in swarms incessantly the whole night long. Both hands were kept going and still they bit us. With his arms tied and his face exposed, I am sure they would kill a man in two nights." The only relief they could find was to bury themselves in sand on the shore, or wrap up in the sail aboard the boat. "I am glad I did not take Cabell with me," the general mused; "he would have died of brain fever." [19]

For the next two days Breckinridge and company made good progress, though one time engulfed in the hardest rain the general had ever seen. The night of June 2 they stealthily slipped past a small Federal guard post at Indian River Inlet near Fort Pierce. "Approaching cautiously, with muffled oars," wrote the general, "we saw a fire on the bank, which we supposed to be the guard fire. The night was dark, and keeping the middle of the stream, we glided past without being challenged." The following day they moved on to a point twenty miles above Jupiter Inlet, where the strip separating them from the ocean was barely fifty yards wide. Hauling their craft across a sand dune, they put it into the Atlantic at 5 P.M. and continued on south, keeping close to shore, and watching with anxious eyes the one or two

18. Breckinridge, Escape Diary, May 31, 1865, in Prewitt Collection.
19. *Ibid.*, June 1, 1865; Cincinnati *Enquirer*, June 2, 1865; Maltby, *Mary Cyrene Breckinridge*, 10.

steamers that passed by. They coasted past Jupiter Inlet that night, making camp some fifteen miles below.

Here the travelers remained most of the day, resting and searching for food. With their cornbread and sweet potatoes gone, they were forced to hunt for turtle eggs, which abounded on the beaches. Fresh water came from a nearby lake, and by late afternoon, after Wood read prayers, they were ready to attempt the crossing to Grand Bahama Island, seventy miles due east. The wind blew against them, however, and they did not even get out of sight of land by next morning. Then they saw a United States steamer heading directly toward them. Quickly they rowed to shore, turned over the boat on the beach in the hope that it would look like flotsam, and hid in the brush behind a dune. The steamer passed within a half mile without stopping, but Breckinridge and his companions were too quick about returning to their boat. The steamer sighted them. As it turned to investigate, Breckinridge proposed that they take to the brush and leave the lifeboat in the hope that the ship's crew would not disturb it. Wood, more experienced at this, knew that the Federals would destroy or carry off the craft, which would result in sure death from exposure and starvation for the fugitives.

Finally it was decided that Wood, Russell and O'Toole would sail out to meet the Federals. While Breckinridge hid in the brush, pistols in his hands, they quieted the enemy's suspicions by looking stupid and claiming to be salvaging along the coast. Breckinridge was greatly relieved to see the steamer move off.

Strong winds continued to hamper attempts to get away from the coast so that on the morning of June 6 Breckinridge was still sailing along in sight of land. About 8 A.M. he saw a group of Seminole Indians on shore, from whom, after smoking a pipe and exchanging some gunpowder, he and his companions received a quantity of *kuntee*, a bread made from ground roots. When cooked, the general found, it "was a little thicker than a pancake and ten times as tough." [20]

Later that day Breckinridge saw a boat approaching. At first the fugitives feared capture, but soon they saw the other craft change course to avoid them. Suspecting that they might be deserters, Wood immediately attempted to overhaul the boat, which he did after sending a pistol shot across its bow. Upon seeing the boat's occupants, the general was sure that

20. Breckinridge, Escape Diary, June 2–5, 1865, in Prewitt Collection; Wood Diary, June 2–5, 1865, in Wood MSS; Wood, "Escape," 114.

they were Federal deserters, and decided to appropriate their boat, much larger and more seaworthy than the *Columbine*'s lifeboat. Turning pirates, Breckinridge and Wood stepped into their intended prize and ordered the leader of the deserters to step forward. When he hesitated, Breckinridge drew his revolver and said, "Wilson, disarm that man." That done, the general "put on a bold air and threatened the rascals with all sorts of dreadful things, but finally relented so far as to offer to let them go with an exchange of boats!" The deserters must have been delighted to get off so lightly, for Breckinridge and his companions looked barbaric. The general, unshaven, browned by the sun and growing gaunt from exhaustion and malnutrition, was the very picture of a buccaneer. Dressed now in an old blue flannel shirt, he wore a straw hat with a brim so huge that it "flapped over his head like the ears of an elephant." Then, after going through the delicate process of switching men and supplies between the boats, Breckinridge gave the deserters a token payment of twenty dollars, and set sail again.

Everyone came out of the encounter pleased, the deserters with their lives, and the fugitives with a better boat. No longer than their lifeboat, the appropriated craft was much more broad, well suited for sea travel. Its acquisition lifted the spirits of all aboard, especially the overenthusiastic Colonel Wilson, whose bumbling misadventures on this arduous trip often gave the others the few moments of mirth so necessary to keep up their courage for the dangers ahead. He was so pleased with the exchange, wrote Breckinridge, that "he expressed a strong conviction that we would soon trade ourselves into possession of a steamer." The colonel was a little disappointed, however, that they had passed up the opportunity to play their role as pirates to the fullest, by making the deserters walk the plank.[21]

That evening Breckinridge and Wood decided to try for Cuba instead of the Bahamas. First, though, they would need more supplies. Working slowly south, they sailed all night for Key Biscayne and Fort Dallas, an abandoned Seminole war post where there was known to be a small trading store. It was nearly daylight, June 7, before they reached the key and sighted Fort Dallas. As they neared the wharf, Breckinridge and party were met by about thirty men of all nationalities, Spanish and Cuban renegades, mixed with deserters from the armies of both North and South. After some parley, Wood and Breckinridge decided not to risk landing among the outlaws, and again moved off down the coast. Soon, a look behind revealed

21. Breckinridge, Escape Diary, June 6, 1865, in Prewitt Collection; Wood Diary, June 6, 1865, in Wood MSS; Wood, "Escape," 115–16; Rowland, *Jefferson Davis*, VII, 16; James A. Wilson to Breckinridge, August 1, 1868, in B. MSS.

four or five canoes filled with renegades giving chase, apparently intent on attack.

Although outnumbered probably more than three to one, the Confederates determined to stand and fight. Russell opened fire on the canoes, breaking two paddles and felling one of the pursuers. Thereafter, Russell, Breckinridge, Tom and Wilson, all aimed shots at the renegades, the general directing their fire. Ironically, these were the only shots that Breckinridge is known to have fired during his service, and yet the war had been completely over for several days. The renegades soon broke off the engagement. After more negotiations, they finally agreed that O'Toole could come ashore to purchase provisions. The general gave him one hundred dollars in gold for that purpose, and as tribute money, charging him to return in two hours.

After two and a half hours, when the sergeant had not yet returned, Breckinridge and Wood gave him up for dead and robbed. Just as they were setting sail to continue, however, they saw O'Toole approaching in a canoe. With him he brought flour, salt pork, yams, two jugs of water, and a small keg of rum. They cooked some of the pork in the boat as they sailed off, overjoyed at O'Toole's return. Then, with a little rum and water, the fugitives had a meal "more enjoyable than any ever eaten at Delmonico's or the Cafe Riche." [22]

Proceeding south that afternoon, the party had gone but a few miles when they sighted a Federal patrol launch approaching. There ensued a chase of three or four hours in which, thanks to their lighter draft, the Confederates outdistanced their pursuers, but not before most of their supplies had to be thrown overboard to lighten the load and enable them to pass over shallow reefs. Breckinridge was at first dismayed to find that the keg of rum was among the items jettisoned, until Tom pulled it out of the transom locker, having been careful to save it. That night, after a most eventful day, the fugitives halted at Key Elliott, twenty miles south of Fort Dallas, and spent the night in the boat shielding themselves from the ever-present mosquitoes. [23]

22. This encounter with the renegades is slightly suspect, since neither Wood nor Breckinridge mentions it in their diaries in any detail. It is taken from Wood's 1893 article "Escape," 116–18, and may have been highly embellished. Wood Diary, June 8, 1865, does mention finding tories and renegades at Fort Dallas, but that is all it says. Hanna accepts the story and, in the absence of evidence to the contrary, so does this author.

23. Wood Diary, June 8, 1865, in Wood MSS; Wood, "Escape," 119. Here again Wood may be embellishing the story. Breckinridge makes no mention of this chase.

The next morning, with the prospect of a voyage on the open sea ahead of them, the Confederates began hunting for food to provision their boat. A quantity of turtle eggs formed the staple of their diet, and Ferguson gathered a number of coconuts to supplement it. Breckinridge wandered off into the brush to try to knock over something more substantial. He soon returned, exhausted, with two pelicans and a crane. Tom Ferguson immediately cooked the birds, and soon placed one of the pelicans before Breckinridge, his being the right of the hunter to the first bite. It proved a dubious honor. After a good deal of exertion, the general cut off a portion, swallowed it, and then, while the others looked on, quietly disappeared into the brush without a word. When he returned, he told Ferguson to remove the fowl. "His tone and expression satisfied us," wrote Wood, "that pelican would not keep us from starving." [24]

Setting sail again, the party finally cleared the keys that evening. Making their course due south, they passed the Carysfort beacon light opposite Key Largo at 10 P.M. Russell and O'Toole had been reluctant to leave Florida, but Breckinridge used some eloquent persuasion to get them to go along to Cuba, convincing them that they could hardly be charged with aiding an enemy of the United States since, in all probability, the North no longer had any organized southern foe. They gave in, finally, and rode on with the general, Wood, Wilson, and Ferguson, as the boat passed slowly out of sight of land. By midnight they were out in the open sea. [25]

If Breckinridge reflected on his unhappy situation as the boat moved farther out into the Gulf Stream, he could not have done so long. For two or three hours they threaded their way through submerged reefs, and then they broke free. During the remainder of the night the sea was rough, water frequently breaking across the bow of their little craft. Then before dawn the sailors met near disaster. O'Toole and Russell were lying in the bottom of the boat, sick, while Tom Ferguson was asleep and Wood sat up forward. Breckinridge recalled:

> I was tired and just losing myself in a daze—and the celebrated Colonel Wilson was steering. Suddenly I was roused by a wave going over me and half filling the boat, which leaned over untill the gun wale was under the water. At the same moment I observed that Capt Wood was overboard, and looking round I saw Col Wilson as stiff as a staunchion holding on like grim death

24. Johnston, "Sketches of Operations, No. 3," p. 390; Wood, "Escape," 120. Breckinridge and Wood have confused the number of days in their accounts of this period, Wood adding one or two, and Breckinridge accounting for too few. Consequently, this account is based on a reconstruction of June 6–8 using both diaries.

25. Breckinridge to Dickison, June 26, 1865, Dickison, *Dickison and His Men*, 227.

to the rudder and sail rope. It was his grip on the latter that was about to sink us. I knew just enough to shout to him to let go the rope which he did, and the strain being taken off, the boat finally righted. Capt Wood fortunately caught a rope as he went and had scrambled on board. Col Wilson expressed his gratification at the general result and explained that he had thought it his duty to hold every thing lest "it might get some advantage of him."

For the next twelve hours Wood took the helm and would trust it to no one else.[26]

They sailed fairly into the Gulf Stream on June 9, with a good breeze behind them and a relatively calm sea, steering by the general's pocket compass. All of the men suffered from exposure now, especially on their feet, which were blistered from constant immersion in the salt water. The sun beat down incessantly, tormenting them with thirst. Breckinridge took charge of the water, guarded it strictly, and doled out rationed amounts, a little at a time. Their meager provisions were exhausted.

That night the wind worked up to gale force. As the seas rose to twenty feet and more, Wood gave Breckinridge the sail and took the helm to ride out the storm. He found himself unable to steer the craft, however, and finally let it bob about at will, while Russell and O'Toole bailed and Ferguson huddled at the general's knees. Somehow the boat remained afloat. By morning, the storm was gone and the fugitives found themselves across the Gulf Stream. Wood later privately admitted to Breckinridge that chances were against them that night, and that "in 19 years experience of the sea he had never felt in so great peril."

Later that morning they sighted several sails on the horizon, and about daylight found themselves heading directly for a United States merchant ship, the *Neptune* out of Bangor, Maine. Breckinridge and his companions, by this time desperate for food and water, decided to take a great chance and hail the steamer. The vessel's captain, leary of the piratical looking men in the small boat, refused to allow them alongside his ship, but after some persuasion threw over to them a keg with five gallons of water and a bag of biscuits or hardtack. The fugitives then parted company with the *Neptune*, though Breckinridge was ever after grateful to its captain. Indeed, he believed that he and his men were kept alive that day thanks only to the generosity of this Yankee skipper.[27]

Breckinridge was very tired that morning. Lying down in the boat, he

26. Breckinridge, Escape Diary, June 7, 1865, in Prewitt Collection; Wood, "Escape," 121.

27. Breckinridge, Escape Diary, June 8–9, 1865, in Prewitt Collection; Wood, "Escape," 121; Rowland, *Jefferson Davis*, VII, 16.

slept for several hours. All of the men were worn out from the rigors of their voyage, and the fact that there was room in the boat for only one of them to lie down and sleep. The hot sun shone on the general all day as he rested, and he awoke terribly sick, an illness that did not entirely leave him for several days. Then, late that night, Wood sighted the Double-headed Shot Keys, small islets off the Cuban shore east of Cárdenas. Their spirits elevated by this discovery, the fugitives hoped to reach the coast that same evening. Nightfall overtook them first, though, and they were forced to steer by the North Star.

Several hours after dark they saw the beam from a lighthouse on shore and headed toward it. Then Breckinridge and Wood fell asleep, leaving Colonel Wilson at the rudder. "That enterprising officer," wrote the general, "ran the boat nearly on the lighthouse and then concluded to wake us up for consultation." The craft was immediately steered clear, but a few minutes later, the colonel still at the helm, the boat struck a coral reef and nearly overturned. With much trouble they got her off the reef and then steered west for the remainder of the night.

On the morning of June 11, starving and exhausted, Breckinridge sighted a town at the head of a bay some ten or twelve miles away. Heading directly for it, they entered the harbor before noon and stopped at the anchorage. Then, at the general's request, Wood read prayers. "I am sure," Breckinridge would recall, "we all felt profoundly gratefull for our deliverance." Thus, after twenty-eight days of anxiety, privation, and physical torture, John C. Breckinridge at last tasted the sweetness of escape to safety and freedom, and the bitter fruit of exile.[28]

28. New Orleans *Tribune*, July 4, 1865; Breckinridge, Escape Diary, June 10–11, 1865, in Prewitt Collection.

Book III

Symbol

CHAPTER 1

You Have a Mission to Perform

John C. Breckinridge knew that for the time being, and perhaps indefinitely, exile was his lot. To be sure, he still hoped to reach Kirby Smith, but that small army—for such he still thought it to be—could not last long, and with the end of hostilities would come the end of any safety for him in the United States or the Confederacy. From the conditions of surrender of Generals Lee and Johnston, Breckinridge knew that nearly all of the men, officers, and generals of the Confederate armies would be unmolested after giving their paroles. For the high civil officials of the South, however, it would certainly be another matter, as evidenced by the hot Federal pursuit of Davis and himself. Indictments were out. He was wanted.

More important was the general's certain knowledge that, in the immediate future, his very identity as John C. Breckinridge would banish him from his country. He had presided over the United States Senate fully three months after the secession of South Carolina, and later sat in that body for over four months after Fort Sumter. Before it his voice was the loudest in opposition to the war and Lincoln, and sometimes the only voice in defense of the South. In the campaign of 1860 prominent southerners regarded him as their symbol, Davis calling him "the best representative" of their interests. Northerners, in later evaluating their feelings during the Civil War, often decided that it was Breckinridge, and not Davis or Alex Stephens, who was "truly representative of the rebellion as an actual force and its underlying causes." [1]

None of this was lost on Breckinridge. Undoubtedly he felt justifiable fears that, if captured, he might suffer the very harshest treatment. Considering the state of mind of the North in 1865, he considered his execution a real possibility. Consequently, as the general sat in the boat in the

---

1. Louisville *Courier-Journal*, May 20, 1875.

Cárdenas harbor, though his immediate objective was Texas, his regard for his own safety and the welfare of his family would force him into uncertain and agonizing exile.

The arrival of a strange boat filled with armed men caused no little consternation in the Cuban city. While a crowd began to gather on the wharf, rumor got about that President Jefferson Davis had escaped his pursuers and was in the boat. Breckinridge and Wood waited at anchor for the port health officer to come and give them clearance. Finally a port launch towed them in, while the people gathering about still wondered who was in the boat. John Cahill, a resident of Cárdenas but formerly a Kentuckian, went down to the customs house to see what was happening and, as the Confederates approached under tow, he knew immediately that Davis was not the imposing officer in the boat. It was John C. Breckinridge. "As he stepped on the wharf from the little boat on which he and his . . . companions had made their perilous voyage . . . his tall, erect figure, wrapped in a well-worn military cloak, towered above all others on that memorable morning." Making himself known to the general, Cahill offered to act as interpreter; told the Spaniards who Breckinridge was and what he had just come through. They seemed unable to believe that he could make such a trip in so small a craft, and Cahill sadly told Breckinridge that they were reluctant to accept his story. At this, the general unbuckled his sword belt, and proffered his arms to the officer in charge with a few words which Cahill translated. The others followed his lead, and the officials were convinced. Their leader handed back the sword and pistols: "You have fought the most heroic battles of the ages in defense of your country and its institutions. You have won the admiration of my countrymen, and of all brave men throughout the world, and, recognizing your nobility and the sad causes that have brought you to these shores, we return to you your arms and tender you our hospitality." Despite the Spaniard's lofty prose, the Confederates still had to wait at the customs house until the Cuban governor, Domingo Dulce in Havana, could be wired for permission to allow the irregular entry of the fugitives. Then, having no passports, Breckinridge and the others filled out and signed a number of papers and reports. Finally a register had to be drawn up for their as yet unnamed boat. A cursory search of their imaginations brought swift results, and the register was made out accordingly for the sloop *No Name*.[2]

2. [John Cahill], "The Escape of J. C. Breckinridge," clipping from undated issue of the St. Louis *Globe-Democrat*, ca. 1900, in JCB Papers; Wood Diary, June 11, 1865, in Wood MSS; Wood, "Escape," 125.

After a visit to the governor of Cárdenas, the fugitives were finally shown to lodgings at El Hotel Cristobol Colon, where, after coffee and a light breakfast at the Fonda del Almirante Colon near the customs house, they at last retired to their rooms for a few hours, the first time in nearly a month that any of them had enjoyed the luxury of a bed.[3]

While he slept, the general's presence continued to create a stir in Cárdenas, and Wood found that his arrival produced as much of a sensation "as would that of a Liner." Governor-General Dulce wired further instructions that Breckinridge was to be accorded the treatment and honors due to one of his position, and the Cárdenas officials soon fawned over him. Throughout the rest of the day, ruining his much needed rest, Breckinridge received calls from the numerous Americans in town, regardless of their sectional affiliations. Cahill brought in Colonel San Martin, president of the Cárdenas branch of the railroad to Havana, a man whom Breckinridge had known when vice-president. San Martin graciously offered the general the use of his private car for the trip to Havana, and the general gratefully accepted. At the same time, the Spaniard purchased from Breckinridge the little *No Name,* the general sharing the proceeds with Wood and, probably, Wilson. That evening Breckinridge was taken in hand by Gumersindo Pacetti, formerly mayor of St. Augustine, Florida, provided with a new suit of clothes, and treated to a dinner in his honor. Afterwards, in the cool of twilight, some of the Cuban Confederates hired the band of the Cárdenas Volunteers to serenade. It is indicative of the nonpartisan reception given Breckinridge that the band played, by request, "Dixie," "Yankee Doodle," "The Bonnie Blue Flag," and the "Star Spangled Banner," in that order. Breckinridge was asked to make a brief speech, but declined, being much too tired.[4]

The next morning Breckinridge, Wood, and the others, boarded San Martin's car for the trip to Havana, arriving at the Regla station, across the bay from the Cuban capital, at about noon. A crowd had gathered to meet him, many still thinking that he was Davis. Upon crossing the bay to the city, he was met by almost ten thousand curious spectators at the ferry. Cahill had to scream in his best Spanish and enlist the aid of several policemen and soldiers to cut his way through the crowd to get Breckinridge a carriage. Once out of the mess, however, they drove with no difficulty to

3. Wood, "Escape," 123; Hanna, *Flight,* 188; Cahill, "Escape of J. C. Breckinridge," in JCB Papers.

4. Wood Diary, June 11, 1865, in Wood MSS; Wood, "Escape," 123; Cahill, "Escape of J. C. Breckinridge," Cahill to Breckinridge, September 14, 1871, in JCB Papers; New York *Herald,* June 22, 1865; Cincinnati *Enquirer,* June 25, 1865.

the Calle Teniente Rey, and the Hotel Cubano. Run by a southern woman named Brewer, this five-story hostelry was the Cuban headquarters for Confederates, and was known in the North as a place where "secessionists and people of like persuasion do most congregate." [5]

Havana lavished Breckinridge with expressions of friendship. One wealthy merchant put his purse entirely at the Kentuckian's disposal, Mrs. Brewer graciously offered to provide him with a home free of charge for as long as he wished to remain, and his old friends the McHattons from Baton Rouge entertained him often at Desengaño, their plantation outside the city. Of course, Breckinridge had no intention of remaining in Cuba. Having now neither a country nor a cause—for in Havana he certainly heard or read of the surrenders of Taylor and Smith—all that was left to him were his wife and children. Reunited with them, he could face his future. [6]

It would be several days before he could get a ship out of Havana, though, and in the meantime there were things to do. On June 14, with Wood and Colonel Charles J. Helm, Confederate purchasing agent in Cuba, he rode out to the country seat of the governor-general. Dulce warmly received Breckinridge, and they had dinner and a long and pleasant interview together. Expressing great sympathy and sorrow over the circumstances which forced the general to become a "guest among strangers," Dulce assured him that he would not be allowed to feel that he was a stranger in Cuba. It would be for him a safe asylum and home for as long as he wished. [7]

Breckinridge needed the rest and quiet he found in Cuba, for he suffered from the trials of his escape, as well as the mental anguish of the circumstances that brought it about. He was gaunt from starvation, and severely sunburned. The perils of the flight, on top of the rigors of almost four years of war, had considerably reduced his formerly vigorous and robust constitution. He had his photograph made on arriving in Havana, and it showed a man older than his forty-four years, worn and tired. When Mary received a copy of it, his appearance shocked her. Reflection on his situation, and perhaps a sober comparison of his present lot with his position just four years before, often left him lost in deep thought during these first

5. Wood Diary, June 12, 1865, in Wood MSS; Hanna, *Flight*, 188; Cincinnati *Enquirer*, June 25, 1865; Cahill, "Escape of J. C. Breckinridge," John Cahill to Breckinridge, August 10, 1871, in JCB Papers; New York *Herald*, June 27, 1865; Ripley, *Social Life*, 287–88; Ripley, *From Flag to Flag*, 127, 132.

6. New York *Herald*, June 27, 1865.

7. Cincinnati *Enquirer*, June 25, 1865; Wood, "Escape," 123.

days. Newsmen seeking interviews found him "frequently lost in fits of abstraction." Known to be lively and animated in conversation and society, he seemed moody and taciturn, "speaking only to his intimate friends." Although this condition remained with the general only a few days before his customary pragmatism set him to making the best of his situation, some Havana correspondents for the northern press enjoyed wide speculation on his reticence and reserve. Evidently, one said, Breckinridge was "chewing the bitter cud of reflection and repentance for the wounds inflicted upon his country; and though he expresses no opinion publicly, we may well conceive how melancholy must be his thoughts when he considers 'What now he is and what he might have been.' " [8]

Definite news of Breckinridge's arrival in Cuba did not reach the United States until June 22, and for the next two weeks the papers were full of his doings and whereabouts. The reports were largely in his own words, for he and Wood and Wilson gave interviews to a few correspondents. They described their voyage in great detail, even their venture at piracy. The New York *Herald* speculated that "the manner of his escape from the coast of Florida savors of the romantic, and may yet form the groundwork of an exciting novel or thrilling drama." The southern reaction to Breckinridge's escape was joyous and unrestrained. "This eminent gentleman and of all Southern statesmen the most high-toned and irreproachable," said one tabloid, "has made good his escape and arrived in Havana. . . . We earnestly hope he may permanently escape the humiliations that are now befalling Mr. Davis." [9]

The condition of Jefferson Davis formed one of Breckinridge's chief concerns while in Cuba. He learned from the newspapers that the former president was to be arraigned before a civil court on the charge of treason, and that his old friend from New York, Charles O'Connor, perhaps the foremost trial lawyer in the country, had volunteered to defend him. Breckinridge and Helm had a number of discussions on the subject, and it appeared that after closing out his affairs the Confederate agent would still have an undetermined amount of government funds left over. Between them they agreed that this money should be used in Davis' defense. Breckinridge wrote to O'Connor, expressing his confidence in him, and his hope

8. Wood Diary, June 19, 1865, in Wood MSS; Breckinridge, Escape Diary, June 10, 1865, in Prewitt Collection; New York *Times*, June 22, 1865; Maltby, *Mary Cyrene Breckinridge*, 8; New York *Herald*, June 27, 1865. The photograph of Breckinridge taken in Havana is in the Sallie Johnson Breckinridge Scrapbook in possession of Peter H. Ten Eyck.

9. New York *Times*, June 22, 1865; Edgefield (S.C.) *Advertiser*, July 5, 1865.

that there would be "a fair and thorough trial upon the highest and broadest grounds." For the moment, there was nothing more he could do.[10]

Meanwhile, it was time for Breckinridge to look to his own future. At Norfolk, Virginia, another indictment had been handed down against him, and the New York *Herald* implied that Breckinridge would be hanged if caught. Obviously, it might be years before he could return to the United States—if at all—yet he longed to be with his family. He decided to meet them in Canada and then worry about what came next. Since the only way from Cuba to Canada was by way of England, he could also contact prominent southern agents and diplomats along the way, doing what he could in closing the affairs of the Confederacy and raising more funds to aid Davis and other political prisoners.[11]

The other members of his party were already leaving. Wood, whose services had been invaluable, left for Halifax, Nova Scotia, by way of England on June 23, to live out his life a permanent exile. Wilson also departed for Canada, to take up temporary residence in Toronto. Breckinridge divided his share of the money from the sale of the boat between Russell and O'Toole, and arranged for their passage from Havana to Mobile, giving them as well a letter to Dickison which absolved them from all complicity in his escape and explaining that they went along only at his earnest entreaty. Tom Ferguson, so seasick on the escape that he could not face another ocean voyage, wanted to go home to his family with Jilson Johnson. The general gave him money for the trip with Russell and O'Toole, and a letter of recommendation. "On many occasions of peril and hardship," wrote the general, "he has proven himself courageous and faithful." Indeed, only one remnant of the little band would remain in Cuba, the brave little *No Name*. For years, surviving even loss at sea during a hurricane, the boat remained for San Martin a constant reminder of the heroic journey it made with a most unusual complement of passengers.[12]

His affairs in Havana concluded, Breckinridge booked passage for himself on the steamer *Conway*, bound first for St. Thomas in the Danish West Indies on July 7, 1865. There was a rumor in Havana that he intended to

10. Breckinridge to Charles O'Connor, June 26, 1865, in John C. Breckinridge MSS, WRHS.

11. *Ibid.*; Washington *Daily National Intelligencer*, June 29, 1865.

12. Wood Diary, June 23, 1865, Breckinridge to John Taylor Wood, September 17, 1865, in Wood MSS; Breckinridge to Clifton R. Breckinridge, October 26, 1865, Cahill to Breckinridge, September 14, 1871, in JCB Papers; Breckinridge to J. J. Dickison, June 26, 1865, in Dickison, *Dickison and His Men*, 227; John C. Breckinridge, letter of introduction and safe conduct for Thomas Ferguson, July 7, 1865, in possession of Mrs. George Roy Hill; O'Toole to Breckinridge, April 24, 1869, in B. MSS.

go on to Spain, but certainly he had no intention of doing so. It may have been a ruse to throw Federal agents off his tracks, for his movements in Cuba had been carefully watched and reported to Washington. In any case, on July 7 Breckinridge and Helm, accompanied by Russell, O'Toole, and Ferguson, went to the docks of Havana where the *Conway* awaited. Before leaving Cuba, however, he performed a last, unofficial, act for the Confederacy. In an attempt to stop any further resistance and fighting, he counseled all of his friends to throw themselves on the clemency of President Johnson, and ask for pardon. He would not have any more blood shed for an extinct cause, and so expressed himself to the correspondents from the northern press. This done, Breckinridge and Helm boarded their waiting ship, said their farewells to the brave men who had helped in the perilous escape, and steamed off toward St. Thomas and the long voyage to England. For Breckinridge it was to be the first of many voyages.[13]

After he got to London, he hurriedly sought out the leading Confederates to offer his services in concluding their affairs. He met with James M. Mason, diplomat and commissioner to Great Britain during the war, as well as General Colin P. McRae and Caleb Huse, purchasing agents. From Mason and McRae he received the dismaying news that the Confederacy actually died in debt to many of its agents. Nevertheless, Mason assured him that sufficient funds were left over to take care of Davis' defense.[14]

While Mason booked passage for himself and Breckinridge on the *Peruvian*, bound for Quebec on August 24, Breckinridge made a short visit to Paris to see John Slidell and Dudley Mann, the commissioners to France and Belgium. Affairs there were much the same, and he spent most of his brief stay with Mann at his small country place, Mont Po. Mann, though several years his senior, loved him dearly and rejoiced in the general's company. When Breckinridge left, Mann told him frankly that "I can scarcely doubt that your life has been preserved, and for *a purpose*. You have a mission to perform, and that Power (which never long deserts the faithful) will in its own good time distinctly signify it to you." Meanwhile, he counseled, wait and watch.[15]

After a quiet trip across the ocean, the general reached port in the St. Lawrence River, and then switched to a train that would carry him to

13. New Orleans *Daily Picayune*, June 12, 1865; New York *Herald*, June 27, 1865; Washington *Daily National Intelligencer*, June 29, 1865.
14. James Mason to Elizabeth Mason, August 9, 1865, in Virginia Mason, *The Public and Diplomatic Correspondence of James M. Mason* (New York, 1906), 572; Breckinridge to Wood, September 17, 1865, in Wood MSS.
15. A. Dudley Mann to Breckinridge, August 25, 1865, in JCB Papers.

Montreal. He arrived on September 12, passed the night at St. Lawrence Hall, and went on to Toronto the next day. As he parted from one of his party who determined to remain in Montreal for a time, the general remarked that "I hope you will see me in Texas (If they ever let me return) for I expect to make Texas my home, for I do not think I will go to Kentucky to live again." Just what prompted Breckinridge to give up the hope of returning to Kentucky is something of a mystery, but it may well have been his intention to start life all over again in a new frontier, in a growing part of the country where a thousand associations and memories of the past would not arise continually to remind him of happier days.[16]

In Toronto at last, Breckinridge found his family waiting for him. Owen, Fanny, Cabell, and little Mary were all there with his wife; only Clifton was absent. On returning to Kentucky, Mary had stayed with a cousin, Martha McConnell, at Woodford for several months until receiving word from her husband. Now with her husband once again at their lodgings at the Queen's Hotel, she could say happily that the Breckinridges were "once more a united family." [17]

There were those, however, who looked upon the general's arrival with less joyful feelings. On September 13, United States Secretary of State William Seward notified President Johnson that he had received information of Breckinridge's presence in Canada. In a cabinet meeting that same day, Johnson reluctantly decided that his old friend Breckinridge should be arrested if found within the boundary of the United States. The temper of the nation and the indictments against him demanded the Kentuckian's apprehension if possible. The next day Secretary of War Stanton instructed his secret service to be on the watch for Breckinridge if he should cross the border.[18]

Breckinridge had no idea of trying to return to the United States while feeling ran against him. He was with his family, relatively happy, and at peace for the first time in years. They spent their first few weeks in Toronto at their hotel but, late in October, moved to a rented house at the corner of Peter and Aduycide streets, a comfortable home at a reasonable rent. Around them they found a number of fellow exiles, enough, thought

16. Breckinridge to Wood, September 17, 1865, in Wood MSS; Edwin Gray Lee Diary, September 13, 1865, in SHC; E. W. Anderson to Breckinridge, August 2, 1873, in JCB Papers.

17. Hines Diary, September 13, 1865, in Hines MSS; Maltby, *Mary Cyrene Breckinridge*, 9; Mary C. Breckinridge to Ann Johnson, October 22, 1865, Mary C. Breckinridge MSS; Stuart Robinson to Clay, September 20, 1865, in Clay MSS.

18. *O.R.*, Ser. II, Vol. VIII, 747.

Mary, "to form quite a pleasant society among ourselves." Helm, Wilson, the Reverend Stuart Robinson of Louisville, and many others paid calls. Wilson remained several weeks in Toronto, visiting his beloved general often before leaving to go South. The colonel was going to marry a certain lady if he could find her, he told Breckinridge but, true to form, he confessed that he had forgotten her name. This company was a great comfort to the general, its joys augmented by a new family pet, a dog named—unimaginatively—Fido. Mary was happy to write that "the General is in good health and after all is restored in honor if not prosperity." [19]

As the Breckinridges passed their winter in Canada, a movement was already under way in the United States to have him pardoned, or at least to allow him to return to Kentucky. "Could a better, an abler, or a more gallant man be sent to the United States Senate than John C. Breckinridge?" asked the Louisville *Courier*. "Would he not honor that body more than it could possibly honor him? Would he not stand there without a peer in everything that constitutes true greatness?" In the Louisville *Journal* the general's old friend George D. Prentice asked whether any could doubt that "as a loyal citizen, he would be a portion of the intellectual wealth of Kentucky and of the nation." [20]

Prentice did more than editorialize. On October 15 he wrote to the general and expressed his conviction that there was no reason why he should not return to Kentucky. Nevertheless, the editor promised to interview General John M. Palmer, commandant of Federal troops in the state, on the matter. The next day Prentice had a full discussion with Palmer and a guest who happened to be with him, Robert J. Breckinridge. The editor asked whether Breckinridge could safely return to the country and, after a moment or two of hesitation, Palmer replied that he did not think so. Palmer and the general's uncle both cited the indictments against him as their main reasons for thinking as they did. Surely the news did not come as much of a surprise to Breckinridge. Many of his friends agreed. "Gen B. must not come," wrote one. "There is a loud cry for his disgrace & punishment." For the time being he must still watch and wait. "The time has not come yet," he confessed, "when I can properly cherish the hope of returning to my country." He had not ceased to think of it as his country, and he advised his friends to "disabuse mens minds" of the many false preju-

19. Robinson to Clay, September 20, 1865, in Clay MSS; Mary C. Breckinridge to Johnson, October 22, 1865, in Mary C. Breckinridge MSS; Breckinridge to Clifton R. Breckinridge, October 26, 1865, in JCB Papers; Breckinridge to Mary D. Breckinridge, May 13, 1866, in possession of Mr. Walter R. Agard, Chicago, Ill.
20. Cincinnati *Gazette*, October 24, 1865.

dices against him. Never despairing, he would watch affairs in the United States with keen interest, telling those at home, "I trust we shall meet when all these wounds are healed over." Indeed, some in the states believed that "His popularity is . . . increasing & in my opinion, he will yet be our leader. He must abide his time however." Influential men like Horace Greeley agreed.[21]

One of the general's first concerns while he waited was his children's education which had been interrupted by the war. He and Mary were much impressed by the educational advantages offered in Canada for Owen and Fanny, and immediately put their daughter in a school for young ladies. Owen, meantime, received his lessons from Lieutenant Bennett Young, a fellow exile, sometime boarder at the Breckinridge household, and the youthful leader of the celebrated Confederate raid on St. Albans, Vermont. In return, the general gave Young lectures in the law, and everyone found the arrangement most satisfactory, and economical. Breckinridge was quite pleased with Owen's progress, though noting that the boy possessed "a few loose notions in regard to horse trading which I have!!" Meanwhile, little Mary, not yet finished with her elementary schooling, was sent to New York to live with her cousin Susannah Lees. Advantages were better for her there, and she could be with children of her own age. She left in November, taking with her the general's injunction to mind her teachers, never be selfish, never say ill of others if possible to think well of them, admit cheerfully and freely any wrongs done, and exert herself to make others happy. Giving up little Mary was hard for them, and her father wrote to her thereafter so often that he feared she could not read it all.[22]

Cabell continued to worry his father. After leaving Toronto, he took a job briefly with the Cincinnati *Enquirer*, but did not keep it. He seemed lost and confused, was in bad health, and dropped contact with his parents. Breckinridge heard of him indirectly on occasion, and his friends tried to find the boy jobs, but he could not hold them, or did not try. Instead, he wandered, sometimes to Lexington, sometimes elsewhere. At least he had stopped drinking, the general discovered, and he regarded that as a major

21. George D. Prentice to Breckinridge, October 15, 17, 1865, in Breckinridge MSS, FC; Breckinridge to Wood, September 17, 1865, in Wood MSS; Breckinridge to Eli M. Bruce, October 26, 1865, Breckinridge to Katherine Carson, November 13, 1865, in JCB Papers; R. Alston to Thomas Hines, November 26, 1865, in Hines MSS.

22. Mary C. Breckinridge to Ann Johnson, October 22, 1865, March 11, 1866, in Mary C. Breckinridge MSS; Breckinridge to Clifton R. Breckinridge, October 26, 1865, in JCB Papers; Breckinridge to Mary D. Breckinridge, November 13, 20, 1865, in possession of Mrs. Kenneth Kirkland; "The Veteran" and "The Mobile Reunion," *Confederate Veteran*, XVIII (June, 1910), 261.

step in the right direction. "Much as I love him," he told Clifton, "if things continued as they once were I could not desire to see him." Cabell proved one of his father's chief worries during the exile, but Breckinridge never lost confidence that his son would find himself in time.[23]

If Cabell caused him worry, the general found nothing but satisfaction with Clifton. Now nineteen, he was employed by an old friend, Eli M. Bruce in his Cincinnati dry goods house. The boy was somewhat uncertain over his future, whether to remain in business or continue his education, and his father recommended that he do both, since Bruce would let him take time off for school. "Whatever you have to do," Breckinridge told his son, "understand it thoroughly and do it well. . . . Be courteous to all, but choose for your *friends* and habitual associates those of pure and elevated thoughts and conduct. We are never stationary—we are continually sinking to a lower or rising to a higher level. We are affected by the society we keep as by the air we breathe, and may as unconsciously contract a low and immoral tone from the one, as inhale disease from the other." And to all of his children, Breckinridge recommended one more study. "The longer I live for," he told them, "the more I am convinced that you will derive great good from the regular reading of your bible." [24]

During this winter in Toronto, Breckinridge made another attempt to aid the imprisoned Jefferson Davis. The president stood charged with responsibility for the poor treatment of Federal prisoners of war, and especially those infamous operations at Andersonville, Georgia. For the purpose of gathering information on the subject, Judge George Shea of New York, a friend and counsel of Davis', went to Montreal in January 1866 to examine Confederate diplomatic archives stored there. Advised by the president's nephew General Joseph R. Davis that Breckinridge was nearby in Toronto, Shea requested that the former secretary of war come to Montreal and furnish what pertinent information he had on the subject. Breckinridge immediately offered his full cooperation and reached Montreal on January 8, 1866. Precisely what he told Shea is unknown but, from his own intimate connection with the prisoner of war problem in the last months of the war, he well knew that Davis was not responsible for any injustices. Breckinridge's chief concern had been Salisbury prison camp, and his experience with the inefficient camp officers there may have served as a good

23. Bruce to Breckinridge, October 17, 1866, Breckinridge to Clifton R. Breckinridge, June 17, 1866, in JCB Papers.
24. Clifton R. Breckinridge to W. C. P. Breckinridge, May 30, 1866, in B. MSS; Bruce to Breckinridge, October 17, 1866, Breckinridge to Clifton R. Breckinridge, October 1, 26, 1865, in JCB Papers.

example to Shea of what had happened at Andersonville. Whatever the case, the judge came away from Canada convinced that Davis had no part in the horrors of that prison hell in Georgia.[25]

It was a severe winter in Toronto, the snow remaining on the ground well into spring. Breckinridge, still practicing the strictest economy, expanded somewhat his small law class, lecturing not only to Young, but to Captain Thomas H. Hines, Confederate secret agent, and Lieutenant George B. Eastin as well. All three had been at one time with Morgan, and the time spent with these young men did the general much good, for he chafed at his inactivity in exile. He needed, thought Mary, "to be actively employed as he has always been." He looked well now, though older. He needed rest.[26]

Toronto did not bring Breckinridge the peace and quiet that he desired. Also Mary's health was in its usual poor state, and her doctor prescribed a less busy environment as a cure. Consequently, Breckinridge decided to move to a more suitable location. Hoping to move in May, he began looking in April, and soon found a perfect place for the summer at Niagara on the lake. For twelve dollars a month Breckinridge rented a small, but comfortable house for the summer, with a yard, shade trees, and a little garden. Owen and Bennett Young preceded the general and Mary a few days to move in the little furniture they had, and then on May 7 they came on to live in the little house on Front Street. As they rode the steamer up to Niagara to take over their new home, they probably did not know that in Washington their old house on I Street finally had an occupant, General Ulysses S. Grant.[27]

The Breckinridges were happy with their new surroundings, rejoicing in the beauty of Lake Ontario, the fresh fish brought to their door, the economy of living, and the friends and relatives who surrounded them. Owen resumed his studies and took up raising poultry—"We are promised great numbers of chickens in due time," the general wrote Cliff. Breckinridge and Helm enjoyed the fishing in nearby streams; one afternoon they caught

25. McElroy, *Jefferson Davis*, II, 533; Breckinridge to Jefferson Davis, January 8, 1866, in Bryan Family MSS, Virginia State Library, Richmond; Shea to the editor of the New York *Tribune*, January 15, 1876, in *SHSP*, I (April, 1876), 321; Cincinnati *Enquirer*, October 27, 1866.

26. Headley, *Confederate Operations*, 449; Mary C. Breckinridge to Johnson, March 11, 1866, in Mary C. Breckinridge MSS; Hines Diary, January 20, 1866, in Hines MSS.

27. Mary C. Breckinridge to Johnson, March 11, 1866, in Mary C. Breckinridge MSS; Breckinridge to Clifton R. Breckinridge, April 5, 1866, in JCB Papers; William Kirby, *Annals of Niagara* (Toronto, 1927), 300; Cincinnati *Enquirer*, October 27, 1866; Adam Badeau to Elihu B. Washburne, November 9, 1865, in Elihu B. Washburne MSS, LC.

This photograph was made in the summer or fall of 1868 at Niagra, Ontario, Canada. It shows Breckinridge, at left, with family and friends. Mary stands next to him, and his son Clifton is fourth from left. In the background the American falls are faintly visible in this picture. Nothing better shows his fervent hope to return to his country than his taking up residence within sight of the United States. (Courtesy Mrs. Kenneth Kirkland)

Joseph Cabell Breckinridge, *ca.* 1870. In December of 1869 he had married Sallie Johnson, daughter of his father's friend, Senator Robert W. Johnson of Arkansas. General and Mrs. John C. Breckinridge attended the wedding in Washington. (Courtesy Peter H. Ten Eyck)

Clifton R. Breckinridge as a student at Washington College, Lexington, Virginia, 1869. (Courtesy Mr. and Mrs. John M. Prewitt)

two hundred in five hours. Walking underneath the great cataract of beautiful Niagara Falls, Breckinridge could see, carved years before on a honeymoon, a brief reminder of home and loved ones. The inscription read: "R. J. Breckinridge and Lady." Their house sat isolated on a rise near the mouth of the Niagara River, overlooking the lake. Immediately opposite the house, on the New York side of the river, sat Fort Niagara. Breckinridge looked across at it often, "with its flag flying to refresh our patriotism." It was both a comfort and a taunt, his only real contact with the country he longed to return to, and a constant reminder that he could not.[28]

Society in Niagara was enhanced considerably that summer by the arrival of several important Confederates. Mason came in July, lured to the village by Breckinridge's description of its "quiet seclusion and the great economy of its simple village life." Lieutenant-Colonel George T. Denison, commander of the Canadian governor-general's Body Guard, was a frequent visitor with Breckinridge, as was his beloved old adjutant, J. Stoddard Johnston. Another welcome guest was Jubal Early, here after a disappointing stay in Mexico. He and the general had not met since the days in the Valley two years before. Now in Canada, Early, Breckinridge, Mason, Helm, and others, met often in the shaded yard in front of Mason's house, discussing military matters and the practice of the soldier's art under the modern conditions inaugurated by the Civil War. Breckinridge's military acumen so impressed Denison that the Canadian sent him a copy of his recently published manual of outpost duties, asking for an opinion on the work. Breckinridge heartily approved it, much to Denison's delight.[29]

The Kentuckian was spending a good deal of time now with history, particularly concerning the late war. Lee, now a paroled prisoner of war, living at Richmond, was contemplating writing a history of his Virginia campaigns, and had asked Breckinridge for pertinent information of his operations in 1864–1865. Breckinridge, in turn, had Johnston prepare a report of his campaigning in the Shenandoah and southwestern Virginia from memory, most of the originals of his reports and documents having been

28. Maltby, *Mary Cyrene Breckinridge*, 9; Breckinridge to Clifton R. Breckinridge, May 13, 1866, in JCB Papers; Letitia Breckinridge to Sophonisba Breckinridge, July 18, 1839, in B. MSS; Breckinridge to Mary D. Breckinridge, May 13, 1866, in possession of Mr. Walter R. Agard.
29. Mason, *Correspondence*, 586; George T. Denison, *Soldiering in Canada* (London, 1900), 58–59; J. S. Johnston to Simon B. Buckner, March 15, 1867, in Simon B. Buckner MSS, HL; Millard K. Bushong, *Old Jube: A Biography of General Jubal A. Early* (Boyce, Va., 1955), 287.

lost or destroyed during the war. In addition, Early had recently completed his *A Memoir of the Last Year of the War*, covering the Shenandoah operations, and now he submitted it to Breckinridge for his comments and corrections. They had discussions and correspondence over the work, and Breckinridge approved of it, making several suggestions which his old commander incorporated in the manuscript.[30]

All of this study of the recent past impressed the general with the historic importance of the era, and of his own role in it. Perhaps with the dim goal of writing his own memoirs in mind, he began gathering available materials from his own career, political as well as military. He found in writing—a discipline which he never enjoyed—a way to pass the time on his hands just now. Whatever the case, he would continue to pull together these relics of his past for the rest of his life.[31]

And it looked as though John C. Breckinridge would continue to have time on his hands. Prospects for his return were as slim as ever. Back on January 18 seventy-seven of Kentucky's legislators, some of them the same men who had demanded his resignation in 1861, sent a petition to Johnson requesting a pardon for the general. Nothing came of it, but it was an encouraging sign. Men's minds were slowly getting disabused.[32]

At the same time, Mary's health failed to improve at Niagara and, by late July, her doctor suggested that Breckinridge take her to the more temperate climate of France. The general agreed, and decided to take Owen and Fanny with them. After settling affairs at Niagara and bidding farewell to their beloved friends, the Breckinridges left on August 8, and took the boat to Toronto. Clifton and James B. Beck, both then in Canada for a short visit, went with them. Arriving that same evening, they immediately boarded a steamer for Montreal. From there, the next evening, they moved on to Quebec, arriving late in the morning of August 10. Breckinridge and Mary passed a final quiet day with their son and their friend, the general taking them to the heights overlooking the Plains of Abraham. There, where so many warriors had fallen a century before, this old warrior spent his last hours in Canada.

30. J. Stoddard Johnston, "Reports of Gen. Lee after the War," *Confederate Veteran*, X (August, 1902), 305; Jubal Early to Samuel Early, August 8, 1866, Breckinridge to Early, August 5, 1866, in Jubal A. Early MSS, LC.

31. Mention of collecting copies of letters, speeches, and reports, will be found throughout the B. MSS. and JCB Papers for the postwar years.

32. Richard T. Jacob and others to Andrew Johnson, January 18, 1866, Records of the Adjutant General's Office, Amnesty Papers, 1865, Kentucky, John C. Breckinridge, RG 94, NA.

The next morning they boarded the *Peruvian* bound for Liverpool and, saying goodbye to Cliff and Beck, were on their way down the St. Lawrence. Sailing on the great river, they passed the next two days quietly, seeing the freshly cut wheat on the banks and the playful white porpoises that frolicked in the ship's wake. Breckinridge, perhaps as a step toward that memoir, began to keep a diary. As the *Peruvian* sailed through the Gulf of St. Lawrence on the evening of August 13, past the Belle Island Light, and moved out into the dark and stormy Atlantic, carrying Breckinridge farther from his home and deeper into exile, he may well have wondered what the uncertain days ahead would bring to fill all of those empty pages.[33]

33. Jubal Early to Samuel Early, August 8, 1866, in Early MSS; Breckinridge Diary, August 8–13, 1866, in Prewitt Collection.

CHAPTER 2

On You, Sir, the Eyes of All True
Southern Men Are Now Fixed

As Breckinridge crossed the ocean that summer, he was one of many exiles wandering about the world, trying to remake their lives, or waiting for the opportunity to return to the scene of their former careers. Europe and the Americas, and the sea routes between them, were alive with former Confederates, civil and military. In all, there may have been as many as ten thousand southerners wandering the globe after the war for various reasons, all of them bound together by the single bond of exile from homes and families. Some, ruined by the war, left to seek new lives and fortunes. Others, like Breckinridge, fled indictments and hostility. And many, like Early and Toombs, exiled themselves out of bitterness. Toombs, when a loyal Union man asked him why he did not seek pardon, replied, "Pardon for what? I have not pardoned you all yet." The majority of the exiles, however, wanted to return to their country as soon as the passions of the North and its courts died down. Of all of them, no one desired this more than John C. Breckinridge, a posture which was made the more significant by the fact that, with Davis and Stephens in prison, he was in effect the highest ranking official of the Confederacy still at large. The only other cabinet officer to escape had been Benjamin, but he had already become a barrister in London, and had put his American past behind him to live out his life a British citizen.

This left the full responsibility of leadership, for setting some kind of an example for the thousands of other exiles, squarely with Breckinridge. All sides would want him; the militants who would begin the war anew, the bitter ones who chose to remain exiles for life, and the homesick Confederates who wanted to return when it was safe, or when they could do so without having to stoop to ask for pardon. As a result, he became a symbol, a distinction he did not seek, but which he could not refuse. To those at home he would come to represent the exile, the Confederate without a country; to those abroad he was one of them, a great leader suffering their same privations and longings, bringing dignity to their exile. To all, he would be a symbol of the unbeaten Confederate, independent despite adversity, and disdaining to curb and woo for clemency from his former foes. As he steamed across the Atlantic, Breckinridge did not yet fully realize this new burden that he must bear, but he had been warned, and knew that he was, and would remain, the object of ever-increasing attention. One year to the day before the general and his family reached London, Edwin DeLeon, Confederate propaganda agent in France, told him plainly: "On you, Sir, the eyes of all true Southern men are now fixed, as the destined head of any future movement." The responsibility attendant to this was one not to be taken lightly.[1]

The *Peruvian*'s crossing was an unpleasant one, everyone on board suffering seasickness except Breckinridge, whose experiences in the little *No Name* left him virtually immune to the hazards of sea travel. By August 22 they reached London where they found a warm welcome from Benjamin, Wigfall, Burton Harrison, Sanders, and other former Confederates. The British press noticed his arrival and commented that Breckinridge looked "old and careworn." The general and family left London on August 30, crossed the Channel, and took the train to Paris and the nearby home of old Mann, Mont Po, where they would remain until Breckinridge could arrange for rooms in Paris.[2]

Breckinridge looked forward to taking advantage of the opportunity that exile now afforded him to see first hand all of the places of history and antiquity that he heretofore could see only in his books, but first there was work to be done, another step to take in his quest to give the Confederacy an honorable demise. The government had died in debt, not only to many of its agents, but to foreign creditors as well. A year before, during his brief stay in England after the escape, Breckinridge proposed the appointment of a commission to liquidate all remaining Confederate assets in Europe, using the proceeds to redeem as much as possible of the national debt of the lost cause. Although some funds became available for the defense of Davis, the main object of his suggestion remained unfulfilled. There was

1. Clifford Dowdey, *Experiment in Rebellion* (New York, 1946), 538; Edwin DeLeon to Breckinridge, August 22, 1865, in JCB Papers. No adequate study of the expatriation movement as a whole has yet been produced.
2. Breckinridge Diary, August 14–September 10, 1866, in Prewitt Collection; undated clipping *ca.* August, 1866, from an unidentified London newspaper, in Wigfall MSS.

still a substantial amount of Confederate money and goods not accounted for, and the general and Benjamin assumed the responsibility of collecting what they could. It would hardly do the Confederacy honor if it died leaving scores of bitter investors wailing loudly over their losses. However, as the work of collection began, Breckinridge soon discovered that there was a much more pernicious and potentially damaging source of scandal.[3]

Accusations started at the top and, what was more dismaying, some of these charges had been made public. Upon Breckinridge's arrival in London, one newspaper seemed to speak upon authoritative information when it said that "He has come to look after some funds which are supposed to have been smuggled away by some of the Rebel agents." Then, in the next breath, the tabloid accused Benjamin of having appropriated some three or four thousand pounds of this money just the week before, claiming it as unpaid salary. There were others who suspected the former secretary of state as well, among them Wigfall. He hated Benjamin, and charged that he had set aside some two hundred bales of cotton in England during the war, taking his profits upon making his escape. In addition, Wigfall charged that Benjamin was making deals with other Confederate agents, splitting between them the funds remaining in their hands. In the absence of evidence, it is impossible to say with certainty that Benjamin himself was guilty of this, though it was recalled that many years before, he had been expelled from Yale supposedly for theft. However, even if he was not involved in this disgraceful business, others surely were.[4]

Potentially very embarrassing was the fate of State Department funds in Canada. While in London the year before Breckinridge received a disturbing letter from Captain Wood in Montreal. Beverly Tucker and George Sanders, ex officio members of the mission to Canada, were complaining that Jacob Thompson, commissioner to that country, had gone to Europe with some $300,000 left in his care at the end of the war. Although the general probably did not hear of it for some time, if at all, the trial of the Lincoln assassination conspirators brought out evidence that Thompson actually took considerably more, citing $649,873.20 withdrawn from Confederate accounts in the Bank of Ontario. Whatever sum he took, he was not entitled to it, especially since Benjamin had already sent requisitions for

3. DeLeon to Breckinridge, August 22, 1865, in JCB Papers.
4. Undated clipping, *ca.* August, 1866, from unidentified London newspaper, Lewis Wigfall to Clement Clay, October 17, 1866, in Wigfall MSS; Alvy L. King, *Louis T. Wigfall: Southern Fire-eater* (Baton Rouge, 1970), 224; Meade, *Benjamin*, 24–30, 342–43.

some of it to be applied to debts before the Confederacy fell.

Upon hearing this, Breckinridge may have tried to contact Thompson in Paris, but seems not to have seen him. He also missed seeing Benjamin, but wrote to him after receiving a suspicious letter from Thompson a few days after arriving in Canada. The commissioner told him of an interview held with Benjamin in Paris early in September and claimed to have turned over to Benjamin all of the funds in his hands. "I feel freer and more independent since I have his receipt in full for all monies in my hands or which I had had." Thompson went on to explain his conviction that these receipts would absolve him of all possible charges of the kind made by Tucker and Sanders, concluding, "I have been unwilling to do aught which might seem or be construed to have resulted from selfish considerations." A letter from Benjamin, however, put the lie to all this. The secretary of state, in company with Slidell, had "a somewhat stormy interview with him," during which Benjamin presented evidence that Thompson should have accounted to him for at least £35,000. Thompson, however, claimed the right to retain all of it as due him for the cotton that Federals had burned on his Mississippi plantation. Benjamin showed that he had already appropriated £25,000 of it to pay a London banker, but Thompson stood fast. After consulting with Slidell, Benjamin finally compromised by taking £12,000, and leaving the remaining £23,000—the equivalent of $113,780—with the commissioner, promising to make no further claims on him. It was the best that could be done, Benjamin explained, for a scandal must be avoided at all costs. "This is a most repulsive subject," he told the general. Upon reaching Paris, Breckinridge himself called on Thompson, where the commissioner freely exhibited his receipts from Benjamin, unaware that the general recognized in them the proof of what Benjamin had said. There are hints that Thompson may have misappropriated even more funds, but on this charge alone there was proof enough of his larceny. Breckinridge concluded from his investigations that, as Benjamin suggested, there was nothing to be done without making the disgrace public. It was, indeed, a most repulsive subject.[5]

While Breckinridge oversaw several of these transactions, the sources of his own funds would become the subject of some speculation. A host

5. John Taylor Wood to Breckinridge, July 5, 1865, in Breckinridge MSS, FC; Jacob Thompson to Breckinridge, September 14, 1865, Judah Benjamin to Breckinridge, November 30, 1865, in JCB Papers; Breckinridge Diary, September 4, 1866, in Prewitt Collection. See William C. Davis, "The Conduct of Mr. Thompson," *Civil War Times Illustrated*, IX (May, 1970), 4-7, 43-47. The originals of Thompson's receipts are in the John B. Castleman MSS, FC.

of friends in the United States offered to help him, and reports did circulate that he was living from "huge contributions of money made him by friends." The general himself emphatically denied this, however. He was living off of several thousand dollars saved from his salary as a general which, apparently, he had transferred in gold to Cuba sometime before the war was over, probably as a safeguard against defeat. This he deposited with the Toronto banking firm of W. B. Phipps, from which he would make periodic withdrawals during the exile. In addition, his old friend Beck offered to make some sales of his property at St. Paul and Superior to finance him, and Breckinridge may well have taken advantage of the opportunity. Whatever the case, the money on which the general and his family lived during these years was unquestionably his own.[6]

With these last vestiges of official business concluded, Breckinridge was free to indulge his interests. Two months before, on July 3, the Battle of Sadowa had decided the Seven Weeks War between Prussia and Austria, and the Prussian victors, in celebration of their triumph, organized a gala military review to be held in Berlin late in September. Although he never regarded himself as primarily a military man, Breckinridge felt a keen interest in the art of war and decided to attend. Leaving on September 12, he arrived before the spectacle was to take place, and wandered through the strange streets of Berlin looking on as the preparations were made. Cannon and garlands of flowers were everywhere, the children swarming over both in a manner which induced the general to reflect a bit on the militaristic state. "How alike are civilized and savage man. In Africa when a slain Lion is brought to the village, the Elders call up the little boys to look upon him and encourage them to bend their tiny bows upon the monster, to accustom them to his aspect and to prepare them for the chase. Here the Prussian boys may be seen marching in military order—shouting the names of their generals—clambering over the captured guns—placing their little ears against the muzzles, and fancying that they hear in the echoed noises of the city, the sounds of successful battle at Sadowa."

When the procession was over, he left by train to join Mary and Fanny at Vevay, Switzerland, where they had gone for his wife's health. On the way he stopped in Cologne, and was dismayed by the proliferation of holy relics and, especially, the "immense number of bones." He left somehow unsatisfied, noting that "there is a great deal of interesting antiquity here, on which has been engrafted much superstition and trash." [7]

6. Cincinnati *Enquirer*, October 27, 1866; M. B. Phipps to Breckinridge, October 10, 1867, James B. Beck to Breckinridge, May 14, 1867, in JCB Papers.
7. Breckinridge Diary, September 10–25, 1866, in Prewitt Collection.

In Vevay, Breckinridge found friends, among them Colonel Andrew Polk of Tennessee. Together, one day, they went to the Hotel Byron to pay a visit to another old acquaintance, Major General George B. McClellan, former commander of the Federal Army of the Potomac. McClellan was surprised by their visit, but glad to see Breckinridge, whom he found "had not changed at all & was as cordial as ever. I cannot see that any bitterness is left in him—he seems to accept the result [of the war] in a truly manly spirit, & I believe that he would make today a good & loyal citizen." [8]

The Breckinridges left Switzerland for Paris in early November and took an apartment at the Grand Hotel after spending several weeks with the William Gwins. Meanwhile the general, having received a number of invitations, decided to go to London for a visit. Parliament would be opening in March, and he had always wanted to witness the attendant ceremonies. This would be the perfect opportunity. Leaving on January 31, 1867, the general arrived in London the next day, and spent two months in the pleasant company of friends and fellow exiles. Lord Campbell did make arrangements for a Parliament pass for Breckinridge to see the opening but, due to a misunderstanding over the time, he missed the event. Nevertheless, the general sat in on the debates often thereafter, hearing all of the great statesmen of the day, including Gladstone, Disraeli, Rosebuck, Lagand, and others. His only disappointment was in missing John Bright.

London was alive with southerners in midwandering, and Breckinridge saw many. Benjamin had him to dinner occasionally, and there he met McRae, who now spoke of emigrating to South America to make a new start. Wigfall was still there, bitter as always, and so was Longstreet's old adjutant, Colonel Osmun Latrobe. The general was often in their company, and called on a number of other friends and former acquaintances, including some enemies in the late war. And occasionally there was a reminder that feelings still ran high with many. When he called on Francis Young, whom he had known as one of Colonel Edwin Baker's aides, the gentleman, who was at Baker's side when he fell at Ball's Bluff, refused to see him. [9]

The British public was as hospitable as Young was rude. Breckinridge found himself socially in demand on all sides. Lieutenant Colonel James Fremantle, Coldstream Guards, who spent three months with Lee in 1863, introduced himself immediately by presenting Breckinridge with a copy of

8. George B. McClellan to C. H. Wright, November 14, 1866, in Huntington Miscellaneous Collection, HL.

9. Breckinridge Diary, November 8, 1866–April 1, 1867, in Prewitt Collection; H. Fuller to Breckinridge, January 30, 1867, L. H. Gregory to Breckinridge, February 12, 1867, Judah P. Benjamin to Breckinridge, February 12, 1867, Francis Young to Breckinridge, March 30, 1867, all in JCB Papers.

his widely read and acclaimed book *Three Months in the Southern States, April–June 1863*. He dined frequently with the general, and arranged for him a temporary membership in the Traveller's Club. Members of Parliament had the Kentuckian to dinner at the Commons, and the Royal United Service Institution made him an honorary member. Among the most prominent of those seeking his company was Alexander J. Beresford-Hope, M.P. for the University of Cambridge, and formerly a champion of the Confederate cause. He and his wife became most fond of Breckinridge, having him as their guest in their city and country homes. Personal acquaintance with the general, wrote Hope, produced "a warm esteem and respect, and a vivid impression of his eminent abilities. I have often since remarked that out of the persons of distinction with whom, in the course of my life, I have in various ways been thrown, General Breckinridge was among those who had most irresistibly struck me with a feeling of ability and ready power." Indeed, Hope was so impressed by the Kentuckian that he expected him to resume his former position of prominence in the public affairs of the United States. And to cap the list of notables with whom the general dined were Prime Minister William Gladstone, and the Archbishop of Canterbury, both of whom Breckinridge found most engaging.[10]

Despite the excellent reception given Breckinridge by most of the English, there was at least one case in which the welcome was somewhat less than cordial. While there he received a luncheon invitation from a countess who, as it happened, had also advertised for a new footman, the requirements being primarily a stately figure. Breckinridge, mistaking the appointed time, arrived too early, and was accidentally ushered into her presence unannounced, the countess mistaking him for a prospective domestic.

"Have you a reference from your last place?" she asked.

Breckinridge, taking in the situation and determined to have some fun with it, answered with studied calm, "Yes, my lady."

"What were your duties?"

"Well, my lady, in the last three places I held, I was Vice-President of the United States, Major General in the Confederate Army, and Secretary of War of the Confederate States of America!"

The countess, stupified, could only utter, "Oh! General Breckenridge." The general did not get the job.[11]

10. Arthur Fremantle to Breckinridge, February 11, March 7, 26, 1867, B. Buefss to Breckinridge, March 7, 1867, Gregory to Breckinridge, March 17, 1867, Francis Lawley to Breckinridge, March 27, 1867, Archbishop of Canterbury to Breckinridge, March 25, 1867, all in JCB Papers; Louisville *Courier-Journal*, November 13, 1875; A. J. B. Hope to A. Patterson, June 5, 1875, in Prewitt Collection.

11. Louise Giraud Wright, *A Southern Girl in '61* (New York, 1905), 28–29.

Breckinridge visited extensively in England. The insane asylum at Bedlam interested him particularly, and he toured it late in February, his curiosity over its practices sparked by his earlier association with the Danville Asylum. Lords gave him reviews of their pet regiments, the noted portraitist B. F. Reinhart wanted to paint him and submit the painting to an exhibition of the Royal Academy, he gathered stamps to send to Cliff for his collection, found time to play cupid for a young lady in Paris who admired one of his London friends, and continued his dormant Masonic work, taking some new degrees not available in America, and becoming one of the highest ranking of American Masons. He seemed to have but two goals for the moment: to gratify his long curiosity about the places he had always wanted to see; and to pass the time. Time lay heavy on his hands.[12]

The general returned to Paris in April, to remain for the next six weeks. It was a busy time, and a pleasant one, for the weather in France turned warmer that month, and the exiles took full advantage of the outdoor beauty of a Paris spring. A typical day for Breckinridge began with breakfast at his hotel followed by a long walk which often took him to the general agency office of Major James Weston, who was with the general at Missionary Ridge. Weston's was a meeting place for many old Confederates, and there Breckinridge usually saw Mann, Major Caleb Huse, ordnance agent in Europe, the noted legal writer Judge Samuel Perkins, and General Ripley of South Carolina. Weston got most of the American newspapers, and here the general read of affairs at home, though the consistent run of sad news from the South soon gave him a distaste for reading the tabloids.

Breckinridge passed his afternoons calling on friends, driving a carriage through Paris, or walking. It was not unusual for him to meet the Emperor Napoleon III on his jaunts, finding the ruler "a short, stout, heavy looking, colorless man, but one of intellect." And he did not neglect the ladies. Breckinridge always delighted in the company of women, young or old, and they in turn sought his wit and conversation to pass the long afternoons. A not untypical day found him dining with Mrs. Hunt, Mrs. Colquitt, Mrs. George, and Estelle Carson, then calling on Miss Cumming and Miss Jameson, Mrs. Battle and Mrs. Barnwell, Miss Rankin, Mrs. Swan and daughter, her sister Mrs. MacKensie, Mrs. Lowe, Mrs. Walker and Mrs. Rice. All of this Breckinridge regarded as "a pretty good day's work."

12. James Weatherby to Breckinridge, February 20, 1867, Lord Sandys to Breckinridge, February 4, 1867, B. F. Reinhart to Breckinridge, March 1, 1867, John W. Breckinridge to Breckinridge, February 15, 25, 1867, Julia Colquitt to Breckinridge, May 15, 1867, all in JCB Papers; Cincinnati *Enquirer*, May 18, 1875.

The general's evenings he devoted to dining with friends, receiving callers at his hotel, or playing whist and eucre with partners ranging from Weston and Thomas Courtenay, organizer of a select secret service in the Trans-Mississippi, to General Benjamin S. Roberts, United States Army. Not infrequently, Breckinridge escorted his guests home, and then went off by himself for a long walk in the park, where he found that "nothing could be more clear, calm and lovely than the moonlight night." It was on these solitary walks, often late into the night, that he thought most of his exile, and his longing to go home.

One of the more pleasant diversions in Paris that spring was the International Exposition. Breckinridge went often, where his interest took him consistently to the industrial exhibits. There he spoke at length with the designers and engineers, among them Scott Russell, builder of the world's largest ship the *Great Eastern*, and Cyrus W. Field, who was using that same ship to lay a telegraphic cable across the Atlantic. Cyrus McCormick, then exhibiting his reapers, found the general quite interesting, and called on him often thereafter. At the same time, Breckinridge found the exposition an excellent means of meeting visiting Americans, often with humorous results. Once, when being introduced to a "demme saint-like person from Boston," he scarcely concealed his amusement at beholding the shock the New Englander felt at seeing the famous traitor Breckinridge face to face. When not viewing the exhibits at the exposition, the general spent a good deal of his time at his rooms writing to his children. Cliff was now entering Washington College on a scholarship provided specifically for a son of Breckinridge's by Lord Ashburton. Young Mary was still in New York, and Cabell's whereabouts were something of a mystery. He did not write to his parents for nearly a year after leaving them in Canada, and Breckinridge worried over his son, earnestly hoping that he might find himself before it was too late. In May there finally came a letter from him, and the general's faith was restored, a burden lifted from his mind.[13]

Other events that spring left Breckinridge more troubled. Europe teemed with people, many of them United States agents trying to locate the remnants of Confederate assets, and several of these approached Breckinridge. One April evening while walking home from the Louvre, he stopped at a café for an ice and was joined by George Sanders and General Herbert

13. Charles Helm to Breckinridge, January 5, 1867, John T. Pickett to Breckinridge, December 24, 1866, Breckinridge to Clifton R. Breckinridge, November 19, 1866, June 10, 1867, J. Cabell Breckinridge to Breckinridge, May 12, 1867, in JCB Papers; Breckinridge Diary, April 3–May 2, 1867, in Prewitt Collection; Breckinridge to Mary D. Breckinridge, April 21, 1867, in possession of Mrs. Kenneth Kirkland.

Titus, a supposed agent for the United States Treasury Department. Sanders left, and Breckinridge and Titus went to call on Courtenay. There the general's host spoke at length about Confederate property in Europe, and it soon became evident to Breckinridge that the former secret agent had designs on any such wealth. "I think he and Titus understand each other," the general confided to his diary, "but I told him I had no knowledge on the subject and would have nothing to do with it." Soon thereafter Breckinridge learned that another person, a Mrs. Whittaker Bush, was trying to get money in London by using his name. Now she happened to be at the Grand Hotel in Paris, and the general confronted her with what he had heard. She denied it, but did admit that she had mentioned his name among others as needing money to buy arms to continue the conflict in America. She acted by direction of a Colonel Howell, she said, giving the general "a long rigmarole." "She I think an adventuress," he decided, "and Howell a great rascal—the whole thing a lie from end to end.—Shall settle Howell." Unfortunately, Breckinridge never caught up with the enterprising Colonel Howell.[14]

As late as the summer of 1867, while the exiles still preserved something of the old southern society, there were those who sought to revive the Confederacy militarily as well, and not all of them were unselfishly motivated. To all who proposed schemes for rejuvenating the "lost cause" Breckinridge turned a deaf ear. However, he did have several discussions with those who sought the economic rebuilding of the South. General Robert V. Richardson had a plan to get capital to lend southern planters. With Mann, Breckinridge talked over the ways to initiate a southern export trade to Europe, and spoke with James Bulloch on a proposal for a southern carrying trade. With General Ripley he talked over a scheme to boost southern manufacturing, and on his own the general looked into mining in Nevada and Colorado. Although nothing came of any of these ideas, they aptly represent the difference between the exiles in Mexico and South America, and those in Europe. While the former sought new, permanent homes, the latter looked ever toward returning to their beloved South, never losing touch with its growth and development. Of these hopefuls, Breckinridge was the archetype. No matter where he was, home was always on his mind, and, if he could not be there, he could at least plan for its future in the hope that he might one day return. No exile better symbolized this longing

14. Breckinridge Diary, April 26, May 15, June 6, 1867, in Prewitt Collection; J. L. O'Sullivan to Breckinridge, June 4, 1867, in JCB Papers.

to return than did Breckinridge, and few wandered farther than he in the waiting.[15]

This summer there came news which might have given him cause to hope that the day was not far off when he could go back. Jefferson Davis, still untried, had been released on bail. Beck wrote hopefully to Breckinridge, "I never thought until now that there was any propriety or chance in any move for you. I have never had the courage to write to you before because I never till now saw a ray of hope. I feel now that all you ought to expect can be done." [16]

Breckinridge must have had the prospects for his return on his mind ever since February, when interesting news came from Kentucky. At the meeting of the Ballard County Democracy in January, Colonel O. Turner offered a resolution nominating Breckinridge for the governorship. A roar went up from the delegates, and the resolution was adopted unanimously by acclamation. At the state convention the next month, when Ballard County put the general in nomination, the cheers nearly disrupted the conduct of business, and were not soon stilled. Those in the party who disliked Breckinridge were seen almost to shudder at the mention of him, and the president of the convention, John W. Stevenson, admitted to the mass that the general's name trembled on his lips. Nevertheless, the convention thought it inadvisable to nominate a former Confederate so soon after the war, and Clifton wrote to his father explaining that the reaction to his name going before the Democrats was evidence that he was too popular for the Radicals to allow him to return yet. This was confirmed by William Preston sometime later, when he wrote that "in my opinion, you are more respected and loved by the people than you ever were in your hours of youthful popularity." [17]

Several people in the United States had taken an interest in Breckinridge's case, among them the widely known editor of the New York *Tribune*, Horace Greeley. In April he wrote to George Shea that "it seems to me a pity that the presence and counsel of Gen. Breckinridge are wanting. We need them, not in the South proper, but in his own Kentucky." The

15. A. Dudley Mann to Breckinridge, October 1, 1866, in B. MSS; Wood to Breckinridge, July 13, 1865, in Breckinridge MSS, FC.

16. Beck to Breckinridge, May 14, 1867, in JCB Papers.

17. Charles Ivey to Breckinridge, February 17, 1867, in Breckinridge MSS, FC; O. Turner to Breckinridge, January 1867, R. W. Woolley to Breckinridge, March 3, 1867, Clifton R. Breckinridge to Breckinridge, March 23, 1867, William Preston to Breckinridge, August 6, 1867, all in JCB Papers; Coulter, *Civil War and Readjustment*, 319.

United States was still Breckinridge's country, said the editor, and he did
not believe that the general would be molested if he returned. Furthermore, he believed that Breckinridge did not need a pardon. Upon learning
that President Johnson had expressed an interest in the general's affairs,
Greeley was displeased over the publicity that it might attract. "Let him
come quietly home and go to work and let the fools who wish to befriend
him simply hold their peace and let him alone." Greeley even wrote to
Breckinridge himself. "Come back," he said, "go to your own beloved
Kentucky; aid in restoring the shattered fortunes of the South and your
country, and I will be responsible for your safety, and assure your immu-
nity from molestation or arrest." The general remained grateful for Greeley's interest for the rest of his life and two years later commented, "Shall
I ever cease to respect and cherish him?" Senator Reverdy Johnson showed
a similar concern, "For Mr. B.," he wrote, "I entertain the kindest feelings,
& am willing to forget the few past sad years & remember only those which
preceded them." He too believed that Breckinridge could, and should, return without fear of interference.[18]

Indeed, it appears that the general might well have heeded Greeley's and
Johnson's call, and returned without incident, and Kentucky might have
been greatly aided by his presence during a critical time. Experience had
shown by now that he would not meet with treatment any worse than
short imprisonment and, indeed, he could probably have surrendered himself at the war's end and suffered nothing more than a year or two behind
Federal bars as Davis had. Indications now pointed to dismissal of all of the
treason cases pending against Confederates, and some like Toombs had already gone home. However, no one else's case was quite like Breckinridge's. Kentucky did not secede; he went South on his own. Many felt
that he had treacherously used his position in the Senate during 1861 to aid
the Confederacy, preaching his heresy even after Bull Run. And his expulsion as a "traitor" could not be forgotten. Even Davis was not as hated as
Breckinridge in some circles, especially among the Radicals in Kentucky
who saw in his return a threat to their hold on the state.[19]

Breckinridge did want to go home, so much so that now it was becoming
public knowledge, though to the mention of the governorship he turned a
deaf ear. "I would not accept any office within the gift of the people, if I

18. Horace Greeley to George Shea, April 8, 1867, in B. MSS; Greeley to "Mrs.
Henningson," May 26, 1867, Reverdy Johnson to Henningson, May 22, 1867, all in JCB
Papers; Baltimore *Baltimorian*, May 22, 1875.
19. Jonathan T. Dorris, *Pardon and Amnesty under Lincoln and Johnson* (Chapel
Hill, N.C., 1953), 274–75; Dorris, "Pardoning John C. Breckinridge," 319–24.

could get one," he declared. "I am growing in years, and I have been losing in fortune. My family is increasing—I need money, and look to my profession, not only as the surest, but as the most suitable and available means of providing it." For several months the press on both sides of the ocean had been speculating on a statement that he made to a British correspondent, supposedly admitting that the North had been more magnanimous than the laws of nations required, and that the South should submit to the Reconstruction acts being passed, as they were more merciful than they had a right to expect. Friends urged him to issue a denial of the report but, since no such retraction was forthcoming, it may well have been accurate. This summer, talking with an old friend Kate Coyle, he admitted that he was very anxious to return and, furthermore, that he would "*submit* to, and *urge* the *reconstruction* of the Union upon any *basis or terms*." Her husband John Coyle saw President Johnson on the subject when she reported her conversation, and the president promised that, while he could not pardon Breckinridge with the indictments still against him, the general would not be molested if he returned.[20]

The reasonably certain knowledge that he could safely go home made more difficult for Breckinridge his decision to remain an exile. To go back with the sufferance of the authorities was not enough. He had to return free, with no necessity to ask or receive official pardon. It was the only way that he could go back without tacitly admitting that he and the South had been wrong, that he was truly a criminal guilty as charged, and that he felt that by acting according to the dictates of his conscience he had truly been in error. If he did this—he who had been the representative of the entire South in 1860, and now her chief official still uncaptured—he would be letting down not only himself, but all those Confederates who now looked to him as the symbol of their conviction of right, and one of their few remaining tokens of independence. Clifton never admired his father more than when he saw the general's resolution when "the question was painfully presented whether you should compromise your principles and return to a comfortable home, or remain in exile and possibly in great want, and preserve your manhood and honor untarnished." Breckinridge could not come home until all Confederates could return free from fear of indictments or recriminations. Indeed, many of his friends, much as they wanted

20. New York *Times,* January 2, 1869; Blanton Duncan to Breckinridge. January 9, 1867, Fuller to Breckinridge, January 26, 1867, Ivey to Pickett, August 8, 1867, Ivey to Breckinridge. August 10, 1867, clipping from an unidentified newspaper *ca.* January 1867, all in JCB Papers.

him back, did not want the general to seek pardon or return under any cloud. "I would not like to see the General here," said Stoddard Johnston, and Colonel O. Turner, who nominated Breckinridge in Ballard County, expressed to the general that "I have been gratified that there was one heroic Patriot that preferred honorable exile, to prostrating himself at the feet of power to ask for favors." Of course there were a few who disapproved of the general's exile, like his friendly foe Humphrey Marshall, who declared that Breckinridge's "present status is willfully absurd," but Charles Ivey, Breckinridge's former clerk in Washington, spoke for most when he wrote, "I hope dear General that . . . you will remain an exile to the day of your death rather than return here to suffer the humiliation all have had to suffer. No dear General, God forbid that you should ever ask pardon." [21]

Obviously, De Leon had been right when he said that all southern eyes were going to be fixed on Breckinridge, and the general sensed the importance he had unwittingly assumed in the postwar mind of the South. That importance was still growing this summer of 1867 as he entered his third year of exile and, even if his longings might have persuaded him to return to his country, his conscience would never have allowed it. Breckinridge had an important role to play and he would live up to it. Sadly, all he could do now was to congratulate Davis on *his* good fortune, express the hope that they might soon meet again, and wait.[22]

21. Clifton R. Breckinridge to Breckinridge, May 13, 1874, J. Stoddard Johnston to Mary C. Breckinridge, November 10, 1867, Turner to Breckinridge, January 1867, Ivey to Breckinridge, August 10, 1867, all in JCB Papers; Humphrey Marshall to Edward O. Guerrant, June 20, 1867, in Guerrant MSS, FC.

22. Breckinridge to Jefferson Davis, June 15, 1867, in Jefferson Davis MSS, Museum of the Confederacy, Richmond, Va.

CHAPTER 3

Thank God You Are Free

"Aug. 26 to 30 Col. Burbank came, with David, on 26th. . . . Have agreed to go with him, on his invitation, to Constantinople, the Holy Land, Egypt, Greece and Italy. We think of starting about Nov. 1st." [1]

Breckinridge was excited. At last he would see the ancient sites that had for so long filled his reading hours with fascination, the scenes of the great dramas of history, the fountainhead of democracy, and the lands of the Bible. The anticipation he felt was not just that of a history enthusiast. During the years of war and exile, Breckinridge pondered continually the waste and destruction, not only of life, but of the products of the efforts of generations of builders as well, the men who, in his eyes, had left a worthwhile mark of their passing. From the perspective of that little boat crossing to Cuba, his own life seemed in retrospect anything but successful, hardly productive of lasting good. Now, when Clifton intimated a desire to go into the law, his father was not enthusiastic. "I confess," he told the boy, "that if I were beginning life and felt an aptitude for those pursuits which develop the material resources of the world as Engineering and the like, I would adopt one of them both for usefullness to Mankind and profit to myself. But one must find out what he is suited for, and then strive to excell in it." Thus the Breckinridge who toured the Old World would be more than a man interested in history. He would be as well one profoundly aware of what the men of the past had left for the future, their spiritual, social, and architectural legacy, their lasting contribution, their "usefullness to Mankind." [2]

The general's companions on the trip would be an old friend from Henderson, Kentucky, Colonel David Burbank, and James Shepard of North

1. Breckinridge Diary, in Prewitt Collection.
2. Breckinridge to Clifton R. Breckinridge, October 7, 1867, in JCB Papers.

Carolina. Breckinridge had actually planned to return to Canada in August or September, but the prospect of the trip, Mary's still frail condition, his pleasure with the progress of his children in their French schools, and the state of his own health, persuaded him to postpone his return until the coming spring. The inactivity and burden of exile were telling on Breckinridge. He was graying more now, and chafed at the boredom of life without occupation. He needed this trip to take his mind away from his situation. Mary saw it, and heartily approved of the journey.[3]

The two months before his departure passed slowly for Breckinridge, though he found much to occupy his time. The unceasing social calls and visits continued unabated, and he widened his circle to include one Henry Given of Georgia, a former slave, "a bright mulatto and worthy fellow." He and Given exchanged calls, and the general even took time to help the Negro with a marital difficulty. He had married a white woman from Boston whom Breckinridge found "rather good looking and very intelligent," who, nevertheless, seemed unaware of the then unnatural aspect of her interracial marriage. At her husband's request, the general spent an afternoon with them, speaking "very plain with her about the singularity of such unions," advising her of the derision she must expect. Breckinridge had spent three years on the battlefield risking his life largely to keep Given a slave, regardless of his own hostility to slavery. Now that he, unlike so many others, accepted the verdict of Appomattox, the Negro was a man, perhaps still not a biological equal, but a man just the same.[4]

With the prospect of several months' traveling before him, Breckinridge made a last visit to London. He toured the ironworks of the Laird brothers of Birkenhead, builders of the great Confederate privateers *Florida* and *Alabama*, boarded and inspected the *Great Eastern*, and rode and dined with all the old friends. The high point of the visit, however, came on his last day in England when he and Latrobe went to Chelsea for a quiet afternoon with one of the greatest intellectuals of the century, Thomas Carlyle. The two found each other kindred spirits in their thoughts on war and the human condition, and the general and the writer enjoyed their conversation. Breckinridge found Carlyle "rather tall, slender, stooping, iron-gray hair matted carelessly over a forehead of great pones; shocking old dressing gown." Indeed, the writer's whole appearance betrayed a carelessness which was, nevertheless, somewhat neat. Most impressive, however, was

3. Mary C. Breckinridge to Ann Johnson, December 11, 1867, in Mary C. Breckinridge MSS; Clifton R. Breckinridge to W. C. P. Breckinridge, July 21, 1867, in B. MSS.
4. Breckinridge Diary, September 9, 1867, in Prewitt Collection.

his face. As the general sat with him, Carlyle bore "the aspect of one,—half sorrowful, half disgusted. . . . A great sad thinker rises now before me like a serene, mournful apparition of supernatural power, at once pointing out, swearing at, and bewailing the short comings and notably the shams and hypocrisies of the world. But a good heart withal, and a love for the manly and the true. We talked of the Reform Bill (so called), of some of the public characters of England, of the Jamaica insurrection [of 1865] and Gov. [Edward J.] Eyre, of the condition of things in America, etc. His remarks about Disraeli and Gladstone were anything but complimentary." For Breckinridge, this meeting with Carlyle would remain one of the memorable occasions of his life.[5]

Once back in Paris, the general spent the month of October in attending the Exposition, gathering his money, and making final preparations for the trip. Finally, on November 13, Mary and Mrs. Burbank made a warm early breakfast for their husbands, and then saw them off at the Paris depot, bound for the Rhine. With him Breckinridge took his diary and a resolve. For some time now journals in the United States and Europe had been imploring him to write for them, anything that he wished, and for handsome sums. One editor in England offered to pay him £20 a month just for sending in a letter each week for publication. Though he refused all of these offers, still retaining his old dislike of writing, Breckinridge seldom let up his preparations for a book, constantly collecting his military and political papers and reports. Now, at last, he was resolved. He would write a book. But somehow it was not to be the book that most would expect and want of him. Characteristic of his ever-temperate view of himself, he chose not to write of his vice-presidency or the tumultuous but romantic years as a general. He was proud of them, but relatively unimpressed. Instead, in cooperation with James Shepard, this man who had lived and known intimately the most important years of his century chose another topic for his book, its title: "Travels in the East." [6]

All that day they rode, and the next dawn found them passing along the Rhine to Strasbourg, where Breckinridge immediately began his inspection of the old ruins and a climb up the Strasbourg Cathedral, supposedly the

5. *Ibid.*, September 11–28, 1867; Breckinridge to Mary C. Breckinridge, September 15, 1867, in possession of Walter R. Agard. Curiously, this letter is the only one known to exist written by Breckinridge to his wife. Since she counseled him to destroy her letters to him—which he did not do—she very likely did so with his letters to her.
6. Breckinridge Diary, November 11–13, 1867, in Prewitt Collection; Colin MacKensie to Breckinridge, October 29, 1867, A. M. Atwood to Breckinridge. October 11, 22, 1867, Frances Breckinridge to Breckinridge, November 26, 1867, in JCB Papers.

tallest stone spire in the world. With an awe not unmixed with irreverent wit, he pronounced it "a wonderful pile," and then left for Munich. Here for two days he enjoyed the statuary in the museums, and the three pints of fine beer that five cents bought at the Royal Brewery. Another two days' travel put him in Vienna, and here his first call was on the American consul who, as it happened, was Brigadier General Sidney Post. Back in December 1862, Post fought Breckinridge and Bragg at Stones River. Now he extended every courtesy to Breckinridge, entertaining him as his guest a few nights later for a concert of Strauss waltzes. Breckinridge and the consul became close enough in these few days in Vienna that the Kentuckian could unburden himself of the pain his exile caused him despite the excitement of the trip. He never forgot his situation. "In fact, Gen. Post," he confided, "I am a man without a country." [7]

From Vienna it was but a few hours by rail to Buda and Pest, Hungary, where the general, Burbank, Shepard, and their courier, booked passage on the *Jusef Carl* for the trip down the Danube to Ruschuk. The voyage proved slow and tedious, the river was filled with floating cakes of ice, and the captain barely competent to manage the ship. Nevertheless, the scenery was exquisite, the weather mild for that season, and inside the cabin a German entertained the passengers with card tricks. However, Breckinridge found his chief amusement, as he would throughout the trip, in the infinite variety of the different nationalities on board. In an argument the day after leaving Pest, the captain tried to persuade his passengers to transfer to another boat, while they steadfastly refused. German, French, Hungarian, and Arabic, were banded about freely in the melee, while the pompous, though harmless, Burbank added to the confusion some energetic English. Breckinridge, relishing the scene, stood back aloof, "silent but observant," in his amusement. Then in another obscure corner of the cabin he noticed two Turks, "composed and happy in being still." They remained to him a constant source of amusement, winning his respect for their dignified reserve. They were, too, something of a humbling influence. When the boat passed into the Drave and reached Belgrade, the passengers transferred to another vessel. Only Breckinridge and the Turks remained undisturbed by the change, but then they accidentally occupied his place in the cabin of the new boat and, seeing them there, he first grew impatient and began "to think of them as nothing but Turks, etc., having no rights." Then he caught himself, realized what he was thinking, and was forced to "laugh out at the

7. Breckinridge Diary, November 13–24, 1867, in Prewitt Collection; Superior (Wis.) *Times,* May 1875.

mean feeling." For the remainder of the trip to Ruschuk, Breckinridge spent the bulk of his time in silent observation and admiration of their simple dignity. Through more changes in ships, crowding, and tension, he marveled at them. While everyone else hustled and argued through the twelve-day journey, as tempers flared and voices screamed in confusion, Breckinridge watched them as they sat quietly smoking, looking "gratified at the existing state of things." [8]

From Ruschuk, the general's party took a train to Varna on the Black Sea, and here they boarded another steamer for the trip to Constantinople, arriving at last on December 15. He spent two days in the ancient city, and here bid a silent farewell to his beloved Turks, though not before noting wryly that they as well as their fellow countrymen "have room in [the] seat of their breeches for a bushel of meal." Then the general boarded ship once more, passed through the Dardanelles, and found himself in the Aegean. Finally, on the morning of December 20, he sighted a piece of land he had read about and wished to see since childhood, "The coast of Greece!" [9]

That evening he arrived in Athens and, the next day, on a "morning lovely beyond expression," he rode up to the base of the Acropolis and ascended to the Parthenon. The majesty of the scene was awesome. "This is no place for description," he told his diary. "Now the sun is rising over the range of Hymettus (famed for bees), beyond which, but invisible, is the plain of Marathon . . . the whole scene surpassingly picturesque and beautiful." Breckinridge went over the ruins of the Temple of Jupiter, the Theater of Bacchus, Mars Hill where St. Paul spoke, and paid particular attention to the hill where his boyhood models Democrites and Pericles addressed the assembled citizens of Athens. Nearby he found the prison of Socrates, where the ancient thinker gave his life for the right to think freely. As he sat in the crumbling cell chamber, Breckinridge perhaps felt a bond between himself and the philosopher, for just such a prison cell might be awaiting him now in his own homeland.

Later that day the general boarded the *Persia* and, after a rough night, reached the port of Siros. Moving on, they spent Christmas at Smyrna, Turkey, and then set out for the Mediterranean. Aboard the ship was about as mixed a complement of religions and nationalities as he could have wished for. There were Arabs from Algiers bound for Mecca, Turks going to the same destination, three Russian pilgrims heading for Jerusalem, a Mussel-

8. Breckinridge Diary, November 28–December 8, 1867, in Prewitt Collection.
9. *Ibid.*, December 9–20, 1867.

man praying every sunset while the ship's officers argued over the direction
to Mecca, and a fat Turk who was "heaving and pitching at his devotions,"
much to the delight of some other Russians and an Armenian Christian. In
this sea of confusion, Breckinridge thought he saw an island of sanity, a
Frenchman. But here his own intimate knowledge of the Bible and ancient
history caught him up, revealing that those who lived nearer than he to
the scenes of the great past civilizations, did not necessarily know as much
about them. He asked the Frenchman if the ship would pass within sight
of Patmos.

"Patmos? Patmos?"

"Yes. The island to which Apostle John was banished, and where he
wrote the book of Revelation."

"Oh, did he?"

The general saw Patmos, all right, but thereafter was a little more careful
of asking strangers for directions. There was too much danger of missing
what he wanted to see.[10]

Going on to Rhodes, Breckinridge and Shepard looked over the ancient
ruins, noting that there was no sign of the Colossus, and in the following
days sailed farther east past Cyprus to Mersin and Alexandretta, Turkey,
then south, past Latakia, and down the rugged coast of Syria to Tripoli.
While on ship by the old pirate city, Breckinridge made a New Year's
resolution, pledging to give up drinking. He had never had a liquor problem, though he enjoyed a good whiskey when it was available, but seeing
the drunkenness so widespread in the army during the war turned him
against drinking almost completely. He continually advised his sons against
it, and probably felt that his own health would be improved by abstinence.
Now, it promised to be a very dry New Year indeed.[11]

The next morning they arrived in Beirut and spent the remainder of the
day making arrangements for the overland journey to Damascus. They
hired a guide, Nejim Bocharte, for five dollars per day, and put him in
charge of getting the pack animals and provisions ready for the trip. Setting out on January 2, they went over the old Damascus road, crossing the
Lebanon Mountains. Along the way, Breckinridge could not help but be
amused by Bocharte's array of armament, an old double-barreled shotgun,
a revolver, and what the general described as "something between a bowie
knife and Roman short sword." The guide promised earnestly to protect
them from all dangers, and appeared bent on doing so.

10. *Ibid.*, December 22–26, 1867.   11. *Ibid.*, December 27–31, 1867.

That same evening they reached Baalbek where, after passing the night, Breckinridge spent most of the next day among the ruins of the ancient city, awestruck. The day before he had measured the supposed tomb of Noah at El Casak, and now he wielded his measure again on the city walls, explored its temples of the Sun and Jupiter, and marveled at the enormity of their stone pillars. The fluted columns throughout the ruin he found "grander and equal in grace and beauty to those at Athens." Indeed, the size and splendor of the ruin as a whole impressed Breckinridge more than anything else he would see on his tour. "There is nothing so vast in all the world," he wrote of Baalbek. "The united efforts of Christendom could not replace the whole on that spot, in its original perfection, in forty years." Breckinridge the armchair historian was rapidly becoming Breckinridge the amateur archaeologist.[12]

Continuing westward, the party finally reached Damascus on January 6, and the Kentuckian found the city fascinating. He visited the House of Judas, the place of Paul's conversion and the spot where he was let down the wall in a basket, and the tomb of Mohamet's wife. Walking through the city streets, he visited the bazaars, a Turkish bath, and saw the fine art of "*making* antiques" displayed, just as the craftsman was finishing "one of the time of Solomon." In the evenings he took in the coffee houses, and tried his hand at a hookah. It involved "much sucking and little smoke," he found, and went back to a dependable cheroot. Then, after four days in the ancient city, Breckinridge boarded a train for the trip back to Beirut.[13]

A steamer, after considerable delay, took them on to Jaffa, and on January 16, 1868, the general's forty-seventh birthday, they rode after a day's journey into the city of Jerusalem. On the way Breckinridge came upon an Arab soldier in the act of stealing a peasant's donkey. Immediately he stepped in "with as strong [an] air of authority as I can muster," and sent the thief on his way.

For the next three days the general toured the Holy City in company with a completely useless guide named Jacob who confused names, dates, and places indiscriminately and, when confronted with his errors by the much better versed Breckinridge, became indignant and silenced all doubts "by saying this is his country and his ancestors were Jews indefinitely." But the general found that Jacob had an annoying habit of mislocating towns and important sites in places where they should not have been and, whenever questioned on a particular discrepancy, "solves it at once with an earthquake."

12. *Ibid.*, January 3, 1868.   13. *Ibid.*, January 6–10, 1868.

Breckinridge saw all of the sights, and everywhere he found confusion between what he saw and what he had read. The Arabs residing in the city had no particular regard for historical accuracy, and often relocated monuments. When not looking at the antiquities, the general was struck by the miserable condition of the people, particularly their health. The women especially, homely and wrinkled, reminded him of the "weeping patients in the female wards of lunatic asylums." He visited two or three mosques, including the Mosque of Omar, wherein stood two stone columns through which one supposedly must pass to be saved. Breckinridge attempted the passage, found that "I was too stout," and went away rather unconcerned over the proven hopelessness of his salvation.

After three days in the Holy City, the party went out to Bethlehem for a day, and then on south to the Pools of Solomon where Breckinridge once again began taking measurements of the ruins. They moved on to Hebron, then east, back through Bethlehem, over the rugged mountains and valleys to the convent of Mar Saba overlooking the valley of Jehoshaphat. The whole scene looked unspeakably desolate to Breckinridge. There was danger now from robbers that infested the hills, and Bocharte engaged the services of a Bedouin sheik, "a subsidized thief, who protects travelers if paid not to rob them." Breckinridge disliked the Bedouin, "who at various times inspected my cuff buttons, watch and other things, with longing fingers," and was happy to see him ride off ahead with Bocharte, who "rode intrepidly down the pass with the air of a man resolved to die, if necessary, in defense of his charge."

They reached the Dead Sea and, traveling north along its shore, came to the Jordan, where Breckinridge took a cold bath in its holy waters. Another hour's journey brought them to Jericho. The general found and studied ruins which indicated that a very large city had once stood on the spot, but nothing now remained other than a few piles of stones. After spending a day examining the ancient site, he returned to Jerusalem, and then went on to Jaffa to take a steamer to Suez. On the way they discharged their courier, a drunken and surly fellow who argued continually with Burbank, and went on by themselves.[14]

At Suez, Breckinridge, Burbank, and Shepard boarded a light draft steamer and went through the recently completed upper half of the Suez Canal to Ismailiya. There they transferred to another boat and went the rest of the way to Suez over a still uncompleted portion of the waterway. Everywhere Breckinridge saw activity. He found a number of obstacles

14. *Ibid.*, January 16–24, 1868.

still in the way of completion of the great canal, but nothing unsurmountable. Here was the kind of work that he would have liked to be doing, active, useful, lasting. The next day he went down the Gulf of Suez a few miles to the place where Moses supposedly crossed the Red Sea. He found the gulf six miles across and quite deep. At a glance, he saw that the widely accepted theory of an ebb tide and strong winds to account for the parting of the sea would not hold. "Besides, Exodus says the waters were a wall unto them on their right hand and on their left." If this was really the place, he decided, then there was "no escape from disbelief or a miracle." [15]

On February 1, Breckinridge and Burbank, having gone on to Cairo, crossed the Nile, hired some comically small and stubborn donkeys, and rode the short distance to the great Pyramids. The colonel's steed ran too fast, urged on by a flock of yelling donkey boys, while Burbank himself, reins in hand, flailing his cane in the air, held on for his life while a boy whipped the beast from behind. And all of this to the accompaniment of a "wild Irishman from Australia, dashing along and remarking cheerfully, these are shabby things to look at sir, but good ones to go." Burbank seemed too intent on staying in the saddle to venture a reply.

Breckinridge did not come through the trip unscathed. Someone called him "general," and instantly he found himself surrounded by a crowd of donkey boys. Were they Americans? Yes? Ah! good. Hurrah—Yankee, Doodle, Dandee! One of the boys placed his hand on Breckinridge's leg to keep him from falling from a donkey barely tall enough to keep his legs off the ground, patted him occasionally on the back, and reassured him that "I man carry you up the Pyramid ten minnits. Yankee Doodle come to town." When at last they reached the tombs, Breckinridge was not allowed to dismount without the aid of three of his followers, and all to the tune of "bravo, great General." Such devotion could not go unrewarded. "Touched by these spontaneous outbursts of admiration," he wrote, "I engage the three to help me up the pyramid, (one to each hand and one to push from behind in emergencies)."

Despite these hardships, Breckinridge did get up the side of the main Pyramid and, entering it and examining its central chamber and numerous passageways, pronounced it a "prodigious pile." Then he went on to the Sphinx and the other smaller pyramids. Along the way he encountered an enterprising Arab who, for five francs, ran from the top of the chief Pyramid to the top of the next in ten minutes. In general, however, he thought the Arabs a lazy, importunate lot, and finally shooed them all away. That

15. *Ibid.*, January 25–31, 1868.

evening the travelers limped back to Cairo, but not before Burbank's donkey inflicted the final indignity. Falling down, it threw him over its head. Burbank, catching himself on his hands, was left in a ridiculous posture with his legs still astride the animal behind its ears. This was finally too much for the noble steed, who rolled over helplessly on its side.[16]

After four days in Cairo, Burbank and Breckinridge parted with Shepard and went on to Alexandria to meet a steamer for Italy. Here one morning, he went to pay his respects to the American consul. As he walked toward the consulate, which was near the bay, he suddenly beheld the Stars and Stripes floating over a ship at anchor. The unexpectedness of seeing that old banner on this side of the world only heightened the feelings that swelled within him at the sight of it. "I thought," he later said, "in an ecstacy I never before felt, there is *my* flag. I had followed it up the heights of Chapultepec; it had waved over my home; my children had played among its folds; it had been raised in my honor, and in the momentary rush of feelings it was again my flag, and the dearest and most beautiful thing upon the earth." Almost immediately, however, the reality of his exile banished the joy at seeing the banner. "I realized in all its terrible force the fact that I had no flag, no country, but was an outcast and a wanderer over the earth." In a burst of emotion, he confided for the first time to anyone that, in spite of his feeling that the states' rights cause of the South had been just, he nevertheless regretted that the section had ever tried to secede, and that he had had to fight against "his country." Here in Alexandria he now decided to return to Canada as soon as he completed his tour. "I had...no right to set my foot on any part of the soil of the United States," he would recall, "but I said the rest of my life shall be lived in sight of it even if I may never more have right in it." [17]

After five days in Alexandria, Breckinridge took a steamer to Messina, Sicily, from which he subsequently caught another ship for Naples, arriving on February 16. Here Mary and Mrs. Burbank were waiting for them, having been told to come ahead to meet them. After a happy reunion, they spent the next several days touring Naples, Pompeii, Vesuvius, and Capri. Then they all got on a road that led to Rome.

The Breckinridges fell in love with the Eternal City. The general was especially delighted with its archaeological wonders, and he planned a cam-

16. *Ibid.,* February 1, 1868.

17. Undated clipping *ca.* 1890 from an unidentified newspaper in the Sallie Johnson Breckinridge Scrapbook; John Ten Eyck to ?, n.d., paraphrasing an article from a Lexington newspaper, in author's possession.

paign that would take in all of them. For two days he looked around in a general way, and then began to examine the antiquities in more detail. Indeed, he worked in such detail that he and Mary moved out of their hotel, took an apartment on the Via Della Croces, and remained in Rome well into April. When Fanny finished her school in March, she came to join them.

Life in Rome was wonderful. Many old friends were there for the season, including General Myers, Judge Samuel Perkins, an associate from Breckinridge's Iowa days, and Charles Wesson, one of the New Market cadets. Breckinridge went riding, watched a fox chase, attended a masked ball—"pleasant and curious, but one will do"—and devoted himself to the history of the ancient city. He spent days in the catacombs, found one of them to be six galleries deep, and read and translated several old Christian inscriptions, "and some that savor of paganism." Perhaps the most memorable occasion in his visit came late in March when he had an audience with the Pope. Breckinridge and Perkins had letters of introduction from an abbe in France, the general's saying that he, "like all who shared in the Confederate forces & fortune, [is] very much attached to the Holy Father & all around him, seeing that you had sympathy and kind words for them in the hour of their trial." Pius IX had been somewhat sympathetic towards the South during the war, but his influence was minimal, with no diplomatic bearing of any consequence. Still, as the only European head of state who "recognized" the Confederacy, he was dear to many in the lost cause. Breckinridge had his audience with the aging Pope, though it was Fanny who came away from the Vatican with the greatest impression, for she met and formed an attachment for a handsome young Papal guard.[18]

Through it all, Breckinridge could not forget his longing to return to Niagara. In mid-April they left Rome and, traveling north, made brief stops in Florence and Venice before moving through Austria and into Prussia. As he passed through the Germanies, Breckinridge would have been amused to see the report then circulating in the United States that he was in New York *incognito*. When he reached Berlin for a final brief visit, he found himself honored by King William and presented with a handsome jeweled sword. Then late in April the Breckinridges finally reached Paris, gathering their belongings and mementos of twenty months in Europe, and pre-

18. Breckinridge Diary, February 5–March 3, 1868, in Prewitt Collection; C. Rogerson to "Monsignor Vardi," November 20, 1867, in B. MSS; Mrs. Kenneth Kirkland to the editor, Lexington *Herald-Leader*, November 18, 1956; Mrs. Kenneth Kirkland to the author, March 18, 1969.

pared for the long voyage to Canada. They left Paris on May 18, spent two and one-half weeks in London in an apartment provided by Wigfall, made a final tour of the sights, and departed aboard the *Moravian* for Quebec on June 4. Mary and Fanny both fell ill again, so seriously that when they passed through Montreal, Breckinridge was forced to go on without stopping to see Davis, then visiting in the city. By the end of the month they were once more in Niagara. Breckinridge could again look for his old country "and see it over the river which I might not cross, and there the first thing in the morning and the last thing at night I watched it, and longed for it with a hunger few men may comprehend." [19]

Almost immediately upon his arrival, Breckinridge had brief hopes that he would shortly be able to do more than just look at his homeland. While in Rome he had received a letter from Beck. Montgomery and Francis P. Blair, Sr., both insisted that he could return to the United States then without fear of molestation. Indeed, the elder Blair offered to go to the president and obtain a pardon for Breckinridge if only he would ask for it. Johnson "felt kindly towards you," Beck reported, and several prominent northern politicians in Congress assured Beck that the general could be pardoned if a united effort was made. Now, only a few days after reaching Niagara, Breckinridge received news of Johnson's July 4 amnesty proclamation, and his hopes soared that he was included in its provisions. This would enable him to go home without asking for a pardon, thereby not violating his unwritten trust with all other unpardoned Confederates.

It was not to be. Although many of his Republican friends like Orville Browning favored including Breckinridge and others still under indictments in the amnesty, Johnson was forced to give in to the more ultra of the Radicals. Consequently, his proclamation excluded those who still faced indictments in the Federal courts. Breckinridge was sorely disappointed, and, what was rare, he showed it. His friend John S. Daniel of Virginia wrote to raise his spirits. "Nothing to be gained by despondency," he said, "so cheer up my friend. I pray for better times for you." [20]

19. Cincinnati *Enquirer*, March 26, 1868; Mrs. Kenneth Kirkland to the author, March 18, 1969; interview with Mrs. Kenneth Kirkland, New York, N.Y., September 1, 1968; Breckinridge to Louis T. Wigfall, May 12, 1868, in Wigfall MSS; Mary C. Breckinridge to Johnson, May 31, 1868, in Mary C. Breckinridge MSS; New York *Times*, June 30, 1865; undated clipping *ca.* 1890 in Sallie Johnson Breckinridge Scrapbook in possession of Peter H. Ten Eyck; Breckinridge to Jefferson Davis, November 23, 1869, in Davis MSS, Museum of the Confederacy.

20. James B. Beck to Breckinridge, January 9, 1868, in JCB Papers; Pease and Randall, *Diary of Browning*, II, 3–4; John M. Daniel to Breckinridge, August 10, 1868, in B. MSS.

The fact that he was not included in the amnesty did not stop others of the general's friends from urging him to come home anyhow. Ivey assured him that, "After you once get here, I do not believe the people would permit you to be taken before any court." William C. P. Breckinridge added his own conviction that it would be safe for him to return, and went so far as to extend the hospitality of his own home for the general's arrival. However, the general would not go home until all could go. He would not accept a special pardon, nor would he live under the sufferance of the government. He had to be free under the law from all indictments before he felt he could honorably return. Until that time, he would remain in Canada. Back in Lexington, his friends missed his presence and wisdom. "The day when Gen. Breckinridge can return to us in safety," said the press, "will not be more joyful to him than to thousands who love and honor the exiled soldier and statesman. Kentucky, the South, the Democratic party, the whole country sadly needs the aid of his eloquence and counsel." For the time being, though, they would all have to wait.[21]

After the years of anxiety during the war, Mary thought their Niagara home to be "like the peace of Heaven," but the general was restless in his waiting. It helped that the whole family was reunited for the first time in years when Clifton, Cabell, and little Mary, came for a summer visit. "I cannot tell you how happy we were," wrote Mary, "as it was the first time we had been together since the war." The reunion was short, for Clifton was called back to his summer job after a few days, but not before the whole family went to Niagara Falls to have their picture taken with the American falls in the background. Ironically, the general appeared in the picture with the United States just over his shoulder, beyond the river he could not cross.[22]

Breckinridge did his best to fight off despondency during these trying months. He continued gathering his papers and accounts of former days from Ivey and others but never quite found time to follow through with his intention to write a book. "Travels in the East" never got out of diary form. His time was too much taken up with the few pleasures available to him, chiefly the company of Early, Mason, Preston, and others. For hours here in the warm summer afternoons, the Confederates sat together once

21. Charles Ivey to Breckinridge, July 4, 1868, in B. MSS; W. C. P. Breckinridge to Breckinridge, July 5, 1868, in JCB Papers; Lexington *Observer and Reporter*, August 22, 1868.

22. Bullock, "Breckinridge," in Prewitt Collection; Mary C. Breckinridge to Johnson, July 15, 1868, in Mary C. Breckinridge MSS; photo in possession of Mrs. Kenneth Kirkland.

again in the shade of Mason's trees. Their faces often turned grave and anxious when some one of them heard word from home of the plight of the South. More usually, however, their discussions were gay as they recalled amusing incidents from the war, often at the expense of one another, and punctuated their stories with peals of laughter that Mason's daughter thought would have "done justice to a party of schoolboys." When discussion failed to conclude a matter, Breckinridge and Early, in the best southern fashion, fought their differences to a finish on Beverly Tucker's croquet lawn. Early remained the general's particular friend, and often the two exchanged visits of several days with each other. Mary could see that Breckinridge felt his idleness weighing upon him, greatly in need of some employment, but she rejoiced that there were so many friends here, as "he enjoys their society exceedingly." Still, receiving friends in rented rooms in Canada was hardly the same as seeing them in his own home, in his own country.[23]

After little Mary returned to New York and Owen left to enroll with Cliff at Washington College, Breckinridge, Mary, and Fanny moved to more comfortable lodgings in a small cottage in Niagara. As always, they were economical. The house cost them five dollars a month, and friends donated enough furniture to make the cottage livable. They hoped to remain here until the winter cold forced them back to a hotel. The days passed slowly and quietly as winter approached, and all the while the general waited for better news from the United States. It was well into November before he began to hear hopeful rumors of another, full, amnesty. While waiting, he continued to receive cheerful letters of hope from home. His brother-in-law J. J. Bullock, reminded Breckinridge that "the Bible is a great book. In your leisure time it would be profitable every way to make yourself thoroughly acquainted with its teachings." Thus, said Bullock, Breckinridge might be better able to bear the burden of exile. Hopeful for the future, he reminded him that many great men performed their best works only after a period of great trial. "You belong to a race of noble witnesses for the truth," wrote the Reverend Mr. Bullock, "you are the child of a proud ancestry. . . . Trust in God & all will be well." [24]

The general was already well acquainted with the Bible and its teachings,

23. Mason, *Correspondence*, 588; Memoranda of Mary Breckinridge, December 8, 1947, in Prewitt Collection; Jubal Early to Samuel Early, August 7, 1868, in Early MSS; Mary C. Breckinridge to Johnson, October 18–19, 1868, in Mary C. Breckinridge MSS.

24. Bullock, "Breckinridge," in Prewitt Collection; Thomas Bullock to Breckinridge, November 20, 1868, in B. MSS.

much more so than Bullock thought. And he did trust in the Lord, but it was Andrew Johnson of Tennessee who finally brought John C. Breckinridge back to Kentucky.

In the United States the clamor for Breckinridge's pardon had become an uproar. The Louisville *Daily Courier* hopefully expected that "the oblivion of past differences will soon restore to our State a son so endeared to her citizens by his many shining and noble qualities." Meanwhile the general's friends sent him letter after letter, asking him to defy the Federal authorities and come home. "You should come back as soon as you can," they told him. "Come here at all hazards"; "you ought to come"; "come *immediately* home." Some grew impatient. "Quit your foolishness and come home," wrote one. "For God Almighty's sake come home and quit your blame foolishness." Everyone assured him that he would not be arrested or interfered with. Indeed, even some of the influential Kentucky Radicals so expressed themselves.[25]

Many outside Kentucky took up his case. Old Blair remained anxious about him and felt that he could get the cooperation of the Radicals in Washington to get Breckinridge a pardon. His old friend Browning offered to present the general's case to the president, confident that "President Johnson would, before leaving office, grant you a full pardon." Indeed, Johnson himself, in conversation with Kate Coyle, told her to write to Breckinridge and "tell *you to come home, you need not have any apprehension.*" The president assured Mrs. Coyle that even though Breckinridge was excepted from the General Amnesty of July 4, "whatever might occur, he would interpose; he desired *you to trust him and come home.*"[26]

What a change had taken place in the North since 1865. During the war and at its end the attitude of the Union toward Breckinridge was vicious. The New York *Times* had applauded the erroneous report of his death, and people throughout the North expected him to receive the most severe punishment after the war. In 1865 Johnson had ordered his arrest if he should step within the boundaries of the United States. Yet now that same Johnson was willing to take an active part in helping Breckinridge return unmolested to his home. He had moved from an attitude of hostility, first to one of noninterference if the general should return, and now to active support of his case. His secretary of the interior, Orville H. Browning, was

25. Frankfort *Yeoman*, September 18, 1875; John Viley to Breckinridge, October 18, 1868, Paul Rankin to Breckinridge, October 22, 1868, D. Howard Smith to Breckinridge, December 11, 1868, all in B. MSS.

26. Beck to Breckinridge, November 25, 1868, Sarah Waller to Breckinridge, October 16, 1868, John Coyle to Breckinridge, August 30, 1868, all in B. MSS.

Mary Cyrene Breckinridge, *ca.* 1890. She outlived John C. Breckinridge by thirty-two years and was buried beside him in the Lexington cemetery in 1907. (Courtesy Mr. and Mrs. John M. Prewitt)

This last known photograph of John C. Breckinridge was made in Lexington in 1873, two years before his death. He was fifty-two. (Courtesy Robert J. Younger)

willing to work for Breckinridge, along with the entire influential Blair family, members of Congress, Radical Republicans throughout the country, and even the New York *Times*, which would shortly laud the general for his integrity and prudence during his exile. All agreed with Greeley that "we need him." What they needed even more was a country that was united in spirit as well as in body, and this was almost impossible as long as thousands of southerners were denied the presence and counsel of their own revered leaders, especially the moderate ones like Breckinridge. All exiles had to be allowed to come home before the nation's wounds could truly be bound.

Still Breckinridge waited. He would not seek pardon, nor would he go home while there were still indictments against him. He must be completely free. Stoddard Johnston implored him not to accept a special presidential pardon if proffered, but to go to Kentucky and take his chances, or remain an exile until all Confederates were free. At last, however, he did not have long to wait.[27]

In mid-December there came a letter from Beck, who had just seen the president on his behalf. When Breckinridge's case was mentioned, Johnson's first reaction was to ask whether the exile had yet petitioned for pardon, implying that it would be granted. Johnson "expressed the kindest feelings toward you," wrote Beck, "spoke of the kindly relations that always existed between you & him & said you ought to come to the United States at once & send up your petition for pardon." Johnson did not precisely say that he would grant the pardon, but Beck received the impression that he earnestly wanted to do so. Johnson realized that the general's two main reasons for not making application while in Canada were, in Beck's words, "because you hoped for a general amnesty & because you recognized the fact, while beyond the jurisdiction of the country, you feared that he might be embarrassed in granting you a special pardon." Johnson admitted that there would be some embarrassment in doing the latter, and that it might have kept him from granting such pardon to the general. But then he gave Beck a tantalizing hint as to the possibilities for the future. As Beck related it, Johnson said: "I want to say this to you & I want to say it in a way not to be distinctly understood as indicating anything decidedly, because I am not settled about it . . . that before the holidays are over something will be done in a general way that will have a decided influence on Mr. Breckinridge's case." [28]

27. J. Stoddard Johnston to Breckinridge, December 13, 1868, in B. MSS.
28. Beck to Breckinridge, December 11, 1868, in B. MSS.

Beck was positive that Johnson meant an all-inclusive general amnesty. A week later, when John Coyle of Washington went to the president and read a letter from Breckinridge concerning the matter, this belief was confirmed. Coyle told the general that "a proclamation of full pardon without reservation" would be issued on Christmas morning, December 25, 1868. Coyle's wife Kate wrote immediately to Breckinridge, joyful that "the seal of Amnesty renders you again free and unshamed." Five days later, on Christmas, Beck wrote again immediately upon hearing the Universal Amnesty declared. "President Johnson has at last done what we have so long begged him to do," he wrote. "*Thank God* you are free." [29]

Just how much influence Breckinridge's own case may have had on Johnson's decision to proclaim the amnesty is uncertain, though the general, as the chief exile, and one whose case was almost constantly before the president, thanks to his many friends in Washington, must have been much on his mind. However, it is doubtful that Breckinridge gave this much thought this Christmas. It was a happy time. After over three years as an exile, a wanderer, he could see the end in sight. Those years had told on him. Mary was still frail and weak, and would not recover her health for some time. The general, too, was unwell. The exile aged him, just as the war had seriously impaired his once vigorous constitution. Indeed, he would suffer recurrent illness for the rest of his life. Breckinridge, despite the joy of this Christmas in Niagara, was nearly worn out.

Back in the United States speculation sprang up almost immediately that, now that Breckinridge could return, he would once again assume an important role in the nation's politics. They were in for a surprise, however, for he denied all interest in again holding office. This was the first hint that he gave of his intentions upon his return to the country. It had been, and still would be, hoped that he would go back to public life to aid his state and nation in the trying years of Reconstruction ahead. Now, however, it looked as though he had put politics behind him forever. His old enemy, the New York *Times*, commented that even his foes must "give him credit for a keen, discriminating judgment, for the strictest personal integrity, and for remarkable prudence." It would require more from the general, however, to convince his friends at home that he could not be lured back into the public arena, and they would never give up hope.[30]

Congratulations came from many quarters, along with offers for a vari-

29. Coyle to Breckinridge, December 20, 1868, Kate Coyle to Breckinridge, December 20, 1868. Beck to Breckinridge, December 25, 1868, all in B. MSS.
30. New York *Times*, January 2, 1869.

ety of positions upon his return. William Preston Johnston urged him to come to Washington College and select one of the three or four professorships in the new law department to be inaugurated. If he did not wish such a position, however, he could name political philosophy, political economy, or even American history, if he wanted, and such a position would be created for him, at a good salary of $2,500 a year or more. A more lucrative offer came from the newly chartered Elizabethtown, Lexington and Big Sandy Railroad, which proposed to run a line from Elizabethtown east to connect with the Chesapeake and Ohio. They wanted him to assume the presidency of the road, at not less than $5,000 per year. Meanwhile, friends opened their homes to him for his return. William C. P. Breckinridge offered to give the general lodgings at his Lexington house indefinitely, should he decide to make Kentucky again his home. The years of exile had mellowed Breckinridge on that point. The old hurt of rejection by his native state, and the resolve to begin life farther west, had been replaced by a yearning for the old places, the old scenes of his youth. "Of course I will return to Ky.," he told the colonel on accepting his invitation, "first because I have nowhere else to go, but chiefly because my heart is there." [31]

Much as he wanted to, however, Breckinridge could not go home at once. When he first heard of the amnesty, he proposed to leave immediately, and had wired ahead to Colonel Breckinridge to meet him at Louisville. However, he saw shortly that returning too soon after the proclamation would cause an uproar, and probably several demonstrations for him when he reached Kentucky. This was the last thing he wanted. A commotion over his return might stir up the Radicals, who had so far been acquiescent toward him, and he wanted to take no chances. There was another reason as well, aptly stated by Early. "I would not be in too great a hurry," advised his old commander, "but take it coolly. Don't act as if you felt like a pardoned criminal, but after giving a little time, go back quietly and tell everyone that you knew of course it must come to this." [32]

Breckinridge decided to postpone his return until early February, 1869. However, he sent Fanny off ahead of him on January 4 to Washington to stay with the Becks. For Breckinridge himself, the last weeks in Canada were ones of farewell. Moving out of their comfortable little cottage, he and Mary took a room at Moffatt's Hotel, had old Early over as their guest

---

31. William Preston Johnston to Breckinridge, January 8, 1869, P. Woodfield to Breckinridge, January 27, 1869, Breckinridge to W. C. P. Breckinridge, January 8, 1869, all in B. MSS.

32. Breckinridge to W. C. P. Breckinridge, December 26, 1868, Early to Breckinridge, n.d. [December, 1868], in B. MSS; Cincinnati *Enquirer*, January 9, 1869.

for a final visit, and saw for the last time in exile their friends the Masons, Beverly Tucker, Mrs. Helm, and others. Early in particular was sad at the parting, since Tucker had "discovered a keg of Bourbon" in his cellar. It was good whiskey, "though not equal to the 'Old Crow,'" and he coveted the hope that the general would join him in savoring it before leaving.[33]

Finally, early in February, the Breckinridges crossed the suspension bridge over the Niagara. For the first time in three and one half years they set foot on their native soil. They went to Buffalo, boarded the New York Central, and hurried on towards Baltimore and waiting friends. Behind them lay years of memories and a host of friends, and not just among their fellow exiles. "They leave this town with the sincere respect and best wishes of all classes," wrote the Niagara *Mail*, "which they deservedly won by the invariably kind and friendly manner in which they have lived among us."[34]

The general spent a week or more in Baltimore, buying some much needed new clothes, and visiting a host of former friends and associates. Here, too, began the invitations to dinners, some in his honor, which he had to expect on his return. He would turn down as many as possible, but some he could not refuse and, once there, he had to face the further pressures to get him to comment on current politics. Whenever he could, he declined such requests but, here in Baltimore, he did give vent to another link in his developing chain of conviction that the southern states had been wrong—or at least mistaken—in their attempt to secede. During remarks at a dinner attended by at least one other old Confederate, Colonel John S. Mosby, he declared that if the Confederacy had been successful in establishing itself, "there would have been such a spirit of self-assertion that every county would have claimed the right to set up for itself." Indeed, he had seen evidence of this as secretary of war in the obstinacy and harmful independence of North Carolina and Georgia, thanks primarily to their governors.[35]

On February 16, the general went north to New York, his principal object being to see Horace Greeley to thank him for his heartfelt interest in

33. C. C. Rogers to Breckinridge, January 5, 1869, Early to Breckinridge, January 12, 30, 1869, Beverly Tucker to Breckinridge, January 20, 1869, all in B. MSS; New York *Times*, March 14, 1869; Breckinridge to Early, January 14, 1869, in Early MSS; Clifton R. Breckinridge to Breckinridge, January 22, 1869, receipt of Moffatt's Hotel, January 1869, in JCB Papers.

34. Niagara (Ont.) *Mail*, February 10, 1869.

35. Receipt of Hopkins & Eichman, February 10, 1869, in JCB Papers; New York *Times*, February 12, 1869; John S. Mosby, *Memoirs of Colonel John S. Mosby* (Reprint; Bloomington, Ind., 1959), 380.

his case. He called first on Judge George Shea, who brought the two together the next day at the *Tribune* office. Breckinridge was delighted to
meet the editor, remarking the next day, "Never have I made a visit that
afforded me more genuine pleasure, for never was visitor more cordially
received." The affection he felt for Greeley was cemented at this meeting,
and, though the two never became intimates, nor even correspondents, the
reverence that Breckinridge felt for him remained undimmed for the rest
of his life.[36]

Shea's club, the Manhattan, honored Breckinridge with a dinner, but,
carefully, the general declined to respond to the cheers and toasts, sat down,
and did not allow himself to be drawn into any political discussion. Leaving
New York, he went on to Washington for a brief visit, made a quick trip
to Petersburg, visited with Fitzhugh Lee in Alexandria, and then crossed
the Blue Ridge to Lexington to see Clifton and Owen at Washington College. General Lee had sometime before invited Breckinridge to stay with
him on his visit, and now the Kentuckian accepted his hospitality. Breckinridge was very much impressed with the college, thinking it one of the best
in the country. He spent two days with Lee, and his old commander found
that he "seems cheerful, and talks hopefully." While here in the Valley,
Breckinridge also called at the Virginia Military Institute. Its graduating
class, upon hearing that he would be returning to the country, had invited
him to give their commencement address and, though he had to decline, the
general was happy to see the familiar faces of their officers. The boys themselves were all new, but he was hardly a stranger to any of them. He and
New Market had given them and the school their finest tradition.[37]

Breckinridge returned to Baltimore on March 1, spent a last few days
with friends there, and then boarded a train with Mary and set off for Cincinnati, arriving on March 5. He stayed in the city for several days as the
guest of McLean, the editor of the Cincinnati *Enquirer*, who had employed
Cabell briefly. He stayed secluded, and McLean helped keep his presence
a secret from all but a few friends, for Breckinridge wished to avoid any
sort of demonstration, even though W. C. P. Breckinridge had spoken with

36. New York *Tribune*, February 17, 1869; George Shea to Breckinridge, February
16, 1869, Horace Greeley to Shea, April 8, 1867, in B. MSS; Louisville *Courier-Journal*,
February 18, 1869; Baltimore *Baltimorian*, May 22, 1875.

37. Lexington *Observer and Reporter*, March 6, 1869; Louisville *Courier-Journal*,
February 23–24, March 3, April 3, 1869; Clifton R. Breckinridge to Breckinridge, January 30, 1869, in JCB Papers; R. E. Lee to R. E. Lee, Jr., February 27, 1869, in R. E.
Lee, Jr., *My Father, General Lee* (Reprint; Garden City, N.Y., 1960), 340–41; Committee of Invitation to Breckinridge, January 17, 1869, in B. MSS.

many Radicals who felt that such an outpouring on the general's return would not anger anyone. The word got out after three days, however, and a decoy dispatch was given out that he would be leaving from the Covington depot for the trip to Lexington on the afternoon of March 8. A large crowd assembled there to see him, when word was sent that he had already gone. Actually, the general did not arrive at the station until 6 A.M. the next morning. With very little demonstration he and Mary boarded the rear car for the trip home.

At all of the stations between Covington and Cynthiana, crowds were waiting to see him. At the latter place he came out on the platform briefly, shook hands with many, inquired about old friends, and explained, "You must excuse me for being quiet; I am here by permission, and it is my request that I be allowed to pass quietly. I am glad to get to my home once more. It is nearly eight years since I was here." There was another demonstration at Paris, and again he came out of the car. He was glad to be back, he said, but he felt older. Somehow, someone got him to make a brief political allusion with regard to the new president, Ulysses S. Grant, and his cabinet. Grant had tried to appoint A. T. Stewart, owner of New York's largest department store, secretary of the treasury. However, an old law had been discovered which prohibited a man engaged in trade or commerce from holding that portfolio, and now Charles Sumner, irate at not being tendered a position in the new administration, was clamoring for Stewart's rejection. Breckinridge could not pass up the opportunity to make a subtle dig at his old foe Sumner. Stewart might make a good secretary, he said—Breckinridge was one of his customers—but he was surprised that no one had thought of that law before. "Sumner would never forgive himself for not being the first to find that out," he said, then boarded the car once more for the last part of the journey home.

Night was gathering about the Bluegrass now, and rain threatened. From the dim car, Breckinridge peered out the window, lost in thought and memory as familiar places from his old life passed by the speeding train. Each brought its own recollection, the nostalgia of days gone forever, of a world that had disappeared in the smoke of war. "Nearly eight years ago," he said softly to himself. "Nearly eight years ago."

And then he was silent.[38]

---

38. Louisville *Courier-Journal*, March 9–11, 1869; W. C. P. Breckinridge to Breckinridge, January 16, 1869, in B. MSS; William Hesseltine, *Ulysses S. Grant, Politician* (New York, 1935), 146–47.

CHAPTER 4

We Address Ourselves to the Duties of the Future

"It has been a long time," Breckinridge wrote to Davis shortly after his return, "and to both of us, a weary one. For myself, I was sustained throughout by the conviction that there was one spot on earth where I had friends who did not believe I deserved the obloquy that was heaped upon me." That one place was Lexington, and the general was not disappointed.[1]

Although it was raining when his train pulled into the depot, a crowd was there to raise three cheers when he alighted on the platform. He shook hands with a few, told reporters that he wanted no publicity but only quiet, and then entered a waiting carriage that took him to Colonel Breckinridge's home at 211 West High Street. A serenade had been planned, but the heavy rain postponed it until 10:30 when, despite the downpour, the crowd gathered, somehow managed to get bonfires and rockets going in the street, and called for "Home, Sweet Home," "Dixie," and "Hail to the Chief" from the band. The rain came in torrents now, but when Breckinridge finally appeared on the steps of the house, a cry of "down umbrellas" went out. The crowd stood cheering and drenched waiting for him to speak.

Breckinridge was still acutely conscious of the potential danger of such demonstrations in his honor. His words were cautious and guarded. He felt deeply this mark of esteem from his old friends, and thanked them sincerely. He had not desired it, and they understood his reasons, but he accepted it nonetheless with gratitude as a purely personal expression, "and containing no particle of political significance." Indeed, he went on, "I can and will say that the tremendous events of the past eight years have had a tendency to deaden, if not destroy, old party feelings, and for myself I can

---

1. Breckinridge to Jefferson Davis, November 23, 1869, in Davis MSS, Museum of the Confederacy.

say that I no more feel the political excitements that marked the scenes of my former years than if I were an extinct volcano." [2]

Great hopes were entertained for Breckinridge on his return. His stated withdrawal from all political activity made little difference. "He is more potential in that State to-day than any of the men in Kentucky," wrote a Cincinnati editor the week after his arrival. "If he wishes to be Governor of that State, Representative or Senator in Congress, he has only to say the word, and at the first opportunity he will be gratified." Consequently, it was in his power to lead Kentucky for better or for worse, to keep her in the civil disorder and confusion that had reigned since the end of the war, or to lead her "on the high road to commercial and industrial enterprise." Greeley's *Tribune* speculated that he came back animated only by hopes for the future of the Union, and that he desired "the acceptance in good faith that the result of the war is final, the secession of strife, the growth of fraternal feeling, the dismissal of old subjects of dispute, and a new political departure." [3]

Greeley and the others could not have been more correct. Breckinridge did hope for all of this, but he knew that first he must rebuild himself, and he was not yet completely sure where and with what he would start the construction. For a few months yet he would be undecided whether to settle permanently in Lexington once more, and he toyed at least briefly, with the idea of starting anew in California. There was also his occupation to consider. He was deluged with offers and proposals. Johnston wrote again reporting the unanimous vote of the board of trustees of Washington College instructing him to invite the general to take a position in their contemplated law department. Lee endorsed their action, hoping that Breckinridge would accept, and Echols—one of the trustees—wrote what Lee could not, that "Marse Robert" was exceedingly anxious to have the Kentuckian with him. The Mound City Life Insurance Company of St. Louis wanted Breckinridge to take their Kentucky agency, his old friend C. G. McHatton urged him to take charge of that same company's southern department including four states, John B. Gordon wrote to offer him the presidency of the Kentucky branch of the Southern Life Insurance Company, and friends from Texas tried to interest him in a position with the new Southern Pacific Railroad. [4]

2. Louisville *Courier-Journal*, March 11, 1869.
3. *Ibid.*, March 14–15, 18, 1869.
4. Milton Latham to Breckinridge, June 7, 1869, J. Stoddard Johnston to Breckinridge, June 25, 1869, R. E. Lee to Breckinridge, June 28, 1869, John Echols to Breckin-

Added to these offers, Breckinridge also considered his primary profession, the law. He could do a handsome business at it if for no other reason than the respect and loyalty of thousands of former friends and supporters who would bring him their business. Then too, he had accepted the presidency of the proposed Elizabethtown, Lexington and Big Sandy Railroad, still being organized, and that would take up much of his time. Finally, he had accepted in June the proposition from General Charles W. Field that he take the presidency of the Kentucky branch of the Piedmont and Arlington Life Insurance Company of Virginia. It would pay $5,000 a year and, combined with his salary from the E.,L. & B.S., would make him financially secure. For the time being, Breckinridge decided to hold his business down to these two presidencies, neither of which occupied him much yet during the summer and fall of 1869, and then began to look to his holdings in the Northwest.[5]

The general still owned his lands in St. Paul, Bass Island, and Superior, though they remained under deed of trust with Madison C. Johnson. Early in June he went to Chicago with Beck and Magoffin, and looked over his properties and their prospects. Word came from Bright that Corcoran and others thought that at last a railroad connection between Superior and some main line could be effected; lots in St. Paul seemed salable; and the red sandstone quarry at Bass Island had enough potential that the general had it tested for durability as a building stone. On the whole, however, he did not believe that much could be expected of his land holdings at present, but had high hopes that they would yet turn profitable enough to pay off his debts for taxes and yield some income.[6]

Even while visiting in Wisconsin, Breckinridge could not avoid the notoriety that he hoped to escape. While staying at the Newhall Hotel in Milwaukee, a number of old Democratic friends called on him, and the conversation and the memories mingled for many pleasant hours. He was reticent about the war, but seemed to feel more secure after three months in the country without trouble, and spoke rather freely on politics. When asked his opinion of Grant and his administration, Breckinridge replied that

ridge, July 23, 1860, Simon B. Buckner to Breckinridge, July 15, 1860. Charles G. McHatton to Breckinridge, July 26, 1869, John B. Gordon to Breckinridge, July 27, 1869, Hall & Baum to Breckinridge, August 24, 1869, all in B. MSS.

5. Louisville *Courier-Journal*, February 23, 1869; Charles Field to Breckinridge, June 13, 1860, in B. MSS.

6. Jesse D. Bright to Breckinridge, June 13, 1869, J. Peter to Breckinridge, August 18, 1860, in B. MSS; Bill from the Tremont House, June 2, 1869, Breckinridge to Clifton R. Breckinridge, July 24, 1869, in JCB Papers.

Grant was smart enough to take care of himself, and that his cabinet men, while hardly the best of statesmen, were nevertheless what he needed to achieve his object of a useful, if not distinguished, regime. He believed that Grant would succeed, though the people might not be completely content. Breckinridge did not believe that the country would be engaged in a foreign war with Great Britain, as was then much speculated. After four years of civil conflict, he felt that the Union would require exceptional provocation to bring it back to the battlefield, adding that if it did come to war, the South would furnish enough men to do the fighting. There were many, he said, who still resented the failure of the European powers to aid the fledgling Confederacy. Clearly, the Breckinridge of old was emerging once more, still reserved and not as outspoken as once he was, but secure, and concerned for the welfare of his country.[7]

When he returned to Kentucky in late July, he had decided to make Lexington his permanent home once more. He and Mary took rooms at the Broadway Hotel, and sometime later moved to the old Phoenix, where eight years before he had received the message that sent him out of Kentucky, and the Union. In August he paid the $8.35 occupational tax to the United States Internal Revenue required of a lawyer, and began once more the practice he had left so long ago. After the years of exile, it was good to be at work again.[8]

Life settled down to a normal pace with surprising ease. The general attended the theater often, resumed his Masonic interests, was seen often at the Kentucky Association racetrack, and once more appeared before the bar. As in the days before the war, he found himself in constant demand by fairs, expositions, societies, and commencements, as a speaker, and as he had in times past, he declined almost all. Breckinridge did give some consideration to a proposed lecture tour, but set it aside for the indefinite future.[9]

One invitation came, however, which he could not have denied if he had wanted to. "Sweet Owen" wanted him to make an appearance at its county fair in October, and he accepted with pleasure. It would be his first public address since returning from exile. Once more he saw the old faces, a little older, and some that he remembered were gone forever. Nevertheless, it

7. New York *Times*, June 8, 1869.

8. Clifton R. Breckinridge to Mary C. Breckinridge, August 9, 1869, Cabell Bullock to Breckinridge, August 24, 1869, check to the Phoenix Hotel, April 15, June 8, 1872, April 15, 1873, receipt of U.S. Internal Revenue, August 21, 1869, all in JCB Papers.

9. Clark, *My Quarter Century*, I, 99; check to Webber, July 16, 1873, in JCB Papers; Breckinridge to R. C. Ackley, October 27, 1867, in Abraham Lincoln MSS, Brown University Library, Providence, R.I.

was a happy occasion, especially since one member of the audience, though ailing and ill, had made a special trip to see his old friend. Seventy-eight years old now, General William O. Butler came out to see Breckinridge again. The speaker was profoundly moved by the evidences of undimmed devotion, and his brief speech betrayed his feelings.

He had heard, he said, that during the war, Owen was never wholly conquered by the Federals, and perhaps it was so. "However this may have been," he went on, "I am sure that now we all desire amity and peace. The growth of a kind and genial nature has effaced the material ravages of war; it will be well if older scars can be covered by the verdure of the heart. If, with minds elevated by experience and chastened by misfortune, and with spirits free, on the one hand, from base subservience and the cowardly abandonment of our honest convictions, and on the other from an irrational obstinacy, we address ourselves to the duties of the future, what brave and true heart can doubt that there yet remains for us and our children a career full of prosperity and honor!" Breckinridge had made his declaration, modest though it was. His position in the coming years of Reconstruction and reunion would be one of reconciliation. He would not dwell on the old hatreds and differences. They must be forgotten. John C. Breckinridge felt only hope for the future.[10]

That hope was encouraged by his children. Cabell had settled down to steady, though not remunerative, occupation; Clifton progressed well at Washington College and earned the admiration and compliments of Lee himself; Mary and Fanny continued their schooling in Kentucky. Only Owen now presented a problem. In December he suddenly left the college without warning or application, and only General Lee's kind intercession prevented him from being expelled. Owen was sick of school, craving the adventure that his youth had denied him during the war, and wanted to go to Cuba. Finally he took a position with a hardware firm in Kentucky, and this, at least, kept him occupied until the desire to finish his education took hold of him. In December, Cabell married Sallie Johnson, daughter of the general's old friend Senator Robert W. Johnson of Arkansas. The Breckinridges went to Washington for the wedding, and while there the general took the opportunity to visit New York once more, and to stay with other recently returned exiles like Mason.[11]

10. James Orr to Breckinridge, September 2, 1869, T. Gale to Breckinridge, October 5, 1869, in B. MSS; New York *Times*, October 17, 1869.
11. Lee to Breckinridge, June 26, 1869, in B. MSS; Clifton R. Breckinridge to Breckinridge, December 1869, J. Cabell Breckinridge to Breckinridge, January 23, 1870, re-

It was a new world, now, a fast-moving one, and wherever Breckinridge went he could see the evidences of the change. Indeed, he first sensed it while still in exile himself. In Paris in October, 1867, he picked up a copy of a new work by the American intellectual writer John William Draper, *Thoughts on the Future Civil Policy of America*. Draper, though not a profound thinker, reflected well enough the tenor of times to come in the United States, and Breckinridge was much distressed. There were "many striking and valuable thoughts" in the book, he believed, but they were without suitable application. What struck him the most, though, was its "intense materialism." In the book he saw "a constant effort to bind, etc., with bands of iron, the very soul and mind of man to the inanimate world." Sadly, he saw this same materialism, grasping and greedy, in America when he returned. Viewing it, he would say, "The world is progressing more rapidly than it used to do, and in some respects progressing in a direction not very agreeable to many of us." Expansion was everywhere and in every facet of life. Breckinridge had always been a friend of growth, but the expansion of postwar America seemed without form or system to him, bent not so much on benefit to the nation as to the accumulation of personal fortunes. The grace and public spirit he fondly recalled from earlier days seemed gone out of public and business life. He might have believed that he could look in vain for a public man today who was willing to sacrifice his career, as the general had done in 1860–1861, for a principle.[12]

His own role as a man of the old world thrust into the new, however, was never in doubt with him. He had a duty to himself and his country. Though he would not hold office, he still saw a part to play. His name, his conscience, and his self-respect, would not allow him to sit by in repose and let others do the rebuilding. It was a question of dignity, honor, and duty. "Gentlemen," he said in January, 1870, "as to the question of dignity, my idea is that that man is dignified in the true sense who tries to do something in life. If a man who has held public position, and has gone again into the shades of private life, instead of sitting with his hands folded, in stupid affectation of dignity, an incubus upon the bosom of society, a mere drone in the human hive, attempts to do something and be useful to himself, and

---

ceipt of the Ebbitt House, December 3, 1860, bill of the Clarendon House Hotel, December 9, 1869, James Mason to Breckinridge, December 30, 1869, all in JCB Papers; newspaper clipping in Sallie Johnson Breckinridge Scrapbook in possession of Peter Ten Eyck.

12. Breckinridge Diary, October 28, 1867, in Prewitt Collection; John C. Breckinridge, *Cincinnati Southern Railroad: Memorial of Trustees and Speech of Hon. . . .* (N.p., 1871), 28.

his friends, and his State, and his country—by my standard of honor and duty, such a man deserves rather the praise than the blame of his fellow men." Breckinridge would attempt to "do something." [13]

He began with himself. The general soon found that there would be no dearth of business for his law practice. Now, as before, he would accept trial cases only when he could act in the defense, and he was much in demand. Slander, robbery, and particularly murder cases, kept him much in court in Fayette and Scott, and his success brought more business than he could handle alone. His fees ran to $350 or more for a defense, and this alone provided a good income. Often he was consulted by people outside Kentucky, and he numbered among his clients a few persons of note in the state and the nation. General Abraham Buford, a classmate at Centre College, engaged his services for defense in a civil suit. Another general, now a lieutenant colonel in the United States Cavalry, later hired Breckinridge in a suit against Buford over a bad horse. George A. Custer, who had battled Early and Breckinridge at Winchester, turned to the Kentuckian when Buford refused to make good on an unsound horse. Custer entertained a high regard for Breckinridge, and in January, 1872, particularly solicited his attendance at a ball in Louisville in honor of the Grand Duke Alexis of Russia. In all, for the next three years, Breckinridge's practice went far toward rebuilding his modest financial fortunes. [14]

Beyond the law, the general looked to his property at Bass Island for some profitable return. The results of the tests he had made showed that the stone in the quarry there which he owned in partnership with Magoffin, was of very high quality, and quite desirable for building purposes. They decided in January, 1870, to form a joint stock company to work the quarry, but found this arrangement easier said than done. Delays ensued and by 1873 the quarry still lay unexploited. [15]

13. Breckinridge, *Cincinnati Southern Railroad*, 6–7.

14. Trusten Polk to Breckinridge, August 3, 1869, A. Frank Brown to Breckinridge, October 12, 1871, James B. Beck to Breckinridge, February 21, 1870, John Donnellan to Breckinridge, November 26, 1870, John Loveley to Breckinridge, January 12, 1871, Abram Buford to Breckinridge, September 2, 1871, G. A. Custer to Breckinridge, September 6, 1872, all in JCB Papers; Breckinridge to Lewis Payne, October 24, 1878, in Prewitt Collection; Breckinridge to W. C. P. Breckinridge. July 24, 1871, in Breckinridge MSS, DU; Custer to Breckinridge, January 25, 1872, Jilson P. Johnson to Breckinridge, January 25, 1872, Thomas Hines to Breckinridge, November 20, 1869, all in B. MSS.

15. Peter to Breckinridge, August 18, 1869, W. Knight to Breckinridge, January 21, 1870, J. Palmer to Breckinridge, October 11, 1870, in B. MSS; Beriah Magoffin to Breckinridge, January 4, February 10, 1872, H. Warden to Magoffin, December 31, 1871, January 12, 1872, in JCB Papers.

On a broader scale, Breckinridge worked for his own future and that of Kentucky and the South through the Piedmont and Arlington. Following the war, a score and more life insurance companies sprang up in the former Confederate states, headed by the generals and civil leaders of the lost cause, designed to rebuild their own fortunes, and give impetus to the shattered southern economy. Most set about their duties with conviction and will, and none more so than Breckinridge.

His first months with the insurance company were good ones, and Kentucky showed a fine annual report for 1869. The next year was more troublesome, though, and the company as a whole lived out a shaky existence along with most of the other life combines. There was simply not enough capital in the South for most of its people to pay out money against death when they had barely enough for life. Breckinridge believed in the Piedmont and Arlington and worked hard for it. He continued with that firm when the Mound City approached him again and offered substantially more than he was then being paid.[16]

There were other ways to work for the southern economy as well. In October, 1869, Breckinridge served as a delegate-at-large appointed by Governor John W. Stevenson to the Southern Commercial Convention at Louisville. Following it, he helped prepare a report on the whiskey industry for Stevenson's use. At the same time, he encouraged a new organization, the Southern Land and Immigration Company. Many in the South's new ruling class had little faith in the old plantation aristocracy or in the newly freed slaves who worked their land. The section needed new blood to develop its agricultural resources, and they hoped to encourage northern farmers and capital to come south. Breckinridge enlisted the aid of other prominent Confederates in promoting the scheme, being specially anxious to demonstrate that the southern climate was not hostile to white labor, but he took little other active part in the movement.[17]

If Breckinridge spent no energy on the immigration scheme, he poured the best efforts of his remaining years into another field which produced

16. A. Duvall to Breckinridge, September 20, 1869, W. Crutchen to Breckinridge, October 18, 1869, W. C. Carrington to Breckinridge, November 10, 1860, June 27, July 2, 1872, all in JCB Papers; Charles G. McHatton to Breckinridge, May 24, 29, 1870, in B. MSS.

17. John W. Stevenson to Breckinridge, September 3, 6, 1869, Blanton Duncan to Breckinridge, September 22, November 12, 1869, T. Osborn to Breckinridge, August 26, 1869, Matthew F. Maury to Breckinridge, December 1, 1869, all in B. MSS; Breckinridge to Stevenson, September 4, 1869, in Stevenson MSS; Breckinridge, *Cincinnati Southern Railroad*, 28, 30; Jack P. Maddex, Jr., *The Virginia Conservatives, 1867–1879* (Chapel Hill, N.C., 1970), 179–83.

greater real and potential benefits to the South than any other enterprise of the postwar period—railroading. His interest in transportation dated back to the 1840s and 1850s with his investments in the several short-line roads in central Kentucky. Not only had he accepted the presidency of the Elizabethtown, Lexington and Big Sandy; in the summer of 1869 he was engaged as general counsel for the proposed Cincinnati Southern Railroad. Louisville had for some time enjoyed a monopoly on the rail trade between the Ohio River and the deep South via its connection with Nashville, Memphis, and Paducah. As a result, the city was not anxious to give up this corner on the trade, and consistently blocked Cincinnati's attempts to effect a rail link. Thus thwarted, Cincinnati sought to build its own road south, through Kentucky, to Chattanooga. To do so, it needed the approval of the Kentucky legislature, and a heavy battle with the Louisville interests was anticipated. It was with this in mind that the Cincinnati managers brought out the biggest gun they could find, John C. Breckinridge.[18]

Many thought Breckinridge's acceptance of the Cincinnati case unbecoming a Kentuckian. He should be fighting with Louisville instead of against her. The general took a different view of the matter. Although Louisville was connected indirectly with the southern roads, the city had failed repeatedly to put through a direct southern route to eastern Tennessee, to connect with Georgia, or the Carolina coast, and the Gulf ports. Cincinnati, however, had raised the necessary bonds to construct such a road, would put it through Kentucky at relatively little cost other than a right-of-way, would thereby bring the incalculable benefits of a massive North–South trade to the state, and with it one more means to relax the sectional tensions by mutual enterprise on a national scale.[19]

In early December, Breckinridge went to Frankfort at the same time that the legislature convened. He stayed with Stoddard Johnston, now editing the *Yeoman* and, though the visit was unannounced and his intentions supposedly secret, it was soon known that he was there to present Cincinnati's case to the General Assembly. By the first of the New Year, it was common knowledge, and the Louisville forces knew that they would face powerful opposition. Their leader was Basil Duke, chairman of the house committee on railroads. At Breckinridge's suggestion, the Board of Trustees of the Cincinnati Southern had their friends in the legislature present their bill

18. E. Ferguson to Breckinridge, August 3, 1869, in B. MSS; Leonard P. Curry, *Rail Routes South: Louisville's Fight for the Southern Market 1865–1872* (Lexington, 1969), 56–58.

19. Henry Watterson to Breckinridge, January 5, 1870, in B. MSS; Breckinridge, *Cincinnati Southern Railroad*, 7, 8, 16.

simultaneously to both the House and the Senate, and each body immediately referred it to the railroad committees. Then, on January 25, the committees of house and senate met in joint session to hear Breckinridge present Cincinnati's case.[20]

Strangely enough, the general's first expression on taking the floor was one of embarrassment. He had expected to speak only to the two committees, and instead found the hall filled with a large, packed audience. He did not plan to make a set speech, and would use no ornaments of eloquence "for which, indeed, long disuse has quite unfitted me." Then, after a brief personal explanation in answer to the criticism of his emergence from quiet private life to appear on behalf of Cincinnati against Louisville, he dove into the subject at hand.

Kentucky needed the connection with the southern railroad system; there was no doubt of that, but she could never get it done herself. Now Cincinnati could do it for her and, without further elaboration, he took up the proposed bill and went through it section by section. He opposed the legislature imposing any special restrictions on the line that were not applied to other roads; asked that, instead of mortgaging the entire assets of the road, that the rolling stock not be included in order that the company would own that portion of its equipment that would enable it to pay for the road itself; and called preposterous the hollow cry of opponents that such a connecting link between great termini, with such vast earning potential, could ever be insolvent. Further, besides providing all of the capital for building the road, Cincinnati was willing to abide by whatever restrictions Kentucky wished to impose. Consequently, because he did not believe it wise that such things be left open to continual legislation, he advised that a maximum freight rate be set in advance, and asked as well that some safeguards should be reserved to insure that passengers and freight coming from North or South on the main trunk, would not be discriminated against by limitations that would prevent either from going off on some side road in the state, a practice growing common with some of the great northern lines.

He appealed to the committees not to try the case as a partisan issue, but to view the benefits it would bring to the state. "I did not come here to appeal to any prejudice for us or against us," he said. "Perhaps mine are as strong as any man's. I do not call them prejudices. I call them just and

20. Louisville *Courier-Journal*, December 18, 1869; Watterson to Breckinridge, January 5, 1870, J. Green to Breckinridge, January 5, 1870, in B. MSS; Curry, *Rail Routes South*, 76–77.

strong resentments, which I feel as deeply as any man, for what I consider the wrongs inflicted upon my people. But at the same time I would desire, by every means in my power, whatever the Lord may have in store for us in future, to make our State great, and strong, and prosperous." Kentucky had more railroad charters and fewer miles of track than any state in the Union. Freight had some depots so crowded that they could not take any more until cleared out. This proposed road would solve both problems, bring new tax revenues to the state's educational needs, induce immigration "of the right sort—of the right origin—of the white race," into Kentucky, and make the land for twenty miles on either side of the road bloom like a garden. So far as railroads were concerned, he said, "We cannot have too many." And they should not be just east-to-west lines, "if you are going to have friendly, social, and commercial intercourse, but you must have lines North and South; and without these girders so to speak, the whole system would fall by its own gravity."

Finally, as an officer of the Elizabethtown, Lexington and Big Sandy, he hoped that the proposed road would come through Lexington. "But, Sir," he concluded, "if I cannot get it myself, I want my neighbors to have it. I want that road built through the State so as to benefit the people, and whether it runs to the east or to the west of any particular town, it will be a great thing for the whole Commonwealth; and therefore I would be glad to see it built. I trust, however, Sir, that in the consideration of this matter, every question of local rivalry and selfish feeling will be put aside, that every thought and every emotion of that sort will be driven out by higher feelings, and that all of us, and particularly the friends of this measure, will, in the future, as they have in the past, pursue such a course that whether successful or unsuccessful, they will not be disturbed by that consciousness of having employed one unworthy argument or appealed to any unworthy motive." As always, success or no, Breckinridge would have truth and moderation. He may have been an "extinct volcano," but within the mountain a fire yet burned.[21]

The general made other, less important presentations, then returned to Lexington. The board of trustees kept him well apprised of the progress of the bill in the legislature and, despite some heavy inducements to woo the Louisville men, it failed in the senate on March 1, and the house mutilated its bill, then tabled it two days later. Everyone of the friends of the proposed road was sadly disappointed, including Breckinridge. The trustees called him hastily to Frankfort again to consult over what should be done,

21. Breckinridge, *Cincinnati Southern Railroad*, 5–33 *passim*.

but it was obvious that a long fight lay ahead. Thereafter, the general took little part in the further battle, though the Cincinnati Southern continued to consider him its counsel. He had accepted the position only on condition that his services would be rendered if and when it would not conflict with his other engagements, and from 1870 on he was much engaged. Cincinnati would not finally get her road until 1872.[22]

The reason Breckinridge was so occupied was that he was building railroads of his own. His trip to Superior in June, 1869, yielded no definite results, but he did find that Bright, Corcoran, Riggs, and others, had already drawn up a plan for the State Line and Superior Railroad subscribing for a total of $28,000 of capital stock. The proposed line was to run from Superior to a point on the Lake Superior and Minnesota Railroad near Duluth, just five miles north across St. Louis Bay, and the proprietors were enthusiastic in their hopes that at last Superior would be able to realize the hopes they had for it so many years before.[23]

Their hopes fell through, however, because of the unwillingness of some to subscribe to that amount of stock and, by the end of the year, the only hope seemed to lie in enticing some other company to build the road. Finally, in early September, 1873, after four years of work with nothing concrete to show for it, and not a mile of track laid, they all but gave up hope.[24]

Breckinridge had a saying that "a man worried by a hundred stings cannot give very thorough consideration to any one of them," and some might have expected this to be the case with him, for while worrying over the Cincinnati Southern and the Superior difficulties, he was also trying to build a road more personally his own, the Elizabethtown, Lexington and Big Sandy. It was planned to extend from the Chesapeake and Ohio head at the mouth of the Big Sandy River on the Ohio, near Catlettsburg, through Mt. Sterling to Lexington, and then on west to Elizabethtown, where it

22. T. Bishop to Breckinridge, February 8, March 1, 1870, Ferguson to Breckinridge, February 8, March 4, 1870, Green to Breckinridge, February 28, March 4, 1870, O. Greenwood to Breckinridge, December 9, 1872, all in B. MSS; Curry, *Rail Routes South*, 136.

23. E. W. Anderson to Breckinridge, March 9, 1874, Breckinridge to Clifton R. Breckinridge, May 23, 1869, copy of agreement, May 26, 1869, Samuel Clay to Beck, August 7, 1869, in JCB Papers; Knight to Breckinridge, June 13, 1860, all in B. MSS.

24. Anderson to Beck, December 18, 1872, G. Cass to Anderson, December 12, 1872 (copy), Magoffin to Breckinridge, November 6, 1872, Agreement, 1873 (copy), Anderson to Beck and Magoffin, March 22, 1873, Anderson to Breckinridge, April 7, August 11, 15, 1874, Jesse D. Bright to Breckinridge, July 7, 1873, Anderson to Magoffin, September 10, 1873, all in JCB Papers.

would connect with the Elizabethtown and Paducah, giving access to the Mississippi Valley.

The general's first concern as president was to get approval of the road and rights-of-way passed by the voters in the counties the line would cross. Woodford, Anderson, and Nelson, the three counties between Lexington and Elizabethtown, posed little problem, and he took some hand in promoting the cause in those counties east of Lexington. At the same time, amendments to the charter had to be routed through the legislature, and this too was entrusted to his care. The work progressed slowly, hampered by James Tracy who, in a reorganization of the company, superseded Breckinridge as president, while the Kentuckian assumed the vice-presidency. Tracy, living in New York, did next to nothing for the road and, by late 1870, the Elizabethtown, Lexington and Big Sandy had only its charter and some right-of-way to show for the work of a year and a half.[25]

Chafing under the inaction, Breckinridge began sounding out Collis P. Huntington of the Chesapeake and Ohio about buying into the Elizabethtown, Lexington and Big Sandy and building the line. By December, he had a definite proposal from Huntington, though it was much too steep. The Chesapeake and Ohio would build the road at $40,000 per mile, requiring a total of $6,700,000 in bonds, stock, and county surety subscription to finance the project. He required that he own the controlling interest in the company, and specified that Breckinridge remain as an officer, as "I should regard it very important to have the active cooperation of so efficient a gentleman as I know you to be." In June, 1871, Breckinridge went in person to New York to confer with Tracy and Huntington, and the result, that same month, was the purchase of 52 percent of Elizabethtown, Lexington and Big Sandy stock by the Chesapeake and Ohio. The general and Tracy remained as officers of the company, and operations began almost immediately, the first object being the leg between Lexington and Mt. Sterling. Returning from New York, Breckinridge made a tour of the entire line from the Big Sandy to Lexington in company with General Echols, soon to be president of the Louisville, Cincinnati and Lexington, a road the Chesapeake and Ohio would acquire in October. Throughout the northeastern Kentucky counties, Breckinridge tried to persuade the mountaineers that this road held the key to their future. There was some opposition to the road because of uncertainty as to its exact route, causing rivalries

25. Beck to Breckinridge, May 2, 1870, R. Fulton to Breckinridge, December 20, 1869, G. Bates to Breckinridge, February 19, 1870, all in JCB Papers; Louisville *Courier-Journal*, February 23, 1869; J. Woolfolk to Breckinridge, January 26, 1870, in B. MSS.

between communities, but he energetically spread his balm in hopes for the coming bond elections. He sponsored barbecues, distributed campaign funds, had handbills printed, shook hands, and did everything but take the stump to promote the road, and his efforts met with success. Almost continually engaged in campaigning for the line during the last half of 1871, he hastily wrote to Early in January, 1872, that "I am busy making a RR to the Big Sandy to meet the C & O in order that I may go to see you." [26]

Breckinridge took his position seriously and put his faith in the road. Between June, 1871, and January, 1874, a month did not go by that he did not, when well, travel from Nashville to New York to West Virginia to Frankfort in working for and promoting the road. Several times he covered its proposed route on horseback. He made appointments, oversaw employees, kept a close watch on company property, searched out valuable deposits of necessary raw materials in counties through which the road would pass, studied the routings and construction of other new lines like the Denver and Rio Grande, guarded against Louisville's jealousy and fear of Lexington stealing the main southern traffic through its Paducah connection, and directed reports on progress and a personal inspection by Huntington. Hopefully, he boasted that the line would be completed to the Virginia border by the spring of 1874, and expected that Early would be the first to come over it to visit him, promising that Fanny would continue the matchmaking she had practiced on the old bachelor in Canada by finding in Kentucky "a lady who will fill the measure of your taste." [27]

But while building a law practice, an insurance company, and three railroads, there was yet another way, perhaps more effective, in which Breckinridge worked toward rebuilding himself, his state, and his country. From the day of his return, the general was a quiet champion of reconciliation between the sections, an unyielding opponent of extremism in any form, North or South.

Breckinridge was, and would always remain, proud of the Confederate

26. Sarah Lees to Breckinridge, September 1, 1870, M. Bowman to Breckinridge, December 8, 1870. Collis P. Huntington to Breckinridge. December 20, 1870. all in B. MSS; Curry, *Rail Routes South*, 128; Lexington *Daily Press*, June 16, 1871; Memoranda of personal expenses in service of the Elizabethtown, Lexington & Big Sandy R.R. Co., June 9, 1871, in JCB Papers; Breckinridge to Jubal A. Early, January 21, 1872, in Early MSS; Breckinridge to R. Beckman, July 1, 1873, in Gratz MSS.

27. Memoranda, 1–8, in JCB Papers; James Field to Breckinridge, June 7, 1872, M. Kafer to Breckinridge, March 2, 1872, R. C. Wintersmith to B eckinridge, July 3, 1872, Breckinridge to W. C. P. Breckinridge, July 15, 1872, I. M. St. John to Breckinridge, October 11, 1872, all in B. MSS; Breckinridge to Early, January 25, 1873, in Early MSS.

epic, however much he may have deplored its coming about. He took pride in his own part in the war. Like most former Confederates, he felt a reverential respect for Jefferson Davis despite the fact that he had been with the president and had seen him in his last, and in many ways least commendable, days in office. Few in the Confederate government would have been in a better position to level severe charges against Davis' conduct of the government than Breckinridge, yet he never uttered a criticism of his old chief. It was part of a credo that he followed for the remainder of his days. Criticism, controversy, the opening and aggravating of old wounds and inflicting of new ones, served only to demean the former Confederate in his own eyes and in those of his former foes. Thus, while he freely gave his aid and his memory to a dozen or more historians of the war—J. Thomas Scharf, Alfred T. Bledsoe, Early, Davis, Leonidas Polk's son and biographer William Polk, Lee, and old Mann who was writing his memoirs—Breckinridge would help only on points of fact, generally regarding affairs in his sphere of operations. He would commend, but never berate, and steadfastly declined to give any aid in personal battles or controversies. Much as he loved and respected William Preston Johnston, the general frustrated him repeatedly by his refusal to add his own opinion to Johnston's fight with Beauregard to prove that Albert Sidney Johnston, and not the Creole, had planned the battle at Shiloh.[28]

Early would chide Breckinridge that he was too busy with his professions to care much for preserving Confederate history. "You will know better some day," replied the Kentuckian. Actually, Breckinridge kept steadily active at the preservation of the history of the war as he had known it. In August, 1869, he was elected vice-president for Kentucky of the newly formed Southern Historical Society and, though he was never able to deliver the address or write the papers that the society wanted from him, he took a keen interest in its activities. The active work that he did for preserving Confederate history was the gathering and collection of his own reports and papers, undoubtedly with a view toward someday preparing his own memoirs, or making the documents available to someone else who would do the writing. He had been getting copies of his papers even while in exile and continued the endeavor during most of the rest of his life. Very

28. Breckinridge to Jefferson Davis, November 23, 1860, in Davis MSS. Museum of the Confederacy; Davis to Breckinridge. December 17, 1860. in Breckinridge MSS. FC; A. Dudley Mann to Breckinridge, April 26, 1860. in B. MSS; J. Thomas Scharf to Breckinridge. February 15, 1873, William Polk to Breckinridge, September 22, 1874, in JCB Papers; A. T. Bledsoe to Davis, April 14, 1872, William Preston Johnston to Davis, December 8, 1874, in Rowland, *Jefferson Davis*, VII, 311, 413.

likely, he looked forward to his retirement as the best time to compile the work, and, meanwhile, having no home of his own, nor any room to keep the documents, he stored them in the attic of John Viley's house on the Leestown Pike. His books he kept at Beck's. The Viley house suddenly caught fire and burned, destroying entirely his papers from his vice-presidency, his uniforms, flags, mementos, and all of the materials he had gathered for his Confederate years. Fortunately, his papers prior to 1858 were preserved elsewhere, but this loss killed permanently any idea of writing his own history.[29]

In the study of the history of the recent conflict, as in nearly everything else that he did after the war, Breckinridge saw a means to reconciliation. The bonds of bravery between former soldiers were, he felt, wider than the chasm of sectional prejudice. Nowhere did he display this better than in Louisville in October, 1870. Robert E. Lee died on October 12, worn out, a casualty of the war as much as if he had perished on the battlefield. All over the South demonstrations were made in respect to the departed leader, and one of the larger ones took place in Louisville. For the occasion, Breckinridge broke with his rule of silence and accepted the invitation to deliver a brief address.

From first to last, his speech on Lee had but one theme—reunion. The vast assemblage at the meeting he characterized as being without distinction of party or section, saying, "It is in itself the omen of reunion." North and South, the mourning cry was being heard for the departed great, and he believed that the observance of formal ceremonies such as this throughout the South was a manly request to the North to join in the grief. "It is an invitation on their part to the people of the North and South, East and West, if there be any remaining rancor in their bosoms, to bury it in the grave forever." It pleased him to see that this demonstration gave evidence of no repining, no recriminations over the loss of the war; Confederates accepted the result, and now employed themselves in the useful work of rebuilding their country. "If the spirit which animates the assembly before me to-night shall become general and permeate the whole country, then may we say the wounds of the late war are truly healed." He did not ask of the North wailing sorrow at Lee's passing, but only the same regard that he would accord the Federal dead. He spoke of Thomas and James B.

29. Breckinridge to Early, August 10, 1873, in Early MSS; D. Jones to Breckinridge, August 12, 1869, Isaac Caldwell to Breckinridge, January 15, June 27, 1872, in B. MSS; Charles Ivey to Breckinridge, June 2, 1869, Beck to Breckinridge, October 3, 1871, in JCB Papers.

McPherson, both now gone. "What Confederate is there who would refuse to raise his cap as their funeral train went by, or hesitate to drop a flower on their graves? Why? Because they were men of courage, honor and nobility; because they were true to their convictions of right, and soldiers whose hands were unstained by cruelty or pillage." [30]

It was hardly a conventional eulogy. Breckinridge did not trace Lee's career in the war and, indeed, spoke more on the symbolism of such demonstrations as this one in Louisville, and the hope they contained for the future, than on the dead general. He used the occasion for an expression of his hope and faith in the reconciliation of the nation, a hope which he and Lee shared fully. Thus it was no surprise that when the Lee Memorial Association was organized on October 24, 1870, and its founders looked for someone to head it who was representative of the great general's own search for reunion and harmony, they chose Breckinridge as its president.[31]

Almost immediately a rival group sprang up, led by Early, which sought to have the Lee monument in Richmond rather than Lexington, Virginia. Breckinridge was appointed chairman of the executive commission for Kentucky in this organization as well, though he declined. Indeed he was ready to decline both positions unless the two movements could be combined or harmonized, for, as Confederates should not fight amongst themselves in life, neither should they engage in any controversy over one in death, especially Lee.[32]

The general never ceased taking an interest in the welfare of Confederates and their orphans. He helped with the schooling of one young orphan, invented a fictitious loan during the evacuation of Richmond as an excuse to send money to the widow of another dead soldier, and often lent money and advice to those who still suffered from the crippling wounds and ill fortunes imposed by the war. More and more now he was thinking on what he felt may have been mistakes in his early "political notions," and old timers would later declare that in the 1870s Breckinridge was heard to express regret that he ever joined the Confederacy. Sorry or not, he was proud and concerned. The best hope that he would express to all old Confederates was that "we are all busy and doing something—to express the

30. Louisville *Courier-Journal*, October 15, 16, 1870; Morris and others to Breckinridge, October 19, 1870, in B. MSS.

31. William Pendleton to Breckinridge, October 24, 1870, in B. MSS.

32. Early to Breckinridge, November 21, 1870, St. John to Breckinridge, November 1, 1870, S. Hays to Breckinridge, November 8, 1870, in B. MSS: Breckinridge to Early, December 20, 1870, in Early MSS; "Sketch of the Lee Memorial Association," *SHSP*, XI (August–September, 1883), 390–91.

hope that we all feel that an idle, whining, repining man demands neither the respect of gods, men or women." As for his pride in his service, he told Early that "I seek no man's society who speaks of us as 'Traitors,' nor will I associate with our former adversaries upon the basis of mere sufferance." He was a champion of reconciliation, but not at the cost of honor or self-respect.[33]

The truest measure of Breckinridge's commitment to peace, harmony, and reunion through moderation, lies in his influence in that one realm which he so steadily eschewed, yet which could never ignore him, politics. He would never again hold public office, yet no man in Kentucky could wield his political power. Kentucky had been in a turmoil since the war, and the quip went the rounds that the state had waited until after Appomattox to secede. The Democrats who had remained loyal to the Union, men like Stevenson and Beck, in company with a number of former Whigs and Republicans whose slaves had been lost to the Emancipation Proclamation, seemed singularly unable to accept the result of the war they had supported. In the Federal victory they refused to recognize the death of the states' rights doctrines which had led men like Breckinridge across the line. Called Bourbons, they clung tenaciously to the past, filled their public offices with former Confederates, denied the newly freed Negroes their rights under the Thirteenth and Fourteenth amendments to the Constitution, and strove to maintain a social, economic, and political system which had been dead for a decade.[34]

Breckinridge was totally out of sympathy with the Bourbons. Although he never declared an affiliation, it was obvious that his attachment lay with the other portion of Kentucky's divided Democrats, the new Liberals. "There are many indications that the Democratic party in Kentucky is splitting," reported one tabloid late in 1870, "into two sections which may be called Liberal and Bourbon and it is reported that John C. Breckinridge and a few other old time leaders sympathize with the former, and think that the results of the war should be recognized, and a new departure taken." The general's commitment to the new Liberal policy is easily seen in his not universally popular stand for the Cincinnati Southern, his declin-

33. Fannie Chapman to Breckinridge, October 27, 1869, E. M. Bruce to Breckinridge, June 13, 1870, in JCB Papers; undated clipping ca. February 13, 1872, from unidentified newspaper, in B. MSS; Dorris, *Pardon and Amnesty*, 275n; New York *Times*, October 26, 1871; Breckinridge to Early, August 10, 1873, in Early MSS.

34. For a good résumé of the situation in Kentucky, see Watterson, '*Marse Henry*,' I, 161–85.

ing to take active part in the numerous Confederate monument movements organized by militant former rebels, and his constant refusal to address the many reunions of former Confederate units that sought him.[35]

More obvious evidence of his liberalism lay in Breckinridge's attitude toward the chief object of Bourbon hatred and scorn, the freed slaves. Consistently, the Bourbons had ignored the new amendments, denying the Negroes the vote, and refusing to allow courts to accept their testimony against whites. The general, as he showed in his address for the Cincinnati Southern, still was not sanguine over the future of white and black living together, fearing the same inequities and resultant degradation of both races which before the war had made him an adherent of African colonization. He preferred that any future immigrants to Kentucky should be white. Nevertheless, the war decreed that the Negro was free and entitled to certain rights, and, never wavering from his fervent attachment to the letter of the Constitution, he would see those rights respected. As a result, Breckinridge went on record as favoring the acceptance of Negro testimony in cases against whites, the foremost Kentucky lawyer to do so. It would not be until 1872 that the Bourbons were finally overcome on the point. While Breckinridge did not actively campaign on the issue, it is obvious that the simple knowledge that he was opposed to this form of discrimination carried great weight in moving Kentucky to living up to the Constitution. What makes it obvious is the destruction that this same kind of undemonstrative but widely known hostility visited upon another unsavory force in the state, the Ku Klux Klan.[36]

Kentucky was the only state outside the seceded South that provided a fertile spawning ground for this vigilante vestige of white supremacy. Formed in 1866 as a social club, the Klan soon fell into the hands of the bitter, malcontented, unreconciled former Confederates who saw in it a covert means of resistance to their Federal conquerors. The agent of this resistance, its victim, was the Negro. Through intimidation, violence, and sometimes murder, the Klan kept the former slave subjugated, in constant terror, too fearful to assert himself or claim his rights. The Bluegrass was particularly infested, and Lexington saw its share of violence and lynchings. Stevenson and the legislature did next to nothing to curb the outlawry, and it enjoyed wide support among the people. To those who did oppose the

35. Sarah Waller to Breckinridge, December 5, 1870, in B. MSS.
36. Cincinnati *Commercial*, May 18, 1875; Louisville *Courier-Journal*, March 18, 1869.

organization, their physical safety seemed to demand silence, or at least a refusal to take any active part in combating the Klan.[37]

For Breckinridge, however, the outrage was too great, and he was not home for long before he spoke his mind. Arguing a case in Lexington on March 13, 1870, he loudly denounced the Ku Klux Klan as despicable banditti, "idiots or villains," and offered his assistance in any attempts to arrest them and bring them to justice. His denunciation was widely reprinted throughout the state, and the most influential paper in Kentucky, the *Courier-Journal*, boldly took its stand with him. "Gen. Breckinridge was a fighting Rebel," declared its editor Henry Watterson, "but neither a brigand or an assassin." The general's pronouncement brought down some hot criticism from former Confederates now active in promoting the Klan, but he never wavered from his position. Even Beck disagreed with him, but he stood firm. Breckinridge was not called upon to take the further action that he offered, but the extent of his hostility to the Klan is evident from the fact that his Lexington declaration was the only instance in the years after the war in which he agreed to act in, and indeed initiate, the prosecution.[38]

The effect of the general's statement was, by the testimony of those who observed its action, truly great. Cassius M. Clay believed it decisive. "He denounced and effectively killed in Kentucky, at least, the remorseless 'Ku-Klux-Klan,'" wrote the general's old foe. Old Crittenden's nephew Thomas in Missouri, soon to be Congressman and governor, believed that "had it not been for Gen. B. [there] would have been much trouble in Ky. immediately after the war with Ku Klux. His bold and defiant stand against such desperadoes intimidated the whole band and dispersed the organization." Breckinridge could make such a denunciation and get away with it, for his position in the state was too high for the Klan to risk retaliation. At the same time, the prestige and respect that he commanded surely turned much of the popular support or acquiescence which the "idiots and villains" had previously enjoyed. The Klan, though easily begun in Kentucky, was never highly organized there, and the advent of Federal arrests and prosecution in 1871 slowed its operations drastically, but there is no denying that the opposition of Breckinridge was a large factor in discrediting it in the eyes of thousands of Kentuckians.[39]

37. Allen W. Trelease, *White Terror: The Ku Klux Klan Conspiracy and Southern Reconstruction* (New York, 1971), 3–6, 125.

38. Louisville *Courier-Journal*, March 14, 1870; Trelease, *White Terror*, 260, 281; Beck to Breckinridge, March 8, 1871, in JCB Papers.

39. Clay, *Memoirs*, I, 220; Thomas T. Crittenden to W. C. P. Breckinridge, May 22, 1875, in B. MSS; Trelease, *White Terror*, 313–17.

Despite his repeated refusals to reenter public life, every gubernatorial election in Kentucky brought out a new cry for Breckinridge to emerge from retirement, and just as often he renewed his refusal. Indeed, he would not allow his friends in Congress even to attempt the waiving of his political disabilities under the Fourteenth Amendment, which required a two-thirds vote of Congress to enable him to hold public office. Furthermore, in keeping with his resolution to avoid all controversy, he even declined to allow friends like Beck to defend him when assailed. When one senator referred in seeming disparagement to the general's flight from Kentucky in 1861, and Beck asked permission to explain the situation, he was refused. This course was not without its toll, and Breckinridge paid much. Clifton could see it.

> The wisest, most unselfish, and noblest part of your life is your conduct since the war. I venture to say that it has called for greater restraint, and caused you more suffering, to sit by and see every vital taken from your country, by fanatics and scoundrels, than every other part of your life put together. A single word of pity or condemnation, or a single suggestion from you, would only have made them more cruel and insane. . . . It takes the highest greatness not to needlessly offend these people, and at the same time not to assist them; but simply to wait, through weary years, knowing that "Truth crushed to Earth *will* rise again."

Clifton gauged his father well. "In regard to public affairs, & my personal fortunes," wrote his father, "you are quite right in supposing that I am not without feeling, yet for years, I have seen no other course to pursue, than to be silent, and uncomplaining." [40]

In national affairs, this uncomplaining attitude revealed itself in the uncommonly moderate terms in which he spoke of the Republican administration. He gave it no praise but, as in his 1869 statement in Wisconsin, spoke his mind plainly. Indeed, his old friend Forney believed that Breckinridge was trying to show his devotion as a Democrat turned Republican. This was a little extravagant, but the general did, in truth, view his old foes with far more tolerance than most Confederates. One evening, at a gathering of friends who were bewailing the crimes of the party in power, one of them turned to the general and asked "What do you say about it, John?" His answer startled them. "I have this to say: Let the republican party do the worst it can; let the republicans do fifty times worse than they are doing, and then we shall have the best government any people in the world ever

40. Undated clipping *ca.* 1871, Beck to Breckinridge, April 19, 27, 1874, Clifton R. Breckinridge to Breckinridge, May 13, 1874, Breckinridge to Clifton R. Breckinridge, May 22, 1874, all in JCB Papers; Joseph Lewis to Breckinridge, April 1, 1872, in B. MSS.

had." Of course, Breckinridge would have been pleased to see the Republicans out of power. In 1872 he almost reentered politics in an active way upon the nomination of Horace Greeley for the presidency to run against Grant. The general could not forget the attachment he felt for the old editor, despite his eccentricities so flagrant that the convention which nominated him was called the "convocation of cranks." Within days after the nomination, Breckinridge sent Greeley a telegram announcing that he would support him, even offering to speak in Lexington under the auspices of the Liberal Republicans, actually the Liberal wing of the state's Democrats. He agreed to one invitation from a Greeley club, but illness prevented his meeting the engagement. Greeley planned, if elected, to remove Breckinridge's political disabilities. Of course, Greeley died during the campaign, and Grant won another term.[41]

Toward the real men in power themselves, the Grants and Sumners, Breckinridge felt no animosity. Here, more than anywhere else, is displayed his ability to put aside the past, to associate with his former enemies. Former friends who had fought against him during the war found nothing but warmth in him, and even to those he had not met Breckinridge showed respect, if not admiration.

In the summer of 1872, while spending a few weeks at the fashionable health resort at Long Branch, New Jersey, on the Atlantic coast, he struck up once more an old acquaintance with Colonel John A. Joyce, a Kentuckian who fought for the Union. One day the general heard that President Grant was staying at a cottage nearby and, never having met him, decided to pay his respects. He and Joyce first called on General Orville E. Babcock, Grant's private secretary, and then went on to see the president. They found him sitting alone smoking a cigar on his porch. Joyce introduced Breckinridge, and Grant asked them to sit down. For an hour or more, he and the general spoke of the past and present. The Kentuckian did not know it but he had been on Grant's mind. The president recognized the influence and potential for good that Breckinridge possessed, and thought it could be put to excellent use in Kentucky by his being elected governor. "Breckinridge was most anxious to restore the Union to good relations," Grant stated, and he considered relieving him of his disabilities in order that

41. Forney, *Anecdotes*, I, 344; undated clipping in Sallie Johnson Breckinridge Scrapbook in possession of Peter Ten Eyck; Watterson, '*Marse Henry*,' 206; R. Blount to Breckinridge, May 15, 1872, S. Carlisle to Breckinridge, September 14, 1872, Paul Rankin to Breckinridge, September 14, 1872, all in B. MSS; New York *Times*, August 10, 1872.

he might run, not as a Republican, but as an anti-Bourbon. "The influence of a man like Breckinridge at this time would have been most useful." However, Grant's Senate managers would not consent to such a move, and he was forced to abandon it. Grant, the Grant of Shiloh, Vicksburg, Chattanooga, the Grant whose terrible attack at Cold Harbor died its bloody death in front of the Kentuckian's line, recognized as well or better than anyone the spirit which animated his former foe. This feeling was confirmed when they finished their conversation. Grant's servant brought in mint juleps. Breckinridge arose, the others following, and proposed a toast to the United States.[42]

That night, Breckinridge sat on the verandah at the West End Hotel, listening to the roar of the ocean, and looking up at the stars. He asked Joyce to join him. "His heart was seemingly surcharged with the memories of vanished years," thought the colonel, and he sat for more than an hour listening to the general's recollections of the past. Joyce, too, spoke, and at last asked Breckinridge of his true feelings on the result of the war.

"Ah, Joyce," replied the weary Kentuckian, "it is all right and far better that we still live as one people, than be torn into fragments by the minions of princes, kings, and emperors. Many a lonely hour I have spent in midnight moments on the streets of London and Paris, awaiting the time that I could once again catch a glimpse of the Stars and Stripes, the flag of my fathers, and all I now wish is to sleep forever beneath its God-given folds." [43]

42. George A. Custer to Breckinridge, January 25, 1872, in B. MSS; Washington *Post*, March 18, 1894; Young, *Around the World*, II, 461–62.

43. Washington *Post*, March 18, 1894.

CHAPTER 5

There Is Now No North and No South

The general was ill. It had been a curious paradox that during his lifetime, despite his robust and vigorous frame and constitution—a student of physiognomy reportedly declared that Breckinridge was better formed than any of the world's current athletes that he had studied—he spent much of his life battling recurrent illness. He was susceptible to disease, especially chest colds, and the years of bad food, exposure, and little rest during the war, had seriously undermined his already low resistance. As a result, all through the exile, and even more in his first four years at home, he had one bout with sickness after another. No one of them had been remarkably bad, but their cumulative effect was noticeable, and 1873 gave them the upper hand.[1]

The year was a disaster. One of the nation's periodic financial panics hit with devastating force, precipitated largely by overspeculation in railroads, and by the chicanery of Jay Cooke. The depression that followed, one of the worst in American history, lasted for five years. Breckinridge felt it almost as severely as he had the 1857 slump, though his personal losses were comparatively small. His Bass Island quarry venture was stopped indefinitely, the St. Paul investments were unsalable, and the report came from Superior that "Matters appear very gloomy." Worse yet, the Piedmont and Arlington began to fail. "We are not making a cent," groaned his chief agent, "on the whole losing day by day." What hurt Breckinridge the most, however, was the serious threat to the Elizabethtown, Lexington and Big Sandy. The Chesapeake and Ohio was forced to halt work on the line's construction, railroad agents began resigning because of nonpayment of salaries, fewer and fewer contracts came in, and, by January, 1874, the company was almost bankrupt. As a result, the line fell into some disrepute, and

1. New York *Turf, Field and Farm*, May 21, 1875.

this mortified Breckinridge, so much so that Stoddard Johnston believed that the Elizabethtown, Lexington and Big Sandy's embarrassment "tended much to wear his constitution." In the fall of 1873, the general went to New York to confer with Tracy and others concerned with the failing road. On his return to Kentucky, his friends first noticed a decided change in his health. He would never be well again.[2]

The general passed a quiet winter in Lexington. His illness was not alarming, and Mary and Fanny took advantage of his being confined to the house to tease him good-naturedly, and he complained to Clifton that "indeed at the present I am of very small repute here." He got back at his wife by carefully poking fun at her weight. "She is getting quite stout," he told his son, "but the fact has to be alluded to with great caution." His family, now well settled, was a comfort to him. Little Mary went to school in New York, Fanny was at home, Owen—who had decided that it was time for him to be called by his real name, John—was starting a good law practice in San Francisco, one that would eventually lead to a seat in the California senate. Cabell and Clifton were in Arkansas struggling to make a living growing cotton. In later years Cliff would represent the state in Congress and serve as Grover Cleveland's minister to Russia. After a winter in Kentucky, Breckinridge went down to Arkansas—"a robber ridden country"—in March, 1874, hoping that the change in climate would do him good. It did not, but he did get to see for the first and only time a very special namesake, his first grandson, Cabell's boy John C. Breckinridge.[3]

A month later, back in Lexington, the general took a sudden turn for the worse after spending a week almost completely shut in the damp courthouse working on a murder case. The close atmosphere aggravated a latent pneumonia and put him in bed almost immediately. He grew rapidly worse, was unable even to write a letter, and seemed near death. Clifton, who shared his father's belief in facing facts squarely, wrote to express his own love and admiration for the general, to comfort him, and to voice the hope that Breckinridge was resigned to what might come. "I shall meet you at

2. D. Mitchell to Beriah Magoffin, January 27, 1873, Breckinridge to Clifton R. Breckinridge, May 31, 1873, E. W. Anderson to Breckinridge, September 30, 1873, February 25, 1874, J. Kirksey to Breckinridge, March 23, 1874, John Echols to Breckinridge, January 2, 1874, James J. Tracy to Breckinridge, January 8, 1874, R. Hannah to Breckinridge, January 1, 1874, all in JCB Papers; Frankfort *Tri-Weekly Yeoman*, May 18, 1875.

3. Breckinridge to Clifton R. Breckinridge, March 31, December 25, 1873, John W. Breckinridge to Breckinridge, August 12, October 18, 1874, Sal Franklin to Breckinridge, March 12, 1874, all in JCB Papers; Breckinridge to Jubal A. Early, January 25, 1873, in Early MSS.

the Bar," wrote his son, "and I can see you now, standing up like a man, as you have always stood, an example to us all. Making no denials and no equivocations, but stating, as God knows, however bright our guiding star or level our way, that our path has been a crooked one." The general's special pride in Clifton was well founded.[4]

But his son need not have worried quite so much, for Breckinridge rallied remarkably. His doctor was amazed at the general's rate of recovery, and confided that, but for his "extraordinary constitution," he would be dead. By late May he was able to sit up and walk about his room. He discovered his appetite and was resolved to go to some resort in the East for the summer. In June he was able to go to Frankfort for a brief visit, and Johnston, though finding him very thin, thought he looked much better. Late that month he and the family went to Hazelwood, New York, near White Plains, for several weeks. The peacefulness was what he needed most, and his mind was "calm and free from care." When he found that there was another retired celebrity in the neighborhood Breckinridge, though still not well, dragged himself from his quarters to pay a visit. The great Dexter, one of the finest race horses of the age, was there spending his twilight years. The general stood fully ten minutes in quiet admiration of the white-legged trotter. "The scene was suggestive," thought a racing enthusiast who witnessed the silent meeting. "Two lions, fretting in retirement, were standing face to face. The applause of the world had been music to their ears, but now they were shut out from it, and the loss of it had brought a shade of melancholy to each." [5]

Breckinridge went on to spend a few days in Virginia, where a friend from former days found that "increasing age, disappointed hopes, and his varied experiences in life had changed his appearance from the well-proportioned, handsome, and erect physical manhood that excited my admiration when I saw him as Vice President in Washington." The general found that, despite his hopes, the trip had done his health no good, and he returned to Lexington in the autumn, disappointed. Needing quiet, the Breckinridges rented a small two-story house on Second Street. The general grew steadily worse. His stomach was delicate, there was little that he could eat, and he began coughing up clotted blood. "I have everything that

4. Frankfort *Tri-Weekly Yeoman*, May 18, 1875; Breckinridge to Clifton R. Breckinridge, May 22, 1874, Mary Bullock to Breckinridge, April 22, 1874, Clifton R. Breckinridge to Breckinridge, May 15, 1874, all in JCB Papers.

5. Breckinridge to Clifton R. Breckinridge, May 22, 1874, Clifton R. Breckinridge to Breckinridge, July 13, 1874, in JCB Papers; Frankfort *Tri-Weekly Yeoman*, June 4, 1874; Breckinridge to L. C. Handy, June 29, 1874, in Breckinridge MSS, FC.

love and attention can give," he told Clifton; "I have not given up hope of recovery." Just the same, though, he decided to prepare his will.[6]

One chief pleasure remained to Breckinridge. Although he was more and more confined to his room as fall moved on toward winter, he was still able to be driven out to the race course in the afternoons. Since 1872 he had been president of the Kentucky Association at Lexington, the oldest racing and breeding organization in the nation. The general never lost his love of horses. When a Congressman, he had often declared that his highest ambition was to own three hundred acres of Bluegrass and do nothing but raise fine stock. Now he owned five bay animals, all thoroughbreds. "The admiration of the blood-horse was a paramount consideration, if not a passion, with him," wrote a professional stock journal. "On the race course, as everywhere, he appeared the uncompromising gentleman." He would not, and never did, wager on the horses but enjoyed them for the pure beauty of the animal and the race. Out of respect and love, Lexington's horsemen named the Breckinridge Stake for him, and preserved fond memories of his last visit to the track "as he stood, wan and weak, in the October sunshine, leaning against the white fence of the quarter stretch on the grounds of the Lexington course, watching, with a gleam of pleasure in his weary eyes, the movements of the horses around the course." He was almost completely gray now, thin, his face showing the years of hardship and sadness, yet still handsome, still majestic. From his tired visage those eyes still burned brightly. He was, friends thought, "a magnificent wreck."[7]

Breckinridge rallied briefly in December, but one of his lungs, which had hemorrhaged sometime before, gave him no peace. He was unable to leave the house after October. Meanwhile, he turned all of his law business over to a new partner, R. A. Thornton, and dissolved his connection with the struggling Piedmont and Arlington. However, he did not cease to take an interest in state and national affairs. He promoted the new law department at the young University of Kentucky in Lexington by sending its curriculum catalogs to friends, and was anxious for the spread of higher education

6. Thomas D. Jeffress, "Escape of Breckinridge and Benjamin," *Confederate Veteran*, XVIII (January, 1910), 27; Johnston, "Sketches of Operations, No. 3," p. 392; John Viley to Breckinridge, August 4, 1874, Clifton R. Breckinridge to Breckinridge, September 12, 1874, Gustavus W. Smith to Breckinridge, October 18, 1874, Breckinridge to Clifton R. Breckinridge, October 7, 1874, all in JCB Papers.

7. Ranck, *History of Lexington*, 133; Louisville *Courier-Journal*. May 18, 1875; New York *Live Stock Record*, May 21, 1875; Joseph Robinson to Breckinridge, August 15, 1874, in JCB Papers; New York *Turf, Field and Farm*, May 15-18, 1875; Inventory & Appraisement of the Personal Estate of Jno. C. Breckinridge, Will Book 4, p. 272, Fayette County courthouse, Lexington, Ky.

in the rest of the South. In general, he still felt solicitous for the welfare of the section. "I regard the future in the South and especially in La, Ark, and Miss as full of uncertainty." He feared the measures Grant would take to subdue Arkansas and Louisiana especially, since rioting had broken out in Little Rock, New Orleans, and elsewhere. Grant appeared to be trying to bind Arkansas to his administration rather than showing any concern for its peace or prosperity. "If you can get peace and stability there would be great and immediate prosperity in the South," Breckinridge counseled; "untill then, you can only hold fast." He believed that rioting, whatever the grounds or justification, served only to hurt the South and encourage the Radicals.[8]

At last, it seemed that his work for reconciliation might be recognized. The 1876 Centennial Exhibition was coming up. As early as 1872 the United States Mint in Philadelphia asked his advice on it, and back in March, 1874, its managers had consulted Breckinridge on the advisability of including a Civil War artifacts exhibit. Significantly, they turned to him to find out if former Confederates would be willing to contribute to it, believing that such a gesture would promote good feeling. Shortly afterward, his close friend from former days, John W. Forney, renewed their acquaintance. The Finance Committee of the Centennial had asked him to go to Washington to help seek a $3 million appropriation for the event, and he agreed only on the condition that he might invite Breckinridge to accompany him. Illness prevented the general from going, but, if he had gone, he would have seen Beck and Stevenson fighting against the appropriation bill. They would not support it until a universal amnesty act should free Breckinridge, Davis, and others, of all their political disabilities. In return for this support, Forney agreed to back the desired amnesty in his paper, the Philadelphia Press. Nothing came of it, but Breckinridge was still spoken of by many in connection with the Centennial. The conviction gained some currency that he should be chosen as the chief orator for the opening ceremonies at Philadelphia on July 4, 1876. Significantly, the suggestion came predominantly from southern newspapers, indicating the extent to which those in his own section looked to the general as a symbol of reconciliation. "If Philadelphia would bridge the bloody chasm with perdurable stone and put the final seal upon the bond of union . . . and give most eloquent expression to

8. Breckinridge to Clifton R. Breckinridge, December 24, 1874, January 3, February 16, 1875, J. Kirksey to Breckinridge, February 15, 22, 1875, James G. Leach to Breckinridge, January 18, 1874, L. Edwards to Breckinridge, July 12, 1874, all in JCB Papers; New York Times, April 25, 1875; Breckinridge to Handy, June 29, 1874, in Breckinridge MSS, FC.

the assertion of American brotherhood and unity," wrote one Texas tabloid, "let John C. Breckinridge occupy worthily, as he would, the position which the world at this moment believes could alone be properly filled by a Daniel Webster." Such a concession to southern intelligence and patriotism, it said, would be more flattering to Breckinridge than would be the presidency to him who should succeed Grant, and it would be far more indicative of the return of fraternal feeling between North and South. If the general had been so chosen, and if he could have been in Philadelphia for the occasion, it would have been the most fitting capstone of all to his ten-year quest for peace, moderation, and reunion.[9]

But Breckinridge would not be going to Philadelphia in 1876. He was slowly dying. He seemed to sense it, but the knowledge caused him little remorse; he made jest of it. Early in 1875, when discussing current affairs with friends over breakfast, the conversation turned inadvertently to death. For an hour or more it went on, Breckinridge listening silently until, "with a twinkle of a rather whimsical mirth," he said, "Come, come, let's put an end to this. It is really getting to be personal." [10]

The family and his doctors had hoped that the coming of spring and warmer weather would improve his condition, but it did not. By the beginning of May, his cousin W. C. P. Breckinridge, who earlier believed he would recover, sadly told Clifton, "Now I do not." Grant's vice-president, Henry Wilson, an old friend and political foe, made a special trip to Lexington to see Breckinridge. It was a happy reunion for both. Significantly, Wilson went despite the heavy criticism from members of his own party. He left the general's bed convinced that it was impossible for him to recover. Friends from all over Kentucky were crowding into Lexington now, and he met them, propped up on pillows in his sickroom. Telegrams came in from all points, asking daily reports of his condition. Little Mary and Clifton hurried to Lexington; Cabell and Owen were unable to come.[11]

The general's exact illness had been variously diagnosed as emanating

9. O. C. Bosbyshell to Breckinridge, March 3, 1874, John W. Forney to Breckinridge, March 19, 1874, James B. Beck to Breckinridge, May 18, 1874, clipping from Austin (Tex.) *Daily Democratic Statesman*, n.d., all in JCB Papers; Forney, *Anecdotes*, II, 198; R. Snowden to Breckinridge, December 19, 1872, in B. MSS. Richard Henry Lee was chosen after Breckinridge's death, though not as chief orator.

10. Clipping from unidentified newspaper of May 19, 1875, in John W. "Owen" Breckinridge Scrapbook in possession of the late Lee Breckinridge Thomas, Berkeley, Calif.

11. W. C. P. Breckinridge to Clifton R. Breckinridge, May 1, 1875, in JCB Papers; Louisville *Courier-Journal*, May 19, 1875; Ernest McKay, *Henry Wilson: Practical Radical, a Portrait of a Politician* (Port Washington, N.Y., 1971), 238; Cincinnati *Enquirer*, May 18, 1875.

from the liver or the lung, but no one seemed sure. Dr. Louis A. Sayre of New York, a cousin of one of the general's long-time Lexington friends, was called in by his doctor, John R. Desha, and he arrived on May 9. There he found Desha, Dr. Luke Blackburn, and a Dr. Gross from Philadelphia. In company with William Preston they all went to Breckinridge's house and proceeded to get involved in a rather petty misunderstanding over who was actually *the* attending physician, meanwhile barely concealing their desire to be at the races instead of with the patient. The general, looking on in silence, finally interceded, weary of their professional pedantry. "Let *me* settle this matter," he said, "if I am a sick man. You all want to go to the races, and it is now 12 o'clock. Desha, go with Preston and take your lunch with Gross, and then go to the races; and Blackburn, you go with Sayre, and, after the races, come and overhaul me at 4 o'clock." That finished the controversy.[12]

At 4 P.M. that afternoon the doctors gathered once more at Second Street, received from Desha a history of the case, and from Breckinridge his own account of his condition, and then proceeded to a complete examination. They found him emaciated, anemic, almost bloodless. The trouble was centered in his right lung which, when sounded by the stethoscope, proved to be two thirds full of fluid. Sayre tried to mark on the general's chest the line to which his lung was full, and Breckinridge looked on, interested, commenting whenever the pencil was applied, "that's it; there you are; you are right on the line." Going outside for consultation, Desha showed the others a spittoon containing the general's expectoration for the past eleven hours, nearly two quarts, and they were informed that sometimes it went to nearly a gallon for a whole day. Microscopic examination revealed that the fluid originated in the liver, and this confirmed their diagnosis. Breckinridge's chief malady was cirrhosis of the liver, brought on initially, they felt, by his injury at Cold Harbor when his horse fell on him, killed by a shell which may have somehow struck the general's side as well. The cirrhosis, in turn, caused adhesions of the liver, diaphragm, and right lung, as well as abscesses of all three. Death, they decided, was inevitable.

His only hope of temporary relief from the racking cough that produced the fluid—and from the near-suffocation he suffered when it would not come up—was an operation, paracentesis of the abdomen, a means by which an opening would be made in his chest to allow the fluid to drain naturally.

12. This account of the operation and Breckinridge's subsequent condition is drawn from a letter of Dr. Louis A. Sayre published in the Louisville *Medical Weekly*, June 12, 1875, and from the Cincinnati *Enquirer*, May 18, 1875.

Gross explained the whole situation to Breckinridge, who asked a few questions about how the operation was performed, and then sat silent for a few minutes, "looking at each of us most intently with those great eyes," wrote Sayre, "as if he would look us through." Finally he spoke.

> Gentlemen, I am under the greatest personal obligations for this great kindness, for your courtesy and attention in coming this great distance to give me so careful an examination. I wish to express to you my warmest gratitude. I am perfectly satisfied from your address, and Dr. Gross' clear description, and from my own sensations, that you have a perfectly clear and exact conception of my present condition, and that your proposition offers me *all* that science now can do for me. I only wish to add that I am not only willing, but anxious to have the operation performed, and I am now ready to submit to your knife.

The clarity and resonance of Breckinridge's voice somewhat startled Gross, for illness had dulled it much during the past weeks. "General," he exclaimed, "your voice seems as clear and strong as ever."

Suddenly it was the Breckinridge of old, the champion of the stump or the legislative hall. With a gesture of infinite grace and beauty, he waved his arm before them, smiling broadly. "Why, Doctor," he said, "I can throw my voice a mile."

The general wanted the operation performed immediately, but the doctors postponed it until the following morning. Gathering at 10 A.M., they found that a coughing spell had emptied the lung again, thought of waiting another day for it to fill, and then decided to go ahead and operate. Breckinridge was administered chloroform, and a short incision was made into the pleural cavity. After inspection, they agreed to complete the operation, placing a silver tube into the lung on the following Wednesday when it had filled again. The general passed a quiet night, and the next day confided to friends that "I feel so easy and comfortable, and experience such relief from suffering, that I believe mortification has set in." The next day, May 12, he called in Beck and F. K. Hunt to assist in finishing his will.[13]

For the next several days, Breckinridge's condition fluctuated, Desha staying at his side constantly. Finally, on Sunday afternoon, May 16, he believed that death was near, since the general had not coughed for some time, nor passed any fluid. His voice was a shadowy whisper. The next morning, however, Breckinridge was breathing normally, looking bright and cheerful when Sayre called. The doctor found the wound in his side closed by a cotton-like discharge, removed it, and was overjoyed to see the fluid draining freely again. Breckinridge felt better than he had for several

13. Will Book 4, pp. 136–37, Fayette County courthouse, Lexington.

days, washed his hands and face, dressed in clean linen, combed his hair, and took a breakfast of beef tea, toast, milk and cream. He sat up in bed, looking greatly improved, and promptly launched into a spirited discussion of the various newspaper reports on his condition. Sayre soon left, confident that the general would last for some time yet in comparative comfort.

He remained quiet and peaceful for several hours, but at 3 o'clock that afternoon, he took a drastic turn for the worse, and despite stimulants, he steadily sank. A few minutes before five he became speechless. Still conscious, he looked about him and communicated with his eyes. The people he had known and loved were with him. His eyes said his farewells. Little Mary, Clifton, Fanny, his cousin W. C. P., Desha and his wife, a nephew Cabell Bullock, and a few more friends and relations, stood about the bed. And of course, there was Mary. In the gathering dimness, he must have seen others as well, those already gone. Douglas, Lincoln, and Lee, were waiting for him.

For the third time in his life, John C. Breckinridge was ending a career with a journey. Unlike the two before it, this one was not in flight. Unlike them, this one led to an unimaginable unknown, yet one in which the general was confident he would find peace. His life seemed measured by his journeys, and, appropriately, this was the only one over which he felt no regret. It had come when it would, and he was ready. As he lay there, speechless, feeling the growing cold, he may have seen as well that this trip, at last, left the great and central question of his life an answer. A man of moderation, conciliation, and compromise could win out over malice and passion, over his own failures and tragedies and those of a generation, to leave behind a real and potential legacy of reason and peace.

The first journey, that harried flight from Lexington in September, 1861, brought to an end his twenty years as a leading Democrat, the decade he had spent in building his party into the dominant force in Kentucky, and his own unparalleled political career. A simple arrest order brought it all to a head. In an instant his life was totally disrupted, his native state arrayed against him, his family broken up, and his career blasted to nothing at its very peak.

Perhaps his life might have been different if Breckinridge's father had lived. Growing up in a home with only his mother and sisters, he heard little of politics and the nature of government other than that handed down from his grandfather. The principles of John Breckinridge had been appropriate for his own time, but, like all theories of government, they could not remain static and stay in tune with the change and growth in the new nation. They had to undergo the same evolution that was making the United States evermore modern, and in the thinking of John Breckinridge's sons that change was evident. But J. Cabell Breckinridge did not live to pass this change on to his only son, and though the later influence of his brothers liberalized the moral, social, and political thinking of John C. Breckinridge, his concept of the nature of the Union under the Constitution came to him directly from his grandfather almost undiluted.

There was a curious paradox in Breckinridge. He was one of the most well-read and educated politicians of his day, and in another time the depth of his thought on society, morals, science, and philosophy might have classed him as an intellectual. In all of these fields he could see and recognize and understand the natural evolution that time, better education, greater personal freedom, and the necessities of a world rapidly increasing in sophistication, demanded. But at the same time he could not see or he refused to see, that all of this also required a commensurate evolution in the nature of the Federal government and interpretation of the Constitution. The reasons for this lay in his very character. His friend William Preston Johnston found Breckinridge "singularly reticent and cautious in matters of import. He made few promises and broke none, and was truthful and magnanimous. It was difficult to move him to anger, impossible to provoke him to revenge." Preston would build upon this to say that "In the character of Breckinridge there was a great reverence for authority. There was nothing turbulent, discontented or rebellious in the man." And it was generally conceded among his lawyer peers in Lexington that he never "engaged in a dispute without saying that his adversary was wrong." [14]

The sum of all this was a political nature bent toward an extreme conservatism. He was calm, methodical, cautious in forming his resolves, never reaching his decisions without deep thought, and never giving in to emotional or "rebellious" reactions. Once that decision was reached, he was sure he was right, occasionally almost smug, and unyielding in his persistence. Many mistook the time that he spent before acting on a question for indolence or laziness—and it does appear that his energies were erratic—but for the most part it was time spent in weighing all the evidence, taking into account all the variables, and forming a decision to which he would commit himself, and which he believed to be right. By 1861 he had spent over twenty years studying the Constitution from the point of view of his grand-

14. William Preston Johnston, *Johnston*, 297; Louisville *Courier-Journal*, May 26, June 18, 1875.

father and the Kentucky Resolves of 1798 and 1799, which were practically ancestral doctrine, and after that much scrutiny he was sure that he and John Breckinridge were right.[15]

His religious background was no small influence on his conservatism. The strict Calvinism that was his spiritual fare from birth taught him respect for authority, for, among the old school Presbyterians, theirs was an authoritarian God. At the same time, he learned and accepted the basic premise that Man's natural instincts, if not curbed, tended toward evil. This spiritual scheme of things was easily applied to the more concrete world of government, wherein the Constitution was the authority which checked the licentiousness of men, a licentiousness which, subverting that great document by giving it a liberal interpretation not intended at the time of its framing, could only end in the loss of personal and public freedom and rights.

Other influences contributed as well. One was his southern birth and heritage. No northerner ever declared his unbounded elation at being from the North, but a man who came from the South said so, and with pride. In that section, thanks to its uneven competition in population and industrial development with the North, an increasingly conservative stand for states' rights as strictly construed in the Constitution was regarded as its guard against minority standing and northern domination. Breckinridge accepted this doctrine in large part, though hardly in its entirety, and it cannot be denied that his feelings as a man from that section exerted some influence upon his public conduct. However, it was not decisive. As his record clearly shows, Breckinridge did what he did because he believed he was right, not because he was southern.

As for slavery, the principal cause at the heart of the states' rights-secession controversy, Breckinridge's position was hardly that of the typical southerner. His feelings about the institution were well, but not widely, known; his defense of it in spite of his feelings hardly sprang from personal interest. To him slavery, one of the rights of the states, was recognized by and therefore guaranteed in the Constitution. A Federal act of emancipation or restriction of the movement of slaves was unconstitutional because that document did not distinguish between property in Negroes and any other form of property. Any such legislation came naturally in the province of the states as one of the implied powers not specifically enumerated in the Federal compact. This was the only basis on which Breckinridge ever

15. Duke, *Reminiscences*, 193; William Preston Johnston, *Johnston*, 297.

justified or defended the institution, and it set him apart from most other prominent southern politicians. They cried states' rights as a cover, when their real concern was only one of those rights, slavery, an economic mainstay, and a curious symbol of their independence, smug superiority, and chivalrous "cavalier" mythology. Breckinridge, whose only other substantive objection to freeing the slaves was the effect that the sudden mingling of the two races might have upon the society and well-being of both, was truly concerned for the rights of the states in the full meaning of the term. It was a misplaced and largely unnecessary concern, but it was somehow more admirable than a mere desire to perpetuate human bondage and white supremacy.

The result of these influences—family heritage, personality and character, spiritual background, southern sympathies and slavery—was immense, enough so to produce in John C. Breckinridge a brand of states' rights conservatism that had been dated in the days of Jackson, and which was entirely out of touch with the needs and realities of an America that was going through the greatest period of industrial, economic, social, and political change in its history. Yet even all of this, even his myopic view of the scope and nature of the Constitution, still was not enough to put him on that gray mare on the road to Virginia in 1861. The blame for that lies elsewhere, beyond his control, beyond any individual's control, in the realm of national psychology. The people of the North, the people of the South, and perhaps even Breckinridge himself, had been persuaded to believe that his real sympathies did not lie with the Union. This persuasion grew out of his associations, the loyalty he accepted, and the friendship he gave.

Prior to 1854 and the Nebraska bill, Breckinridge's record in Washington had been, with minor exceptions, asectional. In that year, however, he first identified with the doughface Pierce, the then seemingly prosouthern Douglas, and the true ultras like Atchison, Mason, and Phillips. His difficulty with Cutting was widely touted throughout the nation, favorably in the South, not so favorably in the North. Indeed, the effect of this manifestation alone, thanks to the tenor of the publicity given it in the North, was such that a major charge against Breckinridge in the campaigns of both 1856 and 1860 was his predilection for violence and dueling. The combination of this, his still limited associations with radical southern men, and his nomination as vice-president on the relatively mild Cincinnati platform, produced in the mind of more than one editor the same distortion that one in Rochester, New York, put in print when he wrote that Breckinridge "is a large slave owner, and is understood to cordially approve of all the efforts made to extend the institution by fair means or foul, into Kansas. He possesses considerable ability as a popular orator, but more as a marksman, being a noted duellist." The influence that such editorials and irresponsible invectives had on the feeling toward him in the North was considerable, and it would grow.[16]

Even Breckinridge's close friends believed that they saw him going ever southward. Speaking of his initial associations with states' righters, Forney would write that "the fascinating society of the Southern magnates was too much for John. They saw that he had a bright future." The Pennsylvanian would say further that Breckinridge "was too interesting a character to be neglected by the able ultras of the South. They saw in his winning manners, attractive appearance, and rare talent for public affairs, exactly the elements they needed in their concealed designs against the country." He believed that Breckinridge had allowed Buchanan and the ultras to force him into supporting Lecompton in 1858, and that his course thereafter had been dictated by his friendship with the secessionists. Forney was surely not alone in these assumptions. He saw Breckinridge intimately in Washington, saw that he moved socially in circles primarily southern, and knew that the movement to make him the nominee in 1860 was largely backed by the radical states' rights men. This was the same picture that the press presented throughout the North, inaccurate, but influential. Even Breckinridge's highly commendable service as vice-president was twisted. His vote killing the homestead bill was noticed and damned throughout the free states. However, when he made sure that Douglas, or even Seward, received his full rights upon the floor of the Senate, when he polled a casting vote in favor of consideration of a bill to bring in another free state—Oregon, or when he ruled with iron hand over a joint session to preserve order, peace, and the lawful election of Lincoln, his actions received scant mention if any. The same was true of his speeches, and, having already established to their own satisfaction that Breckinridge was a secessionist, it was not difficult for northern editors to dismiss the true intent of his Tippecanoe speech or a stirring Union address before the removal of the Senate, as but hypocritical nonsense—talk, but nothing more. This is not to say that there was a concerted conspiracy among northern editors and speakers to misrepresent John C. Breckinridge, for the same was being done with other southern men, while in the South not a little hatred and mistrust of Seward, Lincoln, and the like, was stirred up without justification. The point is that during

16. Rochester (N.Y.) *Daily Union*, June 12, 1856, clipping in B. MSS.

these critical years, the makers and molders of public opinion saw what they wanted to see and feared to see, and that the mythical image they created became, in the minds of millions, one and the same with John C. Breckinridge.[17]

It all crystallized in the campaign of 1860. He was more attacked as a duelist than ever, called a "demisecessionist" and an "ultra-nigger-driver," charges which had absolutely no foundation in truth, which had never been true, but which, in the emotional temper of the time, it was easy for the people of the North to accept. The fact that the bulk of his influential campaign supporters were southern radicals only added substance to the illusion, and the secession of South Carolina made it nearly final. It was in this state of affairs, the most inopportune possible situation, that Breckinridge stepped down from the vice-presidential chair and once more occupied a seat from which he could speak. Had his incumbency extended for another year, he would not have had the opportunity to speak out, and might not have aroused further feeling against himself. But he spoke, and here it was that his extreme conservatism proved to be his undoing. Beck later aptly described Breckinridge's situation.

> Events he could not control confronted him. He thought he saw civil liberty and the constitutional rights of the States and citizens about to be swallowed up by a consolidated, centralized despotism with only the forms of republican liberty left. He was jealous of the rights of the States and the people. He was deeply read in the political history of the world. The Magna Charta, the Bill of Rights and the struggles for English liberty were with him household words. The Declaration of Independence, the Constitution of the United States and of the States were to him sacred.[18]

The views he expressed were the same that the country had been hearing from the secessionists for years, and for those not convinced already, it must have been difficult not to deduce that Breckinridge was one of them, and that he, like Wigfall and others who remained in Washington after their states seceded, was only maintaining a semblance of loyalty in order to subvert the cause of the Union and promote that of the South. The fact that he was also speaking his treason in pivotal Kentucky made things all the worse. For some time yet the North would put up with men like Bright, Vallandigham, Bayard, Pearce and Henry May of Maryland, men whose opinions and utterances were, in some instances, even more conservative

17. Wilson, *History of Kentucky*, II, 356; Forney, *Anecdotes*, I, 41; Blaine, *Twenty Years*, I, 323.
18. George Templeman Strong, *Diary of the Civil War, 1860–1865* (New York, 1962), 52; Louisville *Courier-Journal*, November 17, 1887.

than Breckinridge's. They, however, were from northern states with no threat of leaving the Union. Kentucky was still precarious and, despite the ending of neutrality, would remain so for another year. The Federal authorities, already convinced that Breckinridge was a traitor, could not allow him to spread his treason.

So he ran, but escape was only temporary for him. The journey to Richmond led only to another escape, a continuation of his flight from the past. Three and one half years of war interrupted the trip but then, once again, Breckinridge was running. This time the flight would take him much farther than his escape from Lexington to Virginia, but its significance was no more or less climactic. As in 1861, Breckinridge was ending a career of particular distinction by running from sure imprisonment and uncertain fate. Of course, he still hoped to meet Smith and Taylor in the West, but he well knew that they would be only long detours from the main road away from Federal hands. Just as the ride on that gray mare over the Alleghenies to Virginia signaled the finish of a great career at statecraft, so did the trip south from Washington, Georgia, to the Gulf Stream herald the end of Breckinridge the soldier.

Considered within the limited sphere of generalship, the management of men in war, the story of Breckinridge the untrained civilian-turned-soldier is one of remarkable success. In after years his friends praised him on this point, and, although some of their enthusiasm can be discounted because of unconcealed partisanship, they were capable soldiers themselves, and their opinions are worth some study. William Preston Johnston would say that while Breckinridge "was the Ulysses of American statesmanship," he also "had many of the qualities of a great soldier." General William Preston went much farther. "Breckinridge was a man formed by nature to shine in disasters," he declared. Sagacious, composed, fearless, he held a magnetic influence over his men, "and could lead troops to desperate enterprises with enthusiasm." Preston thought that Breckinridge's success as a soldier outshone his political attainments. "All men trusted him, for he was honorable; his troops loved him, because he shared their glories and privations; and great generals admired him in the field and trusted him in counsel." Understandably, the general's friend and adjutant Stoddard Johnston was most effusive. "Not bred to the profession of arms, at a period when an education at West Point was regarded as a prerequisite for military success, he was undoubtedly the ablest general from the volunteer service, excelled by few who had the trademark of the profession, and superior to scores who claimed distinction by virtue of their diplomas rather than their merit or success in the field." [19]

More objective were the views of Basil Duke. Writing less than two years after Breckinridge started off down the coast of Florida, the cavalryman asserted, "His great energy and indomitable resolution were fairly tried and fully proven. He could personally endure immense exertions and exposure. If, however, when heavy duty and labor were demanded, he got hold of officers and men who would not complain, he worked them without compunction, giving them no rest, and leaving the reluctant in clover. He could always elicit the affection inspired by manly daring and high soldierly qualities, and which the brave always feel for the bravest." Forty-five years later, after nearly half a century for the maturation of his thoughts, Duke felt much the same

> I have always believed that Gen. John C. Breckinridge's capacity as a soldier was not fully appreciated by his Southern countrymen. . . ; his reputation in the Confederate army was good, and he was ranked among the best of those who held high but subord'nate rank, it was not what I th'nk it should have been. He had unquestionably a remarkable sagacity in all matters pertaining to actual warfare, a rare military aptitude. His courage and resolution were superb. I have never, I think, witnessed an indifference to danger so absolutely calm and imperturbable as I have seen him display under very extraord'nary exposure to personal peril. . . .
>
> Along with his stronger and more virile qualities, not less conspicuous was an exceeding amiability of temper and an admirable self-control. I never saw a man more loath to give or take offence, or one so patient with the, perhaps, over-zealous suggestions of younger subordinates, and the occasional petulance which seems an inevitable concomitant of voluntary military service. His overmastering ability and strength of character enabled him to always command easily, but he never exerted his authority harshly, and was apparently often reluctant to exert it at all. [20]

Others, such as Gordon, A. S. and J. E. Johnston, Early, and Lee felt this same admiration for Breckinridge's capacity as a soldier, and in after years the historians who would follow the generals to chronicle their lives and their war, agreed. Indeed, no one who spoke of it, ever spoke ill of Breckinridge the general, during or after the war, with the inevitable exception of

19. Address of William Preston Johnston before the Kentucky Historical Society, February 11, 1880, clipping in Sallie Johnson Breckinridge Scrapbook in possession of Peter Ten Eyck; Louisville *Courier-Journal*, June 18, 1875; J. S. Johnston, *Kentucky*, 189–90.

20. Duke, *Morgan's Cavalry*, 550–51; Duke, *Reminiscences*, 176, 193–94.

Bragg, and even he felt forced to admit in later years that the Kentuckian was "as gallant and true a man as ever lived." [21]

Breckinridge's record as a soldier fully justified the plaudits of those who sang his praises. Coming from a background which, in effect, left him totally unprepared for war or military command, he rose by trial and error, making mistakes, but learning from them, and seldom making the same ones twice. The Breckinridge who maintained scarcely any overall control over his corps at Shiloh, became the general who, four months later at Baton Rouge, ran an efficient company of staff officers back and forth between himself and his brigades, staying well informed and in excellent control of the situation at almost all times. The Breckinridge who cost Bragg valuable time on December 31 at Stones River by not making sure of a sufficient reconnaissance in his front, became the general who, thereafter "was thorough in his reconnaissance, penetrating even beyond his skirmish line to study the topography of the projected field, and fruitful of resource to avail himself of information thus acquired." The Breckinridge who was fooled into false security by the deceptive slopes of Missionary Ridge, became the general who, at New Market, stood on Shirley's Hill, viewed the land before him, and in a few minutes planned a near-perfect little battle which, but for Imboden, went exactly as he foresaw it. And the Breckinridge whose enthusiasm at Chattanooga caused him to advise Bragg to stand and fight in the face of heavy odds, became the general who dispassionately saw the futility of an attack on Washington and, in spite of the severe disappointment it caused, counseled Early to withdraw. Clearly, on a score of the South's battlefields, John C. Breckinridge displayed an admirable capacity to grow and profit by experience.[22]

In the camp and in the field he showed more than the usual aptitude. Despite heavy obstacles, he kept his men supplied and armed, striving always for uniformity and, thereby, conservation of energy and materiel. Camp sanitation and security became a part of his routine, and discipline, though rarely severe, was enforced to the extent that drinking and gambling were suppressed when possible. At drill and parade his regiments were competent, if not spectacular—at Corinth the Second Kentucky was considered one of the two best-drilled regiments in the army—though he seems to have maintained a casual attitude concerning dress, as evidenced by the old hunt-

21. Braxton Bragg to E. T. Sykes, February 8, 1873, in Polk MSS; Tucker, *Chickamauga*, 231–32; Horn, *Army of Tennessee*, 437n; Edward J. Stackpole, *Sheridan in the Shenandoah* (Harrisburg, Pa., 1961), 29; Freeman, *R. E. Lee*, IV, 97.

22. Cincinnati *Commercial*, November 15, 1887.

ing jacket or blue checkered shirts that sometimes replaced his uniform blouse.

As an administrator, Breckinridge proved to be excellent, as shown in his management of middle Tennessee in the fall of 1862 and, more importantly, his handling of southwestern Virginia and east Tennessee. He kept the civilian populace content, maintained the steady flow of the department's vital supplies to Lee and Richmond, and organized from its seemingly barren resources of manpower, forces sufficient to protect it from all but the last great raid led by Stoneman. "Although this unfortunate department was worse handled by the enemy after he commanded it than before," Duke would say of the general, "he came out of the ordeal, fatal to most other generals, with enhanced reputation." [23]

The only fault that Duke could find with Breckinridge was "a strange indolence or apathy," which sometimes left him idle when he was not threatened. "He rose to his full stature only in the midst of danger and disaster," he said. There is scant evidence of this limitation, however, and what little exists is overridden by the general's record. No general officer in either army in this war saw wider service, in more major battles, in more of the major theaters of conflict, than John C. Breckinridge. It is a simple matter of fact. He fought or led troops in every one of the Confederate states but two—Texas and Arkansas; in three of the four border states, Kentucky, Maryland, and West Virginia; and in the District of Columbia. In the single year from September, 1862, to September, 1863, he moved his command nearly three thousand miles through five states, fighting two of the great battles of the West—Stones River and Chickamauga—and several others of lesser moment. Then to the East he went to save the Valley at New Market, beat back Grant at Cold Harbor and Hunter at Lynchburg, lead half of Early's army in the raid on Washington, fight Sheridan at Winchester, and Burbridge and Stoneman in southwest Virginia, not neglecting to lead a raid of his own back into Tennessee. Where reinforcements were needed, there he was sent; if a supply line needed clearing, or an enemy raid threatened, he seemed always on hand; and when a graveyard department needed someone to pull it together, he was there. Indeed, in this war, Breckinridge was nearly everywhere.[24]

Of course, the final test of a general is how he handles himself and his command in battle. Breckinridge was personally a daring, brave man; there is no doubt about that. What set him apart from many of his rank, however, was that this personal daring carried over into his generalship. When

23. Duke, *Morgan's Cavalry*, 550.   24. Duke, *Reminiscences*, 193.

a subordinate, he led his men under orders in attacks that sometimes smashed the enemy. Nowhere is the tenacity, the ruthlessness, and the force of one of his assaults better illustrated than on Rosecrans' left at Chickamauga. Although heavily outnumbered, he nearly demolished the Federal flank before Cleburne joined the action. At the same time he displayed a good sense for finding and turning an enemy flank, and in the absence of orders, would take responsibility upon himself in situations requiring quick judgments.

In independent command, Breckinridge was truly resourceful, almost brilliant. Although an infantry officer, he acquired a good understanding of the capabil ties and limitations of the other branches of the service. He recognized, at a time when many of his superiors seemed blind to the fact, that the advent of the breech-loading rifle had made cavalry obsolete as an offensive weapon against the foot soldier. As a result, he seldom used cavalry for other than scouting and reconnaissance duties—when other troops were available—and fought them on foot whenever possible. As for artillery, though he sometimes underestimated its movability, as at Marion, he never lost sight of its worth in the fight. Indeed, his use of his guns at New Market, advancing them as though a line of battle, was truly innovative, reminiscent of John Pelham's brilliant use of his battery at Fredericksburg.[25]

Breckinridge was not a strategic or tactical genius. In independent command, he had but one plan of battle, though its conception and execution proved its worth for repeated use, and revealed a military sense far above the average. Simply stated, he would advance his infantry or dismounted cavalry against the enemy's front, concentrating the attack on the Federal right, while his cavalry rode around the enemy left, cutting off retreat or attacking in the rear. Time and again, at New Market, Kernstown—which Breckinridge planned—and Bull's Gap, this arrangement, modified only slightly if at all, soundly defeated forces superior to him in numbers. The fact that he repeatedly attacked enemy forces greater than his own, and that in each case he sent the cavalry around to cut off "retreat," shows perhaps the greatest element of all in his generalship; Breckinridge never thought of defeat. Despite the odds, he went into a battle expecting to win it, and made his dispositions accordingly. Even at Marion, where he faced the greatest disparity of numbers in his career, he constantly tried to push Duke around Stoneman's left. When he felt forced to withdraw during the night, it was not to retreat, but to ride completely around the Federal army with the intention of striking its right rear the next morning. This was the

25. Breckinridge Diary, October 25, 1867, in Prewitt Collection.

daring and resourcefulness that had the people of the Valley hailing him as the new Jackson.

It would be dangerous to assert that Breckinridge was capable of army command, or perhaps even the leadership of a full-sized army corps. His one major attempt at the latter ended on Missionary Ridge, though the blame for its rout can hardly be laid solely to him. The Kentuckian was not a Lee or Grant, and it is possible that the responsibilities and greatly magnified scope of command would have overwhelmed him. However, as a division commander and, later, as head of a territorial department, he found and filled his ideal niche. Breckinridge had no superior among the major generals of the Confederacy when it came to overall service, experience, qualities of leadership, and ability in camp and field. Cleburne proved to be the better fighter, but he never faced the responsibility of independent command. The same was true of Gordon, and the only one to come close to Breckinridge in this category was the erratic Hindman, an excellent combat officer whose administration of the Trans-Mississippi was superb on paper, but a failure in the field. These four men were the premier major generals among the Confederacy's nonprofessionals, and in Breckinridge, the twelfth ranking major general in the army, the other three had a most worthy equal.

The Kentuckian's ability as a general makes all the more difficult the inevitable conclusion that in keeping him in the army the Confederacy wasted his talents. Of course, he contributed significantly to a major victory at Chickamauga, secured the Mississippi to the South by taking Port Hudson, and perhaps saved Lee at New Market. Still, the sum of all these and his other military achievements had no significant effect on the outcome or course of the war, and this, considered in the light of his service from February to May of 1865, makes truly tragic Davis' decision not to appoint him secretary of war when he first considered doing so back in November, 1861.

Of all of the Confederate secretaries of war, John C. Breckinridge was the one most suited, from all vantage points, for the office. He came with the stature to give dignity to his portfolio, command the respect and affection of the people, and stand up to the president without fear. At the same time, he had the courage and foresight not to be a conventional administrator. Where Seddon, Walker, and Benjamin accepted their department as a grand clerkship, Breckinridge, like Randolph to some extent, recognized that in a revolution, a war office must be a bit revolutionary. He left the details to his subordinates, saving his time and energy for broad policy and points of emergency. When necessary, he would assume to himself extraordinary powers, even to the point of stepping on the states' rights toes of some of the Confederacy's governors. Most of all, he saw the situation before him with frank, sometimes brutal, realism, the greatest asset he brought to the War Department. By the time he took over, the war was lost, and he had no opportunity to exert an important influence on the military situation, but the manner in which he recognized from the first that the Confederacy was doomed, and the way he thereafter worked toward the single goal of an honorable demise, shows as well as anything could, his ability to face a situation squarely and devise a plausible plan of action.

And in the end, it was as secretary of war that John C. Breckinridge made his only lasting contributions to the Confederacy. By his constant striving, to the point of repeated and open opposition to President Davis, he worked steadily to keep the nation from falling apart in disgrace. He would not let the Confederate States of America degenerate into roving guerrilla bands devoid of either the dignity or morality of its former days. Through four years of war the South had achieved an enviable reputation. Its "magnificent epic" would go down through the ages as a model of manly heroism, and he wanted nothing to tarnish that image. Seeing the cause to be lost for the present, he set about saving it for posterity. His conferences with Lee, bureau circulars, secret interviews with congressmen, aid in the formation of the far-reaching Sherman–Johnston cartel, frank advice to Vance, payment of the specie to the soldiers, and frequent—and sometimes solitary—resistance to Davis' irrational proposals to continue the conflict, were all directed toward a single goal, and for the achievement of that goal he deserves as much as anyone the credit. The Confederacy died, but it was defeated as a nation, and not crushed as a conglomerate of unorganized partisan bands, devoid of dignity. Add to this Breckinridge's concern for the preservation of the written records of the epic, his realization that they would be safer in enemy hands than in custody of Confederate officials who, like Benjamin and bitter lesser functionaries, burned priceless documents to prevent their capture, and the Confederacy emerges as eternally in the Kentuckian's debt. To the generations to follow, he helped give the lost cause the dignity to invite study and emulation, and the raw materials to do so.

The observer considering Breckinridge's first two careers—statesman and soldier—would be forced to conclude that, in large part, the Kentuckian had been a failure. The reasons lay in contradictions within him which undermined his hopes and ambitions for himself and his two countries. His single goal as a statesman had been peace, compromise between the sections, and mutual conciliation. Yet personally Breckinridge could never compromise. He would not yield a principle whatever the price. He held to his beliefs with an iron grasp, could point with ease to the incongruities and misapprehensions in the credos of others, but was seldom able to recognize or admit the same errors in his own. Though his motives and ideals were of the highest and noblest, his basic character and temperament, his very manliness, left him unconsciously ill-suited to the task. The same, in some degree, proved true of his life in uniform, though for different reasons. His sensitivities were such that he could never have made a premier army commander, for he had not the ability to separate himself as a general from his feeling as a man for the lives of his soldiers. To have to deal impersonally with death on such a large scale as Lee or Grant had to face, could have unnerved him. Yet his abandonment of politics, his commitment to the field until the war was won or lost, kept him from the place where he might truly have exerted to the fullest his talents. His voice in the public affairs of the Confederacy would have done far more to see it to its goal than his sword ever did.

With Congress halls and battlefields behind him, Breckinridge finally found the true field for his talents and his temperament. While he had not the tools to keep the Union from crumbling or to buttress the unsteady walls of the Confederacy, he was an artisan born for the work of rebuilding the two into one. In his exile and his "retirement" from public affairs that followed, he found at last his place.

The exile of John C. Breckinridge fits in the framework of a nation trying to reconstruct itself as a prime example of the absolute necessity of that nation to progress as a whole. There could be little truly harmonious effort between North and South while the leaders of the Confederacy were still prisoners in cells or exile. The Union gave tacit admission of this when it released Jefferson Davis in 1867 and chose not to prosecute him. With the release of Davis, the highest remaining official of the Confederacy who was not free was Breckinridge. Even as the president was released, northerners like Greeley, Blair, Browning, and others, began to see that the general, too, must be free and at home. By 1868 some of the highest officials in Washington and elsewhere reached this same realization, and the realization that all Confederates must be allowed to come home. Thus, from his escape and condemnation in 1865 to his return and commendation in 1869, Breckinridge and his exile stand as the measure of his country's settling passions. By his conduct in exile, the general set an example for all other Confederates. Silent, uncomplaining, above petty accusation and bitterness, he acted with a dignity and reserve that won the respect of his enemies, and with an independence and courage that gave pride to his comrades in adversity. In this respect he was one of the few and significant links between the sections in the precarious years after Appomattox.

After returning to Kentucky, he made this same reserve and quiet moderation an active policy. The fight for the freed slave's rights under the Constitution, the denunciation of the remorseless Ku Klux, and his stand against extremism and keeping alive the old hatreds everywhere were the hallmarks of the desire for peace and moderation and compromise, which, in earlier times, he could not bring to fruition. He avoided every subject which might in some way awaken a spark of hostility, fan unwholesome controversy, and set ablaze once more the old arguments. At the same time, as he worked to rebuild the fraternal spirit of the nation, so did he apply himself to its physical development, seeing in expansion and progress a means to reunion between the sections by working, trading, and growing together.

Of course, the differences would remain long after Breckinridge had gone to dust and been all but forgotten. The Union was not entirely reconstructed when he passed his work on to others, nor would it ever be completely reunited in spirit and soul. And what was done during this last decade of the Kentuckian's life was not done by him alone. But no one else in America, and especially in the South, came so near to realizing the full potential of his capabilities for encouraging and engineering the return of fraternal feeling, the reunion of the nation. No single fact displays this more than the consideration given to him for the post of official orator for the coming Centennial in Philadelphia. A country, divided and now reunited, celebrating its first century of independence, might have looked to him to give expression to its confident hopes for the future as one nation, one people.

The general died at 5:45 P.M., May 17, 1875, his long journey done. All of Kentucky went into mourning, and Lexington grieved sorely at his passing. Two days later, despite his wishes for a quiet funeral—he wanted no demonstration on his behalf to the very last—a massive mile-long procession followed his remains through the city streets to the Lexington cemetery. The outstanding feature of the city's funeral drapery was a gigantic Stars and Stripes, spread out above Main Street, draped in black. He passed under it for the last time as he was carried to his burial place on a lovely slope in sight of the monument to another man of peace and compromise, Henry

Clay. Here, in 1907, Mary would come to rest beside him. He would have his wish; he would sleep forever beneath that flag's "God-given folds." [26]

The general himself passed the best judgment on his own life in his brief eulogy of Lee back in 1870:

> But he failed. The result is in the future. It may be for better or for worse. We hope for the better. But this is not the test for his greatness and goodness. Success often gilds the shallow man, but it is disaster alone that reveals the qualities of true greatness. Was his life a failure? Is only that man successful who erects a material monument of greatness by the enforcement of his ideas? Is not that man successful also who by his valor, moderation and courage, with all their associate virtues, presents to the world such a specimen of true manhood as his children and children's children will be proud to imitate? In this sense he was not a failure.[27]

Clearly, the nation agreed. Although in some places his flight from the Union in 1861 was still remembered with bitterness, his countrymen from every corner had praise for his manhood, virtue, and most of all his work for peace and reconciliation after the war. From North and South came expressions of profound sorrow, even from those sources that once hailed with pleasure his reported death in battle and later called for the utmost punishment for him if captured. Just as he had wanted the nation united to face the future, so did it unite now to grieve his passing. "Our country mourns from St. Paul to New Orleans, and from New York to San Francisco," wrote one Minnesota journal. "There is now no North and no South." [28]

John C. Breckinridge's work was done.

26. Lexington *Daily Press*, May 19–20, 1875; Louisville *Courier-Journal*, May 20, 1875.

27. Louisville *Courier-Journal*, October 16, 1870.

28. A large collection of obituaries of Breckinridge, assembled from all over the country, appeared in the Louisville *Courier-Journal*, May 19–20, 1875.

Bibliography

MANUSCRIPTS

Alexander, Edwin Porter, 1864
  Southern Historical Collection, Chapel Hill, N.C.
Anthony, Alfred W., 1857–59
  New York Public Library
Autograph Collection, 1852–60
  Historical Society of Pennsylvania, Philadelphia
Barlow, S. L. M., 1860
  Huntington Library, San Marino, Calif.
Bayard, Thomas F., 1851–61
  Library of Congress, Washington, D.C.
Beauregard, P. G. T., 1865
  Duke University Library, Durham, N.C.
Bell, John, 1860–61
  Library of Congress, Washington, D.C.
Bennett, James Gordon, 1864
  Library of Congress, Washington, D.C.
Bigler, William, 1857–61
  Historical Society of Pennsylvania, Philadelphia
Birney, James G., 1851–57
  William Clements Library, University of Michigan, Ann Arbor
Black, Jeremiah S., 1857–61
  Library of Congress, Washington, D.C.
Bragg, Braxton, 1861–63
  Library of Congress, Washington, D.C.
Bragg, Thomas, 1860–61
  Southern Historical Collection, Chapel Hill, N.C.
Breckinridge, Clifton R.
  National Archives, Washington, D.C.
    Compiled Service Record, RG 109
  Manuscripts in possession of descendants
    Breckinridge, Clifton R., and John C., in possession of Mrs. John M. Prewitt

Breckinridge, John C.
  Manuscripts in possession of descendants
    Walter R. Agard
    Mrs. J. C. Breckinridge
    Mrs. Wheaton Byers
    Joseph Carter
    Mrs. George Roy Hill
    Mrs. Jeter Horton
    Mrs. Kenneth Kirkland
  Collected manuscripts
    Chicago Historical Society, 1851–73
    Duke University, Durham, N.C., 1851–65
    Filson Club, Louisville, Ky., 1851–73
    Office of Military Affairs, Office of the Adjutant General, Frankfort, Ky.
      Statement of Service, Mexican War
      Statement of Service, Civil War
    Library of Congress, Washington, D.C.
      Breckinridge Family Papers, 1820–88
    National Archives, Washington, D.C.
      Compiled Service Record, RG 94
      Compiled Service Record, RG 109
      Records of the Adjutant General's Office, Amnesty Papers, 1865, Kentucky, RG 94
      Unfiled Papers and Slips Belonging in Confederate Compiled Service Records, RG 109
    New York Historical Society, 1851–73
    New York Public Library
      Miscellaneous Papers, 1857–58
    Historical Society of Pennsylvania, Philadelphia, 1856–72
    Western Reserve Historical Society, Cleveland, Ohio, 1851–65
Breckinridge, John W. "Owen"
    Scrapbook and John C. Breckinridge letter in possession of Lee Breckinridge Thomas
Breckinridge, Joseph Cabell
  National Archives, Washington, D.C.
    Compiled Service Record, RG 109
Breckinridge, Mary Cyrene, 1864–68
  University of Kentucky Library, Lexington
Breckinridge, Sallie Johnson
  Scrapbook in possession of Peter H. Ten Eyck
Bryan Family, 1866
  Virginia State Library, Richmond
Buchanan, James, 1856–61
  Historical Society of Pennsylvania, Philadelphia
Buckner, Simon B., 1862–67
  Huntington Library, San Marino, Calif.

Buford, Charles, 1856–61
    Library of Congress, Washington, D.C.
Butler, Benjamin F., 1860–61
    Library of Congress, Washington, D.C.
Cameron, Simon, 1856–61
    Library of Congress, Washington, D.C.
Campbell, Given (Journal), 1865
    Library of Congress, Washington, D.C.
Campbell, John A., 1865
    Southern Historical Collection, Chapel Hill, N.C.
Castleman, John B., 1862–75
    Filson Club, Louisville, Ky.
Chamberlayne, John Hempden, 1865
    Virginia Historical Society, Richmond
Clay, James B., Jr.
    National Archives, Washington, D.C.
        Compiled Service Record, RG 109
Clay, Thomas J., 1851–73
    Library of Congress, Washington, D.C.
C.S.A. Archives. Army (Military Telegrams), 1864
    Duke University Library, Durham, N.C.
Confederate Collection, 1864–65
    In possession of Stanley E. Butcher
Confederate Miscellany, 1863–65
    Library of Congress, Washington, D.C.
Corcoran, William W., 1852–73
    Library of Congress, Washington, D.C.
Corps of Cadets, Virginia Military Institute, 1864 (various files)
    Alumni File Room, Virginia Military Institute, Lexington
Crittenden, John J.
    Duke University Library, Durham, N.C., 1869
    Library of Congress, Washington, D.C., 1840–62
Cushing, Caleb, 1860–61
    Library of Congress, Washington, D.C.
Davis, Jefferson
    Confederate Memorial Literary Society, Museum of the Confederacy, Rich-
        mond, Va., 1867–75
    Library of Congress, Washington, D.C., 1863–65
    Louisiana Historical Association Collection, Howard-Tilton Library, Tulane
        University, New Orleans, La., 1862–75
Dearborn, Frederick M., 1861–65
    Houghton Library, Harvard University, Cambridge, Mass.
Desha, Joseph and John R., 1851–61
    Library of Congress, Washington, D.C.
Donnelly, Ignatius, 1852–61
    Minnesota Historical Society, St. Paul

Douglas, Stephen A., 1852–61
  University of Chicago
Dreer, Ferdinand J., 1853–65
  Historical Society of Pennsylvania, Philadelphia
Duke, Basil W., 1864–75
  Southern Historical Collection, Chapel Hill, N.C.
Early, Jubal A., 1864–75
  Library of Congress, Washington, D.C.
Edgar, George M., 1864–1912
  Southern Historical Collection, Chapel Hill, N.C.
Eldridge, James W., 1862–64
  Huntington Library, San Marino, Calif.
Erwin, W. G., 1863
  Letters in possession of Ray Marshall
Everett, Edward, 1857
  Massachusetts Historical Society, Boston
Fayette County, Kentucky
  Fayette County Courthouse, Lexington, Ky.
    Deed Book 33, Will Book 4
Flagg, Samuel Griswold, 1862
  Yale University Library, New Haven, Conn.
Fogg, John S. H., 1857
  Maine Historical Society, Portland
Gilmer, Jeremy F., 1865
  Confederate Memorial Literary Society, Museum of the Confederacy, Rich-
    mond, Va.
Gratz, Simon, 1855–73
  Historical Society of Pennsylvania, Philadelphia
Guerrant, Edward O.
  Filson Club, Louisville, Ky., 1864–69
  Southern Historical Collection, Chapel Hill, N.C., 1864–65
Hathaway, Leeland, 1865
  Southern Historical Collection, Chapel Hill, N.C.
Hill, Daniel H., 1863
  North Carolina Department of Archives and History, Raleigh
Hines, Thomas H., 1865–69
  University of Kentucky Library, Lexington
Hoadley, Charles J. and George E., 1856–61
  Connecticut Historical Society, Hartford
Hotchkiss, Jedediah, 1864–65
  Library of Congress, Washington, D.C.
Huntington Miscellaneous Collection, 1859–66
  Huntington Library, San Marino, Calif.
Ingersoll, Charles J., 1855
  Historical Society of Pennsylvania, Philadelphia

Johnson, Jilson P.
 National Archives, Washington, D.C.
  Compiled Service Record, RG 109
Johnston, Josiah Stoddard
 National Archives, Washington, D.C.
  Compiled Service Record, RG 109
 Filson Club, Louisville, Ky., 1862–1912
Kohns, Lee, 1859
 New York Public Library
Lane, Joseph, 1857–68
 Oregon Historical Society, Portland
Lee, Edwin Gray, 1865–66
 Southern Historical Collection, Chapel Hill, N.C.
Lee, Robert E., 1861–70
 Library of Congress, Washington, D.C.
Lincoln, Abraham
 Brown University Library, Providence, R.I., 1864–69
 University of Chicago, 1861
McCalla, John C., 1854
 Duke University Library, Durham, N.C.
Mackall, William W., 1863
 Southern Historical Collection, Chapel Hill, N.C.
Mallory, Stephen R., 1865
 Southern Historical Collection, Chapel Hill, N.C.
Marcy, William, 1851–61
 Library of Congress, Washington, D.C.
Miscellaneous American Autographs Collection, 1861
 Pierpont Morgan Library, New York
Morgan, Charles H., 1863
 Chicago Historical Society
National Archives, War Department Collection of Confederate Records, Washington, D.C.
 MIAC. Endorsements on Letters, Department of East Tennessee, 1862–64, Chap. 8, Vol. CCCLVII
 Military Departments, General Orders and Circulars, Department of West Virginia, 1862–64, Chap. 2, Vol. LXII
 Military Departments, Special Orders, Department of West Virginia, 1864, Chap. 2, Vol. LXIII
 Military Departments, Letters and Telegrams Sent, Army of Northern Virginia, March 1863–March 1864, Chap. 2, Vol. LXXXIV
 Military Departments, Letters Sent, Orders, and Circulars, Department of East Tennessee and Department of Western Virginia and East Tennessee, April 1863–October 1864, Chap. 2, Vol. CCXXXIV
 Military Departments, Orders Received and Orders Issued by the First Kentucky Brigade, 1862–63, Chap. 2, Vol. CCCVIII

Military Departments, Orders Received, Orders Issued, and Morning Reports, First Kentucky Brigade, August 1862–October 1864, Chap. 2, Vol. CCCX

Military Departments, Orders and Circulars Received, First Kentucky Brigade, August 1863–January 1865, Chap. 2, Vol. CCCXIV

Secretary of War, Register of Letters Received, September 1862–April 1863, A–L, Chap. 9, Vol. XXVI

Secretary of War, Register of Letters Received, February 1864–April 1865, Chap. 9, Vol. XXXI

Special Orders Received, First Kentucky Brigade, 1862–1863, Chap. 2, Vol. CCCXV

Special Orders Received, First Kentucky Brigade, November 1861–October 1862, Chap. 2, Vol. CCCXVI

Telegrams Received & Sent by Gen Breckinridge's Command, December 1861–November 1863, Chap. 2, Vol. CCCXI

New Market, Battle of (file), 1864–1964
    Alumni File Room, Virginia Military Institute, Lexington

Norcross, Grenville H., 1852
    Massachusetts Historical Society, Boston

Palmer, William, Collection of Braxton Bragg Papers, 1861–65
    Western Reserve Historical Society, Cleveland, Ohio

Phillips, Philip, 1854–61
    Library of Congress, Washington, D.C.

Pierce, Franklin
    Dickinson College Library, Carlisle, Pa., 1852–61
    Library of Congress, Washington, D.C., 1852–61

Pleadwell, F. L., 1864
    Smithsonian Institution, Washington, D.C.

Polk, Leonidas, 1863–74
    Southern Historical Collection, Chapel Hill, N.C.

Preston, William
    National Archives, Washington, D.C.
        Memoranda of A. S. Johnston's Death and the Battle of Shiloh, RG 94

Regimental Order Book, Fourth United States Infantry, 1848–53
    In possession of Chapman R. Grant

Rhees, William J., 1852–53
    Huntington Library, San Marino, Calif.

Robertson, Felix H.
    National Archives, Washington, D.C.
        Compiled Service Record, RG 109

Ruffin, Edmund (Diary), 1856–61
    Library of Congress, Washington, D.C.

Ruggles, Daniel, 1862
    Duke University Library, Durham, N.C.

Sigel, Franz
    New York Historical Society, 1864–74

Western Reserve Historical Society, Cleveland, Ohio, 1864–1912
Stephens, Alexander H., 1851–65
　Library of Congress, Washington, D.C.
Stevens, Isaac I., 1860–61
　University of Washington Library, Seattle
Stevenson, Andrew and John W., 1851–75
　Library of Congress, Washington, D.C.
Swan, Henry R., 1864
　In possession of Paul W. Williamson
Tayloe, Benjamin O., 1860
　Virginia Historical Society, Richmond
Ulmer, L. B., 1901
　Choctaw County Public Library, Butler, Ala.
Vance, Zebulon B., 1865
　North Carolina Department of Archives and History, Raleigh
Venable, Abraham W., 1851–55
　Southern Historical Collection, Chapel Hill, N.C.
Ward, Jesse Durbin, 1857
　Ohio Historical Society, Columbus
Washburne, Elihu B., 1865–66
　Library of Congress, Washington, D.C.
Wayne, James Moore, 1860
　Georgia Historical Society, Savannah
Welles, Gideon, 1854–65
　Library of Congress, Washington, D.C.
Wheeler, Joseph, 1862–63
　Chicago Historical Society
White, Wellford, Taliaferro, and Marshall Family Papers, 1865
　Southern Historical Collection, Chapel Hill, N.C.
Wigfall, Louis T., 1855–71
　Library of Congress, Washington, D.C.
Wilson, James
　National Archives, Washington, D.C.
　　Compiled Service Record, RG 109
Wood, John Taylor, 1865–66
　Southern Historical Collection, Chapel Hill, N.C.
Worley Family Letters, 1862
　In possession of Stanley R. Levitt
Wright, Hendrick B., 1859–60
　Wyoming Historical and Geological Society, Wilkes-Barre, Pa.
Wright, Joseph A., 1856–60
　Indiana State Library, Indianapolis
Wright, Marcus J., 1861–64
　Southern Historical Collection, Chapel Hill, N.C.
Yerger, William, 1862–63
　Mississippi Department of Archives and History, Jackson

NEWSPAPERS

Augusta (Ga.) *Chronicle & Sentinel*, 1865
Augusta (Ga.) *Tri-Weekly Constitutionalist*, 1865
Baltimore *American*, 1860, 1869
Baltimore *Baltimorian*, 1860
Baltimore, *Weekly Sun*, 1860
Boston *Transcript*, 1865
Burlington (Iowa) *Hawkeye and Iowa Patriot*, 1841–42
Chicago *Democrat*, 1860
Cincinnati *Commercial*, 1856–60, 1869–75
Cincinnati *Daily Enquirer*, 1856–70
Cincinnati *Gazette*, 1856–60
Cleveland *Leader*, 1856, 1860
Cleveland *Weekly Plain Dealer*, 1856, 1860
Columbus *Ohio Statesman*, 1856, 1860
Edgefield (S.C.) *Advertiser*, 1865
Frankfort *Commonwealth*, 1850–70
Frankfort *Tri-Weekly Yeoman*, 1850–60
Frankfort *Weekly Kentucky Yeoman*, 1850–75
Frankfort *Yeoman*, 1850–75
Indianapolis *Indiana State Journal*, 1848
Indianapolis *Indiana State Sentinel*, 1848
Kilmarnock (Scotland) *Standard*, 1947
Lexington *Daily Press*, 1850
Lexington *Herald*, 1850
Lexington *Kentucky Statesman*, 1850–62
Lexington *Morning Herald*, 1875
Lexington *Observer and Reporter*, 1844–51
Lexington *Transcript*, 1875
Little Rock *Arkansas Gazette*, 1865
London *Times*, 1865–68
Louisville *Courier*, 1852–61
Louisville *Courier-Journal*, 1869–75, 1887
Louisville *Daily Democrat*, 1856–60
Louisville *Daily Times*, 1860
Louisville *Democrat*, 1852–60
Louisville *Evening Post*, 1860
Louisville *Journal*, 1852–61
Lynchburg *Daily Virginian*, 1864
Maysville (Ky.) *Bulletin*, 1906
Memphis *Appeal*, 1875
Mobile *Daily Register*, 1875
New Orleans *National*, 1865
New Orleans *Picayune*, 1862–65
New Orleans *Times*, 1865
New Orleans *Tribune*, 1862–65

New York *Courier and Enquirer*, 1856, 1860
New York *Harper's Weekly*, 1857–61
New York *Herald*, 1860–61
New York *Live Stock Record*, 1875
New York *Times*, 1851–75
New York *Tribune*, 1860–61, 1864
New York *Turf, Field and Farm*, 1875
Niagara (Ont.) *Mail*, 1869
Paris (Ky.) *State Flag*, 1858
Petersburg (Va.) *Daily Register*, 1864
Philadelphia *Pennsylvanian*, 1860
Philadelphia *Press*, 1856, 1860
Richmond *Daily Dispatch*, 1861–65
Richmond *Daily Whig*, 1861–65
Richmond *Enquirer*, 1861–65
Richmond *Examiner*, 1861–65
Richmond *Sentinel*, 1861–65
Richmond *Times-Dispatch*, 1895–1910
Richmond *Whig*, 1861–65
Rochester *Daily Union*, 1860
St. Louis *Globe-Democrat*, 1860, 1875
St. Paul *Daily Times*, 1875
Staunton (Va.) *Spectator*, 1864
Staunton (Va.) *Vindicator*, 1864
Superior (Wis.) *Times*, 1875
Washington *Constitution*, 1852–61
Washington *Daily Globe*, 1852–61
Washington *Daily National Intelligencer*, 1851–61
Washington *Evening Star*, 1851–61
Washington *Post*, 1851–61
Washington *Star*, 1851–61
Washington *Union*, 1851–61
Winchester (Va.) *Evening Star*, 1956

OFFICIAL PUBLICATIONS

Congressional Globe, 32nd–37th Congresses, 1851–61.
Congressional Record, 67th Congress, 1921–23.
Journal of the Congress of the Confederate States of America. 7 vols. Washington, 1904–1905.
Journal of the House of Representatives of the Commonwealth of Kentucky. Frankfort, 1849.
Journal of the Senate of the Commonwealth of Kentucky, 1849–50. Frankfort, 1849.
Proceedings of the First and Second Confederate Congresses. Edited by Douglas S. Freeman and Frank E. Vandiver. *Southern Historical Society Papers*, XLIV–LII (1923–59).

Richardson, James D., comp. *A Compilation of the Messages and Papers of the Presidents, 1789–1897.* 11 vols. Washington, 1897.
Statutes at Large of the Provisional Congress of the Confederate States of America. Richmond, 1864.
U.S. Naval War Records Office. *Official Records of the Union and Confederate Navies in the War of the Rebellion.* 31 vols. Washington, 1894–1922.
U.S. Senate. *Senate Executive Document 65, 30th Congress, 1st Session.* Washington, 1848.
U.S. War Department. *The War of the Rebellion: A Compilation of the Official Records of the Union and Confederate Armies.* 128 vols. Washington, 1880–1901.

CAMPAIGN PUBLICATIONS

1856

Derby, H. W. *Buchanan and Breckinridge. Lives of James Buchanan and John C. Breckinridge, Democratic Candidates for the Presidency and Vice-Presidency of the United States with the Platforms of the Three Political Parties in the Presidential Canvass of 1856.* Cincinnati, 1856.
Lives of the Present Candidates for President and Vice-President of the U.S. Cincinnati, 1856.
Old Line Whigs for Buchanan and Breckinridge. N.p., 1856.

1860

Address to the Democracy and the People of the United States by the National Democratic Executive Committee. Washington, 1860.
Lives of the Present Candidates for President and Vice-President of the U.S. Cincinnati, 1860.
Speech of Hon. John C. Breckinridge, Delivered at Ashland, Ky., September 5, 1860. N.p., 1860.

BRECKINRIDGE AND LANE CAMPAIGN DOCUMENTS

While twenty or more of these were published, only those useful to this biography are listed below (all are in the author's possession):
No. 3. *Speech of Hon. J. P. Benjamin, of Louisiana: Delivered in the Senate of the United States, May 22, 1860.* Washington, 1860.
No. 4. *Speech of President Buchanan, on the Evening of Monday, July 9, 1860.* Washington, 1860.
No. 6. *Immense Gathering at the Cooper Institute.* Washington, 1860.
No. 8. *Biographical Sketches of Hon. John C. Breckinridge, Democratic Nominee for President, and General Joseph Lane, Democratic Nominee for Vice-President.* Washington, 1860.
No. 10. *Substance of a Speech of Hon. John C. Breckinridge, Delivered in the Hall of the House of Representatives, at Frankfort, Kentucky, December 21, 1859.* Washington, 1860.
No. 11. *Address of Hon. John C. Breckinridge, Vice President of the United States, Preceding the Removal of the Senate from the Old to the New Cham-*

ber, *Delivered in the Senate of the United States, January 4, 1859.* Washington, 1860.

No. 12. *Relations of the States. Speech of Hon. John J. Crittenden, of Kentucky, on the Davis Resolutions, in the U.S. Senate, May 24, 1860.* Washington, 1860.

Printed Primary Sources

Alderman, Edwin A., and Joel Chandler Harris, eds. *Library of Southern Literature.* 10 vols. New Orleans, 1907–1909.

Alexander, E. Porter. *Military Memoirs of a Confederate.* Edited by T. Harry Williams. 2nd edition, Bloomington, Ind., 1962.

Ambler, Charles H., ed. *The Correspondence of Robert M. T. Hunter, 1826–1876.* 2 vols. Washington, 1918.

Anderson, Frank Maloy. *The Mystery of "A Public Man."* Minneapolis, 1948.

Annals of the War Written by Leading Participants, North and South. Philadelphia, 1879.

Basler, Roy P., ed. *The Collected Works of Abraham Lincoln.* 9 vols. New Brunswick, N.J., 1953.

Bearss, Edwin C., ed. *A Louisiana Confederate: Diary of Felix Pierre Poche.* Natchitoches, La., 1972.

Bigelow, John. *Retrospections of an Active Life.* 2 vols. New York, 1905.

Birney, William. *James G. Birney and His Times.* New York, 1890.

Blackford, Susan Leigh. *Letters from Lee's Army; or, Memoirs of Life in and out of the Army in Virginia During the War Between the States.* 2nd edition, New York, 1947.

Blaine, James G. *Twenty Years in Congress.* 2 vols. Norwich, Conn., 1884.

Brackett, Albert G. *General Lane's Brigade in Central Mexico.* Cincinnati, 1854.

Breckinridge, John C. *An Address on the Occasion of the Burial of the Kentucky Volunteers Who Fell at Buena Vista.* Lexington, 1847.

————. *Cincinnati Southern Railroad, Memorial of Trustees and Speech of Hon. . . . to the General Assembly of Kentucky.* N.p., 1871.

————. *General Butler—The Democratic Review—Judge Douglas—The Presidency. Speech of . . . of Kentucky, Delivered in the House of Representatives, March 4, 1852.* Washington, 1852.

————. *Judge Douglas—the Democratic Review, etc. Remarks of Mr. Breckinridge in Reply to Mr. Richardson of Illinois.* Washington, 1852.

Buck, Irving A. *Cleburne and His Command.* 2nd edition, Jackson, Tenn., 1959.

Butler, Benjamin F. *Autobiography and Personal Reminiscences of Major-General . . . Butler's Book.* Boston, 1892.

————. *Private and Official Correspondence of Gen. . . . .* 2 vols. Norwood, Mass., 1917.

Cade, Wirt A., ed. *Two Soldiers: the Campaign Diaries of Thomas J. Key . . . and Robert J. Campbell.* Chapel Hill, N.C., 1938.

Campbell, John A. *Recollections of the Evacuation of Richmond, April 2, 1865.* Baltimore, 1880.

————. *Reminiscences and Documents Relating to the Civil War During the Year 1865.* Baltimore, 1887.

Carson, James P. *Life, Letters and Speeches of James Louis Petigru, the Union Man of South Carolina.* Washington, 1920.

Castleman, John B. *Active Service.* Louisville, 1917.

Centre College of Kentucky. *General Catalogue.* Danville, 1890.

Chancellor, Christopher, ed. *An Englishman in the American Civil War: The Diaries of Henry Yates Thompson, 1863.* New York, 1971.

Chittenden, Lucius. *Invisible Siege: The Journal of . . . April 15, 1861–July 14, 1861.* San Diego, 1969.

————. *Recollections of President Lincoln and His Administration.* New York, 1891.

Clark, Champ (James Beauchamp). *My Quarter Century of American Politics.* 2 vols. New York, 1920.

Clark, Walter, ed. *Histories of the Several Regiments and Battalions from North Carolina in the Great War, 1861–1865.* 5 vols. Raleigh, 1901.

Clay, Cassius M. *Cassius Marcellus Clay, Life and Memoirs, Writings and Speeches.* 2 vols. Cincinnati, 1886.

Cocke, Preston. *The Battle of New Market and the Cadets of the Virginia Military Institute, May 15, 1864.* N.p., 1914.

Coffin, Charles C. *The Boys of '61.* Boston, 1886.

Collins, Lewis. *Historical Sketches of Kentucky.* Cincinnati, 1850.

Constitution of the Aztec Club of 1847 and the List of Members, 1893. Washington, 1893.

Cox, Samuel S. *Union–Disunion–Reunion: Three Decades of Federal Legislation, 1855 to 1885.* Providence, R.I., 1885.

Corcoran, William W. *A Grandfather's Legacy.* Washington, 1878.

Craven, John J. *Prison Life of Jefferson Davis.* New York, 1866.

Crittenden, Henry H. *The Crittenden Memoirs.* New York, 1936.

Curry, Jabez L. M. *Civil History of the Government of the Confederate States.* Richmond, 1901.

Davis, Jefferson. *Rise and Fall of the Confederate Government.* 2 vols. 2nd edition, New York, 1958.

Davis, Reuben. *Recollections of Mississippi and Mississippians.* Boston, 1889.

Davis, Varina H. (Mrs. Jefferson). *Jefferson Davis, Ex-President of the Confederate States of America: A Memoir by His Wife.* 2 vols. New York, 1890.

De Fontaine, Felix G. *Marginalia; or Gleanings from an Army Note-Book.* Columbia, S.C., 1864.

Denison, George T. *Soldiering in Canada.* London, 1900.

Dickison, Mary E. *Dickison and His Men.* Gainesville, Fla., 1962.

Dixon, Susan B. (Mrs. Archibald). *The True History of the Missouri Compromise and its Repeal.* Cincinnati, 1899.

Donald, David, ed. *Inside Lincoln's Cabinet: The Civil War Diaries of Salmon P. Chase.* New York, 1954.

Dorsey, Sarah A. *Recollections of Henry Watkins Allen.* New York, 1866.

Douglas, Henry Kyd. *I Rode with Stonewall.* Chapel Hill, 1940.

Dowdey, Clifford, and Louis P. Manarin, eds. *Wartime Papers of R. E. Lee.* Boston, 1961.

Drake, Edwin L., ed. *Annals of the Army of Tennessee and Early Western History.* Nashville, 1878.

Duke, Basil W. *A History of Morgan's Cavalry.* Cincinnati, 1867.

————. *Reminiscences of General Basil W. Duke, C.S.A.* New York, 1911.

Durkin, Joseph T., ed. *John Dooley, Confederate Soldier: His War Journal.* Georgetown, D.C., 1945.

Early, Jubal A. *Autobiographical Sketch and Narrative of the War Between the States.* Philadelphia, 1912.

Evans, Clement A. *Confederate Military History.* 12 vols. 2nd edition, New York, 1962.

Fleet, Betsy, and John D. P. Fuller, eds. *Green Mount: A Virginia Plantation Family During the Civil War.* Lexington, Ky., 1962.

Foote, Henry S. *A Casket of Reminiscences.* 2nd edition, New York, 1968.

Force, Manning. *From Fort Henry to Corinth.* New York, 1881.

Forney, John W. *Anecdotes of Public Men.* New York, 1873.

Freeman, Douglas S., and Grady C. McWhiney, eds. *Lee's Dispatches: Unpublished Letters of General Robert E. Lee, C.S.A., to Jefferson Davis and the War Department of the Confederate States of America.* New York, 1957.

Fremantle, Arthur J. L. *The Fremantle Diary.* Edited by Walter Lord. 2nd edition, Boston, 1954.

Gilmor, Harry. *Four Years in the Saddle.* New York, 1866.

Gordon, John B. *Reminiscences of the Civil War.* New York, 1903.

Gower, Herschel, and Jack Allen, eds. *Pen and Sword: The Life and Journals of Randall W. McGavock.* Nashville, 1959.

Graf, Leroy P., and Ralph W. Haskins, eds. *Papers of Andrew Johnson,* II. Knoxville, 1970.

Guernsey, Alfred H., ed. *Harper's Pictorial History of the Great Rebellion.* New York, 1866–68.

Harrison, Constance (Mrs. Burton). *Recollections Grave and Gay.* New York, 1912.

Hayes, John D., ed. *Samuel Francis Du Pont, A Selection from His Civil War Letters.* 3 vols. New York, 1969.

Headley, John W. *Confederate Operations in Canada and New York.* New York, 1906.

Hesseltine, William B. *Three Against Lincoln: Murat Halstead Reports the Caucuses of 1860.* Baton Rouge, 1960.

Holmes, Sarah Katherine (Stone). *Brokenburn: The Journal of Kate Stone, 1861–1868.* Edited by John Q. Anderson. Baton Rouge, 1972.

Hood, John B. *Advance and Retreat. Personal Experiences in the United States and Confederate States Armies.* 2nd edition, Bloomington, Ind., 1959.

Johannsen, Robert W., ed. *Letters of Stephen A. Douglas.* Urbana, Ill., 1961.

Johnson, Adam R. *The Partisan Rangers of the Confederate States Army.* Louisville, 1904.

Johnson, Robert U., and Clarence C. Buel, eds. *Battles and Leaders of the Civil War.* 4 vols. New York, 1887.

Johnston, Joseph E. *Narrative of Military Operations.* New York, 1874.

Johnston, William P. *The Life of Gen. Albert Sidney Johnston*. New York, 1879.

Jones, John B. *A Rebel War Clerk's Diary at the Confederate States Capital*. 2 vols. Philadelphia, 1866.

Joyce, John A. *Jewels of Memory*. Washington, 1895.

King, Horatio. *Turning on the Light*. Philadelphia, 1895.

Kirwan, Albert D., ed. *Johnny Green of the Orphan Brigade*. Lexington, Ky., 1956.

Lee, Fitzhugh. *General Lee*. 2nd edition, Greenwich, Conn., 1961.

Lee, Robert E., Jr. *My Father, General Lee*. 2nd edition, Garden City, N.Y., 1960.

Lindsley, John B., ed. *The Military Annals of Tennessee (Confederate)*. Nashville, 1886.

Longstreet, James. *From Manassas to Appomattox*. 2nd edition, Bloomington, Ind., 1960.

Maltby, Mary B. *Mary Cyrene Breckinridge*. Georgetown, Ky., 1910.

Manarin, Louis, ed. *Richmond at War: The Minutes of the City Council, 1861–1865*. Chapel Hill, N.C., 1966.

Marcus, Jacob R., ed. *Memoirs of American Jews, 1775–1865*. 5 vols. Philadelphia, 1956.

Martin, Isabella D., and Myrta Lockett Avary, eds. *A Diary from Dixie, as Written by Mary Boykin Chesnut*. New York, 1905.

Mason, F. H. *The Twelfth Ohio Cavalry; A Record of Its Organization, and Services in the War of the Rebellion*. Cleveland, 1871.

Mason, Virginia. *The Public and Diplomatic Correspondence of James M. Mason*. New York, 1906.

McClure, Alexander K. *Col. Alexander McClure's Recollections of Half a Century*. Salem, Mass., 1902.

McMurray, W. J. *History of the Twentieth Tennessee Regiment Volunteer Infantry, C.S.A.* Nashville, 1904.

Moore, Frank, comp. *The Rebellion Record*. 11 vols. New York, 1862–68.

Morgan, James M. *Recollections of a Rebel Reefer*. Boston, 1917.

Mosby, John S. *Memoirs of Colonel John S. Mosby*. 2nd edition, Bloomington, Ind., 1959.

Mosgrove, George D. *Kentucky Cavaliers in Dixie; or, The Reminiscences of a Confederate Cavalryman*. Louisville, 1895.

Myers, Robert M., ed. *The Children of Pride: A True Story of Georgia and the Civil War*. New Haven, Conn., 1972.

Nevins, Allan, ed. *Diary of the Civil War, 1860–1865*. New York, 1962.

Oswandel, J. Jacob. *Notes of the Mexican War, 1846-47-48*. 2 vols. Philadelphia, 1885.

Owen, William M. *In Camp and Battle with the Washington Artillery*. Boston, 1885.

Parker, William H. *Recollections of a Naval Officer, 1841–1865*. New York, 1883.

Pease, Theodore C., and James G. Randall, eds. *The Diary of Orville Hickman Browning*. 2 vols. Springfield, Ill., 1925.

Phillips, Ulrich B., ed. *Correspondence of Robert Toombs, Alexander H. Stephens and Howell Cobb.* Washington, 1913.

Poore, Ben Perley. *Perley's Reminiscences of Sixty Years in the National Metropolis.* 2 vols. Philadelphia, 1886.

Porter, Horace. *Campaigning with Grant.* 2nd edition, Bloomington, Ind., 1961.

Putnam, Sallie B. *In Richmond During the Confederacy.* 2nd edition, New York, 1961.

Ranck, George W. *History of Lexington, Kentucky.* Cincinnati, 1872.

Ratchford, J. W. *Some Reminiscences of Persons and Incidents of the Civil War.* Austin, Tex., 1971.

Reagan, John H. *Memoirs, With Special Reference to Secession and the Civil War.* New York, 1906.

Riddle, Albert G. *Recollections of War Times.* New York, 1895.

Ripley, Eliza McHatton. *From Flag to Flag, A Woman's Adventures and Experiences in the South During the War, in Mexico, and in Cuba.* New York, 1889.

————. *Social Life in Old New Orleans, Being Recollections of My Girlhood.* New York, 1912.

Robertson, George. *An Outline of the Life of George Robertson.* Lexington, Ky., 1876.

————. *Scrap Book on Law & Politics, Men & Times.* Lexington, Ky., 1855.

Roe, Alfred S. *The Ninth New York Heavy Artillery.* Worcester, Mass., 1899.

Roman, Alfred. *The Military Operations of General Beauregard in the War Between the States.* 2 vols. New York, 1884.

Ross, Fitzgerald. *Cities and Camps of the Confederacy.* Edited by Richard B. Harwell. 2nd edition, Urbana, Ill., 1958.

Rowland, Dunbar, ed. *Jefferson Davis, Constitutionalist: His Letters, Papers and Speeches.* 10 vols. Jackson, Miss., 1923.

Scarborough, William K., ed. *The Diary of Edmund Ruffin: Volume I, Toward Independence, October, 1856–April 1861.* Baton Rouge, 1972.

Schmitt, Martin F., ed. *General George Crook, His Autobiography.* Norman, Okla., 1960.

Scott, Samuel W., and Samuel P. Angel, eds. *History of the Thirteenth Regiment Tennessee Volunteer Cavalry.* Philadelphia, 1903.

Sedgwick, John. *Correspondence of John Sedgwick, Major General.* 2 vols. New York, 1902–1903.

Sherman, William T. *Memoirs of General William T. Sherman, by Himself.* 2 vols. New York, 1875.

Sorrell, G. Moxley. *Recollections of a Confederate Staff Officer.* Edited by Bell I. Wiley. 2nd edition, Jackson, Tenn., 1958.

Stephens, Alexander H. *A Constitutional View of the Late War Between the States.* 2 vols. Philadelphia, 1868–70.

Stevenson, William C. *Thirteen Months in the Rebel Army.* New York, 1864.

Summers, Festus P., ed. *A Borderland Confederate.* Pittsburgh, 1962.

Sykes, E. T. *Walthall's Brigade: A Cursory Sketch with Personal Experiences of Walthall's Brigade, Army of Tennessee, C.S.A., 1862–1865. (Publications of the Mississippi Historical Society, 477–623)* Jackson, Miss., 1916.

Thompson, Ed. Porter. *History of the First Kentucky Brigade*. Cincinnati, 1868.
_____. *History of the Orphan Brigade*. Louisville, 1898.
Turner, Justin and Linda. *Mary Todd Lincoln, Her Life and Letters*. New York, 1972.
Vandiver, Frank E., ed., *The Civil War Diary of General Josiah Gorgas*. Tuscaloosa, Ala., 1947.
Watkins, Samuel. *Co. "Aytch," Maury's Grays, First Tennessee Regiment*. Nashville, 1882.
West, John C. *A Texan in Search of a Fight*. Edited by Bell I. Wiley. 2nd edition, Waco, Tex., 1969.
Wilcox, Cadmus M. *History of the Mexican War*. Washington, 1892.
Wiley, Bell I., ed. *Confederate Letters of John W. Hagan*. Athens, Ga., 1954.
Williams, Ben Ames, ed. *A Diary from Dixie*. 2nd edition, Boston, 1949.
Wilson, Henry. *Rise and Fall of the Slave Power in America*. 3 vols. Boston, 1872–77.
Wise, John S. *Battle of New Market, Va., May 15, 1864: An Address Repeated by ... before Professors, Officers and Cadets of the Virginia Military Institute, May 13, 1882*. N.p., 1882.
_____. *The End of an Era*. Boston, 1902.
_____. *Recollections of Thirteen Presidents*. New York, 1906.
Worsham, John H. *One of Jackson's Foot Cavalry*. Edited by James I. Robertson, Jr. 2nd edition, Jackson, Tenn., 1964.
Wright, Lou'se Giraud (Wigfall). *A Southern Girl in '61*. New York, 1905.
Wyeth, John A. *That Devil Forrest*. 2nd edition, New York, 1959.
Young, John Russell, *Around the World with General Grant*. 2 vols. New York, 1879.
Young, Lot D. *Reminiscences of a Soldier of the Orphan Brigade*. Louisville, 1912.
Younger, Edward, ed. *Inside the Confederate Government: The Diary of Robert Garlick Hill Kean*. New York, 1957.

Secondary Sources

Amann, William P. *Personnel of the Civil War*. 2 vols. New York, 1961.
Ammon, Harry. *James Monroe & the Quest for National Identity*. New York, 1971.
Andrews, J. Cutler. *The North Reports the Civil War*. Pittsburgh, 1955.
_____. *The South Reports the Civil War*. Princeton, N.J., 1970.
Annual Report of the American Historical Association, 1910. Washington, 1912.
Auchampaugh, Phillip G. *James Buchanan and his Cabinet on the Eve of Secession*. Boston, 1965.
Beers, Henry P. *Guide to the Archives of the Confederate States of America*. Washington, 1969.
Biographical Directory of the American Congress, 1774–1961. Washington, 1961.
Blair, Henry C., and Rebecca Tarshis. *Colonel Edward D. Baker, Lincoln's Constant Ally*. Portland, Ore., 1960.

Boynton, Henry V. *Sherman's Historical Raid, the Memoirs in the Light of the Record.* Cincinnati, 1875.

Breckenridge, James Malcolm. *William Clark Breckenridge: His Life, Lineage and Writings.* St. Louis, 1932.

Brice, Marshall. *Conquest of a Valley.* Charlottesville, Va., 1965.

Brown, Alexander. *The Cabells and Their Kin.* Boston, 1895.

Bushong, Millard K. *Old Jube, A Biography of General Jubal A. Early.* Boyce, Va., 1955.

Butler, Lorine L. *John Morgan and His Men.* Philadelphia, 1960.

Cassidy, Vincent H., and Amos E. Simpson. *Henry Watkins Allen of Louisiana.* Baton Rouge, 1964.

Cohen, Henry. *Business and Politics in America from the Age of Jackson to the Civil War: The Career Biography of W. W. Corcoran.* Westport, Conn., 1971.

Coleman, J. Winston, Jr. *Famous Kentucky Duels.* Lexington, Ky., 1969.

————. *Historic Kentucky.* Lexington, Ky., 1967.

Collins, Lewis. *History of Kentucky.* 2 vols. Louisville, 1924.

Collins, Vernon L. *President Witherspoon.* 2 vols. Princeton, N.J., 1925.

Connelly, Thomas L. *Army of the Heartland: The Army of Tennessee, 1861–1862.* Baton Rouge, 1967.

————. *Autumn of Glory: The Army of Tennessee, 1862–1865.* Baton Rouge, 1971.

Connelly, Thomas L., and Archer Jones. *The Politics of Command.* Baton Rouge, 1973.

Coulter, E. Merton. *Civil War and Readjustment in Kentucky.* Chapel Hill, 1926.

Couper, William. *The V.M.I. Cadets: Biographical Sketches of All Members of the Virginia Military Institute Corps of Cadets Who Fought in the Battle of New Market, May 15, 1864.* Charlottesville, Va., 1933.

Craven, Avery. *Edmund Ruffin, Southerner: A Study in Secession.* New York, 1932.

Crenshaw, Ollinger. *The Slave States in the Presidential Election of 1860.* Baltimore, 1945.

Curry, Leonard P. *Rail Routes South: Louisville's Fight for the Southern Market, 1865–1872.* Lexington, Ky., 1969.

Dew, Charles B. *Ironmaker to the Confederacy: Joseph R. Anderson and the Tredegar Iron Works.* New Haven, Conn., 1966.

Dorris, Jonathan T. *Pardon and Amnesty Under Lincoln and Johnson.* Chapel Hill, N.C., 1953.

Dowd, Clement. *Life of Zebulon B. Vance.* Charlotte, N.C., 1897.

Dowdey, Clifford. *Experiment in Rebellion.* New York, 1946.

Eaton, Clement. *The Mind of the Old South.* Baton Rouge, 1967.

Elliott, Charles W. *Winfield Scott, the Soldier and the Man.* New York, 1937.

Feerick, John D. *From Failing Hands: The Story of Presidential Succession.* New York, 1965.

Fite, Emerson D. *The Presidential Election of 1860.* New York, 1911.

Freeman, Douglas S. *Lee's Lieutenants: A Study in Command.* 3 vols. New York, 1946.

————. *R. E. Lee.* 4 vols. New York, 1934–35.

Gunderson, Robert G. *Old Gentlemen's Convention: The Washington Peace Conference of 1861.* Madison, Wis., 1961.

Hage, George S. *Newspapers on the Minnesota Frontier.* St. Paul, 1967.

Hamilton, Holman. *Prologue to Conflict: The Crisis and Compromise of 1850.* Lexington, Ky., 1964.

Hanna, Alfred J. *Flight into Oblivion.* Richmond, 1938.

Harlow, Alvin F. *Weep No More, My Lady.* New York, 1942.

Harrison, Lowell H. *John Breckinridge, Jeffersonian Republican.* Louisville, 1969.

Hartje, Robert G. *Van Dorn: The Life and Times of a Confederate General.* Nashville, 1967.

Hendrick, Burton J. *Statesmen of the Lost Cause.* Boston, 1935.

Hesseltine, William. *Ulysses S. Grant, Politician.* New York, 1935.

Horn, Stanley. *The Army of Tennessee.* Norman, Okla., 1952.

Hughes, Nathaniel C. *General William J. Hardee: Old Reliable.* Baton Rouge, 1965.

Hunt, H. Draper. *Hannibal Hamlin of Maine.* Syracuse, 1969.

Johannsen, Robert W. *Stephen A. Douglas.* New York, 1973.

Jones, Archer. *Confederate Strategy from Shiloh to Vicksburg.* Baton Rouge, 1961.

King, Alvy L. *Louis T. Wigfall, Southern Fire-eater.* Baton Rouge, 1970.

Kirby, William. *Annals of Niagara.* Toronto, 1927.

Kirwan, Albert D. *John J. Crittenden: The Struggle for the Union.* Lexington, Ky., 1962.

Klein, Philip S. *President James Buchanan: A Biography.* University Park, Pa., 1962.

Klement, Frank L. *The Limits of Dissent, Clement L. Vallandigham & the Civil War.* Lexington, Ky., 1970.

Leach, Margaret. *Reveille in Washington.* New York, 1941.

Lonn, Ella. *Salt as a Factor in the Confederacy.* University, Ala., 1965.

MacBride, Robert. *Civil War Ironclads.* Philadelphia, 1962.

McElroy, Robert. *Jefferson Davis: The Unreal and the Real.* 2 vols. New York, 1937.

McKay, Ernest. *Henry Wilson: Practical Radical, a Portrait of a Politician.* Port Washington, N.Y., 1971.

McKinnon, John L. *The History of Walton County.* Atlanta, 1911.

McWhiney, Grady C. *Braxton Bragg and Confederate Defeat. Volume 1: Field Command.* New York, 1969.

Maddex, Jack P., Jr. *The Virginia Conservatives, 1867–1879.* Chapel Hill, N.C., 1970.

Martin, Asa Earl. *The Anti-Slavery Movement in Kentucky, Prior to 1850.* Louisville, 1918.

Meade, Robert D. *Judah P. Benjamin, Confederate Statesman.* New York, 1943.

Miers, Earl S., ed. *Lincoln Day by Day: A Chronology*. 3 vols. Washington, 1960.

Milton, George Fort. *The Eve of Conflict: Stephen A. Douglas and the Needless War*. Boston, 1934.

Mitchell, Memory F. *Legal Aspects of Conscription and Exemption in North Carolina, 1861–1865*. Chapel Hill, N.C., 1965.

Nevins, Allan. *The Emergence of Lincoln: Douglas, Buchanan and Party Chaos, 1857–1859*. New York, 1950.

———. *The Emergence of Lincoln: Prologue to Civil War, 1859–1861*. New York, 1950.

———. *The War for the Union: The Improvised War, 1861–1862*. New York, 1959.

———. *The War for the Union: War Becomes Revolution, 1862–1863*. New York, 1959.

Nichols, Roy F. *Disruption of American Democracy*. New York, 1948.

———. *Franklin Pierce, Young Hickory of the Granite Hills*. Philadelphia, 1931.

———. *The Stakes of Power, 1845–1877*. New York, 1961.

O'Connor, Thomas H. *Lords of the Loom: The Cotton Whigs and the Coming of the Civil War*. New York, 1968.

Overdyke, W. Darrell. *The Know-Nothing Party in the South*. Baton Rouge, 1950.

Parks, Joseph H. *General Leonidas Polk, C.S.A.* Baton Rouge, 1962.

Patrick, Rembert W. *The Fall of Richmond*. Baton Rouge, 1960.

Peter, Robert. *Transylvania University*. Louisville, 1896.

Poage, George R. *Henry Clay and the Whig Party*. Chapel Hill, N.C., 1936.

Polk, William. *Leonidas Polk, Bishop and General*. 2 vols. New York, 1893.

Ranck, James B. *Albert Gallatin Brown*. New York, 1937.

Rawley, James A. *Race and Politics: "Bleeding Kansas" and the Coming of the Civil War*. Philadelphia, 1969.

Rayback, Joseph G. *Free Soil, The Election of 1848*. Lexington, Ky., 1971.

Reynolds, Donald E. *Editors Make War: Southern Newspapers in the Secession Crisis*. Nashville, 1970.

Roland, Charles P. *Albert Sidney Johnston, Soldier of Three Republics*. Austin, Tex., 1964.

Ross, Ishbel. *First Lady of the South*. New York, 1958.

Sanders, Robert S. *Sketch of Mount Horeb Presbyterian Church, 1827–1952*. Lexington, Ky., 1952.

Seager, Robert. *And Tyler too: A Biography of John & Julia Gardiner Tyler*. New York, 1963.

Sensing, Thurman. *Champ Ferguson, Confederate Guerilla*. Nashville, 1942.

Shewmaker, W. O. *The Pisgah Book*. N.p., n.d.

Smith, Justin H. *The War with Mexico*. 2 vols. New York, 1919.

Smith, Sydney K. *Life, Army Record and Public Services of D. Howard Smith*. Louisville, 1890.

Sonne, Niels Henry. *Liberal Kentucky 1780–1828*. New York, 1939.

Sprague, Dean. *Freedom Under Lincoln.* Boston, 1965.

Stackpole, Edward J. *Sheridan in the Shenandoah.* Harrisburg, Pa., 1961.

Steiner, Paul E. *Disease in the Civil War: Natural Biological Warfare in 1861–1865.* Springfield, Ill., 1968.

Stevenson, Alexander F. *The Battle of Stones River near Murfreesboro, Tenn.* Boston, 1884.

Stewart, George R. *American Place Names.* New York, 1970.

Stillwell, Lucille. *Born to Be a Statesman: John Cabell Breckinridge.* Caldwell, Idaho, 1936.

Strode, Hudson. *Jefferson Davis, Tragic Hero, 1864–1889.* New York, 1964.

Tatum, Georgia L. *Disloyalty in the Confederacy.* Chapel Hill, N.C., 1934.

Temple, Oliver R. *East Tennessee and the Civil War.* Cincinnati, 1899.

Thomas, Benjamin P., and Harold P. Hyman. *Stanton: The Life and Times of Lincoln's Secretary of War.* New York, 1962.

Thomas, Lately. *Sam Ward, "King of the Lobby."* Boston, 1965.

Thompson, William Y. *Robert Toombs of Georgia.* Baton Rouge, 1966.

Townsend, William H. *Lincoln and the Bluegrass.* Lexington, Ky., 1955.

Trelease, Allen W. *White Terror: The Ku Klux Klan Conspiracy and Southern Reconstruction.* New York, 1971.

Tucker, Glenn. *Chickamauga: Bloody Battle of the West.* Indianapolis, 1961.

Turner, Edward Raymond. *The New Market Campaign, May, 1864.* Richmond, 1912.

Vandiver, Frank E. *Jubal's Raid: General Early's Famous Attack on Washington.* New York, 1960.

————. *Ploughshares into Swords: Josiah Gorgas and Confederate Ordnance.* Austin, Tex., 1952.

Van Horne, Thomas B. *History of the Army of the Cumberland.* 2 vols. Cincinnati, 1876.

Warner, Ezra J. *Generals in Gray.* Baton Rouge, 1959.

Wertenbaker, Thomas J. *Princeton: 1746–1896.* Princeton, N.J., 1946.

Williams, Alfred M. *Sam Houston and the War of Independence in Texas.* Boston, 1893.

Williams, T. Harry. *P. G. T. Beauregard: Napoleon in Gray.* Baton Rouge, 1954.

Wilson, Rufus R. *Lincoln Among His Friends.* Caldwell, Idaho, 1942.

Wilson, Samuel M. *History of Kentucky.* 2 vols. Chicago, 1928.

Winters, John D. *The Civil War in Louisiana.* Baton Rouge, 1963.

Wise, Winifred E. *Lincoln's Secret Weapon.* Philadelphia, 1961.

Worthington, Glenn H. *Fighting for Time, or the Battle that Saved Washington and Mayhap the Union.* Baltimore, 1932.

ARTICLES: *Primary and Secondary*

Anderson, Charles W. "Gracey—Chickamauga—Whitaker." *Confederate Veteran,* III (August, 1895), 251–52.

Anderson, J. Patton. "Autobiography." *Southern Historical Society Papers,* XXIV (January–December, 1896), 57–72.

Anderson, T. B. "A Boy's Impression of Shiloh." *Confederate Veteran*, XIX (February, 1911), 72.

Avery, A. C. "The Life and Character of Lieutenant General D. H. Hill." *Southern Historical Society Papers*, XXI (January–December, 1893), 110–50.

Bakeless, John. "The Mystery of Appomattox." *Civil War Times Illustrated*, IX (June, 1970), 18–30.

Battle, Frank. "An 'Old Reb' at Richmond." *Confederate Veteran*, XV (August, 1907), 347.

Bean, W. G., ed. "Memoranda of Conversations Between General Robert E. Lee and William Preston Johnston, May 7, 1868, and March 18, 1870." *Virginia Magazine of History and Biography*, LXXIII (October, 1965), 474–84.

Bearss, Edwin C. "General Breckinridge Leads the Confederate Advance into Middle Tennessee." *Register of the Kentucky Historical Society*, LX (July, 1962), 183–208.

————. "Stone's River: The Artillery at 4:45 P.M., January 2, 1863." *Civil War Times Illustrated*, II (February, 1964), 38–39.

Bell, Patricia. "Gideon Pillow." *Civil War Times Illustrated*, VI (October, 1967), 12–19.

Binkley, H. C. "Shared in the Confederate Treasure." *Confederate Veteran*, XXXVIII (March, 1930), 87–88.

Breckinridge, Clifton R. "Domestic Life of Gen. John C. Breckinridge." *Confederate Veteran*, I, 325.

Breckinridge, John C. "Iowa Territory—Its Condition, Resources, Population and Wants." *Spirit of the XIX Century*, II (April, 1842), 184–88.

Breckinridge, Robert J. "The Civil War." *Danville Quarterly Review*, I (December, 1861), 639–72.

Bringhurst, W. R. "Survivor of President Davis's Escort." *Confederate Veteran*, XXXIV (October, 1926), 368–69.

Brown, Joseph A. "The Confederate Treasure Train." *Confederate Veteran*, XXV (June, 1917), 257–59.

Bruce, D. H. "Battle of New Market, Virginia." *Confederate Veteran*, XV (December, 1907), 553–54.

Burnett, T. L. "Battle of Saltville." *Southern Bivouac*, old series, II (September, 1883), 20–22.

Carpenter, J. N. "Courtesy of the Truly Great." *Confederate Veteran*, XXIX (November–December, 1921), 424–25.

Castel, Albert. "The Fort Pillow Massacre: A Fresh Examination of the Evidence." *Civil War History*, IV (March, 1958), 37–50.

Chalaron, J. A. "Vivid Experiences at Chickamauga." *Confederate Veteran*, III (September, 1895), 278–79.

————. "The Washington Artillery in the Army of Tennessee." *Southern Historical Society Papers*, XI (April–May, 1883), 217–22.

"Children of the Confederacy in Kentucky." *Confederate Veteran*, IX (May, 1901), 227.

Clark, Walter A. "The Boy Cadets at New Market, Va." *Confederate Veteran*, XX (February, 1912), 86.

Clay, H. B. "On the Right at Murfreesboro." *Confederate Veteran*, XXI (December, 1913), 588–89.

Cloutier, Philip R. "John C. Breckinridge, Superior City Land Speculator." *Register of the Kentucky Historical Society*, LVII (January, 1959), 12–19.

Cochrane, John. "The Charleston Convention." *Magazine of American History*, XIV (August, 1885), 148–53.

Colgin, James H., ed. "The Life Story of Brig. Gen. Felix Robertson." *Texana*, VIII (Spring, 1970), 154–82.

"Confederate Love-Taps." *Historical Magazine*, 3rd series, I (May, 1873), 257–74, (June, 1873), 334–51.

"Confederate Rag-Bag." *Historical Magazine*, 3rd series, II (August, 1873), 92–93.

Cooper, William J., Jr. "A Reassessment of Jefferson Davis as War Leader: The Case from Atlanta to Nashville." *Journal of Southern History*, XXXVI (May, 1970), 189–204.

Cunningham, John. "Reminiscences of Shiloh." *Confederate Veteran*, XVI (November, 1908), 577.

Curry, Roy W. "James A. Seddon, A Southern Prototype." *Virginia Magazine of History and Biography*, LXIII (April, 1955), 123–50.

Damon, H. G. "The Eyes of General Breckenridge." *Confederate Veteran*, XVII (August, 1909), 380.

Davis, William C. "The Conduct of Mr. Thompson." *Civil War Times Illustrated*, IX (May, 1970), 407.

_____. "Massacre at Saltville." *Civil War Times Illustrated*, IX (February, 1971), 4–11, 43–48.

Dawes, Henry L. "Two Vice Presidents." *Century Magazine*, L (July, 1895), 463–67.

DeRosset, A. L. "Interesting Statement of Judge Robert Ould." *Confederate Veteran*, XV (October, 1907), 455–56.

Derry, Joseph T. "The Battle of Shiloh." *Southern Historical Society Papers*, XXIX (January–December, 1901), 357–60.

Dinkins, James. "The Battle of Shiloh, April 6, 1862." *Southern Historical Society Papers*, XXXI (January–December, 1903), 298–320.

Donnelly, Ralph W. "The Confederate Lead Mines of Wytheville, Va." *Civil War History*, V (December, 1959), 402–14.

Dorris, Jonathan T. "Pardoning John C. Breckinridge." *Register of the Kentucky Historical Society*, LVI (October, 1958), 319–24.

[Duke, Basil W.] "Editor's Table." *Southern Bivouac*, new series, I (September, 1885), 255.

Dunn, C. Frank. "The Breckinridges." *In Kentucky*, VII (Summer, 1942), 9–13, 42–44.

Eby, Cecil D., Jr., ed. "With Sigel at New Market: The Diary of Colonel D. H. Strother," *Civil War History*, VI (March, 1960), 73–83.

"Federal Veterans at Shiloh." *Confederate Veteran*, III (April, 1895), 104–105.

Flateau, L. S. "A Great Naval Battle." *Confederate Veteran*, XXV (October, 1917), 458–59.

"General Albert Sidney Johnston." *Confederate Veteran*, III (March, 1895), 81–87.

Gibson, W. W. "Reminiscences of Ringgold Gap." *Confederate Veteran*, XII (November, 1904), 526–27.

Gift, George W. "The Story of the *Arkansas*." *Southern Historical Society Papers*, XII (March, 1884), 115–19.

Goggin, James M. "Chickamauga—A Reply to Major Sykes." *Southern Historical Society Papers*, XII (May, 1884), 219–24.

Gow, June I. "The Johnston and Brent Diaries; A Problem of Authorship." *Civil War History*, XIV (March, 1968), 46–50.

Grimsley, Elizabeth Todd. "Six Months in the White House." *Journal of the Illinois Historical Society*, XIX (October, 1926), 43–73.

Groves, Walter A. "Centre College—the Second Phase: 1830–1857." *Filson Club History Quarterly*, XXIV (October, 1950), 311–34.

Hamilton, J. G. deRoulhac. "Heroes of America." *Publications of the Southern Historical Association*, XI (January, 1907), 10–19.

Hanna, Alfred J., ed. "The Escape of Confederate Secretary of War John Cabell Breckinridge as Revealed by His Diary." *Register of the Kentucky Historical Society*, XXXVII (October, 1939), 323–33.

Hart, Albert Bushnell, ed. "Letters to Secretary Chase from the South, 1861." *American Historical Review*, IV (January, 1899), 331–47.

Hay, Thomas R. "Lucius B. Northrop; Commissary General of the Confederacy." *Civil War History*, IX (March, 1963), 5–23.

Heck, Frank H. "John C. Breckinridge in the Crisis of 1860–1861." *Journal of Southern History*, XXI (August, 1955), 316–46.

Hightower, T. H. "Lynch's Battery at Bull's Gap." *Confederate Veteran*, XXV (August, 1917), 345.

————. "Mixin' with the Yankees." *Confederate Veteran*, XXXV (December, 1927), 454–55.

————. "Speech of Col. Frances Lee Smith Before the Constitutional Convention of Virginia." *Confederate Veteran*, XXVI (February, 1918), 82–84.

Hinds, Charles F., ed. "Mexican War Journal of Leander M. Cox." *Register of the Kentucky Historical Society*, LV (January, 1957), 29–52; (July, 1957), 213–36; LVI (January, 1958), 47–70.

Hollyday, Lamar. "Maryland Troops in the Confederate Service." *Southern Historical Society Papers*, III (March, 1877), 130–39.

Horde, H. E. "Recollections of Gen. J. C. Breckinridge." *Confederate Veteran*, XVII (December, 1909), 594.

Howard, John Clark. "Recollections of Battle of New Market." *Confederate Veteran*, XXXIV (February, 1926), 57–59.

Imboden, F. M. "Gen. G. C. Wharton." *Confederate Veteran*, XIV (September, 1906), 392.

Jackman, John S. "Vicksburg in 1862." *Southern Bivouac*, old series, III (September, 1884), 1–8.

Jeffress, Thomas D. "Escape of Breckinridge and Benjamin." *Confederate Veteran*, XVIII (January, 1910), 26–27.

"J. F. T." "Some Florida Heroes." *Confederate Veteran*, XI (August, 1903), 363–65.
Johnston, J. Stoddard. "Reports of Gen. Lee After the War." *Confederate Veteran*, X (August, 1902), 305–308.
————. "Sam Laurence." *Confederate Veteran*, X (May, 1902), 200–201.
————. "Sketches of Operations of General John C. Breckinridge." *Southern Historical Society Papers*, VII (June, 1879), 257–62; (August, 1879), 317–23; October, 1879), 385–92.
Jordan, Thomas. "The Campaign and Battle of Shiloh." *United Service*, XII (March, 1885), 262–80; (April, 1885), 393–410.
Joyaex, Georges J., ed. "The Tour of Prince Napoleon." *American Heritage*, VIII (August, 1957), 65–86.
Joyce, Fred. "The Orphan Brigade at Chickamauga." *Southern Bivouac*, old series, III (September, 1884), 29–32.
Kirwan, Albert D. "The Orphan Brigade," *The Civil War in Kentucky*, Louisville *Courier-Journal*, November 20, 1960, pp. 95–97.
"Last Letters and Telegrams of the Confederacy—Correspondence of General John C. Breckinridge." *Southern Historical Society Papers*, XII (March, 1884), 97–105.
Lathrop, Barnes F. "A Confederate Artilleryman at Shiloh." *Civil War History*, VIII (December, 1962), 373–85.
Learned, Henry B. "Casting Votes of the Vice-Presidents." *American Historical Review*, XX (April, 1915), 571–76.
————. "The Relation of Philip Phillips to the Repeal of the Missouri Compromise." *Mississippi Valley Historical Review*, VIII (March, 1922), 303–17.
Leyburn, John. "The Fall of Richmond." *Harper's New Monthly Magazine*, XXXIII (June, 1866), 92–96.
Long, A. L. "General Early's Valley Campaign." *Southern Historical Society Papers*, III (March, 1877), 112–22.
McKinnery, Mrs. Roy. "Report from the President General." *Confederate Veteran*, XXIX (June, 1921), 232–34.
McNeilly, James H. "In Winter Quarters at Dalton, Ga." *Confederate Veteran*, XXVIII (April, 1920), 130–32.
McWhiney, Grady C. "Controversy in Kentucky: Braxton Bragg's Campaign of 1862." *Civil War History*, VI (March, 1960), 5–42.
Maltby, Mary Breckinridge. "Recollections of Civil War Times in Kentucky." *Register of the Kentucky Historical Society*, XLV (July, 1947), 225–34.
Manarin, Louis H., ed. "The Civil War Diary of Rufus J. Woolwine." *Virginia Magazine of History and Biography*, LXXI (October, 1963), 416–48.
Marshall, Edward C. "Progress of Democracy vs. Old Fogy Retrograder." *United States Democratic Review*, XXX (April, 1852), 289–306.
Melzer, Dorothy Garrett. "Mr. Breckinridge Accepts." *Register of the Kentucky Historical Society*, LVI (July, 1958), 217–32.
New Orleans *Times-Democrat*. "Capt. Charles J. Mastin." *Confederate Veteran*, III (April, 1895), 116–17.
"Notes." *Historical Magazine*, 3rd series, I (February, 1872), 119–20.
"Notes & Queries." *Civil War History*, VI (September, 1960), 304–14.

"Obituary of Col. H. S. Vandeventer." *Confederate Veteran*, XIX (March, 1911), 129–30.

O'Connor, John R. "John Cabell Breckinridge's Personal Secession: A Rhetorical Insight." *Filson Club History Quarterly*, XLIII (October, 1969), 345–52.

"Official Correspondence of Governor Letcher of Virginia." *Southern Historical Society Papers*, I (June, 1876), 455–62.

"Open Letters." *Century Magazine*, XXXVIII (October, 1889), 950–54.

Otey, Mercer. "Story of Our Late War." *Confederate Veteran*, VIII (August, 1900), 342–43.

Packard, Joseph. "Ordnance Matters at the Close." *Confederate Veteran*, XVI (May, 1908), 227–29.

Page, R. C. M. "Diary." *Southern Historical Society Papers*, XVI (January–December, 1888), 58–68.

Park, Robert E. "Diary." *Southern Historical Society Papers*, I (May, 1876), 370–86; II (July, 1876), 25–31.

Parsons, J. W. "Capture of Battery at New Market." *Confederate Veteran*, XVII (March, 1909), 119.

Pickett, William D. "A Reminiscence of Murfreesboro." Nashville *American*, November 10, 1907.

Pippen, W. B. "Concerning Battle of Shiloh." *Confederate Veteran*, XVI (July, 1908), 344.

Pirtle, John B. "Defense of Vicksburg in 1862–the Battle of Baton Rouge." *Southern Historical Society Papers*, VIII (June–July, 1880), 324–32.

Powell, Morgan Allen. "Cotton for the Relief of Confederate Prisoners." *Civil War History*, IX (March, 1963), 24–35.

Powell, Smith. "A Boy Soldier of Alabama." *Confederate Veteran*, XXIX (January, 1921), 22–23.

Reed, C. W. "Reminiscences of the Confederate States Navy." *Southern Historical Society Papers*, I (May, 1876), 331–62.

"Resources of the Confederacy in February, 1865." *Southern Historical Society Papers*, II (July, 1876), 56–63.

"Resources of the Confederacy in 1865." *Southern Historical Society Papers*, III (March, 1877), 97–111.

Ridley, B. L. "Camp Scenes Around Dalton." *Confederate Veteran*, X (February, 1902), 66–68.

Roberts, Deering J., ed. "Service with Twentieth Tennessee." *Confederate Veteran*, XXXIII (March, 1925), 100–101.

Robertson, James R. "Sectionalism in Kentucky, 1855–65." *Mississippi Valley Historical Review*, IV (June, 1917), 49–63.

Robinson, Edgar E., ed. "The Day Journal of Milton S. Latham, January 1 to May 6, 1860." *Quarterly of the California Historical Society*, XI (March, 1932), 3–28.

Rothert, Otto A. "A Glimpse of Alfred Pirtle, 1837–1926." *Filson Club History Quarterly*, XI (July, 1937), 211–17.

Scheiber, Harry N. "The Pay of Confederate Troops and Problems of Demoralization: A Case of Administrative Failure." *Civil War History*, XV September, 1969), 226–36.

Shortridge, Wilson P. "Kentucky Neutrality in 1861." *Mississippi Valley Historical Review*, IX (March, 1923), 283–301.

Shoup, F. A. "How We went to Shiloh." *Confederate Veteran*, II (May, 1894), 137–40.

"Sketch of the Lee Memorial Association." *Southern Historical Society Papers*, XI (August–September, 1883), 388–91.

Smith, George H. "More on the Battle of New Market." *Confederate Veteran*, XVI (November, 1908), 569–72.

Smith, Hal H. "Historical Washington Homes." *Records of the Columbia Historical Society, Washington, D.C.*, XI (1908), 243–67.

Smith, Lee. "Experiences of a Kentucky Boy Soldier." *Confederate Veteran*, XX (September, 1912), 440.

Smithson, P. L., and J. L. Gee. "Comments of Comrades." *Confederate Veteran*, II (February, 1894), 40.

Stevens, Frank E. "Life of Stephen Arnold Douglas." *Journal of the Illinois State Historical Society*, XVI (October, 1923–January, 1924), 248–673.

Stevenson, Carter L. "Report of . . . Jan. 2, 1864." *Southern Historical Society Papers*, VIII (June–July, 1880), 270–75.

Stevenson, Daniel. "General Nelson, Kentucky, and Lincoln Guns." *Magazine of American History*, X (August, 1883), 115–39.

Sullins, D. "Heroic Dead at Shiloh." *Confederate Veteran*, V (January, 1897), 10.

Swain, C. F. "Burning of the Blair House." *Confederate Veteran*, XIX (July, 1911), 336.

Swallow, W. H. "Retreat of the Confederate Government from Richmond to the Gulf." *Magazine of American History*, XV (June, 1886), 596–608.

Swan, S. A. R. "Perilous Service of Joseph R. Mason." *Confederate Veteran*, XIV (December, 1906), 551–53.

Sykes, E. T. "A Cursory Sketch of General Bragg's Campaigns." *Southern Historical Society Papers*, XI (October, 1883), 466–74.

―――――. "Singular Things Done Just Before the War." *Confederate Veteran*, XIX (June, 1911), 305–306.

"Theodore O'Hara." *Confederate Veteran*, VII (May, 1899), 202.

Turner, Wallace B. "A Rising Social Consciousness in Kentucky During the 1850's." *Filson Club History Quarterly*, XXXVI (January, 1962), 18–32.

"Unwritten History Worth Preserving." *Confederate Veteran*, VIII (December, 1900), 534–35.

Upshur, J. N. and others. "New Market Day at V.M.I." *Southern Historical Society Papers*, XXXI (January–December, 1903), 173–85.

Venable, M. W. "On the Way to Appomattox—War Memories." *Confederate Veteran*, XXXII (August, 1924), 303–304.

"The Veteran." "The Mobile Reunion." *Confederate Veteran*, XVIII (June, 1910), 257–61.

Washington, Bushrod C. "Henry D. Beally." *Confederate Veteran*, XII (August, 1904), 399–400.

Watkins, S. R., and John S. Jackman. "Battle of Missionary Ridge." *Southern Bivouac*, old series, II (October, 1883), 49–58.

Webster, Miss Rowe C. "Some Reminiscences." *Confederate Veteran*, VII (July, 1899), 324.

"What was in Front of Us, Early in 1865." *Historical Magazine*, 3rd series, III (February, 1874), 69–75.

"W. M. N." "The Battle of Missionary Ridge." *Southern Bivouac*, old series, II (January, 1884), 193–215.

Wood, John Taylor. "Escape of the Confederate Secretary of War." *Century Magazine*, XLVII (November, 1893), 110–123.

"XYZ." "Hunter's Raid, 1864." *Southern Historical Society Papers*, XXXVI (January–December, 1908), 95–103.

Young, Bennett H. "John Cabell Breckinridge." *Confederate Veteran*, XIII (June, 1905), 257–61.

Index

Throughout this index John C. Breckinridge is referred to as JCB.